THE
DiMaggio
ALBUMS

THE

ALBUMS

Selections from Public and
Private Collections
Celebrating the Baseball Career of
JOE DIMAGGIO

VOLUME 1
1932 · 1941

With an Introduction and Commentaries by
JOE DIMAGGIO

Compiled and Edited by
RICHARD WHITTINGHAM

G.P. PUTNAM'S SONS
New York

PUBLISHER'S NOTE

Some of the clippings and other material collected in these volumes were found or located in scrapbooks, private collections, and other sources, unaccompanied by the identity of the publisher, the author or other source of publication, so as to enable Weldon International Pty Limited to determine the identity of the holders of copyright (if any) in this material. Weldon International Pty Limited has made every effort, through independent research, to identify the sources of these items so that Weldon International Pty Limited could endeavor to obtain any copyright permissions that may be required in order to reproduce these items in these volumes. However, in some cases, this has proved impossible, due to the age of the material and the inability to identify, after a diligent search, the party or parties from whom copyright permission (if required) should be sought. Weldon International Pty Limited, and not Joe DiMaggio, is solely and exclusively responsible for the inclusion of these items in this work. Weldon International Pty Limited would be pleased to hear from any parties who can assist in identifying potential holders of copyright in this material so that necessary corrections can be made in future printings.

A Kevin Weldon Production

Designer Susan Kinealy
Production Manager Dianne Leddy
Endpapers Margo Snape

Published by
G.P. Putnam's Sons
Publishers Since 1838
200 Madison Avenue
New York, NY 10016

In association with
Weldon International Pty Limited
372 Eastern Valley Way,
Willoughby, NSW, Australia 2068

Library of Congress Cataloging-in-Publication Data

DiMaggio, Joe, date.
The DiMaggio Albums: selections from public and private collections celebrating the baseball career of Joe DiMaggio / with an introduction and commentaries by Joe DiMaggio.
p. cm.
Includes index.
ISBN 0-399-13487-5; ISBN 0-399-13501-4 (lim. ed.)
1. DiMaggio, Joe, date. 2. Baseball players — United States — Biography — Miscellanea. 3. DiMaggio, Joe, date — Collectibles. I. Title.
CV865.D5A3 1989 /89-10528 CIP
796.357'092—dc20
[B]

Printed in the United States of America
1 2 3 4 5 6 7 8 9 10

Typeset in Australia by Savage Type Pty Ltd, Brisbane
Printed by R.R. Donnelley & Sons Company, Willard, Ohio

CONTENTS

VOLUME 1

Introduction 9

─────────── 1932 · 5 THE MINOR LEAGUES ───────────

Starting out: 13   First professional ballgame: 16   With the San Francisco Seals: 17   A record-breaking 61-game hitting streak: 23   With Dom DiMaggio: 26   New York Yankees are interested: 29   Bad luck: 30 With Lefty O'Doul: 35   Most Valuable Player in the Pacific Coast League: 37   With Jake Ruppert: 41

─────────── 1936 A YANKEE ROOKIE ───────────

Joining the Yankees: 43   Signs first contract: 45   Speculation about the touted rookie: 47   Spring training: 49 First game as Yankee in Florida: 51   With Lou Gehrig: 53   DiMaggio delivers: 55   The first injury: 60 Debut at Yankee Stadium: 72   DiMaggio's presence is felt: 74   A rookie is established: 82   Year's most talked about rookie: 88   With Dizzy Dean: 90   All-Star game: 91   Joe DiMaggio day: 96   World Series: 102 Champions the first year out: 103   Post-season analysis: 118

─────────── 1937 A YEAR OF HOME RUNS ───────────

Home Run Crown: 121   1936 Player of the Year award: 122   Signs contract: 129   With Jake Ruppert, Tony Lazzeri and Frank Crosetti: 130   Spring training: 131   An arm problem: 135   Tonsil trouble: 136   Back in lineup: 138   Special All-Star game: 141   American League teammates: 146   Three homers in one game: 153 With Lou Gehrig, Bill Dickey and George Selkirk: 154   Hits 25th homer: 158   Hits 35th homer: 159   World Series: 165   Hits first World Series home run: 173   With baseball commissioner Kenesaw M. Landis: 181

─────────── 1938 THIRD WORLD CHAMPIONSHIP ───────────

A troubling year: 185   Holding out on Yankees contract: 187   Receives Baseball Writers' award: 192   Signs contract: 197   His first game of the season: 202   All-Star game: 205   With George Selkirk, Jake Powell, Tommy Henrich and Myril Hoag: 212   On the way to another pennant: 214   With Bob Feller: 215   With Ernie Lombardi: 216   World Series: 220   Player of the Year award: 235

─────────── 1939 A BATTING TITLE ───────────

A year of ups and downs: 237   Spring training: 240   Another injury: 244   Coming back: 245   Three home runs: 250   All-Star game: 251   With Bucky Walters: 252   Historic homer: 256   With Ted Williams and Jimmy Foxx: 259   Batting champion of the American League: 265   World Series: 268   DiMaggio is standout in Series: 280   Most Valuable Player award: 285

1940 A SECOND BATTING TITLE

A year without a pennant: 287   Another contract dispute: 290   Signs contract: 291   Spring training: 293   Awards come and go: 296   Joe DiMaggio Day: 298   With Dom DiMaggio and Ted Williams: 301   All-Star game: 302   With Lefty Gomez: 308   With Charlie "King Kong" Keller: 309   Three homers, 9 RBIs: 310   Batting champion of the American League: 312

1941 THE HITTING STREAK

Fifty-six great games: 315   Signs contract: 317   Spring training: 318   First game of hitting streak: 322   Hits safely in 42 consecutive games to break George Sisler's American League record: 326   *Sporting News* Player of the Month: 328   Hits safely in 44 consecutive games to equal Wee Willie Keeler's major league record: 331   All-Star game: 336   Hitting streak continues: 346   A hit in the 56th consecutive game: 349   Recapping the fabulous Streak: 350   Team tribute to DiMaggio: 371   Anything can happen in Brooklyn: 372   World Series: 373   A close-run victory: 384   All-America selection: 392   With Ted Williams: 393   Most Valuable Player award: 394   Outstanding Male Athlete: 399

PLATES

Facing pages listed

Joe DiMaggio at eighteen, in the San Francisco Seals uniform: 32   Joe DiMaggio's first baseball jersey: 33   With Lou Gehrig and the mayor of New York, Fiorello LaGuardia, in 1936: 48   The glove used by Joe DiMaggio in his first years as a Yankee: 49   The famous DiMaggio swing: 96   Vince, Joe and Dom DiMaggio in the late 1930s: 97   Joe DiMaggio's 1936 World Series ring: 112   Two signed baseball bats: 113   Advertisement for the 1937 motion picture, *Manhattan Merry-go-round*, in which Joe DiMaggio appeared: 176   A DiMaggio poster by Joe Eatalano: 177   Yankee pennants: 192   Cereal advertisements in which Joe DiMaggio appeared: 193   Joe DiMaggio receiving the 1938 Babe Ruth All-America award; the sweater received on the same occasion: 224   An advertisement for cigarettes in which Joe DiMaggio and other baseball stars appeared: 225   A cartoon by Gus Uhlmany showing Yankee players bargaining with Colonel Ruppert: 240   Joe DiMaggio waiting to bat: 241   Joe DiMaggio crossing home plate in 1939: 272   Joe DiMaggio in 1939: 273   A watercolor portrait of Joe DiMaggio by Norman Rockwell: 288   A smiling portrait from the early 1940s: 289   An illustration showing the progress of Joe DiMaggio's 1941 hitting streak: 344   The song "Joltin' Joe DiMaggio", by Ben Homer and Alan Courtney: between pages 344 and 345   A 1941 advertisement for Louisville Slugger baseball bats, naming Joe DiMaggio as Batting Champion of 1940: 345   An envelope and a collector's plate, commemorating Joe DiMaggio's 56-game hitting streak of 1941: 376   The sterling silver humidor presented to Joe DiMaggio in tribute by his Yankee teammates in August 1941: between pages 376 and 377   An exhibit in the National Baseball Hall of Fame honoring Joe DiMaggio's 56-game hitting streak: 377

INTRODUCTION

Anyone who has had the opportunity to forge a career in major league baseball is indeed a fortunate person. I found it to be a special world, filled with challenge and competition, one in which a special camaraderie, an essential and cultivated sense of loyalty, develops among players who are each striving to do their best for the sake of the team.

Baseball is such a unique sport, demanding specialized skills, carefully drawn strategies, intense concentration, and a kind of sixth sense, a call to action, that is triggered at the crack of a bat or the moment a batter sees the ball leave the hand of a pitcher. It is also a fascinating sport whose unending popularity has earned for it the deserved reputation as America's national pastime. It has entertained, intrigued, and excited tens of millions of fans for more than a hundred years. And it is the fans — the faithful, the fretful, the optimists, and the pessimists — who have sustained the game and made it the great sport that it is today.

I never dreamed how much a part of my life the game would become when I first started to play it on a sandlot in San Francisco back in the 1920s. It was just a diversion then, some fun to have when I was not in school, working on my father's fishing boat, or delivering newspapers.

My brother Vince was the first real influence I had in baseball. He played the game a lot and was good enough to be signed by the San Francisco Seals in the Pacific Coast League who then sent him to their farm club in Tucson, Arizona.

It was also Vince who got me my first real break. That was in 1932, and by that time he was playing for the Seals. Their shortstop, Augie Galan, had left on a trip just before the season was to end and they needed someone to fill in for him. Vince told his manager that I could do the job. It got me a start, but Vince was wrong: I could not play shortstop, as everyone soon learned.

I spent three fine years with the Seals, and learned a lot my last year there from our new manager, Lefty O'Doul. He had had a fine career playing in the outfield for various teams in the National League in the late 1920s and early 1930s and was a big help to me before I moved up to the major leagues.

Things went so well in San Francisco that the New York Yankees took an interest in me, and a wonderful relationship was sown. I was signed by the most exciting, charismatic ballclub of the time — the team that had showcased the magnificent Babe Ruth and still stood tall with the great Lou Gehrig.

My years with the Yankees were to be balanced, with the joys of victory on one side, and on the other the pains of a seemingly endless string of injuries to two heels, both legs, and an arm. It was to be an unforgettable experience.

Joining the Yankees in the spring of 1936, I made my first trip east of the Rocky Mountains. Before that I had never seen a major league baseball game, much less played in one. But I got in a car with two fellow San Franciscans, two fellow Italian-Americans, who just happened to be members of the New York Yankees — Tony Lazzeri and Frankie Crosetti — and we drove cross-country to Florida for spring training.

Ahead there were thirteen seasons for me as a Yankee. Eight of them were under a manager bound for the Hall of Fame — Joe McCarthy — and the later five split, two with Bucky Harris and three under Casey Stengel. I played against some of the game's greatest players — Charley Gehringer, Jimmie Foxx, Hank Greenberg, Ted Williams — and faced some of the foremost pitchers ever — Lefty Grove, Schoolboy Rowe, Bob Feller, Hal Newhouser, among many others. I was privileged to play on teams that went to ten World Series, nine of which we won, and with some truly great players. Besides Gehrig, Lazzeri, and Crosetti, there was Lefty Gomez, Red Ruffing, Bill Dickey, George Selkirk, Red Rolfe, Tommy Henrich, Charlie Keller, Johnny Murphy, Joe Gordon, Phil Rizzuto, Vic Raschi, Allie Reynolds, Ed Lopat, Joe Page, Yogi Berra, Hank Bauer, and Whitey Ford, just to name a few of the real contributors to the fortunes of the Yankees from the late 1930s to the early 1950s.

I remember two events in particular. The first was the day Lou Gehrig, dying, said farewell to the ballclub. The second was when the fans held a Joe DiMaggio Day for me in 1949. I had missed the first two months of the season with a heel injury, but made a good comeback, and we were on the way to winning a pennant no one thought we would collect that year. Then late in the season I was struck with a terrible flu virus, which cost me eighteen pounds in weight and two weeks of the season.

I was just coming off that when the fans and the team threw the shindig for me. It was before a game at Yankee Stadium late in the season against the Boston Red Sox; my brother Dom played center field for them, and we

Major league brothers: Vince, with the Boston Braves, and Joe, with the
New York Yankees, in 1937.

It is Joe DiMaggio Day at Yankee Stadium in 1949. The Yankees and appreciative fans presented
him with gifts to honor his then 10-year career in New York. At the microphone is New York mayor
William O'Dwyer.

were fighting them for the pennant. My mother came out from San Francisco for it, and I knew this would be her last trip because she was dying of cancer.

Before the game she was asked who she would be cheering to win. "I'm pulling for both of them," she said. "Only I want Dom to win because Joe wins so much."

Then, during the ceremony, she walked onto the field directly over to Dom first and gave him a big hug and kiss and then to me for another kiss.

Those were two deeply emotional moments at Yankee Stadium that stand out among all the other memories. As I have so often said, I was lucky to be a Yankee and blessed to have a career in the great American game of baseball.

Joe DiMaggio

I would like to thank all those who made available material for The DiMaggio Albums, especially Barry Halper, who maintains such a magnificent collection of baseball memorabilia, as well as the various institutions, newspapers, magazines, and other individual collectors. Their cooperation and generosity have made these albums possible.

Joe DiMaggio

1932 · 1935
THE MINOR LEAGUES

Joe DiMaggio, leading hitter and right fielder for the San Francisco Seals of the Pacific Coast League in 1934.

STARTING OUT

I began playing baseball on a vacant lot in San Francisco with the other kids in my neighborhood when I was about ten years old. In those days I preferred almost anything to working on my father's fishing boat or cleaning it up when the fishing day was over. I hated the smell, that was all. My father, on the other hand, looked on baseball, which he knew very little about, in much the same way as I did on fishing.

We did not play on fancy cut diamonds with base paths and green grass. We played on a cleared space of ground that we called the "Horse Lot" because it was used by a dairy firm as a parking area for its horse-drawn milk wagons. Most of the time the spectators at our games were horses.

We used rocks for bases and most of us played barehanded because we could not afford baseball gloves. The rest of our equipment consisted of an old ball, held together by bicycle tape, and an oar handle for a bat. I ordinarily played third base back then.

Joe DiMaggio

1932–1935
JOE DiMAGGIO'S STATISTICS WITH THE SAN FRANCISCO SEALS

	1932	1933	1934	1935
Games	3	187	101	172
At Bats	9	762	375	679
Hits	2	259	128	270
Doubles	1	45	18	48
Triples	1	13	6	18
Home Runs	0	28	12	34
Total Bases	5	414	194	456
Runs Scored	2	129	58	173
Runs Batted In	0	169	69	154
Stolen Bases	0	10	8	24
Batting Average	.222	.340	.341	.398

Joe DiMaggio crosses home plate after homering for the San Francisco Seals in a game against the Los Angeles Angels on July 13, 1933. In this game, DiMaggio tied the Pacific Coast League record — set by Jack Ness back in 1915 — by hitting safely in 44 consecutive games. DiMaggio also collected two singles that day, then went on to extend the consecutive-game hitting record to 61.

☆☆☆ Dec. 21, 1980   S.F. Sunday Examiner & Chronicle

Down Memory Lane with Joe DiMaggio

The Morning Muse

By Bucky Walter
Examiner Staff Writer

Hall of Famer **Joe DiMaggio** didn't spring full-fledged into baseball, although it wasn't long before the future Yankee Clipper was in full sail with the S.F. Seals.

DiMag, we learned from him a while back, played for **Lefty O'Doul's** Seals in 1932 for nothing — not one red cent — and hadn't even signed a contract.

And he was stationed at shortstop. Eager but scatterarmed.

•

"I played three games at short for the Seals at the tag end of 1932," DiMaggio told us at a Memory Lane game at Oakland Coliseum between members of the 1948 Seals and Oakland Oaks, managed by **O'Doul** and the irrepressible **Casey Stengel**.

The tableau at Oakland goes back a bit. But the story of DiMag's genesis in baseball is worth telling.

•

"Early in the ('32) season," reminisced Joe, "I was watching a game at Seals Stadium by peeking through a crack under the rightfield fence while flat on my stomach.

"My eyes were bloodshot from windblown peanut shells."

The next character in the story is the late **Spike Hennessey**, grand old man of Funston Playground, who schooled generations of kids how to play baseball.

"Spike," recalled DiMag, "was passing down 16th Street and saw me. 'Come on,' he said. 'We'll go up to the office and ask **Uncle Charley Graham** (Seals' owner) to give you a free ticket.' "

•

Later, Mr. Graham gave shortstop **Augie Galan** — later sold to the Chicago Cubs — permission to skip the last three games of the campaign to join a barnstorming all-star team in the Hawaiian Islands.

"Someone — Hennessey, I suppose — recommended me to Mr. Graham," recounted DiMag. "I'd been knocking around Funston Playground, playing third base and shortstop. I was only 17 years old."

Graham asked Joe to finish out the last three games at shortstop. "No contract, no pay," said DiMag.

•

As a short-term shortstop for manager **Ike Caveney**, DiMag quickly educated fans behind first base to move to a safer location.

"I was wild, high," he grinned. "Most of my throws hit about five rows up in the box seats."

But Joe wasn't found wanting with the bat. In his first time at the plate, he cracked a triple off **Ted Pillette**.

•

Between seasons, the Missions (the other team in The City) tried to sign DiMag. But his late brother **Tom**, manager of the Fishermans Wharf restaurant, brought him to Graham and dickered a '33 Seals contract.

In this era where prize rookies are given bonuses that would choke horses, it is quixotic to think that Joe signed for only $225 a month.

•

Galan was firmly established as Seals' shortstop in '33. At the outset, Cavaney used Joe sparingly. His baptism as an outfielder came without warning.

"Early in the season, Ike sent me up as a pinch hitter," said DiMag. "At the end of the inning, I was about to sit on the bench when Ike ordered, 'Grab a glove and go out to rightfield.' Sure, I was surprised. I'd never played the outfield before."

•

As an 18-year-old rookie in 1933, DiMaggio hit safely in 61 consecutive games.

It wasn't until 1935 that Joe was moved to centerfield. It was a switch ordered by the N.Y. Yankees, who purchased him after the 1934 season for a paltry $25,000 and five so-so players and left him with the Seals in '35.

"Having hurt my knee in '34, I was damaged property," DiMag explained the cut-rate price.

"**Bill Essex**, a great Yankee scout, kept plugging for me. He took me to Los Angeles to **Doc Spencer**, famed for treatment of ballplayers. Spencer assured Essex my knee was sound. Bill talked the Yankees into buying me."

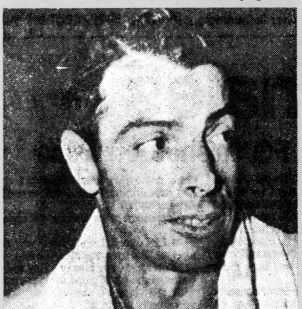

JOE DIMAGGIO
Recalling those days with the Seals   Associated Press

JOE DiMAGGIO'S FIRST PROFESSIONAL BASEBALL GAME
SATURDAY, OCTOBER 1, 1932, AT SAN FRANCISCO

Missions	AB	H	O	A	E	San Francisco	AB	H	O	A	E
Sherlock, 2b	4	3	2	3	1	Donovan, 1b	5	2	12	2	0
Wright, ss	3	1	3	5	0	J. DiMaggio, ss	3	1	2	2	0
Eckhardt, rf	4	2	2	0	0	Garibaldi, 2b	4	3	3	6	1
Almada, cf	3	0	2	0	0	Sulik, lf	4	0	4	0	0
Gyselman, 3b	4	0	2	2	0	Hunt, rf	4	1	2	1	0
Dahlgren, 1b	4	0	11	0	0	V. DiMaggio, cf	4	2	1	0	0
Kelman, lf	3	2	0	0	0	Wera, 3b	4	0	1	2	0
Ricci, c	4	1	3	2	0	Brenzel, c	4	1	0	3	0
T. Pillette, p	3	0	0	1	0	Davis, p	4	1	2	2	0
Totals	32	9	25	13	1	Totals	36	11	27	18	1

Missions	1	0	1	0	0	0	0	1	0	3
San Francisco	0	0	2	0	0	0	1	0	1	4

Two-base hits: Wright, V. DiMaggio, Sherlock — Three-base hits: J. DiMaggio, Kelman — Home run: Donovan — Stolen bases: Garibaldi 2, Sulik — Bases on balls: Off T. Pillette, 1, Off Davis 1 — Struck out: By T. Pillette 3, By Davis 1.

Umpires: Dunn and Fanning

'The Great Di Maggio'

Joe Started at Shortstop

BY JOE CASHMAN

BOSTON, July 5 -- The Yankees had a rookie pitcher named Herman Pilette in camp at St. Pete this Spring. The first pitcher Joe DiMaggio ever faced in the Coast League was an uncle of this boy. And Joe, as shortstop of the Seals, belted out a triple on his first time at bat, first of the more than 2,400 hits he's already made in his pro career.

This happened in San Francisco on the final Saturday of the 1932 season. It wasn't until the following Spring that the Yankee Clipper signed his first contract with the Seals.

That may sound a little confusing to a major league fan. Nobody can now engage in a game in the main tent unless he's under contract. But there was a time in the big show when an unsigned player, being given a look, could be used in not more than three games. Such a rule was in effect in the Coast League in 1932; possibly is to this day.

It hadn't been the intention of President Graham or anybody else connected with the Seals to take an immediate peek at DiMag in competitive action when he was invited to work out with the club.

THOUGHTFUL admirers remembered Joe with gifts on July 21, 1935, which served as real sendoff for the 20-year-old protege who reported to Yankees the following season.

His debut was largely accidental. Augie Galan, later a Cubs' and Dodgers' star, was the Seals regular shortstop that season. He had an invitation to spend a few weeks in Honolulu and was anxious to get started for the land of pineapples and hip-shaking maidens.

Could he be excused a few days early, Augie wanted to know.

"I'd like to let you get away," Manager Ike Caveny told him, "but I'm stuck. We still have three games to play and I haven't anybody who can fill in at shortstop."

Vince DiMaggio heard the conversation. He piped up:

"What's the matter with my brother Joe? He's a shortstop."

That settled it. Galan was given permission to pack up. DiMaggio was told he was to play shortstop.

Vince told us the story a dozen years ago. Joe has frequently confirmed it. But countless other versions have sprung up.

"But don't ever say that I was in any way responsible for anything Joe has accomplished in baseball," Vince admonished. One look at him cutting at a ball in batting practice would have convinced any experienced baseball man that Joe couldn't miss being one of the greats.

Frisco Pilot Shifted Joe to Outfield

By JOE DI MAGGIO.

CHICAGO, May 15.—In the spring of 1933 I reported with some 150 other young men at the school of the San Francisco Seals. I suppose I made a good impression because Charley Graham and Ike Caveney asked if I would sign a contract.

Well, this time I was tough. I told Charley I wanted to play ball and be with Vince, but would have to get far more than they were paying rookies. They were signing youngsters at $125 a month. I got $250.

I went to the training camp of the Seals as a shortstop. Augie Galan, of the Cubs, still owned that position and was making a grand showing.

One afternoon Galan was injured and Caveney

sent me to short. I booted plenty. I was excited. The next day I looked a little better. But I began to get the idea that if I really had some chance as a ball player, it was not at short.

When the Coast League campaign got under way I was just another guy named Joe on the bench. I will say, though, that Caveney gave me a lot of encouragement. And Vince kept telling me that I had the ability, and couldn't miss.

Out in right field the Seals had a new man named Stewart. He had done some remarkable things in training, but when the season opened, Stewart stopped hitting.

One day Caveney sent me in to hit for him. I was so surprised I almost tumbled off the bench. I went up and waited—and walked.

Then Caveney said to me, "Joe, you go to right field."

Well, that was when he really had me floored.

On our bench were two fine outfielders—my own brother and Prince Oana, the Hawaiian. They were experienced players, good hitters. On the other hand, I was just a green kid, who never had played in the outfield.

I thought Caveney was trying to kid me. "Who, me?" I asked. "Yeah, Joe, you go to right field. Stewart needs a little rest. Just go out there and do the best you can."

I ran out to right and never left that San Francisco outfield for three years, except when injured. When I was sold to the Yankees I had to say a sad, yet joyful farewell to the Seals and their park and my folks and friends in San Francisco.

I made good with a bang. That first year, in 187 games, I finished with a batting average of .340. Among my accomplishments was the setting of a Pacific Coast League record by hitting in sixty-one consecutive games.

Don't forget that in sixty years of major league ball, nobody has beaten forty-four straight games. They tell me Willie Keeler set that record with Baltimore in 1897, and that for modern times the best mark is forty-one, made by George Sisler, with the Browns, in 1922.

Buck Newson, pitching for Los Angeles, almost stopped me halfway in the streak, but I finally got to him in my last turn. Ed Walsh broke my string. Newsom was the toughest pitcher for me in that league.

Making good with the Seals filled my cup of joy. And it made me sad, as well. For I was the direct reason for the release of my brother Vince. I had held out for the Seals so I could be with him, and just when I was glorying in success, Vince was cut loose.

Vince laid off for about three months. Then he signed with the Hollywood club, and has been with it ever since. This year the Hollywood team was transferred to San Diego.

In 1935 Frank O'Doul came from the Giants to succeed Caveney. Frank proved a valuable teacher, a fine friend, a sympathetic manager. But I am getting a little ahead of my story.

Joe DiMaggio, with bat, poses with other members of the San Francisco Seals in his rookie year of 1933. From left to right, pitcher Walter Mails, pitcher LeRoy Herrmann, catcher Larry Woodall, DiMaggio, manager Ike Caveney, pitcher Jimmy Zinn, and club president Charley Graham.

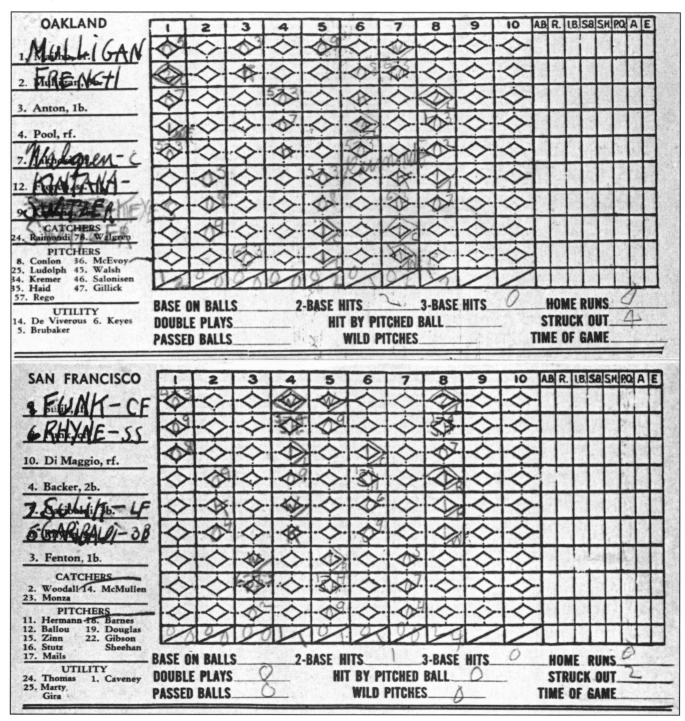

A Seals scorecard. Batting third, right fielder Joe DiMaggio wore number 10 in those days.

THE SPORTING NEWS

MINORS WORTH WATCHING

JOE DE MAGGIO, San Francisco   CHAS. HOSTETLER, Tulsa
★   ★   RUPERT L. THOMPSON, Albany   ★   ★

JOE DE MAGGIO—Age 18. Height, five feet 11 1-2 inches. Weight, 175 pounds. Throws and bats right-handed. Outfielder. San Francisco club. Born in San Francisco.

AN 18-year-old boy, who had never had a day's experience in any kind of professional baseball, started on a batting rampage on May 28 and became the sensation of the Pacific Coast when he hit safely one or more times in 50 games in succession to break the Coast league record of 49, made by Jack Ness in 1915. "Deadpan Joe," so-called because his face remains expressionless while he slams the ball to all parts of the field, tied Ness' record on July 13 and set a new mark by hitting safely in his fiftieth game on the night of July 14.

Two years ago, Joe was a newsboy and played on a Class B semi-pro team. His brother Vincent, two years older, was signed by the Seals and shipped to Tucson, where he performed in promising fashion. Vincent was expected to become a regular this year but failed to hit in the spring and was let out, while Joe was kept. Vincent is now playing with Hollywood.

Joe De Maggio

While hitting safely in his first 49 consecutive games, Joe made a far better record than did Ness in compiling his record 18 years ago. Ness made 61 hits in 184 times at bat for an average of .331, while De Maggio pounded out 84 hits in 201 times at bat for an average of .418.

Joe is a powerful youngster who may weigh 20 pounds more than he does now by the time he reaches voting age. He hits to all fields and he gets plenty of power behind his drives. The day he tied the record he made three hits off Fay Thomas. One of the blows was a home run.

The youngster played shortstop on the sandlots, but when the Seals tried him at that position during the spring he didn't look good, for he fumbled frequently and his throwing was erratic. But when Joe was sent to the outfield he found himself. He had a fine throwing arm and his pegs are usually accurate. San Francisco fans are acclaiming him as the find of the season.

Joe Demaggio, Coast Youngster, Hits Safely in 46 Straight Games

SAN FRANCISCO, Cal.—Joe Demaggio, young outfielder of the San Francisco Seals, with a record of having hit safely in 46 consecutive games up to the morning of July 11, was making a serious threat to eclipse the record for the league set in 1915 by Jack Ness. Ness hit safely in 49 games. Demaggio, who is 18 years old and is doing his first season in league ball, began his streak on May 29. During this period up to July 11 he had gone to bat 187 times and had made 78 hits. His average for the streak stood at .417, while his season's figure was .330.

COAST STAR HITS IN FIFTIETH TILT

SAN FRANCISCO, July 15 (AP).— Joe De Maggio, 18-year-old San Francisco Seals outfielder, whose proud dad pilots a fishing boat, today had shattered a Pacific Coast League batting record which was established the year he was born.

"Deadpan Joe," so called because his face is expressionless as he rifles baseballs to all corners of the lot, last night hit safely in his fiftieth consecutive game.

Way back in 1915, Jack Ness, Oakland first baseman, ran his consecutive games hitting streak to 49, and for 18 years such stars as Paul Waner, Earl Averill, Tony Lazzeri and other swatters have failed to break the record.

A trick of fate tossed young De Maggio into professional baseball. He had played on the sandlots and when the Seals' training camp opened last spring his older brother, Vince, brought him around and pleaded with the team owners to give the kid a chance.

They did and Joe ousted Vince from the Seals' lineup.

It Should Be Di Maggio

SAN FRANCISCO, Cal.—It's all settled now how to spell the name of Joe Di Maggio, sensational young hitter of the Seals. It has been printed "DeMaggio" and "de-Maggio," but it develops that both are wrong. The correct spelling is Di Maggio and that fact was only learned when Vice-President Charley Graham was making arrangements to have Joe's name engraved on the gold watch presented to him for breaking the league's record for hitting in consecutive games.

Joe signed his contract as DeMaggio, but his older brother, who witnessed the signature, signed Di Maggio, so Graham asked Joe: "How do you really spell your name?"

"Spell it any old way," said Joe. But Graham persisted and finally learned that Di Maggio is the proper spelling and that's the way it will be engraved on the watch.

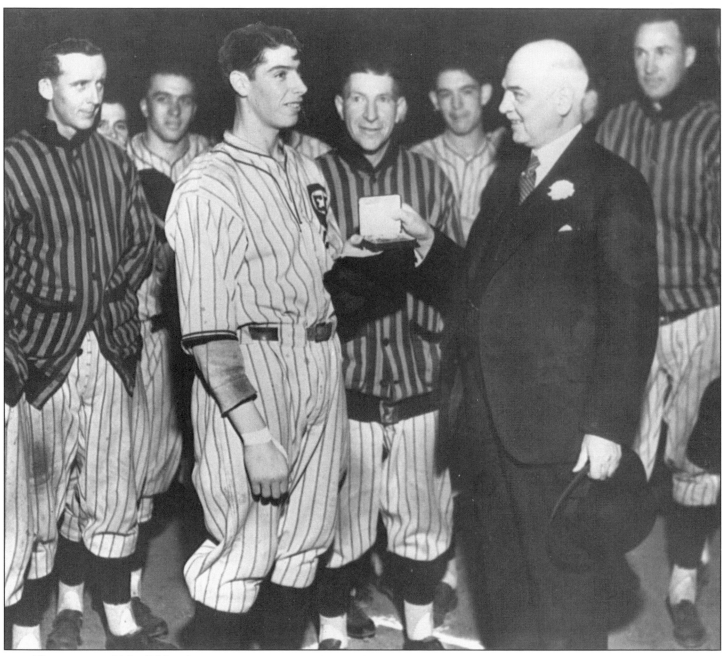

Nineteen-year-old Joe DiMaggio accepts a commemorative watch in honor of getting a hit in his 50th consecutive game in 1933. Presenting it is San Francisco mayor, Angelo Rossi. DiMaggio would extend the consecutive game hitting streak through 61 games.

De Maggio Stops at 61, Mob Charges Scorer

SAN FRANCISCO, Cal.—Joe De Maggio, youthful infielder of the San Francisco Seals, playing his first season in Organized Ball, has set a Pacific Coast League mark of consecutive game hitting at 61 that probably will stand for a long time. He failed in his attempt to equal the world's record of 69, held by Joe Wilhoit of Wichita, but he certainly created a lot of excitement on the Coast while he was hanging up his mark.

Probably no achievement ever had the fans of the Coast so worked up as De Maggio's streak did, because of the manner in which he kept the figure growing toward the end of the run. He wasn't getting the ball to the outfield, but he was placing his hits where they were hard to handle by the infielders, but not hard enough to erase the impression from the minds of some that he was being helped along to a record. He had his partisans and his detractors and the clash of the two as Joe registered at the 60 mark in Sacramento,

brought the unusual spectacle of the official scorer, Steve George, being conducted from the press box by the police to protect him from the fans—which probably never was done before.

Joe was stopped in his sixty-second game, July 26, when the Seals returned home to play Oakland, by Ed Walsh, pitching son of the famous Chicago White Sox spitball hurler. De Maggio went to the plate five times and was turned back each time by Walsh, grounding out and flying out twice and being safe on a fielder's choice another time. The streak started May 28.

In the last four games at Sacramento, the Solon pitchers stopped De·Maggio with an infield single in each game, three of them toward Ray French, shortstop, and one of them a swinging bunt that he beat out. The bunt was made in the fifty-ninth game. Third Baseman Boroja raced in to field it, but his hurried throw to first pulled Camilli off the bag. It came in the ninth inning, as did the one in the sixtieth contest, which French

grabbed for at his right, juggled momentarily and lost, not even attempting to throw the ball, as he figured it was useless. Scorer George said in such cases the batter always is given the benefit of the doubt and he saw no reason to make an exception in this case, although a number of the fans saw differently and stormed the press box.

De Maggio evidently was weakening under the strain at Sacramento. His former clean drives were not getting out of the infield. The adulation and publicity that had been heaped on him and the worry over whether he could set a world's record, apparently, were telling on him, and it became only a question of how soon he would crack.

Jim Oglesby, Los Angeles first baseman, was staging a minor streak at the same time that had gone 44 consecutive games before he was stopped by Roy Joiner, Oakland pitcher, July 24. The irony of Oglesby's break was that he was to be given a "night" the day after his string was broken.   SEAL.

DiMag's 61 Game Streak Top Feat

Joe DiMaggio's feat of hitting in 61 consecutive games is the outstanding achievement in the history of Seal batters.

It began modestly with a single on May 28 and ended on July 25 when Ed Walsh, son of the famous Chicago White Sox pitcher, stopped Di Maggio. Walsh was pitching for Oakland.

The record:

Date	Team	Pitchers	AB	R	H
May 28	Portl.	Jacobs-Boone	4	0	1
May 30	Seatl.	Haid-Sewell	6	1	3
May 30	Seatl.	Caster-Radonits	4	3	3
May 31	Seatl.	Page-Caster	4	1	2
June 1	Seatl.	Sewell-Caster	5	0	1
June 2	Seatl.	Pillette-Haid-Caster	5	1	2
June 3	Seatl.	Radonits	4	3	2
June 4	Seatl.	Page-Caster-Ulrich	4	1	2
June 4	Seatl.	Haid	3	0	1
June 6	Oakl.	Joiner	4	0	1
June 7	Oakl.	Salinsen	3	0	1
June 8	Oakl.	Ludolph-McAvoy	5	1	2
June 9	Oakl.	Gabler	4	1	1
June 10	Oakl.	McAvoy-Joiner-Ludolph	5	2	2
June 11	Oakl.	Walsh-Gabler	5	2	3
June 11	Oakl.	Salinsen-McAvoy	4	2	1
June 13	Seatl.	Haid-Sewell	4	1	2
June 14	Seatl.	Radonits-Caster	2	0	1
June 15	Seatl.	T. Pillette	4	2	2
June 15	Seatl.	Caster	5	0	2
June 17	Seatl.	Page	4	2	3
June 18	Seatl.	Radonits	3	1	1
June 18	Seatl.	Haid	2	0	2
June 20	Miss.	Babich	2	0	1
June 21	Miss.	Phebus-T.Pillette-Osborne	5	0	2
June 22	Miss.	Cole	4	0	2
June 23	Miss.	Johnson-Osborne	4	1	1
June 24	Miss.	Leiber	4	0	2
June 25	Miss.	Pillette-Osborne	4	3	2
June 25	Miss.	Phebus	4	1	1
June 27	Los A.	Newsome-Ballou	4	1	2
June 28	Los A.	Thomas	5	1	2
June 29	Los A.	Hermann	5	0	1
June 30	Los A.	Ward	4	0	1
July 1	Los A.	Newsome	4	1	1
July 2	Los A.	Thomas	4	0	1
July 2	Los A.	Ballou	4	1	2
July 4	Hllyw.	Campbell	5	0	1
July 4	Hllyw.	Wetzel	5	0	2
July 5	Hllyw.	Sheehan	4	1	1
July 6	Hllyw.	Dumovich	5	1	2
July 7	Hllyw.	Page	5	1	1
July 8	Hllyw.	Shellenback	5	2	2
July 9	Hllyw.	Dumovich	3	1	1
July 8	Hllyw.	Campbell	3	0	1
July 9	Hllyw.	Sheehan	6	1	3
July 11	Los A.	Ward	4	0	2
July 12	Los A.	Hermann	4	1	1
July 12	Los A.	Thomas	4	1	3
July 14	Los A.	Newsome-Ballou	5	0	2
July 15	Los A.	Ward	4	1	4
July 16	Los A.	Hermann-Nelson	4	1	1
July 16	Los A.	Wetzel-Ballou	3	1	1
July 18	Sac.	Horne	4	2	3
July 19	Sac.	Bryan	5	1	3
July 20	Sac.	Hartwig	5	0	1
July 21	Sac.	Vinci	5	0	1
July 22	Sac.	Glynn-Sanders-Noonan	4	0	1
July 23	Sac.	Horne-Hartwig	5	0	1
July 23	Sac.	Bryan	4	1	1
July 23	Oak.	Salinsen-McAvoy-Fieber	5	1	1
Totals during streak			257	49	104
Average for streak					.405

The Pupil (Dom) and the Teacher (Joe).

BOY BALL STAR THRILLS COAST

De Maggio Made Money for Seals While in Long Stretch of Hitting.

By SAM MURPHY
(The Old Scout)

For more than two months baseball fans of the Pacific Coast League had been excited about the remarkable batting streak of Joe De Maggio. The eighteen-year-old, first-year rookie had steamed up more interest on the Coast than any player for more than a decade.

The San Francisco Seals will have a profitable season because of the sensational batting of a young player who did not cost the owners one cent to get. He ran his consecutive record up to sixty-one games, within eight of beating the string rolled up by the late Joe Wilhoit, who ran through sixty-nine games before he was stopped.

No such excitement ever was seen on the Coast at ball games when De Maggio was at his top speed. The best of pitchers faced him and gave him all they had, but somehow he managed to get to them for at least one hit. Managers and players tried to find out De Maggio's weakness, but they looked in vain, for he kept slicing off his daily drive until he ran into Ed Walsh, son of the spitballer who was a hero of the old White Sox of more than twenty-five years ago.

Walsh pitched everything he had to De Maggio. Four times he turned him back. With the winning run on the base in the ninth inning he passed a hitter to get at the eager young batter of the Seals. The best that De Maggio could do was to lift a long fly that scored the winning run but stopped his record.

Went Down Fighting.

Young Joe went down gallantly. He was surrounded by admirers when his streak was broken and it was a good thing for the recruit that his streak was stopped. He was getting a bit nervous and was losing weight, the strain was telling on him. Jim Caveney, his mentor, was as happy as De Maggio when he was halted in his sensational rush.

The strain began to tell on him in his last five games. De Maggio, whose deeds have made him famous, was an eight-column headliner every day for a month. His hits toward the end of his streak lacked the old power of his early drives.

Rival players did their best to check the young player because there was some talk that he was being favored. He had to hit clean to get a break after he crossed the half hundred mark.

There was one questionable hit in his entire string and that hit almost caused a riot at the ball field when the official scorer gave him a hit on a long drive in the infield that the shortstop got but could not get to first in time.

Fans who evidently were betting against the young player rushed into the press stand and it was with difficulty that the scorer escaped without a pummeling.

De Maggio was a hero among the fan populace. All over the circuit during his string he was three times presented gifts. On one occasion several of the State legislators paid a visit to the ball park to see him and compliment him on his batting feat. Among his own players he was a hero.

After every hit his teammates gathered around him and patted him on the back. Despite the public clamor and the applause De Maggio is going to be a big leaguer some day to take the place perhaps of Lazzeri or Crosetti, who came from the same part of San Francisco as De Maggio.

Thrills in Sports

"Dead Pan" Joe Di Maggio Prospective Baseball Great

By JACK KOFOED

THE North Beach and Cow Hollow sections of San Francisco have produced some corking good ball players. There was Ping Bodie, for instance, a big slugger and a bigger eater. Even Babe Ruth couldn't slash his way through a menu any better than Ping. There, also was Swede Risberg, a fine shortstop who fell upon evil ways and was banished from baseball for his share in the 1919 World Series scandal. There are still in the big leagues Tony Lazzeri and Frank Crosetti. Three Italians and a Swede, and what ball players!

At North Beach lives a grizzled Italian named Di Maggio. He has five sons and a daughter, and takes his deep sea tug out of Fishermans Wharf every morning. Signor Di Maggio was never intended for fame, nor, for that matter were four of his sons or the black-haired daughter. Fish is their business, and their lives are permeated with the finny odor.

But one son found nothing to intrigue him on the bounding deep. He played baseball whenever and wherever he could. His name is Joe, and no matter how pop bawled him out, he kept swinging the old bat. He made quite a record with the semiprofessionals, so brilliant a record that even his father came to believe there might be a future for his son in this queer American game.

Manager Jimmy Caveney, of the San Francisco Seals, heard that the youngster was worth watching. It didn't cost anything to give the boy a trial, so Caveney invited him to work out with the club.

That was in the Spring of 1933. Joe Di Maggio, rangey, well built, made his professional debut with a Class AA outfit, which is rather unusual in itself. But the really unusual part of this story is still to come.

The kid from North Beach hadn't been with the Seals for more than a few days when his teammates nicknamed him "Dead Pan Joe." He had nothing to say. Fishermen are seldom loquacious. For the sea teaches silence. Probably Joe, who had never gone to sea, absorbed the habit of silence from his sire. Perhaps he didn't know anything to talk about but baseball, and he kept that one subject to himself in the presence of men who were more learned in the lore than he.

As Loose a Swinger as Joe Jackson

BUT it didn't matter to San Francisio whether Di Maggio was quiet or noisy. Not after they had scanned the season's averages. Dead Pan compiled a batting average of .340. He hit safely in sixty-one consecutive games, beating the record of forty-nine that Jack Ness set back in 1915 and drove in 169 runs. He was also a streak in the field and led the league flychasers with thirty-two assists.

That, I submit, is one of the most amazing records ever compiled by an 18-year-old boy in his first year of fast-time baseball.

A few weeks ago when Dead Pan went to the office to sign his 1934 contract he took his father with him. You see, not being of age, he could not legally put his name to any paper. So the puzzled Italian fisherman sat and listened and the young star said hardly a word while Vice President Charley Graham and Jimmy Caveney explained what it was all about. The contract was signed, and they went away.

Graham looked after the loosely built six-footer, who packs 190 pounds on his athletic frame, and said:

"Give him a couple of years Jim, and Di Maggio is going to be one of the greatest ball players in the country."

"I'm sure of it," said Caveney.

"Did you ever see a better natural stance at the plate or a guy who took a freer cut at the ball."

"Yes, sir, he's as loose a swinger as Joe Jackson was, and that's saying something."

I'll pop into the picture and say that if Dead Pan Joe Di Maggio has a swing like Jackson you'll be hearing of him under the big top next season, and he'll be a great star before he's 21. Nobody taught him anything on the North Beach lots. The things he does are instinctive.

He didn't have to learn the fundamentals.

Predictions Are That Joe Can't Miss

FUNNY, isn't it, that many of our great ball players come from the hidden places. Lots of them never had any material advantages at the start. Babe Ruth was found in a Baltimore protectory. Jackson was brought up in the misery of a Southern mill town. And now Di Maggio thrusts his head from a fisherman's shack.

If Dead Pan has a good year in 1934 he's certain of a big-league tryout next Spring. He simply can't miss if all the stories I've heard from the Coast are true. He'll leave the boys at North Beach and the smelly seamen at Fishermans Wharf and come East to see what it's all about. I wonder who will get him? Will he some day be trying to fill the shoes of Babe Ruth, or of Al Simmons or Big Poison Waner? We'll find out more about that later.

Giuseppe Di Maggio! What a name for a baseball hero! It doesn't sound right, but then the cognomens of Sarazen and Turnesa rang queerly in the Scotch game of golf, and to the old-timers who were brought up on the theory that the Irish were the only real fighters, the presence of Carnera, Impellittiere and Canzoneri must seem almost heretical.

The flowers that bloom in the Spring tra-la very often wither by June, and this rather strained metaphor means that young ball players, who earn press notices in the training camp quite frequently are back in the minors before midseason. But, after all, there is no league in the country where Di Maggio can learn more about baseball than he can out there on the Pacific Coast. The players are almost all ex-major leaguers. They are smart and know the answers. Dead Pan Joe will find out what it's all about.

I've a hunch about Joe Di Maggio. I'm predicting now that he will be a great star, and since he is only 19, he should have many years in which to reap the financial rewards of success. But the old weather-seamed fisherman, Di Maggio, pere, probably never will be able to quite figure it out. Why these crazy Americans should pay his boy so much money just for hitting a baseball is quite beyond him. There are fish in the sea to be caught, and Joe goes fishing for curve balls and fast ones. Ah, well, only God in his great wisdom can explain such a mystery.

But I'M telling YOU; keep your eye on Dead Pan Joe Di Maggio.

Red Smith

Quarterback And Outfielder

IT was the start of the football season of 1935, a few weeks more than 46 years ago. Til Ferdenzi was a candidate for quarterback at Boston College but Til isn't a big guy and competition for the assignment was lively. However, on the eve of the opening game a sports page in Boston carried the banner headline: "Ferdenzi to Start at Q.B. for B.C."

Years later when Til was covering the Yankees for The New York Journal-American, a faithful Boston fan sent him the yellowed page with his name in the headline. Looking it over, Til's eye lit on a one-line head at the bottom: "Yanks Buy Coast Star." The item read: "The San Francisco Seals announced today sale of Outfielder Joe DeMagio to the New York Yankees."

Til circled the names, refolded the page and mailed it to Joe DiMaggio with a note: "Just so you know who was the big paisan in Boston in 1935."

Neither Joe nor Til makes the Manhattan scene often these days, but Joe is about to celebrate his 67th birthday, and it is pleasant to recall how he got here in the first place. It is a tale that is repeated frequently, not always with all details accurate.

In the first place, the Yankees had bought his contract some time before Ferdenzi could read about it but had agreed to leave him in San Francisco through the 1934 season, and the announcement wasn't made until after the World Series. It seems incredible today that anyone could have viewed the purchase as a gamble but many baseball men considered it a high-risk venture.

•   •   •

From his first summer as an 18-year-old in the Pacific Coast League, scouts were on DiMaggio's heels. That season of 1933 he played in 187 games, broke the league record by hitting safely in 61 consecutive games, batted .340 with 28 home runs, 13 triples and 45 doubles, batted in 169 runs and led the league's outfielders in assists.

In the Great Depression when owners threw dollars around like manhole covers, bids went to $50,000, $60,000, $75,000 and kept climbing as the Seals' proprietor, Charlie Graham, bided his time. Then the bubble burst.

Joe had a dinner date at his sister's house and he was late. When his taxi pulled up he started to jump out, and his left knee popped like a pistol. He had to be helped into the house and on to a hospital, where he stayed for several weeks.

When he got out there was only one scout in sight — the Yankees' Bill Essick. Bill followed him tenaciously but wasn't always able to see him; one small mishap after another kept taking him out of the lineup, and he missed a total of 87 games that season. Still, when he could stand he could hit; his average was .341.

Studying him closely, Essick was convinced that he still ran as swiftly and easily as before; the leg gave no trouble when he put his weight on it at the plate. The scout called George Weiss, director of the Yankees' new farm system.

"Don't give up on DiMaggio," he said. "Everybody out here thinks I'm crazy but I think he's all right. Let me watch him a couple of weeks more."

"If it had been anybody else but Essick," Weiss said later, "I would have called him off but I had complete faith in Bill."

•   •   •

About two weeks later Essick called again. "Buy DiMaggio," he said. "I think you can get him cheap."

Weiss called Graham, they dickered and settled on $25,000 and five players, conditional upon approval by the New York brass. Weiss presented the deal to Ed Barrow, general manager, who exploded. He said this was exactly what Weiss was hired not to do. George was supposed to develop players, not buy them.

"We had already been burned," Weiss said later, "giving $100,000 for Lyn Lary and Jimmy Reese. But I had faith in Bill Essick."

He packed a bag, called Essick to meet him and caught a train to West Baden, Ind., where Col. Jacob Ruppert, the owner, was on vacation. Ruppert screamed like Barrow.

George showed him the report of an orthopedist who had examined Joe for the Yankees. The leg was sound. He showed Essick's report, written in pencil on stationery of the Brown Hotel in Louisville, where Weiss and Essick had met.

Here is the last paragraph of Essick's report, complete with punctuation: "He hits and throws right handed drives ball hard, fast, good fielder, strong accurate throwing arm and has all qualifications to develop into an outstanding major leaguer."

Reminded again that he had been hired to build a farm system, not buy players, Weiss explained that because of the farm system, only the Yankees could offer five serviceable players to Graham, who wanted help to win a pennant.

Then Ruppert reviewed DiMaggio's playing records, and was sold. One of the first people Weiss encountered during the spring training season was Bill Terry, manager of the Pirates. "You've bought yourself a cripple," Bill said.

There was some ground for suspicion that Bill might have been right. When the season opened, Joe was on the bench nursing an ankle burned by a sunlamp. He didn't get into a major league game until May 3 in Yankee Stadium against the St. Louis Browns.

He got three hits, including a triple. From that day on, he was Joseph Paul DiMaggio, the nonpareil.

BAD LUCK

One evening in June 1934 after a double-header and a dinner at my sister's house in San Francisco, I took a jitney cab home. When I was getting out, I put all my weight on my left leg, and it suddenly buckled. There was no twisting, just sharp cracks at the knee. I couldn't straighten out the leg and when I took a step the pain was awful.

Before the next game I telephoned the manager of the Seals, Ike Caveney, and told him I was in a lot of pain and couldn't walk. Charley Graham, the club president, sent a physician over to see me. He determined it was a torn cartilage. Later he put my leg in an aluminum splint from ankle to buttock, which I wore for what seemed like the longest six weeks of my life. After it was taken off, I tried to come back that season but couldn't.

It was around that time the Yankees were seriously looking at me, as were all the other teams in the major leagues. Most of them now thought I was through and quickly lost interest. If it had not been for the persistency of Bill Essick, one of the Yankee scouts, I would never have become a Yankee or maybe even stayed in baseball. He was positive a kid of nineteen could overcome a bad knee, and in the winter he took me to a specialist in Los Angeles for examination and treatments. He was right; I got over it.

Joe DiMaggio

Joseph (Joe) Di Maggio

He'll Know by His Knee

SOMETHING a little different in deals—sort of an "If coming" transaction—was put over by the New York Yankees, via their Newark farm, at the Louisville meeting, when tentative title was obtained to Joe Di Maggio, sensational young outfielder with the San Francisco Seals. Under the terms of the agreement, Di Maggio is to remain with the Pacific Coast League in 1935, and if he is in sound condition at the end of the season, he will graduate to the Yanks. If not, the deal is to be called off.

These specifications were included in the contract between the two clubs because of a "trick knee" the 20-year-old lad developed during the 1934 schedule. Di Maggio, regarded as a sure-shot for big league suc-cess, went on the sidelines with his injury late in the summer, officials of the Seals explaining that a rest was ordered for him because they did not care to subject the youngster to possible permanent affliction. It is contended that the rest has brought his knee around and that he will be as good as ever in the spring.

As part of the deal, the Yankees will send five players to the San Francisco club, three of them outright. If the final papers are signed, $35,000 in cash will then be turned over to the Seals.

Di Maggio, who has played only two seasons of professional ball, created a stir in 1933, his first year, when he hit safely in 61 consecutive games. He finished with an average of .340. This season, taking part in 143 games, he had a mark of .341 with the bat. The lad is normally fast, a fine fielder and can rifle the ball.

Born in Martinez, Cal., November 25, 1914, Di Maggio played semi-pro ball around the San Francisco bay district and was picked up by an agent of the Seals in the spring of 1933. He made good from the start. He is a six-footer, weighing 185 pounds and a right-handed batter and thrower. His brother, Vincent, two years older, is a member of the Hollywood club in the Coast league.

Yank Rookie Took Helping Brother's Job

Deal for Joe De Maggio Made Under Tentative Terms.

By DANIEL.

Yankee fans today were surprised to learn of the decision of the front office to leave Joe De Maggio, newly acquired outfielder, with the San Francisco Seals, possibly through the 1935 season. Only a year ago Colonel Jacob Ruppert said that he never again would commit the error that had been made with Lyn Lary, Jimmy Reese and other players who had been left in the Pacific Coast League for a year after their purchase had been announced. The sour experience of the Giants with the ill-fated Jimmy O'Connell also counseled against the sort of thing the Yankees are doing with De Maggio.

However, it is explained from the Yankee headquarters at the minor league meeting in Louisville that the De Maggio deal has been made on a tentative basis. Joe injured a knee last July and if he bears any visible reminders of that injury the New York club doesn't want him. Not until Bill Essick, the Yankee agent on the coast, gives the word that De Maggio is sound of limb and wind will the Ruppert checkbook enter the situation and make the purchase definite.

In any event De Maggio is not ready to break in with a club which is hot after the pennant. He is only 20 and has had comparatively little experience. In April, 1932, Joe's older brother, Vince, who was with the Seals, asked permission to bring his kid phenomenon into camp for a trial. Charley Graham told Vince that if Joe had his own shoes, uniform and bats he could join the hundred or more other youngsters who had flocked to the tryouts.

When the Coast League season opened Joe had Vince's job and Vince was on his way to the Hollywood club.

$75,000 Tag on De Maggio; "Greatest Ever," Says Coast.

If the Yankees close the deal for De Maggio, whom they have the right to call in at any time during the 1935 season, the price will come to something like $75,000. Three players will be released outright and two on option to the Seals. Some of the well known Ruppert bankroll also will be included.

Take it from Tom Laird, of the San Francisco News, Joe is the greatest ball player yet developed in a league which has sent up Hal Chase, the Waners, Earl Averill and the Johnson boys.

Joe is a product of the sandlots of the North Beach section of San Francisco, which has taken the place of Telegraph Hill and Cow Hollow as the developing ground of the Italian ball players of the Golden Gate. Joe gained considerable space in the sports columns in 1933 when he set a record by hitting in sixty-four consecutive games.

De Maggio will step in to take care of the Italian vote after Tony Lazzeri, of Cow Hollow, goes from the Yankees.

Private advices from Louisville indicate that the Yankees are almost near the closing point in the deal for Heinie Manush and that Joe McCarthy may succeed in getting Buddy Myer, too.

Di Maggio, New Yankee, Holds Batting Record

SAN FRANCISCO, Nov. 21 (P).—Joe di Maggio, young outfielder, sold today to the New York Yankees by the San Francisco Seals, becomes major league property after two years of professional baseball.

"Deadpan Joe," as he is known throughout the Pacific Coast League, joined the Seals for the last three games of 1932 after his older brother, Vince, had persuaded the club officials he was a "good prospect for shortstop."

In 1933 spring training, Joe was switched to the outfield and made such an impression the Seals made room for him by releasing his brother, also an outfielder.

Playing in 187 games that season, the eighteen-year-old youth set a league record of consecutive game hitting by clouting the ball safely in sixty-one contests. He batted in 169 runs, including twenty-eight home runs, and hit for an average of .340 the same year.

GRAHAM BUDGETS HIS GARDEN

'Frisco Prexy Laying Plans Now to Sell and Replace DiMaggio and Marty.

SAN FRANCISCO, Cal.—President Charley Graham takes issue with the oft-expressed claim that Smead Jolley, Earl Averill and Roy Johnson were the greatest outfielders ever to perform for the Seals. "They were great—no question about it—but when you talk about 'the greatest' it is another case of glorifying the past," said Graham in a recent fanning bee. "Players, when they reach the big league and become outstanding stars, are always appreciated more than when they were performing in the same style before their home crowds.

"Joe DiMaggio and Joe Marty are examples of this," continued Graham. "In my opinion, they rank as the greatest outfielders who ever have played with the Seals. They cover their fields—and I want to direct attention to the vast amount of territory they patrol—with the greatest speed and skill of any outfielders we have ever had in uniform.

"DiMaggio gets balls in almost every game that no other right fielder could reach. I believe it has been definitely established that he has the strongest and most accurate throwing arm in baseball. He has natural baseball instinct. Lefty O'Doul declares that Joe hasn't made a single mistake all season. DiMaggio is also established as a hitter.

"Marty is not as far advanced as DiMaggio, but he is rapidly coming ahead. When he broke in from the sand-lots last year—just as DiMaggio did the year before—he had more faults and corrected them faster than any player encountered in my 35 years of experience in the game. Few outfielders, if any, are faster on their feet. He always gets in position to catch the ball in front of him, no matter how hard the ball is hit. That is a rare art for an outfielder. Joe was slow in getting started at bat this year, but he is going now and has power in his swings. On the bases, he is exceptionally fast and uses keen judgment."

The Seals are already starting to lay plans for a new outfield next year. They expect Charles Laphere, a speedy left-hander from Colusa, recommended by Archie Yelle, to join the club for the next mission series when the Valley League season is finished on July 21, and John Thomas is a cinch to be recalled after his fine work with Des Moines.   SEAL.

At home in November 1934, Joe DiMaggio has kitchen duty peeling potatoes. He is smiling because he has just learned that the deal to make him a New York Yankee has been consummated.

At the age of eighteen, Joe DiMaggio joined the San Francisco Seals. After a brief debut as a shortstop in the last three games of 1932, he signed for the 1933 season, and an incredible baseball career began.

Joe DiMaggio's first baseball jersey. The Seals uniform carried the number 10. He would not become the famed number 5 until joining the Yankees in 1936.

Grooming of Yank Rookie Points to Shift of Chapman

Di Maggio Being Schooled to Take Over Center Field Job—Crosetti Undergoes Successful Operation on Trick Knee.

By TOM MEANY,
World-Telegram Staff Correspondent.

PHILADELPHIA, Sept. 3.—As the Yankees prepared to return to New York today following postponement of their double-header with the Athletics they found themselves in possession of news which reminds them that 1935 is as good as over and that 1936 is occupying the full attention of the front office.

Item No. 1 is that Joe DiMaggio, who will be a Yankee in '36, will play center field with Frisco on the Coast League for the remainder of this season. Di Maggio has been playing right field, where his amazing throwing arm has been of great value. The switch to center comes at the request of the Yanks, and indicates that they are planning to use him there next season.

If Di Maggio goes to center it means that Ben Chapman will be traded or returned to left field, the sun spot at the Stadium. Chapman, hitting under .300 at the moment, never has developed into the ball player that it was hoped he would. Ben, with his speed and throwing ability, should be one of the outstanding outfielders of the American League. Instead, he has shown just enough ability to hold down a regular job and little more.

Di Maggio will come to the majors with plenty of ballyhoo. Only recently Chick Frasier, veteran scout of the Dodgers, declared that of all the minor leaguers he ever has seen Di Maggio, hitting .400 at present, is the tops. And Chick, a scout with Pittsburgh before he came to the Dodgers, has been hitting the scouting trails for twenty years.

The second item is that Frank Crosetti, injured shortstop, underwent a successful operation for the removal of a floating cartilage of the knee at Johns Hopkins Hospital, Baltimore, early today.

Dr. George E. Bennett, who performed the operation, declared that the player would be able to leave the hospital within a week or ten days. He will not be able to play again this season, however.

Crosetti's injury is the most serious blow the Yankee pennant hopes have suffered all year. It was only after Frank had been injured that his true fielding ability was realized. Without Crosetti the Yankees slid out of the pennant picture like a drunk on an escalator.

Obviously the home office took no chances with Crosetti's trick knee. Frank will have to be in tip-top shape if the Yankees are to be in the '36 pennant race. Therefore his transfer to Johns Hopkins.

At present the Yankees are nursing a five-game winning streak, but it serves only to solidify second place, inasmuch as those whooping Tigers have pulled nine games into the clear. There is a good chance of the Yankee string being increased here, for Shibe Park has proved a fruitful stop for them all season. They have lost only one game here and have won eight.

DANIEL'S DOPE

Special to the World-Telegram

CINCINNATI, Sept. 4.—This department's operative in the Pacific Coast League sends a strangely lugubrious report. In past years he radiated enthusiasm and oozed optimism. But this season, he confesses sadly, the circuit beyond the Sierras is low in potential major league talent. However, what his scouting sheet lacks in general ardor it compensates for in unbounded praise of Joe Di Maggio, the 20-year-old right fielder of the San Francisco Seals, who has been bought by the Yankees.

Since the days when they brought Hal Chase from Cincinnati the Yankees have leaned heavily on the Pacific Coast League for reinforcements. Our Coast agent reports that the Ruppert Rifles have purchased not only Di Maggio but Bernie Uhalt, who came up with Stan Bordagaray to the White Sox last year, and Bill Raimondi, a young catcher who has been showing plenty with the Oakland club.

Joe Devine, who has replaced Bill Essick as the Coast League ivory hunter of the Yankees this year, also is watching Gene Lillard, Los Angeles third baseman, and Al Wright, second baseman, who had a trial with the Braves in 1933.

Our man sends word that the showing of Di Maggio this summer has convinced Devine that the knee which the young Italian injured in 1934 had healed completely.

Di Maggio's fine recovery from his injury traces to a cure suggested by Ty Cobb, who lives in Burlingame, near San Francisco, and is very close to Charley Graham, president of the Seals.

* * *

IN 1919 Cobb suffered a severe knee injury. The following winter Ty did a lot of hunting. He wore the heaviest boots he could buy, and loaded the soles with lead strips. For months Ty walked over hill and dale and trudged through the woods, strengthening that knee.

In 1920 Cobb opened the season wearing extra heavy spikes. The experts shook their heads and announced that at last the one and only Cobb had slowed up. But soon Ty discarded the heavy hardware and began to show his old speed all over again.

* * *

McCarthy's First Job Will Be To Teach Di Maggio Bunting.

OUR coast agent tempers his super-enthusiasm over Di Maggio with the admission that Joe has one outstanding weakness. He cannot bunt. That will be Joe McCarthy's first task down at St. Petersburg, Fla., next March—the job of showing Di Maggio the varied uses of the bastinado.

"We believe Di Maggio is even faster than Paul Waner was out here, and has even bigger possibilities," writes our scout. "Di Maggio is hitting around .400 and looks like a sure thing to win the batting championship. He has thirty-five assists, which must be some sort of record for an outfielder.

"Joe stands at the plate without any fancy motions. He holds his bat still and ready, and hits line drives, almost to dead left field. Joe is a right-handed hitter. McCarthy will have to show him how to push a ball into right, and hit behind the runner.

Yankees Send Five Players to Seals In Di Maggio Deal

Three players have been sent outright to the San Francisco club and two others go on option to complete the deal for the young outfielder Joe Di Maggio, it was announced by the Yankees today.

Floyd Newkirk, righthanded pitcher, who was with Newark and the Yankees last season; James Densmore, also a righthanded hurler, who performed for Sacramento last season, and Eddie Farrell, infielder with the Newark Bears, are the players who become the property of the Seals.

Ted Norbert, outfielder, farmed out to Binghamton during the 1934 season, and Leslie Powers, first baseman, who played with Sacramento, go out on option.

Di Maggio is scheduled to report to the Newark Bears next fall to prepare for service with the Yankees.

DANIEL'S  DOPE

WITH Colonel Jacob Ruppert gone to Los Angeles and Ed Barrow resting at a camp in the Adirondacks, things will be very quiet in the offices of the Yankees for the next three weeks. Then things will begin to sizzle. For the front office seems to be determined to do something about a situation which has produced nothing but place money since the big season of 1932.

"We have had some conversations, but nothing has been done, and right now I cannot say that we really have any irons in the fire," said Barrow before he left for the North Woods.

Yankees Turn Down $35,000
Gift for Di Maggio Release

BARROW did talk about Joe Di Maggio, the new outfielder from San Francisco. "If this kid is half the ball player all the scouts insist he is, we certainly have landed a big bargain."

The New York club some time ago declined a profit of $35,000 in the Di Maggio deal. Because of the outfielder's bad leg, Colonel Ruppert was able to buy an option to purchase Di Maggio for $25,000 and five players. Had Di Maggio been sound it would have taken an immediate outlay of $50,000 to swing the deal.

Last August Eddie Collins went out to the Coast and saw Di Maggio. Eddie followed the Seals around for a week and then made an offer of $60,000 for the player. Of course, Collins knew of the conditional sale to the Yankees.

San Francisco then placed the Boston offer before Barrow and Ed's reply was a telegram clinching the original deal.

It is said that this is the first time in the history of baseball that a big league club has had the chance to cash in to the tune of $35,000 on a minor league player who never had seen a major league city, let alone had a trial with a major club.

Di Maggio's travels never have carried him out of the Pacific Coast League. In fact, when he signed with the Seals in 1933 he never had gone so far as Oakland, which is only across the bay from San Francisco.

* * *

COAST Leaguers told the writer at the world series that Di Maggio had only one flaw in his baseball make-up. Joe cannot bunt. However, a batter hitting in the topmost brackets can get along with only an elementary education in the use of the bastinado.

_____

Another sport. DiMaggio gets ready to take the plunge with his longtime friend and manager of the Seals, Lefty O'Doul.

Joe DiMaggio

REMEMBER, I'M STILL YOUNG, TOO!

··HIS OLDER BROTHER, VINCENT, NOW WITH THE HOLLYWOOD CLUB, ALSO IS LIKELY TO MOVE UP TO THE BIG SHOW BEFORE LONG.

- HE, TOO, CAN HIT!!

- JOE WAS THE SENSATION OF THE PACIFIC COAST LEAGUE IN 1933, HIS FIRST YEAR IN PRO BALL.
··HE HIT SAFELY IN 61 CONSECUTIVE GAMES THAT SEASON.

DI MAGGIO 'MOST VALUABLE' IN COAST LEAGUE

Seal Outfielder 'Tops' With Only Three Years' Experience

Joe Almost Unanimous Choice, Being Far Ahead of Veteran Bill Cissell, Runner-Up

By E. G. BRANDS

HAILED as the greatest all-round player produced by the San Francisco Seals in many years, Joe DiMaggio, the youthful outfield star who will graduate to the New York Yankees next year after only three seasons of professional ball, also has received distinction as the most valuable player to his team in the Pacific Coast League for 1935. A committee of sports writers for THE SPORTING NEWS gave DiMaggio that honor by a wide margin over 24 other players considered, in the annual selection, awarding him 46 points out of a possible 48.

DiMaggio was picked by every member of the committee, four of them placing him first and two naming him for second. Richard Barrett of Seattle and Bill Cissell of Portland were the only others getting votes for first place, each being mentioned once. Cissell also drew one vote each for second and third place, which enabled him to become runner-up to DiMaggio, just a point ahead of Jim Oglesby of Los Angeles.

The vote for the most valuable player in the Coast league, based on eight points for first and ranging downward to one for eighth place, follows:

Joe DiMaggio, outfielder, San Francisco Seals, 46.
Bill Cissell, second baseman, Portland, 21.
Jim Oglesby, first baseman, Los Angeles, 20.
Oscar Eckhardt, outfielder, Missions, 15.
Gilbert English, third baseman, Portland, 11.
Cedric Durst, outfielder, Hollywood, 11.
William Outen, catcher, Missions, 11.
Arnold Statz, outfielder, Los Angeles, 10.
John Frederick, outfielder, Sacramento, 9.

Richard Barrett, pitcher, Seattle, 8.
Keith Molesworth, shortstop, Oakland, 6.
Harry Davis, first baseman, Portland, 6.
Gene Lillard, third baseman, Los Angeles, 5.
Clyde Beck, shortstop, Missions, 5.
Emil Mailho, outfielder, Oakland, 5.
Mike Hunt, outfielder, Seattle, 5.
Leroy Anton, first baseman, Oakland, 4.
Frank Shellenback, pitcher, Hollywood, 4.
John Bottarini, catcher, Seattle, 3.
Smead Jolley, outfielder, Hollywood, 2.
Howard Craghead, pitcher, Seattle, 2.
Harry Rosenberg, outfielder, Sacramento, 1.
Bernard Uhalt, outfielder, Oakland, 1.
Paul Gregory, pitcher, Sacramento, 1

It is interesting to note that four of the 25 mentioned will get trials with major league clubs next spring: DiMaggio with the New York Yankees; Eckhardt with the Brooklyn Dodgers; Gilbert English and Gene Lillard with the Chicago Cubs. Harry Davis was recalled by the Detroit Tigers, but later released to Toledo of the American Association. Frank Demaree, who had a big year with the Chicago Cubs as an outfielder the past season, was the 1934 choice for the most valuable player.

Outfielders were more strongly favored by the committee than players in any other position, 11 of the flyhawks being mentioned for a total of 109 points. Three first basemen obtained 30 points and one second baseman gained 21. Two third basemen gathered 16 points, four pitchers 15, two catchers 14 and two shortstops 11.

Deadpan Joe, as DiMaggio is known on the Coast, because he seldom shows any emotion, has enjoyed a meteoric career. Born at Martinez, Cal., November 25, 1914, he played shortstop on the San Francisco sand-lots, where his hitting attracted the attention of Seals officials. When only 19 years old, he was given a trial by the San Francisco club in the spring of 1933, but it was soon evident to Manager Jimmy Caveney that shortstop wasn't his natural position and the youngster was shifted to the outfield, where he made good from the start. That season Joe startled the Pacific Coast League by hitting safely in 61 consecutive games to surpass the league record of 49, made by Jack Ness in 1925. He finished the season with a batting mark of

Trick Knee Seems to Be Only Likely Handicap in Test With Yanks in '36

.340. The following year he boosted his average to .341 and the past season he climbed to .398, only one point behind Oscar Eckhardt, who was the league leader.

Joe's record for the 1935 season is a strong recommendation for his 'fitness to wear the title of the most valuable player in the league. In addition to finishing second in the league in hitting, with the lofty mark of .398, DiMaggio led in runs scored, with 173; in runs batted in, with 154; in triples, with 18; was second in home runs, with 34; fourth in doubles, with 48; eighth in stolen bases, with 24, and first among the outfielders in assists, with 32.

DiMaggio, a young giant in build, possesses a strong throwing arm and covers a lot of ground. When he broke in with the Seals he stood six feet and weighed 185 pounds, but since then he has continued to fill out and now is several inches over six feet and weighs 190 pounds. Broad of beam and knock-kneed, Joe carries a lot more speed than his appearance seems to indicate. He has only one apparent handicap in his forthcoming effort to make good with the Yankees and that is a trick knee, which has forced him to take several vacations from duty. However, his record for his three years as a professional player tends to support the belief he is one of the brightest prospects in years and establishes beyond a doubt his right to be named the most valuable player in the Coast league.

Members of the committee making the selections were: John Connolly, sports editor of the Los Angeles Examiner; L. H. Gregory, sports editor of the Portland Oregonian; Al Vermeer of the Oakland Post-Enquirer; Royal Brougham, sports editor of the Seattle Post-Intelligencer, Ed R. Hughes of the San Francisco Chronicle, and Steve George, sports editor of the Sacramento Union, representing the six cities in the league, two clubs operating in each San Francisco and Los Angeles—the Seals and Missions in the former and Angels and Hollywood in the latter.

COAST LEAGUERS at the world series went daffy about Di Maggio, who is in grave danger of coming into St. Petersburg too highly touted.

"You should have seen Joe hit that one in Los Angeles." "You should have seen Joe throw out Bill Doakes at the plate." "You should have seen Di Maggio run from first to third on an infield out."

Di Maggio throws strikes from center field. But from short he can't reach first base. He likes to fool around shortstop when he isn't shagging flies.

Di Maggio Comes Up With Two Strikes on Him as Innocent Victim of Lavish Newspaper Ballyhoo

REACHES BIG SHOW WITH BRILLIANT RECORD

Fans Expect Recruit from Coast to Be Cobb, Ruth, Jackson in One

Philly Scribe Recalls Highly-Touted Paul Strand Failed to Make Good at Same Time Unknown Simmons Starred

By C. WILLIAM DUNCAN

HEN Joe Di Maggio shoves off from the Pacific Coast in the spring and turns southward to compete against other recruits in the New York Yankees' camp, he'll have youth, ability and ambition on his side. But fighting against the energetic Joe will be the greatest foe of the Double A rookie star—the old ballyhoo.

Di Maggio will probably slug the apple to distant parts of the training camp and circle the bases with tremendous speed. He'll snare long drives and throw rifle-shot returns to the infield. The boys will write columns home about Joe and when he goes around the circuit the fans will be looking for a new Ty Cobb, Joe Jackson and Babe Ruth—all rolled into one!

When the pitchers bear down during the regular season, Joe won't hit .400 and will start to worry. Then will come the deciding point. If he gets a grip on himself, forgets the build-up and howl of the fans and stays in there, he'll become a great major leaguer, like Tony Lazzeri, who overrode the ballyhoo. If he loses his grip on himself, he'll falter and stumble and go back to the minors to sit alongside Paul Strand on the perch of unpleasant memories.

Poor Paul Strand. It is over a decade since Paul came to the Athletics with Al Simmons, but a decade to a man approaching 40 doesn't seem like long ago and I remember it as if it were last week.

Years had passed since Connie Mack had won a pennant with Bender, Plank and Coombs and the famous $100,000 infield of McInnis, Collins, Barry and Baker. The fans were hungry for another winner and Con-nie was "going out and getting them," as they say in football. He was laying the foundation for another great machine, a machine that with Grove and Earnshaw, the mighty Cochrane and others, who came in subsequent years, was to win three titles in 1929, 1930 and 1931.

Connie had fond hopes of what Paul Strand would do and so had the fans who had read all about the fence-busting feats of this outfielder who not only burned up the Pacific Coast League, but had all major and minor managers talking about him.

* * *

Simmons, Up at Same Time, Given Little Attention by Scribes

IT WAS written, incidentally, that another promising outfielder named Al Simmons was coming from the Milwaukee club of the American Association, but nobody paid much attention to the announcement. The fans wanted to see Strand!

Well, they saw him.

I can vision the big fellow, a right-handed hitter, doing his level best to come through. Strand tried, if ever a recruit did try. He tried too hard; that was the trouble. There had been so much ballyhoo about him, the fans expected too much.

He couldn't get going. The Philadelphia fans started their razzberries, known from one end of the circuit to the other, and Paul faltered badly.

What happened is now history. Strand passed out of the American League, back to the minors and we in Philadelphia haven't heard of him since.

By the time Strand had stepped out of the picture, the writers and spectators awoke to find that the fellow who came along the same time as Strand, the outfielder named Simmons, was hitting the ball hard and fielding his position well. Many laughed at his stance and they called him Bucket Foot Al, but he made hits and that was what they paid off on.

Simmons played the entire schedule of games and hit for .308. As the years rolled on, he developed into what many consider the greatest outfielder who ever wore a Philadelphia uniform.

During the championship days, as all fans recall, it was the hitting trio of Cochrane, Simmons and Foxx that wrecked opposing pitchers. As a fielder, Simmons had no superiors in the left garden. He covered worlds of territory and threw accurately.

Suppose the positions of Strand and Simmons had been reversed. Suppose Al had received all the build-up and been hailed as the hitting prospect of the age, while Strand was temporarily forgotten. Would Strand have made good? Would Simmons have failed?

Nobody knows.

We do know that Strand didn't last one season and ballyhoo killed him just as surely as an assassin killed Huey Long.

To me, the Strand case stands out preeminently, but there have been others.

I recall Jimmy O'Connell, also from the Pacific Coast League. His career was cut short by a mix-up in proceedings that didn't meet with the approval of the authorities. But, even up to that time, Jimmy hadn't lived up to expectations and he had been built up plenty.

Remember the case of the late Len Koenecke? He played splendid ball for Brooklyn in 1934, but that was on his second trip to the National League. The first time up he went to the Giants from Indianapolis. John McGraw was reputed to have paid $75,000 for him.

I recall Len with the Giants, at the Phillies' park trying vainly to get a hit or two. "What a lemon for 75,000 bucks," howled the fans. "We can buy all the lemons in California for that much dough."

Koenecke didn't make the grade on that trip. Ballyhoo had killed him. When he came back the second time, the pressure was off and he produced big dividends.

True, his work fell off this year, but in 1934, Len showed enough to indicate a long major league career was ahead of him. It is too bad he didn't live to fully redeem himself.

Al Vermeer in a dispatch to THE SPORTING NEWS from Oakland gave an idea of what's ahead of Di Maggio when he wrote of the meeting between Joe and Jacob Ruppert, who turns out fine ball teams and luscious brew for the folks of old New York.

Al wrote:

"Unfortunately, Joe wasn't so dynamic that afternoon, going hitless in two times at bat and blundering on his only chance in center field. But, as the Colonel said, maybe Joe was pressing too much in his efforts to win the admiration of his new boss.

"Many of the fans here on the Coast believe Di Maggio is being given too much of a build-up in New York and eastern columns. They are confident of his ultimate success in big time, but wish to make clear Joe, after all, is still a boy and will make mistakes, just as do the rest.

"However, he departs from the Pacific Coast League with a brilliant record for the 1935 season. He hit .398, finishing second to Oscar Eckhardt of the Missions. He led all outfielders in assists with 35 and topped the league in runs scored with 173."

What can be done about cutting down the ballyhoo on Di Maggio? The answer is "Nothing." It will surprise Pacific Coast League followers to learn that Di Maggio was unknown to thousands of fans prior to the announcement he would actually join the Yanks in the spring of 1936.

It is true he obtained nation-wide publicity when he created a record out there for consecutive hitting, but such feats are soon forgotten. Fans who are smart enough to read THE SPORTING NEWS are kept in touch with baseball from a national standpoint. Those who do not, know only what is going on in the major leagues. A minor fan follows the majors because he thinks his favorite may some day play there. A **major league fan, as a rule, cares little** about his favorite when he passes out of the big show. For instance, there will be a few items here about the progress of Max Bishop as manager of Portland—that's all. It is rather deplorable, yet true, that stars are so soon forgotten.

Di Maggio as a Coast leaguer was one thing; as a Yankee, another, in the minds of the American League fans.

Now they want to know all about him. What he does is news and it is up to the members of the craft to supply news. News becomes ballyhoo at times and so we are right back where we started.

The newspapermen will not cut down on Di Maggio stories. They can't, because training camp stories are scarce and every move made by the recruit at the conditioning base next spring will be watched.

It's up to Joe.

If he is going to worry and press as did Paul Strand, t.ere are breakers ahead.

If he is the type who can forget outside pressure and go out there and play ball and ride right through the ballyhoo, he is destined for a long career as a big league headliner.

I hope Di Maggio is the latter type and gets by that bad first year. When he can play naturally it will be easy as, with such a record, he must be a great ball player.

Baseball, as a whole, needs new stars to stimulate interest.

Joe DiMaggio

JACKSON
RUTH
COBB

THE OLD BALLYHOO WILL BE DI MAGGIO'S TOUGHEST FOE. FANS WHO HAVE BEEN READING THE NICE THINGS SAID ABOUT HIM. WILL EXPECT A RUTH, JACKSON AND COBB ALL ROLLED IN ONE

SIMMONS

HIGHLY TOUTED PAUL STRAND CRUMBLED ON MACK, BUT "BUCKET FOOT AL" SOARED TO THE HEIGHTS

BALLYHOO BULLETS

ED. MAC.

TOO MUCH BALLYHOO HAS MADE MANY GOOD RECRUITS RETREAT.

High Praise for Di Maggio

California Scribes Rate New Yankee Best Player Developed on West Coast.

By HARRY GRAYSON,
NEA Service Sports Editor.

WITH customary reserve Pacific Coast League baseball writers tell me Joe Di Maggio is the best ball player ever developed out there.

"Offhand I would say there is only one finer ball player alive, and his name is Charley Gehringer," says Tommy Laird, sports editor of the San Francisco News.

"Di Maggio is likely to kill an opposing infielder at any time," asserts Gene Coughlin, of the Los Angeles Post-Record.

"Di Maggio has the strongest and most accurate arm since Long Bob Meusel," testifies Bob Cronin, of the Los Angeles Illustrated Daily News.

"Di Maggio never makes a mistake on the bases," says Rudy Hickey, of the Sacramento Bee.

"You've seldom seen a more accomplished flychaser," reports Cliff Harrison, of the Seattle Star.

"Di Maggio plays ball with grim intensity," asserts Billy Stepp, of the Portland News-Telegram.

With advance notices like that Di Maggio, who reports to the St. Petersburg camp of the New York Yankees next spring, has a lot to live up to.

The Pacific Coast League has turned out some pretty good ones—Roger Peckinpaugh, Dave Bancroft, the Waners, Curt Davis, Franklin Demaree, Stanley Hack, Bob Meusel, Earl Averill, Gus Suhr, Tony Lazzeri, Chic Gandil, Swede Risberg, to mention a few.

Di Maggio, who plays right field, is a right-hand hitter, standing 6 feet 1 inch and weighing 195 pounds. There is tremendous power in his compact swing. He takes a fairly tight grip with his strong hands. He stands firmly in the box, and his batting stride is short. He swats all kinds of pitching. He was the hardest of coast leaguers to fool, and murdered a change of pace.

Di Maggio is so serious that they call him Dead Pan Joe. He is pictured as a ballplayer without nerves. He likes to play ball.

Di Maggio, who is 21, injured a knee a year ago and again during the last season, but his getting in practically every game played by the San Francisco Seals is something in the way of proof that the joint is not of the tricky variety.

Ruppert Gets Acquainted With Di Maggio

OAKLAND, Cal.—Col. Jacob Ruppert, owner of the elaborate New York Yankee organization, perched in a box seat at the Oaks' park here and took his first look at Joe Di Maggio, dynamic Seal outfielder, who next season joins the Ruppert forces in New York.

Unfortunately, Joe wasn't so dynamic that afternoon, going hitless in two times at bat and blundering on his only chance in center field. But, as the Colonel said, maybe Joe was pressing a little too much in his efforts to win the admiration of his new boss.

The occasion of the game, held October 27, was the eighth annual charity game of the Alameda Elks, with many major and minor league stars taking part, including Augie Galan, Stan Hack, Johnny Vergez, Myril Hoag, Joe Cronin, Babe Dahlgren, Dick Bartell, Gussie Suhr, Ernie Lombardi, Bud Hafey, Alex Kampouris, Harry Lavagetto, Bill Brenzel and Tony Freitas.

Considering all these men, along with many others, to be natives of the bay region, it is little wonder why Central California baseball fans are so deeply interested in what happens in the major leagues.

But to return to Di Maggio, many of the fans here on the Coast believe he is being given too much of a build-up in New York and eastern columns. They are confident of his ultimate success in big time, but wish to make clear that Joe, after all, is still a boy and will make mistakes, just as do the rest.

However, he departs from the Pacific Coast League with a brilliant record for the 1935 season. Among his accomplishments are:

Hit .398, finishing second to Oscar Eckhardt of the Missions. Led all outfielders in assists, with 35. Topped the league in runs scored, with 173. Was second in hits, with 270. Eckhardt had 283. Third in two-base hits, with 48. Oglesby of Los Angeles and Clabaugh of Portland each had 56. Led in triples, with 18. Second in home runs, with 29, and that in the huge Seals' Stadium. Gene Lillard of the Angels was tops, with 56. Eighth in stolen bases, with 24. First in runs batted in, with 154.

Ruppert was here with George Weiss, head of the Yankee farm system, and plans were roughly outlined for the 1936 campaign. The Oakland club, while not owned by the Yankees, works with that team as a farm club and last season found close to a dozen young Yanks playing here. Names of players coming here will be announced after November 20. AL VERMEER.

Minor leaguer Joe DiMaggio shown with New York Yankees owner Jake Ruppert in 1935, the year before he moved up to major leagues.

PACIFIC COAST LEAGUE records for the past season no doubt hit Joe Di Maggio, the new boy wonder of the Yankees, right between the eyes when they were announced today. Joe had figured that he was being graduated by the San Francisco Seals with the distinction of having won the 1935 batting championship of the Coast circuit. But the averages prove that Di Maggio was nosed out by Oscar Eckhardt, sold by the Missions to the Dodgers, by a scant point. Oscar took the title with .399.

While Di Maggio failed to acquire the batting championship, he took a lot of other knick-knacks in the league of the Far West. Joe led the organization in scoring runs with 173. He drove in 154 runs and got 34 homers and 24 steals. When the fielding records are announced they will show Di Maggio with the phenomenal total of 37 assists. The pride of North Beach, San Francisco, certainly will be a much publicized young man when he hits the Yankee camp at St. Petersburg.

1936
A YANKEE ROOKIE

Rookie Joe DiMaggio is greeted by New York Yankees owner, Colonel Jacob Ruppert, in 1936. Looking on is manager, Joe McCarthy. Ruppert owned the ballclub through 1939 and McCarthy was its manager through 1946.

JOINING THE YANKEES

I had never been east of the Rockies when we drove from San Francisco to St. Petersburg, Florida, in 1936 for my first spring training session with the Yankees. I was riding with two fellow San Franciscans, Frankie Crosetti and Tony Lazzeri, both already established Yankee stars. We got along well but I had a worry they didn't have — making the team.

We reported to Miller Huggins Field in St. Petersburg in late February. Our manager, Joe McCarthy, greeted me and told me not to worry about anything. Tony Lazzeri introduced me to all the other Yankees and made me feel at ease. I sensed immediately a feeling of loyalty and harmony among the ballplayers.

Frankie Crosetti offered to room with me. And I was, so to speak, off and running.

Joe DiMaggio

1936

JOE DiMAGGIO STATISTICS

Games	138
At Bats	637
Hits	206
Doubles	44
Triples	15*
Home Runs	29
Runs Scored	132
Runs Batted In	125
Bases on Balls	24
Strike Outs	39
Stolen Bases	4
Slugging Average	.576
Batting Average	.323

* Led the American
  League

STANDINGS

	Won	Lost	Percentage	Games Behind
New York Yankees	102	51	.667	
Detroit Tigers	83	71	.539	19.5
Chicago White Sox	81	70	.536	20
Washington Senators	82	71	.536	20
Cleveland Indians	80	74	.519	22.5
Boston Red Sox	74	80	.481	28.5
St. Louis Browns	57	95	.375	44.5
Philadelphia A's	53	100	.346	49

DANIEL'S DOPE

THE postman brought a large, promising envelope into the offices of Ed Barrow, general manager of the Yankees. It bore a San Francisco mark. Ed grabbed it with avidity. He frowned; then he smiled. "It's from Joe Di Maggio," Barrow explained. "It seems he was misquoted. Anyway, he has too many advisers out there."

"Well, somebody is steering Joe in the direction of real dough," the writer suggested. Barrow countered—"Why, there isn't $4 between us and Di Maggio! Those stories out of San Francisco are crazy."

Barrow, of course, declined to let your correspondent take a squint at the letter. From what we can gather, Di Maggio got $750 a month from the Seals—$4,500 for the season. He may have had a bonus arrangement which was not in his contract. Pursuant to baseball law, the Yankees apparently gave Joe the required 25 per cent increase of $1,125 and sent him a contract for $5,625.

Joe wants $8,000. If he is only half as good as Coast League enthusiasts shout he is, Giuseppe is worth at least what he wants.

In any event, it is almost certain that Di Maggio will be on hand when the first squad of the New York club opens training on March 2.

"How fast are those unsigned contracts bouncing back at you?" the writer asked. "We are signing our men as fast as any other club," bridled Barrow.

'Timid' DiMaggio Refuses to Sign Yankee Contract

By ROGER BIRTWELL.

The Yanks stopped worrying yesterday about the bashfulness of Joe DiMaggio. Their slugging acquisition from the Pacific Coast League, who is the most ballyhooed rookie since the days of Kelley and O'Toole, had been pictured as so timid he'd stand with his hat in his hand for an hour before walking through a subway turnstile. They feared he'd be too frightened to play big league ball. But when he became a holdout last night they decided he had plenty of nerve—too much, in fact.

In return for DiMaggio, the Yanks gave four players and $25,000. For more than a year Coast papers have hailed him as the greatest outfielder in Coast League history. When the Yanks sent him a contract for a puny sum, Joe said "nix." Reports from San Francisco indicate he's holding out for $8,000 a year.

While the Yanks were worrying about having to pay DiMaggio a living wage, the Giants absorbed a bit of culture and increased their intellectual batting average by signing Steve Kuk and Clary Anderson, two Colgate products. Anderson is a catcher, while Kuk played both third base and the outfield while performing for Bill Reid, mayor of Hamilton, N. Y., who coaches the Maroon ballchuckers.

One of the Dodgers' two fugitives from Bob Quinn's Boston Bee-hive, Randy Moore, signed with the Dodgers yesterday. Harry Eisenstat, former schoolboy hurler at James Madison, also signed a Brooklyn bill of lading as did Tom Baker, big hurler who joined the late last season.

Di Maggio, Outfield Recruit, Wires Acceptance of Terms to Yankees

Coast Star Ends Threat of Holdout for Sum Said to Be $8,000 —Richardson, Uhalt and Tobin Sign—Jordan in Dodgers' Fold—Big Enrollment at Terry's Baseball School.

By ROSCOE McGOWEN.

Joe Di Maggio, the young San Franciscan who is expected to be one of Manager Joe McCarthy's most important outfielders this year, has deserted the holdout ranks of the Yankees, Business Manager Ed Barrow announced yesterday.

Di Maggio hasn't signed his contract yet but in answer to a wire from Barrow he agreed to terms and the attested document will be filed as soon as the mail can deliver it here. His salary was not revealed, but it is known that the 22-year-old Coast League star was seeking $8,000 or more.

"You know I told you," said Barrow, "that we were not very far apart and when I wired him he came right back with an acceptance." From which it may be inferred that Di Maggio will get close to what he desired.

Three other Yankees returned their signed contracts—Nolen Richardson, shortstop; Bernard Uhalt, outfielder, and James Tobin, right-hand pitcher.

Tobin, Barrow revealed, has just undergone an appendicitis operation in Oakland, Calif., but is recovering nicely and will be on hand with the battery men when they report at St. Petersburg, Fla., March 1.

Jordan Versatile Infielder.

Business Manager John Gorman of Brooklyn weighed in with the announcement that Jimmy Jordan, Casey Stengel's prize utility infielder, has returned his signed contract. Jimmy hit only .278 last year in playing all infield positions except first base but drove in many runs.

Russell Olsen, rookie shortstop, originally acquired from the Davenport club of the Western League,

has been sent on option to that club for the coming season. Olsen played with Sacramento last year and fielded well but hit poorly.

With the Giant offices closed yesterday the only news of that organization came in a special bulletin from Bill Terry's baseball school at Pensacola, Fla.

The bulletin gives the information that there are twenty-four first basemen, seventeen third basemen, seventeen shortstops, fourteen catchers, thirty-seven pitchers and twenty-nine outfielders going through their paces there, with the school only in its second week. Frank Snyder, Tom Clarke, Adolfo Luque, Travis Jackson and Hank DeBerry are the instructors in charge. Mel Ott has been there, but only as a spectator.

Terry's Position Seems Safe.

Despite the two dozen first basemen in his school, there is no indication that Manager Terry intends to bench First Baseman Terry this year.

An Associated Press interview with George Earnshaw in his home at Swarthmore yesterday struck an optimistic note for Stengel. The Big Moose, who finished as a strong first-string hurler for Brooklyn last season, predicts the Dodgers will finish in the first division next Fall.

Earnshaw made his prophecy on his return from Hot Springs for a visit at home before heading for Clearwater to complete his training. He is certain Brooklyn will get a cut of world series cash but would not commit himself on how many games he will win.

"It all depends," he said, "on how the arm feels—and on the rest of the club."

Joe Di Maggio Going to Camp Ahead of Yanks

Ruppert Team Lists Only 28 Spring Exhibition Games.

By DANIEL.

Along with the spring training schedule of the Yankees today came the word that Joe DiMaggio, the new outfielder with an amazing string of Pacific Coast League achievements, would be the first to get his marching orders to St. Petersburg, Fla. The first squad, which will report to Joe McCarthy at Miller Huggins Field on Monday, March 2, will consist almost entirely of pitchers and catchers. But McCarthy has decided to have Di Maggio on the scene early and let him get acquainted by easy stages.

"Colonel Ruppert, who saw Di Maggio in San Francisco some time ago, got the impression that the young man is very shy," said Ed Barrow today. "It would be a mistake to take him into camp all of a sudden, with the second squad, on March 9. Besides, Joe may want to devote a little time to Di Maggio, in particular, before the entire roster starts work."

Barrow examined Di Maggio's record for 1935. He read the reports of his scouts. "If this kid is even half as good as the dope and the scouts insist he is, everything will be grand."

Training Schedule Reduced To Twenty-eight Games.

The Yankee training schedule, opening with the Braves at St. Petersburg on March 14, and closing with the Dodgers at Ebbets Field on April 12, has been reduced to only twenty-eight games. The annual series with the Braves, which ran through nine meetings last spring, has been cut to seven.

The Yankee schedule shows that the club again has adhered to its old system of refusing to play other American League teams during the training season.

Five National League clubs—the Braves, Dodgers, Cardinals, Cubs and Reds—will be met. The Giants are barred, the Phillies do not seem to fit into the list, and the Pirates will be out in San Antonio, Tex.

With the return of the Dodgers to Clearwater, near St. Petersburg, the old home-and-home arrangement has been revived, for March 24 and 25. And, of course, there will be three games with the Dodgers at Ebbets Field, on April 10, 11 and 12. The Yankees will open their league season at home.

Only Six Stops on Way to Series in Brooklyn.

The Yankee schedule is in marked contrast to the list which soon will be issued by the Giants, and which once more will show Bill Terry's men as pretty constant riders of the rattlers of Dixie. With Babe Ruth gone, and no adequate intriguer of Dixie fandom yet developed as a substitute, Barrow appreciates that the time is not yet ripe for returning to extended junkets.

As a result, the jump from St. Petersburg to Brooklyn will be made in nine days, with only six stops. On Tuesday, March 31, the Yanks will meet the Newark Bears. That evening the American Leaguers will break camp and head for Birmingham, where they will linger for two days. A three-day visit to Atlanta will follow.

Nashville, Knoxville, the farm at Norfolk and then Richmond, to be revisited for the first time in many years, complete the itinerary of the Yankees.

While the Yanks are at St. Pete, they will make four trips—to neighboring Bradenton, to tackle the Cardinals; Tampa, to meet the Reds; Sebring, the new camp of the Newark club, and Clearwater, to engage Casey Stengel's hopefuls.

Yanks Pin Hopes on Rookie

Di Maggio, Sensational Outfielder, May Be Deciding Factor in Pennant Problem.

By JAMES M. KAHN.

The Red Sox are looking to their newly acquired high priced stars to lead them to a pennant. The Tigers are counting on their seasoned talent, now supplemented by another veteran in Al Simmons, to carry them to their third straight American League championship. But the Yankees, unsuccessful so far in their trade talks with other clubs, are pinning their hopes on a rookie.

The rookie is Joe Di Maggio. Lou Gehrig, Lefty Gomez and the other old reliables, of course, will have to do their stuff, if the Yankees are to remain in the running. Di Maggio is not looked upon as the answer to all their problems. But if the Coast youngster lives up to his advance notices, they do see in him what might well be the difference between second place, where the Yanks finished last season, and first, where they hope to wind up this year.

There are some in the Yankee family who will be satisfied to see young Di Maggio measure up only partly to his advance notices. That, they concede, will still make him quite an asset. Certainly few rookies have ever been preceded into the big league by a build up as extravagant as that which Di Maggio will have to follow. It has been the unanimous opinion of every one who has seen the San Francisco Italian that he is a great ball player, and no less, in the making.

Di Maggio's Own Ballyhoo.

Di Maggio has made his own ballyhoo with his performances, a la Joe Louis. He is a devastating hitter, runs like a frightened antelope, and his throwing arm struck terror into the hearts of Pacific Coast League base runners last season. In fact, with more than thirty assists, he led all Coast outfielders in this department.

Probably at no other time in the history of the Yankees have they looked to a recruit with so much hope and expectation. Di Maggio's performances have been such that the most conservative of ivory judges cannot see him flopping. Furthermore, they all expect him to come through in his first year, to become that outfielder the Yanks need and whom they have been trying to land by trading with other American League clubs.

It has been the custom of baseball men to discount privately a lot of the Coast league averages. There has been a strong suspicion for some time that the booster spirit rampant on the sun-kissed slope has crept into the baseball averages and that they suffer a bit from inflation. Certainly many loudly acclaimed Coast rookies have failed badly in trying to make the big league grade, which has encouraged this view. But even with considerable deflation, Di Maggio's record last season stamps him as a prospect far above the average.

Heavy Hitting on Coast.

He led the Pacific Coast League in hitting with an average of .399, turning on the pressure in the closing weeks of the campaign to beat out Oscar Eckhardt of the Mission Club, who is going to camp this spring with the Dodgers. Young Joe, who is twenty-two years old and a right-handed hitter, need not fret about the wide open spaces of the left field sector at the Stadium, where right-handed fly ball hitters have met their Waterloo. He hits 'em on a line, and his "totals" show that he banged out forty-six two-baggers, seventeen three-baggers and thirty-four home runs among his 269 hits. He scored 171 runs and batted in 151. He really went to town.

Up to now the Yanks have had pretty fair luck with the ball players they procured from the Coast league. Bob Meusel, Mark Koenig, Lefty Gomez and Frank Crosetti are some of them. At the same time, if it means anything, they have had extraordinary luck with Pacific Coast Italians, Tony Lazzeria and Crosetti of the modern day Yanks, and the unforgettable Ping Bodie of happy days gone by, being the Signors in question. Though the raves which have come on ahead of him have sort of placed Di Maggio on the spot, certainly no rookie ever found such a ready spot to drop into, if it develops that he has the stuff.

O'Doul Says Di Maggio Is Better in Right Field

By the Associated Press.

SAN FRANCISCO, Jan. 24.— Frank (Lefty) O'Doul, manager of the San Francisco Seals, believes reported plans of the New York Yankees to play Joe Di Maggio in left instead of right field this season "would be a terrible mistake."

Di Maggio, who will make his big-league debut this year, played under O'Doul on last season's pennant-winning San Francisco club.

"Maybe when McCarthy sees Di Maggio in action he will change his mind," O'Doul said. "With Di Maggio in left, or even center, field one of his great abilities will be lost. I mean his throwing arm, which I consider the best in baseball."

Yankee Fans! Meet Joe Di Maggio

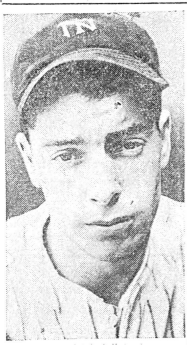

JOSEPH PAUL DI MAGGIO, JR., outfielder. . . . Born at Martinez, Cal., on November 25, 1914. . . . Weighs 195 pounds and stands just half an inch over six feet in height. . . . Has four sisters and four brothers. . . . His dad, 67 and a retired fisherman, speaks English imperfectly, but knows finer points of baseball. . . . When Joe first went into the Coast League with San Francisco, in 1932, his Italian father thought it was football and feared his lad's injury.

Joe began to play ball at 10 and five years later lost interest and went in for tennis. . . . But when brother Vincent landed with Seals, Joe figured he, too, might have an opportunity in the game. . . . In 1932 Joe played the last three games of the season at shortstop for the Seals. . . . The club was going nowhere and Augie Galan, regular shortstop, had left for Honolulu. . . . Joe demonstrated just how not to play the position. . . . However, in his first time up in league ball he got a triple off Ted Pillette.

In 1933 Giuseppe went to the Seal school and was signed. . . . Stewart, in right field, fell off in hitting and Manager Caveney sent Joe in as pinch hitter. . . . Di Maggio walked. . . . Caveney sent the new boy into right field. . . . Joe was amazed. . . . His brother Vince and Prince Oana were on the bench. . . . Joe kept right on playing regularly. . . . Likes the movies, but hasn't much use for books. . . . His brothers, Tom and Mike, are crab fishermen. . . . Nineteen-year-old Dominic is playing bush ball.

Joe's baseball hero is Joe Cronin. . . . The man from whom he got greatest help, Di Maggio says, is Frank O'Doul, who was his manager at San Francisco last year. . . . In 1933 Di Maggio set a Coast League record by hitting safely in sixty-one consecutive games. . . . Young Ed Walsh stopped him. . . . Joe likes spaghetti even if Tony Lazzeri doesn't. . . . Bats and throws righthanded. . . .

In New York, Joe DiMaggio poses with another Yankee legend, Lou Gehrig, within the arms of a certified superfan, the city's beloved mayor Fiorello LaGuardia.

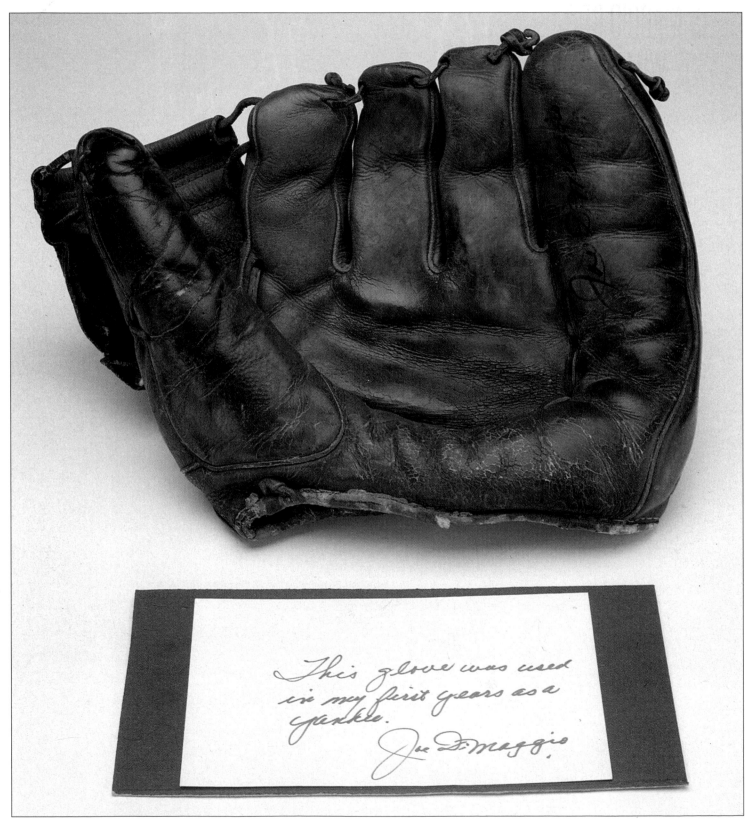

This glove was used in my first years as a Yankee.

Joe DiMaggio

The glove, authenticated. It is hard to believe that DiMaggio made the catches he did with a glove like this.

DI MAGGIO GETS IDEA OF WHAT'S TO COME

FANFARE FRIGHTENS YANK RECRUIT DESPITE HIS ICY VENEER

Coast Star a Quiet Lad, Determined Not

to Let Fan Expectations Down Him;

Hoag Groomed as Pitcher

T. PETERSBURG, Fla.—The Yanks are here! They assembled over the week-end, and started their training with a more or less complete squad of pitchers and catchers, aided and abetted by a few infielders and outfielders who could not wait for the second squad inaugural on March 9, and beat the gun. Among the early comers who hopped right into the limelight were Joe DiMaggio, the most talked-about minor league graduate of the year, and Myril Hoag, the outfielder, who is about to be converted into a pitcher.

DiMaggio was bought conditionally from the San Francisco Seals more than a year ago, and was left on the Coast for a season to improve his technique under Frank O'Doul—and to satisfy the New York office that the leg which Giuseppe injured getting out of a taxi in mid-season of 1934 was okay.

DiMaggio's showing last year was splendid, and the Yanks closed a deal in which San Francisco got $25,000 in cash, and five players, none of them of noteworthy ability. At the time the sale was made, there was some question about Joe's leg. But when the deal was closed, the Seals realized that they had made a poor bargain. The Red Sox offered $60,000 for DiMaggio.

Joe McCarthy says that Giuseppe from the North Beach end of San Francisco is his new left fielder. Present plans call for a fight in right between George Selkirk and Roy Johnson, with Ben Chapman a fixture in center.

Johnson, with Boston last season, outhit Selkirk by a point and there is a feeling that, at least until June 15, the Swedish Indian may keep Twinkletoes on the bench. However, Selkirk, who has plenty of that commodity the players call "moxie," promises plenty of fun and action, and the camp is set for a royal duel.

Much Fanfare Over DiMaggio Debut.

DiMaggio's debut as a Yankee has been celebrated with a fanfare of trumpets and a blowing of bugles. The picture men and the writers all have been giving Joe plenty of attention and, to tell the truth, he is a bit scared over the hullabaloo. Giuseppe is not the easiest guy in the world to get acquainted with. He is determined to keep a sane noggin above his Adam's apple, and not let publicity get the better of him.

Joe is confronted with a tough job. In the first place, there is the proposition of making good in the American League, with a club which gets all the good pitching from the opposition. That is a tremendous factor which must be figured in the showings of all newcomers in the Ruppert livery. Other clubs get the benefit of second and third-string hurling from the other teams. But when the seven other clubs battle the Yankees, the McCarthy gang gets no soft touches.

In addition to being confronted with the task of making good on his six-sheet publicity, DiMaggio is face to face with the fact that in New York there are thousands of fans who believe that the spaghetti kid from the Golden Gate will be the difference between second place, where the Yankees have finished three years in a row, and the pennant. Joe McCarthy, who usually is given to no outbursts, has given weight to the popular notion of DiMaggio's importance.

DiMaggio makes his debut with the New Yorks against a background of failure for so many other Coast league stars who came highly touted. Lyn Lary, who with Jimmy Reese cost $103,000 in cash, could not make the grade with the Yanks. Hoag, who cost $65,000, has yet to make a place for himself off the bench. Other Coast luminaries have failed in the Big City—notably Jimmy O'Connell, who cost the Giants $75,000 in cash.

McCarthy Now Says Di Maggio's Place in Outfield Unsettled.

"If there were anything wrong with Crosetti's leg, now would be the time to find out," McCarthy said, as he exulted over the recovery of Tony Lazzeri's running mate.

"Frank and I agreed that it would be best for him to extend himself as soon as he had limbered up. This he did yesterday, and you saw him in action. Well, that's one worry off my mind. And don't think it wasn't a big one!"

The last two days have seen secret outfield drills for Joe Di Maggio, the budding star from California. McCarthy waits until the general workout is finished and the crowd has gone and then takes Giuseppe in hand. Developments at these private sessions have not lessened McCarthy's estimate of the ability of his new flychaser.

However, McCarthy is not so definite now as to Di Maggio's ultimate destination on the New York picket line. During the winter Marse Joe kept reiterating his intention to send Di Maggio to left, with Chapman in center and George Selkirk battling Roy Johnson in right.

Now the boss of the Yankees insists he wants to wait until Di Maggio has played some exhibition games before talking about Giuseppe's ultimate post. McCarthy often is inscrutable, and it is hard to say just what is in his mind.

Di Maggio continues to impress not only in the field but at the plate. And his bashfulness has given way to a smile and readiness to talk and be one of the boys. Joe has done everything but throw. The camp is waiting for the young man to show his arm, with which he made thirty-six assists in the Coast League last season.

Di Maggio Impresses Yanks

McCarthy Expresses Keen Satisfaction Over First Week's Demonstration of Coast League Star.

By DANIEL,
World-Telegram Staff Correspondent.

ST. PETERSBURG, Fla., March 9.—Though Joe Di Maggio thus far has not driven a single ball to the right of second base, and from all appearance is a dead left field hitter, there will be no effofrt by Joe McCarthy to change the style of the new outfielder of the Yankees. That assurance came today from McCarthy, himself, who expressed keen satisfaction over the first week's demonstrations of the Californian.

"Even with due allowance for Pacific Coast League pitching Di Maggio, on his record, is a great hitter and what we have seen of him has added to that impression," McCarthy said. "So far he hasn't hit to right field. But I am told that he can do it. In the field he ranges well. The other day he made three catches which no outfielder this club has had in the last three years would have accomplished.

"It would be dangerous, and an injustice to the boy, to attempt to change him in any particular. If, under the stress of American League competition, he indicates that he needs some alterations in style there will be time enough then.

"I discussed certain things with him yesterday, and he said that while he was best acquainted with right field he was eager to do anything I wanted."

The writer asked the boss of the Yankees to name the outstanding feature of the first week of training, other than the debut of Di Maggio.

"Sundra," McCarthy replied. "You rarely get a rookie pitcher with that something extra which this big lad has shown us in six days of work. Every time I see him pitch I cross my fingers. He is big and strong and has a remarkable hurling repertoire. And he has style, as well. Will he develop control? Well, if he does we will have one of the most remarkable young pitchers in the big leagues.

Joe DiMaggio Gets Two Hits

Young Outfielder Plays Center as Yankee Regulars Beat Yannigans, 5–1, in First Game.

By DANIEL,
World-Telegram Staff Correspondent.

ST. PETERSBURG, Fla., March 11.—Joe DiMaggio, the expensive young outfielder who is expected to furnish the pennant punch for the New York Yankees this season, was the center of attention today as the Regulars beat the Yannigans, 5–1, in the first of the intra-club games.

DiMaggio, who batted third, Babe Ruth's old position, got two hits and fielded his position in center field faultlessly, but clouting honors went to George Selkirk. The latter hit a home run with one on.

Lou Gehrig failed to connect safely in five trips to the plate. Pat Malone worked the first three innings for the Regulars and was in rare form. The veteran did not permit a safety as he opened up for the first time since the training started.

Manager Joe McCarthy finally located Roy Johnson, his missing outfield candidate. It developed that Johnson was delayed when the airplane in which he was traveling from California was forced down by a heavy fog in a remote section.

Mrs. Johnson phoned the news to Ed Barrow in New York and the latter relayed the message here to McCarthy. Johnson is now en route by train. He was due last Sunday.

Di Maggio swings a bat which weighs forty ounces and is thirty-eight inches long. It may develop that Joe will have to cut down both on the size and weight of the bludgeon. He may not be able to bring the bat around fast enough against the type of fast-ball pitching he will see from Lefty Grove, Schoolboy Rowe, Mel Harder, Tommy Bridges and a few other lads in the American League.

When Babe Ruth hit sixty home runs he swung bats weighing more than fifty ounces. But since then thirty-four ounces is regarded as plenty of wood for any hitter.

Last Fraction of a Second Hitter, Like Tris Speaker.

Di Maggio is a peculiar batsman. He is not a long swinger, but a wrist swinger, with a terrific pull on the ball. He will have to learn to push that ball into right field or he will run into a peck of trouble. The Stadium in the Bronx is tough enough on a right-handed hitter even if he can smack an occasional ball into right. Neither Jimmy Foxx nor Al Simmons has a career average of .300 at the Yankee park.

In stance, one foot from the plate, with feet twelve inches apart, Di Maggio reminds you of Joe Jackson. But in his application of power at the very last fraction of a second Joe is more reminiscent of Tris Speaker. Earl Combs also had something of that knack. How Di Maggio gets so much power on the ball when it is right on top of him is amazing.

In build Joe is another Bob Meusel. The Italian lad has big strong arms, with tremendous wrists. His back muscles ripple in their sheaths.

In temperament Di Maggio is even and pleasant. He is not a mixer, for he sits too much by himself, thinking and looking out into the street. He is no reader of books.

Di Maggio No "Holler Guy," But There Isn't One on Club.

DiMaggio looks like a youngster who rarely gets excited. In that respect he closely resembles two other Italians of the Yankees, Tony Lazzeri and Frank Crosetti. That so-called hot Italian temper doesn't go with the three Romans of the Ruppert legion.

Certainly Di Maggio is no "holler guy." His feats may make him colorful, but his makeup promises no fanfare. The Yankees are sorely in need of what the ball players call a "holler guy"—a man like Leo Durocher. Johnny Allen did considerable hollering, but he is gone. And not one of the newcomers—Roy Johnson and the additional pitching talent included—is known as a jockey of even lesser degree.

Di Maggio came here with a reputation as a bashful boy. At first he fostered that impression. But he can talk. In fact, he insists he knows he can make the grade.

The position Di Maggio should play is right field. He wants to play there and that should be enough. But George Selkirk and Johnson also are right fielders. Placing Joe in the right spot is going to be no soft touch for McCarthy, and he admits it.

While Di Maggio wonders about his destiny, McCarthy is pretty much on the spot with the lad, as he is with so many other factors in the Yankee situation. Di Maggio has come here labeled "a genuine wonder." And it's up to McCarthy to give the fans what the label reads.

McCarthy Sees Shortstop
Ideal Man for First Spot

Di Maggio to Hit Ahead of Gehrig, Who Retains Clean-up Position—Chapman To Be Shoved Into Lower Brackets.

By DANIEL,
World-Telegram Staff Correspondent.

ST. PETERSBURG, Fla., March 12.—Preparing for the opening exhibition games of the Yankees with the Boston Braves here over the week-end, Joe McCarthy today began to evolve the batting order which his club will carry into the American League race.

The manager revealed to the World-Telegram that Frank Crosetti will be his 1936 leadoff man; that Joe Di Maggio will hit third and almost certainly start in left field; and that George Selkirk or Roy Johnson will come up behind Lou Gehrig, who will cling to the No. 4 spot.

"Of course, a training season is made up of a long series of experiments and the manager of a club often is forced to change his apparently definite decision over night," McCarthy opined. "But from the looks of things, our 1936 batting order will be headed by Crosetti, who is an ideal man for the place.

"We had Crosetti in the leadoff spot in 1934 and he did very well, indeed. Last season we sent either Earle Combs or Jess Hill, whichever happened to be playing left field, to bat first. Now, Hill is with Washington and Combs is a coach, and we must make a new arrangement.

"In the second spot, we need a man who can pull that ball into right field. Red Rolfe seems to get the nomination. He is not the ideal man for that position in the batting order, but will answer.

"From what I have seen of Di Maggio, he fits into the requirements of a No. 3 man. I could not let him hit behind Gehrig, as Joe sends too many balls into left field, which would place us in jeopardy of too many double plays.

"So, at this time, it looks like Di Maggio third, followed by Lou, with either Selkirk or Johnson hitting fifth. George and Roy will fight it out for the right field job. Both are well able to beat out those second outs.

"Until Ben Chapman reports, Di Maggio will play in center field. But with Ben on the job, Di Maggio will move over to left. I think it almost certain that Chapman will remain in center."

Dickey Threatens to Move
Up Behind Lou Gehrig.

McCarthy then discussed the possibility of Bill Dickey's moving in behind Gehrig in the batting order. If Bill continues to pull that ball into right field, and develops his old power and that threat for the right field bleachers in the Stadium, he will have to be shifted to the No. 5 spot.

Dickey has recovered from the shyness at the plate which sent him toppling to a .279 average last year, from his .322 mark of 1934. Until the lanky catcher was hit in the head last summer he was his old slugging self. But following that accident he moved so far to the outside of the batter's box that he hit everything to center and was a sucker for a lot of long flies.

Chapman and Tony Lazzeri are destined for the lower brackets in the New York batting order. Ben may not like this. But he got every opportunity in the No. 3 and No. 4 spots last season and wound up with nothing better than .289.

Chapman must rehabilitate himself as a hitter before he can command new consideration for a high post in the batting array. Ben isn't enough of a waiter to lead off, and his righthanded style disqualifies him as a No. 2 man.

With the "Iron Horse", Lou Gehrig.

Only Joe's Hitting in Doubt

Recruit, Still to Be Tried at Plate, May Oust Chapman From Center Field.

By JAMES M. KAHN.

ST. PETERSBURG, Fla., March 17.—If Yankee Joe DiMaggio can hit, he is going to be a recruit who will come up to the extravagant advance notices which preceded him into camp. Thus far he has demonstrated he can do everything else—field and throw—and there now remains only the final test which will be offered by the major league hurling he will have to look at in the scheduled exhibition games.

There is a certain amount of palpitation over this question which the weather has not allowed to be answered up to now, the games with the Bees on Saturday and Sunday having been lost forever by rain and wet grounds. With the resumption of hostilities against the Cardinals here today, there is a recurrent hope that the weather will tame down eventually and that the games which lie ahead for the Yanks will provide the opportunity for DiMaggio to show that he can hit.

Certainly that wonderful throwing arm of his has convinced the last of the camp skeptics in other respects. On a few occasions after the daily workouts were ended, Marse Joe had DiMaggio making deep throws from the outfield to the plate, and the recruit whipped the ball in with swiftness and accuracy. He has an arm which ranks with the best ever seen in baseball, and which will remind old Yankee followers of Bob Meusel and Babe Ruth when they were at the top of their form.

DiMaggio's Mighty Arm.

In the practice game yesterday, which went to the Yannigans by a score of 5 to 3, Joe unloosed one of those prodigious heaves which overshadowed practically everything else in the game. He took a fly in center in the eighth inning and, with the swiftness of an infielder, whammed it back to the plate with such force and accuracy that Jack Saltzgaver, who was trying to score from third, was trapped by fifteen feet. It would have been easier for Saltzgaver to scurry back to third, rather than try to score. But he continued and was easily out.

The excitement created by Joe's arrival here is still present, but is being repressed. Every one is a little afraid to go overboard on him, because he has not had a real test. Still, he continues to look every inch a ball player and a young man who can do everything. If he has a weakness, it has not been discovered, and there seems little doubt, even at this early date, that when the Yanks tee off in the opening game in Washington on April 14, he will be in the starting line-up.

DiMaggio may well regard himself as a fortunate young man. He has come into a baseball camp which badly needs an outfielder with a punch and where a job has been staring him in the face since he first reported. In addition, he finds himself under the wise old wing of the canniest ball player on the Yankee roster, his fellow San Franciscan, Tony Lazzeri. The undemonstrative Tony is only thirty-one himself, but he regards Joe as a kid, and has been guiding him ever since training began. The rookie could not have a wiser mentor.

Competition for Chapman.

It must be said in DiMaggio's behalf that he has responded to the encouragement and guidance he has received since reporting in a modest and judicious fashion. He has tried as hard as he could, but has not been bold or forward. He will talk to every one that talks to him, and answer all questions put to him, truthfully and completely. Nevertheless, he remains a quiet youngster, sticking in the background, and apparently without any other desire than to be regarded as just a rookie, trying to make a job for himself.

Di Maggio Flashes Power

Californian's Smashing Debut Against Big League Pitching Boosts Yanks' Flag Chances.

By DANIEL

World-Telegram Staff Correspondent

BRADENTON, Fla., March 18.— One vagrant robin doesn't make a spring. Neither does one interesting afternoon in March turn a baseball rookie into a second Babe Ruth or a copy of Ty Cobb. But when a major league aspirant with the background and record which are Joe Di Maggio's steps up and delivers, with elan and power that characterized his demonstrations in the 8-to-7 defeat of the Yankees by the Cardinals, you feel like sitting down and writing a postcard home about it.

Di Maggio had been the hot story of the New York camp for more than a fortnight. But when Giuseppe cracked a triple and three singles, scored two tallies, and drove in the two which put the Yankees right back into the game in the eighth inning, in his debut against major league competition, the San Francisco Italian became a veritable Vesuvius of fire and action.

To make the rookie's dream of a resplendent start complete, Di Maggio needed only a home run. And he might have got that if Arthur Fletcher had not stopped him at third when, with two out in the first inning, he drove the ball far over Joe Medwick's head. Mike Ryba was pitching for the Cardinals, and he had sent up a high, hard one on the inside.

In the eighth inning, which was punctured with a four-run rally by the Yankees against Willie Walker, Di Maggio came to bat with the bases filled and two out. The St. Louis southpaw, who had seen Joe get two hits off him on inside pitching, switched. Di Maggio caught the outside curve with the meat of his bat and drove it right into right center. It was this the whole camp had waited for—a Di Maggio hit to the right of second base. It was the first time Di Maggio had pushed a ball, rather than pulled it.

McCarthy Takes Off Wraps
In Talking About Joe.

As the Yankees rode into Bradenton from St. Petersburg today for a return engagement with the Cardinals, McCarthy for the first time removed the wraps and warmed up in a eulogy of his new prize.

"Somebody has written, without foundation of fact, that Di Maggio pulls away from a curve ball," said the manager of the Yankees. "Well, you saw him handle curves. He can hit those as well as fast balls. And remember, he was facing the most advanced pitching you will find in any major league camp. Don't forget that it was the ninth game for the St. Louis club, which, favored by its trip to Cuba, was in splendid shape.

"Di Maggio has everything it takes for success. He has the eye, the arm, the legs. In all sincerity, there is nothing about the young man which suggests any misgivings or doubts."

With George Selkirk in right, Di Maggio in center and Roy Johnson in left, the New York outfield looked good enough to start the season. As George and Roy contributed two blows apiece, McCarthy's picket line delivered eight of the Yankees' fifteen hits.

The Cardinal pitching finally caught up with Roy. Walker's southpaw curve dismissed the left-handed Johnson on strikes in the ninth when he came up with the bases loaded and one out and the ball game in his bat. Selkirk suffered a similar fate in the eighth with two out.

DiMaggio Believes In Carrying Big Stick

Special Dispatch to THE SUN.

BRADENTON, Fla., March 18.— Rookie Joe DiMaggio uses one of the biggest bats in the major leagues. . . . It weighs 40 ounces and is 36 inches long. . . . The average bat is 35 inches and 36 ounces. . . . Al Simmons, who was induced to lighten his bat to 33 ounces by Mickey Cochrane, still swings a 37-inch club. . . . It looks like a fungo stick. . . . Di-Maggio swings a heavier mace than Lou Gehrig, who has been using a 39-ounce war club for the last few seasons.

The first pruning of the Yanks took place today. . . . Bernie Uhalt, an outfielder who played for Oakland last year, and Bill Baker, Newark catcher, were released to the Newark club on option. . . . They will join the Bears at their Sebring, Fla., camp today. . . . A few more noggins will fall before the Yanks break camp here in a couple of weeks.   J. M. K.

McCarthy Says Veteran Will Be Used as Starter

Pilot Points Out Bump Is Particularly Effective Against Tigers—DiMaggio Continues Sensation of Training Camps.

By DANIEL,
World-Telegram Staff Correspondent.

ST. PETERSBURG, Fla., March 19.—The real story in the Yankee family today once more is Joseph Paul DiMaggio, who hit a 420-foot triple in the second defeat by the Cardinals, 6 to 5. However, it looks as if Giuseppe will have to be written about a great deal from now on. So we shall set our song to another key and sing of Irving Bump Hadley, whose three innings against the Redbirds started him on his campaign to gain a place among Joe McCarthy's starting pitchers.

Up to now it had been taken for granted that the manager of the Yankees was grooming Hadley only for a spot on the relief corps. But Marse Joe today announced that he had acquired Bump from the Senators for certain starting assignments, not the least important of which will be against the Tigers.

"Doc Painter has ironed out some kinks in Hadley's back which Bump says had hampered him for three years," McCarthy explained. "Now Hadley is no youngster, but he still has a lot of stuff and still is, in my opinion, a nine-inning hurler. I certainly would not have given up Jimmy DeShong for Bump if I felt that Hadley was just a forlorn hope.

"The records will show that Hadley always has done well against Detroit. Last summer Bump split four games with the Tigers. He beat us twice and the Athletics three times. Only against the White Sox was Bump a real washout.

"Naturally, it would be ridiculous to go into ecstacies over three innings of pitching in a training debut. But in those few innings at Bradenton, in which he gave three hits and one run, our new right-hander proved to me that he has grand possibilities. He's going to be one of my starting pitchers."

This DiMaggio person is getting everybody excited with his power at the plate. After having seen Joe collect six hits in two games against his Cardinals, Frankie Frisch went into quite a delirium over the San Francisco Italian.

John O. Seys, vice president of the Cubs, who is spending a little time in these parts, is just as excited over DiMaggio as McCarthy himself. "Gosh, I wish we had that young man. He'd make a second pennant sure," said John.

Catching one of Marvin Quante's fast pitches on the outside, in the first inning yesterday, DiMaggio drove it to the right center wall, just where a large "420" was set down in whitewash. Soon Lou Gehrig walked and the pair put on a double steal in which the fleet Giuseppe scored.

In the fifth inning, with Bill Hallahan pitching, DiMaggio slugged a long single to center. In the only two games the Yankees have played DiMaggio has hit .666. Experts have come from far and wide to give him a close inspection, but as yet nobody has discovered a real flaw in the 21-year-old outfielder's style, either at the plate or in the field.

In the outfield DiMaggio gets to places without apparent effort. This is in striking contrast with the style of Selkirk. It was George who eased the game to the Cardinals yesterday in the eighth inning by losing Terry Moore's fly in the sun. This mishap, which cost two runs, came on a ball which should have been the third out.

Gehrig Gets Two Hits and Feels He Is on Right Track.

Among the Yankee celebrants is Lou Gehrig, who has been doing some experimentation at the plate for more than two weeks and wishes to announce that he is on the right track. Lou is certain that he is not headed for a dismal spring like that which helped cut down his 1935 batting average to .329.

In two contests Gehrig has made three hits, for a .500 average, and has collected three passes. Yesterday Lou got a triple and a single. His long hit went into deep left center.

McCarthy is quite sure that DiMaggio is the right man to hit in the No. 3 spot, in front of Gehrig. But the manager admits that he is not so sure that Selkirk is the proper choice for the fifth niche in the batting order. It may be that this eventually will go to Bill Dickey, who has developed a stiff arm and has done little work in the last few days.

Another not-so-good arm is that of Red Rolfe, who still has something to learn about throwing and is prone to get his wing into trouble. Sometimes Red's arm gets so kinky that he has to hang by it to get the pain out. That's because Rolfe cannot master the trick of throwing across his body. This trouble recently has hampered Rolfe's all-around work.

While Frankie Crosetti has yet to get the batting range, his job around short leaves nothing to be desired. All doubt as to Frank's complete recovery from his knee operation has been eliminated and it is no longer a club house topic.

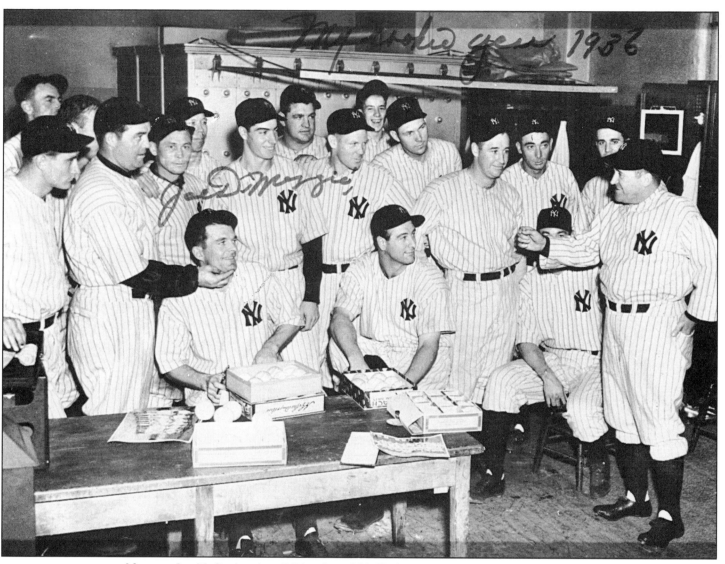

Manager Joe McCarthy gives DiMaggio and his Yankee teammates a little pep talk in 1936.

DiMaggio Big Camp Lure

Sensational Recruit Giving Yanks New Power at Bat and Box Office.

By DANIEL.
World-Telegram Staff Correspondent

TAMPA, March 20.—Writing about the 1936 Yankees is tantamount to being a Boswell for Joe DiMaggio. In all three games played by the New York Club, the Italian lad from San Francisco has been the outstanding performer. With four hits in six tries in the 13-to-8 victory over the Cincinnati Reds at St. Petersburg, Giuseppe made it ten out of fifteen, for an average of .666.

Not only is DiMaggio furnishing most of the power for the New York club, but he has developed into a real attraction. Fans are coming out to se him. Yesterday 2,691 persons turned out—far and away the largest crowd that has seen the Reds in an exhibition game in Florida in many years. They never before had drawn within 1,000 of that total at St. Petersburg.

Each performance of the New star at the plate was the signal for a salvo of applause. Joe came up twice in the long eighth inning. In his first effort in that round he singled to center. As he walked up to the plate again, the fans shouted their encouragement. But the youngster grounded out to Lew Riggs.

Never before in the history of the Yankees has a recruit fresh from the minors created the furore which DiMaggio has stirred up, or intrigued the fans so thoroughly with the magic of his bat and his possibilities in the American League. Tony Lazzeri came in here from the Pacific Coast League in 1926 with a reputation even more resplendent than that of DiMaggio. But even Lazzeri did not arouse the interest which is being evinced in Joe's achievements and potentialities.

DiMaggio Hits to all
Fields Against Red Hurlers.

DiMaggio is very industrious in his determination to break down the impression that he is a dead left field hitter. In three games in the Yankee camp, and in batting practice, DiMaggio did not drive a ball to the right of second base. But in the two meetings with the Cardinals, and yesterday's enocunter with the Reds, Giuseppe sent three hits into left, one in front of the box, three into right, and three into center. In his fourth time up he fouled out to Riggs, but Joe smacked another hit into center in the eighth inning, off Tony Freitas.

The fame of "DiMag" is travelling abroad, and experts are coming in from alien camps to see the Italian in action, and write about his style and their reactions.

His success in competition has acted in a strange way on the lad. He has become quieter, more thoughtful. Perhaps he is beginning to feel the mental weight of striking achievement in the Big Show, and the need for holding to a high standard.

It looks very much as if the Yankees will open the American League season with their current outfield—George Selkirk, in right; DiMaggio, in center, and Roy Johnson in left. With all due respect to the absent Ben Chapman, this arrangement may be the strongest one at Joe McCarthy's command. Johnson wants to play in left, and his .315 batting average with the Red Sox last season cannot be brushed aside. DiMaggio's work in center hasn't developed a flaw.

Colonel Ruppert insists that both Chapman and Red Ruffing, holdouts, will have to sign at terms offered.

Ruppert is particularly sore over Ruffing's attitude. Red has done no training at all, while Ben has been working out with the Birmingham club.

Rookie May Don Ruth Mantle

If Joe Keeps Up Present Pace, Lou Is Likely Again to Be Only Yankee No. 2 Star.

By JAMES M. KAHN.

TAMPA, Fla., March 20.—The baseball fates, being as prankish as any others, may be preparing one of those bitter jokes for Lou Gehrig. A fine ball player in his own right, he was overshadowed through the more spectacular years of his career by the dominant figure of Babe Ruth. Now that the Babe has gone, leaving an opportunity for Lou to step out boldly on his own, a new figure, rookie Joe DiMaggio, is swinging up over the baseball horizon and threatening to obscure him again.

With the Babe's passing last year, Lou ascended to the undisputed position of head man of the Yanks, but his elevation turned out to be an ironic anticlimax. He battled with jinxes and a hitting slump all season and wound up with one of the most disappointing records of his career. This year, when he is in top trim, meeting the ball solidly, and appears to be off to a flying start, he finds a juvenile still to embark on his first major league pennant pursuit stealing most of the preseason thunder.

During the rousing 13 to 8 victory the Yanks scored over the Reds in St. Petersburg yesterday, Lou connected with one of Gene Schott's fast ones in the fourth inning and poled it solidly to the distant left center-field fence for a home run. He legged it for all he was worth to complete the circuit and was unmistakably elated over his first 1936 four-bagger.

Applause Goes to Rookie.

Ordinarily, Lou would have moved off with the hitting honors and the headlines for the day, but as it turned out, DiMaggio drew the enthusiastic applause of the grandstanders and raised the most fuss in the ball game.

Rookie Joe got four hits, all of them whistling blows. Added to the hitting he had done in the first two exhibition games with the Cardinals, they kept him careening along dizzily at the top of the Yankee parade. He has made ten hits in fifteen times at bat, two of them triples, for a .667 average, leaving Lou, who boasts a .400 figure for his own three game batting, no doubt wondering just what a fellow has to do, anyway.

Every one knows, of course, that DiMaggio is not going to continue to hit .667, while Gehrig very likely can stick close to the .400 figure if he has one of his olden, golden years. But the fact remains, nevertheless, that this Coast youngster is no ordinary ball player, and that Gehrig, even with Ruth now gone, may have to share top billing with a rookie. DiMaggio has simply overshadowed the whole works since the Yanks started playing their exhibitions.

In continuing to demonstrate that he can hit, Joe yesterday stuck his wallops into all fields, left, right and center. It was feared that he might turn out to be a dead left field hitter, and that fielders, moved over for him, might knock his average down, much as the infields and outfields used to shift for Ruth and rob him of base hits. But opposing clubs now are playing Joe right down the middle, and he is belting them to all sides, to keep them guessing. Of his ten hits, three have gone to left field, three to right and four to center.

Batting Ace Out of Game

Yankee Sensation May
Be Kept Out of Action
For Ten Days.

By DANIEL,
Staff Correspondent.

ST. PETERSBURG, Fla., March 23.—Joe DiMaggio, outfielder of the Yankees, the most talked about recruit of the major league training season, was in bed here today, his baseball demonstration halted for the club's final week at this base.

DiMaggio is suffering from a first degree burn on his left foot, and has been ordered by Dr. John H. Strickland to remain in bed for forty-eight hours. The doctor was inclined to believe it would be ten days before DiMaggio would be able to resume serious training. By that time the Yankees will be on their trip toward New York. Joe must be guarded carefully against blood poisoning.

The manner in which DiMaggio suffered the burn was as fantastic as his batting feats in the four games he has played have been amazing. Joe's foot was blistered by twenty minutes of diathermia treatment administered yesterday by Dr. Earle V. Painter, trainer of the club. This period of electric baking is not considered unusual, but it develops DiMaggio has a super-sensitive skin.

The super-heterodyne hipper-dipper gave DiMaggio's foot so complete a baking that the pedal broke out with two gigantic blisters. Dr. Strickland punctured and drained these and put the little Bambino into bed, where he has been having a gay time with his radio. Joe says there is no pain except the mental one of being forced to lie on his back while he could be out there adding to his feats as a hitter.

The super-heterodyne oven was lashed on the DiMaggio hoof because it had become sore and swollen after Joe Coscarart, second baseman of the Bees, had stepped on it in the second innings of Saturday's contest.

DiMag Lays Off with
Dozen Hits in Twenty Tries.

"After I had made my second hit on Saturday, George Selkirk grounded to short and I was forced at second," DiMaggio related. "As I slid into the bag, Coscarart stepped on my foot and I figured I had been spiked. I took off my shoe, but when I found there was no cut I played through the game. At night the fun began. The foot swelled and I remained up bathing it in Epsom salts.

"Yesterday I went out in uniform, but soon found that it was impossible to hit or run. It was then that Doc Painter examined the injury again and decided to give it some diathermic treatment. And here I am. Well, it's tough. I hope that doctor was wrong when he said I would be out for ten days."

DiMaggio's absence from the New York line-up in the second victory over the Bees, 4 to 3, came as a disappointment to some 2,500 persons. Among them were quite a few experts from other camps who had come to see the much discussed San Francisco Italian in action. Babe Ruth, seeing his first game of the year and eager to get a line on the little Bambino, was quite put out.

DiMaggio has been forced out with twelve hits in twenty times up, for a batting average of .600. He has not fanned, he has not walked. Joe has hit the ball every time up in his four games.

DiMaggio had counted on adding to his feats and his fame in this week's games with Newark, the Dodgers, Braves and Cubs.

DiMaggio Views Life from
A Bed in Yankee Hotel.

As he lay in bed today young DiMaggio reviewed the past three weeks here, and said:—"It's just a dream."

The 21-year-old Italian chuckled. "Just imagine being in the big league and being able to play against such men as Averill, Foxx, the Ferrell boys, Myer and the rest! Imagine being a teammate of Gehrig, Roy Johnson and Gomez! When I was out in the Coast League I used to wonder how it felt to be in such company."

Setting the Pace

By FRANK GRAHAM

Tony's Boy Joe Is Making Good.

The way Joe DiMaggio had been whaling away at the ball in the Yankees' training camp must have made Tony Lazzeri very happy and Tony must feel very badly about Joe being out of action for the next week or ten days with a burned foot. Tony had nothing to do with Joe coming up to the majors or even setting out in baseball. Indeed, since Tony has spent the last ten baseball seasons as a Yankee, bounding around from town to town in the American League, and since Joe was only eleven years old when Tony broke in with the Yanks, the chances are Tony never saw Joe play ball until they reached St. Petersburg a couple of weeks ago. But because Joe is an Italian kid from San Francisco, Tony naturally is interested in him just as he has been interested in Frank Crosetti ever since Frank began to make his mark as a ball player. He took Joe in hand this spring and delivered him to Joe McCarthy and has been watching over him at the camp.

This is a fortunate arrangement for DiMaggio who, what with one thing and another, is a very fortunate young man. The sandlots of San Francisco have sent many good ball players to the big leagues but they never sent a better one than Lazzeri. And no grander guy ever dug himself in at the plate. Everybody in baseball likes him. More important, everybody respects him.

DiMaggio is right where Tony was exactly ten years ago this spring; at St. Petersburg with the Yankees—and trying to make good on all predictions inspired by his remarkable performances in the Pacific Coast League. Some of the critics are saying that if Joe makes good the Yankees may win the pennant. Tony knows what a load that puts on the kid's shoulders. Ten years ago they were saying that if he made good the Yankees might win the pennant. And by way of making that viewpoint authentic, Miller Huggins said the same thing. In fact, Miller said if his second base combination of Lazzeri and Mark Koenig stood up, the Yankees would win and if it didn't the Yanks would go down with a crash. He knew about what Koenig could do, because he had seen him through the last few weeks of the 1925 season. But he didn't know about Lazzeri except by hearsay. He was gambling on the square shouldered kid—and the kid delivered and the Yankees won the pennant.

Lazzeri, Crosetti and Now DiMaggio.

The Yankees have been pretty lucky with these San Francisco Italians. Lazzeri not only made them champions again after they had blown up in 1924 and fallen apart in 1925, but with John McGraw looking about desperately for a Jewish star who could add to the drawing power of the Giants, Tony captured the large Italian vote which no one had thought of up to that time. Crosetti, although not in Lazzeri's class as yet, is a good ball player and is getting better all the time. DiMaggio, by all accounts the best ball player in the minor league for the last couple of years, apparently has an attractive personality to match his rare ability and, as Jim Kahn pointed out in a story from St. Petersburg the other day, may take the play away from Lou Gehrig as the No. 1 man among the Yankees in public appeal.

It would not be surprising if this came true. He already is the No. 1 man in the baseball news. True, he hasn't had much competition except from Dizzy Dean, who is achieving his effects by an exchange of threats with Branch Rickey, but of late even Dizzy Dean has been running a very poor second to him. His failure to hit anywhere but to left field—and to hit there only infrequently—in the practice games among the Yankees, and his dynamic hitting to all fields once the Yanks began to trade blows with outsiders, plus his skill on defense and the obvious pull he exerts at the turnstiles, have made the most interesting reading that has come out of the Southland.

One marked detail of his play, as reflected in the reports from St. Petersburg, is the smoothness of it. He seems, while in the minors, to have achieved the major league stride. Well, Lazzeri was that way, too. He came up to join a club loaded down with fellows who had been in the big leagues for years and had won pennants and world series, yet he was so far from being the crude busher that he stepped right out in front of them and they had to hustle to keep up with him.

DiMaggio swings for the camera at his first spring training camp with the Yankees in 1936.

Enforced Idleness Due to Injury Seen Blessing in Disguise for Joe Di Maggio

Yankee Mates Believe Rest Will Prove Good Thing for Youngster.

By DANIEL,
Staff Correspondent.

ST. PETERSBURG, Fla., March 24.—Joe Di Maggio's enforced idleness with a burn on his left foot today was translated into a blessing in disguise by nearly everyone in the Yankee family except the Italian outfielder himself. It was felt that unless his injury developed septic complications the layoff would prove a good thing for the Little Bambino. Joe's vacation also would help the veterans of the club, who, perhaps, had been irked by their having been shoved into the background by the socker from San Francisco.

Di Maggio had been going at too rapid a pace for a 21-year-old rookie. He had made a dozen hits in twenty times at bat and had attracted the attention of baseball writers from all the other camps in this part of the country. His off-the-field hours were devoted largely to interviews. Now he lies in bed and listens to the radio. Joe can't dance a step, but he's goofy over hotcha music.

It must not be inferred that success had gone to Di Maggio's head or that he was in need of readjustment of values. "I don't see any reason for all that excitement over my twelve hits," the young man said today. "They come to me and ask me how it feels to hit big-league pitching. And I say, 'How do I know?' I haven't seen very much major-league hurling so far. In the four games I have played Bill Hallahan and Bill Walker, of the Cardinals, were the only class shooters I faced.

"One thing has impressed itself on me. The umpiring is different. Comparing the work of Harry Geisel with the type of umpiring I saw in the Coast League is like putting Gehrig alongside that kid who plays first for the Braves. You aren't afraid to take a ball, because you know the chances are high the umpire will agree with you. In that way, hitting is not so complicated as it is in the minors."

Not the least interesting by-product of the Di Maggio uprising has been the response of Lou Gehrig. There is no getting away from the fact that Joe has been a challenge to Lou, who came into camp with a panacea for his 1935 batting ills and figured on grabbing the headlines, the drug-store camera fiends from Sioux City and the autograph hunters from Topeka in the old Ruth manner.

Gehrig has accepted the challenge and has stepped out. Contrary to his training-camp habit of other years, Lou is hitting over .300 for six games. He got his second home run yesterday when, in the course of a 5-to-2 victory over the Newark Bears at Sebring, he lifted a ball over the right field fence at the 350-foot mark. Roy Johnson scored in front of him.

Not all the serious fighting on this Yankee club is going on in the front trenches. For example, there is Don Heffner, second baseman, who looked good here last year but was shipped to Newark. He is determined to stick this time. His four hits against the Bears yesterday are only part of the evidence.

The arrival of the Dodgers here today will put Dixie Walker in the showcase in center field. Joe McCarthy cannot keep Dixie. At least so it looks right now. Walker's arm makes him the No. 6 outfielder, and McCarthy plans to carry only five. Joe would like to sell Dixie out of the American League and Brooklyn looks like a reasonable spot for the lefthanded socker.

DANIEL'S  DOPE

Special to the World-Telegram.

ST. PETERSBURG, March 24.—In the Pacific Coast League last season Joe Di Maggio, of the Seals, and Oscar Eckhardt, of the Missions, were keen rivals for the batting championship and for the fealty of the fans of San Francisco, in which both clubs are located. The final figures showed Eckhardt the winner, .399 to .398. After having hit only .302 in the first half of the season Di Maggio went along at close to a .500 clip, but he could not quite overhaul the big Texan of the Missions.

Joe Di Maggio.

Now Di Maggio is with the Yankees; Eckhardt is in the outfield of the Dodgers. The Brooklyn club came into St. Petersburg today to start a series of five games with the Yankees, three of which will be played at Ebbets Field. The Yanks go to Clearwater tomorrow. It had been expected that the Di Maggio-Eckhardt rivalry would be resumed today. But Joe is out of action with a bruised foot, so we will have to wait until they clash in Brooklyn.

Oscar Eckhardt.

In the meantime what is Di Maggio's reaction on Eckhardt? What does Eckhardt think of Di Maggio? Here is what the rivals from San Francisco had to say about each other today:—

Eckhardt Says:—

"Joe Di Maggio was far and away the greatest ball player in the Pacific Coast League for several years. He has everything it takes to star in any company. Wait until he cuts loose with that arm of his. He made thirty-six assists in the Coast League, and don't forget that in seven of the eight ball parks out there he had to throw through a wind that cut across the field.

"Di Maggio has the greatest arm I ever saw, and he will prove a sensation in that department as well as in hitting and fielding.

"To my mind Di Maggio has only one failing. You simply cannot make that kid sore. I think if he could get a hate on you he could hit better. But he never loses his temper. No matter what you holler at him—and we hollered plenty—he just looks at you so sweet, and he hits another double.

"Don't worry about that big, heavy bat of his. He'll bring it around fast enough. He hasn't far to bring it.

"Joe is the most settled young ball player I have ever seen. And you cannot pitch to him.

You may fool him once, and then when you try that pitch again he's likely to knock it out of the park.

"The pitcher never catches Di Maggio off balance. He's ready and with those lynx eyes of his watches the ball from the delivery to the break.

"American Leaguers seeing Joe for the first time will get the impression he has been around for two or three years. No, they can't stop Joe!"

Di Maggio Says:—

"Of course, Ossie Eckhardt is no kid. He is, I should say, around 34. And he is not the most graceful outfielder in the business. But he can do things, and I can see no reason why he should not stick with Brooklyn.

"He is a strange sort of ball player. In the field he gives you many thrills. A fly ball over his head makes plenty of trouble for Ossie, but you don't get a chance

to hit it over his noodle. He plays deep enough to take everything in front of him. How this would work out in the National League is a question. His arm is good.

"In hitting Eckhardt, who is a lefthanded batsman, pushes everything into left field. I doubt that I ever saw Ossie pull a ball. Last season the San Francisco pitchers began to toss it up to him, but he kept right on shoving the ball into right field.

"As he meets the ball Oscar is off to first base. And in getting down to first he is about as fast as anything you ever saw. In the field and around the bases he is not what you would call a jack-rabbit.

"Eckhardt hits nothing but singles, and he gets a lot of those beating out balls to first base. In addition to being a strange ball player he is a funny guy.

"With that Texas drawl of his and a fine sense of humor he brings a story into the park every day and a wisecrack to the plate every time he comes up. He is a good guy to have on a ball club."

Daniel, Sizing Up Joe DiMaggio in Camp, Calls Him a Throwback to Joe Jackson

Like Famous Sox Slugger, He Stands One Foot Behind Plate, With Feet 12 Inches Apart; Swings Large Bat

By DANIEL M. DANIEL

JOSEPH PAUL DI MAGGIO, JR., faces no easy task with the Yankees. Hailed as the greatest minor league star of 1935, flattered with the announcement that but for his having been sold to New York, the Red Sox would have paid $60,000 for him, confronted with the fact that Yankee fans regard him as the Moses who is to lead their club out of the second-place wilderness, in which it has wandered for three years, he is more in the limelight than any other major league recruit. In fact, Giuseppe, as Bill Duncan pointed out in his comparison of similarly highly touted phenoms from the Coast, in a recent issue of THE SPORTING NEWS, is decidedly on the spot, but from early indications, it appears he will live up to his boosters' predictions.

DiMaggio certainly created a furore in his first two games with the Yankees, against the Cardinals. Sam Breadon and Frankie Frisch went into ecstacies over Giuseppe, and so did John O. Seys of the Cubs. In the pair of contests with the Redbirds, DiMaggio got six hits for .666, smacking a tremendous triple in each. At Bradenton, the three-bagger went to the 420-foot mark on the right-center field fence. Joe followed this performance by getting four hits in a game against the Reds, March 20, giving him a total of ten hits in 16 times at bat, for the impressive mark of .625 for three games. During that period he faced three right-handers and three southpaws, getting five hits against each style of flinging, and his drives went to all fields.

In his next appearance, against the Braves, Joe made two hits in four times at bat, running his total to 12 hits out of 20 trips to the plate. Then he went on the shelf for ten days, with a burn on the left foot, suffered when the diatherma treatment was applied to an injury received in a game.

The Yankees bought DiMaggio at the minor league meeting in Columbus in November, 1934. Joe had injured a knee getting out of a taxicab the previous summer, and this left his future in doubt. The New York club purchased an option to take DiMaggio for $25,000 in cash and five players. DiMaggio was left with the Seals. Last summer, the deal was closed—much to the chagrin of the San Francisco club, which had that offer from Eddie Collins before it.

DiMaggio was born in Martinez, Cal., November 25, 1914, which makes him just past 21. He weighs 190 pounds and stands half an inch over six feet in height. He hits right-handed and throws right.

Joe is one of nine children. He has four sisters and as many brothers. Dominic, 19, plays bush ball around San Francisco and Joe says he is a comer. Vincent is an outfielder with the San Diego Padres of the Pacific Coast League. Vince is Joe's senior and was with the Seals when Joe broke in.

When Joe was only a year old, the family moved from Martinez to San Francisco.

Joe's dad was a fisherman. Now, at 67, he is retired, and a close student of baseball, about which he knew nothing until a couple of years ago, when he became a hot fan.

Joe began playing ball when he was ten. He was a shortstop then. In fact, DiMaggio did not become an outfielder until 1933.

At 14, Joe lost interest in baseball. He went in for tennis in a big way, and played basket ball, and "touch" football. When his

HE BULGES WITH POWER

JOSEPH PAUL DIMAGGIO

brother Vince hooked up with the Seals, and made good, Joe began to think things over and went back to baseball intensively. He joined the San Francisco Boys Club, then played for the Mission Red A's, all at short.

With his brother on the Seals, Joe began to haunt the knotholes at the San Francisco park. However, he had aroused the interest of Spike Hennessey, scout, who hauled Joe into the Seals' office, where Charley Graham told him there was no need of his peeking through knotholes, and handed him a bunch of passes.

Graham asked Joe to work out for a few weeks with the Seals. Near the close of the season, Augie Galan got permission to go to Honolulu, so Joe played in Augie's place in three games. That was in 1932. Joe got two hits in nine tries, and remembers that his first safety, off Ted Pillette, was a triple.

In 1933, the Seals asked Joe to attend their school. Then Joe signed and went to camp. He was given his chance at short, but proved a failure. About that time a young man by the name of Stewart had developed into something of a sensation in right field, when suddenly he stopped hitting. One day Manager Caveney sent DiMaggio in to bat for Stewart. Joe got a base on balls. The following day Caveney sent Joe to right field.

Young DiMaggio was amazed. His own

Coast Graduate Hits .666 in Two Exhibitions Against the Cardinals, Then Gets Four Blows in Game With Reds

brother, Vince, and Prince Oana both were on the bench. But Joe got the call over the pair. And he remained in the outfield from then on.

In his second season with the Seals, DiMaggio set a Coast record by hitting in 61 consecutive games. Buck Newsom, who was the toughest pitcher for Joe, almost stopped that streak right in the middle. Young Ed Walsh was the pitcher finally halting DiMaggio.

In 1935, DiMaggio and Oscar Eckhardt, now with the Dodgers, had a great battle for the Coast batting title. Ox won with .399. Joe hit .398. In the first half, DiMaggio batted only .320. He hit over .500 the second half.

Joe reminds one of Joe Jackson at the plate—standing with one foot back, with his feet 12 inches apart. He swings a 40-ounce bat, 36 inches in length—one of the biggest bats used by any major league player, even heavier than that of his teammate, Lou Gehrig, whose club weighs 39 ounces. Al Simmons, who was induced by Mickey Cochrane to lighten his bat to 33 ounces, uses a 37-inch length. The average mace weighs 36 ounces and is 35 inches long. Joe meets the ball at the last possible fraction of a second. Most of his hits are pulled. He has a remarkable arm, as evidenced by his 36 assists last season. That total was achieved in spite of the fact that for the last month of the campaign he was handicapped by a cold in his arm. His throwing and fielding has measured up to expectations in exhibition work this spring.

Among his 1935 feats was a drive over the 420-foot left field fence in San Francisco—the longest in Coast league records. He scored 171 runs and drove in 151. Joe got 34 homers and was voted the most valuable player in the league.

Joe likes movies, but hasn't much use for books. He also likes spaghetti, even though his new teammate, Tony Lazzeri, doesn't care much for Italy's favorite dish. Although DiMaggio regards Joe Cronin, another Californian, as his baseball hero, he credits Frank O'Doul, his manager at San Francisco last year, with giving him his greatest help in the game.

Prize rookie of the New York Yankees, Joe DiMaggio, laces a hit in an exhibition game against the Cincinnati Reds during spring training at St. Petersburg, Florida, in March 1936. It was one of four hits DiMag got in that game.

Di Maggio Sent To Hospital as Chapman Signs

By STUART ROGERS.
(Staff Correspondent of The News)

Atlanta, Ga., April 4.—Glad tidings that Ben Chapman had seen the error of his holdout ways and would join the

Joe DiMaggio, the Yanks' prize rookie, packs his bags in Atlanta before leaving for New York. Joe's injured foot failed to respond to treatment, so Manager Joe hustled him North for special attention.

Yankees upon their arrival at Nashville, Monday, were somewhat offset today by the discovery that Joe DiMaggio's foot injury is more serious than at first supposed.

Failure of DiMaggio's left foot to respond to treatment is giving Manager Joe McCarthy real concern now, and this afternoon, following cancellation of the game with Atlanta because of cold, he decided to send his highly prized rookie to New York for special treatment. Business Manager Ed Barrow told McCarthy over the phone today that the club will spare no expense to cure the injured extremity and save one of the most promising young baseball careers.

Made Worse by Treatment.

DiMaggio had been going like a house afire and was leading the club with a batting average of .600 when Joe Cascarart of the Boston Braves stepped on his arch during an exhibition game at St. Petersburg, March 21 Joe thought little of the injury at the time and walked off the field without a limp.

After the game and the next day Earle Payntor, club trainer, subjected the member to therapeutic treatment. It appears now that the hyper-sensitive skin could not withstand the intense heat of the baking process and the treatment aggravated rather than helped the injury.

Joe did not complain and appeared in uniform off and on. But Thursday it was noticed that blood seeped through the bandage and heavy woolen sock.

The reticent young outfielder walks normally and says the burns do not pain him much except when he laces up his shoes. He will leave town at 9:15 tonight and arrive at Pennsylvania Station at 4:10 tomorrow afternoon.

McCarthy said he hoped Joe's pedal would be healed in time for him to appear in the opening game with the Dodgers at Ebbets Field, April 10.

Ben Chapman capitulated to Yankee terms — $10,000 plus $2,000 if he's a good boy. Ben was meek and mild as Millie De Stross when he surrendered to McCarthy by phone from Birmingham and promised to don his uniform for the first game at Nashville.

McCarthy's decision to call off today's ice carnival was prompted by his experience of a year ago, when under similar conditions in this same city he contracted the case of pneumonia that put him into the hospital and kept him from his duties the first fortnight of the season.

Setting the Pace

By FRANK GRAHAM

Joe DiMaggio Comes to Town.

Joe DiMaggio doesn't look much like Tony Lazzeri. As a matter of fact, he looks more like Milton Berle. But he makes you think of Tony, at that. Probably because he's a slim Italian kid off the San Francisco sandlots, and because he's a good ball player. He must be a good ball player. Everybody says so.

Joe's left foot still is encased in a soft slipper he has been wearing ever since the day a diathermic contraption, applied to his foot to bake the soreness out of it, left him with a first degree burn. That was at St. Petersburg more than two weeks ago. Maybe he will not be able to play when the Yankees open the season in Washington on April 14, but if he isn't it will not be long after that before he is in the line-up. Dr. Jacoby, who is treating him, said last night he thought Joe would be ready to play within ten days or so. This is good news for the Yankee fans, who have read so much about him and are so eager to see him. In fact, it will be all right with them if he doesn't play in Washington—just so long as he plays on the opening day at the Stadium.

DiMaggio says he never stopped to measure his height, but he thinks he is about six feet one-half inch. And winter or summer, he weighs about 180 pounds.

"All I do is loaf around all winter," he said in his room in the New Yorker. "All I do is loaf, but still I don't put on a pound."

He didn't always loaf. He worked once. One day. He got a job peeling oranges in an orange juice plant in San Francisco, but they didn't pay him enough.

"So I quit," he said. "I was aiming at big dough, and I knew after one peek at that pay check I wasn't going to get it there."

Didn't Mean to Take Vince's Job.

He didn't think, when he was a kid, that he ever would be a ball player.

"I always liked to play the game," he said, "and I was pretty good at it, but I never thought about playing it in the Coast League. That was a game for grown-ups, and I was only a kid."

But when his brother, Vince, landed with the Seals, Joe thought maybe he could get somewhere.

"I figured I was pretty near as good as he was, so if he could get money for playing ball, maybe I could, too," he said.

So he took Vince's job away from him? Wasn't that it?

He looked uncomfortable.

"Well," he said, "I don't know as I took his job away from him."

But he did succeed Vince in his post in the Seals' outfield, didn't he?

"Well," he said, "he was playing left field, and I went to center."

And Vince was benched?

"Yes. But I didn't have anything to do with that."

Of course not. And is Vince still with the Seals?

"No. He's with the San Diego Padres. They used to be the Hollywood club, but they moved the club to San Diego."

He Wanted to Meet the Babe.

Had he seen anything of New York save his hotel, the doctor's office and the Yankees' office?

"I went out to my cousin's in the Bronx last night," he said. "I had a steak this big. It was too big for me."

Had he seen the Stadium?

"Just from the outside. It looks like a big oval. I stood outside the left field fence and looked up at those three decks of the stand. It looked pretty big."

What was his impression of New York, based on his brief excursions and the view from his window on the thirty-second floor?

He looked out at the murk of the late afternoon.

"Right now it looks a lot like San Francisco," he said. "This is our kind of weather. It makes me feel right at home. But of course the buildings are higher and better."

Did he think he was going to like it?

"I sure do. It may sound funny, but I always wanted to play with the Yankees. I guess maybe it was on account of Babe Ruth. Everybody was rooting for the Babe, and I was like all the rest. I thought if I ever came up to the big leagues I would like to play on the same team with him, although I didn't think I ever would. I almost made it, at that, didn't I?"

Did he meet the Babe at St. Petersburg?

"No," he said. "I wish I had. The only place I've ever seen him was in the news reels, taking batting practice or something. I was hoping I would meet him at St. Petersburg. But I didn't. I wanted to meet him the worst way."

Dutch Was Right, After All.

He fell to talking about ball players and newspaper men in the Coast League. Tommy Laird . . . Abe Kemp . . . Frank O'Doul.

"Frank was one of my heroes when I was a kid," he said. "I liked him and Babe Ruth best. What a swell fellow Frank is to play for! All he thinks about is the kids playing for him. He will do anything for them."

He mentioned Dutch Ruether, and you told him about the Seattle newspaper man who came to your room in Detroit during the world series last fall to tell you Dutch wanted you to know that DiMaggio was a great ball player in the making and not to go wrong on him.

"Here's a funny one about Dutch," Joe said. "The first year I was in the league he watched me run, and then he went to the trainer of our club and asked him if there was anything the matter with my left leg. The trainer said he didn't think so, and Dutch said he was sure there was, because I dragged it a little when I ran. Naturally, the trainer came and told me about it.

" 'He's crazy,' I said. 'There is nothing the matter with my leg, and there never was, and I don't drag it, either.'

"He told Dutch what I said, and Dutch said he didn't care. There was something the matter with it. And, by golly, there was. I was invited out to my sister's house to dinner one night, and I took a cab from the ball park, and when I got to the house I was getting out of the cab just like this, as though I was getting out of this chair, and pop! went the knee. It hurt like the dickens. I never did find out what was the matter with it. One doctor said it was broken cartilage and another said there was something the matter with the bone. I didn't care what it was, just so long as it mended. It mended all right. I never have had any trouble with it since."

He Never Played the Sunfield.

How did he like Joe McCarthy and the rest of the Yankees?

"Fine."

What did Joe say to him when he reported?

"Nothing much."

Did Joe tell him where he was going to play?

"No. I told him I would play anywhere he wanted me to. I played center field down there, but I have been reading that when the season opens Chapman will play in center field and I will be in left."

How does that strike him?

"All right. I never played in left field, and I never played the sunfield, but I want to do whatever they want me to. You know, I never played in the outfield at all until I joined the Seals. I was a shortstop. But now I like the outfield better."

Did he feel even a little bit anxious when he reported to the Yankees?

"Yes. I wanted to get there and see Florida. I had heard it was such a beautiful place, but I was disappointed. I guess it was on account of the weather. And I guess I would have been a little anxious about my ball playing, too, only I had company all the way. Tony Lazzeri and Frank Crosetti and I drove there, and they were a big help to me. I roomed with Frank. This will be his room, too, when the ball club gets here on Friday."

How many games had he played against other major league clubs before he was hurt?

"Four. One with the Reds and one with the Bees and two with the Cardinals."

Had he been able to form any impression of major league pitching in view of the scant experience he had with it?

"No. The only real good pitchers I faced were Walker and Hallahan. The others were just young fellows like myself, trying to make places for themselves. It wasn't a fair test. But I think the umpiring up here will help me. The fellows like Babe Pinelli and Harry Geisel, who worked for us down there, really call them as they are. That gives a hitter confidence that he can wait for a good one and not have to swing at a ball over his head because he's afraid the umpire might call a strike."

He doesn't know, offhand, of any reason why he shouldn't succeed in the majors, does he?

"The only thing that worries me is the weather," he said. "They tell me it gets very hot in St. Louis."

Joe DiMaggio Reluctant To Discuss Foot Injury

By LEWIS BURTON,
N.Y. American Staff Writer.

Let's have this nonsense over with. The last name of the Yankees' $75,000 outfielder is "Dee-mah-gee-oh." None of the syllables is accented. The "g" is soft, as in "regime."

And who's the didactic author of this opinion? Not, your blushing correspondent wishes to point out, himself, but the rightful owner of the name.

SEEKS MEDICAL AID.

His damaged left foot encased in a soft brown slipper Joe DiMaggio came to New York late yesterday afternoon seeking expert medical attention. A diathermy burn has left his left instep raw and prevents him from wearing a shoe. Ed Barrow, business manager of the Yankees, today will take him to a specialist in the hope that something can be done about it.

The most expensive rookie of the year is in a serious plight. It worries the front office. DiMaggio is reluctant to discuss the ailment. He was delighted to forget about his troubles and go Vizetelly.

ORTHODOX PRONOUNCIATION.

"I pronounce 'DiMaggio' in the orthodox Latin way," he said. "Any Italian will tell you how to pronounce it as well as myself."

But that did not settle the condition of his foot. He returned reluctantly to that phase of the discussion.

"It is just because I can't put my shoe on that I'm here ahead of the team," he said with affected unconcern. "I'll be all right in 10 days—for the beginning of the season."

STOCK OBSERVATION.

You could tell it was just a stock observation that he doesn't quite believe. He looked out pensively from under ebony brows that come together in a thin line over his nose. In 1934 he was kept out of baseball three and one-half months by a knee injury suffered getting out of a bus. Can it happen again?

In mufti DiMaggio is far from a prepossessing figure. He is decidedly not a second Babe Ruth. In his hotel room at the New Yorker, among a group that included Paul Krichell and Gene (White Necktie) McCann, Yankee scouts, DiMaggio was not readily distinguishable. You had to look twice for his youth, his new Southern tan, his glistening black hair.

He doesn't look big, though he weighs 187 pounds and measures 6 feet ½ inch up. He is just another chap seeing New York.

"It's my first visit here," he said, "but I'll take everything in stride. The thing I'm most interested in seeing is—no! not the Empire State Building—the Yankee Stadium.

"But I'll wait till the Yanks come to town on Friday to do it."

Yankees Turn Superstitious as Hard-Luck "Room 819" Claims Second Victim

By DANIEL,
Staff Correspondent.

HIGH POINT, N.C., April 8.—"The hard luck of Room 819," which first claimed Joe Di Maggio and his fried foot for a victim, and now has sent Frankie Crosetti to join Joe in New York with a broken nose, today was the chief topic of conversation among the Yankees. Like all other groups of professional ball players, they are highly superstitious.

"The hard luck of Room 819," would have made a subject for a story by a Gaboriau or the mystic Conan Doyle. Di Maggio and Crosetti teamed together in 819, at the St. Petersburg Hotel of the Yankees. When the recruit outfielder went to the hospital list with a singed hoof, the camp got set. Something was bound to happen to the other inmate of 819! And it was a fortunate thing that there hadn't been three in the room.

That "something which was bound to happen" hit Crosetti before yesterday's 11-6 Yankee victory over the Knoxville Smokies. Johnny Murphy was pitching to batters, Tony Lazzeri was swinging, Frankie was standing near the cage, waiting for his turn. Tony offered at a fast ball, and fouled it right into the face of the astounded—and take it from the other players, doomed—Crosetti. Down went Frankie, and the others rushed to his aid.

Crosetti was sent to the offices of Dr. Sam Hodge, who found the nose chipped, but could discern no dislocation. Last night Crosetti, chaperoned by Pat Malone, a sore throat patient, left Knoxville for New York.

Crosetti has not been liked any too well by Dame Fortune for the last two years. Last summer she put him on the shelf with a bad knee just when the club needed him most. An operation was necessary, and Frankie was out of the last sixty-two games played by the Yankees.

Malone reported sick yesterday morning and was sent to a throat specialist, who found an infected tonsil, with danger of quinsy. He advised Blubber to go to New York.

Injuries and illnesses rarely scare Joe McCarthy, who is a disciple of the old Oriole school on that subject, and takes the pollyanna attitude.

"Crosetti will be in our lineup in Brooklyn on Saturday or Sunday, and certainly will play in the opener in Washington," said Marse Joe. "Malone may work in Brooklyn, too. I get word from New York that Di Maggio's foot is coming along in fine shape and that he will be ready next Tuesday if I need him. However, Joe will want some hitting before he goes back into the lineup."

The Knoxville game gave Ben Chapman a chance to make his 1936 debut in the Yankee lineup. Ben batted sixth, behind Bill Dickey, and in front of Tony Lazzeri.

Chapman came up four times and got a hit and a pass. He used his old stance at the plate, looking over his left shoulder, and hit the ball to the third baseman on three occasions. His safe drive knocked the third sacker down and bounded away.

Lou Gehrig lifted his average with a two-run homer, and a single. The four bagger went over the distant rightfield fence, and was his fifth round tripper of the training season. Gehrig never before hit so many home runs during the conditioning term.

Red Rolfe got back his batting eye and made two doubles off Brooklyn pitchers of yore, old Jess Petty, who is manager at Knoxville, and Ray Moss. Roy Johnson also socked a pair of two baggers, and what with homers by Red Ruffing and Steve Sundra, the Yankees had quite a time.

Ruffing allowed five hits and four runs in five innings. Red is being groomed for the second game in Washington. Lefty Gomez still has the call for the opener.

BY JOE WILLIAMS

Dopester's Day Spoiled
Blames Easter Broadcast
Guesses Tigers and Cubs

I AM picking the Detroit Tigers and the Chicago Cubs to do it all over again in the two big league races this year, but my confidence is hardly what you might call sublime. It might be different if I hadn't had my meditations interrupted yesterday.

Always when the time comes around to pick the baseball winners I take my meditations and go for a long walk. I am forced to admit the results haven't been uniformly satisfactory and there have been complaints from two elements: (1) that the walks were not long enough, (2) that I always came back.

Anyway, I was walking down Park Ave. immersed in my meditations yesterday when suddenly I found myself being elbowed vigorously by a copper. . . . "Get back there. Can't youze see they're making moon pitchures?". . . .

This was in front of the fashionable St. Bartholomew's Church, and they were doing more than making moving pictures. They were broadcasting a play by play description of the worshippers. Mr. George Hicks, the old fight announcer, was giving it the "Oh, boy, folks-you-ought-to-be-here" stuff.

Mr. Hicks wore a cutaway coat, striped trousers and a silk hat, out of the top of which protruded something that resembled a steel fishing rod. It was a part of the broadcasting apparatus. The effect was to make the gentleman look like a hitch-hiker from Mars.

* * *

What, No Hot Dogs?

A TALL blond young man similarly dressed, save for the fishing rod gadget, and the young lady in navy blue who clung to his arm, seemed to be the main objects of Mr. Hicks' excited oratory; he described their stroll past the church, step by step, and at the end gave them the microphone to address the great unseen audience.

Worshippers coming out of and going into the church paused to view the odd Easter Sunday ceremonials. A copper yelled. . . . "Say, youse guys got all you want?" . . . It seemed that unfortunately they hadn't. The sound men wanted a retake. So the tall blond young man and the lady in navy blue did it all over again, he very sedately, she very demurely.

This time it seemed to be the Malarkey, for Mr. Hicks beamed into the microphone at his vast invisible gallery and while the rugged stone features of St. Bartholomew's looked down on the scene in hushed horror, the announcer thanked the two strollers for making the happy Easter day what it was.

There isn't any particular point in this except that it may help the outsider better to understand some of the bizarre behaviors of the country such as, for example, the mannerly conduct of the Hauptmann trial. It was either very comical or very shocking depending on how you regard such things.

The old flower woman whose business had been cut short by th showy antics was bitter in her fury and when she cried that next yea they were going to have the Lord Himself there to go on parade and sa a few words over the network nobody seemed to think she was especiall impious.

* * *

Getting Down to Cases.

SPEAKING for myself, I have no cause to remember the episode with an great happiness because, as I have said before, it cut into my baseba meditations and if it so happens that either the Tigers or the Cubs, o both, should lose, I shall insist upon a suspended sentence because o extenuating circumstances.

But seriously, in my book these two teams figure as the class of th league. The Tigers spotted the rest of the league a month's run of medioc rity last year and then won going away, coming from nowhere. They ar stronger now than they were when they won the world series, particu larly in reserves.

The veteran Al Simmons, purchased from the White Sox, for $75,00 can help the Tigers a lot but it may not make any difference whether h does or doesn't. They won without him last year, didn't they? True fev clubs ever manage to win three championships in a row. The Tigers c 1907, '08 and '09 did, so plainly there is no law against their moder prototypes doing the same thing.

The St. Louis Cardinals are the popular choice to win the Nationa League pennant and of course this club with its vast minor leagu resources is always a fairly safe selection. But it should be kept in min they had a better ball club last year and yet failed to win. If nothing els this proves they can be beaten.

The rap against the Cubs is that they took twenty-one straight game to win the championship and the percentage is heavy against their doin that again. Of course, it is. But who says they'll have to? As a matter o fact, and this is a point generally overlooked, the Cubs probably coul have won if they had taken no more than seven straight games.

Naturally they would have had to do this three successive times t account for the twenty-one games they ultimately accumulated. The effec in the standings would have been the same but the fan tumult and critica acclaim would not have been as great. The Cubs, you know, scored 10 victories all told and won the pennant by four games. They didn't jus stagger in.

* * *

Yanks Seen as Threat.

WHAT I'm trying to say is that I think too much stress has been place on the Cub's streak in relation to its pennant victory and prospects fo 1936. As a rule 93, 94 or 95 games will prove more than enough to wi a pennant. The Cubs, to repeat, won with 100 games, the third Nationa League team in twenty-two years to win as many as a hundred games.

Theoretically the Cubs can slow up to the extent of from five to eigh games and still repeat. It is worth remembering, too that the Cubs wer handicapped for fully half the season by the indecision of their manager Charley Grimm, the old gas meter reader. He had a pennant winnin team at his command all the time but the great white light didn't dawn o him until July. Which is to say it wasn't until midseason that he figure out a winning combination. With a whole winter to think it over, it mus be assumed that even Mr. Grimm knows what he's got by now.

This explains my leaning toward the Cubs. Of course, the Cards mus be listed next, despite the precarious second base situation involvin Frankie Frisch. It's my guess the third base spot will produce a ma scramble, with the figures slightly favoring the Giants. The delightfu Dodgers will do well to top the second division again.

Getting back to the American League, if any team overtakes th Tigers I have a hunch it will be the Yankees. This is a well balanced outfi and the addition of Joe Di Maggio gives the club the power it needs. don't see how a mere shift in managers makes the Indians a pennant win ning team. The Red Sox may do it—but they seem shy on pitching to me

Don't forget these estimates could be slightly out of line. I don' usually function well when my meditations are smacked around. I wonde if they'd let me do my Tennessee strut for the movies in front of St Bartholomew's next Easter Sunday if I put on a silk topper?

Mystery in Origin Of Di Maggio's Name

THE entrance of Joe Di Maggio into the baseball arena has created considerable interest in the origin of his family name. Various authorities offer divers explanations.

An Italian padre says that Di Maggio refers to the Magi, or the Wise Men of the East. Another offers the explanation that it means Man of Magic.

A third authority insists it is a place name and that the family originally came from Lake Maggiore.

Joe Di Maggio Finally Ready To Play Again

Interest in Tomorrow's Game Centers Upon Young Outfielder.

By DANIEL.

Joseph Paul Di Maggio, Jr., Yankee outfielder who has yet to play in the Yankee outfield in the American League, finally is ready to return to the wars. The New York club has announced that Di Maggio will start in left field against the St. Louis Browns in the Stadium tomorrow.

Never before has there been so much interest in a new player at the Stadium. The Yankee front office has had at least 100 telephone inquiries each day for the last fortnight, and the question has been unvaried, "When will Di Maggio play?"

Di Maggio's left foot, which was injured and then burned by a diathermia machine, is not entirely healed. However, the doctors who have been treating Joe have told him he can go to work. Whether Di Maggio will be able to play nine innings and remain in the lineup remains to be seen.

It was on Saturday, March 21, that Di Maggio was hurt. Joe Coscarart, of the Braves, stepped on Joe's left foot in a force play at second base. The next afternoon Di Maggio got the diathermia treatment and twenty minutes of this burned the skin off his foot. When Joe was almost ready to return to the lineup in Washington a foul tip hit the left foot in batting practice and sent the lad to bed.

Di Maggio played in seven exhibition games with the Yankees and hit an even .600.

Rookie Joe Comes Through

Joins in General Bombardment of St. Louis Hurlers With Three Hits, One a Triple.

By JAMES M. KAHN.

As evidence that the fickle fortune which had given the Yankees a cold shoulder for so long a time is now turning the warm beneficence of her sunny smile upon them, witness the debut of rookie Joe DiMaggio. It was a veritable triumph. Given a terrific buildup, young Joe came through and inaugurated himself as an American Leaguer and a Yankee with a .500 batting average.

Having stepped off to such a happy start, DiMaggio will continue in left field, a spot which is new to him but which, unless future developments dictate a change, will be his regular niche from now on. In his first appearance he was not called upon to exhibit any extraordinary skill in the field. He had only a few chances, which were commonplace, and he handled them in routine fashion.

But his hitting, which has been the more widely ballyhooed phase of young Joe's short career, and upon which the Yanks are counting heavily in their pursuit of a pennant, completely satisfied the 25,430 Sunday visitors who watched the Yankees hammer the Browns down to their eighth straight defeat that the youthful San Franciscan was no ordinary recruit. A lot was expected from him and DiMaggio gave the fans a lot to look at.

DiMaggio's Three Hits.

He got three hits, two of them singles, in six times up. His first single was thoroughly undistinguished. It looped out to center field and fell just short of Ray Pepper. His other single, in the eighth, was an honest blow into right field and was clouted off Russ Van Atta, the former Yankee lefthander, on a low outside pitch which he caught on the end of his bat.

Between them was sandwiched a three-base belt, made off Elon Hogsett in the sixth, which completely satiated the clamoring customers who were beseeching Joe really to smack one. It was a vicious swipe which zoomed like a rifle shot into left center between Pepper and Julius Solters and bounded with a few hops to the bleacher fence. It was good for three bases and it scored Red Rolfe, who had opened the inning with a double.

Thus, young Joe showed the power he has at the plate, batted in a run, started off with a luxurious average and altogether added to the mounting impression that the Yanks are the team which will have to be beaten in this year's American League flag scramble. They are getting the breaks, and the successful unveiling of their spectacular young rookie is but further evidence of it. It is a year in which things are clicking for them.

Unless every baseball man of any experience who has had a chance to see DiMaggio in action is a lunatic, young Joe is destined to move right along in the same manner in which he has started. The opinion is unanimous, without one dissenting voice, that he is a great ball player and needs only to play to prove it. Certainly, if he comes through, the Yanks will continue their campaigning with a battle front even more formidable than they had in 1932, when they won their last pennant.

In Ruth's Old Role.

Aside from the actual help DiMaggio promises to lend the Yanks with his power at the plate and his defensive strength in the field, he is bound to be a tremendous psychological factor in keeping the McCarthymen pennant-minded. Inserted in the third spot in the batting order, just ahead of Lou Gehrig, he is being relied on to worry the pitchers and take some of the power-house responsibilities away from Larruping Lou. Joe is inheriting the pace-setting role which the Babe played for Gehrig when the Bam was the most illustrious No. 3 batter in baseball.

Whether the fine Italian hand of DiMaggio had anything to do with it or whether the whole business can just be charged up to the ineffectiveness of the Brownie pitchers, Gehrig had his best day of the young season up at the plate yesterday, as he banged out four hits in five official tries and scored five runs. He and Ben Chapman, who had an ultra-perfect day with two triples, a double and a single, did as much as they could to make the literally thunderous debut of DiMaggio a glittering triumph, by driving in half of the Yankees' fourteen runs.

The whole jubilant occasion was the biggest run-scoring spree the Yanks have been on this year. With the incentive to turn the springing of Rookie Joe into a holiday, they took advantage of every opportunity shoddy St. Louis pitching offered them to score runs. At the same time, now brought up to their full strength by the presence of DiMaggio, they served notice on the rest of the league that it will take an awful lot to stop them as they keep hammering at the portals of first place.

JOE DiMAGGIO'S FIRST GAME IN THE MAJOR LEAGUES AT YANKEE STADIUM, NEW YORK, MAY 3, 1936

St. Louis Browns	AB	R	H	O	A	E
Lary, ss	5	1	1	1	2	0
Pepper, cf	5	1	3	5	1	0
Solters, lf	5	1	2	3	0	0
Bottomley, 1b	3	1	1	4	0	0
Bell, rf	4	1	1	2	0	0
Clift, 3b	3	0	2	0	3	0
Hemsley, c	1	0	0	1	1	0
Giulani, c	3	0	0	6	1	0
Carey, 3b	4	0	3	2	1	0
Knott, p	0	0	0	0	0	1
Caldwell, p	2	0	0	0	1	0
*Coleman	1	0	0	0	0	0
Hogsett, p	0	0	0	0	0	0
**West	1	0	0	0	0	0
Van Atta, p	0	0	0	0	0	0
Totals	37	5	13	24	10	1

New York Yankees	AB	R	H	O	A	E
Crosetti, ss	5	1	1	2	4	0
Rolfe, 3b	5	3	2	0	0	1
DiMaggio, lf	6	3	3	1	0	0
Gehrig, 1b	5	5	4	7	0	0
Dickey, c	3	1	0	8	1	0
Chapman, cf	4	0	4	1	0	0
Hoag, cf	0	1	0	2	0	0
Selkirk, rf	3	0	1	4	1	0
Lazzeri, 2b	5	0	1	2	2	0
Gomez, p	2	0	0	0	0	0
Murphy, p	3	0	1	0	1	0
Totals	41	14	17	27	9	1

*Batted for Caldwell in 6th inning

**Batted for Hogsett in 8th inning

St. Louis	3	0	1	0	1	0	0	0	0	5
New York	4	3	0	2	0	4	1	0		14

Runs batted in: Bell, Clift 2, Chapman 5, Lazzeri 2, Gehrig 2, Dickey, Pepper 2, DiMaggio, Selkirk — Two-base hits: Clift, Chapman, Pepper, Rolfe, Larry — Three-base hits: Crosetti, Chapman 2, DiMaggio — Home run: Pepper — Bases on balls: Off Knott 3, Off Caldwell 1, Off Hogsett 3, Off Gomez 1, Off Murphy 1 — Struck out: By Gomez 3, By Murphy 4, By Caldwell 4, By Van Atta 1 — Hit by pitcher: By Hogsett (Hoag) — Wild pitch: Hogsett.

Winning pitcher: Murphy

Losing pitcher: Knott

Umpires: Summers, Johnston and Owen

Di Maggio's Heave to Plate to Nip Fox
Recalls Bob Meusel Heyday in Stadium

Titanic Throw from Outfield in Ninth Saves Triumph for Yanks.

By DANIEL.

JOE DI MAGGIO, the new Duce of the diamond, who has helped the Yankees to revive Murderers' Row of the 1927 offensive, today had added another outstanding achievement to the list of feats he has put on display since he made his American League debut last Sunday. Having proved to the complete satisfaction of even the most carping critics that he could hit and field, Joe yesterday cut loose with his arm and made one of the most remarkable throws seen in the Stadium since the Bob Meusel heyday.

Di Maggio's heave, which cut down the fleet Pete Fox at the plate in the ninth inning, wasn't just an exhibition throw. It was the smashing climax of a dramatic ball game. It saved victory for the New Yorks, by 6 to 5, after Bill Dickey's second homer had driven in three runs in the eighth, and reclaimed the contest from the clutches of the Tigers.

Examination of the official score shows that to Ted Kleinhans, successor to John Broaca and Bump Hadley, went the credit for having pitched the triumph. But the best strike of the battle was thrown by Di Maggio in that thrilling ninth.

Yankees Headed for West Determined to Keep Lead

Oust Red Sox from First Place by Conquering A's In Final Game of Brilliant Home Stand, in Which Di Maggio Hits Homer.

By DANIEL,
World-Telegram Staff Correspondent.

WITH THE YANKEES, bound for St. Louis, May 11.—In first place nearly a month earlier than they achieved that position last year, and determined not to fritter away their advantage again, the Yankees today were headed for the Mississippi, and their first invasion of the West.

It was a 7 to 2 victory over the Athletics, before the biggest Stadium crowd of the season—32,034 paid—that sent the Broadway boys into the pacemaking position. While Johnny Murphy was making his first pitching start of the year a winning one—even though Pat Malone had to dash in and hurl him out of a tight situation in the eighth inning—the Red Sox were being knocked off by the Senators, 4 to 0.

The entire Sabbath program tended to increase the confidence and elation of the Yankees. They rolled along the highway toward the sunset in glee over the fact that in Washington yesterday Lefty Grove, their nemesis, had been knocked out of the box. After having allowed only one earned run in forty-eight innings, Robert Mose finally got his comeuppance, and Boston sank into second place.

The Yankee valedictory in the Stadium, which was marked by Joe DiMaggio's first home run in the American League, ended a home stay in which the New Yorks won ten out of twelve, losing only to the White Sox and the Athletics, and sweeping the series with the Indians, Browns and Tigers.

Joe McCarthy's club has demonstrated remarkable strength on its home field, where it has won fourteen games out of seventeen, for an .824 gait. Not only did the Yanks win consistently at home, but they drew remarkably well, particularly when one considers the average temperature for the seventeen contests. The total attendance was 277,000. It looks as if old times have come back in the Ruppert arena.

Babe Ruth Sees DiMaggio Hit Ruth Homer, Fan Like Babe.

Among those who saw the new York victory yesterday was Babe Ruth. He had not seen DiMaggio in action at St. Petersburg, and he was eager to watch Joe against American League pitching.

The Babe saw the little Bambino hit a Ruth homer, and he also saw Giuseppe swing three in one of those enthusiastic Ruth strikeouts.

DiMaggio swatted that bulls-eye in the first inning, after Red Rolfe had worked George Turbeville for a pass. Jolting Joe jounced George's first pitch—a ball far on the outside—into the right field bleachers to send the fast increasing DiMaggio Marching and Rooting Club into a frenzy.

The Babe smiled with satisfaction, and sat back to see some more of the little Bambino. But Joe did not get another hit. He flied out in his next two tries. Then he came up in the sixth innings with the bases loaded, and two out.

The lefthanded Whitey Wilshere was pitching for the Mackmen. Whitey has a pretty good curve ball. He showed it to DiMag thrice in succession, and Joe took three of those gorgeous, healthy Ruth swings to fan in the approved, copyrighted Ruth manner. The Bam grinned, and started for the exit.

In left field, DiMaggio's most important contribution was a splendid catch on Frank Higgins with two out and runners on first and third in the sixth inning.

Dickey's Seventh Home Run Settles Issue in Fifth.

It looks very much as if Bill Dickey intends to grab the home run championship of the Yankees away from our Lou Gehrig. On Saturday, Gehrig blasted his fourth and served notice of intention to overhaul the lanky catcher. But yesterday, while Larruping Lou was getting on base only through being hit with a couple of pitched balls, Dickey blasted his seventh homer into the right field bleachers. Scoring Gehrig in front of Bill, this drive brought the New York run total to six, and settled the issue.

That Murphy was unable to finish what he started may be blamed on the strange light which hampers pitchers in the Stadium at this time of the year. Johnny said in the eighth inning, when he suddenly lost control and issued four passes, the freakish sun slanted over the grandstand roof in such a way as to make it impossible for him to see the plate. Lefty Gomez and Charley Ruffing corroborated this testimony.

Browns First To Face Yanks In Hinterland

McCarthy Taking Nothing for Granted on Jaunt Through West.

By DANIEL,
Staff Correspondent.

ST. LOUIS, May 12.—Out here where the muddy Mississippi rises and falls, but the Browns just keep falling, the Yankees today opened their first invasion of the West. The Broadway Boys set out on their Argosy in first place. The Browns, or more aptly the Blues, staggering under the weight of thirteen successive defeats, were deeply embedded in Mr. Harridge's cellar. But Rogers Hornsby's lads were lusting for red meat, and Joe McCarthy and his entourage confessed that they were taking nothing for granted, and looking for a difficult series.

Buoyed up by fourteen successes in their most recent seventeen games, strengthened by the return of Ben Chapman, and an eager Joe Di Maggio who has had a week's American League competition and wrestling with divers types of pitching; out in front weeks before they achieved that position in 1935, the Yankees presented a formidable front to the West.

From three games here the New Yorks will pass to a couple of contests in Chicago, three in Cleveland and a climactic duo in Detroit. In New York the Yankees won eight out of nine from the Western contingent. Seven out of ten would satisfy McCarthy on this trip.

Last year, when the Yankees won 89 and lost 60, they had the best road record in the league, with 48 and 27. In the four Western cities the Ruppert Rifles won 24 and lost 20, which was no better than .545. It will take about ninety-five victories to win the pennant this season, and the Yankees will have to pick up those six and three more in this part of the country. The importance of this venture beyond the Alleghenies is manifest.

Malone Assumes New Importance on Staff.

In the past McCarthy never did much maneuvering with pitchers. He held to the idea that going along from day to day was the best plan. But now he is looking ahead and scheming for every one of the ten games scheduled on this tour.

In this scheming Pat Malone assumes a new importance on the Yankee pitching staff. Last year Blubber was a wretched failure. McCarthy's unwavering belief in Pat in the face of repeated collapses had much to do with the ultimate deficit in the standing.

But the Yankees now boast a new Malone, in good shape, determined to regain the place he boasted when he was with the Cubs. Pat has set a dozen victories as his goal. He got off to a fine start with his first complete game in three seasons when he beat the Browns in the Stadium, and he hurled a fine relief job on Sunday. He is slated to start again tomorrow.

McCarthy is trying to arrange the schedule so that Charley Ruffing and Lefty Gomez will pitch the two games in Chicago and come back for the pair in Detroit. Johnny Murphy, whose curve ball behaved famously for seven innings on Sunday against the Athletics, may induce Marse Joe to make a few changes. However, Johnny still finds the eighth inning unfamiliar territory—a habit he must have acquired when he specialized in those seven-inning second games of double-headers in Newark.

McCarthy's chief job on the pitching staff on this trip is to rehabilitate Johnny Broaca, who has finished only one out of five games. Getting Ruffing to forget that home run ball is another task for the pilot of the Broadway Boys.

Di Mag Has 'Em Guessing

Pitchers Fail to Find Yank Star's Weakness as Average Nears .400.

By DANIEL,
World-Telegram Staff Correspondent.

CHICAGO, May 15.—Lo and behold, when the Yankees arrived here today from St. Louis, they found Joe Di Maggio perched on the top rung of their batting averages! With three doubles and a single in five times up in the parting 6 to 1 victory over the Browns, Jolting Joe lifted his record to a resplendent .400.

When Di Maggio left New York for the first tour of the West in his young life, his average had been whittled from the upper .400's down to .323. It looked as if the opposition might have discovered the hitherto unfound Heel of Achilles of the Italian outfielder from the Golden Gate. It was recollected that in New York, Rogers Hornsby had voiced the suspicion that a low curve ball could baffle Giuseppe, or at least present serious discouragements.

But that low curve ball is not the solution to the problem of stopping the Little Bambino. In fourteen times at bat in the three contests in St. Louis, Di Maggio made seven hits, for an average of .500. He was the only Yankee who improved his batting record in the jousts with the Browns.

In five encounters with St. Louis pitching, Di Maggio has accumulated thirteen hits in twenty-five tries, for .520.

Di Maggio has made eighteen hits since he broke into the New York line-up two weeks ago Sunday. He has walloped a homer, and he has crashed a triple and a flock of doubles. He hasn't made a single mistake in the field. On the contrary, he has flashed a fine burst of speed, cool, calculating and a marvelous arm. Jolting Joe harbors the unannounced ambition to lead the club in hitting in his first season. Stranger things have happened.

DiMag Center Of New Break In Tribe Park

Clubs Near Warfare in Ninth Inning of New Yorkers' Victory.

By DANIEL,
Staff Correspondent.

DETROIT, May 20. — Vendetta! Not to mention a few vivas. The feud between the New York Yankees and the Indians was on today in earnest. Interesting developments were promised in the remaining seventeen meetings of the American League contenders. It is to be regretted that the schedule forced the New Yorks to quit Cleveland last evening, after the small riot threatened in the ninth inning of the Yankee victory, by 10 to 4.

Joe Di Maggio was the unconscious storm center. Billy Knickerbocker was the enemy aggressor. Stalking to avenge Di Maggio, Tony Lazzeri walked from the New York dugout like Wyatt Earp proceeding down the main stem of Tombstone for the bloody battle that still is the talk of the Arizona metropolis. Tony was Billy the Kid, ready for the draw. Close behind him came Fankie Crosetti, attended by fifteen other Yankees, nobody running, everybody with shoulders hunched up, perhaps ready for a fight, perhaps intending just to look on.

Here's how it all happened. Di Maggio opened the ninth with his second hit, a single to right. At this time the New Yorks were leading by 7 to 4 in their fifth consecutive victory over the Indians. The populace was giving the well known tribe the buzzer. The Redskins were sore and sour.

Up came Lou Gehrig. He grounded to Boze Berger, who flipped the ball to Knickerbocker, apparently starting a double play. However, as Di Maggio sprawled in the dirt, the ball came flying at him. It missed its mark. Then the fun began, with Signor Lazzeri in the van.

Knickerbocker practically admitted he had tried to hit DiMaggio. When Earle Combs said to Billy, "You can't take it," Knickerbocker replied, "Well, that guy has been trying to cut me down."

Lazzeri Rushes to Defend Joe. Who Wonders What It's About.

As Di Maggio picked himself up, he had no idea of what had happened. All he knew was that Gehrig was safe, and the ball had got away from Knickerbocker. Giuseppe looked up, and there was Lazzeri shouting at him for having failed to visit merited punishment on Knickerbocker. On the other side of the bag was Knickerbocker, being shoved about by Umpires Basil and Kolla.

From the New York dugout streamed the Yankees. From the Cleveland bench came the entire tribe of Indians, ridiculously unwarlike. For a short while there was high and pleasant promise of a repetition of the Battle of Washington, started in similar circumstances by Ben Chapman and Buddy Myer in 1933.

But in the case which here is being recorded for posterity, Lazzeri seemed to be the only really outraged citizen. There was a tremendous lot of jawing on the field, and there were tentative gestures which encouraged the belief that the American League at last would grab the 1936 brawling championship away from the Nationals.

Joe McCarthy was one of those who eased into the arena. He was a mission of peace. Umpire Kolls got into the melee and threw a damper on it by hollering, "Boys, be careful! It costs at the rate of $100 a punch in this league."

After some six or seven minutes, the non-combative combatants dispersed, and the aroused Yankees heaped three more runs on the helpless Indians. It was great while it lasted.

Knickerbocker and Hughes Riding For a Fall, Says the League.

The ill-feeling between the Yankees and the Indians traces to the three straight defeats which the tribe suffered some time ago in the Stadium. Knickerbocker and Roy Hughes got quite funny. The New Yorks had been told about the pranks of the Cleveland midway duo. The whole league is talking about Billy and Roy, and predicting that they are riding for a fall. Men who play short and second live in glass houses.

There were a few ugly clashes in the Sunday game in Cleveland. Di Maggio rolled Knickerbocker, and Johnny Allen tried to knock Lou Gehrig into right field.

In the seventh inning yesterday Bad News Hale kicked the ball out of Crosetti's hands in a hot play at third base. In that same frame, Frank Pytlak charged Monte Pearson like the wild bull of Bashan, in a close encounter at first base.

Behind these divers encounters lay New York's jubilation over Pearson's second victory against Cleveland and Johnny Allen's two setbacks by the Broadway Boys. Behind Cleveland's combative attitude was chagrin over the sour turn taken by the much discussed Pearson-for-Allen exchange of last December.

Di Maggio, Hero and Goat in Yankee Loss, Finds Major League Fates Treacherous

Jolting Joe Fans Twice With Winning Run On Base.

By DANIEL,
Staff Correspondent.

DETROIT, May 21.—Joseph Paul Di Maggio Jr. today appreciated that playing baseball in the American League was not one round of pleasure. For the first time in his short and meteoric career as a Yankee, the Little Bambino was confronted with the poignant realization that while the fates of the diamond may be jolly builder-uppers, they may turn treacherous in the flash of an eye and become sour knocker-downers.

The intricate philosophy of major league life was driven home to Di Maggio in the 4 to 3 defeat which the Yankees suffered at the hands of the Tigers yesterday, when Marvin Owen lifted one of Red Ruffing's fast balls over the left center wall in the tenth inning. Into the overtime session Ruffing held Schoolboy Rowe better than even. But when it was all over it was found that the Schoolboy had scored his tenth triumph, as against four defeats, over the New York in three years, and that they had yet to achieve a second victory over him at Navin Field.

Di Maggio kept riding a heavy ground swell all afternoon. First he was the goat, then he was the hero. He fanned with the tying tally on second and two out in the eighth. And in the tenth, with Ruffing on third and two gone, Jolting Joe once more found himself on the spot. Again he struck out. He was enveloped in excitement all through this most dramatic battle of the six-

Fothergill Calls Turn When Di Mag Whiffs

Special to the World-Telegram.

DETROIT, May 21.—Among the 18,000 who gloried in the discomfiture of the Yankees at Navin Field yesterday was Fat Fothergill, one-time outfielder for the Tigers. When Di Maggio fanned the first time, Fat announced:—"That's the ball with which to stop this kid. He strides all wrong."

When Ruffing and Rolfe were on the bases, with two out in the tenth, and Di Maggio strode to the plate, Fothergill predicted:— "The kid will strike out on three slow curves."

And so today Fat's weight as a prophet stood as high as his poundage, which has become too enormous to compute.

teen in which he has competed in the American League.

Standing out in black ink in the day's accounts for Di Maggio was his second home run as a Yankee. He drove it 370 feet against the iron base of the new upper right field stand. In the fourth inning Giuseppe had crashed a hit like a rifle shot through Charley Gehringer—a single which soon blossomed into New York's first run, and tied the score. But in his two chances with men on the bases Jolting Joe became Dour Di Maggio. Life suddenly rose up and punched him right on the nose.

To be sure, Giuseppe had not gone through his fifteen previous games without some sour looks from fickle fortune. He had had three hitless games—two against the Athletics, and one against Ted Lyons, of the

Coast Star Clouts Rowe's Speedball, but Falls For Curve.

White Sox, last Saturday. Nor was striking out a new experience for the Little Bambino. He had been fanned four times—by Vernon Wilshire, George Blaeholder, Lyons and Earl Caldwell. But the sum total of all these untoward developments did not approach the grief which heaped itself on Giuseppe as Rowe fanned him twice yesterday.

Detroit believes that in those two strikeouts Rowe solved the problem of stopping this 21-year-old phenomenon from the Golden Gate. The Schoolboy did it with slow curves. Three of them in the eighth, three more in the fatal tenth. And let it be said that Rowe's let-up ball is not exactly the easiest in the league to gauge.

Whether Rowe really made an important discovery, or whether his solution, like others, will be blasted the next time he faces Di Maggio, the fact remains that Giuseppe showed he could hit red hot speed and Rowe as well.

As he drew a pass his first time up, Joe had an even .500 afternoon against the Schoolboy. Only four other hits were made off Rowe—Lou Gehrig's grand triple, which hit the right field screen and led to a tie in the ninth; George Selkirk's run-making double in the fourth, and singles by Rolfe and Ruffing.

Di Maggio has been up 68 times and has made 27 hits, a dozen of them for extra bases. He is hitting a gaudy .397, with two homers, a triple and nine doubles. His first homer was off George Turbeville, of the Athletics, on May 10.

Joe DiMaggio is considered one of the most graceful fielders the game has ever known.

Tour Triumph for DiMaggio

Rookie Joe Retains Spotlight as Yanks Move Back East in First Place.

By JAMES M. KAHN.

BUTLER, Pa., May 22.—The Yankees concluded their first Western trip with a spiraling nose-dive in Detroit after smooth sailing through the other outposts of the midland circuit. By dropping the final two games to the Tigers they wound up with a total of five victories against four defeats.

It wasn't a bad showing, and they are heading back into the East still in first place. That is not only something. If they can do that on every one of their junkets it will be everything. However, if the let down at the finish deprived the Yanks of becoming conquering heroes in the West, at least one of their members turned the invasion into a tour of triumph. As might be expected, said member is Rookie Joe DiMaggio, and he has given the answer to those who wanted to see what young Joe would do after he had been "once around."

What did he do in the West? Here are some figures that tell the story, at least about his batting. What they don't show is the general excitement he aroused among fans and rival players alike, the fine fielding he contributed to what success the Yanks had and the inspiring effect his proficiency at the plate has had on his teammates.

Nobody stopped him. He hit .500 in St. Louis, .400 in Chicago, .444 in Cleveland and .556 in Detroit. For the nine games played with the four Western clubs he compiled a batting average of .476. He made twenty hits, and just half of them were for extra bases. He clouted nine two-baggers and a homer, in addition to ten singles. He was a wow.

His Batting Average .411.

Joe is returning East after having appeared in sixteen games, with a batting average of .411, which leads the club. Only Washington remains for him to face, and that

Holiday Twin Bill.

The Dodgers and Giants will play a double-header at Ebbets Field on Memorial Day, instead of morning and afternoon contests as originally scheduled. Tickets will be put on sale next Monday. The holiday contests will open a three-game series between the interborough rivals, after which they will start on their second western invasions. The Giants will go to Chicago and the Dodgers to St. Louis.

will not come off until the Fourth of July. Every one else, however, has had a crack at him, and the summation is that Rookie Joe is quite a hitter and quite a ball player and that he is going to get better as he goes along.

The effervescent Mickey Cochrane, who is a square shooter and ever ready to deal out credit where it is due, said after the windup of the series in Detroit yesterday "that young DiMaggio is quite a ball player."

"He's a real good hitter," says Iron Mike, who has looked at a lot of them from his post back of the plate. "I've never seen a hitter with a nicer free swing than that kid has."

Up in the lofty Detroit press box, which is perched on top of the roof off to one corner, is a radio announcer who broadcasts the games. He is a former ball player and in his day was a powerful right-handed hitter. With the passing of time it has come to be acknowl-edged that he was one of the great right-handed hitters of all time. His name is Harry Heilmann. What does he think of a youngster who may become the greatest right-handed hitter the game ever knew?

"Marvelous," chirps Harry. "He's simply great. Why, he looked better to me striking out twice against Rowe than he did hitting that home run. Why? Well, because of the way he swung at the stuff Rowe was tossing. Rowe got him with outside curves. They were honeys. But don't let that throw you off. You say Hornsby says an outside curve is going to stop DiMaggio. Well, tell me what hitter a real good curve, kept low and outside, won't fool. That's the pitch they're all suckers on. Hornsby isn't coming up with anything new when he says DiMaggio can be stopped with that."

Not Like Babe Ruth.

Having been "once around," Di-Maggio has justified everything his Coast boosters said about him. Fans and baseball men have been lying back, hoping for a successor to Babe Ruth to come along as a magnet and a provoker of excitement. DiMaggio is not going to be another Babe Ruth. No one is going to be another Babe Ruth, because there was only one like him, and Rookie Joe isn't that style of ball player, anyway.

Instead of being the second Babe Ruth, here is a young man who is going to be the first Joe DiMaggio, and that may turn out to be something just as glamorous and exciting. With his continued playing he is coming up to the physical trim and spryness of those who had weeks of playing and training while he was doctoring his injured foot. He is picking up speed rather than slowing down.

Altogether, he is a powerhouse clouter and a fine defensive fielder who is adding tremendously to the pennant chances of the McCarthy-men. Not the least of their successes in the West was finding out that Rookie Joe, off to a great start, is not inclined to stop suddenly, and that they have acquired a player in him who is generally coveted throughout the league.

Yanks Home for 17 Games

Di Maggio Vital Figure in Keeping Ruppert Flag Contenders at Top Throughout Trip.

By DANIEL.

BACK in New York with the American League lead, which they held without a break throughout their trip of sixteen games, of which they won ten, the Yankees today got set for a home stay in which they are scheduled to play seventeen contests. They tackle the Senators in tomorrow's holiday double-header and the Red Sox in a single meeting on Sunday. After a Monday picnic at West Point the Ruppert Rifles will dig in for a long series against the West. The White Sox will be in the Bronx on Tuesday.

The Yankees left the Stadium on Sunday, May 10, with Joe Di Maggio their big story. They came back with the Italian outfielder a more vital figure than ever in their pennant-winning scheme.

When Di Maggio hit the road for his debut in all the other American League cities, except Washington, he had made eleven hits in thirty-one times at bat, for an average of .323. The sceptics predicted that the broad and difficult highway would take care of the youngster's aspirations and drop him under the .300 mark.

Di Maggio returned here today with his batting average a gay .375—a gain of fifty-two points. In nine games in the West he hit .467. In the sixteen contests on the road he made thirty-one hits in eighty-one tries, for .383. The kid must be good.

Giuseppe hit three of his four home runs in enemy parks. When the customers in Philadelphia will rear up and holler "Viva!" for a Yankee rookie that newcomer must be credited with an allure that can overcome one of the most violent municipal prejudices in baseball.

Two Singles, Triple and Steal Climax Boston Feats.

Di Maggio took charge in yesterday's 10-to-6 victory in Boston. He got two singles and a triple, and achieved his third stolen base. His first hit, in the fourth inning, soon became New York's entering wedge. His second single drove in two runs and helped to pump vitality into the Yankee rally for six tallies in the seventh inning. He stole third in that frame. In the next inning Joe tripled to the center field fence and scored on a passed ball. His drive went 410 feet on the fly.

The Yankees pulled hard for Di Maggio to stretch that hit into a home run. But Doc Cramer made a fast recovery and Art Fletcher stopped the Little Bambino at third.

Because a strong wind blew in over the left field fence and carried fly balls toward right, the home run orgy of the Yankees, which had stretched through nine consecutive games in which they made twenty-one circuit drives, was stopped. They were shooting at the home run streak of eleven straight games of the 1922 Browns, who hit twenty bullseye in that stretch. It is believed that twenty-one in nine contests is a record. The New Yorks have forty-five homers in all, with Bill Dickey leading with nine.

One of the blushing heroes of yesterday's gale-swept, chilled imbroglio, was Pat Malone, who managed to go the route for the Yankees. Malone has made four starts and has won three and lost one.

This Morning . . .

With Shirley Povich.

New York, May 30.

Certain New Yorkers, you know the type, can almost turn a guy against the town. With them anything that bears the New York label is no·less than great; at least they'll argue that it has no superior. To hear 'em tell it, it's unthinkable that New York doesn't boast the best, be it subways, traffic lights or Spaghetti Caruso.

So, naturally, when New Yorkers boasted to this department that young Joe DiMaggio is the best-looking rookie outfielder·to break into the big leagues since a fellow named Ty Cobb put in his appearance in 1905, why, as far as I was concerned, great suspicion attached to DiMaggio's talents.

POVICH.

But I got an eyeful of DiMaggio this afternoon in those two games against Washington, and, brother, methinks they haven't overrated him much. If there's anything that DiMaggio can't do on a baseball field, I dunno what it is. That .380 batting average he's sporting around is no myth (as three consecutive doubles off Buck Newsom's pitching in the second game attest) and the only thing that will stop that guy from dragging down every ball hit into his field is the fences.

I saw him light out after a tremendous wallop off Jake Powell's bat in the first game and the way he was loping along, you'd a-thought he was giving up on the ball, but there's where you'd a-been wrong. The guy apparently is a great judge of pace. Anyway, he meandered over there onto the running track and gathered the ball in as if by appointment, with no more lost motion than you'd have found in Dillinger's trigger finger.

He's got poise. The last thing you'd be willing to believe about DiMaggio is that he's a Johnny-come-lately in the big leagues. Up at the plate he oozes confidence. Not an unnecessary waggle, ... any kind of a waggle, in fact, is discernable in his statuesque stance. He just holds his bat where he likes to hold it, a bit out in front, and waits for the pitch he likes.

And he doesn't shorten up any on that bat handle, either. He did tolerably well when he led the Coast League hitters for two years with his hands way down on the handle, and he isn't figuring the big league pitchers as much tougher, apparently. Anyway, he seems to be doing very well for himself.

He got one lucky hit today—that was the bat-handle double to rightfield that he knocked against Newsom in the fourth inning of the second game, but there was nothing illegitimate about those other two doubles or that single that he whacked. But his hardest sock of the day didn't even get into the hit column. That was the prodigious line drive that he walloped up against the stands in leftfield in his last turn at bat when Johnny Stone, who was playing back in Westchester County, dragged the ball down with a one-hand running catch.

I had heard that the guy could run, but I saw the evidence today, that was in the fifth inning of the second game when he skimmed a hit over second base into centerfield. Jake Powell came up with that ball as clean as a whistle, and his throw to second was well-nigh perfect, but DiMaggio was picking himself up out of the dust at second base by that time. He had stretched an ordinary single into a two-bagger with a greyhound burst of speed.

The tip-off on the guy apparently is Buck Newsom's lack of success against him today. Newsom had been claiming ever since DiMaggio came into the big leagues that he had a batting weakness that Newsom had discovered while pitching against him in the Coast League. Newsom found his weakness all right. In the boxscore it is identified as a weakness for two-base hits (3).

You don't have to take my word for his greatness. Bucky Harris, the last rival manager to view DiMaggio in action. thinks he's the best-looking rookie that ever stepped into a big-league outfield,, and Clark Griffith, who has given 50 years of his life to baseball, says he's a wonder. no less.

Every club in the league has now seen something of DiMaggio, to their sorrow. Only the A's have been able to check his mad batting streak, and Connie Mack did that by running into some luck in the placing of his infielders and outfielders whenever the new Walloping Wop appeared at the plate. But other managers confess frankly that they don't know how to play a guy who hits to all fields. If you're interested, here's his record against each club this season:

	G.	A.B.	R.	H.	R.B.I.	Ave.
St. Louis	5	25	6	13	5	.520
Washington	2	8	2	4	1	.500
Detroit	4	17	5	8	4	.471
Cleveland	2	9	2	4	1	.440
Chicago	2	10	2	4	0	.400
Boston	3	16	4	5	8	.313
Philadelphia	7	35	9	8	7	.229
Totals	25	120	30	46	26	.383

Rookie Hero As Yankees Trip Boston

Triple in Twelfth Beats Red Sox—His Average Is Now .381.

By DANIEL.

HAVING won five straight and stretched their lead to four and a half games, the Yankees today stopped for a little picnic at West Point before starting the reception of the Western clubs in the Stadium.

As the players disported themselves in a welcome respite from league competition, Joe McCarthy and Ed Barrow foregathered with Colonel Jake Ruppert in the marble halls of the brauhaus and felicitated each other over the grandest bargain and one of the most inspired purchases in Ruppert's twenty-two years of Yankee ownership. The subject of their jubilation was Joseph Paul Di Maggio, Jr., of North Beach, San Francisco.

That Di Maggio is a really great ball player, and one of the most remarkable first-year outfielders of the last twenty years, already has been proved beyond debate. If there still were any lingering doubters, they were won over to the side of the Italian lad in the twelfth inning yesterday, when his triple beat the Red Sox by 5 to 4.

That Di Maggio is a tremendous factor at the box office now also is an established fact. The 71,754 who saw the Yankees take the Memorial Day double-header from the Senators, with the Little Bambino making three successive doubles in the nightcap, and the 41,781 fans who attended yesterday's festivities proved by their acclaim of Jolting Joe that he is second only to Babe Ruth as the most intriguing attraction the Yankees have boasted in the last two decades.

Colonel Ruppert certainly got a bargain when he landed Di Maggio. All sorts of fantastic sums have been named in connection with the purchase. As a matter of record, Jake gave up only $25,000 in real money. He threw in a lot of cast-off players who weren't worth much more than the fare to San Francisco.

Hits in Fourteenth Straight Game, Lifts Average to .381.

In return for those twenty-five grand Jake has an outfielder who has hit in fourteen consecutive games, who has lifted his average to .381, who can field and run, throw and make those turnstiles click. It's the luck of the rich all over again.

Having faced both Schoolboy Rowe and Lefty Grove, Di Maggio now has seen some of the best fast ball pitching of the American League. In Detroit Joe got to the Schoolboy for a homer and a single. Yesterday Giuseppe could not solve Grove until the fourth try, when Di Maggio belted a single into center field and drove in two runs. Those tallies tied the score at 4 to 4.

Di Maggio's solid smack also impressed on Joe Cronin the desirability of removing Grove before Lefty suffered a more severe shock to his finer sensibilities. You know, Grove doesn't like to pitch in the Stadium. In the eighth Cronin let Bing Miller bat for Robert Mose and sent Fritz Ostermueller in to finish the game. Ostermueller pitched hitless, shut-out ball for four innings—and then Frankie Crosetti singled, was forced by Red Rolfe, and Di Maggio sent a low, outside pitch into a crazy careen in right field for the old ball game.

Bump Hadley's Third Victory Shows Him in Regal Splendor.

Di Maggio's were the crashing, obvious accomplishments in yesterday's thriller. The more subtle hero was Irving Bump Hadley, who in registering his third victory as a Yankee hurled nine and two-thirds innings in which he allowed only five hits and one run. The Red Sox scored in the seventh when a screwball got away from Rolfe and a slow ball eluded Bump's too eager effort. Cramer's single to right in the eighth was the only solidly hit ball off Hadley's pitching.

Hadley was rushed to the relief of Johnny Broaca, with one out in the third. Bump then took care of McNair and Werber on strikes. In nine starts Broaca has gone the route only twice. He has been knocked out seven times. Every time he goes into a game he leaves it feeling as if he had met Joe Louis. But with all his ill luck Broaca has been fortunate, nevertheless. His official record is:—Won, 3; lost, 0. Which proves again that all is not gold that glitters.

Setting the Pace

By FRANK GRAHAM

Going About: In the Yankees' Office.

Edward Grant Barrow, who does the Yankees' scouting by remote control and otherwise superintends all the details of the club that do not fall upon Joe McCarthy in the actual management of the young men on the field, leaned back in his big chair and gazed at the crowds sauntering by in the sun on Forty-second street.

"Well," he said, "I guess we fooled you with our ball club this year. You didn't think it was so good, did you?"

You told him you didn't. That you thought it was just a second-place ball club. That it would beat the Red Sox and the Indians, but that it couldn't beat the Tigers. But now——

"Don't say it," he said. "I don't like to hear such things so early in the season. . . . Still, I don't know who is going to beat us, at that."

You fell, rather naturally, to talking of Joe DiMaggio, just as every one else seems to be doing.

"He's a pretty darned good ball player," Barrow said. "I'll tell you a funny one about him. When he first came here this spring in advance of the club I gave him a little friendly talk. I wanted to warn him against overeagerness. I wanted him to know we wouldn't expect him to deliver everything he had every time he went to the plate. I was just trying to make him feel at home and, maybe, soothe his jumping nerves. He listened to me very politely and when I got through he said:

" 'Thanks very much, Mr. Barrow. But don't worry about me. I never get excited.' "

Between You and Me

.... BY ED BANG ....

A "spittin' image" of the late Ed Delahanty, that's what the old boys of baseball are saying about Joe DiMaggio, the kid outfielding and batting phenom of the New York Yankees, touted by many to make the big town fans forget about Babe Ruth.

Bill Dinneen, veteran indicator handler and himself a great pitcher in his day (he won three world series games for the Boston Red Sox against the Pittsburgh Pirates back in 1903) can see the late and lamented "Del" in every move the kid makes.

When Dinneen, who just finished umpiring a series at League park, saw "Di Mag" step to the plate the first time, he said he could scarcely believe his eyes.

His memory went back almost twoscore years. Bill couldn't take his optics off that thin-handled bat with the big bottle effect end and the stance of the individual holding it.

Of course, he knew it was Di-Maggio, but he had to all but pinch himself to realize he wasn't seeing a ghost out of the long ago.

Di Mag's Every Action Reminds of Delahanty

THAT phantom of other years was a Clevelander, the one and only Ed Delahanty, one of the greatest hitters of all time.

Ed was the sort of hitter that once collected four home runs and a single in one game, and they say he hit the single harder than any of his circuit drives.

Del was just as much the idol of the young boys of his day, the grandfathers of the present, as were Lajoie, Cobb, Ruth, Hornsby, Wagner and other stars of the game.

Looking at DiMaggio, watching his every move at the plate, Dinneen said to himself, "There is the closest replica to Del I have ever seen."

The bat he uses, the way he swings, the manner in which he watches balls he doesn't offer at, are reminiscent of Del.

In the outfield, DiMag simply emphasizes on the likeness to the old-time star, the way he catches balls, runs and throws. His every move is taken from the same baseball mold that cast Ed Delahanty.

DANIEL'S DOPE

THIS Di Maggio person at Yankee Stadium is creating quite a stir, even across the seas. Trevor Wignall, London sports authority, who is dividing his time between the fight camps and the ball park, cabled something like 1,400 words to his paper the other day, marvelling at this new phenomenon, who is worth so many thousands of pounds on the hoof and is doing things which even Babe Ruth wasn't accomplishing at 21.

And there is Tom Laird, sports editor of the San Francisco News, dashing into the Stadium to get the latest on "my boy." Tom was the first to tout Giuseppe as a potential big league star. He was hollering "Di Maggio" from Telegraph Hill two years ago, when Jolting Joe was only a yearling with the Seals.

Laird was delighted to learn that Di Maggio was hitting a nifty .379, with sixteen doubles, five triples, four homers and thirty-three runs driven in, and had hit in seventeen straight games.

"That sounds fair, but he hasn't started yet," announced Laird. "He is just feeling his way around the league, getting acquainted with a strange position. Left field isn't his spot. Left—and a terrible sun field —at that! Give him another swing through the West, and then watch that boy! He'll have those pitchers dashing for the exits. He might go on and hit in sixty straight games.

"Has he shown you his arm? You say he made a great throw against the Tigers here? Well, you saw Bob Meusel at his best? Bob was good, wasn't he?" Laird paused for reply. "Well, before the summer is over you'll think Meusel couldn't throw any better than, let us say, Combs!" Gosh!

* * *

WAS there another Di Maggio in the making out in his Pacific Coast League? Laird exclaimed, "Another Di Maggio? Listen, they threw away the mould. Was there a second Michael Angelo? Another Beethoven.

We have a grand prospect in Eddie Joost, who plays third base for the Missions. Only 19, but has been with the club for four years. The Yanks or the Giants are suckers if they don't grab him—either Joost or Dick Gyselman, third sacker for Seattle, who some years ago had a trial with the Braves." * * *

Joe Di Maggio Big Factor In 200,000 Gain Over 1935

Yanks May Pass Record Set in 1932 if Young Star and Club Continue Present Pace— Gehrig Going at Top Speed.

By DANIEL.

EDWARD GRANT BARROW, business manager of the Yankees, sat in his office today with a form chart of the New York players before him. The record of Joe Di Maggio seemed to make especially pleasant reading for Cousin Egbert.

Barrow got quite a scare over the week-end, when Cleveland pitchers stopped Di Maggio in two games and he came up eleven successive times without hitting safely When Giuseppe not only made it an even dozen, but hit into a double play in his first trip to the plate against Jack Knott, of the Browns, yesterday Cousin Egbert got something more than a scare.

But as Barrow pored over that form sheet today, he fairly purred with satisfaction. For in the 12 to 3 drubbing of the Browns yesterday, Di Maggio crashed a 380-foot homer into the left field stands with one on; smacked a 400-foot triple with two mates on the paths, and wangled a simple little single, to lift his batting average back to a decorative .363.

How had Di Maggio affected attendance at the Stadium this year? Barrow cogitated, and then hauled out the records. "Di Maggio has done a lot, but don't forget that we have quite a ball club, which seems likely to win the pennant," explained cautious Cousin Egbert, already visioning a contract debate with Jolting Joe next winter.

"The books show that the New York club is a little more than 200,-000 paid admissions beyond 'he mark set for a similar number of games in the Stadium last season," Barrow announced.

"The records also prove that we are having by far the greatest season at the Stadium box offices we have enjoyed since the Yankees won the pennant and the world championship in 1932.

Yankees Doing Better Than In Babe's Closing Years.

"It would be reasonable to believe that if Di Maggio continues to play great ball and we remain in the race, we will beat the mark we set here in 1932." And cautious Cousin Egbert closed the books.

With Di Maggio intriguing not only all fandom, but a brand new clientele, Lou Gehrig hitting .364 and the entire club geared to a pennant gait, the Yankees are more than likely to outdo all records except those of 1926, 1927 and 1928. Those were the golden years of Babe Ruth, with 1927 the season in which he set his record of sixty homers, and when Murderers Row became a byword in American baseball.

When the Yankees won their pennant in 1932, Ruth had his last good year, hitting .341 and banging forty-one homers. Gehrig also had a grand season. The Yankees of that summer had to fight perhaps the worst year of the depression. But they saved baseball interest in New York.

Gehrig Enjoying Whale of a Season.

Now there is a Di Maggio to impel the customers toward the turnstiles. And hitting is not Giuseppe's sole virtue. His two catches yesterday more than emphasized that fact.

In the third inning, with one on and nobody out, Harland Clift crashed one toward the new left field bleachers. Giuseppe raced back, made a desperate leap and clutched that ball with his gloved hand.

Came the fifth inning, and Beau Bell hammered an even tougher offering into the Di Maggio sector. That time the bases were loaded, with two out. Once more Joe leaped, once more he grabbed that leather in its wild flight. It was the break of the ball game.

This season Gehrig is playing remarkable ball in the field. He is hitting with consistency and run-making effectiveness. His average is .364. His home runs are not numerous, for Gehrig, but they add up to eleven. He stroked the eleventh into the little parking space in front of the scoreboard with one on in the fifth inning yesterday. In short, Gehrig is enjoying one whale of a season.

Joe Di Maggio Leads Race for All-Star Berth

By the United Press.

BOSTON, June 12.—Outfielder Joe Di Maggio, of the New York Yankees, is almost certain of a berth on the American League nine which opposes a National League aggregation in the all-star game here July 7.

Latest returns in the nationwide poll of fans for the selection of players today showed the young Italian sensation far ahead of all left fielders in the junior circuit. He also has polled more votes than any other outfielder, even surpassing Earl Averill, center fielder of the Cleveland Indians.

Whether Manager Mickey Cochrane, of the Detroit Tigers, will recover in time to lead the American League team is headache No. 1 of officials in charge of the game. Cochrane not only is manager of the team, but is almost a unanimous selection for the all-star catching job. He is in Henry Ford Hospital in Detroit suffering from hyperthyroidism.

Worry about the status of Van Lingle Mungo, second choice for a National League hurler, appears at an end with announcement the one-man strike of the big right-hander was over.

Di Maggio May Also Get Into Contest

Joseph Paul Di Maggio, Jr., of the San Francisco Di Maggios, via Sicily, also is a Yankee nominee for the All Star imbroglio. To be sure, it would be breaking precedent to smithereens to put a yearling into the classic. But this looks like the year.

With a single and a three bagger —his fifth triple of the season—Di Maggio was quite active in the chastisement of Ray Phelps, who in two previous starts against the Yankees had beaten them.

That three-baser was not just one of your garden variety wallops. It came with the bags loaded and crashed off the right field wall. Explaining that he sought protection for himself and his family in his third base berth, Jimmy Dykes told Phelps to pitch outside to Joe.

Di Maggio, with an average of .382, has hit safely in sixteen consecutive games. Tricks of that sort are quite common with Giuseppe, who in 1933 set a Pacific Coast League record by socking in sixty-one straight contests.

Jolting Joe has hit four homers. With sixteen doubles, he is hot after the league leadership in that specialty.

Yanks Win, DiMaggio Tying Mark With Two Homers in One Inning

Drives Feature McCarthymen's Ten-Run Attack in Fifth as White Sox Lose, 18-11—Gehrig's Four Hits Give Him 101 for Season—Powell Connects With Bases Full.

By JOHN DREBINGER
Special to THE NEW YORK TIMES.

CHICAGO, June 24.—With Colonel Jacob Ruppert viewing the spectacle and wearing at the same time his best smile, the only one, indeed, that could be seen in the gathering of 7,000, the Yankees today put on a gorgeous show for the edification of their employer.

Joe DiMaggio hit two home runs, and Frank Crosetti, Jake Powell and Bill Dickey each exploded one. Even if our own pitching was not of the best, the twenty-four blows that sailed off the Yankee bats sufficed to bring down the White Sox with a grand crash and a final score of 18 to 11.

Yankees Extend Lead

That gave the McCarthymen the lead in the current series, two to one, restored their hold on first place over the Red Sox to five and a half games and gave our Colonel, here essentially to attend a brewers' convention, a marvelous appetite for an excellent repast.

DiMaggio's two homers, his seventh and eighth of the season, came in one inning to tie a major league record and supply the highlight of a 10-run rally which the Yanks touched off in the fifth to wreck the encounter for the Sox beyond repair.

The first DiMaggio clout, made off Babe Phelps, came with one on, and the second one, off Russell Evans, found two on the bases, to give Joe credit for driving in five tallies in a single round, only one behind the all-time record. DiMaggio also hit two doubles.

In the same inning, Powell unfurled his homer and bagged four on the shot, the clout coming with the bases full.

Lou Still Has the Range

Dickey, prior to unloading his homer in the ninth, had warmed up on three singles, while Crosetti, who opened the first with his four-master, subsequently contributed two more singles.

Lou Gehrig's home run bludgeon

The Box Score

NEW YORK (A.)	ab.	r.	h.	po.	a.	e.
Crosetti, ss.	6	3	3	4	1	0
Rolfe, 3b	6	3	3	0	2	0
DiMaggio, rf	6	3	4	1	1	0
Gehrig, 1b	5	4	4	9	0	1
Dickey, c	5	2	4	6	1	0
Selkirk, lf	4	1	1	3	0	0
Powell, cf	6	1	1	3	0	0
Heffner, 2b	5	0	2	1	7	0
Gomes, p	2	0	1	0	1	0
Malone, p	3	1	1	0	1	0
Total	48	18	24	27	14	1

CHICAGO (A.)	ab.	r.	h.	po.	a.	e.
Radcliff, lf	5	3	3	4	0	0
Rosenthal, cf	4	2	2	1	0	0
Hass, rf	4	2	0	0	0	0
Bonura, 1b	2	1	1	9	1	0
Appling, ss	4	0	2	2	2	0
Hayes, 2b	5	0	1	3	5	0
Dykes, 3b	5	0	0	0	7	0
Sewell, c	2	1	1	4	1	0
Shea, c	1	1	0	2	0	0
Cain, p	1	0	0	0	1	0
Phelps, p	1	0	0	0	1	0
Evans, p	1	0	0	1	1	0
aKreevich	1	0	1	0	0	0
Chelini, p	1	1	1	1	0	0
Total	37	11	13	27	18	0

aBatted for Evans in eighth.

New York .... 2 3 0 0 10 0 2 0 1—18
Chicago .... 3 0 1 3 0 0 0 2 2—11

Runs batted in—Crosetti, Dickey 4, Appling 3, Gehrig, Selkirk 3, Hayes 2, Sewell, Bonura 3, DiMaggio 5, Powell 4, Rosenthal 2.

Two-base hits—Rolfe, Bonura, Gehrig 2, Heffner, DiMaggio 2. Three-base hit—Radcliff. Home runs—Crosetti, Sewell, DiMaggio 2, Powell, Dickey. Double plays—Gomes, Crosetti and Gehrig; Appling, Hayes and Bonura; Hayes, Appling and Bonura; Dykes, Hayes and Bonura. Left on bases—New York 7, Chicago 10. Bases on balls—Off Gomes 6, Cain 2, Phelps 1, Malone 5, Evans 1. Struck out—By Gomes 3, Cain 3, Phelps 1, Malone 3, Evans 1, Chelini 1. Hits—Off Gomes 6 in 3 2-3 innings, Cain 7 in 2 3-3, Phelps 7 in 1 1-3, Evans 9 in 4, Malone 6 in 5 1-3, Chelini 1 in 1. Winning pitcher—Malone. Losing pitcher—Phelps. Umpires—Dineen, Geisel and Hubbard. Time of game—3:30.

was a little out of working order, but nothing serious. All Lou did was to pound out four hits, two of them doubles.

On taking an inventory this morning McCarthy found he had lost something more than the ball game in yesterday's bruising encounter. Tony Lazzeri reported on deck with a badly damaged finger that may keep the veteran second sacker on the sidelines for several days.

When Gehrig fetched up with his third blow it gave Lou the distinction of being the first player in the majors this year to gain his one hundredth hit. His seasonal total at the close of the day was 101.

By hitting two homers in one round DiMaggio tied a major league record held jointly by four others, Ken Williams, Hack Wilson, Bill Regan and Hank Leiber.

Rookie Joe DiMaggio acknowledges the cheers after hitting a home run against the St. Louis Browns in late June 1936.

Gehrig and Di Maggio Driving Yanks at Faster Gait Than '27 Murderers' Row

By DANIEL,
Staff Correspondent.

CHICAGO, June 25.—Headed by Larruping Lou Gehrig and Jolting Joe Di Maggio, the Yankee clouting circus today had picked up a gait which, if persisted in, will lift the current club above even the Huggins power magnets of 1927 in the modern ranking of run riot and hit hilarity.

In the 18-to-11 trouncing which the New Yorks heaped on the White Sox yesterday, achievements which not even the famous Murderers Row of nine years ago crashed into the record book, spattered all over Comiskey Park like hail on a tin roof. For one thing, the Clouting Circus got twenty-four hits, including five home runs and six doubles, for a total of forty-five bases.

The Yankees fell just one base behind the forty-six they accumulated on only nineteen hits in that early season 25-to-2 victory in Philadelphia.

Di Maggio, who had been somewhat quiescent in Chicago and had made the Italian colony on the South Side grieve no little over his local conservatism, put on a show which will give the sons of Romulus and Remus plenty to gloat over for some time to come.

In the first place, Di Maggio crashed two terrific home runs in one inning, bringing his four-base total to eight. For another thing, Jolting Joe drove in five runs in that one frame, and with those two drives matched a couple of league records. He also maced a couple of doubles and lifted his average to .363.

Giuseppe's home run exploits marked the fifth inning, in which the New Yorks got ten runs on as many hits for twenty-one bases. Jake Powell's circuit stroke with the bags loaded aided no little in raising the hilarious pitch of one of the most notable innings in the history of the Yankees.

For a club to gather three home runs in one inning is a trick, but not a really rare one. It had been done no fewer than eight times by the Yankees, particularly in the Ruth, Gehrig and Meusel heyday.

But never before in the annals of baseball had any team got three homers in one frame with one man accounting for two of them.

In walloping that pair of homers Di Maggio performed a feat which had been accomplished only twice before in the American League and seven times in the sixty years' existence of the National. Not even Babe Ruth, in his palmiest days, or the lethal Gehrig could get a brace of four-baggers in one frame.

In the American League, the stunt had been done by Ken Williams, of the Browns, in 1922, and Billy Regan, of the Red Sox, in 1928. Hank Leiber did it for the Giants last August. But when Di Maggio drove in five runs in one inning—two with his first homer and three with the second—Joe did something which had not been seen in his circuit since 1929, when Al Simmons was the proud hero.

Only three other American Leaguers—Ty Cobb, in 1909; Ray Bates, of the Athletics, in 1917, and Chick Gandil, of the White Sox, in 1919—had been able to sock in so many tallies in so short a space of time.

As Di Maggio's first double scored Red Rolfe, Joe drove in six runs for the afternoon. Both of his homers went into the left-field pavilion. His second drive traveled at least 400 feet on a line into the upper tier.

Di Maggio enjoyed his gala day with Colonel Jacob Ruppert looking on and getting his biggest kick of the season. It was extraordinary that two such exploits as that of Di Maggio and Gehrig should come on the same afternoon. Lou made four consecutive hits—two doubles and two singles—and with 101 drives has the distinction of being the first major leaguer to pass the century mark this season.

Gehrig is batting .404. He does not recollect such offensive opulence at this time of the year in the past. But the 33-year-old Iron Horse predicts that this will be his greatest season.

With Frankie Crosetti hitting his eighth homer and Bill Dickey his thirteenth—and not forgetting Jake Powell's first circuit smack in a Yankee uniform—the New York club has made seventy-seven four-baggers and is likely to outdo its record of 160, made in the world championship season of 1932.

The rise of Joe DiMaggio has focused attention on Italian players with major league clubs of the present and the past, writes Daniel M. Daniel in the New York World-Telegram, who points out that the New York Yankees, more than any other club, seem to have had a penchant for descendants of the Romans. "With Tony Lazzeri, Frankie Crosetti and DiMaggio, the Ruppert Rifles boast three regulars of Italian parentage, more Latins than any other combination ever has harbored at one time since major league began in 1876," Daniel observes.

"In the past, the Yankees had three other Italians, chief among them Ping Bodie, the pudgy outfielder, born Francisco Pizzola, Peoli Smith and Jack Smith, both catchers, came in later years. Neither amounted to very much. Jack was a better fighter than he was a ball player—and he wasn't much of a fighter.

"It is strange that Italian players of the major leagues have had so strong a trend towards second base. In addition to Lazzeri, we find Ed Abbaticchio of the champion Pirates of the Fred Clarke regime; Oscar Melillio of the Red Sox; Tony Cuccinello of the Bees; Louis Chiozza of the Phillies, who this season has been shifted to the outfield, and Joe Coscarart, third sacker of the Bees, who came up from the Coast league as a second baseman.

"Italian first sackers are Phil Cavarretta of the Cubs; Zeke Bonura, White Sox, and Dolf Camilli of the Phillies. At short, the legions of Rome are represented by Frankie Crosetti. At third, there is no current incumbent, but the past presents Babe Pinelli of the Reds, now a National League umpire. There are three Latin catchers—Gus Mancuso of the Giants, Ernie Lombardi of the Reds and Angelo Giuliani of the Browns. Reaching into the ranks of the flychasers, we find George Puccinelli of the Athletics and Ernie Orsatti, who was released by the Cardinals last winter.

"Our Italian delegation in baseball has yet to develop a first-class pitcher. Emile Meola, who started the season with the Browns; Joe Cascarella, Red Sox; John Pezzullo, formerly of the Phillies; Harry Coppolla, just optioned by Washington; Italo Chelini, White Sox; Bill Ferrazzi, who was with the Athletics, and Pete Daglia, who hurled for the White Sox, complete the list."

JOLTING JOE DI MAGGIO OF THE YANKEES, THE YEAR'S MOST TALKED ABOUT ROOKIE

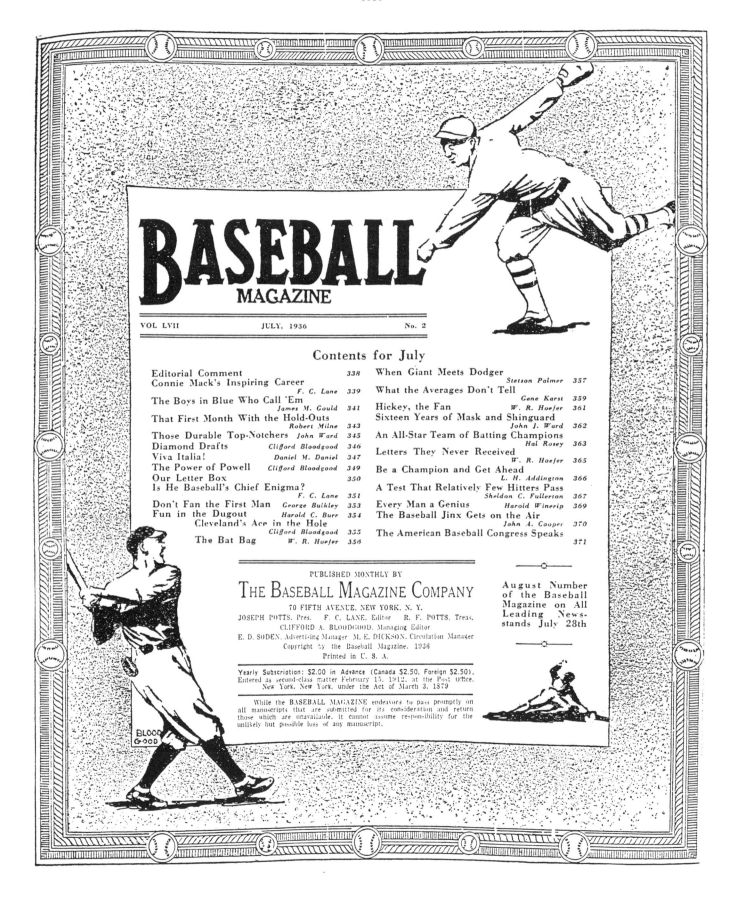

BASEBALL
MAGAZINE

VOL LVII   JULY, 1936   No. 2

Contents for July

Editorial Comment	338
Connie Mack's Inspiring Career *F. C. Lane*	339
The Boys in Blue Who Call 'Em *James M. Gould*	341
That First Month With the Hold-Outs *Robert Milne*	343
Those Durable Top-Notchers *John Ward*	345
Diamond Drafts *Clifford Bloodgood*	346
Viva Italia! *Daniel M. Daniel*	347
The Power of Powell *Clifford Bloodgood*	349
Our Letter Box	350
Is He Baseball's Chief Enigma? *F. C. Lane*	351
Don't Fan the First Man *George Bulkley*	353
Fun in the Dugout *Harold C. Burr*	354
Cleveland's Ace in the Hole *Clifford Bloodgood*	355
The Bat Bag *W. R. Hoefer*	356
When Giant Meets Dodger *Stetson Palmer*	357
What the Averages Don't Tell *Gene Karst*	359
Hickey, the Fan *W. R. Hoefer*	361
Sixteen Years of Mask and Shinguard *John J. Ward*	362
An All-Star Team of Batting Champions *Hal Rosey*	363
Letters They Never Received *W. R. Hoefer*	365
Be a Champion and Get Ahead *L. H. Addington*	366
A Test That Relatively Few Hitters Pass *Sheldon C. Fullerton*	367
Every Man a Genius *Harold Winerip*	369
The Baseball Jinx Gets on the Air *John A. Cooper*	370
The American Baseball Congress Speaks	371

PUBLISHED MONTHLY BY

THE BASEBALL MAGAZINE COMPANY

70 FIFTH AVENUE, NEW YORK, N. Y.

JOSEPH POTTS, Pres.   F. C. LANE, Editor   R. F. POTTS, Treas.
CLIFFORD A. BLOODGOOD, Managing Editor
E. D. SODEN, Advertising Manager M. E. DICKSON, Circulation Manager
Copyright by the Baseball Magazine, 1936
Printed in U. S. A.

Yearly Subscription: $2.00 in Advance (Canada $2.50, Foreign $2.50).
Entered as second-class matter February 15, 1912, at the Post Office,
New York, New York, under the Act of March 3, 1879

August Number
of the Baseball
Magazine on All
Leading News-
stands July 28th

Posing here with St. Louis Cardinal pitcher Dizzy Dean, DiMaggio is perhaps telling the masterful hurler what he plans to do to the ball with his bat. In the All-Star game of 1936, however, DiMaggio went hitless against Dean.

18 Will Make Bow Tuesday In Star Game

EXAMINING the lineups for the All-Star game to be played in Boston next Tuesday, we find that the American League has afforded an opportunity to seven newcomers.

For the first time, freshmen will play in the inter-league contest, as the American League has designated Joe Di Maggio and the National Stu Martin. These are the outstanding rookies of the year.

The American League has eleven veterans of former games, plus three who have been named before but haven't seen service. The National has thirteen vets and eight newcomers, making eighteen new men in all.

Here are the line-ups for Tuesday:—

NATIONALS	AMERICANS
OUTFIELDERS	**OUTFIELDERS**
Medwick, Cards	*Di Maggio, Yanks
Ott, Giants	Averill, Indians
Berger, Braves	*Selkirk, Yanks
*Demaree, Cubs	*Radcliff, White Sox
J. Moore, Giants	*Goslin, Tigers
*Galan, Cubs	Chapman, Senators
INFIELDERS	**INFIELDERS**
Herman, Cubs	Gehringer, Tigers
Vaughan, Pirates	Gehrig, Yanks
*Suhr, Pirates	*Appling, White Sox
*Riggs, Reds	Foxx, Red Sox
Whitney, Phillies	†Higgins, Athletics
Collins, Cards	*Crosetti, Yanks
*Durocher, Cards	
*S. Martin, Cards	
PITCHERS	**PITCHERS**
J. Dean, Cards	Grove, Red Sox
Hubbell, Giants	Gomez, Yanks
Mungo, Dodgers	*Pearson, Yanks
Warneke, Cubs	†Rowe, Tigers
*Davis, Cubs	†Bridges, Tigers
	Harder, Indians
CATCHERS	**CATCHERS**
Hartnett, Cubs	Dickey, Yankees
*Lombardi, Reds	Hemsley, Browns
	Ferrell, Red Sox

*First time selected on All-Stars

†Picked previously on All-Stars but didn't play.

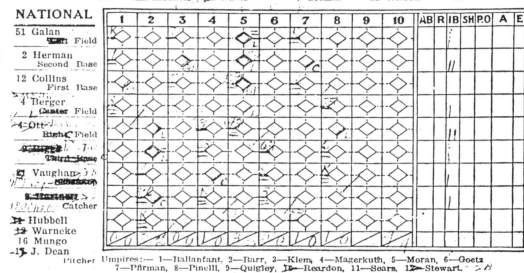

OFFICIAL 5¢ SCORE CARD

BOSTON NATIONAL LEAGUE

NATIONAL LEAGUE FIELD   SEASON 1936

1 Moore   6 S. Martin   24 Suhr   7 Grimm   12 Wilson   33 McKechnie
2 Lombardi   24 Davis

NATIONAL

51 Galan Left Field
2 Herman Second Base
12 Collins First Base
4 Berger Center Field
4 Ott Right Field
Third Base
Vaughan Shortstop
Catcher
Hubbell
Warneke
16 Mungo
J. Dean

Pitcher   Umpires:— 1—Ballanfant, 2—Barr, 3—Klem, 4—Magerkuth, 5—Moran, 6—Goetz, 7—Pfirman, 8—Pinelli, 9—Quigley, 10—Reardon, 11—Sears, 12—Stewart.

3. Selkirk   16 Pearson   4 Chapman   31 Schulte
25 Keefe   11 Hemsley   Ferrell   3 Fox   6 Cronin   29 Fletcher   McCarthy

AMERICAN

Crosetti Short Stop
2 Gehringer Second Base
9 Di Maggio Right Field
4 Gehrig First Base
Averill Center Field
Base
Goslin Left Field
Catcher
10 Bridges
11 Gomez
Harder
Rowe
Pitcher   Information as to Postponed Games Broadcast Daily at 12.59 p.m. by WNAC and WAAB

The Sporting News
THE BASE BALL PAPER OF THE WORLD

VOLUME 101, NUMBER 21   ST. LOUIS, JULY 9, 1936   TEN CENTS THE COPY 15c in Canada.

Pitching Carries N. L. All-Stars to First Triumph

A. L. STRING BREAKS IN FOURTH CONTEST

Dean, Hubbell and Warneke Effective, but Davis Is Punished; DiMaggio Misses Many Chances to Star

BOSTON, Mass.—After three long years, the worm turned here, July 7, and the National League representatives in the fourth All-Star game broke the string of the American Leaguers at three straight victories, by winning, 4 to 3. Superior pitching proved the fulcrum on which the National triumph was swung, the losers being held hitless in all but four innings, their lone threat being made in the seventh inning at the expense of Curt Davis.

Dizzy Dean, Carl Hubbell and Hal Warneke were effective throughout their tenures on the mound, the trio striking out seven, with the St. Louis hurler getting three of the whiffs and the Giant and Cub twirlers accounting for two each. The American League hurlers fanned six, Bob Grove, Schoolboy Rowe and Mel Harder each getting two. While Dean walked two, he was the most effective pitcher of the game, yielding no hits during the three innings he worked. Grove was a victim of one two-run attack by the Nationals and Rowe of the other assault that yielded a pair of tallies.

The Nationals took the lead early, scoring twice in the second inning before an out was made. Demaree led off with a single to left and Hartnett scored him with a hit that went for a triple, when DiMaggio failed to make a shoestring catch. Pinky Whitney then lofted a long fly to Averill to send Hartnett across the plate.

The second cluster of two runs for the Frick circuit came in the fifth inning,

when Augie Galan led off with an unusual home run. The ball hit the flag pole in right field and glanced off into the right field stands, in foul territory. The ruling giving Galan a round-tripper brought protests from the American Leaguers, until they were assured that it was a standard ground rule in the Boston Bees' park. The hit seemed to unsteady Rowe and Billy Herman singled sharply to left, going to second, when DiMaggio fumbled the ball. Jimmy Collins then drew a walk, after which Joe Medwick singled to left, scoring Herman.

After being almost completely throttled for six innings by Dizzy Dean and Carl Hubbell, the American Leaguers staged a real threat in the seventh inning, pounding Curt Davis, who had just gone to the mound, from the box. Lou Gehrig greeted him with a terrific home run that traveled at least 420 feet, and which was the New York first baseman's first hit in the All-Star games, none of which he had missed. Davis settled down and forced Earl Averill and Bill Dickey, who batted for Rick Ferrell, to roll out, but a barrage of hits then followed that drove the Cub pitcher out. Goose Goslin, batting for Rip Radcliff, singled past second. Jimmy Foxx, who batted for Higgins, sent a sizzler to Durocher that the shortstop knocked down, but the throw to second was too late to get Goslin, and the Red Sox first baseman was credited with a hit. Selkirk batted for Rowe and walked, filling the bases. Luke Appling then produced a single to right that scored Goslin and Foxx and the American Leaguers appeared to be on their way to a fourth straight victory. However, Lon Warneke was summoned from the bullpen at this point to take charge of the proceedings. He refused to give Charley Gehringer a good ball at which to hit, and consequently walked him to get at DiMaggio, who lined out to Durocher.

The game was cleanly played, the only error being charged to Joe DiMaggio, the rookie sensation of the New York Yankees, who had a bad afternoon. He hit into a double play in the first inning, popped out to Durocher in the fourth, rolled out in the sixth, and lined out in the seventh and popped out in the ninth to end the game. Thus, he had chances to advance runners five times and failed on each occasion. The Yankee rookie tried to make a shoestring catch of Hartnett's short liner in the second inning and permitted it to go for a triple and drive in a run, while in the fifth he played Herman's single poorly and was charged with an error when the Chicago

Cub second baseman went on to second base.

Luke Appling, Charley Gehringer and Lou Gehrig were the leading performers for the Americans and Augie Galan, Billy Herman and Dizzy Dean played stellar roles for the Nationals. Out of the squads of 21 players, Manager Charley Grimm used 14 and Pilot Joe McCarthy 17.

The crowd numbered 25,534, nearly 20,000 short of the expected attendance. The usual pre-game predictions that seats would be hard to obtain were held responsible for the failure to attract a full house.

The game in detail:

First Inning.

AMERICANS—Appling walked. Gehringer popped to Durocher. DiMaggio hit into a double play. Whitney to W. Herman to Collins. No runs, no hits, no errors.

NATIONALS—Galan fanned. W. Herman lined to DiMaggio. Collins strolled. Medwick flied to Averill. No runs, no hits, no errors.

Second Inning.

AMERICANS—Gehrig walked. Durocher went back to short left for Averill's fly. R. Ferrell struck out. With Radcliff at bat, J. Dean picked Gehrig off first base. No runs, no hits, no errors.

NATIONALS—Demaree singled to left field. Hartnett was credited with a three-base hit when DiMaggio missed a shoestring catch, Demaree scoring. Whitney hoisted to Averill. Hartnett scoring after the catch. Durocher singled, but was out trying to stretch it into a double. Averill to Appling. J. Dean fanned. Two runs, three hits, no errors.

Third Inning.

AMERICANS—Radcliff tapped to J. Dean. Higgins fanned. So did Grove. No runs, no hits, no errors.

NATIONALS—Galan lifted to Averill. W. Herman walked. Collins flied to Radcliff. Medwick popped to Radcliff. No runs, no hits, no errors.

Fourth Inning.

AMERICANS—Hubbell went in to pitch for the Nationals. Appling fouled to Demaree. Gehringer singled to right. DiMaggio lifted an infield fly to Durocher. Gehringer went to second on a passed ball. Collins knocked down Gehrig's grounder and threw to Hubbell, who covered first base. No runs, one hit, no errors.

NATIONALS—Rowe went in to pitch for Americans. Demaree fouled to Gehrig. Hartnett bounced to Appling. Whitney singled to center. Durocher struck out. No runs, one hit, no errors.

Fifth Inning.

AMERICANS—Averill popped to W. Herman. R. Ferrell fanned. Radcliff dropped a Texas leaguer into center field. Higgins fanned. No runs, one hit, no errors.

NATIONALS—Hubbell popped to Gehringer. Galan's drive, which hit the flagpole in right field, went for a home run, when it bounced into the right field stands. W.

NATIONAL LEAGUE ENDS AMERICAN STREAK

Herman singled to right, going to second when DiMaggio fumbled the ball. Collins strolled. Medwick singled to left, W. Herman scoring. Demaree hit into a double play. Higgins to Gehringer to Gehrig. Two-runs, three hits, one error.

Sixth Inning.

AMERICANS—Rowe popped to Hubbell. Appling flied to Galan. Gehringer walked. DiMaggio tapped to Hubbell. No runs, no hits, no errors.

NATIONALS—Goslin replaced Radcliff in left field. Appling tossed out Hartnett. Whitney struck out. Durocher flied to Gehrig. No runs, no hits, no errors.

Seventh Inning.

AMERICANS—Davis went in to pitch for the Nationals. Gehrig poled a home run into the right field bleachers. Averill bounced to W. Herman. Dickey batted for R. Ferrell and tapped to Davis. Goslin singled past second base. Foxx batted for Higgins and was credited with an infield hit

when Durocher stopped his sizzler but threw to W. Herman too late to get Goslin. Selkirk batted for Rowe and walked to load the bases. Appling singled to right, scoring Goslin and Foxx. Warneke replaced Davis. Gehringer walked to load the bases again. DiMaggio lined to Durocher. Three runs, four hits, no errors.

NATIONALS—Harder went in to pitch, Chapman to center, Foxx to third base and Dickey behind the bat for the Americans. Harder tossed out Warneke. Galan fanned. W. Herman singled to center. Collins flied to Goslin. No runs, one hit, no errors.

Eighth Inning.

AMERICANS—Gehrig walked. Chapman grounded to Whitney, Gehrig stopping at second. Dickey was tossed out by W. Herman, Gehrig going ot third. Goslin strolled. Foxx struck out. No runs, no hits, no errors.

NATIONALS—Foxx tossed out Medwick, Ott batted for Demaree and singled to left.

Hartnett lined to Appling. Riggs batted for Whitney and fanned. No runs, one hit, no errors.

Ninth Inning.

AMERICANS—Ott went to right field and Riggs to third base. Crosetti batted for Harder and fanned. Appling bounced to W. Herman. Gehringer doubled to left. DiMaggio popped to W. Herman. No runs, one hit, no errors.

The next All-Star game, fifth to be played between the luminaries of the two leagues, will be staged in Washington, the date to be determined when the 1937 schedules are made up. Selection of the nation's capital city was made at a joint meeting of the club owners of the leagues the night before the Boston dream game.

Lou Gehrig walked on four straight pitches from Dizzy Dean in the second inning. Jerome Herman pitching inside to him. Then Diz caught Lou off first with a lightning throw.

Vernon Kennedy, White Sox pitcher, substituted for Tommy Bridges, Detroit, on the American League team, the latter being indisposed.

Charley Grimm showed a preference for Cubs and Cardinals in his starting line-up. He employed four Cubs—Galan, Herman, Hartnett and Demaree—and four of Frisch's Gas House Gang—Collins, Medwick, Durocher and Dizzy Dean. Whitney was the only stranger in their midst.

Both Charley Grimm, Cub pilot, and Joe McCarthy, pinch-manager of the American forces, looked at each other with an odd twinkle in their eyes when they posed for a picture. It was a case of Cub chief and former Cub chief. When McCarthy was manager of the Cubs, Charley was one of his most faithful players.

Al Schacht, Red Sox clown and coach, put on a new act. Half of him was in black face, the other half white. He put on an imitation of the Louis-Schmeling fight and the Schmeling part of himself eventually knocked out the Joe Louis side.

Under regulations this year, no pitcher was permitted to go more than three innings, thus the fans were given a chance to see most of the aces in action.

Clark Griffith, Washington's energetic executive, was present in flawless linen, which fitted the Potomac better than the Charles. Griff said next summer's show in the national capital would be "the greatest of them all."

When the game started, Gehrig, Gehringer, Averill, Rick Ferrell, Hartnett and Medwick were the only players of the starting 1933 game in Chicago appearing in the two line-ups. Of these six, Gehringer and Gehrig had not missed a single inning of the three previous All-Star games.

Augie Galan's home run in the fifth inning was a drive to right that hit the flag-pole and bounced into the right field pavilion in foul territory, and for a time there was some question whether it would be counted as a four-bagger. Under the National League rules, a hit bounding off the flagpole into the stands is scored as a homer and this rule prevailed.

Rip Radcliff's single in the fifth off Carl Hubbell was a Texas leaguer which fell in short center. It was the second American League hit.

The first half of the game was played with a National League ball and the second section with the official American League ball.

Dizzy Dean made a strong start on Luke Appling, whipping over two quick called strikes. Luke then ran the count to three and two, and refused to offer at a fourth fooler that gave him a walk. He was wiped off the base lines when DiMaggio smacked into a double play.

Del Baker, manager pro tem of the Tigers, who was selected by Manager Joe McCarthy of the A. L. team as one of his

HE'S A 'NATIONAL' HERO

AUGUST JOHN (AUGIE) GALAN

coaches, begged off from the assignment and League President William Harridge named Joe Cronin, pilot of the Red Sox, in his place. Baker has heavy responsibilities, filling in as director of the Tigers during Mickey Cochrane's illness, and felt he would better serve his club's interests by remaining closer to his own important duties.

Luke Appling's single chased Curt Davis in the seventh. The blow drove in Goslin and Foxx, with the American League's second and third runs of the inning. Then Lon Warneke took Davis' place and walked Gehringer. With the bases full, DiMaggio lined to Durocher, ending the scoring.

The best catch of the game, and one of the finest of the four All-Star games played, was Rip Radcliff's play on Medwick in the third. Ducky-Wucky sent a drive screeching to deep left near the foul line. The ball apparently was tagged for three bases, but Rip was off like a deer and caught it near the fence.

The umpires shifted when the All-Nationals went to bat in the fifth, Bill Summers moving from first base to behind the plate. Immediately he had a tough decision to make as Augie Galan's drive into the right field bleachers grazed the foul pole before it curved foul. Bill Stewart, at first, motioned that it was a fair ball, a decision in which he was upheld by Summers, despite the oratory of Joe McCarthy and Art Fletcher.

A glittering stop by Pinky Higgins saved Schoolboy Rowe additional punishment in the fifth. Two runs were in and National Leaguers were perched on third and first, when Connie Mack's star got in front of Demaree's hot smash and converted it into a double play.

Gabby Hartnett couldn't acquaint himself with the American League rule which requires the umpire to throw to the pitcher a ball being put into play. He kept reaching back to get the ball from Bill Summers every time a sphere went out of play, but Summers ignored him and tossed the pellet to the pitcher.

After popping out his first time up, Charley Gehringer helped his hefty All-Star average with a double and single and two walks.

The Box Score

AMERICAN LEAGUE.

	AB.	R.	H.	TB.	PO.	A.	E.
Appling, shortstop	4	0	1	1	2	2	0
Gehringer, second base	3	0	2	3	2	1	0
DiMaggio, right field	5	0	0	0	1	0	1
Gehrig, first base	2	1	1	4	7	0	0
Chapman, center field	1	0	0	0	0	0	0
Averill, center field	3	0	0	0	3	1	0
R. Ferrell, catcher	2	0	0	0	4	0	0
*Dickey, catcher	2	0	0	0	2	0	0
Radcliff, left field	2	0	1	1	2	0	0
Goslin, left field	1	1	1	1	1	0	0
Higgins, third base	2	0	0	0	0	1	0
†Foxx, third base	2	1	1	1	0	1	0
Grove, pitcher	1	0	0	0	0	0	0
Rowe, pitcher	1	0	0	0	0	0	0
Harder, pitcher	0	0	0	0	0	1	0
‡Selkirk	0	0	0	0	0	0	0
zCrosetti	1	0	0	0	0	0	0
Totals	32	3	7	11	24	7	1

NATIONAL LEAGUE.

	AB.	R.	H.	TB.	PO.	A.	E.
Galan, center field	4	1	1	4	1	0	0
W. Herman, second base	3	1	2	2	3	4	0
Collins, first base	2	0	0	0	9	1	0
Medwick, left field	3	0	1	0	0	0	0
Demaree, right field	3	1	1	1	1	0	0
§Ott, right field	1	0	1	1	0	0	0
Hartnett, catcher	4	1	1	3	7	0	0
Whitney, third base	3	0	1	1	0	2	0
xRiggs, third base	1	0	0	0	0	0	0
Durocher, shortstop	3	0	1	1	4	0	0
J. Dean, pitcher	1	0	0	0	0	2	0
Hubbell, pitcher	1	0	0	0	2	1	0
Davis, pitcher	0	0	0	0	0	1	0
Warneke, pitcher	1	0	0	0	0	0	0
Totals	31	4	9	13	27	11	0

*Batted for R. Ferrell in seventh.
†Batted for Higgins in seventh.
‡Batted for Rowe in seventh.
§Batted for Demaree in eighth.
xBatted for Whitney in eighth.
zBatted for Harder in ninth.

American .... 0 0 0 0 0 0 3 0 0—3
National .... 0 2 0 0 2 0 0 0 *—4

Runs batted in—Hartnett, Whitney, Medwick, Galan, Appling 2, Gehrig.
Two-base hit—Gehringer.
Three-base hit—Hartnett.
Home runs—Galan, Gehrig.
Double plays—Whitney, W. Herman and Collins; Appling, Gehringer and Gehrig.
Pitching records—Grove, 2 runs, 3 hits in 3 innings; Rowe, 2 runs, 4 hits in 3 innings; J. Dean, 0 runs, 0 hits in 3 innings, Hubbell, 0 runs, 2 hits in 3 innings; Davis, 3 runs, 4 hits 2-3 inning.
Struck out—By Grove 2 (Galan, J. Dean), by Rowe 2 (Durocher, Whitney), by J. Dean 3 (R. Ferrell, Higgins, Grove), by Hubbell 2 (R. Ferrell, Higgins), by Harder 2 (Galan, Riggs), by Warneke 2 (Foxx, Crosetti).
Bases on balls—Off J. Dean 2 (Appling, Gehrig), off Hubbell 1 (Gehringer), off Grove 2 (Collins, W. Herman), off Rowe 1 (Collins), off Davis 1 (Selkirk), off Warneke 3 (Gehringer, Gehrig, Goslin).
Wild pitch—Hubbell.
Winning pitcher—J. Dean.
Losing pitcher—Grove.
Left on bases—American League 7, National League 6.

Umpires—Reardon (N. L.) home plate; Summers (A. L.) first base; Stewart (N. L.) second base; Kolls (A. L.) third base for the first four and one-third innings; Summers (A. L.) home pate; Stewart (N. L.) first base; Kolls (A. L.) second base; Reardon (N. L.) third base for remainder of game.
Time—2:00.

Rings Bell for A. L.

Henry Louis Gehrig

LOU GEHRIG, hardy perennial of All-Star game competition, had to wait four years before he registered his first hit in the annual mid-summer classic, but the Yankee iron man distinguished himself with the most telling blast registered by the American League team in the July 7 interleague clash. Larrupin' Lou caught hold of one of Curt Davis' pitches in the seventh inning and rammed the ball something like 420 feet for the first run scored by the junior loop in the tilt. The blow paved the way for the ultimate rout of Davis, who did not finish the inning.

Gehrig had been in the three preceding All-Star games and had gone to the plate nine times without coming through with a bingle, so the blow was more than welcome to the Yankee first base star, who has been piling up various and sundry records in the American League. Besides having broken all marks for consecutive games played in, Lou also is the possessor of one of the most impressive home run records outside of those of Babe Ruth. On June 3, 1932, he smacked four in a row for the circuit and also holds the distinction of having made six circuit drives in six consecutive games. In 1933, he hit 49 for the circuit, as the leader, and in 1931 tied Ruth, with 46.

Joe Di Maggio Day Tomorrow

He Will Receive Trophy as Most Valuable on Coast Last Year.

Joe Di Maggio, of the Yankees, gets a trophy tomorrow. . . . He won it last season as the most valuable player in the Pacific Coast League. . . . The statuette will be given to Di Maggio between games of a double-header with Detroit. . . . Mayor Fiorello La Guardia will give the trophy to Di Maggio. . . . And so it will be Di Maggio Day, and the Yanks hope he snaps out of his slump.

The New Yorks went fishing today. . . . They went swimming. . . . They went by land and they went by sea, and Joe McCarthy told them to stay away from baseball. . . . Johnny Murphy, who did not look so good in his return on Sunday, pitched much better ball yesterday. . . . He relieved Pearson in the third, and in five and one-third innings gave only three hits and one run. . . . The tally came with Jimmy Dykes' homer into the right field sector, close to the foul line.

Tony Lazzeri put on the play of the day when, in the sixth inning, he dashed behind second, grabbed Appling's hot grounder, and flipped to Crosetti to force Bonura for the third out.

Roy Johnson hit for Murphy, and in the ninth Pat Malone pitched and forced in a run. . . . Rolfe and Powell got two hits apiece and Gehrig his homer. . . . That was all the hitting the Yankees did during the afternoon. . . . Lefty Gomez and Red Ruffing will pitch the double-header against the Tigers tomorrow. . . . The Yankees and the Sox now are even for the season, seven games each.

Di Maggio Day Is a Bust with Mayor Missing

Joe Fails to Get His Prize —Cochrane Is Back, Still Ailing

It was Joe Di Maggio Day in the Stadium. . . . And yet, it wasn't Joe Di Maggio Day. . . . Mayor Fiorello La Guardia was detained by an important meeting of the Board of Estimate. . . . As a result the presentation of the Pacific Coast League most valuable player trophy was postponed for a few days. . . . Di Maggio was stopped in the first game but got a double, a single and three walks in the night cap. . . . Since the All-Star game Di Maggio has hit only .219. . . . He seems to be taking it too hard.

Schoolboy Rowe pitched great ball in the first game and very easily could have had a shutout. . . . It was Ruffing's seventh defeat, as against eleven victories. . . . In the second battle Mickey Cochrane played a hunch and started Vic Sorrell. . . . In an important doubleheader here last July Mickey called Vic out of a month's retirement, and Sorrell pitched the most important victory of the season. . . . Yesterday it was a different Yankee club Vic faced. . . . Two hits and two passes in the third, stretching the Yankee total to four runs, ran Vic out of the park. . . . Joe Sullivan and Lem Phillips finished.

Cochrane is eight pounds under weight and looks none too chipper. . . . He complains of a throat ailment. . . . On his return to Detroit he found his doctors away for a vacation, so he came on here and took charge again. . . . There will be a hospital checkup on Cochrane in Detroit next Monday.

The best play of the doubleheader was Gehrig's grand catch of Goslin's low liner near the bag in the third inning of the second game.

Di Maggio Ace Among Rookies With Willow

Coast Star Holds Distance Hitting Record For Newcomers.

By DANIEL,
Staff Correspondent.

WASHINGTON, Aug. 18.—Joseph Paul Di Maggio, Jr., the well-known home run collector from San Francisco, today had completed the most remarkable set of distance hitting records yet completed by a freshman in the major leagues. Up to now the Washington Park had defied his most ardent efforts at anything measuring more than 400 feet. But in the 7-to-5 defeat with which the Yankees opened their series of three jousts with the Senators, Joe accomplished a 450-foot classic into the middle row of the center field section of left bleachers the Old-timers said they never had seen anything like that before.

Not until he came up with two out in the ninth, and Sid Cohen pitching did Clouting Joe jounce that Homeric four bagger, which carromed off the wooden target like a bullet against armor plate. Di Maggio had got two hits off Earl Whitehill, but they were mere singles.

Now every city in the circuit has seen Di Maggio achieve an out-of-the ordinary homer. In the Stadium he has landed one in the extreme corner of the left field stand, a distance of some 410 feet. In St. Louis he has lashed a circuit drive into the upper rows of the center field bleachers for a distance hitherto unmatched.

In Philadelphia, on Sunday, he blasted one into the far center field sector of the upper pavilion. From the classic Charles to the muddy Mississippi, Joe has made them all sit up and gasp.

Di Maggio now owns twenty home runs, and has tied Bill Dickey for the runner-up distinction on the Yankees. Lou Gehrig, of course, is the head man in the four-bagger industry with 38. Joe's contribution brought the club total to 141 with the Yankee record at 160, and forty-one more games to be played.

Joe Di Maggio

The famous DiMaggio swing, a sculpture of grace.

The DiMaggio brothers in the late 1930s: Vince, Joe, and Dom.

TIPS FROM THE SPORT TICKER
By James C. Isaminger

IN LESS than one season Joe DiMaggio, the California falcon, has done these two rare things:

1—Proved that he can cover centre field like Speaker.

2—Proved that as a drawing card he approaches Ruth.

The drum-beaters were energetic when the olive-skinned slugger from San Francisco joined the Yankees last spring, but the season was not very old when he justified everything.

If he keeps on advancing in the next few seasons he seems certain of equalling or topping Babe Ruth as a powerful and popular player and a drawing card.

His resemblance to Tris Speaker is plainly seen. In that last series at Shibe Park with the Yankees, DiMaggio, gracefully and without effort, made catches that seemed unbelievable.

His tumbling catch of Chubby Dean's liner at the scoreboard last Sunday was about the most audacious bit of outfield work seen at Shibe Park this year.

DiMaggio had to go far for this ball. It looked as if he had given up in his last strides, but he justified his sub-title by swooping on it like a falcon. He caught and fell at the same time, but the ball stuck in his glove like a burr.

That was only one of many catches in a four-game series that crippled the Athletics' attack. Placed in centre, he is a daily reminder of Speaker, the best compliment that can be paid to him.

Through the years when Speaker was active and not a memory he did some gorgeous fielding at Shibe Park, but never in his best day did he look any better than DiMaggio in that last visit of his here.

DiMaggio is rapidly becoming one of the standout drawing cards of the league. When you have a good Italian ball player you have someone whose presence will be felt at the turnstiles.

When you have an ace Italian like DiMaggio, a wonder in every department, you have a magnet that means a steady flow of gold into the exchequer of a club.

Certain the Ruth-bereft Yankees needed a stalwart figure, an idol, since the old Bambino threw his bat into the corner.

It came this year in this San Francisco Italian, six-foot son of a deep sea fisherman. The Yankees have owned him for several years while he was a minor. They decided not to bring him up to the majors until they were sure.

He batted .399 last season for San Francisco and that percentage eloquently cried: "I'm ready."

So he joined the Yankees this year, and from the start galvanized the team into a championship band. DiMaggio was just the divine spark to set the team off.

Yankee attendance this season rates with their best years of the past, far above the last five seasons. In four straight Sunday games from July 26 to August 16 the Yankees have attracted 194,617 spectators.

On other days their attendance has been uniformly good and they now face the windfall of another World Series.

The Yankees are anything but a one-man team, but without DiMaggio this season who will say that the team would have its present position in the percentage table and that the financial position of the club would be as strong?

DiMaggio, who will not be 22 years old until next November 25, has proved in his major league freshman year that he is as good a centre fielder as Speaker and that he is the best drawing card in baseball today.

The soon-to-be-famous number 5.

DiMaggio's Average Mounts

Jolting Joe, Now Hitting .340, May Set Highest Mark for First-Year Player.

By EDWARD T. MURPHY.

It wouldn't be a surprise if Jolting Joe DiMaggio reaches the end of his first sensational year in the major leagues with a batting average of .350. The Yankees' prize rookie, worth all of the $75,000 paid for his release from San Francisco, is banging the ball savagely.

Today his average for the season was up to .340. He has picked up six points since the Yankees opened their home stay. It is not a cinch for a batter to keep adding points to a high-powered percentage. To gain he must crack out two or three hits in every game. That's the way Joe has been going, and he is likely to continue his heavy slugging right up to the finish line. DiMaggio is too good a hitter to fall into a slump that will last beyond two or three games. He hasn't had a long hitless spell this year. Just before the all-star game he fell off in his stickwork, and when he failed to connect for a hit in the mid-season baseball Mardi-Gras t h e r e were some who predicted he would stay in his slump and fade into an ordinary first-year performer.

DiMaggio didn't do that. Immediately after the all-star contest he recaptured his real batting form and he has played through few games in which he didn't make at least one safe wallop. Joe had hit eleven home runs when the all-star game was played on July 7. Since that afternoon he has cracked out twelve more. That doesn't sound as though his hitting was affected because he had failed to click in the interleague clash.

Jolting Joe was playing under a physical handicap for several days before the all-star game. Two corns on his right foot knocked him out of his stride at the plate and slowed him up on the base paths. The day after the game he had them removed and soon he was back in his natural hitting form.

May Create New Record.

DiMaggio has firmly established himself as one of the best right-handed batters to break into the major leagues. It would require much research to discover the highest batting mark ever compiled by a first-year right-hander. Perhaps the average DiMaggio will have at the end of the season will be the highest of all.

Before DiMaggio came along Rogers Hornsby and Al Simmons were considered the best right-handed hitters of recent years. Hornsby's first complete season in the majors was 1916. He played in 139 games for the Cardinals and batted .313. Simmons batted .308 in 1924, his first season with the Athletics. Later on both developed into league batting champions. It would be unwise to wager DiMaggio will never capture an American League title. He might be next year's champion.

Through the years in which Hornsby was the king of big league hitters he never had much to say about the way he tormented pitchers. DiMaggio is like that now. He doesn't talk about his hitting. In fact, he doesn't talk much about anything. He seems to be content to throw a blanket of silence over his batting achievements.

There is only one set of pitchers in the league who have had success against Joe. That is the Athletics' staff. The rookie has made some hits, even some home runs, against Philadelphia, but he hasn't had many big days. Joe has hit savagely against St. Louis all season. The seven hits he made in the last two games against the Browns boosted his total number of wallops off Hornsby's hurlers up to forty-two. In getting them Joe made eighty-six trips to the plate. His average against the St. Louis staff is a sizzling .488.

Pearson's Streak Ends.

The decision Monte Pearson dropped to Ivy Andrews yesterday was the first reversal the curve ball artist encountered since the White Sox took his measure on July 13. Monte had won five games in a row, but it was a winning streak somewhat marred, because he appeared in other games in which he was knocked off the mound but escaped defeat. In his string of successes Monte beat the Browns and A's twice apiece and the Red Sox once. Pearson generally is backed up by numerous tallies, but yesterday the Yankees were unable to give him more than two runs and didn't score after the second inning. Monte yielded four runs in the fifth and that attack, climaxed by a triple with the bases filled, brought about his undoing. The triple, a drive over Jake Powell's head, was struck by Beau Bell. In the fourth Bell knocked in the first Brown tally with a single.

Andrews allowed nine hits, but kept them well scattered, and as he moved along to victory he fanned Red Ruffing and Roy Johnson, both of whom were sent to the plate as pinch hitters.

DANIEL'S DOPE

"Now, about this Di Maggio," opened George Moriarty, American League umpire, keen judge of ball players, vociferous scrapper and once a truly great third baseman. "Joe is the most remarkable ball player I have seen come up in the last thirty years. He is the best outfielder in baseball today."

With a sense of the dramatic, Moriarty let the pronouncement sink in. "He is great now. He will be more amazing next season. And by 1938 or 1939, the baseball world will be embroiled in violent dispute as to whether the accepted all-time outfield of Babe Ruth, Ty Cobb and Tris Speaker should not be broken up to make room for Di Maggio. Nothing but Fate—I mean injuries—can stop him."

The writer suggested that Morey might have forgotten about an outfielder by the name of Joe Jackson, who as a freshman in 1911, with Cleveland, set a yearling batting mark with .408, and stole some forty-one bases.

"No, I haven't forgotten Jackson, and my estimate of Di Maggio stands," Moriarty replied. "Di Maggio is a greater ball player than Jackson was. The Italian boy has everything, including a high sense of responsibility to himself, his team and the game. Jackson was a happy-go-lucky guy who played baseball by instinct. Di Maggio studies everything out. He corrects his mistakes.

"Jackson was somewhat illiterate. And of course you know how he went for that sucker stuff in the 1919 world series."

* * *

"I want to make another prediction about Di Maggio," Morey continued. "He will be an outstanding star in the world series. There is no book on the young man. He may fan on a pitch in one inning and hit it out of the park the next.

"True, he did not look so good in the All Star game.

"That experience in Boston will make him all the more determined and all the more successful in the series."

* * *

Joe Has Power and Then
Something Extra, Says Morey.

"Di Maggio has power, and then something extra," Moriarty went on. "And he is all baseball. You never see him lazy out in his position. You never see him walk back. And he isn't found hanging around talking on the field. He always finds something to do. As for that arm of his—well, it's in a class by itself.

"You watch Joe day in and day out, and yet you perhaps do not appreciate fully his remarkable speed. If he set out to run bases he would win the major league championship.

"He is the fastest runner in the

International League

STANDING OF THE CLUBS.

	W.	L.	Pct.		W.	L.	Pct.
Buffalo	92	55	.626	Toronto	73	73	.500
Newark	83	63	.568	Montreal	67	76	.469
Rochester	82	63	.566	Syracuse	56	90	.361
Baltimore	77	69	.527	Albany	53	94	.361

Games Today.

Newark at Syracuse.
Baltimore at Albany.
Buffalo at Montreal.
Rochester at Toronto.

Yesterday's Results.

Buffalo, 9; Montreal, 7.
Newark-Syracuse (2), rain.
Rochester-Toronto, threatening weather.
Baltimore-Albany, wet grounds.

American League in the last four or five strides going to first base. Ben Chapman, Bill Werber and a few others are fast from the drop of the bat. Joe is quick, too. But when he nears that bag he picks up his greatest speed. You've got to be extra careful umpiring at first base, because, as the saying goes, he is sure to steal a few decisions away from you.

"In the outfield he is so nimble that he is paced by the ball. He makes remarkable catches look simple because when that ball comes down he has arrived.

"We have two other fine freshmen in the league in Roy Weatherly, of the Indians, and Buddy Lewis, of the Senators. But Di Maggio is out alone. He has no weakness. Weatherly, being a lefthanded hitter, must yet prove that he hasn't the handicap of so many young men who hit from the first base side of the plate—a letdown against southpaws."

* * *

Moriarty then shifted to a discussion of American League hitting —and the ball. He indicated that those who look for crafty National League hurling to stymie the Yankees may be disappointed more than sorely.

"The ball is okeh," said George. "We have had a hot, dry Summer and that sort of weather makes the leather lively. Now, with damp weather, the ball sounds and acts punk. Let the ball alone."

DANIEL'S DOPE

Special to the World-Telegram.

CLEVELAND, Sept. 9.—What with Babe Ruth rehearsing for his radio debut as a comedian and Joe Di Maggio signing for a post world series vaudeville tour, the baseball situation today was somewhat loaded with air waves and redolent with the old-fashioned flavor of the stage.

The Babe, we are informed by the press bureau of the Columbia System, will team with Kate Smith in an act which will go into the ether a week from Thursday and will boost the products of a grocery chain. Since Ruth and Miss Smith themselves are living boosts for groceries of all sorts, the sponsors seem to have picked a proper representation—at least, physically.

The press agent says:—"This is a very interesting story. Ruth is not going to talk baseball. In fact, it is goodby to baseball. He stipulated that the broadcasts say nothing about the game. He wants to forget it."

This is all very interesting. For Ruth to forget about baseball would be Lindbergh erasing airplanes from his recollection. For the Babe to forget about home runs, the Stadium and the roar of the crowd would be Jack Dempsey wiping away memories of the title, Carpentier, Firpo, the Tunney fights and those opulent million dollar gates of the Rickard dynasty.

For Ruth to make a conscious effort to move out of the game which owes so much to him, and to which he owes so much, would be not only inconceivable but as impossible as an election minus campaign speeches.

In other words, the story sounds interesting but cannot approach fact closer than the equator can come to the North Pole.

* * *

The Ruth radio extravaganza is to be labeled "Kate and the Babe" and will mark the home run record holder's first secondary booking of his mature life.

Kate will warble. It is hoped that Ruth does not ditto. We have heard the Babe sing in the shower, and we don't think the air waves will stand the strain.

Ruth apparently will put the stinger on the jokes which will be fed to him by Miss Smith. Maybe the Bam will be the moon coming over the mountain.

* * *

**Di Maggio to Team
With Brother in Act.**

Joe Di Maggio's entry into the realm of Thespis will make drama history. Joe is to be teamed up with his brother Vince, who plays in the outfield of the San Diego Padres, and they are to roam the Pacific Coast circuit. Vince will sing and furnish the patter.

As for Joe—well, he can't sing and he can't patter. So he has decided on one of the most drastic experiments yet seen on any stage. He will hit fungoes into the gallery!

Somewhere in Follies or Scandals or something on Broadway we have seen chorines toss tennis balls into the crowd. But hitting fungoes into the gallery comes under the head of bold venture, unmatched since the good old days of Booth, Macready and Forrest. Not even the effete John Drew ever hit a single fungo, even into the parterre.

Since a league ball coming into contact with a schnozz leaves a stinging imprint and a lasting memory, it is conceivable that the Di Maggio experiment will have to be toned down with tennis balls. There are outfielders even in the American League who have found handling Di Maggio fungoes no mean job. And, of course, there may be additional hazards in the act of the Brothers Di Maggio, connected with Vince's singing.

* * *

Judging from reports, a world series on a five cent fare would be followed by a veritable cloudburst of stage effort by classic heroes.

You see, the new rule forbids their baseball barnstorming, so we shall be regaled with uncertain vocalizations and fumbling recollection of stirring moments in the battles of the Giants and the Yankees.

At the 1936 World Series, in which the Yankees beat the New York Giants in six games, Joe DiMaggio poses with teammates, Frankie Crosetti, far left, and Tony Lazzeri, far right. To DiMaggio's right is Ripper Collins, and to his left is Tony Richardson.

CHAMPIONS
THE FIRST YEAR OUT

Sportswriters had been predicting that the Detroit Tigers, who had stars like Hank Greenberg, Charlie Gehringer, and Al Simmons, would win the American League pennant in 1936, just as they had the two previous years. But they were wrong. The records show the Yankees that year were one of the greatest teams of all time.

We had six players who hit above .300. Bill Dickey led the team with a .362 average, Gehrig was right behind him at .354, and I batted .323. Red Rolfe, George Selkirk, and Jake Powell also were above the .300 mark. And five of us drove in more than 100 runs: Gehrig led the team with 152, I had 125, Tony Lazzeri 109, and Dickey and Selkirk rapped in 107 each.

We won 102 games that year and were 19½ games ahead of the second-place Tigers at the end of the season. Then we went out and beat the New York Giants in six games to win the World Series.

Joe DiMaggio

1936

The Sporting News

THE BASE BALL PAPER OF THE WORLD

VOLUME 102, NUMBER 7　　　ST. LOUIS, OCTOBER 1, 1936　　　TEN CENTS THE COPY 15c in Canada

11 SERIES' VETS GIVE GIANTS EDGE IN EXPERIENCE

Represent New York in First All-Gotham Cast for Series Since 1923

Lou Gehrig

Tony Lazzeri

Frank Crosetti

Bob Rolfe

Joe DiMaggio

Sam Leslie

Mark Koenig

George Selkirk

Roy Johnson

Bob Seeds

Jake Powell

Jack Saltzgaver

Eddie Mayo

Mel Ott

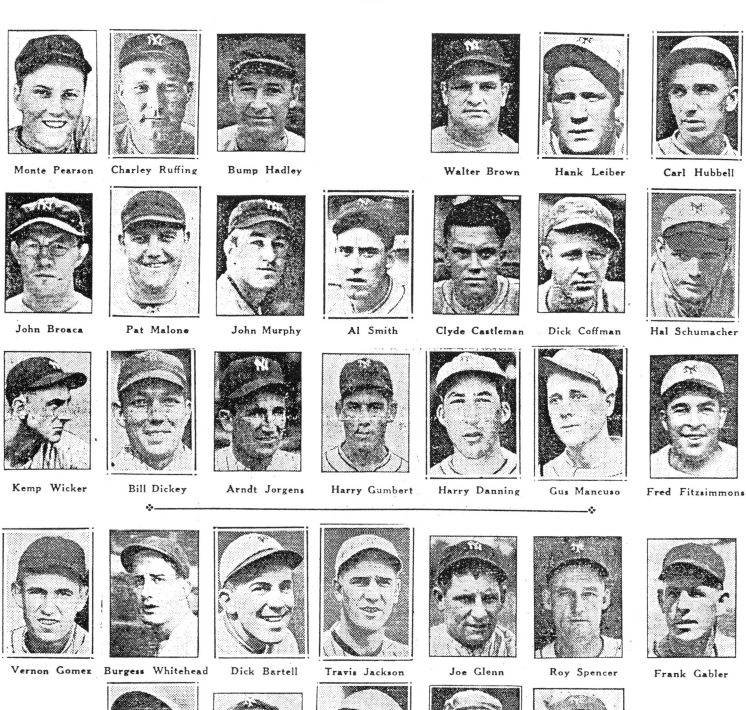

Monte Pearson   Charley Ruffing   Bump Hadley   Walter Brown   Hank Leiber   Carl Hubbell

John Broaca   Pat Malone   John Murphy   Al Smith   Clyde Castleman   Dick Coffman   Hal Schumacher

Kemp Wicker   Bill Dickey   Arndt Jorgens   Harry Gumbert   Harry Danning   Gus Mancuso   Fred Fitzsimmons

Vernon Gomez   Burgess Whitehead   Dick Bartell   Travis Jackson   Joe Glenn   Roy Spencer   Frank Gabler

Joe Moore   Jim Ripple   George Davis   Joe McCarthy   Bill Terry

ONLY SIX YANKS HAVE PLAYED IN BIG EVENT

GEHRIG, KOENIG AND LAZZERI TOP ALL OTHERS IN PARTICIPATION

Absence of Heffner Leaves A. L. Champs
With Only 22 Players Against 23
for the Polo Grounders

NEW YORK, N. Y.—A fourth World's Series confined to New York! Pop Knickerbocker, sitting in the arena at the Polo Grounds, tired from rushing around for tickets, fatigued from finding hotel accommodations for his brothers and sisters from San Diego to Newfoundland, wonders if it isn't all a dream. Of course, Pop got all set for the Yankee half of the classic as far back as July 4, when the Bronx Bombers had a lead of 11 games. But the Giant section of the series still has him wondering, exulting over a miracle baseball had not seen since the 1914 Braves crashed from the cellar to the world championship.

The time for speculating as to the winner is past. The series is under way. The professional betting gentry made the Yankees 2 to 1 favorites, then went to 3 to 2, and finally 8 to 5. Carl Hubbell became the favorite to win the opener. There is more betting on this series than ever before in the history of the classic, and it is not so much professional as man-to-man wagering, with surprising support for the Giants.

A comparison reveals that the Giants have an edge over the Yankees as far as players with previous World's Series experience are concerned. Eleven of the 23 Giant eligibles have participated in previous classics, as contrasted to six members of Joe McCarthy's club.

Among the Giants who have had their baptism of fire in baseball's big event are Manager Bill Terry, Travis Jackson, Gus Mancuso, Mark Koenig, Carl Hubbell, Hal Schumacher, Fred Fitzsimmons, Mel Ott, Joe Moore, George Davis and Burgess Whitehead.

Gehrig, Koenig, Lazzeri Real Veterans.

The real series veterans, however, are Lou Gehrig, Mark Koenig and Tony Lazzeri, who are playing in the post-season classic for the fifth time. Other Yankees with series experience are Pat Malone, Bill Dickey, Vernon Gomez and Charley Ruffing.

Commissioner K. M. Landis certified the following eligibles for the series:

YANKEES: John Broaca, Walter Brown, Frank Crosetti, Bill Dickey, Joe DiMaggio, Henry L. (Lou) Gehrig, Joseph Glenn, Vernon Gomez, Irving D. Hadley, Don Heffner, Roy C. Johnson, Arndt Jorgens, Anthony Lazzeri, Perce Malone, John J. Murphy, Monte Pearson, Alvin J. Powell, Robert A. Rolfe, Charles Ruffing, Jack Saltzgaver, Robert Seeds, George Selkirk and Kemp Wicker, players: Manager Joseph V. McCarthy, and Coaches Earle B. Combs and Arthur Fletcher.

GIANTS: Manager William H. Terry, Richard Bartell, Clydell Castleman, Richard Coffman, Harry Danning, George Davis. Fred Fitzsimmons, Frank Gabler, Harry E. Gumbert, Carl Hubbell, Travis C. Jackson, Mark A. Koenig, Henry Leiber. Samuel A. Leslie, August R. Mancuso, Edward Mayo, Joseph G. Moore, Melvin T. Ott. James Ripple, Harold Schumacher, Alfred J. Smith, Roy Spencer and Burgess Whitehead, players, and Coaches Frank Snyder and Adolfo Luque.

President William Harridge of the American League named Umpires Harry Geisel and William Sommers to officiate in the series, while President Ford Frick of the National League appointed Umpires Cy Pfirman and George Magerkurth.

The Yanks got a bad break when Monte Pearson tore a muscle in his back, September 24. As I write this, there seems to be little chance that Monte will be able to work in the series. He did not go to Philadelphia and Washington but remained in his quarters under the care of Dr. Edwin Spies, the club surgeon. It appears Monte previously suffered the same kind of mishap. He is not very robustly put together for a big league pitcher.

Plenty of Room for Everybody.

The general set-up for the series is marvelous—two big parks, with lots of room for everybody. The man in the street got what he wanted and speculators were not very active. There was considerable squawking from Gus II. Fan over the sale of tickets in blocks of three, but it just could not be done any other way. Besides, the general arrangements at the Polo Grounds and the Stadium, with plenty of $3.30 grandstand unreserved, made the squawk sound vapid.

The Yankees were praised all over town, and along way stations as well, for the most generous split of the money in the history of the World's Series. The boys voted 36 persons into the divvy, with 26 full shares.

The most generous action was voting a full share to Ted Kleinhans, who finished the season with Newark, and had no claim, other than a moral one. When Kemp Wicker, voted half a share with Bob Seeds, came to the Yanks, Kleinhans was shipped back to the Bears. Yet the Yankees voted him between $5,000 and $7,000 for the single game Ted had won for them.

Myril Hoag, retired for the season, naturally got a full share. So did Don Heffner, who had his appendix removed before the close of the season and was out of the series.

The Yankees tried to get permission to place Nolen Richardson, veteran infielder from Newark, on their World's Series list in place of Heffner. But Landis refused. He said that Richardson was not eligible, as the Yanks had recalled him some time previous, only to release him outright to Newark 24 hours later. The Yankees then decided to go into the series with only 22 players, leaving Jack Saltzgaver as the only extra infielder.

The series developed a lot of interesting sidelights. It was discovered that never before had the Yankees gone into a classic without Babe Ruth. And never before had the Giants played a World's Series without John McGraw as manager or spectator. In 1933, he was just an onlooker.

The Giants were rather liberal in their cutting of the World's Series melon, 27 full slices being pared off by the vote of the players. In addition to Manager Terry, Coaches Frank Snyder and Dolph Luque were given a full share, as were Secretary Eddie Brannick and Trainer Willie Schaeffer. The groundskeeper, Henry Fabian, clubhouse boys and other Polo Grounds attendants also were remembered.

DANIEL M. DANIEL.

WORLD SERIES
Giants vs Yankees
1936
Official Program 25¢

Game 1 September 30 at Polo Grounds

NY Yankees	Pos	AB	R	H	RBi	PO	A	E
Crosetti	ss	4	0	1	0	1	3	1
Rolfe	3b	3	0	1	0	2	1	0
DiMaggio	cf	4	0	1	0	3	0	0
Gehrig	1b	3	0	0	0	7	0	0
Dickey	c	4	0	0	0	8	0	1
Powell	lf	4	0	3	0	2	0	0
Lazzeri	2b	3	0	0	0	1	2	0
Selkirk	rf	4	1	1	1	0	0	0
Ruffing	p	3	0	0	0	0	1	0
Totals		32	1	7	1	24	7	2

Doubles—Crosetti, Ott, Powell
Home Runs—Bartell, Selkirk
Sacrifice Hits—Ripple 2, Rolfe
Double Play—Whitehead to Terry
Hit by Pitcher—Gehrig (by Hubbell)
Left on Bases—Yankees 7, Giants 7
Umpires—Pfirman (N), Geisel (A),
Magerkurth (N), Summers (A)
Attendance—39,419. Time of Game—2:40.

NY Y	0 0 1	0 0 0	0 0 0		1
NY G	0 0 0	0 1 1	0 4 x		6

NY Giants	Pos	AB	R	H	RBi	PO	A	E
Moore	lf	5	0	0	0	0	0	0
Bartell	ss	4	1	2	1	1	2	0
Terry	1b	4	2	2	0	12	2	0
Ott	rf	2	2	2	0	0	0	0
Ripple	cf	2	0	0	0	0	0	0
Mancuso	cf	3	1	1	1	9	1	0
Whitehead	2b	3	1	0	1	3	4	0
Jackson	3b	4	0	0	1	1	1	0
Hubbell	p	4	0	2	1	1	2	1
Totals		31	6	9	5	27	12	1

Pitching	IP	H	R	ER	BB	SO
Yankees						
Ruffing (L)	8	9	6	4	4	5
Giants						
Hubbell (W)	9	7	1	1	1	8

1st Inning
Yankees
1 Crosetti grounded to third.
2 Rolfe grounded to first.
3 DiMaggio grounded to short.
Giants
1 Moore flied to left.
2 Bartell lined to left.
   Terry singled beyond short.
   Ott walked
3 Ripple popped to short.

2nd Inning
Yankees
1 Gehrig grounded out, Terry to Hubbell.
2 Dickey grounded to second.
   Powell singled to center.
3 Lazzeri struck out.
Giants
1 Mancuso struck out.
2 Whitehead grounded to short.
3 Jackson struck out.

3rd Inning
Yankees
   Selkirk homered into the upper right
   field stands
1 Ruffing grounded back to the pitcher.
2 Crosetti popped to second
   Rolfe singled past second
   DiMaggio singled to right with Rolfe
   falling after rounding second (he got
   back safely)
3 Gehrig grounded back to Hubbell.
Giants
   Hubbell singled to center
1 Moore struck out.
   Bartell singled to right, advancing
   Hubbell to third
2 Terry fouled out to Dickey
   Ott walked to load the bases
3 Ripple struck out.

4th Inning
Yankees
1 Dickey struck out.
   Powell doubled to left
   Lazzeri walked
2 Powell was caught attempting to
   steal third, Mancuso to Jackson
   with Lazzeri going to second.
3 Selkirk struck out
Giants
1 Mancuso popped to third
2 Whitehead struck out
3 Jackson grounded to second.

5th Inning
Yankees
1 Ruffing struck out.
2 Crosetti fouled to Mancuso.
3 Rolfe popped to second
Giants
1 Hubbell grounded to second.
2 Moore fouled to Dickey
   Bartell homered into the left field
   stands.
3 Terry grounded to second

6th Inning
Yankees
1 DiMaggio struck out.
2 Gehrig struck out.
3 Dickey grounded to first.
Giants
   Ott doubled to left
1 Ripple sacrificed Ott to third,
   Ruffing to Lazzeri.
   Mancuso singled beyond third, scoring
   Ott
2 Whitehead popped to third.
3 Jackson flied to center.

7th Inning
Yankees
   Powell singled to left.
1 Lazzeri struck out.
2 Selkirk forced Powell at second, Terry
   to Bartell
3 Ruffing struck out.
Giants
1 Hubbell fouled to Gehrig.
2 Moore flied to center.
3 Bartell popped to Dickey.

8th Inning
Yankees
   Crosetti doubled to left.
   Rolfe bunted and was safe on Hubbell's
   error with Crosetti stopping at
   second
1,2 DiMaggio lined to Whitehead who
   threw to Terry to double up Rolfe
   with Crosetti still holding second.
   Gehrig was hit by a pitched ball.
3 Dickey grounded to first.
Giants
   Terry singled to right
   Ott bunted safely, Terry to second.
1 Ripple sacrificed Terry to third and
   Ott to second, Rolfe to Gehrig
   Mancuso intentionally walked to load
   the bases
   Whitehead walked forcing in Terry with
   a run, bases still jammed
2 Jackson flied to DiMaggio, Ott scoring after
   the catch
   Hubbell singled past Lazzeri scoring
   Mancuso and when Crosetti made a bad
   throw to the plate Whitehead scored,
   Dickey threw wildly to catch Hubbell
   who reached third on the two errors.
3 Moore grounded to short.

9th Inning
Yankees
1 Powell grounded to short.
2 Lazzeri grounded to second.
3 Selkirk also grounded to second.

Game 2 October 2 at Polo Grounds

NY Yankees	Pos	AB	R	H	RBI	PO	A	E
Crosetti	ss	5	4	3	0	0	1	0
Rolfe	3b	4	3	2	1	2	0	0
DiMaggio	cb	5	2	3	2	6	0	0
Gehrig	1b	5	1	2	3	6	0	0
Dickey	c	5	3	2	5	8	0	0
Selkirk	rf	5	1	1	0	2	0	0
Powell	lf	3	2	2	0	2	0	0
Lazzeri	2b	4	1	1	5	1	3	0
Gomez	p	5	1	1	2	0	0	0
Totals		41	18	17	18	27	4	0

Pitching	IP	H	R	ER	BB	SO
Yankees						
Gomez (W)	9	6	4	4	7	8
Giants						
Schumacher(L)	*2	3	5	4	4	1
Smith	⅓	2	3	3	1	0
Coffman	1⅓	2	1	1	0	1
Gabler	4	5	3	3	3	0
Gumbert	1	5	6	6	1	1

*Faced 3 batters in the 3rd.

		2	0	7	0	0	1	2	0	6	18
NY Y											
NY G	0	1	0	3	0	0	0	0	0		4

NY Giants	Pos	AB	R	H	RBI	PO	A	E
Moore	lf	5	0	0	0	2	0	0
Bartell	ss	3	0	1	1	2	2	0
Terry	1b	5	0	2	2	6	1	0
Leiber	cf	4	0	0	0	7	1	0
Ott	rf	4	0	0	0	4	0	0
Mancuso	c	2	2	1	0	3	2	0
Whitehead	2b	4	0	0	0	2	1	0
Jackson	3b	4	1	1	0	0	2	1
Schumacher	p	0	0	0	0	0	0	0
Smith	p	0	0	0	0	0	0	0
Coffman	p	0	0	0	0	0	1	0
a Davis		1	1	1	0	0	0	0
Gabler	p	0	0	0	0	1	0	0
b Danning		1	0	0	0	0	0	0
Gumbert	p	0	0	0	0	0	0	0
Totals		33	4	6	3	27	10	1

a Singled for Coffman in 4th.
b Struck out for Gabler in 8th.

Doubles—Bartell, DiMaggio, Mancuso. Home Runs—Dickey, Lazzeri. Sacrifice Hit—DiMaggio. Stolen Base—Powell. Double Play—Leiber to Jackson to Bartell. Wild Pitches—Gomez, Schumacher. Left on Bases—Yankees 6, Giants 9. Umpires—Geisel (A), Magerkurth (N), Summers (A), Pfirman (N). Attendance—43,543. Time of Game—2:49.

1st Inning
Yankees
Crosetti singled to center.
Rolfe walked.
DiMaggio singled on a bunt to fill the bases.
1 Gehrig flied to right, Crosetti scoring after the catch and Rolfe going to third on the throw to the plate. DiMaggio to third on a wild pitch, Rolfe holding.
2,3 Dickey flied to Leiber scoring Rolfe but DiMaggio was doubled up trying for third, Leiber to Jackson to Bartell.
Giants
1 Moore struck out.
2 Bartell struck out.
Terry singled over second.
Leiber walked.
3 Ott flied to center.

2nd Inning
Yankees
Selkirk walked.
1 Powell lined to right.
2 Selkirk was caught stealing, Mancuso to Whitehead.
3 Gomez struck out.
Giants
Mancuso walked.
1 Whitehead flied to right.
2 Jackson flew out to right.
Schumacher walked.
On a wild pitch Mancuso scored and Schumacher reached third.
3 Moore fouled to Rolfe.

3rd Inning
Yankees
Crosetti singled to left.
Rolfe walked.
DiMaggio was safe at first on Jackson's error filling the bases.
For the Giants—Smith pitching
Gehrig singled over first, scoring Crosetti and Rolfe and moving DiMaggio to third.
Dickey singled to right, scoring DiMaggio and moving Gehrig to third.
1 Selkirk flied to Leiber in short left.
Powell walked loading the bases again.
For the Giants—Coffman pitching.
Lazzeri hit a grand slam into the lower right field stands (only the second in Series history tying Elmer Smith's mark of 1920).
2 Gomez struck out.
3 Crosetti grounded to short.
Giants
Bartell walked.
1 Terry struck out.
2 Leiber struck out.
3 Ott popped to third.

4th Inning
Yankees
1 Rolfe was tossed out by Coffman on a bunt to the mound.
2 DiMaggio flied to Moore.
Gehrig singled past first.
3 Gehrig was caught stealing, Mancuso to Bartell.
Giants
Mancuso walked.
1 Whitehead fanned.
Jackson singled beyond second.
Davis, batting for Coffman, singled over second filling the bases.
2 Moore fanned.
Bartell forcing in Mancuso.
Terry singled to left, scoring Jackson and Davis, Bartell stopped at second.
3 Leiber lined to left.

5th Inning
Yankees
For the Giants—Gabler pitching.
1 Dickey rolled out to first.
2 Selkirk flied to left.
Powell singled off the left field wall.
3 Lazzeri flied to center.
Giants
1 Ott grounded to second.
2 Mancuso struck out.
3 Whitehead grounded to second.

6th Inning
Yankees
1 Gomez grounded to short.
Crosetti walked.
Rolfe singled, sending Crosetti to third.
2 DiMaggio flied to left, scoring Crosetti.
3 Gehrig flied to right.
Giants
1 Jackson popped to second.
Gabler walked.
2 Moore lined to center.
3 Bartell lined to left.

7th Inning
Yankees
Dickey walked.
Selkirk singled to center, Dickey stopping at second.
Powell singled to left, filling the bases.
1 Lazzeri flied to deep center, Dickey scored and Selkirk went to third after the catch.
2 Gomez grounded to second, scoring Selkirk.
3 Crosetti flied to center.
Giants
1 Terry grounded to second.
2 Leiber grounded to short.
3 Ott flied to center.

8th Inning
Yankees
1 Rolfe popped to second.
DiMaggio doubled off the left field wall.
Gehrig walked.
2 Dickey flied to right.
3 Terry grounded out, Terry to Gabler.
Giants
Mancuso doubled to left.
1 Whitehead fouled to Gehrig.
2 Jackson fouled to Gehrig.
3 Danning, pinch hitting for Gabler, struck out.

9th Inning
Yankees
For the Giants—Gumbert pitching.
Powell walked.
Powell stole second.
1 Lazzeri flied deep to center, advancing Powell to third.
Gomez singled to center, scoring Powell. Crosetti singled to left, moving Gomez to second.
Rolfe singled off Jackson's glove, scoring Gomez, Crosetti moved to second.
DiMaggio only singled off the left field wall, scoring Crosetti with Rolfe stopping at second.
2 Gehrig grounded to third, advancing both base-runners.
Dickey hit a three run homer into the lower right field stands.
3 Selkirk struck out.
Giants
1 Moore flew out to center.
Bartell doubled to left.
2 Terry flew out to center.
3 Leiber also flew to DiMaggio who got all three putouts in the final inning.

YANKS 1-2 CHOICE TO CAPTURE SERIES

Slate Revised by Doyle After Overwhelming Triumph— Giants Now 8 to 5.

When the Yankees turned in their record-breaking performance to even the world series with the Giants yesterday they ascended immediately into higher favoritism in the books of Jack Doyle, Broadway commissioner.

"On the series now," said Doyle, "it is 1 to 2 against the Yankees and 8 to 5 against the Giants."

For today's game, in which Freddy Fitzsimmons will try to put the Giants ahead once more, with Bump Hadley as his opponent, the price was fixed at 3 to 5 against the Yankees and 6 to 5 against the Giants.

"But," said Doyle, "this price is contingent upon Carl Hubbell not pitching. If Fitz is certain to pitch the figures stand; if Hubbell should go a sharp revision must be made."

Doyle also said that a big play on the day's game might drive the price down to 1 to 2 against Joe McCarthy's "Murderers' Row."

Schedule for the Series

Today—At Yankee Stadium.
Tomorrow—At Yankee Stadium.
Monday—At Yankee Stadium.
Tuesday—At Polo Grounds (if necessary).
Wednesday—At Polo Grounds (if necessary).

All games start at 1:30 P. M., with the exception of Sunday's contests, which begins at 2 P. M. Postponed games will be played at the park for which they were scheduled and dates of the remaining games will be shifted accordingly.

YANKS CRUSH GIANTS, 18-4, A WORLD SERIES RECORD; 45,000 SEE SECOND GAME

SERIES TIED, 1 GAME EACH

Fans Cheer Roosevelt and Remain Till He Leaves at End.

4-RUN HOMER FOR LAZZERI

He and Dickey Equal Mark, Sending Five Home—Score Highest in Classic.

FIVE HURLERS BATTERED

Schumacher Starts and Paves Way to 7 Tallies in Third— Gomez Staggers Through.

By JOHN DREBINGER

With President Roosevelt casting a keen, critical and, beyond question, an appreciative eye on the thoroughness of the spectacle, Marse Joe McCarthy's Yankee juggernaut rolled out on the hard, smooth terrain of the Polo Grounds yesterday and put on the most amazing exhibition of devastating power in all world series history.

For with no Carl Hubbell or slippery underfooting to distract and derail them, the American League champions emptied broadside after broadside into the riddled defenses of Colonel Bill Terry's Giants and, in a final shower of records, individual and collective, bagged the second engagement of the Fall classic by the overwhelming score of 18 to 4.

It was the most decisive, humiliating defeat ever suffered by a contender in the thirty-one years of world series warfare and left a crowd of 45,000 stunned and awed at the finish, while the President and James A. Farley exchanged significant glances. For they had observed a truly remarkable steamroller in action.

Italian Triumvirate Shines

Behind the somewhat erratic pitching of their Castilian comrade, Lefty Vernon Gomez, the Italian battalion of the Yankees swung magnificently into action as first Tony Lazzeri, then Frankie Crosetti and finally Joe DiMaggio ripped and slashed five hapless Giant hurlers to ribbons.

Tony, providing the high spot of a fearful seven-run explosion in the third inning, cracked a homer with the bases full, subsequently pushed another run across the plate and with this equaled a series record for runs batted in, a total of five.

Crosetti, blazing a trail with three singles and a pass, carried four runs across that severely dented plate to tie another mark.

And DiMaggio, the latest addition to this singular array of Latins from far off Telegraph Hill in San Francisco, touched off two singles and a double, then brought the uneven struggle to a dramatic close by making a spectacular catch of a towering shot directly in front of the Eddie Grant Memorial tablet in center field.

Bewildered by Catch

Hank Leiber had stroked that blow with an effort born of despair and wound up standing on second base in utter bewilderment, unable to comprehend why all the other players were rushing past him to the clubhouse.

Nor were Marse Joe's three most extraordinary Latins the only members in his cast who made the afternoon one of total misery for Colonel Terry as first Hal Schumacher, then Al Smith, Dick Coffman, Frank Gabler and finally Harry Gumbert stumbled and fell in an endless succession of bruising rounds.

"So they said we can't hit, eh?" muttered these aroused Yanks as they came up for the ninth with the score already 12 to 4.

And with that they tore into the luckless Gumbert for a final cluster of six, three riding home on a circuit smash by Bill Dickey. Previously Bill's war club had accounted for two other tallies, so he, too, finished the long afternoon with five runs batted in to his credit to match the record equaled by Lazzeri.

Lou Gehrig, the most destructive force the Yankees own, took a modest part in the general battering. He merely unloaded two thundering singles into the helpless Giants, driving in three runs, and that wasn't anything at all.

Every member in the Yankee lineup helped himself to one or more blows in this assault of seventeen hits, to which Gomez himself contributed a single that drove in the first run in that ninth-inning jolt.

Their grand total of eighteen runs surpassed by five the highest previous mark for a single world series game, set by the Athletics in 1911 against another Giant team. Subsequently that mark of thirteen was tied by the Giants against the Yankees in the first all-New York series in 1921, and in 1932 the Yanks took a turn at matching this figure when the Cubs the victims.

And so, with their present mastery as the greatest clouting team of all time firmly and most convincingly established, the Yanks stand this morning on even terms with their battered National League rivals, each holding a victory apiece as the struggle for this afternoon moves into the Stadium for the third engagement.

In sharp contrast to the wretched conditions which prevailed for the first game, when the still invincible Hubbell held back those Ruppert Riflers in a three-hour drenching rain on Wednesday, the weather yesterday was excellent for baseball.

A brilliant sun shone and scarcely a breeze caused a flutter among the flags over the grand stand. Folks who, still a trifle distrustful of it all, brought overcoats, were soon perspiring freely and looking rather ridiculous.

Crowd Short of Capacity

The crowd arrived early and seemed bent on enjoying itself, although it again failed to touch the capacity mark, which had been set at 52,500. The paid attendance totaled only 43,543, with the receipts $184,982, and the baseball people last night were shaking their heads and wondering. For there seems to be something radically wrong with the present manner of selling world series tickets.

The clock atop the center-field clubhouse had passed 1 by a few minutes when the center-field portals swung open and, amid a great scurrying of police and Secret Service agents, who seemed to view with suspicion Yanks and Giants alike, four large, shiny automobiles rolled onto the field.

The crowd rose and cheered—all but Henry Fabian, venerable ground custodian of the Polo Grounds, who just rose and glared. Old Hennery wasn't disrespectful, but his greatest concern is for his velvety grass, and these mammoth machines were putting some terrible ruts in that outfield. It would have pained him less had they ridden over his feet.

In the first one, an open touring car, sat the President, who presently removed his large tan fedora to flash the famous Roosevelt smile. Senator Robert F. Wagner and Mr. Farley accompanied the Chief Executive. On the running board clung the ever-watchful Secret Service agents, looking more like somebody who just hopped on to get a lift down to the next corner.

Roosevelt Near Giants

With the President and his retinue safely and comfortably lodged in the boxes alongside the Giant dugout, the scene moved on to its closing number.

The President, scarcely discernible from above amid the battery of cameras which flanked him on all sides, rose with a white ball in his hand, and with Managers Terry and McCarthy standing before him, he tossed it for a perfect wild pitch well over the heads of the perspiring, jostling photographers.

Then he shook hands with the rival pilots and also insisted that McCarthy and Terry likewise exchange greetings to make it look like a real happy family all around. Little, however, did the unsuspecting Colonel Bill realize at that moment what terrible intent was in the usually affable Marse Joe's breast.

Presidential automobiles rolled away, though it might have been more thoughtful had they been allowed to remain in order to give those three Giant outfielders a little more help later on. That outfield on Wednesday had something of a record by not being called on to catch a single fly. Yesterday the trio simply wore out their shoes and caught plenty.

That grand and gorgeous offense which the Yanks were to unloose was something no world series game had ever seen before. The McCarthymen simply showered the premises with runs and in a moment of great magnanimity actually gave the Giants a couple as well.

Game 3 October 3 at Yankee Stadium

| NY G | 000 010 000 | 1 |
| NY Y | 010 000 01x | 2 |

NY Giants	Pos	AB	R	H	RBI	PO	A	E
Moore	lf	5	0	1	0	2	0	0
Bartell	ss	3	0	1	0	0	1	0
Terry	1b	4	0	1	0	5	1	0
Ott	rf	4	0	2	0	4	0	0
Ripple	cf	4	1	1	1	2	0	0
Mancuso	c	4	0	1	0	7	0	0
Whitehead	2b	4	0	0	0	3	4	0
Jackson	3b	2	0	1	0	1	0	0
a Koenig		1	0	0	0	0	0	0
Fitzsimmons	p	3	0	2	0	1	1	0
b Leslie		1	0	1	0	0	0	0
c Davis		0	0	0	0	0	0	0
Totals		35	1	11	1	24	8	0

NY Yankees	Pos	AB	R	H	RBI	PO	A	E
Crosetti	ss	4	0	1	1	4	5	0
Rolfe	3b	4	0	0	0	3	4	0
DiMaggio	cf	3	0	1	0	2	0	0
Gehrig	1b	3	1	1	1	10	1	0
Dickey	c	2	0	0	0	3	2	0
Selkirk	rf	3	0	1	0	2	0	0
Powell	lf	2	1	0	0	1	0	0
Lazzeri	2b	2	0	0	0	2	2	0
Hadley	p	2	0	0	0	0	3	0
d Ruffing		1	0	0	0	0	0	0
e Johnson		0	0	0	0	0	0	0
Malone	p	0	0	0	0	0	0	0
Totals		26	2	4	2	27	14	0

Pitching	IP	H	R	ER	BB	SO
Giants						
Fitzsimmons (L)	8	2	2	2	2	5
Yankees						
Hadley (W)	8	10	1	1	1	2
Malone (SV)	1	1	0	0	0	1

a Grounded out for Jackson in 9th.
b Singled for Fitzsimmons in 9th.
c Ran for Leslie in 9th.
d Hit into fielders choice for Hadley in 8th.
e Ran for Ruffing in 8th.

Double—DiMaggio. Home Runs—Gehrig, Ripple. Sacrifice Hits—Bartell, Lazzeri. Double Plays—Crosetti to Gehrig, Bartell to Whitehead to Terry. Umpires—Magerkurth, Summers, Pfirman, Geisel. Left on Bases—Giants 9, Yankees 3. Attendance—64,842. Time of Game—2:01.

1st Inning
Giants
Moore singled past third.
1 Bartell sacrificed Moore to second, Hadley to Gehrig.
Terry singled to center with Moore stopping at third.
2,3 Ott grounded to Crosetti who stepped on second to force Terry and threw to Gehrig to get Ott in a double play.
Yankees
1 Crosetti flied to right.
2 Rolfe grounded to first.
3 DiMaggio popped to second.

2nd Inning
Giants
1 Ripple flied to right.
2 Mancuso flied to center.
3 Whitehead grounded to second.
Yankees
Gehrig homered into the right field stands.
Dickey walked.
1 Selkirk fouled to Mancuso.
2,3 Powell grounded into a double play, Bartell to Whitehead to Terry.

3rd Inning
Giants
1 Jackson grounded to third.
2 Fitzsimmons struck out.
3 Moore flied to right.
Yankees
1 Lazzeri struck out.
2 Hadley flied to right.
3 Crosetti struck out.

4th Inning
Giants
1 Bartell fouled to Rolfe.
2 Terry grounded to short.
3 Ott fouled to Rolfe.
Yankees
1 Rolfe grounded to second.
DiMaggio doubled to left-center.
2 Gehrig flied to right.
3 Dickey grounded to second.

5th Inning
Giants
Ripple homered into the right field bleachers.
Mancuso blooped a single over short.
1 Whitehead forced Mancuso at second, Gehrig to Crosetti.
2 Whitehead caught stealing Dickey to Crosetti.
Jackson walked.
Fitzsimmons bounced a single over Rolfe's head, advancing Jackson to third.
3 Moore grounded back to the pitcher.

5th Inning (continued)
Yankees
1 Selkirk struck out.
2 Powell struck out.
3 Lazzeri flied to left.

6th Inning
Giants
1 Bartell fouled to Rolfe.
2 Terry flied to center.
Ott singled over second.
3 Ripple struck out.
Yankees
1 Hadley struck out.
2 Crosetti flied to center.
3 Rolfe lined to center.

7th Inning
Giants
1 Mancuso grounded to short.
2 Whitehead bunted and was out, Dickey to Gehrig.
Jackson singled to center.
Fitzsimmons singled to left, Jackson stopping at second.
3 Moore lined to second.
Yankees
1 DiMaggio lined to left.
2 Gehrig flied to right.
3 Dickey grounded to second.

8th Inning
Giants
Bartell singled to left.
1 Terry bunted but forced Bartell, Hadley to Crosetti.
Ott singled to center, Terry to second.
2 Ripple grounded to second, both runners advancing.
3 Mancuso flied to left.
Yankees
Selkirk singled to right.
Powell walked.
1 Lazzeri sacrificed Selkirk to third and Powell to second, Jackson to Whitehead.
Ruffing, batting for Hadley, tapped to
2 Fitzsimmons and Selkirk was trapped at the plate, Fitzsimmons to Mancuso. Johnson ran for Ruffing.
Crosetti singled off Fitzsimmons' glove, scoring Powell with Johnson stopping at second.
3 Rolfe grounded out, Terry to Fitzsimmons.

9th Inning
Giants
For the Yankees—Malone pitching.
1 Whitehead struck out.
2 Koenig, batting for Jackson, grounded to short.
Leslie, batting for Fitzsimmons, singled to center.
Davis ran for Leslie.
3 Moore forced Davis, Crosetti to Lazzeri.

Game 4 October 4 at Yankee Stadium

| NY G | 000 100 010 | 2 |
| NY Y | 013 000 01x | 5 |

NY Giants	Pos	AB	R	H	RBI	PO	A	E
Moore	lf	3	1	1	0	2	0	0
Bartell	ss	4	0	1	0	3	4	0
Terry	1b	3	0	0	0	10	1	0
Ott	rf	4	0	0	0	0	0	0
Ripple	cf	4	0	2	1	3	0	0
Mancuso	c	4	0	0	0	3	0	0
Whitehead	2b	3	0	0	0	2	5	0
c Koenig		1	0	1	0	0	0	0
Jackson	3b	4	0	0	0	0	3	1
Hubbell	p	2	0	0	0	1	0	0
a Leslie		1	0	1	0	0	0	0
b Davis		0	1	0	0	0	0	0
Gabler	p	0	0	0	0	0	0	0
Totals		33	2	7	2	24	13	1

NY Yankees	Pos	AB	R	H	RBI	PO	A	E
Crosetti	ss	4	1	2	0	4	1	0
Rolfe	3b	3	1	2	1	1	2	0
DiMaggio	cf	4	0	0	0	1	0	0
Gehrig	1b	4	2	2	2	7	0	0
Dickey	c	4	0	0	0	8	2	0
Powell	lf	4	1	1	2	1	0	0
Lazzeri	2b	4	0	0	0	3	4	0
Selkirk	rf	3	0	1	0	0	0	1
Pearson	p	4	0	2	0	1	2	0
Totals		34	5	10	5	27	11	1

Pitching	IP	H	R	ER	BB	SO
Giants						
Hubbell (L)	7	8	4	3	1	2
Gabler	1	2	1	1	1	0
Yankees						
Pearson (W)	9	7	2	2	2	7

a Singled for Hubbell in the 8th.
b Ran for Leslie in the 8th.
c Singled for Whitehead in the 9th.

Doubles—Crosetti, Gehrig, Pearson. Home Run—Gehrig. Double Play—Bartell to Whitehead to Terry. Wild Pitch—Hubbell. Left on Bases—Giants 6, Yankees 7. Umpires—Summers, Pfirman, Geisel, Magerkurth. Attendance—66,669 (**New Series record**). Time of Game—2:12.

1st Inning
Giants
Moore walked.
1 Bartell struck out.
2 Terry struck out.
3 Moore was out attempting to steal, Dickey to Crosetti.
Yankees
1 Crosetti grounded to third.
Rolfe singled past Jackson.
2 DiMaggio popped to first.
3 Gehrig grounded to second.

2nd Inning
Giants
1 Ott struck out.
Ripple singled between first and second.
2 Ripple caught trying for second, Dickey to Crosetti.
3 Mancuso fanned.
Yankees
1 Dickey fanned.
Powell reached first on Jackson's error.
2 Lazzeri grounded to second with Powell going to second.
Selkirk singled to left, scoring Powell.
3 Pearson flied to center.

3rd Inning
Giants
Whitehead safe at first as Selkirk dropped his short fly.
1 Jackson flied to center.
2 Hubbell grounded to the pitcher, Whitehead advancing to second.
3 Moore fouled to Rolfe.
Yankees
Crosetti doubled to right.
Rolfe singled to center, scoring Crosetti.
1 DiMaggio fouled to Mancuso.
Rolfe went to third on a wild pitch.
Gehrig hit a two-run homer into the right field bleachers.
2 Dickey lined to left.
3 Powell lined to Ripple who made a good low catch.

4th Inning
Giants
Bartell singled to right.
Terry walked.
1 Ott forced Terry at second, Crosetti to Lazzeri with Bartell going to third.
Ripple singled to left, scoring Bartell with Ott stopping at second.
2 Mancuso forced Ripple at second, Ott to third, Lazzeri to Crosetti.
3 Whitehead popped to short.
Yankees
1 Lazzeri flied to center.
2 Selkirk fanned.
Pearson singled to left.
3 Crosetti forced Pearson at second, Bartell to Whitehead.

5th Inning
Giants
Jackson beat out a bunt.
1 Hubbell flew out to left.
2 Moore struck out.
3 Bartell popped to short.
Yankees
Rolfe walked.
1 DiMaggio flied to left.
2 Gehrig forced Rolfe at second, Whitehead to Bartell.
3 Dickey forced Gehrig at second, Bartell unassisted.

6th Inning
Giants
1 Terry struck out.
2 Ott flied to left.
3 Ripple popped to short.
Yankees
1 Powell grounded to third.
2 Lazzeri grounded to short.
3 Selkirk grounded out, Terry to Hubbell.

7th Inning
Giants
1 Mancuso popped to Dickey.
2 Whitehead grounded to the pitcher.
3 Jackson struck out.
Yankees
Pearson doubled to right-center.
Crosetti singled to right, advancing Pearson to third.
1 Rolfe popped to short.
2,3 DiMaggio hit into a double play, Bartell to Whitehead to Terry.

8th Inning
Giants
Leslie, pinch hitting for Hubbell, singled to left.
Davis ran for Leslie.
Moore singled to left, moving Davis to second.
1 Bartell grounded out, Lazzeri to Pearson, both runners advancing.
2 Terry grounded to second, scoring Davis and Moore going to third.
3 Ott grounded to third.
Yankees
For the Giants—Gabler pitching.
Gehrig doubled to left.
1 Dickey grounded to short, moving Gehrig to third.
Powell singled to left, scoring Gehrig.
2 Lazzeri grounded to second, advancing Powell to second.
Selkirk walked.
3 Pearson grounded to third.

9th Inning
Giants
1 Ripple grounded to short.
2 Mancuso grounded to third.
Koenig, pinch hitting for Whitehead, singled to right center.
3 Jackson fouled to Gehrig.

Game 5 October 5 at Yankee Stadium

NY Giants	Pos	AB	R	H	RBI	PO	A	E
Moore	lf	5	2	2	0	1	0	0
Bartell	ss	4	1	1	1	2	2	1
Terry	1b	5	0	0	1	6	2	0
Ott	rf	5	1	0	0	1	0	1
Ripple	cf	2	1	1	1	2	0	0
Mancuso	c	3	0	2	0	14	2	0
Whitehead	2b	4	0	1	1	3	4	0
Jackson	3b	4	0	0	0	1	1	1
Schumacher	p	4	0	0	0	0	2	0
Totals		36	5	8	4	30	13	3

Pitching	IP	H	R	ER	BB	SO
Giants						
Schumacher (W)	10	10	4	3	6	10
Yankees						
Ruffing	6	7	4	3	1	7
Malone (L)	4	1	1	1	1	1

		NY G	3 0 0	0 0 1	0 0 0	1		5
		NY Y	0 1 1	0 0 2	0 0 0	0		4

NY Yankees	Pos	AB	R	H	RBI	PO	A	E
Crosetti	ss	5	0	0	1	2	3	1
Rolfe	3b	5	0	2	0	3	1	0
DiMaggio	cf	4	0	1	0	4	0	0
Gehrig	1b	4	0	1	0	5	1	0
Dickey	c	5	0	1	0	8	0	0
b Seeds		0	0	0	0	0	0	0
Selkirk	rf	4	2	2	1	2	0	0
Powell	lf	4	1	1	0	2	0	0
Lazzeri	2b	3	1	1	1	3	1	0
Ruffing	p	1	0	0	1	1	2	0
a Johnson		1	0	0	0	0	0	0
Malone	p	1	0	1	0	0	2	0
Totals		37	4	10	3	30	10	1

a Struck out for Ruffing in 6th.
b Ran for Dickey in 10th.

Doubles—Bartell, DiMaggio, Mancuso, Moore 2. Home Run—Selkirk. Sacrifice Hits—Bartell, Mancuso. Double Plays—Schumacher to Terry to Mancuso, Bartell to Whitehead to Terry, Mancuso to Whitehead, Crosetti to Lazzeri to Gehrig. Wild Pitch—Schumacher. Left on Bases—Giants 5, Yankees 9. Umpires—Pfirman, Geisel, Magerkurth, Summers. Attendance—50,024. Time of Game—2:45.

1st Inning
Giants
Moore doubled to left.
Bartell doubled to right, scoring Moore.
1 Terry struck out.
2 Ott grounded to short, moving Bartell to third.
Ripple singled to left, scoring Bartell.
Mancuso singled to right, moving Ripple to third.
Whitehead singled to right, scoring Ripple with Mancuso stopping at second.
3 Jackson flied to center.
Yankees
1 Crosetti struck out.
2 Rolfe flied to center.
3 DiMaggio grounded to third.

2nd Inning
Giants
1 Schumacher flied to second.
2 Moore popped to third.
3 Bartell struck out.
Yankees
Gehrig singled to right and got all the way to third as Ott erred.
1,2 Dickey was thrown out by Schumacher to Terry who pegged to Mancuso getting Gehrig trying to score for a double play.
Selkirk homered into the right field seats.
3 Powell flied to center.

3rd Inning
Giants
1 Terry grounded out to short.
2 Ott flied to left.
3 Ripple looked at a called third strike.
Yankees
Lazzeri walked.
Ruffing walked.
Lazzeri went to third and Ruffing to second on a wild pitch.
Crosetti was safe on first on Bartell's low throw scoring Lazzeri with Ruffing holding second.
Rolfe bunted for a single, loading the bases.
1 DiMaggio struck out.
2 Gehrig struck out.
3 Dickey flied to right.

4th Inning
Giants
Mancuso doubled to left.
1 Whitehead hit back to the pitcher who caught Mancuso off second throwing to Crosetti.
2 Jackson popped to short.
3 Schumacher struck out.
Yankees
Selkirk walked.
Powell walked.
1 Lazzeri attempting to sacrifice forced Selkirk at third, Schumacher to Jackson.
2,3 Ruffing grounded into a double play, Bartell to Whitehead to Terry.

5th Inning
Giants
1 Moore grounded out, Gehrig to Ruffing.
2 Bartell struck out.
3 Terry fouled to Rolfe.
Yankees
1 Crosetti struck out.
Rolfe bunted safely for a single.
2,3 DiMaggio struck out and Rolfe was doubled up going for second, Mancuso to Whitehead.

6th Inning
Giants
Ott singled over Crosetti's head.
Ripple walked.
1 Mancuso sacrificed both runners up, Ruffing to Lazzeri.
Whitehead made it to first on Crosetti's fumble, Ott scoring and Ripple going to third.
2 Jackson struck out.
3 Schumacher struck out.
Yankees
1 Gehrig grounded to second.
2 Dickey struck out.
Selkirk singled to right.
Powell grounded to Jackson who threw over Terry's head scoring Selkirk with Powell reaching third.
Lazzeri singled past second, scoring Powell.
3 Johnson, pinch hitting for Ruffing, struck out.

7th Inning
Giants
For the Yankees—Malone pitching
1 Moore flied to right.
2 Bartell flied to left.
3 Terry grounded back to the pitcher.
Yankees
1 Crosetti struck out.
2 Rolfe struck out.
DiMaggio doubled to left-center.
Gehrig walked.
3 Dickey fouled to Mancuso.

8th Inning
Giants
1 Ott flied to center.
Ripple walked.
2,3 Mancuso hit into a double play, Crosetti to Lazzeri to Gehrig.
Yankees
1 Selkirk popped to Mancuso.
2 Powell struck out.
3 Lazzeri grounded to short.

9th Inning
Giants
1 Whitehead flied to right.
2 Jackson out back to the pitcher.
3 Schumacher struck out.
Yankees
Malone singled to left.
1 Crosetti bunting forced Malone at second, Terry to Bartell.
2 Rolfe forced Crosetti, Whitehead to Bartell.
DiMaggio walked.
3 Gehrig grounded to second.

10th Inning
Giants
Moore doubled to left.
1 Bartell sacrificed Moore to third, Rolfe to Lazzeri covering first.
2 Terry flied to center, Moore scoring after the catch.
3 Ott popped to third.
Yankees
Dickey singled through first.
Seeds ran for Dickey.
1 Selkirk fouled to Mancuso.
2 Powell flied to left.
3 Seeds was caught stealing Mancuso to Whitehead.

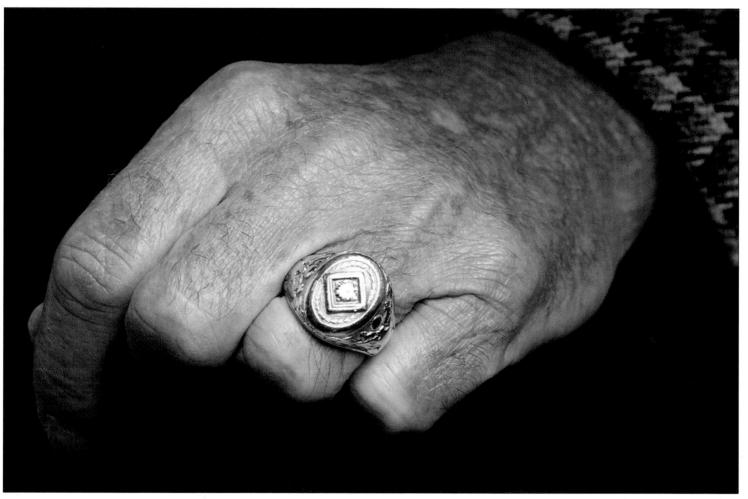

The 1936 World Series ring on the hand of Joe DiMaggio in 1989. It was the first of ten World Series rings he earned during his thirteen years with the Yankees.

Two bats bearing Joe DiMaggio's signature. On the left is one he used in his later years with the Yankees; the other is a commemorative bat from the 1936 World Series, signed by all members of the victorious Yankees.

Game 6 October 6 at Polo Grounds

NY Y											13
	0	2	1	2	0	0	0	1	7		
NY G	2	0	0	0	1	0	1	1	0		5

NY Yankees	Pos	AB	R	H	RBI	PO	A	E
Crosetti	ss	4	0	0	1	0	1	0
Rolfe	3b	6	1	3	2	3	2	1
DiMaggio	cf	6	1	3	1	2	0	1
Gehrig	1b	5	1	1	1	10	0	0
Dickey	c	5	2	0	1	3	0	0
Selkirk	rf	5	2	2	0	3	0	0
Powell	lf	5	3	3	4	3	0	0
Lazzeri	2b	4	2	3	1	3	5	0
Gomez	p	3	0	1	1	0	3	0
Murphy	p	2	1	1	1	0	0	0
Totals		45	13	17	12	27	11	2

Pitching	IP	H	R	ER	BB	SO
Yankees						
Gomez (W)	6⅓	8	4	4	4	1
Murphy (SV)	2⅓	1	1	1	1	1
Giants						
Fitzsimmons (L)	3⅓	9	5	5	0	1
Castleman	4⅓	3	1	1	2	5
Coffman	*0	3	5	5	1	0
Gumbert	1	2	2	2	3	1

*Pitched to 5 batters in 9th.

NY Giants	Pos	AB	R	H	RBI	PO	A	E
Moore	lf	5	2	2	1	2	0	0
Bartell	ss	3	2	2	0	0	2	0
Terry	1b	4	0	1	0	6	0	0
Leiber	cf	2	0	0	0	6	0	0
Mayo	3b	1	0	0	0	0	0	0
Ott	rf	4	1	2	3	3	0	0
Mancuso	c	3	0	0	0	4	0	0
a Leslie		1	0	0	0	0	0	0
Danning	c	1	0	0	0	3	0	1
Whitehead	2b	3	0	0	0	1	2	0
b Ripple	cf	0	0	0	0	1	0	0
Jackson	3b	3	0	1	0	0	0	0
c Koenig	2b	1	0	0	0	1	0	0
Fitzsimmons	p	1	0	0	0	0	1	0
Castleman	p	2	0	1	0	0	0	0
d Davis		1	0	0	0	0	0	0
Coffman	p	0	0	0	0	0	0	0
Gumbert	p	0	0	0	0	0	0	0
Totals		35	5	9	5	27	5	1

a Fouled out for Mancuso in 7th.
b Walked for Whitehead in 7th.
c Struck out for Jackson in 7th.
d Flied out for Castleman in 8th.

Doubles—Bartell, Ott. Triple—Selkirk.
Home Runs—Moore, Ott, Powell.
Sacrifice Hits—Leiber, Terry.
Left on Bases—Yankees 11, Giants 10.
Umpires—Geisel, Magerkurth, Summers,
Pfirman. Attendance—38,427.
Time of Game—2:50.

1st Inning
Yankees
1 Crosetti popped to second.
2 Rolfe popped to first.
3 DiMaggio flied to center.
Giants
  Moore singled to left.
  Bartell walked.
1 Terry sacrificed Moore to third and
  Bartell to second. Rolfe to Gehrig.
  Leiber walked filling the bases.
  Ott doubled to right, scoring Moore
  and Bartell and advancing Leiber to
  third.
2 Mancuso fouled out to Rolfe.
3 Whitehead grounded to second.

2nd Inning
Yankees
1 Gehrig flied to center.
2 Dickey flied to left.
  Selkirk tripled to right-center.
  Powell homered into the upper left
  field stands.
  Lazzeri singled.
3 Gomez grounded out to the pitcher.
Giants
  Jackson singled through the box.
1 Fitzsimmons flied to right.
2 Moore flied to left.
  Bartell walked.
3 Terry flew out to center.

3rd Inning
Yankees
1 Crosetti fanned.
  Rolfe singled to left.
  DiMaggio singled to left, Rolfe
  advancing to third.
2 Gehrig flied to right, Rolfe scored
  after the catch.
3 Dickey flied to left.
Giants
1 Leiber fouled to Dickey.
2 Ott's hit was deflected by Gomez to
  Crosetti who threw him out.
  Mancuso safe at first on Rolfe's
  fumble.
3 Whitehead fouled to Selkirk.

4th Inning
Yankees
1 Selkirk flied to center.
  Powell singled between third and
  short.
  Lazzeri singled through short, Powell
  stopping at second.
  Gomez singled over Bartell's head,
  scoring Powell with Lazzeri going to
  second.
2 Crosetti flew out to center.
  Rolfe singled to right-center, scoring
  Lazzeri with Gomez going to third.
  For the Giants—Castleman pitching.
3 DiMaggio flied to right.
Giants
1 Jackson grounded to second.
  Castleman singled to right center.
2 Moore flied to right.
  Bartell beat out a bunt along the third base
  line, Castleman moving to second.
3 Terry grounded to second.

5th Inning
Yankees
1 Gehrig grounded to first.
2 Dickey grounded to second.
3 Selkirk flied to center.
Giants
1 Leiber struck out.
  Ott homered into the upper tier of
  the left field stands.
2 Mancuso flied to center.
3 Whitehead grounded back to the pitcher.

6th Inning
Yankees
1 Powell struck out.
2 Lazzeri struck out.
3 Gomez struck out.
Giants
1 Jackson popped to second.
2 Castleman grounded back to the pitcher.
3 Moore grounded to second.

7th Inning
Yankees
1 Crosetti grounded to short.
  Rolfe singled past second.
2 DiMaggio flied to center.
3 Gehrig grounded to second.
Giants
  Bartell doubled to left.
  Terry singled to center and on
  DiMaggio's bobble Bartell scored
  and Terry went to second.
1 Leiber sacrificed Terry to third.
  Rolfe to Lazzeri.
  Ott walked.
  For the Yankees—Murphy pitching.
2 Leslie, pinch hitting for Mancuso, fouled
  to Rolfe.
  Ripple, pinch hitting for Whitehead,
  walked to load the bases.
3 Koenig, pinch hitting for Jackson, fanned.

8th Inning
Yankees
  For the Giants—Koenig to second, Mayo
  to third (batting fifth), Ripple to
  center, Danning in as catcher (batting
  seventh).
  Dickey walked.
  Selkirk singled to right, Dickey
  stopping at second.
1 Powell fanned.
  Lazzeri singled to center, scoring Dickey
  and advancing Selkirk to second.
2 Murphy struck out.
  Crosetti walked filling the bases.
3 Rolfe flied to right.
Giants
1 Davis, pinch hitting for Castleman, flied
  to left.
  Moore homered into the upper deck of
  the right field stands.
2 Bartell popped to second.
3 Terry grounded to second.

9th Inning
Yankees
  For the Giants—Coffman pitching.
  DiMaggio singled over third.
  Gehrig singled to right, DiMaggio going
  to third.
  Dickey bounced to Terry and DiMaggio
  was trapped between third and home but
  scored when Danning dropped Mayo's
  throw to the plate. Gehrig got to
  third and Dickey to second.
  Selkirk intentionally walked loading
  the bases.
  Powell singled through the hole to score
  Gehrig and Dickey as Selkirk moved
  to third.
  For the Giants—Gumbert pitching.
  Lazzeri walked again loading the bases.
  Murphy singled to right, scoring Selkirk.
  Crosetti walked forcing in Powell (**For
  Powell his 8th run of the Series tying
  the 6 game record set by Babe Ruth in
  the 1923 Series**).
1 Rolfe forced Crosetti at second, Bartell
  to Koenig, scoring Lazzeri with Murphy
  going to third.
  DiMaggio got his second single of the
  inning, scoring Murphy and moving Lazzeri
  to second.
  Gehrig walked to again load the bases.
2 Dickey struck out.
3 Selkirk flied to center.
Giants
1 Mayo fouled to Rolfe.
2 Ott flied to left.
3 Danning bounced to Gehrig, unassisted.

NEW YORK, WEDNESDAY, OCTOBER 7, 1936.

Yanks Win Series, Routing Giants With 7 Runs in Last Inning, 13-5

Take Title, 4 Games to 2, After Losers Miss Big Chance to Tie Exciting Battle—Powell, Ott, Moore Hit Homers—Gomez and Fitzsimmons Fail—Record Gate for 6 Contests.

By JOHN DREBINGER

The overpowering force behind the Yankee bludgeons, which crushed the entire American League this year, reigns supreme in the baseball universe today.

There was no checking it, and the end to the 1936 world series came under a gray and murky sky that hung over the Polo Grounds yesterday as the Joe McCarthy juggernaut battered Colonel Bill Terry's Giants into submission in the sixth and final game by a score of 13 to 5. That clinched the classic by a margin of four games to two.

Seven of those thirteen runs came hurtling over the plate in the ninth after the last desperate but gallant stand of the Giants had failed by one of bringing about a tie, and sent a crowd of 38,427 on its way convinced there had been a miscarriage of justice.

As late as the seventh and eighth innings that all-New York gallery had, in characteristic manner, given its undivided vocal support to the plucky fight of the underdog to prolong the struggle into a seventh game. At the finish it remained just long enough to give one rousing salute to the triumphant Yanks and then, again in typical New York fashion, it filed hurriedly out of the arena to concern itself with other matters of interest.

It was the second world championship to fall to the Yankees under the leadership of the square-jawed but affable enough Joseph V. McCarthy, who never played a game of ball in the major leagues in his life, and the fifth title to come to roost under the Ruppert banner.

The crowd, the smallest of the series, nevertheless brought the aggregate to 302,924, a record for six games and the second highest figure ever attained in world series history. The receipts for the day, $169,213, brought the grand total to $1,204,399, which also sets a six-game record and falls short by only a few thousand dollars of the all-time mark of $1,207,864.

That record was set in the seven-game series between the Yankees and Cardinals in 1926, when the paid attendance totaled 328,051.

That year the Yankees lost, but it was to be their last defeat for baseball's highest honors, though they appeared in four classics since. They even entered the clash just ended with the amazing record of three series triumphs scored in twelve straight games without a single reversal.

That streak ended when the seemingly invincible Carl Hubbell stopped them in the first game of the series exactly a week ago today and they were thrown for a loss again on Monday by a superb effort of sheer grit on the part of one Harold Schumacher.

But when the final drive for the championship came there was no halting that surging Yankee horde, though the Giants threw everything they had into as desperate and gallant a fight as ever a game but thoroughly outclassed contender in a world series could make.

For until that final cataclysm of runs crashed down on the heads of the Giants in the ninth this final game was as tense and dramatic as any of the series.

Ott Sends in First Two

There was an opening charge by Terry's men upon the left-handed Vernon Gomez in the first inning that for a few minutes promised to assure almost immediately that a seventh game would be needed to decide final honors. Mel Ott exploded a two-bagger with the bases full and two runs whirled over the plate to give the stout-hearted Freddy Fitzsimmons a lift in his second appearance in the series.

Fat Fitz had pitched a four-hit classic in the third game, only to lose in heart-breaking fashion, and the chance to square accounts seemed to have been provided for him almost at the start.

But it took those long-range guns of the Yanks only two innings to stride abreast of the luckless Giants, who seemed to be fighting howitzers with cap pistols.

George Selkirk sent a towering smash clear down to the Giant bullpen for three bases in the second and a moment later Jake Powell rifled a home run into the upper left stand. It was the sixth consecutive game of the series in which some member of that murderous array of Yankee clouters had unloaded a homer, and in a jiffy it had tied the score at 2—all.

In the third the American Leaguers wrenched another run away from the toiling Fitz and in the fourth they routed the pudgy knuckleballer with a four-hit barrage that yielded two more runs.

Still the Giants fought back. They called on Clydell Castleman to replace the twice vanquished Fitz, and the young right-hander, called Slick, making a tardy entry in the series, turned in a brilliant piece of relief pitching for the next four innings while his comrades strove with might and main to draw even once more.

First Homer for Mel

In the fifth, the youthful veteran Ott, whose home run proclivities up to then had been restrained by a studied campaign of the Yankee pitchers to prevent him from pulling his favorite shots into right, amazed the crowd by stroking a powerful smash into the upper left tier, a sector in which he had never been known before to hit a homer. But the circuit smack came with the bases empty and left the Giants still two runs shy.

In the seventh they launched another mighty effort, rammed another run across and routed Gomez. Terry himself lashed this tally home with a line single to center which went right through Joe Di-Maggio for an error and came perilously close to leaving this otherwise brilliant rookie the goat of the afternoon.

Here, too, was unfolded the dramatic highlight of the entire battle. For with two on the bases, only one out and only one run needed to bring about a tie, Marse Joe called on the youthful Fordham Johnny Murphy to stem this Giant tide.

And Fordham Johnny made it, though the despairing Terry threw every ounce of his reserve power into the fray. Failure to carry the day with this fierce sally finally broke the hearts of the Giants.

Giants Still One Short

In the eighth the bruising Yankee attack clipped even the surprisingly fine-working Castleman for a run, and though Jo-Jo Moore negatived this tally in the same inning with a homer that again had the Giants only one count short, the crowd felt the final verdict was in.

For with Castleman replaced by a pinch-hitter in the eighth and the last vestige of his fine defenses stripped in a futile quest for power that simply was not there, Colonel Terry had nothing left in the ninth to hold that swarming Yankee legion.

Seven runs streaked across the plate in riotous profusion as the McCarthy forces in a final outburst of unrestrained might and power raked the blond Dick Coffman and the dark-haired Harry Gumbert for five hits, which, mingled with four passes and a woeful error, shot like darts into the broken hulk of a sorely wounded bull.

Limp and dejected, though perhaps not altogether greatly surprised, Colonel Terry limped off the field, his exit from the scene being his last as an active ball player. To the end he had spared neither himself nor his men and now the fight was over.

Team Rebuilt Since 1932

There simply was no stopping that amazingly powerful baseball machine which the canny McCarthy had reconstructed since 1932 and which, with little regard for the subtleties of technical play on the ball field, he just rolled out to flatten all opposition.

Those Yanks had wrecked their own circuit to win by eighteen games on the earliest date an American League pennant had ever been clinched and they had now finished smashing the stoutest defenses the National League could muster.

For the second successive year the might of the American circuit's flag winner triumphed. Last year the Tigers outsmacked the Cubs. This year the Yanks fairly annihilated the Giants.

••

38,427 Paid $169,213 To See Sixth Contest

Final Standing of the teams

	W.	L.	P.C.
Yankees	4	2	.667
Giants	2	4	.333

Sixth Game Statistics

Attendance (paid)	38,427
Gate receipts	$169,213.00
Commissioner's share	25,381.95
Clubs' share	71,915.52
League's share	71,915.53

Total Series Statistics

Attendance (paid)	302,924
Gate receipts	$1,204,399.00
Commissioner's share	180,659.85
*Players' share	424,737.18
Clubs' share	299,500.98
Leagues' share	299,500.99

Radio Receipts

Players' share	$35,265.48
Commissioner's share	15,000.00
Clubs' share	24,867.26
Leagues' share	24,867.26

*Players share in gross receipts of first four games only.

The official paid attendance at the sixth game of the 1936 world series was about 10,000 less than that for the corresponding game in the 1935 series. However, the gross receipts here exceeded those at Detroit by more than $20,000. The gross receipts for the series fell short of the record set in 1926 by the Yankees and Cardinals by $3,465. The 1926 series lasted the full seven games. While the total paid attendance for that series was 328,051, the 1936 classic attracted 302,924. The 1935 total attendance was 286,672 and the gross receipts were $1,173,794.

Highlights

- The Yankees and the Giants met for the fourth time in an intracity Series, and the Yanks' triumph evened the record at two successes apiece.
- Red Rolfe's 10 singles for the Yankees set a record for a six-game Series.
- The Yankees' 43 runs scored and 41 RBIs set marks for a six-game Series.
- The Yankee loss in Game 1 ended their 12-game Series winning streak.
- Rookie Joe DiMaggio got the first of what would be 54 career World Series hits when he singled in Game 1.
- The Yankees set a Series standard when they scored 18 runs in Game 2, one that has never been bettered.
- In Game 2, Tony Lazzeri became the second slugger to hit a grand-slam homer in the World Series (Elmer Smith of the Cleveland Indians hit the first back in 1920). Lazzeri and Bill Dickey also drove in five runs each in the massacre of the Giants.
- The four runs Frank Crosetti scored for the Yanks in Game 2 tied a Series mark.
- Crosetti singled to drive in Jake Powell with the game-winning run in the bottom of the eighth of Game 3 to give the Yankees a two-to-one edge in the Series.
- In Game 4, the Yankees scored three runs in the third, two of them off a Lou Gehrig homer, to gain the winning margin.
- Hal Schumacher fanned 10 Yankee batters in Game 5.
- Bill Terry's sacrifice fly in the tenth inning of Game 5 scored Joe Moore and won the game for the Giants.
- The Yankees exploded for seven runs in the top of the ninth of Game 6 to clinch the Series. Their 17 hits matched the total they ran up in Game 2.
- Four Yanks got three hits apiece in Game 6: Red Rolfe, Joe DiMaggio, Jake Powell, and Tony Lazzeri.

Best Efforts

Batting

Average	Jake Powell .455	Runs	Jake Powell 8
Home Runs	Lou Gehrig 2	RBIs	Lou Gehrig 7
	George Selkirk 2		Tony Lazzeri 7
Triples	George Selkirk 1	**Pitching**	
Doubles	Joe DiMaggio 3	Wins	Lefty Gomez 2-0
Hits	Jake Powell 10	ERA	Bump Hadley 1.12
	Red Rolfe 10	Strikeouts	Red Ruffing 12
		Innings Pitched	Carl Hubbell 16

NEW YORK YANKEES
NEW YORK GIANTS
1936

Reprinted, with permission, from
The World Series, A Complete
Pictorial History, by John Devaney
and Burt Goldblatt (Rand McNally
and Company, Chicago, © 1972).

From FDR To DiMag, a Wave

This was the pit of the depression, and a man of his time was Tony Albano, an unemployed Brooklyn chauffeur. For 12 days he stood in line outside the Polo Grounds to be the first to buy a ticket. On the 12th day he offered to sell his spot for $150. This also told of the times: He got no offers.

Despite the hard times, big crowds filled the two ball parks that squatted across from each other on the Harlem River—the double-decked Polo Grounds and the triple-tiered Yankee Stadium. The receipts, counting a radio fee of around $100,000, came to $1,204,399, the highest ever. This was the fourth "nickel" Series, 5¢ being the cost of a subway ride to the Polo Grounds or to Yankee Stadium. For the second time the Yankees won, beating the Giants in six games.

This was the first Series for the Yankees without Babe Ruth in their lineup. And it was the first Series for a lanky, shy centerfielder, then only 21, named Joe DiMaggio. As in almost every Series he played in, Joltin' Joe distinguished himself, this time hitting .346.

The Giants' King Carl Hubbell halted the Yankee machine in the first game with a 6-1 victory, his 17th straight triumph. He had not lost a game since the Cubs' Bill Lee beat him 1-0, in July. The Yankees evened the Series with an 18-4 massacre, the most lopsided win in Series history. The Yankees then rolled to victory, even beating Hubbell on the way. With President Franklin Roosevelt watching from a box seat at the Polo Grounds, the second game ended with Hank Leiber hitting a soaring drive to deep centerfield. Joe DiMaggio raced toward the bleacher wall and speared the ball for the final out. Then he stood at attention as Mr. Roosevelt, in his limousine, was driven out of the ball park through the centerfield exit, the President waving to DiMag as he passed by.

Carl Hubbell:
Suppose a fan saw me talking to Gehrig

Carl Hubbell, the Giant pitcher and now that team's director of player development, recalled that: *We had a book on all the Yankee hitters. Our scouts had watched the Yankees and they told us the usual things: pitch so-and-so inside, that sort of thing. But I have always thought that those books on hitters were vastly overrated. Before each World's Series you will hear how one team is going to pitch so-and-so high and tight and this other guy low and away. But no two pitchers can pitch alike. A book could have told me and [Fred] Fitzsimmons to pitch tight to a certain hitter. But a hitter might murder a tight pitch by me while a tight pitch by Fitz might get him out.... In those days we didn't talk to the players on the other team—especially before a Series. I never believed in it. Suppose a fan saw me talking to Lou Gehrig before a game. Then in a game Gehrig hits one up into the seats off me. The average fan, he's got to think, Hey is there something going on here or what?*

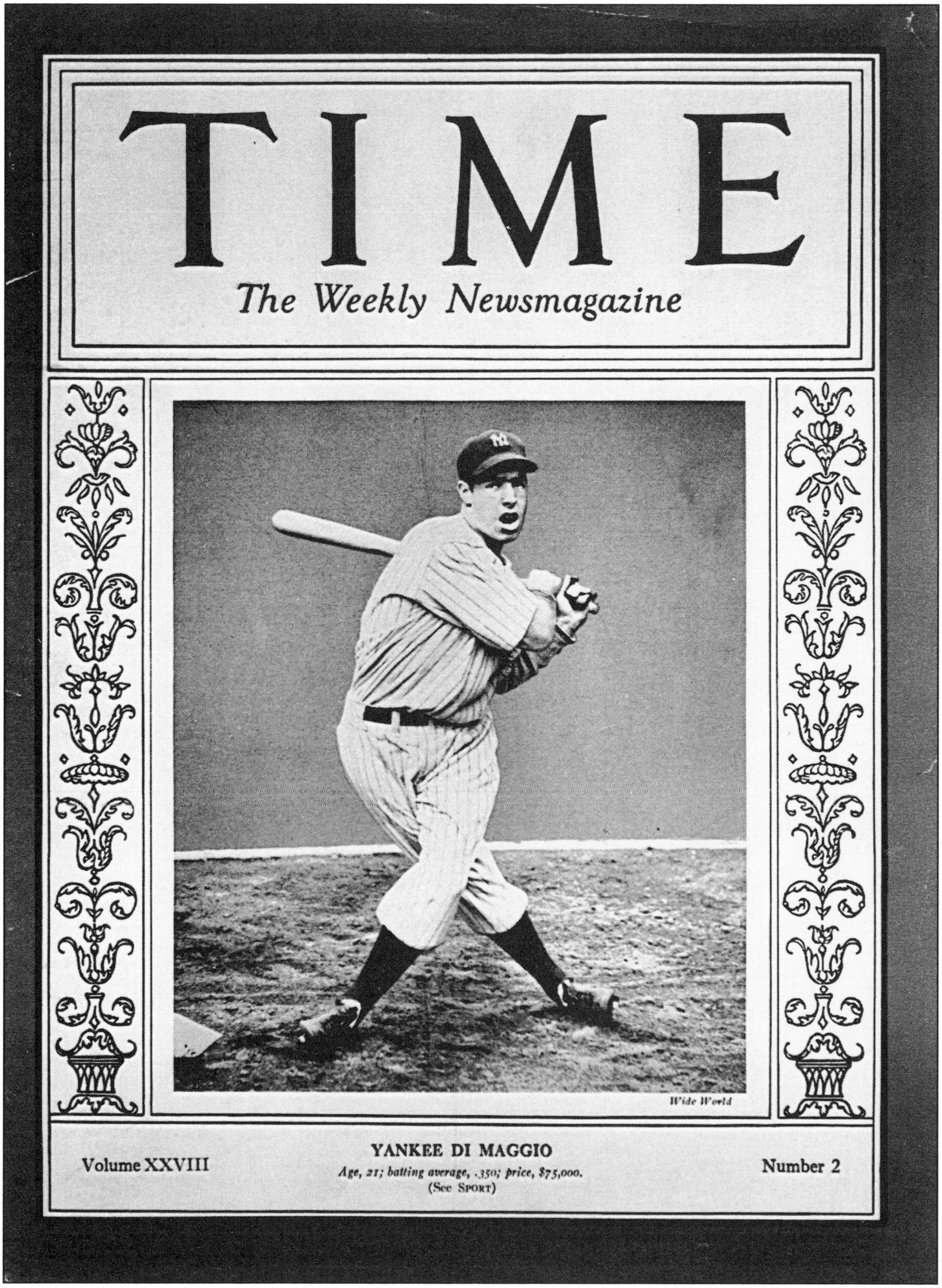

TIME

The Weekly Newsmagazine

Wide World

YANKEE DI MAGGIO

Age, 21; batting average, .350; price, $75,000.
(See SPORT)

Volume XXVIII

Number 2

Making the cover of *Time* magazine after the 1936 World Series.

DIMAGGIO WINS OVER SKEPTICS IN RIVAL LEAGUE

Coast Rookie's Speed Is Praised Along With His Hitting and Throwing.

By JAMES M. KAHN.

The world series may be over, but the conversation about it still goes on. Few, if any, of the brighter moments of the big battle have been neglected by those conducting the verbal post-mortem, including a thorough dissecting of Col. Bill Terry's master-minding in the final game.

However, out of all the controversial conversation emerges one item around which no controversy rages. It is that Joe DiMaggio is a fine ball player. It took the world series to make it unanimous, for that furnished National Leaguers with an opportunity to give the Coast rookie a thorough inspection under testing conditions. The American League, after watching him all season, already was agreed on his stature as an outfielder.

The Giants, who played against him, and many other National League players and managers who watched the series from the stands and the press box, have nothing but admiration for his talents. The Giants learned early to have respect for them, too, particularly his throwing arm. They made no attempt to run on him.

Joe's Only Misplay.

The only misplay Joe made in the series came in the final game. In his eagerness to field Bill Terry's single and make a throw home to head off Bartell, who had started from second, he let the ball go through him. Otherwise, he was perfection, roaming far and wide to make more putouts than any other outfielder in the series, and to turn in the most spectacular catch of the classic when he speared Hank Leiber's terrific drive in the second game up against the center field bleacher wall.

National Leaguers had only heard of DiMaggio, first as the Coast league's most brilliant graduate who was coming up to the Yankees, and later as the rookie sensation who was whizzing through his first year in the big leagues at a pace that was swifter than they could easily believe. He was quite a hitter, they knew from reading the box scores, but it took the series for them to discover how skillful a fielder he was and how natural and accomplished a base runner.

Joe Devine, who scouts the Coast territory for the Yankees, was busy throughout the series answering the questions that National Leaguers were putting to him about DiMaggio. It was Devine who was in favor of bringing Joe up in 1935, when the Yankee outfield was unsettled early in the year and the team had difficulty in getting started. The Yanks were in favor of letting Joe stay out there and play another season and establish that his injured knee was completely mended. But Devine insisted that DiMaggio was ready for the big league then.

Star After One Season.

Off what he showed during the past season, he probably was. At any rate, no one denies now that he already is entrenched as a star after only one season.

One of the things Devine pointed out to his National League inquirers was to watch DiMaggio's speed. It is deceptive, but he has it, and it comes from his long stride. Devine revealed for the first time during the series that he had taken DiMaggio down to the University of Southern California for a few test runs after his injured knee had healed. They measured Joe's stride and found it to be seven and a half feet when he is in full flight. It is a coincidence that this is the exact stride of Jesse Owens.

It was DiMaggio's all-around play, however, and his natural baseball savvy which evoked the enthusiasm of those National League men who were seeing him for the first time, rather than any single outstanding talent. They see in him just a splendid natural ball player who will get even better as he goes along.

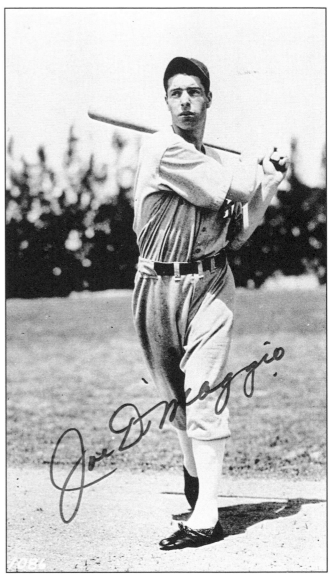

DiMaggio batted .323 in 1936, with 29 home runs and a league-leading 15 triples.

DANIEL'S DOPE

Joe Di Maggio, perhaps the greatest first-year ball player in the history of the major leagues, has gone home to San Francisco, and it is believed that he has taken with him a Yankee contract for three years.

Joe, his mother and older brother, Tom, visited Ed Barrow in the Yankee offices the other day. While Ed has made no announcement, it is reported that he got Joe's signature to an agreement calling for $15,000 a year for the next three seasons. Barrow soon leaves for Hadley, N. Y., to rest on the farm of his friend, Joe McCarthy—not the manager of the Yanks, but a song writer.

After the sour experience which he suffered with Lefty Gomez, whom he signed for two years at $20,000 a season, Colonel Jacob Ruppert told Barrow never again to give anybody on the club a contract for more than a year. But as soon as a club owner makes a resolve, somebody usually happens along to make him change his mind.

Di Maggio aroused the excited praise and abounded envy of Bill Terry in the world series. Bill had heard a lot about Di Maggio, but having seen him only in the all star game, in which Jolting Joe made himself the goat without a dissenting vote, the manager of the Giants was just a mite skeptical. That is, he was until he got a load of Joe in the classic. Then Terry announced "that Di Maggio is the greatest player on the Yankees."

The final figures of the American League show that Di Maggio finished with an average of .323, for 138 games. Joe scored 132 runs and made 206 hits, of which 45 were doubles, 15 triples and 29 homers. He drove in 125 runs and stole four bases.

Joe can run, and would have liked to run, but McCarthy put the wraps on him right at the start. "You get on and we'll take care of driving you around," Marse Joe warned his young star. You see, Di Maggio suffered a serious leg injury in 1934, and McCarthy wanted him to take no chances.

* * *

Di Maggio was headed for a .350 average until he ran into a slump in the last fortnight. In that stretch there were a lot of games with the Athletics. Strangely enough, Joe could not hit Connie Mack's pitchers. They held him to an average of worse than .200.

Di Maggio did his best hitting against the Browns. When Roger Hornsby first saw Joe he said that the young man could be pitched to. But Di Maggio wound up with a .525 record against the St. Louis slingers.

* * *

Di Maggio's Career Meteoric; Got Highest Rookie Salary.

Di Magigo has yet to celebrate his twenty-second birthday. But his career already has been a meteoric one. His salary with the Yankees this year was $8,500. That's the highest stipend yet paid to a rookie by the New York club. Very likely it set a record for both circuits.

Di Maggio did phenomenally well not only on the field, but at the turnstiles. He proved the biggest attraction the major leagues had seen since Babe Ruth's heyday. And his influence on the ball club as a whole cannot be overestimated.

When a pole on the American League race was taken early in April, not a single writer who had reported the Yankeee doings in their training camp at St. Petersburg, Fla. nominated them to win the pennant. You see, the scribes had only a glimpse of Joe Di Maggio.

After Di Maggio had played in four exhibition games, he suffered a foot burn and had to remain on the sidelines until the Yankess had played seventeen contests in the league race. As soon as Di Maggio went into the outfield, the Yankees became a different ball club. He pulled up the entire outfit.

Without Di Maggio, the New Yorks looked like a second place outfit, at best. Colonel Ruppert only the other day confessed that when the Yanks left St. Petersburg he did not rate them definite pennant contenders.

For a kid just out of the Coast League to pull a ball club right into a contending position, and keep it in the Number One spot, is a feat which not even so great a rookie as Joe Jackson, who set a record for freshmen when he broke in with .408 with Cleveland in 1911, could approach. The Indians finished third that season.

* * *

It surely was a case of "Viva Italia" on the Yankees of 1936. Frank Crosetti hit .288 and drove in 78 runs, with 15 homers, and Tony Lazzeri hit .287, driving in 111 tallies and making 14 home runs.

1937
A YEAR OF HOME RUNS

A pensive Joe DiMaggio. He led the major leagues with 46 home runs in 1937, and in runs scored with 151 while batting .346.

HOME RUN CROWN

In the early part of 1937, for me, it hardly looked like it would be a base-ball year worth remembering. From the day I reported to spring training down in St. Petersburg, my arm bothered me. I couldn't throw without pain.

Then, while we were on the exhibition trail, a doctor in Knoxville, Tennessee, found I had enlarged tonsils, which he determined had to go. I was sent back to New York ahead of the ballclub and checked into Lenox Hill Hospital.

My ailments were taken care of by May 1, the day I got back into the lineup. The rest must have helped because I was stronger than ever. In late July, I hit a home run off Howard Mills of the St. Louis Browns that travelled 450 feet into the left field bleachers at Yankee Stadium — at the time it was the longest ever hit in that area of the ballpark. On August 1, I hit my 31st homer of the season, which put me ahead of the 1927 pace of Babe Ruth, the year he hit 60. I didn't keep up the Babe's pace, however, but did end with 46 to win the home run crown that year.

Joe DiMaggio

1937

JOE DiMAGGIO STATISTICS

Games	151
At Bats	621
Hits	215
Doubles	35
Triples	15
Home Runs	46*
Runs Scored	151*
Runs Batted In	167
Bases on Balls	64
Strike Outs	37
Stolen Bases	3
Slugging Average	.673*
Batting Average	.346

* Led the American
  League

STANDINGS

	Won	Lost	Percentage	Games Behind
New York Yankees	102	52	.662	
Detroit Tigers	89	65	.578	13
Chicago White Sox	86	68	.558	16
Cleveland Indians	83	71	.539	19
Boston Red Sox	80	72	.526	21
Washington Senators	73	80	.477	28.5
Philadelphia A's	54	97	.358	46.5
St. Louis Browns	46	108	.299	56

DiMaggio Named Player of Year By New York Baseball Writers

Yankee Star, Here Today, Will Receive Award at Dinner on January 30

By Rud Rennie

The eighth annual "player of the year" award by the New York chapter of the Baseball Writers' Association of America has been voted to Joe DiMaggio, the slugging Yankee center fielder. He will receive a suitable plaque at the baseball writers' dinner at the Commodore on January 30.

The writers selected DiMaggio as the player of the year in spite of the fact that Charley Gehringer, second baseman of the Detroit Tigers, had been voted the most valuable player in the American League and Joe Medwick, of the St. Louis Cardinals, had been similarly honored in the National League. The New York writers could not help thinking DiMaggio was the best ball player there was last year.

Joe arrives in town today from San Francisco, where, in the off-season, he operates a restaurant. He came East to see the Farr-Braddock fight, to attend a sports dinner in Philadelphia and the writers' banquet at the Commodore and, mayhap, to discuss his contract with Ed Barrow, the Yankees' business manager.

The Yankee contracts have not been sent out yet, but if Joe drops around to the Yankee offices and inquires about his salary the reply may cause a difference of opinion. The Yankees may think that is what Joe should receive this year but Joe

Herald Tribune photo—Acme
Joe DiMaggio

may disagree with them.

The popular Italian received $15,000 for his work last year. He had a good year.

Joe has been reported as thinking he should get $30,000 this year for playing ball and being a drawing card. Colonel Jacob Ruppert, owner of the club, has given him a raise in salary, but the chances are he did not give him a $15,000 raise. And that's what Joe wants. So they may have to talk this matter over a bit.

Contract Let For Enlarging Yank Stadium

Addition Will Give Bronx Bowl Seating Capacity Of 75,000 for Baseball.

Contracts for the construction of a right field addition to Yankee Stadium having been let today, Colonel Jacob Ruppert announced that by July 1 he would have a plant seating 75,000 for baseball, and more than 85,000 for football. The set-up for boxing will accommodate something like 107,000 persons.

Di Maggio New Impetus To Bigger Yankee Stadium.

While, with contract negotiations soon to be resumed with Joe Di Maggio, there is no official confirmation, the impetus to a bigger Yankee Stadium for 1937 was furnished by the 22-year-old Italian outfielder.

When Colonel Ruppert announced his plans for stand changes in his ball park last winter he said something about a new right field wing, but was somewhat hazy as to when he would enter upon that costly venture.

However, the Yankees last season went over the 1,000,000 mark in attendance at home and, with more than 900,000 on the road, finished the year with a total of more than 2,000,000 paid admissions.

When Babe Ruth slid down the toboggan and then quit to go to the Braves it was believed the old attendance records never would be approached in the Bronx park. But with the amazing development of Di Maggio last summer the old marks were threatened. The old enthusiasm was rekindled. With an even more adroit and efficient Di Maggio next season, the new right field wing will be needed.

The effort to get Di Maggio on board the Yankee bandwagon is slated for resumption soon after New Year's Day.

Yankees Team To Lick, Says Joe Cronin.

By the Associated Press.

SAN FRANCISCO, Jan. 7.—Joe Cronin, youthful manager of the Boston Red Sox, tabbed the world-champion New York Yankees today as "the team to beat" this year.

Cronin, who leaves Sunday for Boston, said most clubs are out to "knock down the Yankees," but "it's not going to be an easy job. McCarthy has a powerful club."

"Still," he philosophized, "baseball is a funny game. Last year most observers picked our club as the one to beat. Of course we got nothing, but if some of the players we purchased had delivered we would have caused the Yankees a lot of trouble."

The Red Sox pilot said he's satisfied with his club, "though if I had an outfielder just one-half as good as Joe Di Maggio I wouldn't fear the Yankees half as much as I do. What a ball player that fellow is!"

Aside from the Yankees the two strongest American League clubs in 1937 loom as Detroit and Cleveland, he said.

"The Red Sox may come out on top, however, if some of the other boys help out Foxx in hitting," he warned.

YANKS RENEW EFFORT TO SATISFY DiMAGGIO

New Contract Reported at $15,000 Sent to the Coast Star— Other Holdouts Silent

There was a decided lull yesterday on the Yankees' capital-labor battlefront. Herr Lou Gehrig, for one, seemed to feel no crying need for issuing another public proclamation and Colonel Jacob Ruppert seemed to feel he already had said the last word the first time when he broadcast an emphatic no, and so likewise maintained a dignified silence.

However, from a source close to the Yankee frontier it was learned that the period of conciliation already has set in, with the first move consisting of sending a new contract to Joe DiMaggio.

The prize rookie of 1936, it is understood, is now being offered $15,000, which doubtless would have been the figure the first time but for a practice adopted a number of years ago whereby the previous year's pay is always offered in the opening batch of contracts in order to start negotiations, so to speak, "from scratch."

Only in the case of Vernon Gomez, left-handed hurler, was there an exception made to this rule this year, for his salary was slashed from $20,000 to $7,500.

Gomez, incidentally, is due in New York today, returning from a vacation trip to Bermuda.

An early settlement is now being confidently expected in DiMaggio's case. The brilliant young Coast Italian was originally offered $8,500, the amount he received last year and which the Yankees, of course, never expected him to accept anyway.

DiMaggio Yearns for Florida To Feel and Crack 'Old Apple'

Yankee Outfielder Craves Return to Baseball After Winter of Crab-Fishing

By The Associated Press

SAN FRANCISCO, Jan. 26.—Joe Di-Maggio already is getting itchy feet.

The New York Yankees' outfielding star of 1936 is straining at the leash. Springtime can't come too soon for the long-legged Italian youth who carved his name in bold letters in his major league debut last year. The Florida spring training grand may be a pain in the neck to the oldsters, but it's a lark for Joe.

"I sure have missed the feel of that old apple," says DiMaggio with almost as much feeling as if he had been away from the sport for three years instead of three months. "That blistered foot at training camp last spring cost me a lot of time and I missed the first seventeen games of the season. This year I want to play in every game."

Since he helped the Yankees ring down the curtain last fall with a world championship, Joe has taken things as easily as is possible for a twenty-two-year-old youngster who thinks and talks in terms of baseball.

His daily routine is simple and his diversions few. He doesn't play golf, neither does he hunt. He floated placidly through a football season that had the rest of the community standing on its collective ear.

A sand-lot baseball game between teams of grammar school kids attracted and held his attention on a day when 90,000 pigskin maniacs were blotting out the seats of a college football stadium miles away. His chief pleasure is crab fishing, which is part of the DiMaggio family's business. It is up at 3 o'clock in the morning, a trip through the Golden Gate on his older brother Tom's boat and then twelve hours pulling nets from the bottom of the Pacific Ocean. Some fun!

Formerly a bashful boy, whose conversation consisted mainly of "yes" or "no," and whose expressionless face earned him the nickname of "Deadpan," Joe has developed into an after-dinner speaker of considerable force.

His presence has been in great demand at boys' clubs and civic organizations throughout northern California. Naturally, his subject has been baseball. He tells about the Yankees; the club's hitting power, and what an "Iron Man" Lou Gehrig is.

If they ask about DiMaggio, he tells how he broke in as a shortstop with the San Francisco Seals in the last three games of 1932, went in as a pinch hitter in the third game of the 1933 season, was sent to right field the next inning and has been a regular outfielder since.

Ranked as one of the greatest throwers in the game, he is frankly puzzled over his ability to rifle the ball with so little effort.

"All the time I played shortstop, my arm would go lame after throwing three or four balls," he says. "When I switched to the outfield the whip came on all of a sudden. I haven't had a sore arm since."

DiMaggio finished his first big league season with a batting average of .323. He thinks he'll boost the mark this year; says he knows the ropes better and has the pitchers sized up.

The toughest pitcher he found to hit was Mel Harder, of Cleveland, and the most difficult park to play, the Cleveland Stadium.

"Too much acreage in the left and center fields at Cleveland; they run you ragged there. And all the pitching is tough if you're not on your toes," he said.

DiMaggio's Unsigned Contract
Lands Back in Yankee Office

*Sensational Rookie of Last Year Reported Seeking $17,500, but
Barrow Expects Early Agreement—Gehrig Demands
$40,000—Luque and Sheehan in Line With Giants*

By ROSCOE McGOWEN

One signed contract was deposited on the desk of Business Manager Ed Barrow of the Yankees yesterday, but an unsigned one accompanied by a letter which arrived at the same time, was far more important.

The unsubscribed document came from Joe DiMaggio, most sensational rookie of a decade. The satisfied Yankee was Jack La Rocca, right-hand pitcher, who was born on St. Patrick's Day, 1914, and who won seventeen and lost twelve games with the Oakland club last season. Jack personally delivered his contract to Barrow.

DiMaggio, according to Barrow, will be no problem child in entering his second major league season, but will be given a salary that will start him out as a completely contented player.

"I received as nice a letter from Joe as anybody could get," said Barrow, and his broad smile was evidence that he wasn't "whistling through the woods."

Yanks, Too, Are Eager

"I don't anticipate any difficulty whatever in signing Joe, because I know we're not very far apart on terms," Barrow continued. "He is ready to continue playing ball for us and we're certainly willing to have him do so."

The Yankee official, of course, offered no figures for publication. DiMaggio, who was reported to have received $10,000 last year, his first in the majors, recently was alleged to have said he wanted $17,500 for 1937.

He had a remarkable first year, batting .323, hitting 29 home runs and driving in 129 runs, this last feat making him one of the five Yankees to go over the century in that respect. He made the All-Star team, too, although his experiences in that contest were not too happy.

Others Still Unsigned

But whether he gets $17,500 or less, there seems to be no doubt that he will be signed up and ready to report with the second squad of Yankees at St. Petersburg, Fla., on March 8.

Barrow has some other unsigned contracts on his desk and, although he refused to name the players, it is understood that among them are Jake Powell, George Selkirk, Vito Tamulis and Fordham Johnny Murphy.

No trouble in signing these players is anticipated by Barrow. He indicated that Selkirk's modest demands would be met without argument, and as for Powell, he remarked:

"There was a vast difference in the letter Jake wrote to me and his quoted remarks from his home a few days ago. We'll get along, all right."

As for Lou Gehrig's demands, Barrow said he had nothing to do with that, because Colonel Jacob Ruppert was handling all negotiations with the Iron Horse. Gehrig didn't see the colonel yesterday, as he spent the afternoon visiting a school in Greenwich, Conn., and later reported at the parental home in New Rochelle.

Gehrig's Price Goes Up

The $33,000 estimate on a two-year contract, however, appears to be much lower than Lou's ideas. He wants a great deal more than that and will put up a stiff argument with Ruppert in his effort to get what he wants. Gehrig's demands will go up to $40,000, and he is not especially concerned about a two-year contract, being willing to take the usual one-year document if the figures are acceptable.

Gehrig will entertain the press this afternoon at a "tea party" at the Hotel Commodore, but if he follows his previously announced policy will have nothing definite to say about his contract difficulties. He doesn't believe such arguments should be aired in public.

Yankee Rosters Released

The Giants came up yesterday with the signed contracts of a grizzled veteran and a verdant rookie. Señor Adolfo Luque forwarded his contract from Havana, while Jimmy Sheehan, rookie catcher from Fordham, dropped into the Giant offices and handed his papers to Secretary Eddie Brannick.

Reverting to the Yankees, it should be reported that the world's champions' rosters were released yesterday, once more bearing the familiar posed "dugout" picture of Manager Joe McCarthy on the cover.

Only thirty-one players are listed—fifteen pitchers, four catchers, six infielders and six outfielders. The new name among the outfielders is that of Ernest Koy, who played with Newark last year. The first squad is to report March 1, and the others a week later.

BIXLER

Five Revolters Warned
To Get Into Line or Quit!

Recalcitrants Told They'll Sign and Be Satisfied or Be Replaced—Ultimatum Directed at Gehrig, Ruffing, Gomez, DiMaggio and Powell.

Colonel Jacob Ruppert today reiterated his refusal to meet the salary demands of five revolting Yankee players, and advised them to sign at a reasonable figure or suffer the consequences.

"I'll put a ball club on the field this spring no matter what happens," the Colonel told the Associated Press. "I've taken a definite stand on this and I'll see it through."

Disregarding, for the moment, the demands of Joe Di Maggio for something like a 100 per cent boost in his 1936 freshman year salary Ruppert revealed that First Baseman Lou Gehrig had been offered $31,000 and was asking $50,000; Pitcher Red Ruffing had been offered $15,000 (a $3,000 raise) and wants $30,000; Outfielder Jake Powell, $7,500, and demanded $14,000, and Pitcher Vernon (Lefty) Gomez, $7,500 (a $12,500 cut). Gomez sent his contract back without comment.

"I can understand how a man and his employer can be a few thousand dollars apart on a single year's salary," said Ruppert of his world champion holdouts. "But when a man asks $19,000 a year more, that's another thing."

When Ruppert revealed the extent of Gehrig's demands, Lou pointed out in a formal statement that the Yankees haven't needed a reserve first baseman for twelve years, and because of this they were in a position last year to sell three first basemen for a reported price of $105,000.

Furthermore, Gehrig added, "I yielded to the Colonel's wishes during the depression years, and now that recovery is well on its way, as the past season's near-record attendance indicates, I feel I am only asking what I believe to be my value to the club."

Coming out of a brewers' meeting late in the day, the genial Ruppert shot verbal holes in Gehrig's statement.

"In the first place, it's none of Gehrig's business what I do with my ball players," he insisted. "I've spent a fortune to develop the system which develops these players. And as far as Lou's salary is concerned, I gave him what he wanted two years ago.

"When I sent him his contract at that time, it was for $30,000. He asked for $31,000 and got it."

Ruppert pointed out that Jimmy Foxx was said to be getting only $18,000 from the Boston Red Sox, but quickly added:—

"Of course, I don't think Jimmy's as good as Gehrig. But he's good, just the same."

He also said that when Gehrig conferred with him about salary originally, he (Ruppert) reminded Lou that Mickey Cochrane was only getting around $28,000 for catching

Jake Ruppert.   Lou Gehrig.

and managing the Detroit Tigers.

"I'm not trying to beat these players down," he added. "I think anybody in baseball will tell you I've never been measly. But there has to be a limit somewhere."

Ruppert pointed out that Jake Powell had been given a $1,000 rise when he came from Washington to the Yanks last year at a $5,000 salary.

"In addition to this, he got into the world series and got a cut of the series money," Ruppert went on. "And now he asks for $14,000, exactly $8,000 more than his 1936 salary."

The Yankee owner conceded Di Maggio "was probably ill-advised," but said he could not understand Ruffing's request for $30,000.

"He was a holdout last year, and he had a good year," Ruppert said, "but he wrote a letter saying he was dissatisfied and mentioned $30,000 as an equitable figure."

Ruppert described such demands as "ridiculous," and didn't quibble over what will happen if the players insist in their demands.

"They'll make those demands reasonable, sign and convince me they're satisfied—or else!" he stormed. "And they'll play their best ball, too. I'm not going to start the season with any dissatisfied ball players on my team, even if I have to bring a lot of youngsters in from other clubs. There's isn't a man on the team who can't be replaced."

Ruppert Praises Gehrig, But Ridicules Demands.

Returning to Gehrig's $50,000 demand, Ruppert explained that Lou had asked for a $40,000 contract with the stipulation that he receive another $10,000 if he plays 100 games this coming season.

"Recently Gehrig outlined his plans for playing 2,500 consecutive games (he has played 1,808 now), and the way it looks I'm being asked to pay $10,000 a year extra to see him do this," the Colonel commented.

"I think his record is admirable, but personally I think when I pay him $31,000 a year I have a right to expect him to play as many games as he can without paying him extra for it."

Angry as he was, however, Ruppert didn't neglect to pay his respects to Gehrig. "He's a fine player and a splendid young man," the Colonel conceded, "but I don't think he realizes there were many years when my business didn't even make $31,000."

Of the five holdouts Ruppert mentioned, only Gomez was conceded any sort of argument. The Colonel described his $7,500 offer as "just a starter." Ruppert said he knew nothing about Pitcher Monte Pearson, but admitted that in the confusion "I may have missed him."

DiMaggio in Fold At Record $15,000

By Bob Brumby.

Joe DiMaggio gave up the holdout ghost yesterday. The Yank outfielder wired from San Francisco that he would accept the club's offer of $15,000. It was a $6,500 increase for the popular Italian slugger who made good sensationally his first year in big time. Jake Ruppert, usually about as garrulous as a sphinx with laryngitis, was so pleased he actually verified the terms.

With DiMag in the herd, only Lou Gehrig and Red Ruffing remain unroped. Ruffing is asking $18,000, which is $3,000 more than the Yanks are willing to pay. Gehrig craves $40,000 and a two-year contract. Ruppert has offered him $36,000 for one-year. Joe asked for $17,500.

DiMaggio is reported in great shape. He has gained poundage and tips the beam at about 200. Last year he collected 206 hits for

Here Joe DiMaggio signs last year's contract which gave him $8,500. Yesterday he accepted Jake Ruppert's offer of $15,000 and became highest paid second-year man in baseball's history.

an average of .323. He belted 15 triples, 44 doubles and drove in 125 runs in 138 games played. He was third in fielding averages and first in assists with 22.

The 15 grand pay check makes Joe the highest salaried second-year man in baseball as well as top money man among Yank outfielders. He'll leave today by plane for St. Pete.

Three illustrious Yankees face the camera with their employer, Colonel Jacob Ruppert: from the left, second baseman Tony Lazzeri, center fielder Joe DiMaggio, and shortstop Frankie Crosetti. All three hailed from San Francisco.

Di Maggio to Follow Advice of Cobb And Shift Scheme of 1937 Campaign

Young Star to Switch to Lighter Bat Late in Season.

By DANIEL.

Staff Correspondent.

ST. PETERSBURG, March 20.—Tutored over the winter by the immortal Ty Cobb, Joe Di Maggio, latest arrival in the camp of the Yankees, today revealed plans for changes in his scheme of campaign for 1937.

"In the first place, I cannot go through the season swinging a forty-ounce bat," Di Maggio said. "I intend to start the new campaign with a forty, but after August I intend to switch to a thirty-seven or thirty-six ouncer. Last summer I found myself getting tired lugging that heavy stick through August and September. In the last two weeks I got so fagged out I fell off 18 points in my hitting.

"Another thing I must do is to lay off those bad balls I went after with the count three and two. I was too anxious. Now I appreciate that the percentage is altogether with me. The pitcher must satisfy me, because right behind he sees Lou Gehrig and behind him Bill Dickey.

"Cobb wised me up to another trick. He told me that after August 1 a good outfielder is crazy to spend fifteen minutes shagging flies. He said to me, 'Joe, the trick of conserving your energy and pacing yourself is one of the most important things a young fellow has to master. Don't spent your hitting energy chasing flies. Grab a few and then sit down in a cool, shady spot. The flies you catch in practice never show in the records or the salary, because the fans don't pay to see that sort of thing.'

"Still another thing I've got to do is to prevent getting so heavy in hot weather. Last season I gained eighteen pounds from the day I broke into the line-up until the world series. I was astonished when I weighed myself during the series and found I tipped the beam at 205 pounds. That has got to stop.

Double-Play Ball in First With Giants Toughest Blow.

"While on the subject of the games with the Giants let me say that in the first contest I suffered the worst blow of my life," Joe continued. "I had a chance to upset Hubbell, but hit to Whitehead, starting a double play. I had some tough breaks in the All-Star game, but they didn't bother me at all. This blow upset me plenty."

The interviewer asked the real reason for the ability of Connie Mack's pitchers to hold him around .200 for the season.

"It was a matter of plain luck," Di Maggio replied. "Those Philadelphia pitchers didn't have a thing that other pitchers, whom I hit, did not have. Mack did not have a secret trick for stopping me. Kelley's slow curve and Ross' fast ball were tough, at times, but there were a lot of better pitchers around the circuit. It just happened that way. In Shibe Park I can remember at least four marvelous catches that robbed me of hits. I had no luck there.

"The guy who really stopped me was Mel Harder, of the Indians. I thought I went twenty-one for nothing against him, but they tell me it really was eighteen times at bat, and that I actually made two hits. I don't recollect either of them. Harder has what it takes. Cousins? Nothing doing, man, I don't want a couple of guys gunning for me this year!

In Line-Up Inside Week, It's Mine Host Joe Now.

"I weigh 198 pounds now and should take off a little weight inside a week, when I expect to be in the line-up," Joe went on. "I got all the way to 207 during the winter, but long walks and less sleep turned the trick.

"I don't diet. I believe in three square meals a day and I am not ashamed to say I am nuts about spaghetti. No vino, though. No gals, no dancing, but give me music and singing.

"Soon Di Maggio's place, a restaurant seating 400 people on Fisherman's Wharf, in San Fran-

Also Planning to Hold Weight Down During Hot Weather.

cisco, will open. That's in case I don't make the grade in baseball, or get old some day. I have $25,000 invested in this place—every dime I own in the world. My brother Tom is running it for me."

Di Maggio got his first workout at Tampa yesterday, while the Yankees had their winning streak broken by the Reds, 7 to 3. Joe went to a distant part of the big race track and worked with Jake Powell, John Schulte and some of the pitchers. In the sixth inning Joe McCarthy called him in to hit for Rube Wicker and Giuseppe belted a long fly to right against Paul Derringer.

Last year Di Maggio was hitting around .600 for the first four exhibition games, when his foot was burned by a diathermia machine and he had to lay off until the eighteenth American League contest of the Yankees. Now he finds he missed the first four exhibitions, and is likely to get into all the rest—into the next four as a hitter, anyway. Joe was 22 on November 25, and he says he is not a bit awed by the new contract for $15,000, the record salary for a second-year player.

During the winter Di Maggio posed for movies which Frank O'Doul is using to teach his San Francisco Seals. Joe had a reunion with his 24-year-old brother, Vince, last night. Vince is trying out at third base with the Bees. A 19-year-old brother, Dominick, is with the Seals.

Yankees Break Camp and Head North After .800 Average in Citrus Belt Games

Di Maggio and Dickey Stars at Bat as Cards Are Beaten.

By DANIEL,
Staff Correspondent.

ST. PETERSBURG, Fla., April 1. —Happy over their final exploit here—a 5 to 4 victory over the Cardinals—the Yankees today broke camp and soon after nightfall will be on their way to Tallahassee, Mobile, Houston and other cities to the westward. The world champions will take with them the pleasant experience of having won all twelve games they played in this city. Their three defeats of the current training season—by the Dodgers, Reds and Bears—were suffered away from here.

At the climax of their stay in St. Petersburg the Yankees found Joe Di Maggio, Vernon Lefty Gomez and Bill Dickey the men of the moment. In so far as the pennant destinies of the club are concerned, the things which Gomez did in five innings of pitching against the Gashouse Gang were of the greatest interest and importance.

To Di Maggio went the distinction of having got a triple, two singles and a walk; to Dickey fell the satisfaction of driving in the tying and winning runs with a double in the ninth inning. Giuseppe also exulted over having hit a long single off the first pitch served up to him by the famous Dizzy Dean.

Fastening his grip on the opening game assignment in the Stadium, Gomez blanked the Cardinals with only two hits in his second five-inning stretch of the spring. Lefty faced just sixteen men and let go with all the fire and speed he ever had in 1935.

"There's nothing wrong with that bird now," said Frankie Frisch as he moved his Redbirds over to the bailiwick of the Dodgers. "I'd like to have Lefty on my ball club. I'd say he showed us about as much speed as he ever has had—more than we had seen this year in ten games with major league teams."

One Earned Run Off Gomez In Sixteen Innings of Pitching.

Gomez has pitched a total of sixteen innings spread over four contests. He has allowed only eight hits and just one earned run. Another tally was achieved against Vernon on an error.

When the Yankees played the Cardinals at Daytona Beach Di Maggio had not yet reported. Last spring, when the New Yorks tackled the Redbirds, Giuseppe was on the hospital list with a burned foot. As a result yesterday's game afforded the Californian his first opportunity to joust with the colorful troupe from the Kerry Patch.

In his first time up, with one on

Gomez Shows Gashouse Gang Real Fireball Hurling.

and one out, Di Maggio lit on Dizzy's first pitch, a fast ball a trifle high, and drove it right down the fairway. The next time Jolting Joe came up Bob Weiland, lefthander, was pitching, and Di grounded to short. Weiland walked him in the fifth.

The seventh innings saw Di Maggio face the southpaw with Frankie Crosetti on first and one out. Joe lashed his fourth triple in eight games to the left field fence and soon was driven in by Gehrig with the run that gave the Yankees a 3 to 2 lead.

Di Maggio was a force in the winning rally as well. After Red Rolfe had singled to second with one down, Giuseppe crashed one to left to put the tying run on third. Gehrig walked, to fill the bases, and then Dickey slugged that double into the crowd in left center.

Di Maggio has made a dozen hits in thirty-one times at bat and, with an average of .387, presses George Selkirk for the leadership of the club. Twinkletoes got a horse collar against the Gashouse mob and his record was whittled thirty-nine points to .405.

Dickey's two hits and general deportment were particularly pleasing to McCarthy, as Bill has been handicapped by a bad leg.

With one of his first swings of the bat at spring training in 1937, Joe DiMaggio connects easily. This was a pinch-hit single in late March at the Yankee training site in St. Petersburg, Florida.

BY JOE WILLIAMS

About the Two Di Maggios
Joe Has Competitive "It"
But Brother Vince Hasn't

Special to the World-Telegram.

EN ROUTE NORTH, April 10.—You get to talk with a lot of baseball people in the South—managers, scouts, old players, current stars. There were two things most of the baseball people I talked with agreed on unanimously. One was that Joe Di Maggio was going to be an enduring sensation in the majors. The other was his brother Vincent wouldn't last beyond mid-season.

And the odd part of this is the baseball people concede Brother Vincent has almost as much mechanical ability as Joe. It seems to be a question of temperament. One brother's got it and the other hasn't. Nothing ever seems to disturb Joe. On the other hand, Vincent is addicted to nervous moods. Joe plays as if he knows he's good, Vincent as if he isn't sure.

The two brothers are alike in mannerisms at the bat and in the field. In the unimportant practice maneuvers, it is difficult to tell them apart. But when the game starts and the pressure is on, Joe stands out and Vincent doesn't. The baseball people say this is a mental condition. They say Joe has made himself a great player because he has confidence in himself, something Vincent lacks.

*   *   *

Bought as Box Office Bait?

I recall talking with Lefty O'Doul in New York last winter shortly after the Boston Nationals had bought Vincent. O'Doul managed San Francisco, was instrumental in the development of Joe and was familiar with Vincent, who played in the same league. . . . . "He has got the stuff to make good in a big way," said O'Doul, "but I'll be surprised if he does. Something happens to him in the pinches."

The baseball people have had two months to look over Vincent and they are now saying the same thing O'Doul said last winter. Some men have the temperament to be great competitive athletes. Others haven't. This seems to be the difference between the two Di Maggio brothers, who are by all accounts equally gifted in most other respects.

Old Bob Quinn, who operates the Bostons, is a wise baseball head. It isn't easy to sell him a gold brick. The chances are he knew all about the peculiarities of Vincent when he bought him from San Diego. Old Bob also happens to be a wise box office man. The Di Maggio name became widely publicized last season. He probably reasoned that even a thin carbon copy of the original would excite his clientele. At least for a while.

As for Joe, there were some baseball men who were disposed to reserve judgment on him last season, and even after the season had ended. They recalled a number of other young players who had come to the majors, had a sensational first year, then faded into obscurity when subjected to the test of time. They said, "We want to take another look at him."

Well, they have taken another look and while it has been limited to exhibition games, they have capitulated. They are saying now he is one freshman phenom who can't miss being a great star. They are saying he will be even better this year than last, when it was generally agreed he was the No. 1 rookie of the season.

*   *   *

Bad Breaks Make Him the Goat.

Besides electrifying the customers with his gaudy fielding exploits and dramatic throwing, Joe, his first year up, took his place alongside the established sluggers in the Yankee batting order and hit .323. He was a vital factor in the team's championship success. Had he been more experienced, his record would have been even more impressive.

No first-year player could have asked for a more satisfying year than Joe had. Yet if the breaks had been with him, his fame would have been even greater. He might easily have been the hero of the world series if Burgess Whitehead hadn't made an incredible stop at his expense in the first game. All credit to Whitehead, but the fact remains he did happen to come up with one of those 100 to 1 stops.

Joe was the goat of the All-Star game. He could just as easily have been the hero. To begin with, it was a tough spot for a youngster who had been in the league only two months. There were some baseball people who questioned the wisdom of using him in the game at all. They argued this was a game that should be played by seasoned players, accustomed to unusual responsibilities. But the fans of the country had voted the rookie a place in the lineup and Joe McCarthy who directed the American Leaguers, abided by their sentiment. Left to his own judgment, he probably wouldn't have started him; possibly he wouldn't have called on him at all.

The young Italian's failure in the All-Star game was complete. But, as I have said, if he had gotten the breaks he would be known today as the man who won the game, instead of lost it. In five times at bat he failed to hit the ball out of the infield and did not reach first base once. He had chances to drive in seven runners and he left seven on the bases.

He gave the National Leaguers two runs in the second inning when Gabby Hartnett's drive skipped off the heel of his glove, and rolled to the fence. It was generously scored a three-base hit. He made the only recorded error of the game when he fumbled Bill Herman's single and permitted the Chicagoan to take an extra base.

*   *   *

Came Back Better Then Ever.

Despite all this, he should have been the hero of the game. In the seventh inning with the bases full and the winning run on second, Joe hit the first ball Lon Warneke pitched and rifled it to Leo Durocher at short. Durocher made the same sort of miracle catch that Whitehead did in the world series. No ball could have been harder or more perfectly hit. Nine times out of ten it would have gone safe. This time it went for an out, decided a ball game and cast Di Maggio in the undeserved role of goat.

Before the game was over the customers were booing the young man. They had cheered him wildly when he stepped to the plate in the first inning. When he popped feebly to Herman to end the game in the ninth the customers let him have it. Seasoned players are accustomed to the fluctuating passions of the crowd. It is always a new experience for the rookie.

Even Manager McCarthy was concerned as to how Di Maggio would react to the reception he received in Boston and the way the fates had frowned on him. But not for long. Di Maggio took up where he had left off, as if nothing untoward had come into his life, and went on to even greater success as a first-year major leaguer. He proved he had the competitive temperament so necessary to stardom in the big leagues. And you can believe the baseball people, he has a monopoly on this quality in the Di Maggio family.

In This Corner . . . By Art Krenz

BASEBALL'S NEWEST IDOL

KRENZ
AFTER CHARLES DANA GIBSON'S FAMOUS PICTURE,
"THE CHAMPION"....

Di Maggio Arm Causes Worry

Fielder Still Can't Throw and Yankees Miss His Heavy Slugging.

Special to the World-Telegram.

CHATTANOOGA, Tenn., April 12. —The week's rest, which Trainer Doc Painter prescribed for the ailing arm of Joe Di Maggio, the Yankees' young slugger, hasn't brought the desired results.

Di Maggio still can't throw or raise his arm above his head without considerable pain, but Painter thinks he'll be ready for duty again by Friday.

"If we run into some real warm weather, I would advise Di Maggio to go out and throw out the soreness," Painter said. "But in the sort of weather we have been having for more than a week, it would be unwise to try this heroic treatment."

Di Maggio smiles and replies, "I dunno" to questions as to when he will be back in the game. He doesn't seem to let it get him. McCarthy, too, says he hasn't the faintest notion when his star fly chaser will begin to thrill the customers again. "Maybe tomorrow, maybe not until next Tuesday," Marse Joe replies.

The Yankees suddenly have indicated a need for Di Maggio in his best slugging form. The club is hitting spasmodically, and its defenses have taken to acting up in non-championship manner. The chances are the boys have begun to show the effects of that bouncing around on the railroads of Dixie and the Southwest.

Di Maggio Faces Tonsil Operation

By CHARLES SEGAR

KNOXVILLE, Tenn., April 13—With a tonsilectomy recommended by a local throat specialist, Joe DiMaggio, outfield star of the Yankees, left here this afternoon for New York, definitely considered a non-starter in the opening game of the season next Tuesday.

DiMaggio, perturbed by an ailing arm that failed to respond to the baking treatment of Doc Painter, Yankees' trainer, this morning visited Dr. Reese Patterson.

After a thorough examination, Dr. Patterson found DiMaggio suffering from enlarged tonsils. While these were said not to be diseased, Dr. Patterson recommended that they be removed, believing that they may be causing DiMagg's trouble. The throat specialist also recommended that a tooth which has been annoying DiMagg be removed.

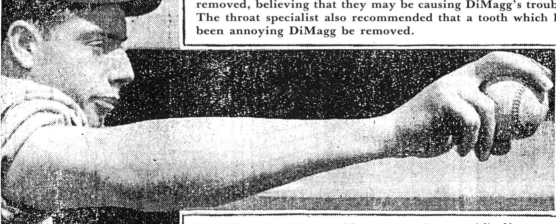

Joe Di Maggio's whip, one of best in game, is cause of Yank's worry.

When DiMaggio brought this news to Manager McCarthy the latter got in communication with Ed Barrow, Yanks' business manager. Barrow suggested that DiMagg be sent to New York for another examination by the Yanks' physician. If the New York surgeon agrees that the tonsils should come out, the operation will take place.

LONG THROW RESPONSIBLE.

If such a step is necessary, DiMagg not only is expected to be lost to the Yankees for the opening game, but isn't likely to start for about three weeks, approximately the same time that he was out of the 1936 campaign when he had a blistered ankle.

Joe's current trouble started the day after the Yankees left their St. Petersburg training camp. On April 2, in Tallahassee, he made a long throw from the outfield and the whip has bothered him since. He hasn't started in a game since that day though he has been a pinch hitter in 12 games, getting six hits in 12 times at bat.

Last week DiMagg revealed that he had trouble with his arm in the Spring of 1935 when he was with San Francisco. But it improved with the advent of warmer weather and DiMagg figured that this year it would do the same. Trainer Painter exhausted every known means, trying to bring the arm around and, when it failed to respond, the visit to the specialist here today was suggested.

Times Wide World Photo.

AILING YANKEE STAR ON ARRIVAL HERE
Joe DiMaggio being greeted by Scout Paul Krichell at Penn Station

DECIDE TO OPERATE ON JOE DIMAGGIO

Tonsillectomy Is Ordered to Correct Lame Arm—Goes Under Knife Tomorrow

APPEARS FIT ON ARRIVAL

Physician Feels That Cause Will Be Removed—To Resume Workouts in 10 Days

Joe DiMaggio, Yankee outfielder who has been troubled with a lame throwing arm during the training season, will be operated on tomorrow for the removal of his tonsils. This was decided on yesterday following an examination by Dr. Girard Oberrender, personal physician to Colonel Jacob Ruppert, owner of the club.

DiMaggio arrived in town shortly before noon from Knoxville, Tenn., where he left the team. He was whisked to Dr. Oberrender's office where, except for the enlarged tonsils, he was found to be in excellent condition. Dr. Oberrender thought the removal of the tonsils would correct the condition which has caused the lame arm.

The Yankee outfielder weighed 197 pounds, which is about ten more than he scaled last season, and looked very fit. It was said that he would be able to take part in practice ten days after the operation and would be able to get back into the line-up within two weeks.

Much as he regretted having to miss taking part in the opening game, DiMaggio was pleased to know that he would be ready to play within two weeks. "If the doctor thinks the tonsils should come out, it is all right with me," he said. "The sooner the better."

World Champs Hail Di Maggio Back in Lineup

Return of Star Outfielder Should Pep Up Sagging Extra-Base Hitting

By DANIEL.

Di Maggio is back. That was the big news in the Yankees camp today. Joe returned to action in Washington yesterday. He came up as a pinch hitter and acquired his first blow of 1937—a corking drive into center field. In the two games with the Red Sox in the Stadium over the week-end, Giuseppe will be seen in his old spot in center. With Di Mag on the job, the world champions should perk up. Their extra-base drive has fallen off.

Last year Di Maggio missed the first seventeen games of the American League season. He did not come back until May 3—the season opened a week earlier in 1936—and punished the pitching of the Browns for two singles and a triple.

Di Maggio's return to the outfield will act as a tonic on the whole Yankee club. Not that the champions, who won five straight before they were stopped in Washington yesterday, 4 to 1, have not played championship ball. But with Di Mag in there, it will be a different kind of ball club.

Di Maggio last was seen in the Yankee outfield on April 2 at Tallahassee, Fla. He strained his arm making a long throw that afternoon and a few days later was rushed home for the removal of infected tonsils. This operation has proved eminently successful.

Johnson, Hoag in Left; What's Wrong with Powell?

With Di Maggio back in center, Myril Hoag will move into a left field partnership with Roy Johnson. When the opposition pitching is righthanded, Roy will get the call. Hoag will work against southpaws.

Because Joe McCarthy is giving Hoag the call over Jake Powell, his world series batting star, there is a feeling something is wrong in the Powell situation. In other clubhouses they insist that Powell will be traded. This report was particularly persistent in Washington.

The fate of Tommy Henrich who got $20,000 from Jake Ruppert for signing, has been decided. Tommy goes to Newark for further seasoning.

The Yankees faced the first Western trip, to be opened in Detroit next Tuesday, with Kemp Wicker, lefthander, more or less installed as a starting possibility. In his first major league start, in Washington yesterday, Kemp took a beating, but his showing merited another chance.

Wicker was taken out to let Di Maggio hit for him in the seventh. In six innings, the Carolina tobacco planter allowed six hits and four runs, two of which were earned, with the other two tracing to a wild throw by Frankie Crosetti.

Di Maggio Arm Again Causing Yanks Concern

The Di Maggio situation is giving McCarthy far more concern than he will admit. Joe played through that 6-to-5 defeat by the Indians yesterday, but his throwing was far from impressive. Before the game McCarthy had Myril Hoag listed for center field. But after Giuseppe had tossed in a few he asked to return to the batting order.

It developed that Di Maggio's arm never really went back to form even after the removal of his tonsils. He injured his wing Wednesday when he was seen to make a peculiar flip return of a hit he had taken on the first bounce. Joe jumped into the air and tossed the ball as if it had been a hot potato. It was apparent that he had been hurt, but he denied it. On Thursday, when he took two tumbles at Detroit, he hurt his shoulder again. His second somersault, after he had charged Pete Fox's liner and let it go through for three bases, was the more painful.

Di Maggio Hitting .346, But Arm Has Him Down.

Di Maggio still is among the batting elite, with an average of .346. But his arm has the lad down. He mopes around the hotel and he comes to the plate like a mourner. In his most recent nine tries he has made only two hits. Yesterday he was held to an infield single.

It may be that Joe is hurting himself by playing. It is possible that working the arm will bring it around. In the meantime, McCarthy is worried, and then some.

DiMaggio Hits 3 Homers in Row While Clift Drives 3 for Browns

Champions Win First, 16-9, With 7 in 9th; Final called in 11th With Score at 8-8

By Rud Rennie

ST. LOUIS, June 13.—In two wild and thrilling ball games, one of which the Yankees won, 16 to 9, with a seven-run rally in the ninth, and the other going eleven innings and being called with the score of 8 to 8, the Yankees held the league leadership today and ended their second Western trip with five victories and six defeats.

There were nine home runs in the two games. Joe DiMaggio hit three in succession in the second game, tying the score with his third with two out in the ninth. Hamond Clift, of the Browns, hit three, two in the first game. Lazzeri, Dickey and Joe Vosmik were the other home run hitters.

The Yankees had their biggest scoring and hitting game of the season in the opener making twenty hits and sixteen runs.

It was a wild day with forty-one runs and fifty-seven hits. Frank Makosky, of the Yankees, pitched in both games and Julio Bonetti went the route for the Browns in the second game. The Yankees made fourteen runs in their last four innings to win the opener.

Murphy Knocked Out

The first game was loosely played and filled with base hits and poor pitching.

Vosmik hit a home run in the first inning with a man on base and the Browns got off to a two-run lead. Johnny Murphy, the Yankees' starting pitcher, tied the score with a double in the second.

The score was tied three times. The Browns made a run in the third and three more in the fourth, knocking Murphy out of the box. Frank Makosky came in to pitch for the Yankees.

Clift belted a home run in the fifth with no one on. That was directly after Oral Hildebrand, the first St. Louis pitcher, had walked three men with one out and the Yankees' two biggest hitters, DiMaggio and

FIRST GAME											
NEW YORK (A. L.)						ST. LOUIS (A. L.)					
	ab	r	h	po	a	e		ab	r	h	po a e
Crosetti, ss.	5	1	2	1	4	0	Davis, 1b..	4	1	2	7 0 0
Rolfe, 3b...	5	1	3	3	2	0	West, cf..	5	0	1	2 0 0
DiMaggio,cf	5	1	1	2	0	0	Vosmik, lf.	5	1	3	2 0 0
Gehrig, 1b.	6	3	3	9	0	1	Bell rf....	5	1	1	1 0 0
Dickey, c...	4	3	2	6	0	0	Clift, 3b...	5	2	2	1 2 0
Selkirk, rf.	6	3	4	1	0	0	Kn'ker, ss.	4	1	0	4 4 0
Henrich, lf.	5	1	0	3	0	1	Huffman, c.	4	1	2	5 0 0
Lazzeri, 2b.	6	2	2	2	3	0	Carey, 2b..	4	1	1	2 1 0
M'PHY, p..	1	0	1	0	2	1	H'BR'D, p.	2	1	1	0 0 0
MA'SKY, p	4	1	2	0	0	0	BLAKE, p..	0	0	0	0 0 0
							KNOTT, p.	0	0	0	0 0 0
							W'LKUP, p	0	0	0	0 0 1
							KOUPAL, p	0	0	0	0 0 0
							*Allen	1	0	0	0 0 0

Totals..47 16 20 27 11 3 Totals....39 9 13 27 8 8

*Batted for Knott in eighth inning.

New York.......... 0 2 0 0 0 3 2 2 7—16
St. Louis.......... 2 0 1 3 1 0 2 0 0— 9

Gehrig, had come up with the bases filled and flivvered. DiMag struck out and Gehrig fouled to the catcher.

So the Browns were leading, 7 to 2, going into the sixth. With one out, Selkirk started a three-run rally with a triple. With two out and men on first and third in the seventh, Clift made a foolish attempt make a force play at second. One run scored and then Makosky singled and drove in another, tying the score.

Clift Hits Another

Immediately, the Browns untied it. DiMaggio lost Bell's pop fly in the sun, folded his arms around his head and let it fall for a single. Then Clift hit his second homer, a prodigious wallop which cleared the left-field bleachers.

Blake and Knott pitched in the seventh. The Yankees tied the score off Knott in the eighth with two out. Gehrig singled. Dickey tripled and Selkirk doubled and the thing was done.

Then, with a final flourish, the champions made seven runs off Jim Walkup and Lou Koupal in the ninth. Ten men batted, starting with Makosky. Crosetti, DiMaggio, Gehrig, Dickey and Selkirk hit singles. Rolfe tripled. And Lazzeri hit a home run with two men on bases.

Makosky fanned Bell and Clift in the ninth and won his second game of the year.

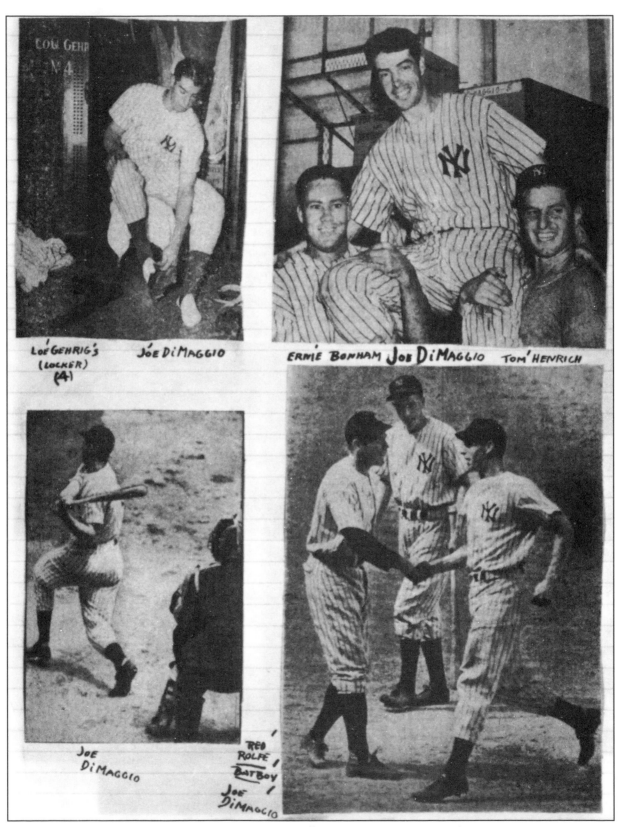

A scrapbook look at The Yankee Clipper and various teammates.

1937

A SPECIAL ALL-STAR GAME

I have more than a certain fondness for the 1937 All-Star game. It was not my first: I had been to the one the year before. But the All-Star game of 1937 was a personal triumph for the Yankees as a team and for our manager Joe McCarthy.

There were an unprecedented five Yankees in the starting lineup that year for the American League. I was in center field, Lou Gehrig was at first base, Red Rolfe at third, Bill Dickey was catching, and Lefty Gomez was the starting pitcher.

Gomez allowed the National Leaguers only one hit in a scoreless three innings. Gehrig smashed a home run, and Rolfe a triple. I got my first All-Star hit, a single off Dizzy Dean of the St. Louis Cardinals. And the American League, thanks to the Yankees aboard, was victorious by a score of 8–3.

Joe DiMaggio

Joe Di Maggio Best Outfielder in League

Yankee Star Continues Heavy Hitting with Twentieth Homer.

By DANIEL,
Staff Correspondent.

WASHINGTON, July 6.—On his way to the All-Star game with the home run leadership, at 20, and a batting average of .346, Joe Di Maggio, of the Yankees, today stood out as the greatest outfielder in the American League and Joe Medwick's lone rival for the major supremacy.

Giuseppe stressed his strident position with the home run which gave the world champions a sweep of the holiday double-header with the Red Sox before 61,146 enthusiasts in the Stadium. It was his first circuit drive with the bases loaded in his two years with the Yankees and accounted for the nightcap, 8 to 4. The Yankees, with Red Ruffing turning in a remarkable six hit shutout, had overwhelmed the Boston club in the first game, 15 to 0.

Di Maggio's knockout punch was delivered with two out in the sixth. Chandler, Heffner and Rolfe were on the bases and the game was deadlocked at 4-all. With the count one and one, Giuseppe lit on one of Rube Walberg's lefthanded fireballs and drove it 425 feet into the Yankee bullpen between the left field stand and the bleacher.

As it crashed into the area it sent Yankee reserve pitchers and catchers scampering for cover. It was Jolting Joe's second homer in two days and brought the club's total to 79.

There have been homers and homers in the bailiwick of the Yankees since it was opened in 1923. But only one hit into the left side of that park compared with that with which Giuseppe rang up four runs and drove Walberg to the showers. Some years ago, when Foxx was with the Athletics, he drove a tremendous homer into the extreme corner of the upper left field stand. Two years later Tony Lazzeri hit a fair ball into the bullpen, but under a ground rule, since eliminated by the construction of a fence, Tony was held to a couple of bases.

Last year Di Maggio was the first rookie to attain a starting position in the All Star game. As matters turned out, he was the goat of the American League defeat. Had his high line drive with two out and the bases loaded gone just a couple of inches above the outstretched glove of Leo Durocher, Giuseppe would have been the shining hero.

Now Di Maggio heads for his second All Star game with the determination to make up for his failure in Boston, and add to the interleague laurels he achieved in the world series against the Giants last October.

Hit with Three Men On Stops Boston—Red Ruffing Victor.

Di Maggio's wallop yesterday was the chef d'oeuvre of a cluster of four homers, two of which went to Lou Gehrig, who now owns 13. He got one in each game. The other was contributed by Bill Dickey in the first contest, giving him 13. In this early demonstration of power the Yankees enjoyed their fattest inning of the year, with nine runs on seven hits, two of them homers.

The Yankees face the second half of the season, which gets under way in the Stadium on Friday, against Washington, with a lead of five and a half games. Not as big an edge as they had at this stage last season, when it was eleven games, but big enough to make New York confident of another world series.

The work of the world champions in the Stadium has been phenomenal. They have won twenty-six and lost seven there.

Ruffing's pitching in scoring his ninth victory, as against two defeats, was superb. Boston's six hits were scattered over as many innings. In scoring his fifth victory Chandler allowed only seven hits and ran into some tough breaks. But after the first inning he was in complete command.

DANIEL'S DOPE

Developments clustering around the All-Star game have given new impetus to an intriguing discussion—the relative merits of Joe and Joe—Di Maggio, of the Yankees, and Medwick, of the Cardinals. Giuseppe has made himself the greatest outfielder in the American League. Ducky Wucky has achieved a similar distinction in the National. To whom the major league laurel?

Maintaining an even and brilliant pace over the 400 mark, Medwick has established himself as one of the greatest righthanded hitters the game has seen. Some of the more enthusiastic Boswells who cover the National League insist Medwick is an even grander hitter than Rogers Hornsby of his glittering prime. But that is something the writer is not conceding.

It must be remembered that in his heyday Hornsby won the National League batting championship six times in a row, and in seven years out of nine, his conquering records running from .370 in 1920 to .424 in 1924. Thrice the Rajah went over the .400 mark. Medwick, on the other hand, never has hit better than .353 for a season with the Cardinals.

Students of the zodiacal and astrological will tell you there is something of the gift of the stars and the planets in the batting skill of the two Joes, as their birthdays are close to each other. Di Maggio's is November 25, Medwick's November 24. Di Maggio is three years younger than the pride of Carteret, N. J. Giuseppe was born in 1914, and will be twenty-three in the fall.

Di Maggio is the better gifted, physically. He stands 6 feet 1½ inches in height and weighs around 200 pounds. His wrists are steel shafts, his arms could swing the hammer of Thor. Medwick's height is 5 feet 9 inches and his best weight is 180.

* * *

It is more than interesting to find that these outstanding exponents of the great American game are sons of immigrant parents. Both Joes picked up baseball on the wrong side of the tracks.

The Di Maggios came from Italy to San Francisco, and went fishing. From Martinez to the Golden Gate, to North Beach, the Little Italy of San Francisco.

The Medwicks—that is an Americanized version of the name—shipped here from Hungary and landed over on the slums side of Carteret, among the factories and the daily turmoils of hard, unlovely battle for a living.

* * *

Medwick Hits Bad Balls;
Di Maggio Getting Choosier.

Whether Medwick is better than Di Maggio—whether the Italian Joe is superior to the Hungarian version—the writer is not prepared to say. Di Maggio boasts two important advantages over his National League rival. One, a superior arm. Two, a better grasp of the mental angle. Medwick still likes to throw to the wrong base occasionally.

In batting method, they are exponents of divergent schools. Di Maggio has become very choosey this year. Last season, when he hit .323 and drove out 29 homers, he was a bit over-anxious. Now he makes the boys pitch more.

Medwick is distinctly a bad ball hitter. He showed that in the All-Star game. He will clout one off his ear, and then go fishing for an outside curve and push it into right for two bases.

Many of the experts say that when Medwick learns not to hit the bad ones he will move along as a steady .400. But we are of the opinion that if Medwick stops hitting the bad ones he will descend to a somewhat ordinary level. Part of his batting genius lies in the ability to convert waste balls and wild ones into hits.

Last year Medwick tried to pull everything. He batted .351. Now he hits with the pitch and finds he gets most of his power on the ball. Hornsby hit that way, too. And did it amazingly, from the extreme rear corner of the batter's box.

* * *

The Yanks got Di Maggio by risking $25,000 when all other clubs thought Giuseppe's bad knee would get worse.

The Yankees could have had Medwick, as well. But they ignored the tip about a boy wonder in Carteret, N. J. They heard he played football better than baseball. The Dodgers were urged to grab Ducky Wucky. The Giants passed him up, as well.

Branch Rickey walked in while the local clubs snoozed and started Joe off with Scottdale, as a Mr. King. Mr. King initiated his career with a neat .419. He's catching up with it again.

JIMMY FOXX, 3   WES FERRELL, 12   JOE DIMAGGIO, 5   ROGER CRAMER, 8

AMERICAN LEAGUE PLAYER SKETCHES

JAMES FOXX—One of the longest right-handed hitters in the majors today. Starred for the A's since 1928 but was sold to the Red Sox before the 1936 campaign. Was batting champion in 1933 with .356 mark and batted 58 home runs in 1932, missing a tie for Babe Ruth's record by only two. Born, Sudlersville, Md., 1907. Lifetime average, .339. 1937 average as of June 27, .258.

WESLEY CHEEK FERRELL—Half of the most famous brother battery in major league history. A headliner ever since he broke into the American League with Cleveland in 1929. Was traded by Red Sox, along with Brother Rick, to Washington Senators in June of 1937. Pitched no-run, no-hit game against Browns in 1931. Rated one of the better hitting pitchers. Born, Greensboro, N. C., February, 1908. Lifetime record—won, 161; lost, 96. 1937 record as of June 27—won, 6; lost, 7.

JOSEPH DIMAGGIO—Most highly-touted rookie in years when he came up from San Francisco last year to make good. First recruit to be named on an All-Star team. Has one of the best arms in business and in 1933, playing in Coast League, he hit safely in 61 consecutive games. Born, Martinez, Calif., 1914. Lifetime average, .323. 1937 average as of June 27, .335.

ROGER (DOC) CRAMER—Another Athletic star who was sold to Boston, going to the Sox in 1936 after five years of fine service at Philadelphia. Started career as a pitcher. Born, Beach Haven, N. J., 1906. Lifetime average, .305. 1937 average as of June 27, .308.

HOWARD EARL AVERILL—Batted .330 in first season in American League and has been going strong for Cleveland ever since, which covers more than eight years. Bought from San Francisco for $50,000. Made 230 hits last year to lead league. Born, Snohomish, Wash., 1903. Lifetime average, .325. 1937 average as of June 27, .308.

CHARLES (BUDDY) MYER—Staging fine comeback this season after bad 1936 campaign, due to illness. Was batting champion of American League in 1935. Starred at Mississippi A. & M. College. Born, Ellisville, Miss., 1904. Lifetime average, .302. 1937 average as of June 27, .293.

MELVIN (MEL) HARDER—Possesses one of finest curve balls in majors and the top pitching record for All-Star game competition. Has worn a Cleveland uniform steadily since 1930. Born, Beemer, Neb., 1909. Lifetime record—won, 112; lost, 94. 1937 record as of June 27—won, 4; lost, 5.

CHARLES GEHRINGER—Almost unanimously regarded as standout second baseman of his era. Also ranked high among hitters in American League. Graduated from U. of Michigan in 1924 and joined Tigers after spending one year in minors. Born, Fowlerville, Mich., 1903. Lifetime average, .325. 1937 average as of June 27, .360.

EARL AVERILL, 3   "BUDDY" MYER, 1   MEL HARDER, 18   CHARLIE GEHRINGER, 2

Murderers Row is what this lineup of American League sluggers was dubbed when they queued up for a publicity photograph before the 1937 All-Star game at Griffith Stadium in Washington. From the left: Lou Gehrig of the Yankees, Joe Cronin of the Red Sox, Bill Dickey and Joe DiMaggio of the Yankees, Charley Gehringer of the Tigers, Jimmy Foxx of the Red Sox, and Hank Greenberg of the Tigers. They lived up to their reputation and pounded the National League All-Stars 8–3.

A. L. Victory in All-Star Game Glorifies Power System as Compared to National Loop's Strategy and Defense

N. Y. CALLS DIMAGGIO 'RIGHT-HANDED RUTH'

YOUNGSTER APPEARS TO BE HEADED FOR 50 HOMERS THIS YEAR

Yankee-Senator Feud Boils After Powell
Fracas With Kuhel; Giants Hopeful
of Catching Cubs on Home Stand

NEW YORK, N. Y. — The writer could do this whole piece about New York's pride in the achievements of the Yankees in the All-Star game. But Fred Lieb was on the job to tell readers of the family bible what happened. So we will let him give the details. In any event, what the world's champions accomplished in the inter-league interlude in Washington has been covered amply and ably in other columns, so we will dispense with further euloguim and go on to things that have to do with the pennant races.

The Yankees did a fine job before and after they went to the All-Star battle. They gave the Red Sox a double beating on July 5 and whittled down Joe Cronin's aspirations. From the Washington classic, the Yankees moved back to the Stadium and belted the Senators, 16 to 2 and 12 to 2. On that 16 to 2 afternoon, Joe DiMaggio enjoyed the greatest day of his career and proved that he is on his way to becoming a right-handed Babe Ruth.

In hitting for the cycle against Carl Fischer and Ed Linke, DiMaggio did something handsome. He had two homers, a triple, double and single for 14 bases, seven runs driven in, four scored, with an average that day of .359 and 65 runs driven in for the season. Well, no wonder Yankee fans are all excited and DiMaggio is being called the Player of the Year.

The fans here think DiMaggio the greatest outfielder in the major leagues. They know all about Joe Medwick and his .400 average, with a fine home run total and a mess of two-baggers. But New York thinks DiMaggio can do more things than Joe the Medwick with a baseball, that he can give the job a better mental going-over, can

and does throw better. Anyway, it's something to talk about, and you will find the fans here tough to argue down on that subject.

Hit Only 29 Circuit Blows in '36.

With 22 home runs in 69 games—the Yankees had 82 as a club—DiMaggio seems to be on his way to 50 for the season. He hit 29 last year, with an average of .323.

The visit of the Senators reopened old wounds. You will recollect that Washington for years was the feud club for the Yanks. The A's used to have that position, but when the Mackmen were broken up and the team slipped, Washington moved into the vendetta.

In 1932, Bill Dickey broke Carl Reynolds' jaw, and in 1933, Ben Chapman and Buddy Myer started the riot which enveloped the entire Washington park.

On July 3, this year, in Washington, Jake Powell ran into Joe Kuhel at first base, knocked Joe down and raced for second as the ball rolled off.

The fans hurled pop bottles at Jake. The next afternoon it was more glassware and fire crackers. Jake got out of his old bailiwick alive and then went to the shore for a couple of days to do some fishing and swimming.

He came back to the Stadium covered with sunburn blisters. All through the afternoon the Senators tried to get Jake and in the sixth inning, as he ran to first on a close play, being thrown out by Lewis, Kuhel stuck out his arms and let Jake have it.

They tangled and Catcher Walter Millies ran out and held Jake's arms, as he explained it, to stop the fight. Anyway, those sunburn blisters were mashed. It was a poor fight, but a fight just the same. The scrappers were stopped and both were thrown out of the game and fined $25.

Joe McCarthy rushed to the support of Powell, and announced in no uncertain terms that he was all for Jake and the way he plays ball.

George Selkirk is being missed in right field. He was going marvelously well when he hurt his shoulder in Philadelphia. The surgeons say he will be out a month. There is no guarantee that George will be back even then, as he tore the tendons in his right shoulder and in his back—and, you know, he is a right-handed thrower.

New Assurance From Pearson.

Monte Pearson, who had not gone nine innings since his one-hit shut-out against the White Sox on May 10, lasted the route against the Senators on July 9, and while they hit him freely, he could bear down when necessary.

The Yankees have gone West, for the third time. If they are to be hampered and impeded and a race is to develop, the West will have to turn the trick on this tour. In their first trip westward, the Yankees won four and lost five. On their

second journey, they won five and lost six, showing a western deficit, as against a better than .700 pace in the Stadium, where, at this writing, they have won 28 and lost seven.

The Giants are doing a marvelous job of hanging on to the pace in the National League. It was just too bad that Terry's men selected July 9 to take a terrific pasting from the Dodgers. For on that day the Cubs got a lacing from the Pirates and the way was open for the Giants to move up. But they didn't move that afternoon.

Terry's problems are many and they are varied. He is worried now about Hal Schumacher. There is talk of buying Hi Vandenberg from Baltimore to bolster the hurling.

Bartell and Whitehead continue their fine work in the infield. But Terry has his troubles at first and third. The newspapers in New York get letters asking why Terry does not go back to work, but the fact remains that Bill is absolutely finished as a player and the letter writers are wasting their time.

New York appreciates that the Cubs are tough hombres, with plenty of pitch and catch and hit, and that it is going to be no picnic stopping them.

However, that's what was being said at this time last year. On July 17, 1936, Hubbell got off on his winning streak, and carried the Giants with him, right into the World's Series. DANIEL M. DANIEL.

'Contest, Dominated by Yanks, a Repetition of McCarthy's Success in World's Series of Last Fall', Says Lieb

By FREDERICK G. LIEB.

WASHINGTON, D. C.—Yankee batting power, which devastated the National League in last fall's World's Series, also proved too much for the senior major league in All-Star competition in Clark Griffith Stadium here on July 7, the American League representatives crushing their opponents by a score of 8 to 3. It was the fourth American League victory in five All-Star games and seven of the eight runs, which brought joy to the hearts of Will Harridge and his cohorts, rode home on smashing drives from the cudgels of athletes wearing the New York livery of Col. Jacob Ruppert.

In many respects, it was the most colorful and dramatic of the All-Star series. President Franklin Delano Roosevelt threw out the first ball and remained until the last ball was pitched. Postmaster-

TWO PLAYS IN ONE INNING THAT SNUFFED

N. L. CHANCES

❖THE stage was set for a big rally by the National leaguers in the sixth inning of the All-Star game, but two❖ plays snuffed out their best opportunity of the game and they had to be content with only one run, although favored with three hits and an error. Had the breaks been different in that inning, the American leaguers might have found the going close. Medwick, first up in the sixth, singled and went to third on Demaree's hit. Mize flew out and Medwick scored. Then Hartnett rolled to Gehringer, who tossed to Cronin at second, forcing Demaree, the Boston Red Sox manager and shortstop being seen in the picture at the left above, ready to throw, in trying to turn a double-play, but Hartnett reached first safely. Had Demaree beaten the throw, too, the Nationals would have had two runners on the bases and only one out. Bartell was safe on Rolfe's error and Jimmy Collins, as a pinch-hitter, singled to right, but DiMaggio made a great throw to catch Whitehead, running for Hartnett, at the plate, the New York Giants' infielder's fruitless sprint ending the rally. Whitehead is shown in the picture as he was touched out by Catcher Bill Dickey.

General Farley and most of the Cabinet occupied ringside seats, while members of the Senate forgot the Supreme Court squabble as they munched peanuts and watched the parade of America's foremost baseball stars. A delegation of Boy Scouts, holding their annual pow-wow in Washington, acted as an escort for the President as he entered the park and assisted in the picturesque flag-raising ceremonies.

However, for the 31,391 spectators, from the President down to the merest office boy, the game was the thing. Fought in a city which has known only American League ball since the turn of the century, the crowd yelled lustily as the team commanded by Joe McCarthy lambasted one National League pitcher after another. Except for the three-inning pitching tenure of Vernon (Lefty) Gomez, southpaw ace of the world's champion Yankees, it was strictly a game of hitters.

Twenty-six rousing wallops, evenly divided, whistled from the war clubs of the mighty aggregation of hitters, but there were greater length and more timeliness to the 13 American League blows than the 13 entered into the Ford Frick side of the scoring ledger.

Gehrig Drives in Four Runs.

Whereas the 13 National League hits ran largely to singles, the American League hits totaled 21 bases. The most lethal of these extra-base knocks were furnished by members of Joe McCarthy's famous Yankee wrecking-crew. Held to one hit, a homer, in his four previous All-Star games, Lou Gehrig, Yankee powerhouse, broke forth with a homer and double and banged in half of the eight American League runs. Two others came in on a triple by Red Rolfe, Yankee third baseman, and a seventh was prodded in by Bill Dickey, who smacked a double and single and drew a walk in four attempts. The only run driven in by an American leaguer not connected with the Yankees was sent in by Charley Gehringer, who singled Rolfe home after the Dartmouth collegian's fourth-inning triple. Gehringer, who started the game with a .500 batting average for his previous four All-Star games, increased his average to .529 by lashing out three hits in his last three times up.

There was plenty of small gun fire from the National leaguers, with the powerful Gas House contribution, Joe Medwick, pacing Bill Terry's brigade. After Gomez retired the Cardinal left fielder in the first inning, there was no stopping the rampaging Jerseyman. Tommy Bridges and Mel Harder were as impotent in halting Medwick as National League pitchers have been this season. Joe rapped out two doubles and a brace of singles.

Arky Vaughan and Billy Herman were the only other National leaguers to get more than one hit. Both players collected a pair of singles in five attempts. The biggest batting failures in the National League camp were Paul Waner, 1936 National League batting champ, and Johnny Mize, slugging first sacker of the Cardinals. Paul had five hitless times at bat, while Mize fell down four times, twice in the pinches.

Pitchers have dominated in most of the previous All-Star games, but of the eight twirlers used this year, only Vernon Gomez and Mel Harder added to their reputations. These two pitchers have done the bulk of American League pitching in All-Star games of the past and 1937 saw no lessening of their effectiveness. Pitching in his fourth All-Star game, Gomez started the contest against Dizzy Dean and received credit for his third victory in this type of pitching. Gomez warmed up for the dream game with low-hit contests against the Athletics and Washington and was the outstanding pitcher of the classic, as only ten men faced him in his three innings, Vaughan straightening out a fast one for a single with two down in the first.

Tommy Bridges, Tiger ace, pitched the next three innings for the American League team and was stung hard and often. The National leaguers got to him for seven hits in his three-inning term, and picked up a run in each of these frames. Good support and Tommy's own stout heart saved him from worse punishment.

Harder was not as effective as in former experiences against the National League, yielding five hits. However, at the end of his three innings, the National League had still to score a run on him. Harder pitched five innings in the game of 1934, three in 1935, two in 1936 and three this year, and the National League never learned the scoring combination. One run was scored on him in 1934, but it was put on base by Charley Ruffing, and after that the going for the National League became harder and harder.

Dizzy Dean, whisked to Washington by airplane after he gave an early indication of ducking the All-Star game, was charged with the defeat, inasmuch as the score was 2 to 0 against the National League, when Dizzy surrendered the mound. Dizzy would have shared honors with Gomez if he had retired one more batsman, but that batsman was Lou Gehrig. Diz walked DiMaggio in the first and yielded two singles in the second, but escaped unscathed. He also retired the first two hitters in the third, when Joe DiMaggio low-bridged him with a hot shot through the box, his first and only hit in two All-Star games. The count to Gehrig was worked to three balls and two strikes and Diz tried to shoot through a fast one. Lou had hit one dangerous foul, and he was ready for this pitch. He drove it well over the high right field fence, one of the most difficult home run socks in the major leagues.

King Carl Far From Himself.

Tragedy for the National League stalked in the wake of Gehrig's homer. Dean was followed by Carl Hubbell, who only recently completed a run of 24 straight National League wins and who struck out Ruth, Gehrig, Foxx, Simmons and Cronin in succession in the 1934 All-Star game at the Polo Grounds. Hub gave an early indication that it wasn't his day, as his control was poor and he constantly was in back of his hitters. Bill Terry, his New York manager, lifted him after he was prodded for three runs on two singles, a triple and a walk.

Rolfe hit the most damaging clout, a three-bagger that sailed deep into right-center, far above the heads of Demaree and Paul Waner. Cy Blanton of the Pirates was rushed to Hubbell's relief and lingered long enough to strike out Joe DiMaggio. The Buccaneer gave way to a pinch-hitter, and Lee Grissom, freshman Cincinnati left-hander, was the next National League victim. Lee started brilliantly, fanning both Gehrig and Earl Averill, but Joe Cronin and Bill Dickey bunched doubles on him for the A. L.'s sixth run.

Lee, too, gave way to a pinch-hitter, and Van Lingle Mungo, wearing the Kelly green cap of the Brooklyns, next was trotted to the mound. Van supposedly was out of the game because of a lame back, and Clydell Castleman of the Giants had been rushed in as a replacement. However, Mungo reported well enough to pitch and Clydell appeared in a seat in the press box, instead of in the National League dugout. It might have been better for the National League if Terry had stuck to Castleman. Van wasn't much more effective than when the American League guns roared against his fast one at the Polo Grounds in 1934.

Mungo walked Rolfe in the sixth and Gehringer lashed him for a single. Gehrig brought them in with a long double to center. Lou lost a triple and helped Mungo out of a hole by over-sliding the base. The big Columbian was nailed after Umpire McGowan had first ruled him safe.

Bucky Walters of the Phillies was the sixth National League pitcher, and just managed to get by in the eighth. Rolfe and Gehringer reached him for singles, but DiMaggio left them stranded, fouling to Vaughan for the last National League putout of the game.

DiMaggio's Great Throw Nips Run.

If Yankee hitters excelled and a Yankee pitcher, Gomez, turned in the best pitching job, so it was a Yankee, DiMaggio, who turned in the best fielding plays. Joe held doubles to singles all afternoon, but his prize play was one of his famous throws to the plate to squash a National League rally in the sixth. The Nationals were pecking away at Bridges in this round; they had one run in and runners on first and second, when Ripper Collins, batting for Grissom, drove a sharp single to right. Terry had sent in Burgess Whitehead, one of the fastest men in the National League, to run for Gabby Hartnett in this inning. Whitey looked like a cinch to score from second on the hit, but Joe's great peg, which came to Dickey on a high, first bounce, beat him by several feet. Burgess looked like the most surprised man in the park when Dickey nestled the ball against his ribs. Red Rolfe, Yankee third baseman, was guilty of a pair of errors, the only marks against the great play of the Yankee detail.

Cocky, aggressive Dick Bartell of the Giants made the best fielding play for the National League, in the sixth inning, when he grabbed Cronin's hot shot about an inch off the ground and converted it into a double play. The always-brilliant Gehringer and Cronin played nice ball around second base for the American League. Charley pounced on Waner's awkward grounder in the seventh, after it squirted away from Harder, and got his man.

As in the 1934 All-Star game, Bill Terry called on most of his forces. In the game of three years ago, Terry used 20 players, and employed five pitchers, including Hubbell, Mungo and Dean, who also served in this game. In this Washington encounter, Bill used 19 players and rushed in six pitchers. When the game was over, he had only Billy Jurges of the Cubs, Pepper Martin of the Cardinals, Gene Moore of the Bees and Ernie Lombardi of the Reds left on the bench. However, unlike 1934, Terry made no attempt to see how many faces he could show the fans. He rushed in pitchers, pinch-hitters and replacements, as he thought they would

do his team the most good.

Joe McCarthy, managing his second All-Star game, did not lift a player of his original line-up, with the exception of a pitcher. He used only one pinch-hitter, Jimmy Foxx, batting for Bridges in the sixth. At that time, Tommy had finished his three innings.

Starting Sam West Surprise.

Joe sprung a surprise when he started Sammy West of the Browns in left field. The original selection from the St. Louis club was the hard-hitting Beau Bell, West having been added to the American League squad when Gerald Walker of the Tigers became incapacitated. It was believed that Joe would rush in Bell after Left-Handers Hubbell and Grissom took up the pitching burden for the National League, but Joe believed he had sufficient hitting strength and wished to avail himself of West's defensive ability as an outfielder.

No criticism of tactics can be made against Terry, the losing manager. Bill played the cards which were dealt to him. Oddly enough, the game and score represented in some degree the types of ball which is played in the two major leagues. In the National League, there is more or less of an inclination to play for one run and have the pitchers protect that lead. In the American League, especially in the Yankee system of play, the battle campaign still is to play for a batch of runs and overpower opponents by brute strength. That has been the World's Series strategy against the National League. In this great game of 1937, the top-ranking pitchers of the National League, Dean, Hubbell and Mungo, failed to check the American League bats. It was a victory for American League power over the best National League defense that Bill Terry and his assistants, Frankie Frisch and Chuck Dressen, could throw against them. The game in detail:

First Inning.

NATIONALS—Paul Waner grounded to Rolfe. Herman fouled to Dickey. Vaughan singled to center. Medwick forced Vaughan, Cronin to Gehringer. No runs, one hit, no errors.

AMERICANS—Rolfe popped to Herman. Gehringer lined to Bartell. DiMaggio walked. Gehrig struck out. No runs, no hits, no errors.

Second Inning.

NATIONALS—Demaree flied to Averill. Mize flied to West. Gehringer threw out Hartnett. No runs, no hits, no errors.

AMERICANS—Averill singled to right. Cronin flied to Demaree. Dickey singled off Herman's glove, Averill stopping at second. West flied to Demaree. Gomez struck out. No runs, two hits, no errors.

Third Inning.

NATIONALS—Cronin threw out Bartell. J. Dean flied to Averill. P. Waner flied to West. No runs, no hits, no errors.

AMERICANS—Bartell threw out Rolfe. Gehringer was out, Herman to Mize. DiMaggio singled to center. Gehrig hit a home run over the right field fence, scoring behind DiMaggio. Averill's drive caromed off Dean's foot to Herman, who threw him out. Two runs, two hits, no errors.

Fourth Inning.

NATIONALS—Tommy Bridges went in to pitch for the Americans. Herman singled to left. Bridges tossed out Vaughan. Medwick doubled to left, scoring Herman. Demaree popped to Gehringer. Cronin threw out Mize. One run, two hits, no errors.

AMERICANS—Carl Hubbell went to the mound for the Nationals. Cronin flied to Medwick. Dickey walked. West singled off Mize's glove, sending Dickey to third. Bridges fanned on three pitched balls. Rolfe tripled to the scoreboard in right center, scoring Dickey and West. Gehringer singled to right, scoring Rolfe. Hubbell was taken

out, Cy Blanton replacing him. DiMaggio struck out. Three runs, three hits, no errors.

Fifth Inning.

NATIONALS—Hartnett slashed a single through the box. Bartell flied to West. Ott batted for Blanton and doubled to right. Hartnett pulling up at third. P. Waner flied to West, Hartnett scoring. Rolfe muffed Herman's liner for an error. Ott going to third and Herman reaching first. Vaughan fouled to Gehrig. One run, two hits, one error.

AMERICANS—Lee Grissom was the fourth National League pitcher. Gehrig was called out on strikes. Averill fanned on three pitches. Cronin doubled to right. Dickey doubled to the scoreboard, scoring Cronin. West popped to Vaughan. One run, two hits, no errors.

Sixth Inning.

NATIONALS—Medwick singled to right center. Demaree singled off Rolfe's glove, sending Medwick to third. Mize flied to Averill in deep center. Medwick scoring after the catch. Hartnett forced Demaree at second, Gehringer to Cronin. Whitehead ran for Hartnett. Bartell was safe when Rolfe booted his grounder. Collins batted for Grissom and singled to right, but Whitehead was out at the plate, DiMaggio to Dickey. One run, three hits, one error.

AMERICANS—Mungo and Mancuso formed the new National League battery. Foxx batted for Bridges and grounded out, Mungo to Mize. Rolfe walked. Gehringer singled to left, Rolfe stopping at second. DiMaggio fanned. Gehrig doubled to center, scoring Rolfe and Gehringer, but was out at third attempting to stretch it into a triple. Demaree to Bartell to Vaughan. Two runs, two hits, no errors.

Seventh Inning.

NATIONALS—Mel Harder went to the mound for the Americans. Waner was out, Gehringer to Gehrig. Herman singled to left. Vaughan forced Herman, Gehringer to Cronin. Medwick doubled down the right field line for his third straight hit, sending Vaughan to third. Demaree grounded to Cronin. No runs, two hits, no errors.

AMERICANS—Averill walked. Bartell made a diving catch of Cronin's low pop fly and threw to Mize, doubling Averill off first. Dickey flied to Demaree. No runs, no hits, no errors.

Eighth Inning.

NATIONALS—Mize flied to West. Rolfe threw out Mancuso. Bartell beat out a scratch hit to Cronin. Joe Moore batted for Mungo and forced Bartell, Cronin, unassisted. No runs, one hit, no errors.

AMERICANS—Walters was the sixth National League pitcher. West popped to Herman. Herman threw out Harder. Rolfe singled to left. Gehringer singled to center, for his third hit, sending Rolfe to third. DiMaggio fouled to Vaughan. No runs, two hits, no errors.

Ninth Inning.

NATIONALS—Harder threw out P. Waner. Herman was out, Gehrig to Harder. Vaughan singled to center. Medwick's fourth hit was a line single to right-center, Vaughan going to third. Gehringer threw out Demaree. No runs, two hits, no errors.

NOTES OF THE GAME.

CLARK GRIFFITH, venerable owner of the Washington club, put on a fine show. Griff, dressed all in white and beaming from ear to ear, led the presidential parade which preceded the game. First came the Old Fox, then the Boy Scouts, followed by the two cars bearing the President and his party.

Joe Engel, former Washington pitcher and now Griffith's farm club overseer and scout, played host to the several hundred writers present for the game in the haven of rest and refreshment under the right field pavilion. Buck O'Neill, head of the Washington chapter of the Baseball Writers' Association, awarded the press cards.

President Roosevelt was accompanied by his son and secretary, James, and, while he occasionally wiped beads of July perspiration from his forehead, he apparently had a good time. Commissioner Landis called on the nation's head between innings and paid his respects. Landis sat

Each Team Makes 13 Hits, But American Drives Go for 21 Bases; Lefty Gomez Notches Third Dream Win

with Jesse Jones, head of the Reconstruction Finance Corporation.

Senator Pat Harrison of Mississippi sat with Russian Ambassador Troyanovsky. The Soviet envoy is keenly interested in our national game and wishes to see it popularized in Russia. He says the game has been introduced in Moscow, but there are not enough Russians who understand it.

The official scorers, Charley Segar, Buck O'Neill and Shirley Povich, did a good job. Most writers were in agreement on the two errors for Rolfe, though some felt Cronin should have had a fumble in the eighth, which was scored as a hit for Bartell. Joe went down for the ball, but didn't come up with it.

There was some Washington criticism of Joe McCarthy for his failure to employ a single member of the Washington squad in the game. Three members of the Senatorial squad. Second Baseman Buddy Myer and the brother battery, Wesley and Rick Ferrell, were members of the American League brigade. Rick caught the entire All-Star game of 1933 and divided the catching assignments with Bill Dickey in 1936. However, Joe McCarthy played strictly to win. He refused to disturb Charley Gehringer and Bill Dickey, both of whom were going great guns, and with Gomez, Bridges and Harder handling the pitching, he had no occasion to call on Wes Ferrell.

All three of the outfielders employed by Joe McCarthy—Joe DiMaggio, Earl Averill and Sammy West—are center fielders. He couldn't play them all in center field, so West went to left and DiMaggio to right. However, Joe still was playing center in the sixth when he got in front of Medwick's smash over second and held it to a single.

In the first inning, Bill McGowan, American League umpire, had some difficulty in getting onto the hang of Arky Vaughan's unorthodox batting stance. Arky is inclined to keep his right foot out of the box and Bill wanted him to keep it in. After the conversation was over, the Pirate infielder drove back Gomez' first pitch for a clean single. But, he was the only one to dent Vernon's armor.

Joe Medwick played them all over the board. His first hit went between the third base bag and Red Rolfe and whistled down the left field foul line for a double. His second hit tore over second base. No. 3 sailed between Gehrig and the first base bag for a double down the right field foul line. Having played all the bases, Medwick wafted his fourth hit to right-center.

Paul Waner, batting terror of the National League and three times its hit champ, went through his fourth hitless All-Star game. He shouldn't feel discouraged. Lou Gehrig failed to hit until his fourth game, but since then he has knocked out two homers and a double and driven in five runs. Incidentally, both Gehrig and Joe Medwick set a new high for total bases for an All-Star tilt. Medwick's two doubles and brace of singles, giving him six bases, the same as Larrupin Lou. Medwick's four successive hits also was a record.

Some 46 pair of hands were stretched out to catch the ball which the President threw out from his box before the start of hostilities. It was like a ball hit into the stands; several youngsters scuffle for it and a third gets the prize. While big Hank Greenberg of the Tigers and Bill Jurges of the Cubs were battling for the precious pellet, Joe Moore of the Giants grabbed it.

Babe Ruth, who played in the first two All-Star games, winning the first one in

Chicago with a homer, had a front row box with Mrs. Ruth. The Babe showed his usual patience in autographing scorecards and baseballs. Aided by Walter Johnson, former pitching star of the Senators, he put on a broadcast from Washington after the game.

Connie Mack, 74-year-old manager of the lowly Athletics, who commanded the American League team in the first All-Star game four years ago, was an interested spectator. "I'm scouting for talent," said Mr. Mack, with a sly grin. "After the way we slid from first to last, I guess we could use a few of these fellows."

Two players who would have represented the American League in many All-Star games had the custom prevailed earlier—Walter Johnson and Eddie Collins—talked of old times before the game. "Who would McCarthy play at second if Eddie Collins and Charlie Gehringer were in the league at the same time?" some one asked. Fortunately for Joe, he had no such choice to make. It was difficult enough having such first base slugging stars as Gehrig, Greenberg and Foxx on his team.

Back from a vacation trip to Hawaii, John Heydler, former National League president, came down from his Garden City, L. I., home for the tiff. John and his former secretary, Harvey Traband, took advantage of their Washington visit to call on John B. Foster, former writer and Giants' secretary, who is a semi-invalid in the national capital.

Arch Ward, sports editor of the Chicago Tribune, who conceived the idea of the All-Star game in Chicago, was given a chance to address the crowd over the loud speaker. He thanked Commissioner Landis and the big league presidents, Will Harridge and Ford Frick, for taking up his brain child and rearing it.

Many of the All-Stars were accompanied by their ladies. Mrs. Lou Gehrig, Mrs. Bill Dickey, Mrs. Vernon Gomez and Mrs. Robert Rolfe cheered for their illustrious husbands. Mrs. Joseph Michael Medwick also got quite a kick out of her mate's contribution to the fun.

Three former American League umpires, Tommy Connolly, now chief of staff for Will Harridge, Billy Evans, head of the Red Sox farm system, and Dick Nallin, had an old-time fan-fest Dick came over from his farm at Frederick, Md., to renew old acquaintances.

Dressed in his familiar high hat and frock coat, Al Schacht, baseball's famous clown, returned to the scene of his former conquests. Al led the famous Army Band, which looked after the musical end of the program.

Ways and means of subduing Dizzy Dean without detracting from his drawing powers was said to be the leading topic at the National League meeting, which preceded the All-Star game. Commissioner Landis is reported to be "all fed up" on Dizzy and he would have exploded if the eccentric twirler had run out on baseball's biggest show.

Judge William Bramham, head of the minors, came up from his Durham, N. C., headquarters to see the game and talk things over with Landis. He reports a great season all along the minor league front, with more leagues, teams and players in action than at any time since the pre-Federal League days. "Among our players," said the Judge, "are the All-Stars of tomorrow."

Judging by Dizzy Dean's facial expressions, he didn't think much more of Bill McGowan's umpiring than he does of that administered in the National League. Dean gave Bill an outraged look in the first, when he called a ball on Rolfe, and an even more painful expression when he called a ball on Gehringer. Diz felt better when Rolfe rolled to Herman and Gehringer lined to Vaughan.

NATIONAL LEAGUE.

	AB.	R.	H.	TB.	O.	A.	E.
P. Waner, right field	5	0	0	0	0	0	0
Herman, second base	5	1	2	2	1	4	0
Vaughan, third base	5	0	2	2	3	0	0
Medwick, left field	5	1	4	6	1	0	0
Demaree, center field	5	0	1	1	3	1	0
Mize, first base	4	0	0	0	7	0	0
Hartnett, catcher	3	1	1	1	6	0	0
†Whitehead	0	0	0	0	0	0	0
Mancuso, catcher	1	0	0	0	1	0	0
Bartell, shortstop	4	0	1	1	2	3	0
J. Dean, pitcher	1	0	0	0	0	1	0
Hubbell, pitcher	0	0	0	0	0	0	0
Blanton, pitcher	0	0	0	0	0	0	0
*Ott	1	0	1	2	0	0	0
Grissom, pitcher	0	0	0	0	0	0	0
‡Collins	1	0	1	1	0	0	0
Mungo, pitcher	0	0	0	0	0	1	0
xJ. Moore	1	0	0	0	0	0	0
Walters, pitcher	0	0	0	0	0	0	0
Totals	41	3	13	16	24	10	0

AMERICAN LEAGUE.

	AB.	R.	H.	TB.	O.	A.	E.
Rolfe, third base	4	2	2	4	0	1	2
Gehringer, second base	5	1	3	3	2	5	0
DiMaggio, right field	4	1	1	1	1	1	0
Gehrig, first base	4	1	2	6	10	1	0
Averill, center field	3	0	1	1	2	0	0
Cronin, shortstop	4	1	1	2	4	3	0
Dickey, catcher	3	1	2	3	2	0	0
West, left field	4	1	1	1	5	0	0
Gomez, pitcher	1	0	0	0	0	0	0
Bridges, pitcher	1	0	0	0	0	1	0
§Foxx	1	0	0	0	0	0	0
Harder, pitcher	1	0	0	0	1	1	0
Totals	35	8	13	21	27	13	2

*Batted for Blanton in fifth.
†Ran for Hartnett in sixth.
‡Batted for Grissom in sixth.
§Batted for Bridges in sixth.
xBatted for Mungo in eighth.

National	0	0	0	1	1	1	0	0	0—3
American	0	0	2	3	1	2	0	0	*—8

Runs batted in—Gehrig 4, Rolfe 2, Gehringer, Dickey, P. Waner, Medwick, Mize.

Two-base hits—Medwick 2, Gehrig, Cronin, Dickey, Ott.

Three-base hit—Rolfe.

Home run—Gehrig.

Double play—Bartell and Mize.

Pitching records—J. Dean 2 runs, 4 hits in 3 innings; Hubbell 3 runs 3 hits in 2-3 inning; Blanton 0 runs, 0 hits in 1-3 inning; Grissom 1 run, 2 hits in 1 inning; Mungo 2 runs, 2 hits in 2 innings; Gomez 0 runs, 1 hit in 3 innings; Bridges 3 runs, 7 hits in 3 innings.

Struck out—By J. Dean 2 (Gehrig, Gomez), by Hubbell 1 (Bridges), by Blanton 1 (DiMaggio), by Grissom 2 (Gehrig, Averill), by Mungo 1 (DiMaggio).

Bases on balls—Off J. Dean 1 (DiMaggio), off Hubbell 1 (Dickey), off Mungo 2, (Rolfe, Averill).

Earned runs—American League 8, National League 3.

Left on bases—National League 11, American League 7.

Winning pitcher—Gomez.

Losing pitcher—J. Dean.

Umpires—McGowan (A. L.) home plate; Barr (N. L.) first base; Quinn (A. L.) second base; Pinelli (N. L.) third base for the first four and one-half innings; Barr (N. L.) home plate; Quinn (A. L.) first base; Pinelli (N. L.) second base; McGowan (A. L.) third base for the remainder of game.

This Morning

DiMaggio Can Hit, But He Has No Color.

By Shirley Povich.

Joe DiMaggio, with his free swing and solid stance, may conceivably displace Babe Ruth as the all-time home run champion of the big leagues, but Giuseppe will never make the turnstiles click as merrily as did the Babe.

Because DiMaggio is news only when he hits a home run. Modesty may be a virtue in other walks of life, but in the big leagues they pay off on braggadocio, color and showmanship. In that league DiMaggio couldn't hit .029.

POVICH.

The Yankees' young Italian boy is seemingly too goldarned content to hit his home runs and those long triples and let it go at that. He has none of Ruth's flourish and gusto, none of Dizzy Dean's self-admiration. And because of that, he will set no salary records no matter how many slugging records fall before the power of his bat.

* * * *

Down here last week at the all-star game Giuseppe scarcely broke into print, despite the fact that he was leading both leagues in home run production and was the batting sensation of the season. This reporter abandoned all ideas of an interview when DiMaggio emitted a couple of unintelligible grunts in answer to what we thought were some well-put questions.

* * * *

On the days that he hits a home run or two they can't keep DiMaggio out of the news, but apart from that he is no more noteworthy than another birth in China. And you know, dear reader, that publicity is very vital to outstanding success in baseball.

* * * *

The fellow can smite that apple, of course. And he can cover acres of ground in the outfield, and he has positively the greatest throwing arm in either league, but when he isn't hitting those home runs he has no more fan appeal than a foul tip. He doesn't even crab at the umpires. The even tenor of his ways is killing —killing his chances to really cash in on the big money in baseball.

* * * *

Sure, he's done pretty well so far for a rookie. Made the Yankees come through with $8,000 last season —his first in the majors—and forced 'em to up it to $15,000 this year. But that's far, far from the $80,000 Ruth commanded or the $165,000 he once received for a three-year contract.

* * * *

Whatever salary heights DiMaggio does reach he will achieve with the power in his bat. But even Col. Ruppert admitted that Babe Ruth, owner of the most murderous bat of all time, wasn't being paid for his home runs. The Babe, as you know, was paid off on his magnetism at the gate.

* * * *

Fellows like Ruth and Dizzy Dean, as you know, didn't have to hit a home run or pitch a winning ball game to get their names in the headlines. Dean merely has to praise himself and deride others, but Ruth commanded the headlines in any number of ways.

* * * *

There was the time when the Babe, en route from Southern training, gorged himself on a half-dozen hot dogs and a half-dozen bottles of pop at one sitting and came up with the most celebrated tummy ache in the history of the Nation. The Babe's eating proclivities were well known and the sympathy of a Nation was with him when he was rushed off the train to a hospital with doctors issuing hourly bulletins on his condition.

* * * *

He didn't get away with it, but the Babe back in 1922 set himself up as a bigger man than Judge Landis in baseball by openly defying Landis and taking himself off on a barnstorming tour after the World Series of 1922. That cost the Babe a 38-day suspension at the start of 1923 and a $5,000 fine. And it kept his name in the papers.

* * * *

In some ways, he was just a great big kid, with no particular idea that his thorough naturalness was a powerful asset. He didn't stop to think sometimes and one of those times was on a September day at Griffith Stadium in 1927 when the Babe refused to pose with Secretary of Commerce Herbert Hoover, Republican nominee for the Presidency.

Ruth waved away the photographers who went out into right-field before the game and asked him to pose with Hoover in a box seat. "G'wan away from here," the Babe yelled. "I'm an Al Smith man. I ain't posing with Hoover." The Babe didn't get a home run that day, but he was very much in the news just the same. Those quotes of his were priceless.

* * * *

To date, the extent of DiMaggio's extra-curricular publicity has been his admission that he is saving his money. I would say that isn't calculated to excite the Nation's fans.

Yankees Rout Browns by 16 to 9, Then Draw, 8-8, in Eleven Innings

DiMaggio Smashes 3 Homers in Nightcap, Which Is Called to Make Train—Clift, St. Louis, Also Gets 3 for Day—Seven Runs in 9th Win Opener—New York Lead Now Half Game

By JAMES P. DAWSON
Special to THE NEW YORK TIMES.

ST. LOUIS, June 13.—More than five hours of baseball ended at Sportsman's Park today with the Yankees gaining a decision over the Browns in one end of a double-header and getting a tie in the other.

The Yanks romped off with the first game by 16 to 9 in their biggest hitting and scoring splurge of the season. They were battling the Browns tooth and nail in the nightcap when the skirmish was called with the score 8-all after eleven innings because dusk was fast enveloping the field and the necessity for making even belated train connections was imperative.

The season's biggest American League crowd here, 12,249, left without grumbling as both clubs rushed for their trains.

Drop Part of Lead

The day's doings cost the Mc-Carthymen part of their lead. They now show the way to the second-place White Sox by a half game.

Joe DiMaggio stood out pre-eminently in this day of weird play which saw the Yankees smite six of Rogers Hornsby's pitchers for thirty-one hits that held five homers, three of them in a row by DiMaggio, and were good for fifty-eight bases.

DiMaggio struck his three round-trippers in the nightcap and drove in five runs. The blow boosted his total of homers to fourteen, gave him the honor of striking nine over a stretch of as many games, five of them in four skirmishes, and extended the string of contests in which he has hit consecutively to fifteen.

Bill Dickey also hit a homer for the Yankees in the nightcap, a blow that was good for two runs in a six-run fifth inning which jarred Julio Bonetti, young Brown hurler.

More Destructive Blows

DiMaggio's blows were the more destructive. His first fashioned three of the first four Yankee runs in the fifth. His second brought the Yanks within striking distance of the Browns in the seventh after they had hammered Bump Hadley to shelter and feasted generously on the offerings of Pat Malone. His third, struck in the ninth, brought the Yanks even with the enemy.

Not all the home-run hitting was done by the Yankees. Harland Clift hit one clean out of the park on Hadley in the fourth. He also smashed two in the opener.

Twenty hits in the opener established a season's high for the New Yorkers. The Browns added thirteen to the general bombardment. Fourteen runs in the last four innings, seven of them in the ninth, pulled the Yanks through. Joe Vosmik and Tony Lazzeri also connected for the circuit.

Johnny Broaca, it was revealed today by Dr. Robert F. Hyland, is handicapped by a torn ligament in the socket of his right arm, and the condition has ossified. It is a complaint somewhat similar to that which overtook Paul Dean, and there is little that can be done about it.

Monte Pearson, an X-ray examination showed, has a spur, a callous growth, on his right elbow, which must be subjected to intensive diathermic treatment. During the treatments Pearson must not undertake to do too much throwing.

George Selkirk was back in action for the first time since he pulled up lame in Cleveland more than a week ago. He made four hits in the opener.

The Box Scores

FIRST GAME

NEW YORK (A.)	ab.	r.	h.	po.	a.	e.
Crosetti, ss.	5	1	2	1	4	0
Rolfe, 3b.	5	1	3	3	2	0
DiM'gio, cf.	5	1	1	2	0	0
Gehrig, 1b.	6	3	3	9	0	1
Dickey, c.	4	3	2	6	0	0
Selkirk, rf.	6	3	4	1	0	0
Henrich, lf.	5	1	0	3	0	1
Lazzeri, 2b.	6	2	2	3	3	0
Murphy, p.	1	0	1	0	2	1
Makosky, p.	4	1	2	0	0	0
Total	47	16	20	27	11	3

ST. LOUIS (A.)	ab.	r.	h.	po.	a.	e.
Davis, 1b.	4	1	2	7	0	0
West, cf.	5	0	1	2	0	0
Vosmik, lf.	5	1	3	2	0	0
Bell, rf.	5	1	1	1	0	0
Clift, 3b.	5	2	3	1	2	0
Knickb'r, ss.	4	1	0	4	4	0
Huffman, c.	4	1	2	8	0	0
Carey, 2b.	4	1	1	2	1	0
Hildeb'd, p.	2	1	1	0	0	0
Blake, p.	0	0	0	0	0	0
Knott, p.	0	0	0	0	0	0
Walkup, p.	0	0	0	0	1	0
Koupal, p.	0	0	0	0	0	0
aAllen	1	0	0	0	0	0
Total	39	9	13	27	8	0

aBatted for Knott in eighth.

New York	0	2 0	0 0 3	2 2 7	—16
St. Louis	2 0 1	3 1 0	2 0 0	—9

Runs batted in—Vosmik 4, Murphy 2, Carey, Clift 3, Selkirk, Dickey 2, Henrich, Crosetti, Rolfe 2, Lazzeri 4, Makosky, DiMaggio, Davis. Two-base hits—Murphy, Hildebrand, Gehrig, Selkirk. Three-base hits—Selkirk, Dickey, Rolfe. Home runs—Clift 2, Vosmik, Lazzeri. Stolen base—Crosetti. Sacrifice — Hildebrand. Double plays—Knickerbocker and Davis; Rolfe, Lazzeri and Gehrig. Left on bases—New York 11, St. Louis 6. Bases on balls—Off Murphy 2, Hildebrand 5, Blake 1, Knott 1. Struck out—By Murphy 1, Hildebrand 2, Knott 3, Makosky 4, Koupal 2. Hits—Off Murphy 7 in 3 2-3 innings, Makosky 6 in 5 1-3, Hildebrand 8 in 6, Blake 1 in 0 (pitched to two batters in seventh), Knott 4 in 2, Walkup 5 in 1-3, Koupal 2 in 2-3. Winning pitcher—Makosky. Losing pitcher—Walkup. Umpires—Kolls, Basil and Summers. Time of game—2:26.

SECOND GAME

NEW YORK (A.)	ab.	r.	h.	po.	a.	e.
Crosetti, ss.	5	1	0	2	3	0
Rolfe, 3b.	6	1	3	1	2	0
DiMaggio, cf.	6	3	3	5	0	0
Gehrig, 1b.	3	1	2	10	0	0
Dickey, c.	4	1	2	10	0	0
Selkirk, rf.	4	0	0	1	0	0
Henrich, lf.	4	1	1	3	0	0
Lazzeri, 2b.	5	0	0	1	4	0
Hadley, p.	1	0	0	0	0	0
Malone, p.	1	0	0	0	1	0
Makosky, p.	1	0	0	0	2	0
aRuffing	1	0	0	0	0	0
Total	41	8	11	33	12	0

aBatted for Malone in eighth.

ST. LOUIS (A.)	ab.	r.	h.	po.	a.	e.
Davis, 1b.	5	2	2	14	0	0
West, cf.	5	1	2	3	0	0
Vosmik, lf.	5	0	0	4	0	0
Bell, rf.	4	2	2	3	0	0
Clift, 3b.	6	1	2	0	4	0
K'knocker, ss.	6	0	2	2	2	0
Hemsley, c.	5	0	1	5	2	0
Carey, 2b.	5	1	2	2	2	0
Bonetti, p.	3	1	0	0	1	1
Total	44	8	13	33	11	1

New York | 0 0 0 | 0 6 0 | 1 0 1 | 0 0 —8
St. Louis | 0 0 0 | 3 5 0 | 0 0 0 | 0 0—8

Runs batted in—Clift 3, DiMaggio 5, West 2, Vosmik, Bell, Knickerbocker, Lazzeri. Two-base hits—Gehrig 2, Davis 2, West 2, Knickerbocker. Home runs—Clift, DiMaggio 3, Dickey. Stolen base—Henrich. Sacrifices—Vosmik, Bonetti. Double plays—Hemsley and Knickerbocker; Clift, Carey and Davis; Lazzeri, Crosetti and Gehrig. Left on bases—New York 7, St. Louis 10. Bases on balls—Off Hadley 3, Bonetti 7, Makosky 2. Struck out—By Hadley 3, Bonetti 5, Malone 2, Makosky 3. Hits—Off Hadley 4 in 4 innings (none out in fifth), Malone 5 in 3, Makosky 4 in 4. Umpires—Basil, Summers and Kolls. Time of game—2:41.

Murderers' Row. They perpetrated the crime against opposing pitchers with their bats: from the left, Lou Gehrig, Joe DiMaggio, Bill Dickey, and George Selkirk.

New Stance Aids Di Maggio

Heavier Hitting Traced by Yankee Mates to Freer Stride and Better Pivoting.

By DANIEL,

World-Telegram Staff Correspondent.

DETROIT, July 15.—Joseph Paul Di Maggio, Jr., having become a truly celebrated case with his twenty-third home run, in an eighth consecutive Yankee triumph, 10 to 2, over the Tigers, baseball anatomists and power biologists today put Giuseppe's slugging scheme on the dissecting table.

Last season Di Maggio accounted for twenty-nine circuit drives altogether. With eighty-four games yet to be played, the dynamo from the Golden Gate is not only a mere half dozen homers behind his output for his freshman campaign, but eleven beyond the total he boasted on July 15, 1936.

Taking a generous and apt slice out of Shakespeare, diamond clinicians today asked: "On what meat hath this, our Caesar, fed that he hath grown so great?" And they added, "What is this bird doing now that he did not do last season, and how come he is socking those homers with such precision and frequency?"

Questioning the subject, himself, failed to satisfy investigators. Di Maggio smiled. He stretched out his hands and gave his shoulders a Sicilian shrug. "I dunno! Must be the old confeedence. Maybe the pitchers don't fool me so easily. I pick a ball better. Perhaps I'm stronger. I've grown in a year. My diet is unchanged. I eat heavy and hearty. But nothing during a game. No hot dogs. I never have indigestion. My family would be insulted if I had."

Fellow Yankees Declare It's in Joe's Stride.

Inquiry among Di Maggio's teammates supplied an interesting clue. They agreed Giuseppe was hitting more homers mainly because he had changed his stance. He is striding better, has more mobility, stands with feet farther apart, with right pedal a bit behind the left, and he pivots much better than he did last summer. The weight of his bat is unchanged—38 or 39 ounces, and the heaviest on the club.

Last season Di Maggio stood about a foot away from the plate. Inside pitching gave him a little trouble. Now he hits everything because he isn't so rigid at the plate. And he has been around. That counts, too.

He's never undecided, hardly ever starts after a ball he eventually lets go by. His eye is fine, and take it from his fellow Yankees, he has only started to develop his power. He hits the hardest ball in the American League, perhaps in the majors. In a park better suited to a righthanded hitter than is the Stadium, Joe would be up around the thirty mark in homers right now.

Di Maggio has hit only seven of his twenty-three home runs in New York. His blow off George Coffman in the seventh inning yesterday was his fourth circuit drive in Detroit. Fenway Park in Boston, and League Park in Cleveland, though favorable to righthanded hitters, thus far have baffled Giuseppe's home run schemes.

Giuseppe has hit eight homers with men on bases. One came with the bases loaded, another with two on, six with one mate on. Here's how he has distributed the twenty-three:—New York, 7; St. Louis, 5; Detroit, 4; Washington, 3; Chicago, 3; Philadephia, 1.

Di Maggio Again On Hitting Streak

Special to the World-Telegram.

DETROIT, July 16.—Joe Di Maggio today was enjoying another hitting streak. . . . He has belted the ball safely in fifteen consecutive games. . . . He kept the skein going with two singles in that 13 to 6 passing of the Tigers. . . . Di Maggio got his hundredth hit in the first off Rowe and No. 101 off Jack Russell in the sixth. . . . Lou Gehrig got two doubles and made his hit total 102.

Thanks to Caster's pitching, after the A's had dropped fifteen straight, the Yankees picked up another game on the White Sox, who are seven and a half games behind. . . . Greenberg's homer, No. 20, left him three behind Di Maggio. . . . The Yanks now have an even balance in the West, 11 to 11. . . . The crowd of 22,500 hooted Powell all day, but Jake could not make a stronger comeback than a double. . . . In two days here the Ruppert Rifles drew 48,500. . . . This is the grandest week-day baseball city in the league for single games.

An Italian delegation brought a band and whooped things up for Joe, Tony and Frankie. . . . The Tigers refused to roll over and play dead, and kept trying all day. . . . In the third, they pulled a double steal, Greenberg and Walker doing the streak act. . . . Roxie Lawson has gone absolutely sour. . . . He had no more than Rowe. . . . Gill pitched two good innings, and then the Yanks got to him, too. . . . The Yanks close here today and go to Cleveland for three games.

DiMaggio Steals the Show

Yankee Sophomore's Hitting Overshadows Pitching of Youthful Bob Feller.

By EDWARD T. MURPHY.

CLEVELAND, July 19. The batting prowess of Joe DiMaggio, the Yankees' super-sophomore, today is more amazing than ever. In a dramatic setting here yesterday before a gathering of approximately 60,000, of whom 58,884 were cash customers, in the vast Municipal Stadium, Jolting Joe hammered out a double, a triple and a home run off the eighteen-year-old Bob Feller, heralded as the major league's new wizard of the mound, to bring, almost single handed, the Yanks' latest triumph in their flight toward another championship.

DiMaggio's home run, his twenty-fourth of the season, was exploded in the ninth inning with the bases filled, to break a 1 to tie. It brought defeat to Feller, the farmer boy out of Van Meter, Iowa, and victory to the more experienced Charley Ruffing, ace righthander of the Yankees' mound staff. It was Feller's fourth consecutive reversal of the season and Ruffing's twelfth success.

The crowd came to see Feller pit his youthful pitching skill against the batting power of the Yankees, heaviest hitting aggregation in the major leagues. They filed out of the great stadium talking, not of Feller's pitching skill, nor of the Yankees' tremendous batting power as a unit, but of DiMaggio's remarkable ability to hit a baseball. DiMaggio stole the show from Feller, from Lou Gehrig and from Bill Dickey.

Feller Not Fastest.

It was the first time this season the Yanks and Feller had clashed; in fact, the first time they had crossed each other's path since one day last season when the young pitcher was trotted out to the mound in the Yankee Stadium. In that game the Yankees blasted a nervous kid pitcher off the slab in one inning, scoring five runs off him. They didn't see enough of him that day to form an opinion of his skill.

In yesterday's game, however, Feller stood up before them for nine innings. He became the first pitcher to last that long against them since June 29, when Edgar Smith, a young lefthander of the Athletics, went the route, only to be beaten in the ninth inning just as Feller was.

After Feller had been beaten, members of the Yankees were asked to compare the farmer boy's skill against other pitchers. DiMaggio, hero of the New Yorkers' triumph, was the last of the Yankees to be interviewed when the athletes had returned to the hotel from the stadium.

More Speed Than Feller.

"There are several pitchers in the American League who have showed me more speed than Feller did today," said Joe. "Tommy Bridges of the Tigers for one. Jack Wilson of the Red Sox is another, but I wouldn't say Feller isn't swift. He is."

"What pitcher has the most speed?"

"I would say the pitcher who showed me more stuff than any other I hit against this year was Van Mungo," answered DiMaggio. "He did that in the all-star game. The curve he threw to strike me out was the best I have seen this year. He has more speed than any other pitcher I have hit against."

DiMaggio was asked what Feller had pitched to him in the ninth inning.

"It was a curve ball," he said. "The count was two and nothing against me and he got the strikes with fast balls. I expected him to pitch a ball wide of the plate. He threw a curve and I swung my bat. As soon as I hit the ball I knew it was on its way into the grand stand. It felt that good when I connected."

What did Lou Gehrig, who didn't make a hit off Feller, but drew two of the eight passes Bob issued, think of the youngster's pitching?

"He has speed, but there are several pitchers in the league who have a greater assortment of stuff," replied Lou. "Feller was difficult for me to hit because of the background in the stadium. I do not think he would be as effective in the Indians' home park or in other parks in the circuit as he is when pitching in the stadium. The lights and shadows there are a disadvantage to hitters."

Made 172 Pitches.

Red Rolfe agreed with Gehrig and so did Jake Powell.

"He didn't throw many curves during the game, only about five or six," said Powell. "The pitch he made that hit Gehrig was a curve and he struck out Bill Dickey with a hook."

All through the game Feller's lack of experience was against him, particularly when the Yankees had one or more runners on the base paths. Then his effectiveness was decreased because he couldn't take his full wind-up. In the entire game Feller, by actual count, made 172 pitches. He made his greatest number for a single inning in the third when he delivered thirty. In that inning DiMaggio bounced a double off Odell Hale's gloved hand, the hit scoring Frankie Crosetti, who had walked and annoyed Feller once he became a baserunner. In the ninth the youngster made twenty-seven pitches. Nine Yankees came to bat in that session.

Ruffing, who yielded eight hits, one more than Feller, did not burn up nearly as much energy as his rival. Red made only 121 pitches, fifty-two less than Bob. The Yankee pitcher clearly demonstrated the value of good control. He did not walk a batsman and the only run he allowed came in the seventh inning on three singles. The Indians didn't make an extra base hit off Red.

Mack Visions Joe Di Maggio As Super-Ruth

Has Excellent Chance to Set Home Run Mark, Says Veteran.

Special to the World-Telegram.

CLEVELAND. July 20.—"Joe Di Maggio, of the Yankees, is the greatest baseball player of the year and has an excellent chance not only to draw as well as Ruth did but even to beat the Babe's home-run record."

This surprising statement to the World-Telegram came today from Connie Mack, septuagenarian manager of the Athletics, who sees in Di Maggio one of the most amazing ball players in the history of the game.

"Di Maggio already is packing them in," Mack continued. "He has attracted a new type of fan to our games. He has made the Italian population baseball conscious.

"I know it is asking a lot of any hitter to beat Ruth's home-run record of sixty. To expect that of a righthanded batter seems too much. But I really do think it lies within the ability of Di Maggio to turn the trick, even if we do adopt a less lively ball for 1938.

"In my opinion, the Yankees are 100-to-1 shots to win the pennant," Mack went on. "I can't see anybody in this league to even impede the power of Joe McCarthy's team."

Athletics Hard Hit by Injuries.

Connie has been busy the last twenty-four hours trying to get a couple of infielders. Wayne Ambler, second baseman who joined the club this year from Duke University, suffered a jaw fracture in a head-on crash with Catcher Huffman in St. Louis on Sunday.

Skeeter Newsome, shortstop, is out for the year with a fractured skull. He was hit by a spitball pitched by a semi-pro in a recent exhibition game.

Mack's scouts are combing the higher minors for players. He figures he pulled a wise move in getting Jess Hill from the Senators. His greatest need, apparently, is a catcher. He said a first-rate backstop could do a lot with his young pitchers, especially Buck Ross, who is learning slowly it is very difficult to fog the ball by the hitters consistently.

Shifting to the National League, Mack said:—"I am convinced Bill Terry really is a great manager. He must have something to maneuver around and stick like a leech to the Cubs, who seem to be the strongest club in that circuit, with power and pitching."

Joe Di Maggio Still Dazzles Fans in West

Yankee Star Makes Great Throw—Hits 25th Homer.

By DANIEL
Staff Correspondent.

ST. LOUIS, July 21.—In the days of old when ball players chewed tobacco, Ty Cobb was king and Jack Murray used to fling them in from the outer reaches at the Polo Grounds, outfielders really could throw, we are told by the Old Guard time and again. But the old boys never saw Murray or any of those other storied autocrats of the arm excel the throws with which Joe Di Maggio and Baby Face Henrich made it possible for the Yankees to sweep their double-header with the Browns and stretch their lead over the unfaltering White Sox to six and a half games.

The Homeric heaves by Giuseppe and Baby Face featured the first game, which went to the world champions in ten innings on only five hits, 5 to 4. The nightcap was a sour and dreary affair that saw Blubber Malone stagger through nine heats to win by 9 to 6.

Henrich's throw saved the opener in the tenth, Di Maggio's great peg cut off grief in the seventh. It was preceded by an amazing shoestring catch and climaxed with a double play. When you consider that Giuseppe embellished his performance with his twenty-fifth home run and got two blows in the nightcap to stretch his streak of hitting games to twenty-one, it becomes apparent that none of the eulogies which Connie Mack and others have uttered lately about Joe have been extravagant.

Henrich Heads Off Knickerbocker From Right Field Wall.

In the seventh, with one out, Harry Davis walked. Sam West singled to third, and then came the hard-hitting Joe Vosmik. Giuseppe was playing him deep. Low and with the speed of a projectile came one of Monte Pearson's fast balls into center. Di Maggio charged in, made a grand catch not six inches from the grass and hurled the ball to Lou Gehrig to double West off first. It was the sort of play they have started to call a Di Maggio.

Having taken the lead on a hit by Gehrig in the tenth, the Yankees saw Frank Makosky's victory threatened as Beau Bell opened the home half with a single and dashed to third on a double by Billy Knickerbocker. Jim Bottomley, pinch hitter, was passed intentionally to fill the bases. Rogers Hornsby, hitting for Tom Carey, tapped in front of the plate and forced Bell.

Then came Ethan Allen, a third straight Minute Man. He sent Henrich back to the right field wall for his fly, and as Knickerbocker darted for the plate Baby Face doubled him with a throw which Jack Murray might have made—and then again, might not. Those knights of old, who had their pictures in cigarette boxes and their wooden effigies in front of cigar stores, never had to cope with that jackrabbit ball and play up against the fences.

With his twenty-fifth homer, Di Maggio retained his lead of four over Hank Greenberg.

As two were on when Giuseppe lifted a Hildebrand pitch into the left field bleacher in the fifth inning of the opener, Di Maggio had the satisfaction of winning the battle both on offense and defense.

It was Di Maggio's tenth homer with somebody on the bases, his sixth in St. Louis, as against only seven in the Stadium, and his fourteenth in a Western park. He has driven in eighty-six runs, of which forty-one have been accounted for by his circuit drives.

Since the New York club boasts a total of ninety-one homers, Di Maggio owns better than a quarter interest in the production.

Children Mob DiMaggio
At Playlot Appearance

Yankee Star Needs Police Escort in Sullivan Street

Joe DiMaggio, star outfielder of the New York Yankees, was almost mobbed by enthusiastic youngsters yesterday when he made a brief appearance at the Clarence Hubert playground of the Children's Aid Society, 219 Sullivan Street, to present autographed baseballs and bats to boys leading in the sports tournament at the playground.

DiMaggio, who was voted the most popular player in the American League in a poll of the Children's Aid Society Yankee Sandlot League, passed the afternoon at Jimmy Kelly's Restaurant, 181 Sullivan Street, autographing 500 baseballs presented by Kelly to the neighborhood children. It took four patrolmen to get DiMaggio to the playground a block away, where he presented bats and balls to Frank Lavenia, eleven years old, 125 Sullivan Street; Benny Urgola, eleven, 240 Sullivan Street, and Phil Pardini, eleven, 217 Thompson Street, the leaders in the junior division, and to Joey Urgola, eight, 240 Sullivan Street; Bob Barbieri, eight, 208 Sullivan Street, and Ralph Gentile, ten, 225 Sullivan Street, leaders in the midget division.

Afterwards DiMaggio was escorted through a crowd of 500 cheering children to Sullivan Street where several hundred more persons awaited him. He tossed the remainder of the 500 baseballs into the crowd who scrambled wildly for them. The last ball was thrown far down Sullivan Street and in the ensuing confusion DiMaggio made his escape.

Boosts Home Run Total
To 35, Highest in Career

Hopes to Raise Mark to 50 by End of Season—Dickey's Third in Two Days Gives Him 24 to Date.

Di Maggio Reaches New Home Run High for His Career.

In the clubhouse, a jubilant Yankee gang. Loaded with victories, gorged with laurels, they still become exuberant over every success, disconsolate over every setback.

Di Maggio held court along the back row, next to Lou Gehrig's locker. "That's a new high in home runs for my baseball career," smiled Jolting Joe.

"In 1935, with San Francisco, I hit thirty-four, which was tops for my experience in the Pacific Coast League. Last season I got twenty-nine with the Yankees. With forty-eight games to go, I want to hit about fifteen more. I ought to get fifty, which is a fair bunch of home runs for a righthanded hitter who has to work seventy-seven games in the Stadium."

With a double and single in addition to that fourmaster, Giuseppe poked his batting average to a gaudy .374 and breathed heavy defiance to Cecil Travis, Charley Gehringer and Gehrig in the struggle for the league batting championship.

Di Maggio's runs batted in total of 117 tops that of the Iron Horse by only one. With Gehrig owning twenty-eight homers, the rivalry between Lou and Joe is a most intriguing one.

Joe and the once mighty Ruth have much in common.

Illustration by Sam Berman.

Di Maggio Story Book Hero

By DAVIS J. WALSH

MAYBE it was a bad case of intellectual jaundice. Maybe the fellow had what the English lady called an "overhang," having been out the night before absorbing atmosphere and needled beer and having returned, betimes, well filled with both. And maybe it was only rare, good sense.

Anyhow, somebody who must have felt so low that he could have made an umbrella out of a thumb tack once said that "life is short and fame is fleeting," and while most of us, having spent a lifetime wooing mediocrity, just wouldn't know about that, it must mean something to Babe Ruth. Mr. Ruth, you know, is the gentleman with the double or spare bosom who is currently endeavoring to bear up bravely on the interest on his annuities and is thinking quite seriously of publishing his memoirs, entitled "How to Be Happy on $25,000-a-year."

Nevertheless, he still remembers with a pang the day they sent the vigilantes after him in Boston where he had been employed as vice president, in charge of right field. As blousy by that time as an old soubrette, he was doddering around in his athletic dotage and couldn't run fast enough to overtake a wheelbarrow. So they compromised. The Boston Bees agreed not to pay him, if he'd agree not to play any more baseball. It was a simple decision, after all. He just couldn't play any more baseball.

It was a melancholy moment, the end of a career so gaudy and fabulous as to impinge upon the thin, wavering borderline of fantasy.

"There he goes," everybody said, morosely. "There was only one Ruth and you'll never see his like again."

That was only two years ago. Today, "never" seems to be just another misleading word in the dictionary, for it is defined as meaning "not at any time." Today, we have the patriarchal Connie Mack, of Philadelphia, as conservative as a frock coat, bursting into paens of praise for Joe Di Maggio, whom he manages to see not only as another Babe Ruth, but possibly, and probably, as a better one.

And, if you think Mr. Mack is talking just to play a castenet solo on his bicuspids, give a glance to the gate receipts and the home run records for the first two-thirds of the current season.

"Di Maggio is the greatest ball player of the year," says Mr. Mack with pardonable gusto, "and has an excellent chance not only to draw as well as Ruth but even to beat the Babe's home run record. He is one of the most amazing players in the history of the game."

There will be quite a few who will disagree on some counts, some on all. There will be those who contend that Di Maggio is the athlete of the year, not accepting Don Budge, the tennis player who did so much to bring the Davis Cup back to America, or Joe Louis, the Lenox Avenue beige who won the heavyweight championship.

There will also be those who feel that he isn't even the ball player of the year, at least not with Mr. "Ducky" Medwick, the ingenuous young man from St. Louis, leading the National League in almost everything except fielder's choices.

But, if Di Maggio is at all close to Ruth, he is —per se, ad. lib. and automatically—a better man than the likes of Medwick. And, beyond a doubt, the old home run hitter and the new are a duo who have at once so little in common and so much.

"He (meaning Di Maggio) waits until the ball is right on top of him and then hits it a mile,"

said Gus Mancuso, Giant catcher, during the last World Series. He might have been talking about Ruth. It remains a never-ending source of technical amazement to this day, in fact, that Ruth—

Di Maggio makes 'em forget Ruth.

with that tremendous swing—was even able to get a fairly audible foul.

So, both know the virtue of extraordinary timing, although it's worth mentioning in this connection that Di Maggio fanned only fifteen times in the first 79 games this year. Both have great personal appeal, although Ruth's was such that he gave the people in the stands a definite place in his joys and sorrows, which were equally acute. Still, Di Maggio, in spite of a retiring disposition, stands out over the rest.

He doesn't need outward showmanship. It's something within. It's probably a trait that's not without what is known as annoyance-value.

There was the story early this year, for instance, that Di Maggio and the Yankees' other Italians from San Francisco, Tony Lazzeri and Frank Crosetti, were not exactly pals any more. If so, neither Lazzeri nor Crosetti would admit it and, as for "Di Mag," he just sits on the Yankee bench and apparently falls into a profound reverie, speaking only when spoken to and then mostly in the one-syllable manner.

His reserve with the rest of the club—and the rest of life—is probably his outstanding characteristic; that, and his appetite.

"He's always eating," those who travel with the club say. Otherwise, they know little about him personally, because the fellow seems to be a "loner," the ball player's word for the man who plays his off-hours strictly on his own. Di Maggio recently acted a small role in a movie. He had been spending his mornings at the studio for a week before the Yankee office or his fellow players ever heard about it. But his reticence hasn't kept him from being an idol of the fans. The Yankee "front office" admits that he is drawing even greater crowds than the mighty "Babe" did.

Joe's movie debut, however, resulted in one of his few bursts of garrulousness. When the news that he was making a film got around, "Di Mag" confirmed it and let slip sundry remarks on life, love and the world in general. "The smart thing I do is never fall in love," he said solemnly. "I just talk a good game with women."

The self-confidence that helped to make Joe a great ball player was reflected in his attitude as he watched a scene being played prior to his own screen attempt. One of the actors "blew up" in his lines 16 times. "I won't make as many errors as that guy," said Joe.

"The toughest part about this whole business of acting is being nonchalant," he said after he had tried his hand at the movie game. "It's easy to be nonchalant on a baseball diamond because then you know what you're supposed to do next."

Hollywood hype: the treatment of a movie matinee idol. Joe DiMaggio gets a touch of eye make-up from Kay Thompson, center, his co-star in the 1937 movie *Manhattan Merry-Go-Round*, and a little manicuring, daubing, spraying, and combing from other members of the cast. It was the only motion picture DiMaggio ever made.

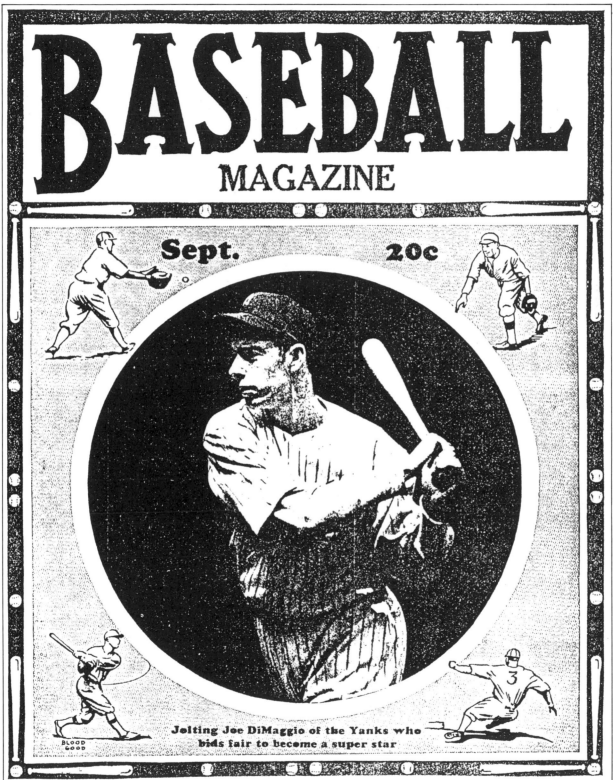

BASEBALL
MAGAZINE

Sept.　　　20c

Jolting Joe DiMaggio of the Yanks who
bids fair to become a super star

BLOOD
GOOD

I REMEMBER, I REMEMBER—F. Graham　　LEE GRISSOM—C. Bloodgood　　THEY'RE ON THE AIR—H. C. Burr
THE POWER OF THE YANKEE PUNCH—F. C. Lane　　DON'T SELL SEPTEMBER SHORT—L. H. Addington

Daniel Calls Di Maggio Outstanding of Season

Hitting and Fielding of Yankee Star Put Him at Top.

By DANIEL.

The Yankees are in. The Giants, back from their big adventure in the West with a lead of three and a half games, also are regarded as certainties. For the second consecutive year, and the fourth time in the history of the major league, New York today faced a world series on a five-cent fare, with the opener set for Yankee Stadium on Wednesday, October 6.

Now talk has shifted from teams to individuals. Who will pitch the classic opener? Joe McCarthy had two stars at his command, Lefty Gomez and Red Ruffing. It remained to be seen whether he would pick Gomez, even though the power of the Giants had gone to right-handed hitting. In the camp of the Giants there was a definite impression that if Bill Terry got into the series he would pass up Carl Hubbell, who won the first game last fall against Ruffing, and send Cliff Melton after the inaugural victory.

Fans debated over the Yankees and argued about the Giants, and conversation spread to the entire field of 1937 All-America candidates. Going over the list of availables, we are struck with the fact so many stars of 1936 had either faded out of the picture or had been forced to the sidelines with injuries.

Al Simmons, Kiki Cuyler, Goose Goslin and Tony Lazzeri had dropped from robust contention on the way out. Injuries had claimed Dizzy Dean, Schoolboy Rowe, Van Lingle Mungo, Monty Stratton, Monte Pearson, George Selkirk and Hank Leiber. Bob Feller, whose spring showing had promised a leap into All-America company in one season, had been hampered most of the year by a sore arm. Mickey Cochrane had suffered a fractured skull and retired from service as a catcher.

Di Maggio's Arm Best in Baseball.

For player-of-the-year distinction we have four outstanding candidates—Joe Di Maggio, of the Yankees; Charley Gehringer, Tigers; Joe Medwick, Cardinals, and Hank Greenberg, Tigers.

Di Maggio has hit .347, driven in 149 runs, slugged 44 home runs, and turned in plays which have astounded men who had watched major league baseball for a generation. His arm is regarded as the best in baseball.

Gehringer is sure to win the American League batting championship. His current record is .380. He is far and away the best second baseman of the year and may be the greatest in the history of his league.

Medwick's average is .376, his runs-batted-in total 148. Most of the season he hit better than .400. He already is being hailed as Paul Waner's successor to the batting championship of his circuit. Greenberg has hit .342, with 168 runs batted in.

Everything considered, Di Maggio deserves the high honor. He is the most valuable player on the most valuable team in his league. All this in his second season in the Big Show.

· DiMaggio ·

1937

The Sporting News

THE BASE BALL PAPER OF THE WORLD

VOLUME 104, NUMBER 8   ST. LOUIS, OCTOBER 7, 1937 ▲ ℵ   TEN CENTS THE COPY 15c in Canada

GIANTS AGAIN TEST YANKEE POWER IN WORLD SERIES

World's Series Facts

Meeting in the thirty - fourth World's Series between the pennant-winners of the American and National leagues and the fifth in which only New York teams have been participants, the Yankees and Giants are scheduled to play the first two games at the Yankee Stadium, October 6 and 7, then shifting to the Polo Grounds for three and returning to the American League park for the sixth and seventh games, if necessary. Games will be called at 1:30 EST.

Reserved seats sell for $16.50 for a set of three and box seats for $19.80 for a similar set of three, tickets being sold only on that basis. The seating capacity of the Polo Grounds is 60,000 and that of the Yankee Stadium, 75,000.

Players of the contesting teams share only in the receipts of the first four games and there will be no radio additions to the pool this season, for the first time in three years, because the broadcasts will be sustaining, without sponsors. After 15 per cent is deducted from the receipts, 60 per cent goes into the players' pool, the balance being divided between the clubs and their leagues.

Umpires — Emmett Ormsby and Steve Basil, American League; George Barr and William Stewart, National League.

ELIGIBLES OF NEW YORK CLUBS IN THIRTY-FOURTH BATTLE FOR GAME'S SUPREMACY

Lou Gehrig	John McCarthy	Burgess Whitehead	Dick Bartell	Mel Ott	Sam Leslie
Bill Dickey	Jack Saltzgaver	Don Heffner	Bob Rolfe	Frank Crosetti	Tony Lazzeri
Johnny Murphy	Irving Hadley	Kemp Wicker	Pat Malone	Frank Makosky	Ivy Paul Andrews
Clydell Castleman	Don Brennan	Tom Baker	Dick Coffman	Harry Gumbert	Al Smith
Gus Mancuso	Harry Danning	Ed Madjeski	Cliff Melton	John Ryan	Lou Chiozza

Charles Ruffing

Joe Glenn

Joe Moore

Monte Pearson

Arndt Jorgens

Jim Ripple

Carl Hubbell

Joe DiMaggio

Walter Berger

George Selkirk

Hal Schumacher

Hank Leiber

Jake Powell

Myril Hoag

Tom Henrich

Vernon Gomez

N. L. MUST SPIKE BIG GUNS OF A. L. TO WIN

RUBBER SERIES FOR GOTHAM, EACH LOOP CLUB HAVING TWO WINS

McCarthy Seems to Be Stronger Behind Plate and in Outfield, but in Other Departments Edge Goes to Terry

By EDGAR G. BRANDS
Editor of The Sporting News.

MORE is at stake in the thirty-fourth World's Series, being staged this week by the New York Yankees and Giants, than the world's championship, which goes to the winner of the fall classic, for it is the fifth time that the city's two major league clubs have met in the game's premier event of the year and this is the rubber series, the Nationals having won two and the Americans two. Moreover, the Ruppertmen will be fighting to become the first American League club to be credited with six world's titles.

By capturing the pennant, the Yankees gave New York supremacy for the number of times any American League city has been represented in the series, this being the ninth fall that a Gotham team has carried the hopes of the junior major in the championship battle. The Yanks tied the Philadelphia Athletics for pennants last season, with eight. They also went into a tie with the Boston Red Sox and Athletics for the most series triumphs last year, with five, and should they emerge the winners this fall, the New Yorkers will be the first American League club to be returned champions six times. They have lost three series, as have the A's, while the Red Sox have yet to taste a loss in the inter-league struggles.

In the previous all-New York World's Series, the Giants won the first two, in 1921 and 1922, and the Yankees were winners in 1923 and 1936. Thus, the team which is returned a winner in the present classic, will have the edge of one series in five.

This is the twelfth time a New York National League team has been entered in the modern World's Series. Others won four and lost seven.

Regardless of the result of this year's series, the American League will continue to hold a long lead over its rival circuit, having won 20 of them to 13 by the National. The present series may send to $19,000,000 or over, the total receipts collected during that time and should put the total of attendance at nearly 7,000,000. Receipts up to this year totaled $18,722,685 and the attendance 6,044,206.

First Inter-League Clash In 1903.

History of the World's Series usually dates back to 1903, when the Boston Americans won five games and Pittsburgh three. There was no meeting in 1904, but in 1905, John T. Brush originated the idea of making the clashes between the two major leagues annual affairs, under the auspices of the National Commission, and the rules drawn up at that time have been changed little since then.

The first inter-league series was staged in 1884, when Providence of the National League won three games from the Metropolitans of New York. The championship of 1885 was undecided, as the Chicago Nationals and St. Louis American Association club each won three games and one game was tied, without being played off. In 1886, the St. Louis A. A. club won four out of six from the Chicago Nationals; in 1887, the Detroit Nationals took ten out of 15 from St. Louis A. A.

The New York Nationals first appeared in the championship picture in 1888, when they won four out of six from the St. Louis A. A. club and followed up the next year with a six-to-three triumph over Brooklyn of the American Association. There was no decision in 1890, Brooklyn of the National and Louisville of the A. A. winning three each and one game ending in a tie.

This ended the original period of inter-league battles. National League teams participated in play-offs in 1892, 1894, 1895, 1896 and 1897, the last four being known as the Temple Cup series, New York and Cleveland, runners-up in the regular season defeating Baltimore, and Baltimore, in turn, winning from Cleveland and Boston in next two.

The Yankees enter this year's series as heavy favorites, because of the easy manner in which they won their pennant, and because of their victory over the Giants last fall. While the pre-series odds, favoring the American League entry, might be justified on the surface, there are many factors entering into a short series that could easily upset form and return the under-dogs the victors. On paper, the Giants do not appear to be so badly outclassed as many of the dopesters seem to think.

PAUL ANDREWS

IVY PAUL ANDREWS, righthanded pitcher, is one of the newcomers in the family of the Yankees. New, and yet old to the club, for the Yankees had him as far back as 1929, and again in 1931 and 1932. They sent him to the Red Sox in the MacFayden deal. Boston traded him to St. Louis and last January the Indians got him in a three-for-three trade with the Browns. After the retirement of John Broaca with a sore arm this Summer, McCarthy got Andrews from Cleveland. Paul was born at Dora, Ala., May 6, 1907. Broke into professional ball with Mobile, in 1928. Has a screwball and a knuckler. Learned the screwball from Alvin Crowder.

•

ANTHONY MICHAEL LAZZERI is another Yankee who finds himself in his sixth world series. He broke into the classic company in 1926, the year he joined the club. He found the Yankees in a slough after their 1921, 1922 and 1923 triumphs, and helped to lift them into a proud position. One of the greatest second basemen the game has developed. He was born in San Francisco in 1904 and at eighteen made his professional debut with Salt Lake. With amazing home run feats to his credit in the Coast League, Lazzeri came to the Yankees at an outlay of $55,000 and immediately proved that Huggins had landed a bargain.

TONY LAZZERI

JOSEPH PAUL DI MAGGIO, JR., center fielder, home run hitter, marvelous fielder and grand thrower, maker of runs and terror of pitchers, is one of the greatest picket men the Yankees have boasted. Second only to Ruth and in time may even eclipse some of the Babe's performances. A righthanded hitter, and that makes it tough for him as a home run slugger in the Stadium. In two years, Di Maggio has established himself as one of the most remarkable players of the generation. Born at Martinez, Cal., November 25, 1914. Came to the Yankees from San Francisco, where he set a Coast League record by hitting in 61 straight games. In the 1936 world series he batted .346 against Terry's pitchers.

•

GEORGE ALEXANDER SELKIRK is one of the Yankees who was born out of the country. He is a native of Canada, and traces back to Scotland. Born at Huntsville, Ontario, January 4, 1908. In 1935, when Joe McCarthy announced that Selkirk would succeed to the right field post and the famous No. 3 of Babe Ruth, there was some doubt as to the Canadian's ability to fill so tough an assignment. But Selkirk has come through with flying colors. Badly handicapped this season by an injury. Tore his right shoulder making a diving catch in Philadelphia, July 1st. Broke out as a high school star in Rochester. Spent many years in the minors after he had tried professional wrestling.

JOS. DiMAGGIO

GEO. SELKIRK

FRANK CROSETTI

FRANK PETER CROSETTI, shortstop extraordinary, is one of the many Native Sons from sunny California on the Yankees. Born in San Francisco, October 4, 1910. When he was a youngster the Crosetti's moved to a ranch at Los Gatos. There he learned to play ball. He broke in with San Francisco in 1928, and with the Yankees in 1932, the price paid for him being $75,000. He had plenty of competition for the shortstop job, but finally wore them all down and induced Mc-Carthy to give him the place permanently. In 1935, a knee injury threatened Frank's career, but a successful operation sent him back to work in 1936, a better ball player than ever before.

ROBERT ROLFE

ROBERT ABIAL ROLFE, one of the greatest third basemen baseball has developed in the last decade, is one of the original Yankees on the New York club. He traces back to the Rolfe who married Pocahontas. This particular Rolfe, who also is married and lives in Penacook, N. H., was born there October 17, 1908. He achieved considerable athletic distinction at Dartmouth College. Jeff Tesreau, once pitching star for the Giants, coached Red, and in 1931, sent him out a splendid prospect. Rolfe signed with the Yankee farm at Albany and came up with the Yankees in 1934, as a shortstop. McCarthy soon discovered that Red's true position was third. Red hit a clean .400 in the 1936 world series.

JOHN SALTZGAVER

JACK SALTZGAVER, utility infielder on the McCarthy machine, can play anywhere and is a handy man to have around. While he is called Jack, his true name is Otto. He was born at Croton, Iowa, in 1906, and after dabbling in baseball decided he wanted to make shoes. However, the shoe factory lost its attraction and in 1925, Saltzgaver jumped into league ball with Decatur. In 1931, the Yankees bought him from St. Paul for $42,500. He was slated to become Lazzeri's successor at second base. But Tony decided to hold on and Jack still is waiting for the job. In 1934, Jack played 84 games at third base, but when Rolfe moved over there, Saltzgaver was stopped again.

DON HEFFNER

DON HENRY HEFFNER, utility infielder, specializes in second base play. He is rated one of the best defensive men in the league. Heffner was born at Rouzerville, Pa., on February 8, 1911. Nothing much really happened to Don until this past Summer, when he got married. Then ambition got into his soul, and he made the most of every chance offered, especially when Lazzeri was injured on the last Western trip. Yankees got Heffner from Baltimore in 1934, and used him in 61 games, but sent him to Newark the following year. Was not available for the 1936 series as he was getting over the removal of his appendix.

TOM HENRICH

THOMAS HENRICH, new outfielder of the Yankees, is called Baby Face. Looks like a college sophomore growing out of his clothes rather than a budding star on a great ball club. Born at Massillon, Ohio, February 20, 1916. Has played hard ball for only five years. Was headed for a career as stenographer when he heard the call of the diamond. When Judge Landis last Spring declared Henrich a free agent, the Yankees dashed in with a bonus of $30,000 for signing and obtained a young man who, in a couple of years, is likely to be one of the established luminaries of the Big Show. Bats lefthanded, can run like a deer, has no present intention of ever getting married, he says, and lives with his folks at Massillon.

NEW YORK YANKEES 1937

JAKE POWELL

JACOB ALVIN POWELL, righthanded hitting outfielder, goes into the 1937 world series with a remarkable record of accomplishment in the 1936 classic against the Giants. Last year, his first with the Yankees, Powell did not excite much interest. He had won a place largely because of an accident to Hoag. But Jake stepped out and made himself the batting hero of the series, with ten hits for .455. Born in Montgomery County, Maryland, July 15, 1909. Broke in with Washington in 1930. In June, 1936, the Yankees traded Ben Chapman for Jake. There is one thing Powell does not like. And that is to be called Alvie.

FRANK MAKOSKY

FRANK MAKOSKY, relief pitcher of the Yankees, is a righthander. Born and reared in New Jersey, where he still makes his home, near Boonton. Makosky is twenty-four years of age and a big lad. This is his first season with the Yankees but he was in the Weiss chain-gang for some years before he finally got his chance with the Bronx Bombers at St. Petersburg last Spring. Makosky has a delivery which no other pitcher in the American League boasts the old fork ball, developed by a Yankee hurler of other days, Joe Bush. Frank is married, has a son, and by the other players is called Noisy. Because he isn't.

ARNDT JORGENS

ARNDT JORGENS, catcher, was born in Modum, Norway, on May 13, 1906. Thus Jorgens is the one Yankee who was born across the seas. Really Arndt is Jorgensen. He is rated one of the finest receivers in the majors. When Arndt was a year old the family moved to Chicago. He became a high school star and then went to Little Rock, in 1926. Oklahoma City next saw him. Miller Huggins spotted him there and in 1928, bought him. Jorgens saw service in Jersey City and Newark before coming to the Stadium to help Dickey in 1931. Jorgens did a lot of catching in 1932, when Dickey was out for his wallop at Carl Reynolds. Jorgens is married.

JOSEPH GLENN

JOE GLENN, catcher, was born at Dickson City, Pa., near Scranton, in 1909. He is Polish and his true name is Glenzynski. Glenn spent some time in the Yankee chain, and in 1933, made quite a stir with Minneapolis. In 1934, he came to the Yankees, but not until this year did Joe really establish himself. For a breaker boy from the coal mines, Glenn has done a remarkable job. He has a fine career in front of him and looks forward to the day when he will make Dickson City hang out a banner reading, "Welcome Home, Our Joe."

JOHN SCHULTE
Coach

JOHN SCHULTE, who used to be a great catcher with the Cubs and other teams in the National League, is one of the Yankee board of strategy. Art Fletcher, Earle Combs and Schulte are the coaches. Schulte catches in the bullpen, but he also pitches in batting practice. In May, 1930, Schulte began to do a little pitching for exercise. The Yankees began to win. They insisted that Schulte keep right on pitching, and that's the way it has been ever since. Lives in St. Louis, and is married.

Game 1 October 6 at Yankee Stadium

NY Giants	Pos	AB	R	H	RBI	PO	A	E
Moore	lf	4	0	2	0	4	0	0
Bartell	ss	4	0	1	0	1	2	1
Ott	3b	4	0	0	0	1	2	0
Leiber	cf	4	0	0	0	3	0	0
Ripple	rf	3	1	1	0	2	0	0
McCarthy	1b	4	0	1	0	8	0	0
Mancuso	c	3	0	0	1	4	1	0
Whitehead	2b	3	0	1	0	1	4	1
Hubbell	p	2	0	0	0	0	1	0
Gumbert	p	0	0	0	0	0	0	0
Coffman	p	0	0	0	0	0	0	0
a Berger		1	0	0	0	0	0	0
Smith	p	0	0	0	0	0	0	0
Totals		32	1	6	1	24	10	2

a Flied out for Whitehead in 8th.

Double—Whitehead. Home Run—Lazzeri.
Double Plays—Crosetti to Lazzeri to
Gehrig, Ott to Whitehead to McCarthy.
Left on Bases—Giants 5, Yankees 6.
Umpires—Ormsby (A), Barr (N), Basil (A),
Stewart (N) Attendance—60,573.
Time of Game—2:20.

NY G	000	010	000						1
NY Y	000	007	01 x						8

NY Yankees	Pos	AB	R	H	RBI	PO	A	E
Crosetti	ss	4	1	1	0	0	2	0
Rolfe	3b	4	1	1	1	0	0	0
DiMaggio	cf	4	0	2	2	4	0	0
Gehrig	1b	2	1	0	0	9	0	0
Dickey	c	3	1	1	1	3	0	0
Hoag	lf	4	1	0	0	5	0	0
Selkirk	rf	4	1	1	2	3	0	0
Lazzeri	2b	4	1	1	1	3	2	0
Gomez	p	2	1	0	0	0	2	0
Totals		31	8	7	7	27	6	0

Pitching	IP	H	R	ER	BB	SO
NY G						
Hubbell (L)	5⅓	6	7	4	3	3
Gumbert	*0	0	0	0	0	0
Coffman	1⅓	0	0	0	4	0
Smith	1	1	1	1	0	0
NY Y						
Gomez (W)	9	6	1	1	1	2

*Pitched to one batter in 6th.

1st Inning
Giants
1 Moore grounded to first.
  Bartell singled beyond third.
2 Ott popped to first.
3 Leiber fanned.
Yankees
  Crosetti walked.
1 Rolfe fanned.
  DiMaggio singled past third, advancing
  Crosetti to second.
2 Gehrig flied to center, runners hold.
3 Dickey flied to center.

2nd Inning
Giants
1 Ripple flied to left.
2 McCarthy lined to second.
3 Mancuso lined to right.
Yankees
1 Hoag grounded to short.
2 Selkirk grounded to second.
3 Lazzeri bounced to the pitcher.

3rd Inning
Giants
1 Whitehead grounded to short.
2 Hubbell flied to right.
3 Moore grounded back to the box.
Yankees
1 Gomez grounded to second.
2 Crosetti flied to left.
3 Rolfe flied to left.

4th Inning
Giants
1 Bartell flied to left.
2 Ott grounded to second.
3 Leiber popped to second.
Yankees
1 DiMaggio grounded to second.
2 Gehrig struck out.
3 Dickey grounded to first.

5th Inning
Giants
  Ripple singled to right.
  McCarthy singled past second. Ripple
  going to third.
1,2 Mancuso hit into a double play,
  Crosetti to Lazzeri to Gehrig scoring
  Ripple.
  Whitehead doubled down the right field
  line.
3 Hubbell grounded to first.
Yankees
1 Hoag popped to short.
2 Selkirk flied to right.
3 Lazzeri struck out.

6th Inning
Giants
  Moore singled through the box.
1 Bartell flied to right.
2 Ott fouled to the catcher.
3 Leiber flied to left.

6th Inning (continued)
Yankees
  Gomez walked.
  Crosetti singled to left sending Gomez
  to second.
    Gomez trapped off second on throw
    from Mancuso to Bartell but Bartell
    dropped the ball for an error with
    Gomez safely returning to second.
  Rolfe singled to left loading the
  bases.
  DiMaggio singled to left-center,
  scoring Gomez and Crosetti (Rolfe
  advanced to third and DiMaggio to
  second on the throw to the plate).
  Gehrig intentionally walked.
  Dickey beat out a single to second,
  scoring Rolfe (bases still loaded).
1 Hoag forced DiMaggio at the plate, Ott
  to Mancuso.
  Selkirk singled, scoring Gehrig and
  Dickey and sending Hoag to third.
  For the Giants—Gumbert pitching (A
  mixup as Coffman came in from the bullpen but Captain Mancuso gave Gumbert's
  name to plate umpire Ormsby.
  Lazzeri got on when Whitehead fumbled
  his grounder with Hoag scoring and
  Selkirk going to third.
  For the Giants—Coffman pitching
  Gomez walked filling the bases.
2 Crosetti flied to short left.
  Rolfe walked forcing in Selkirk.
3 DiMaggio flied to center.

7th Inning
Giants
1 Ripple flied to left.
2 McCarthy grounded out to the pitcher.
3 Mancuso flied to center.
Yankees
  Gehrig walked.
  Dickey walked.
1,2 Hoag hit into a double play, Ott to
  Whitehead to McCarthy, Gehrig to
  third.
3 Selkirk grounded to short.

8th Inning
Giants
1 Whitehead flied to center.
2 Berger pinch hit for Coffman and flied
  to center.
  Moore singled to left.
3 Bartell lined to left.
Yankees
  For the Giants—Smith pitching.
  Lazzeri homered into the lower left
  field stands.
1 Gomez lined to right.
2 Crosetti lined to third.
3 Rolfe flied to left.

9th Inning
Giants
1 Ott struck out.
2 Leiber lined to center.
  Ripple walked.
3 McCarthy grounded to first.

61,000 SEE YANKS CRUSH GIANTS, 8-1, IN SERIES OPENER

Hubbell Routed in Sixth as Victors Stage Seven-Run Uprising at Stadium

GOMEZ PITCHES SUPERBLY

Holds Rivals to Six Hits and Yields Only Tally in Fifth—Lazzeri Gets Homer

DIMAGGIO STAR IN RALLY

Singles With Bases Full to Start the Onslaught—Gate Receipts Are $234,256

By JOHN DREBINGER

Bursting out of the misty haze like an enveloping flame such as a man might encounter on locating that leak in a gas pipe with the aid of a match, the Yankee juggernaut exploded only once at the Stadium yesterday, but that once sufficed to blow the opening clash of the 1937 world series virtually into atoms.

It came with cyclonic effect in the sixth inning, toppled Carl Hubbell like a reed in a high gale, tossed Colonel Bill Terry and his Giants into such confusion that they even nominated a relief pitcher who was sitting awed and spellbound in the dugout, and went on to hurtle seven runs across the plate.

Two rounds later the venerable Anthony Lazzeri wafted a towering home run into the stands and the sum total of all this was a smashing victory for Marse Joe McCarthy's amazing American League champions behind their own left-hander, Vernon Gomez. The final score, 8 to 1, left a crowd of 61,000 almost as stunned and bewildered by it all as were the crestfallen National Leaguers.

Clings Tenaciously to Lead

For five innings, Hubbell, ace pitcher of his circuit, strove heroically to repeat his notable triumph in the series opener of 1936. In four of these rounds, in fact, the work of the famous screwball maestro was absolutely flawless as he clung tenaciously to a one-run margin he had gained over his left-handed adversary.

But in this, perhaps, he made a mistake, for it is a matter of scientific knowledge that at times it is extremely dangerous to keep a highly volatile explosive too tightly bottled up. Something simply had to give and in the sixth it was ol' Hub himself.

Confronted by the inviting set-up of the bases full and nobody out but a few less hardy Giant rooters who doubtless already felt what was coming, Joe DiMaggio, he whom they call the wonder player of his time, crashed a single to center field to start the avalanche of Yankee runs pouring across the plate.

More Shells Are Fired

Presently the bases again filled. In fact, those Yankees seemed to keep the bases filled for an almost interminable period while Bill Dickey and George Selkirk fired more shells into the gaunt frame of ol' Hub, who was unmistakably going down with all his comrades on board.

Finally, with the seven big tallies tucked away, the Yankee storm subsided, leaving only Gomez to move serenely on to his fourth victory in world series warfare.

The singular Castillian, who once made the classic remark that he would rather be lucky than good, now reveled in the picture of combining both of these rare qualities so vital to success in any venture.

For not only had fortune smiled on him to the extent of having runs poured in for him in a carload lot, but he was undeniably superb as well. He pitched smoothly and easily, held the straining National League standard bearers to six blows, only two of which did any damage at all, and all in all was a far cry from the Gomez who stumbled badly to two victories last Fall behind a similar withering barrage.

Open Gaps in Stands

As had been half feared, the capacity crowd which was expected to total 70,000 did not materialize. There were a few open gaps in the lower end of the reserved sections and, what was even more surprising, the unreserved upper tier revealed vacant spaces as well.

The paid attendance totaled 60,573, more than 6,000 short of the all-time record set last year, and the receipts were $234,256.

Following a night of heavy rains which for a time threatened to postpone the whole program a day, a clear but intensely humid morning greeted the early arrivals. It assured a ball game, even if the sun remained behind a haze that hung over the arena like a smoke screen throughout the sultry afternoon.

The bulk of the crowd, in fact, was rather tardy in putting in an appearance. It was, too, for the most part, a typical New York gathering, a trifle blasé because this happened to be the city's second successive so-called nickel world series and given to taking only a mild interest in the usual inaugural ceremonies.

Schacht Amuses Crowd

It lent a half attentive ear to the popular airs of Captain Sutherland's Seventh Regiment Band, laughed good-naturedly at the antics of baseball's No. 1 comedian, Al Schacht; respectively stood at attention while the band blared forth the strains of the "Star-Spangled Banner" and then settled quickly down to the more serious business at hand.

In the crowd and, indeed, very much just part of the crowd, sat former President Herbert Hoover. Some distance off sat Postmaster General Farley, representing President Roosevelt as well as himself; but no sooner had our energetic little Mayor La Guardia tossed out the first ball than the entire setting receded like a huge fade out in the movies.

Game 2 October 7 at Yankee Stadium

NY Giants	Pos	AB	R	H	RBI	PO	A	E
Moore	lf	5	0	2	0	2	0	0
Bartell	ss	4	1	2	0	3	5	0
Ott	3b	4	0	1	1	2	1	0
Ripple	rf	4	0	0	0	0	0	0
McCarthy	1b	4	0	0	0	8	1	0
Chiozza	cf	4	0	1	0	3	0	0
Mancuso	c	4	0	0	0	4	0	0
Whitehead	2b	3	0	1	0	2	3	0
Melton	p	1	0	0	0	0	0	0
Gumbert	p	0	0	0	0	0	0	0
Coffman	p	1	0	0	0	0	1	0
a Leslie		0	0	0	0	0	0	0
Totals		34	1	7	1	24	11	0

a Walked for Coffman in 9th.

Doubles—Bartell, Crosetti, Moore, Ruffing, Selkirk Double Play—Bartell to Whitehead to McCarthy
Left on Bases—Giants 9, Yankees 6
Umpires—Barr, Basil, Stewart, Ormsby
Attendance—57,675. Time of Game—2:11.

1st Inning
Giants
1 Moore struck out.
 Bartell doubled to left.
 Ott singled to right, scoring Bartell
 (Ott took second on the throw to plate)
2 Ripple fanned.
3 McCarthy fanned.
Yankees
1 Crosetti fanned.
2 Rolfe grounded to short.
3 DiMaggio popped to short.

2nd Inning
Giants
1 Chiozza grounded to third.
2 Mancuso grounded to short.
3 Whitehead flied to right.
Yankees
1 Gehrig grounded to short.
2 Dickey flied to center.
3 Hoag grounded to short.

3rd Inning
Giants
1 Melton grounded to third.
2 Moore grounded to short.
 Bartell singled past third.
3 Ott flied to left.
Yankees
1 Selkirk popped to third.
 Lazzeri singled.
2,3 Ruffing hit into a double play.
 Bartell to Whitehead to McCarthy.

4th Inning
Giants
1 Ripple popped to short.
2 McCarthy grounded to the pitcher.
3 Chiozza grounded to second.
Yankees
1 Crosetti popped to Bartell in short left.
2 Rolfe grounded to first.
 DiMaggio singled to center.
 Gehrig walked.
3 Dickey took a called third strike.

5th Inning
Giants
1 Mancuso grounded to short.
2 Whitehead grounded to second.
 Melton walked.
 Moore singled to right, Melton to second.
3 Bartell struck out.
Yankees
 Hoag doubled to right.
 Selkirk singled to right, scoring Hoag.
 Lazzeri singled to left, Selkirk to second.
 Ruffing singled past third, scoring Selkirk and moving Lazzeri to second.
 For the Giants—Gumbert pitching.
1 Crosetti flied to left.
2 Rolfe forced Ruffing, Whitehead to Bartell with Lazzeri moving to third.
3 DiMaggio struck out.

NY G		1 0 0	0 0 0	0 0 0				1
NY Y		0 0 0	0 2 4	2 0 x				8

NY Yankees	Pos	AB	R	H	RBI	PO	A	E
Crosetti	ss	5	0	0	0	1	4	0
Rolfe	3b	5	0	0	0	0	3	0
DiMaggio	cf	4	1	2	0	4	0	0
Gehrig	1b	2	1	1	0	11	0	0
Dickey	c	4	1	2	1	8	0	0
Hoag	lf	4	2	1	1	2	0	0
Selkirk	rf	4	2	2	3	1	0	0
Lazzeri	2b	3	1	2	0	0	2	0
Ruffing	p	4	0	2	3	0	2	0
Totals		35	8	12	8	27	11	0

Pitching	IP	H	R	ER	BB	SO
NY G						
Melton (L)	*4	6	2	2	1	2
Gumbert	1⅓	4	4	4	1	1
Coffmann	2⅓	2	2	2	1	1
NY Y						
Ruffing (W)	9	7	1	1	3	8

*Faced 4 men in 5th.

6th Inning
Giants
1 Ott flied to center.
2 Ripple flied to center.
3 McCarthy flied to center.
Yankees
 Gehrig singled on a roller to third.
 Dickey singled to center, Gehrig stops at second.
1 Hoag forced Gehrig at third on an attempted sacrifice, McCarthy to Ott
 Selkirk doubled off McCarthy's leg, scoring Dickey and Hoag.
 Lazzeri intentionally walked.
 Ruffing doubled to left, scoring Selkirk and Lazzeri.
 For the Giants—Coffman pitching.
2 Crosetti flied to center moving Ruffing to third after the catch.
3 Rolfe grounded to second.

7th Inning
Giants
1 Chiozza struck out.
2 Mancuso grounded to the pitcher.
 Whitehead walked.
3 Coffman called out on strikes.
Yankees
 DiMaggio singled to left.
 Gehrig walked.
 Dickey singled over second, scoring DiMaggio and sending Gehrig to third.
1 Hoag flied to center, scoring Gehrig.
2 Selkirk forced Dickey, Bartell to Whitehead.
3 Lazzeri grounded to third.

8th Inning
Giants
 Moore doubled to left.
1 Bartell fanned, foul tipping his third strike to Dickey.
2 Ott flied to center.
3 Ripple grounded to short.
Yankees
1 Ruffing flied to left.
2 Crosetti called out on strikes.
3 Rolfe grounded to the pitcher.

9th Inning
Giants
1 McCarthy flied to left.
 Chiozza singled to left.
2 Mancuso called out on strikes.
 Whitehead singled to center moving Chiozza to second.
 Leslie pinch hit for Coffman and walked loading the bases.
3 Moore grounded to third.

Game 3 October 8 at Polo Grounds

NY Yankees	Pos	AB	R	H	RBI	PO	A	E
Crosetti	ss	4	0	0	0	1	7	0
Rolfe	3b	4	1	2	0	1	1	0
DiMaggio	cf	5	0	1	0	5	0	0
Gehrig	1b	5	1	1	1	12	0	0
Dickey	c	5	1	1	1	5	0	0
Selkirk	rf	4	2	1	1	0	0	0
Hoag	lf	4	0	2	0	0	0	0
Lazzeri	2b	2	0	1	1	3	3	0
Pearson	p	3	0	0	0	0	0	0
Murphy	p	0	0	0	0	0	0	0
Totals		36	5	9	4	27	11	0

Pitching	IP	H	R	ER	BB	SO
NY Y						
Pearson (W)	8⅔	5	1	1	2	4
Murphy (SV)	⅓	0	0	0	0	0
NY G						
Schumacher (L)	6	9	5	4	4	3
Melton	2	0	0	0	2	0
Brennan	1	0	0	0	0	0

NY Y	012	110	000				5
NY G	000	000	100				1

NY Giants	Pos	AB	R	H	RBI	PO	A	E
Moore	lf	4	0	1	0	2	0	0
Bartell	ss	4	0	0	0	3	2	0
Ott	3b	4	0	1	0	1	3	0
Ripple	rf	4	1	1	0	5	0	0
McCarthy	1b	3	0	1	1	7	0	2
Chiozza	cf	3	0	1	0	3	0	1
Danning	c	4	0	0	0	5	0	0
Whitehead	2b	3	0	0	0	1	4	0
Schumacher	p	1	0	0	0	0	1	0
a Berger		1	0	0	0	0	0	0
Melton	p	0	0	0	0	0	0	1
b Leslie		1	0	0	0	0	0	0
Brennan	p	0	0	0	0	0	0	0
Totals		32	1	5	1	27	10	4

a Struck out for Schumacher in 6th.
b Fouled out for Melton in 8th.

Doubles—McCarthy, Rolfe 2. Triple—Dickey Sacrifice Hit—Hoag. Double Play—Whitehead to Bartell to McCarthy. Left on Bases—Yankees 11, Giants 6. Wild Pitch—Schumacher. Umpires—Basil, Stewart, Ormsby, Barr. Attendance—37,385. Time of Game—2:07

1st Inning
Yankees
Crosetti walked
1 Rolfe lined to right
   Crosetti to third on wild pitch
2 DiMaggio struck out
3 Gehrig grounded to second
Giants
1 Moore grounded to short
2 Bartell flied to center
3 Ott flied to center

2nd Inning
Yankees
1 Dickey lined to center
   Selkirk walked
   Hoag singled to left. Selkirk to second
   Lazzeri singled to center, scoring
   Selkirk and sending Hoag to third
   Pearson walked loading the bases
2 Crosetti forced Hoag at the plate, Ott
   to Danning
3 Rolfe fouled to the catcher
Giants
1 Ripple grounded to first
2 McCarthy flew out to center
3 Chiozza fouled to third

3rd Inning
Yankees
1 DiMaggio flied to center
   Gehrig singled off right field fence
   and took second on Ripple's throw to
   first
   Dickey tripled off the left field fence,
   scoring Gehrig
   Selkirk singled to right, scoring Dickey
2 Hoag got a sacrifice hit, Ott to
   McCarthy
   Lazzeri intentionally passed
3 Pearson called out on strikes
Giants
1 Danning popped to second
2 Whitehead fouled to first
3 Schumacher looked at a third strike

4th Inning
Yankees
1 Crosetti grounded to third
   Rolfe doubled to right
   DiMaggio got an infield single, Rolfe
   going to third
2 Gehrig flied to left scoring Rolfe
3 Dickey forced DiMaggio, Whitehead to
   Bartell
Giants
1 Moore grounded to short
2 Bartell grounded to second
3 Ott struck out

5th Inning
Yankees
   McCarthy fumbled Selkirk's grounder
   then threw wild to Schumacher covering
   first, Selkirk on second (2 errors
   charged to McCarthy)
   Hoag singled to center where Chiozza
   fumbled allowing Selkirk to score.
1 Lazzeri fanned
2 Pearson grounded to the pitcher
3 Crosetti flew out to left

5th Inning (continued)
Giants
1 Ripple grounded to short
2 McCarthy grounded to second
   Chiozza singled on a bunt down the
   first base line
3 Danning forced Chiozza, Crosetti to
   Lazzeri

6th Inning
Yankees
   Rolfe blooped a double to short right
1 DiMaggio grounded to short
2 Gehrig popped to second
3 Dickey grounded to second
Giants
1 Whitehead grounded to second
2 Berger, pinch-hitting for Schumacher,
   struck out
   Moore singled to left
3 Bartell called out on strikes

7th Inning
Yankees
   For the Giants—Melton pitching
1 Selkirk flied to center
   Melton threw wildly to first on Hoag's
   hit to the box (Hoag reached second)
   Lazzeri intentionally walked
2,3 Pearson hit into a double play,
   Whitehead to Bartell to McCarthy
Giants
1 Ott popped to second
   Ripple singled to right
   McCarthy doubled off the right field
   fence, scoring Ripple
2 Chiozza grounded to second, advancing
   McCarthy to third
3 Danning grounded to short

8th Inning
Yankees
1 Crosetti lined to center
   Rolfe walked
2 DiMaggio flied to right
3 Gehrig flied to right
Giants
1 Whitehead grounded to third
2 Leslie, pinch-hitting for Melton, fouled
   out to Dickey
3 Moore grounded to short

9th Inning
Yankees
   For the Giants—Brennan pitching
1 Dickey flied to right
2 Selkirk fouled to third
3 Hoag lined to short
Giants
1 Bartell flied to center.
   Ott singled to left.
2 Ripple forced Ott, Crosetti unassisted.
   McCarthy walked.
   Chiozza walked loading the bases.
   For the Yankees—Murphy pitching.
3 Danning flied to center.

Game 4 October 9 at Polo Grounds

NY Yankees	Pos	AB	R	H	RBI	PO	A	E
Crosetti	ss	4	1	0	0	2	3	0
Rolfe	3b	4	1	2	0	2	2	0
DiMaggio	cf	4	0	0	1	2	0	0
Gehrig	1b	4	1	1	1	10	0	0
Dickey	c	4	0	0	0	3	1	0
Hoag	lf	4	0	2	0	3	0	0
Selkirk	rf	3	0	0	0	0	0	0
Lazzeri	2b	3	0	1	0	4	4	0
Hadley	p	0	0	0	0	0	1	0
Andrews	p	2	0	0	0	0	1	0
a Powell		1	0	0	0	0	0	0
Wicker	p	0	0	0	0	0	0	0
Totals		33	4	6	2	24	11	0

a Struck out for Andrews in 8th

Double—Danning. Triple—Rolfe.
Home Run—Gehrig. Stolen Base—Whitehead. Double Plays—Whitehead to Bartell. Hubbell to Whitehead to McCarthy. Left on Bases—Yankees 4, Giants 8. Umpires—Stewart, Ormsby, Barr, Basil. Attendance—44, 293. Time of Game—1:57

NY Y	101	000	001				3
NY G	060	000	10x				7

NY Giants	Pos	AB	R	H	RBI	PO	A	E
Moore	lf	5	1	1	1	1	0	0
Bartell	ss	5	1	1	1	3	2	2
Ott	3b	5	0	1	0	1	0	1
Ripple	rf	2	0	1	0	3	0	0
Leiber	cf	3	2	2	2	3	0	0
McCarthy	1b	4	1	2	0	9	0	0
Danning	c	4	0	3	2	4	0	0
Whitehead	2b	3	1	1	0	3	5	0
Hubbell	p	4	1	0	1	0	2	0
Totals		35	7	12	7	27	9	3

Pitching	IP	H	R	ER	BB	SO
NY Y						
Hadley (L)	1⅓	6	5	5	0	0
Andrews	5⅔	6	2	2	4	1
Wicker	1	0	0	0	0	0
NY G						
Hubbell (W)	9	6	3	2	1	4

1st Inning
Yankees
1 Crosetti popped to second
   Rolfe tripled past Leiber who tried and
   missed a shoestring catch
2 DiMaggio flied deep to right, Rolfe
   scoring after the catch
3 Gehrig fouled to first
Giants
1 Moore flied to left
2 Bartell popped to Dickey in front of
   plate
   Ott singled to right
3 Ripple grounded to short

2nd Inning
Yankees
1 Dickey flied to center
   Hoag singled through the box
   Selkirk walked
2,3 Lazzeri lined into a double play,
   Whitehead to Bartell
Giants
   Leiber singled to center
   McCarthy singled to right, Leiber
   stopping at second
   Danning singled to right, scoring Leiber
   with McCarthy going to third
1 Whitehead's grounder hit Danning for an
   automatic out (Whitehead credited with
   single)
   Hubbell grounded to Lazzeri and was safe
   when Lazzeri threw to the plate to get
   McCarthy but throw was wide and
   McCarthy scored (Whitehead to second)
   Moore singled to center, scoring White-
   head and moving Hubbell to second
   For the Yankees—Andrews pitching
   Bartell singled to center, scoring
   Hubbell and moving Moore to second
2 Ott struck out
   Ripple walked loading the bases
   Leiber hit his second single of the
   inning, scoring Moore and Bartell with
   Ripple going to third
3 McCarthy grounded to Lazzeri

3rd Inning
Yankees
   Andrews was safe on Bartell's throwing
   error to first
1 Crosetti forced Andrews, Whitehead to
   Bartell but Bartell trying for the DP
   threw wildly to first Crosetti going
   to second
2 Rolfe lined to left
   DiMaggio reached second and Crosetti
   scored when Ott threw wildly to first
3 Gehrig grounded to first
Giants
   Danning beat out a hit down the third
   base line
1 Whitehead forced Danning, Lazzeri to
   Crosetti
   Whitehead stole second.
2 Hubbell grounded to Andrews, Whitehead
   to third
3 Moore popped to short

4th Inning
Yankees
1 Dickey lined to right
2 Hoag grounded to second
3 Selkirk flied to center
Giants
1 Bartell lined to center
2 Ott grounded to first
   Ripple walked
3 Leiber flew out to center

5th Inning
Yankees
   Lazzeri singled over second
1 Andrews struck out
2,3 Crosetti hit into a double play,
   Hubbell to Whitehead to McCarthy
Giants
1 McCarthy grounded to second
2 Danning grounded to third
3 Whitehead grounded to short

6th Inning
Yankees
   Rolfe singled to right
1 DiMaggio forced Rolfe, Whitehead to
   Bartell
2 Gehrig fanned
3 Dickey popped to first
Giants
1 Hubbell grounded to short
2 Moore grounded to third
3 Bartell lined to left

7th Inning
Yankees
1 Hoag fanned
2 Selkirk grounded to first
3 Lazzeri grounded to short
Giants
1 Ott fouled to the catcher
   Ripple singled past short
2 Ripple caught stealing, Dickey to
   Lazzeri
   Leiber walked
   McCarthy singled over second, Leiber
   moved to second
   Danning doubled to right, scoring Leiber
   and sending McCarthy to third
   Whitehead intentionally walked filling
   the bases
3 Hubbell lined to left

8th Inning
Yankees
1 Powell, pinch-hitting for Andrews, fanned
2 Crosetti grounded to short
3 Rolfe grounded to the pitcher
Giants
   For the Yankees—Wicker pitching.
1 Moore grounded to second
2 Bartell popped to second
3 Ott popped to second

9th Inning
Yankees
1 DiMaggio fouled to third
   Gehrig homered into the right field
   stands.
2 Dickey flied to right
   Hoag singled past second
3 Selkirk flied to center.

Game 5 October 10 at Polo Grounds

NY Yankees	Pos	AB	R	H	RBI	PO	A	E
Crosetti	ss	4	0	0	0	2	1	0
Rolfe	3b	3	0	1	0	1	0	0
DiMaggio	cf	5	1	1	1	3	0	0
Gehrig	1b	4	0	2	1	8	1	0
Dickey	c	3	0	0	0	7	0	0
Hoag	lf	4	1	1	1	1	0	0
Selkirk	rf	4	0	1	0	3	0	0
Lazzeri	2b	3	1	1	0	1	5	0
Gomez	p	4	1	1	1	1	1	0
Totals		34	4	8	4	27	8	0

Pitching	IP	H	R	ER	BB	SO
NY Y						
Gomez (W)	9	10	2	2	1	6
NY G						
Melton (L)	5	6	4	4	3	5
Smith	2	1	0	0	0	1
Brennan	2	1	0	0	1	1

		NY Y	NY G					
NY Y	0 1 1	0 2 0	0 0 0	4				
NY G	0 0 2	0 0 0	0 0 0	2				

NY Giants	Pos	AB	R	H	RBI	PO	A	E
Moore	lf	5	0	3	0	4	0	0
Bartell	ss	4	1	1	0	3	0	0
Ott	3b	3	1	1	2	0	3	0
Ripple	rf	4	0	2	0	1	0	0
Leiber	cf	4	0	2	0	1	0	0
McCarthy	1b	4	0	0	0	6	0	0
Danning	c	4	0	0	0	11	1	0
Whitehead	2b	4	0	1	0	1	1	0
Melton	p	1	0	0	0	0	0	0
a Ryan		1	0	0	0	0	0	0
Smith	p	0	0	0	0	0	1	0
b Mancuso		1	0	0	0	0	0	0
Brennan	p	0	0	0	0	0	0	0
c Berger		1	0	0	0	0	0	0
Totals		36	2	10	2	27	6	0

a Struck out for Melton in 5th.
b Flied out for Smith in 7th.
c Grounded out for Brennan in 9th.

Doubles—Gehrig, Whitehead.
Triples—Gehrig, Lazzeri.
Home Runs—DiMaggio, Hoag, Ott.
Sacrifice Hit—Rolfe. Double Play—Gehrig
(unassisted). Left on Bases—Yankees 9,
Giants 8. Wild Pitch—Melton.
Hit by Pitcher—Lazzeri (by Smith).
Umpires—Ormsby, Barr, Basil, Stewart.
Attendance—38,216. Time of Game—2:06.

1st Inning
Yankees
1 Crosetti flied deep to Moore.
   Rolfe singled to left.
2 DiMaggio popped to Whitehead in short
   center field.
   Rolfe took second on a wild pitch.
   Gehrig walked.
3 Dickey struck out.
Giants
   Moore singled to left.
1 Bartell flied to left.
2 Ott struck out.
   Ripple singled to right-center, moving
   Moore to third.
3 Leiber fouled to first.

2nd Inning
Yankees
   Hoag homered into the right field
   bleachers.
1 Selkirk grounded to second.
2 Lazzeri called out on strikes.
3 Gomez also took a called third strike.
Giants
1 McCarthy grounded to second.
2 Danning struck out.
   Whitehead doubled into right.
3 Melton struck out.

3rd Inning
Yankees
1 Crosetti grounded to third.
2 Rolfe called out on strikes.
   DiMaggio homered over the left field
   stand.
3 Gehrig struck out.
Giants
1 Moore popped to short.
   Bartell singled to left.
   Ott hit a two-run homer into the upper
   deck of the right field stands.
2 Ripple popped to short.
3 Leiber lined to center.

4th Inning
Yankees
1 Dickey fouled to the catcher.
2 Hoag flied to deep left.
3 Selkirk fouled to the catcher.
Giants
1 McCarthy fanned.
2 Danning fouled to the catcher.
3 Whitehead lined to right.

5th Inning
Yankees
   Lazzeri tripled to center.
   Gomez singled off Whitehead's glove,
   scoring Lazzeri.
1 Crosetti flied to short right.
   Rolfe walked.
2 DiMaggio popped to the catcher.
   Gehrig doubled to center, scoring
   Gomez, Rolfe advancing to third.
   Dickey walked, loading the bases.
3 Hoag fouled to the catcher.

5th Inning (continued)
Giants
1 Ryan, batting for Melton, struck out.
   Moore singled to center.
2 Bartell flied to center.
3 Ott grounded to second.

6th Inning
Yankees
   For the Giants—Smith pitching.
1 Selkirk grounded to first.
   Lazzeri was hit by a pitched ball.
2 Gomez attempting to sacrifice forced
   Lazzeri, Ott to Bartell.
3 Crosetti bounced back to the pitcher.
Giants
   Ripple singled to left.
   Leiber singled to right-center, Ripple
   going to second.
1 McCarthy attempting to sacrifice
   forced Ripple at third, Gomez to
   Rolfe.
2 Danning struck out.
3 Whitehead grounded out to second.

7th Inning
Yankees
1 Rolfe grounded to third.
2 DiMaggio struck out.
   Gehrig tripled (Ripple fell going for
   his hit).
3 Dickey flied to center.
Giants
1 Mancuso, pinch-hitting for Smith, flied
   to right.
   Moore singled to left (his 9th hit of
   a 5 game series tying the record held
   by 4 others).
2 Bartell popped to Crosetti who
   deliberately dropped the ball and
   threw to Lazzeri forcing Moore.
   Ott walked.
3 Ripple grounded to second.

8th Inning
Yankees
   For the Giants—Brennan pitching.
1 Hoag flew deep to Moore at the left
   center field wall.
   Selkirk singled to left.
2 Lazzeri flied to Bartell in short left.
3 Gomez flied to left.
Giants
   Leiber singled to left.
1 McCarthy flied to right.
2,3 Danning lined to Gehrig who stepped
   on first doubling up Leiber.

9th Inning
Yankees
   Crosetti walked.
1 Rolfe sacrificed, Danning to McCarthy.
2 DiMaggio popped to short.
3 Gehrig struck out.
Giants
1 Whitehead lined to center.
2 Berger batted for Brennan and grounded
   to second.
3 Moore grounded out, Gehrig to Gomez.

38,216 Paid $167,747
At Fifth Series Game

Final Standing of the Teams

	W.	L.	P.C.
Yankees	4	1	.800
Giants	1	4	.200

Fifth Game Statistics
Attendance (paid) 38,216
Gross receipts $167,747.00
Commissioner's Share 25,162.05
Clubs' share 71,292.47
Leagues' share 71,292.48

Total for Five Games
Attendance (paid) 238,142
Gross receipts $985,934.00
Commissioner's Share 147,899.10
Players' share 417,305.97
Clubs' share 210,394.46
Leagues' share 210,394.46

Players' share based on receipts of
first four games only.

The official paid attendance for the
fifth and final game of the 1937
world series at the Polo Grounds fell
far below the figures for the fifth contest last year at the Yankee Stadium,
where 50,024 persons paid $202,368.
The six-game series last year drew
302,924 paid admissions and the
gross receipts amounted to
$1,204,399.

CHEERS DIMAGGIO HOMER

Father Rewarded for Trip From
Coast by Son's Big Blow

Papa DiMaggio, who came all the
way from San Francisco to "see
Joe hit some home runs," finally
was rewarded when his big son
catapulted a drive a few feet inside
the left field foul line in the third
inning of yesterday's finale.

It was a terrific shot that, had it
not connected with a flagpole atop
the stands, would have traveled
perhaps 500 feet before hitting anything, and others besides the proud
parent cheered.

"I hit a curve ball off Melton,"
said Joe, grinning happily. "At the
Stadium that one would have
landed in the upper tier. I could
tell the way it felt when I hit it."

The ball would have landed where
Joe claimed, no doubt, but it also
might have been foul. He hit it
with a tremendous pull and, traveling the greater distance, it might
have hooked out of fair territory.

YANKS, WITH GOMEZ, TOP THE GIANTS, 4-2, AND CAPTURE SERIES

Hurler Gains Second Victory to Make Margin 4-1 as the McCarthymen Keep Laurels

LAZZERI STARTS BIG DRIVE

Triples in the Fifth, Lefty Singles, Gehrig Doubles to Break 2-All Tie

THREE SMASH HOME RUNS

Hoag and DiMaggio Connect— Ott Hits One for Losers With Bartell Aboard

By JOHN DREBINGER

With their long-range guns booming once more behind their streamlined lefthander, Vernon Gomez, the Yankees brought the 1937 world series to a swift and decisive close at the Polo Grounds yesterday. They found their target with unerring accuracy and brought down the Giants in the fifth and final game by a score of 4 to 2.

By this victory Marse Joe McCarthy's amazing American Leaguers made off with the classic by a margin of four games to one to bring home to roost under the banner of Colonel Jacob Ruppert the second world championship in a row. It was the third under the personal direction of Marse Joe himself and the sixth in the history of the club.

A gathering of 39,000, which hastily rushed to the arena when word was passed that a morning of drizzling rain would not cause a postponement, witnessed the spectacle and left with the conviction there had been no miscarriage of justice.

For one afternoon Marse Joe's famous juggernaut had been thwarted in its quest for another grand slam triumph. That was on Saturday when the heroic figure of Carl Hubbell had come back to stem the Yankee sweep in the fourth game.

Lasts for Five Rounds

But yesterday Colonel Bill Terry found as he had found many times the past few years that he still has no second Carl Hubbell. He had only another tall, lean left-hander in his freshman star, Cliff Melton, for a second try at the world champions. And though the Giants fought far more determinedly and courageously behind their quaint hill billy from North Carolina than they did the first time, the result was inevitable. The Yanks again polished him off in five rounds.

Two home runs, one by Myril Hoag in the second inning, the other by the matchless Joe DiMaggio in the third, were the opening blasts with which the Bronx Bombers greeted the towering Cliff of Black Mountain as the latter set out to duplicate what Hubbell had accomplished the previous afternoon.

Both shots came with the bases empty and merely opened a lead of 2 to 0. But to the crowd which sat shivering under a leaden sky it looked as if the beginning of the end was coming on with a tremendous hurry.

Use Their Remaining Powder

But the Giants still had powder left and used it. In the same third inning which saw the great DiMag almost snap off a flagpole atop the left side of the grandstand, Dick Bartell, still sparking for the National League forces, unloaded a single and a moment later Melvin Ott, compact little powerhouse of the Giants, exploded a home run high in the upper right-field stands.

That tied the score at 2—all and produced a tremendous cheer from the Giant cohorts in particular and the nonpartisan element in general. For inherent in all New York crowds is the desire to see the under dog make a real fight of it.

But that cheer was the last to be heard for the luckless National Leaguers. For in the fifth those Yankee guns belched fire again and from the Giants there came no answer.

Tony Lazzeri, senior member of the Yanks' famed Italian battalion, and who now was taking part in his fifth world series triumph under the Ruppert colors, opened this final and decisive drive with an inspiring three-base smash that almost carried into the center-field bleachers, 485 feet away.

Straight Down the Center

Gomez himself followed with a single over second that broke the deadlock and sent the venerable Tony over the plate. Presently came a screaming two-base wallop down the center of the fairway by Herr Lou Gehrig. It drove in the Yankees' distinguished leftist.

Again the American Leaguers were two in front and this time they made that margin stand up to the end. Though Colonel Terry, master-minding his cause to the last, unearthed two relief pitchers in Al Smith and Don Brennan, who checked those Yankee maulers the rest of the way, he had no further armaments that could blast another pair of tallies out of Gomez.

The singular Castilian, in fact, pitched almost as well as he did in the first game of the series last Wednesday when he held the Giants down to one run and six hits. For though tapped for ten blows yesterday, including the circuit clout by Ott, he seemed to ride in high command throughout.

Lefty even found time to gape at a passing airplane. He has an overpowering weakness for planes. At the finish, only the Giants were left gaping, for which they too appeared to have a weakness, as Gomez stalked off with his second victory of the series and his fifth since 1932. He has never been beaten in the classic.

Gallop to Swift Destruction

For the second successive year of these all-New York world series conflicts, Terry and his Giants have found that winning a brilliant uphill pennant fight in the National League means in the end only a gallop to a swift and final destruction. Last year the Yankees vanquished them in six games. This time they did it in five, and as they vanished into the mist they left in their wake a maze of astonishing records.

The Yankees have emerged triumphant in the last five world series conflicts they have engaged in, beginning with the 1927 classic. In the matter of games, during that period, they won twenty and were defeated in only three.

Grand slam sweeps had come to them against the Pirates in 1927, the Cardinals in 1928 and the Cubs in 1932. Last year the Giants managed to turn them back twice, but this year the Yanks just missed another sweep by one.

Of their present cast, only Gehrig and Lazzeri hold the distinction of having taken part in all five series. The personnel may change, but the machine rolls on. In 1927 and 1928 the late Miller Huggins was at the helm. In the last three series it was Marse Joe McCarthy.

Fail to Find Weakness

Up to 1932 they had Babe Ruth to awe their rivals. The last two years it has been Joe DiMaggio. Always the McCarthymen seem to have the replacements and if there may be any weakness, their rivals invariably get slaughtered in the search.

With rain dripping from the skies throughout the forenoon, the day began rather dubiously for both factions. In fact, for a time it looked almost certain there would have to be a postponement, but Commissioner Kenesaw M. Landis, whose word is the law in all such matters, held off, and in the end his guess proved correct. The rain finally did cease and at 12:20 o'clock he definitely announced the game would go on.

Highlights

- The Yankees became the first team to win six world championships with their triumph over the Giants.
- Yank Joe Moore's nine hits tied the record for a five-game Series.
- The Yankees erupted for seven runs in the bottom of the sixth of Game 1, the result of five singles, four walks, and two Giant errors.
- Red Ruffing went the distance for the Yanks in Game 2, striking out eight Giants, and helping his pitching efforts with a double, single, and three RBIs.
- Lou Gehrig hit his tenth and last World Series homer in Game 4. Only four players have ever belted more in the postseason (Mickey Mantle, Babe Ruth, Yogi Berra, and Duke Snider).
- In Game 6, Tony Lazzeri tripled in the fifth and scored what proved to be the game- and Series-winning run when pitcher Lefty Gomez cracked a single.

Best Efforts

Batting

Average	Tony Lazzeri	.400
Home Runs	(five players)	1 each
Triples	(four players)	1 each
Doubles	Red Rolfe	2
	Burgess Whitehead	2
Hits	Joe Moore	9
Runs	George Selkirk	5
RBIs	George Selkirk	6

Pitching

Wins	Lefty Gomez	2-0
ERA	Red Ruffing	1.00
Strikeouts	Lefty Gomez	8
	Red Ruffing	8
Innings Pitched	Lefty Gomez	18

NEW YORK YANKEES
NEW YORK GIANTS **1937**

Reprinted, with permission, from
The World Series, A Complete
Pictorial History, by John Devaney
and Burt Goldblatt (Rand McNally
and Company, Chicago, © 1972).

A First for Joe
and a Last Hurrah for Lou

During this Series, Hearst newspaper columnist Bill Corum was talking to Giant manager Bill Terry in Terry's hotel suite. Corum offered Terry a bet that the Yankees would beat the Giants. Terry refused to bet. "I'm no sucker," Terry told him, according to Corum.

Not many were betting on the Giants, who were three-to-one underdogs. The wise money was right. The Yankee hitting demolished the Giant pitching with such methodical force that Terry got a telegram from a Giant fan who informed him, tongue in cheek, to "change your signals. The Yankees know them."

The Yankees served up the bad news early, driving Carl Hubbell, winner of 22 that season, from the mound with a seven-run barrage in the sixth inning of the first game. But only Hub could stop a Yankee sweep, beating the Yankees, 7-3, in the fourth game. Lefty Gomez won the final game, his fifth Series victory without a defeat, matching the record of the Yanks' Herb Pennock of the Twenties.

In this Series there was a demonstration of the passing of strength in the Yankee lineup. Young Joe DiMaggio hit his first World Series home run, a towering drive that struck a flagpole above the leftfield roof of the Polo Grounds. And Lou Gehrig hit his 10th Series home run—his last.

After the final game one wag summed up the Series this way: "The Giants won one game and

the Yankees won the Series and that's the way it should have been."

Joe DiMaggio:
A home run a kid might dream of

Joe DiMaggio was reminiscing not long ago at an Oldtimers' Day game at Shea Stadium in New York City. *When I think about World Series*, said Joe, *I always remember the 1937 Series because that was the one where I hit my first Series home run. It was off Cliff Melton in the Polo Grounds. It was always a dream I'd had, as a kid, you know, standing on the street corner [in San Francisco] and watching while they showed the play by play of a Series game on a big board. It would be a game in a place like the Polo Grounds or the Yankee Stadium or somewhere and I'd stand there and imagine myself hitting a home run in a World Series. I don't know if you remember this, but they had lights that showed the play by play on the boards. . . . And what impressed me always was a home run in a World Series game. And when I hit that home run off Melton, I thought, 'Now it's happened for me.' It was one of the hardest-hit balls I ever hit. It hit the flagpole on top of the roof. But that's not why I remember it, not because it was a hard-hit ball, but because it was my first in a Series.*

Movie stardom: Joe DiMaggio's first and only motion picture appearance was in *Manhattan Merry-Go-Round*, in 1937. He appeared with a bevy of film stars and a variety of orchestra leaders.

A DiMaggio poster, painted by Joseph Eatalano.

The Yankee Clipper drives one out over the wall in the Polo Grounds in the fifth game of the 1937 World Series against the New York Giants. The Yanks won the game 4–2, and with the victory took the Series. The Giant catcher is Harry Danning.

Joe DiMaggio crosses home plate after hitting his first World Series home run. It came in the fifth and final game of the 1937 Series. The Yankees took the Series that day with a 4–2 win over the New York Giants. The Giant catcher is Harry Danning.

World champions.

A little locker-room celebration. The Yankees have just won their second World Series in a row, by defeating the New York Giants, four games to one.

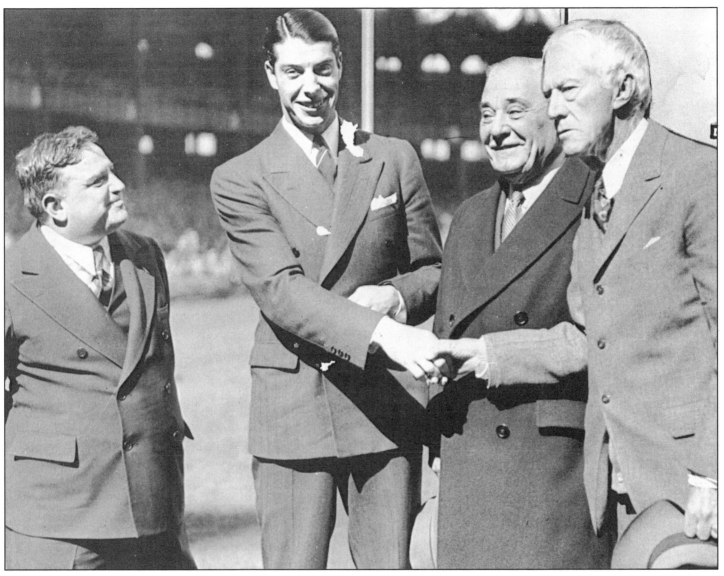

Joe DiMaggio accepts a world championship emblem and congratulations from baseball commissioner, Kenesaw M. Landis, at Yankee Stadium. Standing beside DiMaggio are New York mayor, Fiorello LaGuardia on the left, and Yankee owner, Jake Ruppert, on the right.

Plain Dealing

By Gordon Cobbledick

A political philosopher could find food for disturbing reflection in the fan poll taken by the American Institute of Public Opinion which resulted in the landslide election of Joe DiMaggio as the most valuable ball player in the big leagues.

The institute is a sort of inquiring reporter on a nation-wide scale. Its business is to keep a finger on the public pulse, so that it can tell the public what the public is thinking about in such weighty matters as the business cycle, Justice Black and the president's economic policies. Its venture into baseball was a frivolous interlude, but it may have served to point a moral.

Six hundred institute interviewers asked the fans of 48 states to name the most valuable player. DiMaggio received 29 per cent. of all the votes, Lou Gehrig 17 per cent., Carl Hubbell 16, Joe Medwick 8, Lefty Gomez 7, Charlie Gehringer 6

GORDON COBBLEDICK and Gabby Hartnett 5.

This was an independent, unofficial ballot, of course. The official selection of the most valuable player in each league has been made by committees of baseball writers, one for the American League, another for the National. The winners will be announced shortly.

I don't know what the American Legion committee has decided, but I shall be a little surprised if it hasn't chosen Gehringer, who received only slightly more than one-fifth as many votes as DiMaggio in the institute's fan poll. And I should like to guess that the National League choice was Medwick, who got only half as many votes from the fans as Carl Hubbell.

Why Overwhelming

I believe that a poll of American League players, managers, umpires and writers would find Gehringer and DiMaggio running nearly neck and neck, with probably a slight edge for the Detroit second baseman.

Then why the overwhelming victory of DiMaggio when the issue was taken before that great tribunal, the American peepul?

Why, ballyhoo, my friends. Ballyhoo's the answer, and I don't mean to take anything away from DiMaggio when I say this. He's a great young ball player, the greatest recruit of the last ten years unquestionably, but he still isn't as great as Gehringer, a better hitter who plays a more exacting position.

If DiMaggio were a member of the Detroit Tigers and Gehringer a member of the New York Yankees there would be no question about the most valuable player award. If DiMaggio were a member of the Cleveland Indians he would be recognized as a good young player, but his batting accomplishments probably would be discounted with a well-aimed sneer at the right field wall of League Park.

There's only one sure way to quick and certain fame in the minds of the fans of Podunk and points west, and that's to get a job with one of the New York ball clubs, with the power of the New York press behind you. The exploits of New York ball players are advertised far and wide, since the great agencies for news dissemination center in New York. For a player outside of the big town to win recognition equal to that of the stars of the Giants and Yankees he must be superior by a tremendous margin, or he must possess such great gobs of that quality known as color that even New York is compelled to recognize it.

But we live in a democratic land (with a lower case d) and the basic principle of democracy is that the majority shall determine what is right and what is wrong, what is good and what is bad.

If the power of ballyhoo can so exaggerate the worth of a DiMaggio that he receives five times as many votes as Gehringer, one of the three or four greatest infielders of all time, is it any wonder that some of our public offices are filled by mountebanks, scoundrels, incompetents and plain fatheads?

DiMaggio Barred From Court Play

Business Manager Ed Barrow announced yesterday that Yankees officials will refuse permission to Joe DiMaggio, star outfielder, to take part in basketball games, exhibition or otherwise, this Winter. "It is too dangerous a sport. We can't take chances," said Ed.

DiMag, who has been collecting soft dough via the movies and radio, can play no sports other than baseball, according to a clause which Barrow insists is in every player's contract.

$50 Per Minute.

He had signed to play with the N. Y. pro Jewels against the Whirlwinds at Arcadia Hall Sunday night, after playing baseball

Joe DiMaggio
Barred from basketball.

with Jake Powell and an All-Star team against the Bushwicks at Dexter Park in the afternoon.

DiMag will get $500 for the ball game and was guaranteed $50 a minute for the basketball contest. If he played less than half of the court game, he would have received $1,000. Barrow said Joe had not consulted him before signing the court contract and declared his decision is final.

The Yankee Clipper with baseball commissioner, Judge Kenesaw Mountain Landis.

1938
THIRD WORLD
CHAMPIONSHIP

Two DiMaggios in the major leagues in 1938: Vince of the Boston Braves and Joe of the Yankees. Vince hit .228 that year while kid brother Joe batted .328.

A TROUBLING YEAR

The year 1938 was a troublesome one. It began with a contract dispute. We did not have long-term contracts in those days: I signed a new one each year. I ended up holding out, in fact did not come to terms with the Yankees until the end of April.

Then, when I was finally back on the field, I collided with Joe Gordon, the second baseman we had acquired to replace Tony Lazzeri, who had gone to the Chicago Cubs as a player/coach. Gordon, however, left the field via a stretcher, and I was booed for the first time that I can remember in my baseball career.

It was also a year where we had some very evident competition. The Red Sox gave us a run for the flag through most of the season. Jimmy Foxx was having a great year for them, ended up leading the league with a .349 average and 179 RBIs. He also hit 50 home runs but that was short of Hank Greenberg's 58 that year. If Lefty Grove, Boston's best pitcher, hadn't hurt his arm, it might have been a different story at the World Series. But we made it by winning 99 games, our third American League pennant in a row.

Joe DiMaggio

1938
JOE DiMAGGIO STATISTICS

Games	145
At Bats	599
Hits	194
Doubles	32
Triples	13
Home Runs	32
Runs Scored	129
Runs Batted In	140
Bases on Balls	59
Strike Outs	21
Stolen Bases	6
Slugging Average	.581
Batting Average	.324

STANDINGS

	Won	Lost	Percentage	Games Behind
New York Yankees	99	53	.651	
Boston Red Sox	88	61	.591	9.5
Cleveland Indians	86	66	.566	13
Detroit Tigers	84	70	.545	16
Washington Senators	75	76	.497	23.5
Chicago White Sox	65	83	.439	32
St. Louis Browns	55	97	.362	44
Philadelphia A's	53	99	.349	46

1938

Behind the Box Score

Joe DiMaggio Has Radio Going
Constantly, but He Can't Dance a Step

Joseph Paul Di Maggio, Jr., is 24 and unmarried. . . . When asked if he has any matrimonial plans he protests strongly that a wedding is as far from his mind as a transfer to the Athletics. . . . He weighs about 200 pounds. . . . He is nutty about radio music. . . . The receiver in his room goes on as soon as he wakes and it keeps right on as long as he is around. . . . He cannot dance, not even a step. . . . It is strange but true that ball players, as a class, are not good dancers. . . . Though their work calls for the achievement of rhythm. . . . He is the son of a fisherman who came from Italy and he runs a restaurant specializing in sea food on Fisherman's Wharf in San Francisco. . . . So he comes naturally by his love for fish in preference to meat. . . . Goes strong for spaghetti. . . . Says his favorite dish is chippino, which is an Italian concerto composed of cracked crab and spaghetti sauce. . . . "Our big seller," Giuseppe says. . . . Reads little, and what he does read he finds in pulp and picture magazines. . . . Has intense Italian devotion to family, which is a big one, with three sisters and as many brothers—Vince, with Kansas City; Dominic, with San Francisco, and Tom, the oldest, who is Joe's manager and a converted crab fisherman. . . . Giuseppe insists he has no superstitions. . . . When he came to the Yankees he had one. . . . He always made it a point to touch second base on his way ·out. . . . But he discarded that. . . . And, by the way, he's batting .459 in the Grapefruit League this season.

Two Experts Slight Di Mag

Joe Not Unanimous All-Star Choice

By the Associated Press.

ST. LOUIS, Jan. 5.—Somewhere there are two members of the Baseball Writers Assn. who would leave Joe Di Maggio of the Yankees off an all-star 1937 baseball team, and there are four writers who would pass up Joe Medwick of the Cardinals.

The fact neither of the hard-hitting outfielders was a unanimous choice was surprising about an all-star team named by 247 baseball experts and announced today by the Sporting News. Di Maggio got 245 votes and Medwick 243.

As could be expected, the world champion Yankees dominated the team, although the two leagues divided evenly, with five players each. In addition to Di Maggio, the Yanks placed Pitcher Charles Ruffing, firstbaseman Lou Gehrig and thirdman Bob Rolfe.

The team, with the number of votes each player received for his position, although not necessarily his total vote, was:—

First Base—Lou Gehrig, Yankees (229).
Second Base—Charles Gehringer, Detroit (238).
Shortstop—Dick Bartell, New York Giants (72)
Third Base—Bob Rolfe, Yankees (81).
Right Field—Paul Waner, Pittsburgh (182).
Center Field—Joe Di Maggio, Yankees (240).
Left Field—Joe Medwick, Cardinals (235).
Catcher—Charles Hartnett, Chicago Cubs (135).
Pitchers—Carl Hubbell, Giants (203), and Charles Ruffing, Yankees (142).

Bartell nosed out Joe Cronin of the Boston Red Sox by one vote for shortstop while Rolfe was chosen for third base over fourteen other players, led by Harlond Clift of the St. Louis Browns with 45 votes and Art Whitney of the Philadelphia Nationals with 36.

Vernon Gomez of the Yankees got 57 votes for a pitcher's berth, and Lou Fette of the Boston Bees received 34. Bill Dickey, the Yanks' catcher, trailed Hartnett with 105 ballots.

By Joe Williams

Di Maggio and Greenberg May Head The Holdouts

Mr. Roosevelt covered a lot of territory in his brisk workout on the economic field the other day, but he didn't get around to saying anything about the downtrodden slaves of baseball, and this was an unfortunate omission.

Because any day now you will be reading in the sports pages how some of these oppressed people are having the very juice of life squeezed out of their undernourished carcasses by the tories of the ivory trust, leaving them no alternative but to refuse their contracts and go back to the farm or gas-filling stations.

This is one of the economic miseries we have with us at all times, in prosperity, in depression and in recession, and since Mr. Roosevelt seems determined to get everything fixed up just peachy in this country, it is strange he has neglected to investigate this particular and peculiar problem.

Of course, it may be that some of the problems in the social scheme are more pressing, and that it is difficult for a humanitarian even of Mr. Roosevelt's dimensions to get sweaty about some clover kicker who thinks he ought to have $50,000 instead of $40,000 a year for nudging a baseball into the stands.

I wouldn't know about that, but I do know there is nothing so important to the demon athletes as their pay checks, and come this time of the year they begin to put on the pressure, making all sorts of silly threats as to what they will do with the remainder of their precious lives if they don't get their asking price.

* * *

It's a Monopoly. So What?

These threats are seldom carried out for the simple reason that in the end the demon athletes must take what they are offered or stay out of baseball, a forbidding sort of situation which explains and probably justifies their loud talking and swaggering antics.

If they make good their threats and quit they are just through, because, as every 10-year-old child knows, baseball is the tightest monopoly in existence; an office worker, a sales manager or an automobile worker can quit in rebellion against what he considers unfair trade conditions, and run a fair chance of doing just as well or better elsewhere, but a baseball player can't, because when he quits organized baseball he quits the only kind of baseball there is.

This suggests tyranny in its most suffocating form until you consider that baseball by its very nature must be patterned along monopolistic lines to exist. The business would be reduced to complete chaos with no profit for anybody, including the players, if it were not for the stern contractual arrangements which practically wed the performer to the owner for life.

This is the phase of the business that is always attacked when the anti-trusters start viewing with alarm, yet without it there can be no organized baseball. It seems plain enough that baseball as a monopoly could not have existed as long as it has and not be fundamentally fair and just.

* * *

When Gehrig Asked for $50,000.

Very few people are going to get maudlin over the plight of a hired man who is compelled to spend his winters in Florida or California sunshine, his summers in the open air playing a game—which in most cases amounts to the sum total of his ability—and for which he receives, even as an average player, more than is paid to our leading educators.

You get some faint notion of how brutally the hired hand in baseball is treated by the soulless capitalist when you recall that Babe Ruth was paid $80,000 a year by the Yankees for hitting home runs, and since Ruth left baseball he can't get a job. This wouldn't seem to indicate that the Yankees took advantage of him, would it?

I grant you Ruth wouldn't have got $80,000 if he hadn't fought for it, and wasn't worth it. The point I make is that this is scarcely the case history of a cringing peon in chains. Baseball salaries can't be standardized and shouldn't be. That's why you have the annual holdouts. The boys want to get as much as they can, and you can't blame them for that.

The year Lou Gehrig held out for $50,000 and signed for $36,000 he said, "I knew I wasn't going to get the fifty, but what could I lose by asking?" That's the general attitude. And Gehrig was openly pleased with the $36,000. To him it was a fair price for his services.

The holdout march this year probably will be headed by Joe Di Maggio, of the Yankees, and Hank Greenberg, of the Tigers. Di Maggio, a second-year man, got something like $15,000 last year. The dope is he will ask for $25,000, maybe $30,000. Greenberg got $25,000, himself, last year; as the man who drove in more runs than any other player in the league last year he may consider $35,000 an attractive figure.

* * *

Already Ahead of Ruth in Dough.

Since both Di Maggio and Greenberg have come along to fill part of the outlines of the massive Ruthian picture, it may be interesting to check back and study the Babe's salary scale. What do you suppose he got his second year as a big leaguer? This was in 1916. He was a pitcher then. He won 23, lost 12 and had an earned run average of 1.75 a game. His salary was all of $3,500.

As a second year man Di Maggio was paid $11,500 more, and I am not familiar with Greenberg's second year figures. Now let's take Ruth as a second year man, since pitchers are seldom paid as much as sluggers. This was in 1920. He hit 54 home runs, had a batting average of .376, was one of the leading defensive stars, and was paid $20,000.

Neither Di Maggio nor Greenberg has yet come close to these hitting totals. Di Maggio hit 46 homers and had an average of .346, his best in the league. Greenberg hit 46 homers and had an average of .336, three points under his best. Yet Greenberg is already being paid more than Ruth was at a time when he was the most talked of player in the game, and Di Maggio's new contract is certain to carry him beyond that figure, too.

Colonel Jacob Ruppert said a couple of years back there never would be another $80,000 ball player. This would seem to depend entirely on the individual. As pointed out, both Di Maggio and Greenberg are already far ahead of the early Ruth scale. Just how much higher they will go is up to them. Ruth didn't stop; he was that kind. The Di Maggios and the Greenbergs may be different.

DIMAGGIO ON WAY EAST

Coming Here for Social Affairs and Salary Discussions

SAN FRANCISCO, Jan. 14 (AP).—Joe DiMaggio headed eastward to-day on what he described as a pleasure trip, but he is expected to visit Colonel Jacob Ruppert for a verbal tussle over his 1938 baseball contract.

If he follows the customary procedure, guessers here say he will ask for $35,000 without a smile, then reluctantly let the owner of the Yankees talk him down $5,000 or $10,000.

Before leaving he insisted he had not signed a contract. He revealed he had lost three pounds since last Fall. He now weighs 202.

Joe will reach New York Monday. He will see the Tommy Farr-Jimmy Braddock fight next Friday, then attend the Philadelphia baseball writers' dinner Jan. 25. He will be guest of honor. DiMaggio will attend a similar affair in New York five days later before returning home.

The first thing Joe Di Maggio did on arrival here last night was to dash for the wrestling show in the Hippodrome.... Giuseppe will see the Braddock-Farr fight as guest of Joe Gould, Jim's manager.... The reception Di Mag got in Philadelphia yesterday—mob scene, band, police escort, luncheon at Palumbo's and all the trimmings—was the most remarkable demonstration for any ballplayer in the history of the Quaker City.... Di Mag addressed 1,000 boys at Bartlett Junior High, in the Italian section, and again was mobbed.... Jimmy Foxx also was there and paid high tribute to Giuseppe.

Joe DiMaggio with the man who brought him to New York and the major leagues, Colonel Jacob Ruppert. Ruppert died in 1938.

DiMaggio Wants Big Increase but Withholds Demand Till Yanks Make Offer

COAST STAR HERE FOR SALARY TALK

DiMaggio, Hoping for Quick Closing of Contract, Is Eager to See Barrow

BARS GEHRIG COMPARISON

Will Not Be Guided by What Yanks Pay Lou—McCarthy Accepts Giants' Terms

By JOHN DREBINGER

Looking remarkably fit and weighing four pounds less than when he discharged his final blast into the reeling Giants last October, Joe DiMaggio, wonder player of the Yankees, swept into New York yesterday after attending a luncheon in his honor in Philadelphia earlier in the day.

In fact, attending luncheons and dinners is ostensibly the prime motive which has brought the American League's home-run champion East from his home and lucrative restaurant business in San Francisco, but he made it clear he would be ready to mix business with pleasure if the Yankees cared to invite him to attend a little conference concerning his 1938 contract.

Taken immediately in tow by Joe Gould, Jim Braddock's fight manager and DiMaggio's bosom pal, the young star reiterated his denial of a week ago on the Coast that he already had signed a Yankee contract, a transaction variously reported to have been closed secretly last Summer with Business Manager Ed Barrow.

Times Wide World
JOE DIMAGGIO

Asked Barrow for Tickets

"To tell you the truth," said Joe, "and strange as it may sound, I never saw Barrow once to talk to all last season until just before the world series, when I went to see him about buying two extra world series tickets at the Polo Grounds. I have signed no contract up to now, haven't even seen one, and have no idea what the Yankees intend to offer me.

"I understand they are sending the contracts out this week, and I hope they don't send mine all the way out to San Francisco. Because if they would ask me over to see them I'd go at once and maybe settle the whole business without any further delay."

He even said he would gladly call up Barrow himself except for the hoax he heard somebody had sprung on the Yankee business manager last week on the telephone.

"After that," chuckled Joe, "I'm afraid Barrow would tell me to go to blazes if I told him I was Joe DiMaggio on the phone."

As in his Coast interview, DiMaggio again declined to name any specific salary he would ask for beyond saying he thought he was "entitled to a substantial increase." As a second-year man with the Yanks last season he is understood to have received $15,000.

Waiting for Offer

"While I naturally have an idea what I'm worth," he explained, "I don't think it's up to me to say anything about that now. I'd rather wait until the club has made its offer."

Asked whether he expected to get as much as Lou Gehrig is receiving or "somewhere near" Lou's reported salary of $36,000, Joe replied:

"No. Lou's figure doesn't enter into this thing at all and frankly I don't even know what Gehrig is getting beyond what has been mentioned in the papers. That's really none of my business and my negotiations with the Yankees will be carried on entirely apart from what they pay Lou."

DiMaggio, who recently was voted the "Player of the Year" by the New York baseball writers and will receive their honor plaque at the chapter's annual dinner at the Hotel Commodore on Jan. 30, will attend numerous functions in the interim. He will return for a one-day visit to Philadelphia today and on Jan. 25 will be guest of honor at the annual dinner of the Philadelphia writers, who also have voted Joe as 1937's outstanding player.

Star Sees No Trouble In Arriving at Terms

Again Denies Having Signed For $25,000 Last July

By DANIEL.

Joe Di Maggio, center fielder of the Yankees and new home-run king of baseball, was here today with that 6,000-pound look—thirty grand to you. In from California by way of Chicago and Philadelphia, Giuseppe announced that he had no intention of pressing negotiations for a 100 per cent salary increase to $30,000.

"I am not going to call Colonel Ruppert or Ed Barrow, but if I am wanted I will be around, on and off, until January 31," said Di Maggio as he dashed back to Philadelphia to appear at a showing of the American League's new picture.

Joe professes to believe that his salary expectations are so rational that even so shrewd an organization as that headed by the Colonel will lose no time in clinching the deal before Giuseppe has a chance to develop fancier notions.

"I am not going to make any cracks about what I want because no contract has yet been presented to me," Di Maggio continued. "Contrary to somebody's insistence, I did not sign last July for $25,000 or any other sum. Nor did the club try to sign me.

"My arm is as good as ever and I am down to playing weight right now. In fact, at 202 pounds, I am three pounds lighter than I was in the world series last October. When I went home, Barrow warned me about the old spaghet', and I have watched my diet for the first time in my life.

"Only the other day I got into uniform and worked out at Seals Stadium for something like half an hour, posing for pictures to be used in advertisements. I threw a lot and had no pain.

**Figures Training
Games in Salary.**

"In arriving at a logical salary figure I have considered the Yankee training schedule," Di Maggio resumed. "I think I mean something at the gate in that, too.

"In two years with the Yankees I have learned that to predict what you are going to do is sucker stuff. But it seems to me that with a good break I can win the triple crown—the home run title, the batting championship, and the runs-driven-in leadership.

"In New York, they appear to pay off mainly for homers. Around the circuit, they pay tremendous respect to the batting champion. In my own heart, the reputation as the best run-maker in baseball is the biggest honor.

"As for popping off about matching Babe Ruth's home run record of sixty—well, that's plenty of homers and the longer you are in baseball, the more you appreciate that. I do not forget that I hit only nineteen of my forty-six last season in the Stadium, and that both Lou Gehrig and Bill Dickey beat me at that game on our home field.

"I am a bit sore that I did not get fifty last year. I am sure I can make that grade."

**Glad Gehringer Won
Valuable Player Award.**

Di Maggio said that, in all sincerity, he was glad Charley Gehringer was voted the most valuable player in the American League.

But he was sore Joe Medwick almost had been beaten in the National League by "an outsider," Gabby Hartnett.

"I will report at St. Petersburg on March 6, that is, if everything is settled by then," Giuseppe laughed. "I can't see how they are going to stop us from taking our third straight pennant. Oscar Vitt tells me Joe Gordon will make us forget about Tony. And he adds that when we get Keller in 1939, we will have one of the greatest outfields in the history of the game.

"The one thing I've got to do this year is solve that Philadelphia pitching. I still failed to hit .300 against Connie's hurlers last summer. And I've got to improve against Mel Harder. I got only three hits off him last season—five in two years.

"My one regret right now is that I can't stay to see my pal Apostoli fight Lee. Apostoli is the world's best middleweight."

Di Mag said he had not seen either Lazzeri or Frankie Crosetti all winter. "Business in my restaurant is fine, and I am going to pick up plenty of sugar in advertising and radio."

Ruppert's Conference With DiMaggio on Star's Contract Ends in a Stalemate

DIMAGGIO REJECTS OFFER OF $25,000

Long Hold-Out Is Not Likely, However, With Yankees and Star Only $5,000 Apart

OFFER FINAL, SAYS OWNER

Ruppert Makes Figure Public —Increase Is $10,000—No Later Conference Set

By JOHN DREBINGER

Moving with the deliberation of two great chess masters, each of whom seems to hold a profound respect for the other, Colonel Jacob Ruppert, owner of the Yankees, and his latest diamond luminary, Joe DiMaggio, went into their salary huddle yesterday and emerged with what might be termed a "perfunctory draw."

The Yanks, upon the say-so of Colonel Ruppert, offered their star outfielder, who led the American League in home runs last season, a one-year contract calling for $25,-000, or $10,000 above his 1937 salary.

But in almost less time than it takes the great DiMadge to bring his powerful bludgeon around on a choice pitch, the offer was turned down and, after a session that lasted scarcely a half hour, the two went their separate ways, with not even an agreement when they would meet again.

Silent on Difference

Just how far apart the two are in their negotiations neither party would reveal. In fact, it was only after much persuading that the colonel could be induced to disclose what the Yankees had offered. Later, however, he admitted the difference was "considerable," adding in a jocular vein to an inquiring reporter:

"I think you'd be satisfied with it."

As for DiMaggio, the 23-year-old Coast star deftly parried all attempts to get him to quote any figures at all, an attitude he has assumed since he arrived in the city last Monday.

"I promised the colonel I would not mention any of the amounts we are discussing," he said, "so all information will have to come from him. All I can say is that I have not signed and that their offer is quite a way off from what I think I'm worth."

Despite this, however, and a statement later from the Colonel that the Yankee offer of $25,000 was positively tops, local baseball observers last night were of the opinion that the matter never would reach the proportions of a serious "holdout siege." In fact, from a source close to the renowned slugger it was learned that the "considerable difference" will simmer down to not more than $5,000.

Starts With $40,000

According to this informant, DiMaggio entered yesterday's conference with a demand of $40,000, which, however, he meant to employ only as a preliminary gesture to match the Yanks' opening offer of $15,000 contained in the contract the club had sent him as a mere formality on Thursday.

The conference, which was held in the Ruppert Brewery, was attended also by Business Manager Ed Barrow and was set for 10 o'clock in the morning. DiMaggio was first on the scene. In fact, the Yanks' wonder player was kept cooling his heels all of forty-five minutes before being invited to step into Colonel Ruppert's regal chamber.

Joe, however, accepted the wait good naturedly. laughed and joked with the assembled scribes and posed for innumerable pictures, several of which revealed him tapping gingerly on the colonel's door. According to Barrow, the meeting, unlike some of the far more blustery sessions the colonel used to hold in the same room with Babe Ruth, moved quietly and swiftly.

$25,000 Considered Fair

The colonel himself at first declined to reveal what he had offered, but, after thinking the matter over for a time, said:

"I suppose there'll be no end of wild guessing among you fellows, so I might as well tell. It's $25,000, and I think that is a very fair salary. I don't intend to go any higher."

The colonel also took occasion to deny once again a persistent report that DiMaggio and the Yankees actually came to terms for 1938 in a secret session last Summer.

"I want to say to you on my honor as a gentleman," said the colonel, "that this is the first time that I or any one connected with the Yankees has spoken to DiMaggio about his salary for 1938."

As for DiMaggio, Jolting Joe appeared not at all concerned as he breezed out of the colonel's sanctum. He said he expected to remain in the East until about Feb. 1, attending the Philadelphia baseball writers' dinner next Wednesday and the New York scribes' dinner Jan. 30, at both of which he is to be honored as 1937's outstanding player.

FAMILY OF HOLDOUTS

Three DiMaggio Brothers at Odds With Teams on Salary

SAN FRANCISCO, Jan. 21 (AP).— Salary squabbles of the DiMaggios became a unanimous family affair today. All three DiMaggio brothers are baseball holdouts.

LANDIS, DIMAGGIO HONORED AT DINNER

Commissioner Calls Baseball 'Stronghold of Democracy' as He Receives Plaque

---

800 AT WRITERS' FROLIC

Lehman, Farley, La Guardia in Record Throng—Notables in All Sports Attend

Although occasionally skidding off the base lines in the manner of ardent Dodgers bent upon doing something extraordinary, the baseball writers of New York successfully brought the 1938 "indoor" season to a close on a ringing high note last night at their fifteenth annual dinner and frolic.

The event, held in the grand ballroom of the Hotel Commodore, drew a record crowd of more than 800 enthusiasts who accorded a thunderous ovation to the scribes' two leading guests of honor, Kenesaw Mountain Landis, commissioner of baseball, and Joe DiMaggio, wonder player of the world champion Yankees.

To the judge went the plaque for meritorious services to baseball over a long period of years and there was a rousing reception for the white-haired former jurist who back in 1920 stepped from a Federal bench to embark upon a brilliant career as baseball's guiding genius, following the 1919 world series scandals.

When the presentation was made to Commissioner Landis by President Tom Meany of the writers' New York Chapter, the judge extolled the national pastime as he expressed his appreciation. He termed baseball a "stronghold of democracy in these days of strife."

Because of ill health, which forced him to forego visits North during the Winter, the commissioner had not been able to attend the writers' dinner for several years, but he insisted on making this trip from his retreat in Clearwater, Fla., despite an offer by the scribes that he receive his honors "from a distance" and address the gathering by telephonic arrangements.

The Judge Keeps His Word

"Nonsense," boomed the judge, "it would sound like a voice from the grave. I'll be there, boys, I'll

SOME OF THE NOTABLES AT BASEBALL WRITERS' DINNER

Times Wide World

Kenesaw Mountain Landis, with plaque he received for meritorious services to baseball; Tom Meany, who made the awards, and Joe DiMaggio, holding prize for outstanding player of 1937.

be there." And there he was.

Another boisterous welcome was accorded to DiMaggio when the American League's new home-run champion received the plaque as the outstanding player of last year.

Spurred by the presence of their severest critic and now their most distinguished literary contemporary, Bill Terry, the scribes, in their stage productions, really went to town on the old colonel. Bill looked on as he saw himself in the person of Arthur Daley interview Charlie McCarthy, with Tom Meany playing the part of Edgar Bergen.

Disdainful of Charlie's baseball talents at first, Terry wound up by seeking advice.

"Suppose," he asked, "the Giants and Yankees were in the seventh game of a world series."

"Now, Bill," McCarthy shot back, "I'll answer questions, but don't ask me how to get your Giants into the seventh game of a world series."

Terry Tries Again

Terry tried again. "Suppose the bases were filled and Joe DiMaggio was at bat, and you were the Giants' manager, what would you do?"

"There's always suicide," the dummy suggested. "Then again, you might get DiMaggio to autograph the ball. That would take time. You might have Mr. Stoneham autograph a new five-year contract. That also would take time. Then you might—oh, hell, Bill, I'd catch the next train to Memphis."

From the dais a battery of orators, introduced by Toastmaster Sid Mercer, cut loose with a veritable broadside. Among the speakers were Governor Herbert H. Lehman, Postmaster General James A. Farley, Mayor Fiorello La Guardia and former Mayor James J. Walker, but before the folks had time to run out in order to cast their votes accordingly, Jimmy McWilliams and Joe Cook, noted radio entertainers, barged in

to upset the entire political outlook, along with Warren Brown, Chicago sports writer. Governor A. Harry Moore of New Jersey also was present.

Then one of the greatest ball players of all time—the famous John Honus Wagner—was invited to give his views on the game as played today in contrast with his era of nearly a score of years ago.

Max Kase and Jim Kahn, scriveners, gave an excellent reason why vaudeville went into a permanent recession. A young fellow named John Kieran sang something about "A Vulgar Boatman."

Yankee pennants, from the days when Joe DiMaggio wore his pin-striped number 5. During those thirteen years when DiMaggio starred for the Yankees, 1936-42 and 1946-51, his team collected ten authentic American League pennants.

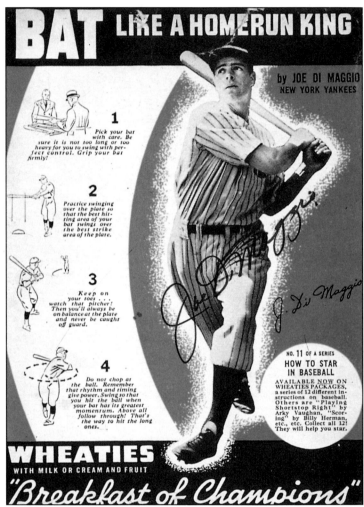

With prominence came the perks. Promoting Wheaties, the ''Breakfast of Champions''.

Di Mag Owes All to Pal

Joe, Off for Coast Unsigned, Reveals How Neighbor Spurred Him On

By DANIEL.

Joe Di Maggio, who can have $25,000 for playing center field for the Yankees next season but demands what, in the vernacular, is called forty grand, today was headed back for Taylor St., San Francisco, unsigned if not unsung.

"I am taking no contract back with me for consideration, and right now I do not know what the next move will be or even whose move it is," protested Giuseppe.

Di Maggio certainly has had a fine time in the East these last two weeks. Nothing that has happened has prompted him to revise his estimate of his abilities and his financial worth to the New York club and the American League.

Before packing his bags Joe divulged the name of the young man who was responsible for the outfielder's start toward stardom. The hitherto unknown hero is Frank Venezia, also of the North Beach section of San Francisco.

Just when Giuseppe had lost interest in baseball, Venezia kept pestering him until he induced him to join a newly organized nine, as shortstop. But for the persistence of Venezia, it is doubtful if Di Maggio would have gone back to the game, in which his previous experience had been confined to softball.

Lest he forget his heritage, DiMaggio clutches a pair of freshly caught crabs during the off-season. His father, of course, made a living by fishing for crabs in the ocean waters off San Francisco.

GEHRIG, DIMAGGIO ALARM YANK CAMP

Continued Silence of Absent Stars on Salary Offers Puzzle to McCarthy

RUPPERT BELIEVED FIRM

Players Fish and Play Golf on Last Off Day Before the End of Baseball Season

By JAMES P. DAWSON
Special to THE NEW YORK TIMES.

ST. PETERSBURG, Fla., March 6.—There was no Yankee baseball activity to disturb the Sabbath calm today. The athletes, on the one Sunday they could expect off between now and October, unless rain comes to upset the playing schedule, gave their attention to fishing expeditions out in the Gulf, patronized some of the near-by golf links, or just idled the time away at movies or playing cards.

Speculation revolved around Joe DiMaggio and Lou Gehrig and their aloofness from contract offers. Every other member of the championship squad is under contract now. Indeed, most of them are accounted for, in homes or hotel quarters here, or are on the way. But DiMaggio and Gehrig are conspicuously missing as Manager Joe McCarthy heads his athletes into another week of intensive training at Huggins Field, and their absence is beginning to cause alarm.

Ruppert and Barrow Silent

More annoying still is the absence of any news on the situation involving the two stars. The Yankee pilot said tonight he had received no encouraging word from Business Manager Ed Barrow in New York, indicating there has been no revision by Colonel Jacob Ruppert, club owner, of the maximum he intends to pay, or by the players, on their own salary appraisals.

DiMaggio has been offered $25,000. Gehrig, seeking $41,400, has been offered a renewal of last year's $36,000 contract. In the case of Gehrig it is suspected he will be made a more attractive offer, particularly in view of the fact the $36,000 figure represents a cut of $750 for Battering Lou, the amount of the bonus he received on signing last season.

DiMaggio, however, is being offered a $10,000 rise, has demanded a boost of $25,000 and has indicated he will settle for a $30,000 contract.

Not in Hold-Out Class Yet

The unsigned stars are not yet considered hold-outs, but they will slide into that category tomorrow if they fail to report for training. After that the quiet negotiations now being conducted can be expected to be superseded by frantic activity by club and players, because the club needs the stars and the stars need the benefit of the exercise those training camps provide.

But for the DiMaggio-Gehrig situation Manager McCarthy was feeling satisfied tonight. The pitchers, catchers, infielders and outfielders who have been going through their paces since camp opened finished the first week of training without major mishap.

Catcher Bill Dickey wrenched his right side, but the pain is expected to disappear completely before tomorrow's workout gets under way and the angular Arkansan is expected to resume hitting. For the rest there has been nothing to worry the Yankee leader but the customary cases of sunburn and blistered feet, which are not allowed to interfere with the activities of the players.

1938

Sleepy-Eyed Joe!

Broken Slumber Bothers DiMaggio More Than His $25,000 Contract

SAN FRANCISCO, April 6 (By International News Service).—It's a snore a caller hears at Joe DiMaggio's home—at 10:30 in the morning, the snoring of the famous New York Yankee holdout.

There can be no doubt that Joe enjoys his slumber as the entire baseball world is puzzled whether he'll weaken and sign Jake Ruppert's $25,000 contract.

Awakened, Joe blinks as he asks:

"What time is it?"

"Ten thirty."

"Nuts, this is the middle of the night for me."

Joe, who clouted 46 homers last year, consents to answer a few questions, although he makes it plain that he would rather sleep.

"If an agreement is reached on your contract, will you be in condition to play on opening day?"

"Yep," he replies, "I'm in condition. I weigh 200 pounds, which is normal for me."

"How do you keep in form?"

"Oh, play a little catch with some of my friends from North Beach and sometimes take a walk."

"How far do you walk?"

"Oh, a few blocks. Say I'm still sleepy."

Joe hasn't been in uniform for more than two weeks. He worked out a few days with the San Francisco Seals at their Hanford training camp. But, the Pacific Coast League race is now under way and the Seals are on the road.

"Are you worried about your contract?"

"Nope! It seems everybody else is more worried about it than I am."

Believe It or Not!

ST. LOUIS, April 18 (AP).—The St. Louis Browns offered the New York Yankees about $150,000 for Joe DiMaggio but failed to swing the deal, it was learned tonight.

Col. Jacob Ruppert was quoted by the Globe-Democrat as saying in a telephone conversation that his star outfielder, at present a stubborn holdout, "is not for sale at any price."

President Don Barnes, of the Browns, admitted he had made an offer—it was learned the offer approximated $150,000 cash.

Barnes said he was "mighty sorry" Colonel Ruppert's stand was so determined, but "the deal isn't dead as far as the Browns are concerned. I would certainly like to get DiMaggio for the Browns."

Yankee Contract Is Accepted by DiMaggio

DIMAGGIO AGREES TO $25,000 TERMS

Ruppert Wins Salary Battle— Pay Starts When Joe Shows He Is Ready to Play

STAR DUE HERE SATURDAY

'Can't Get Back Quick Enough,' He Declares Preparatory to Leaving Coast Home

Joe DiMaggio's hold-out siege against the Yankees terminated abruptly and without much dramatics yesterday, when it was announced that the American League's home-run champion and so-called "wonder player" had notified Colonel Jacob Ruppert from his home in San Francisco that he has accepted terms.

The terms, Business Manager Ed Barrow, who made the announcement, hastily explained, are those laid down by the Yankees. This means that the young Coast star, who has been a sensation with the world champions the past two years, will accept a one-year contract at $25,000, less the time he has lost in reporting.

What is more, his salary will not start with his arrival in New York, but only when he is pronounced ready to play. Manager Joe Mc-Carthy is to be sole judge of this. Marse Joe at present is in Boston, where the Yanks conclude their series with the Red Sox today.

Will Don Uniform

According to Barrow, DiMaggio, who ever since Jan. 21 has stoutly insisted he would not don a uniform this year unless the Yankees met his demand for $40,000, left San Francisco at 3:40 P. M., Pacific Coast time, yesterday. He is due to arrive in the city at 7:30 Saturday morning and will be in uniform when the Yankees face the Senators in the afternoon at the Stadium.

The ultimatum to DiMaggio that he must get ready at his own ex-

Times Wide World
JOE DIMAGGIO

pense is similar to that which was meted out to Charlie Ruffing last year, but if Manager McCarthy follows precedent in that case, DiMaggio's salary is likely to start as soon as he arrives.

McCarthy did this in the Ruffing case, explaining that was the more satisfactory way to handle the matter.

"I don't want to be unfair to a player," he said then, "and I don't want him hustling too fast to get in shape. He may tell me he is ready before he actually is and only harm may result."

Barrow, however, was not so certain McCarthy would adopt this policy again.

At his brewery offices Colonel Ruppert, winner in the salary battle, expressed himself as satisfied his difficulty with his young star had come to an end, though it was not without a touch of irony that he added.

"I hope the young man has learned his lesson. His pay will be $25,000, no more, no less, and it won't start until McCarthy says it should."

A Third-Year Man

The salary dispute ends with DiMaggio one of the highest-salaried players in organized baseball and indisputably the highest-paid third-year man in the game's history. Before coming to the Yankees in 1936, DiMaggio was under a six-months' contract in the Pacific Coast League for $1,800. He received $8,000 as salary from the Yankees in 1936, in addition to a cut of the victors' share in the world series. Last year DiMaggio's salary was $15,000, plus a world series cut which amounted to about $6,000.

Only Lou Gehrig, with his $39,000 contract, tops DiMaggio in Yankee salaries. The 23-year-old Coast player, on a $25,000 basis, outranks even the great Carl Hubbell, Giant pitching ace, whose salary is $22,500.

In one other respect, DiMaggio stands singularly alone. He has yet to open a season with the McCarthymen, as this, his first hold-out period, ends. In his first year as a Yankee, DiMaggio was out of the line-up because of diathermic burns on his right instep. Last year a tonsillectomy kept him on the sideline for the opener.

DiMaggio last year hit .346. He hammered out forty-six homers, batted in 167 runs, second only to Hank Greenberg, and got 215 hits for 418 total bases in 151 of the 157 contests in which the Yanks engaged. All this earned him recognition through the Winter as the player of the year, a distinction accorded him through the award of plaques by the New York Chapter of the Baseball Writers Association and the Philadelphia Sports Writers Association.

Joe Appears Relieved

SAN FRANCISCO, April 20 (AP). —Obviously relieved by termination of his holdout campaign, Joe DiMaggio said today he was "all excited about getting back there and rapping the ball again."

Confirming he had accepted the Yankees' terms, Joe declared he was going to try to get in such a good season that "there won't be any chance of an argument over salary next year. Naturally, I thought I was worth more this year. But I'd rather play ball than hold out. I can't get back quick enough now and I'm rarin' to go."

While completing packing DiMaggio ventured the prediction the Yankees would walk off with the pennant again, "not because I'm through holding out, though. It is a championship club anyhow. My team-mates are a swell bunch of fellows and I'd rather play with the Yanks than any other team in baseball."

His emphasis of the fact he had accepted "the club's terms" led some interviewers to speculate as to whether or not he had received private assurance of a bonus provided he turns in another spectacular season. DiMaggio denied this, however.

Throughout the entire DiMaggio clan there appeared a note of relief that he had capitulated and was ready to leave.

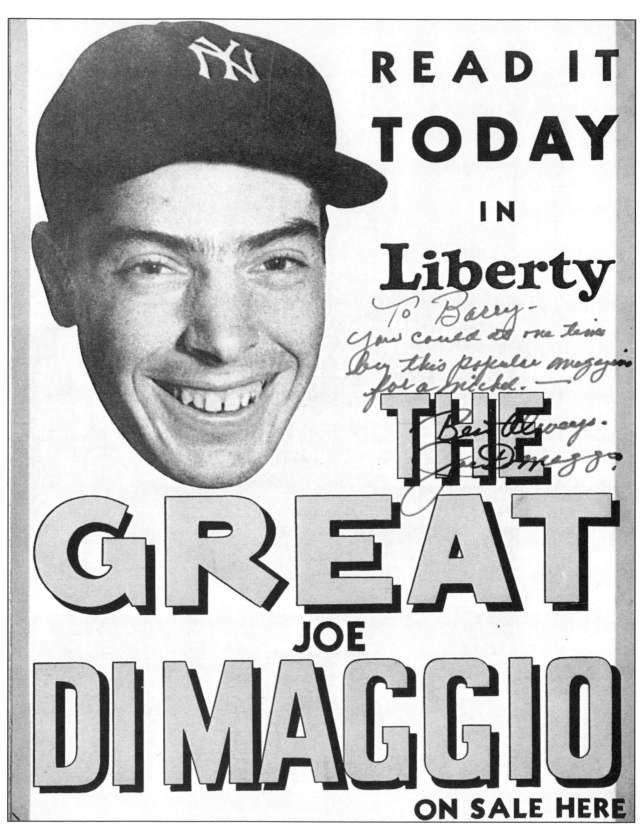

On the cover of *Liberty* magazine, which sold for a nickel in 1938.

Joe In Fold, But Not Forgiven

The brusqueness with which Col. Jacob Ruppert dealt with Joe DiMaggio, when the outfielder signed his contract, April 25, shows that the owner of the Yankees hasn't yet forgiven Joe's hold-out tactics. indicates Paul Mickelson of the Associated Press, who says the Colonel was so riled "he could hardly talk."

"None of the typical Ruppert fanfare and ballyhoo attended the signing and ceremony," reports Mickelson. "Except for the presence of a few baseball reporters, press photographers and newsreel men. it might have been the signing of Joe Foul Ball with Terre Haute.

"'Here's your contract, Joe DiMaggio,' said Col. Ruppert icily. 'Now go ahead and sign it.'

"Giuseppe signed without a word, and handed the papers back to the Colonel.

"'Now go ahead and play ball, Joe Di-Maggio,' ordered the Colonel like a stern country judge. 'Do your best. I hope you have a great year.'

"'Thanks,' said Joe. 'I'll do my best.'

"Someone asked if Joe was getting a bonus for signing.

"'Joe DiMaggio,' barked the Colonel, 'are you getting any bonus for this?'

"'No bonus,' gulped Joe.

"'That's right,' continued the Colonel. 'And furthermore Joe DiMaggio will not get a cent of pay until he starts to play ball. Now go ahead, you fellows (newspapermen), and bet that $2,000 with the fellow (Sports Editor Jimmy Powers of the New York Daily News) who says Joe signed his contract last fall.'

"'Yeah, but where are we going to get the money?' asked a reporter, 'besides, Powers' bet is $5,000.'

"'I'll loan you the money,' offered the Colonel.

"No one made a move to borrow the dough or to try to place the bet with Powers, so the matter was forgotten. However, the Colonel was so riled about the assertion DiMaggio had been signed all along and that his hold-out was a publicity stunt that the old gentleman could hardly talk."

The Yankees, at last, have the services of Joe DiMaggio, who after having missed 12 games, finally got into the line-up on April 30, against Washington. That very same day, DiMag collided with Joe Gordon chasing a fly and both players were taken to a hospital. However, the young Italian was back in the game next day, but Gordon could not play.

Joe Sees Strange Yankee Picture.

DiMaggio walked into a rather disconcerting and unfamiliar picture. He discovered that the famous power of the world champions had not yet shown itself with consistency, that batting totals in double figures had become very scarce, that the pitching was hot and cold, that Lou Gehrig simply could not strike his stride, and Lefty Gomez had lost two in a row and had failed to finish in any of his first three starts.

This put Giuseppe in a rather tough situation. The fans all said, "Well, now that DiMag is in there, things will right themselves."

As a matter of fact, it may take some time for the Yankee situation to achieve its normal. The club got off on the wrong foot. Too many hold-outs. Then Gehrig came in and could not get going.

What's wrong with Gehrig? Well, for one thing, it's not a trip to Japan. In 1935, when he had a tough time getting under way, his trip to Nippon was blamed. This time it may be his work in Hollywood, it may be the 35-year mark in age. It may be just an accident, which, over night, will be eradicated.

The Yankee situation has not been without compensations. Myril Hoag, thrown into DiMaggio's place, hit around .350. And he did a marvelous job in the field, too. Joe Gordon, whose first Yankee homer won a game in Philadelphia, after his speed had carried in the winning tally against Washington, also looks like the real thing.

McCarthy can't seem to make up his mind about the new pitchers and has asked President Harridge to extend the time for cutting down to 23 players from May 15 to May 22. Joe says that with the season starting a week later than it used to open, when the May 15 rule was adopted, there should be a week's grace.

Other managers are of a similar mind and it is believed that Harridge will allow the pilots until May 22 to make up their minds on new material.

Lee Stine has made a good impression, with his fine curve, as a relief pitcher. Atley Donald's speed intrigues McCarthy. Beggs' sinker ball has its moments. Sundra, hampered by a sore arm, may come along late and grab the spotlight. In the meantime, Joe is giving them all a fine chance to show what they can do.

DANIEL M. DANIEL.

DiMaggio and Spring Training

What odds spring training, now that Joe DiMaggio is picking up where he left off last year? Giuseppe didn't report to the New York Yankees until the season had opened, yet he jumped right in after working out a week, and apparently has done as well as if he had put in the entire training period in St. Petersburg.

Of course, the Yankee Bomber not only had the advantage of his youth, but he conditioned himself out in California while waiting for the golden word from Colonel Jacob Ruppert that would summon him back to the Yankees. It was, nevertheless, unsupervised training, without a manager, coach or trainer, yet, he came back seemingly in as good condition as anyone on the team; in fact, he hit his stride sooner than some of the others who had spent the entire training period in Florida.

The answer is that a DiMaggio, under favoring conditions in California, might be able to accomplish results impossible of attainment for others of less ability and in a different climate.

It has been fairly well established that the only way to get players into shape is to bring them together under regulated training conditions and an exception here and there does not prove that the system is either wrong or unnecessary. Until it is demonstrated otherwise—and club owners are not likely to encourage such dilatory tactics as DiMaggio's in order to furnish proof—spring training is going to continue along the extensive lines now followed. Even Class D clubs are establishing training camps these days and the trend seems to be toward more spring prepping, instead of less, with the idea that it is the only way to bring a team into the opening of the campaign, ready to play in what approximates mid-season form.

In his first appearance at the plate for the Yankees in 1938, in late April, Joe DiMaggio hits a looping single to left against the Senators at Griffith Stadium in Washington. The catcher for the Senators is Rick Ferrell.

Takes Girl to Learn DiMag Has Wonderful Brown Eyes

'Goodness, He's Divine! Lovely 198 Pounds,' Dorothy Writes

By DOROTHY KILGALLEN

Baseball experts are always telling me irrelevant things about the game, like how many men on a team, and what is a fly ball, but it took me to discover something really important, which is that Joe DiMaggio has wonderful brown eyes.

Goodness, he's divine!

Maybe there is something in this baseball, at that. Of course I have a lot to learn, but with a little help from Joe, say a couple of hours a day—I think I could catch on to some of the fancier plays.

THE OLD POTATO.

I had lesson one today, but I'm afraid I'll have to go all over it again, because I became rather confused—I might even say flustered—at the part where Joe was helping me hold the baseball.

"This," he said, looking meltingly at the ball, "is what we call the stitched potato, or the apricot, whichever you like."

"I like you," I said dreamily.

He showed me how HE holds the ball, and Mr. Max Kase, our baseball expert, came in just then and remarked: "You're doing fine," although I am not sure whether he was referring to the way I was holding the ball—or what.

LOVELY 198 POUNDS.

Then Joe explained to me how you swing the bat. He says all players have different size bats, depending on the weight that's most comfortable.

"This weighs about 39 ounces," he said.

"How much do you weigh?" I asked.

"A hundred and ninety-eight," Joe said.

Isn't that a lovely weight?

After we practised a while, Joe told me about some of his troubles with the Yankees, who certainly do not pay him what he is worth if he plays ball the way he looks, and Mr. Kase, the expert, who is inclined to be cynical, assures me he plays BETTER than he looks.

THAT $25,000 LOOK.

Joe is about to sign a contract for $25,000 a year, but he says: "I am worth a lot more than that," and I certainly think he is worth more than that if he just stands around on the field and lets the people look at him.

He has black hair that grows in a widow's peak, like Robert Taylor's, and quizzical eyebrows, to say nothing of eyelashes a yard long.

He says he gets a lot of fan mail from little boys, and offhand I could name a few little girls who would be very glad to write him a line, too.

OUTFIELD TOO FAR.

When I left him (reluctantly) Joe was on his way to the ball park to hit a few balls around and do a little catching and throwing.

He says he is an outfielder, and I think it's a shame to put him away out there where nobody can see him.

Joe not only has to hit home runs, but he has to catch fly balls, which are very hard to catch, and he says I will not get up to catching flies until about lesson 11 (goody).

In his spare time, Joe eats steaks, sleeps and goes to the movies. He likes watching movies but not being in them. He just likes to play ball.

HE DOESN'T DANCE.

"And I don't dance," he said to me, rather sternly, I thought. "Some athletes are good dancers, but I'm not. I don't do the dipsy doodle. I get my exercise playing ball."

(That's all right, Joe, we can sit this out.)

Before I left, Joe autographed a real baseball for me—the one he'd been using himself.

"Now take it home and practise," he told me.

And I did. But it's a funny thing. I don't seem to be very good at this game unless Joe is around to help me hold the ball.

Our Dorothy Kilgallen, who's summat of a reporter on things other than baseball, discovers that "there may be something in the game, after all . . ."

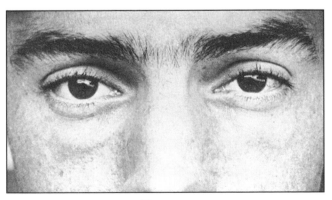

The eyes.

PLAYERS IN CRASH

Gordon Collides With DiMaggio Chasing a Fly—Both in Hospital

YANKS TOP SENATORS, 8-4

Chandler Goes Route to Win —Outfield Ace Gets Safety in His 1938 Debut

By JAMES P. DAWSON
Special to THE NEW YORK TIMES.

WASHINGTON, April 30.—Launching his third year as a Yankee in his first game today, Joe DiMaggio, the celebrated holdout, played a part in a victory for the McCarthymen over Bucky Harris's Senators, 8 to 4, to give the champions the distinction of passing the .500 mark for the first time this season.

Tonight, however, DiMaggio is confined to a hospital cot. Joe Gordon is in an adjoining bed and Myril Hoag narrowly escaped keeping them company as a consequence of an exciting mid-game crack-up which temporarily shocked some 16,000 fans.

DiMaggio and Gordon were taken to Garfield Hospital for observation. They were removed to the institution by ambulance on orders from Dr. Edward Larkin after being assisted off the field at the end of the Senators' sixth inning.

Hurry Call for Ambulances

Colliding under a fly ball hit to left field by Taft Wright, pinch-hitting for Dutch Leonard when the Senators were fighting to overcome a three-run Yankee lead, DiMaggio and Gordon went down in their tracks, lay unconscious on the field as play was interrupted for five minutes, and showed symptoms of brain concussion which led to a hurry call for ambulances.

They were under observation for possible internal injuries. Gordon crashed head-on into DiMaggio as he darted over to left field for a high, short fly for which DiMaggio and Hoag ran simultaneously.

DiMaggio was hit on the left side of the head and a swelling started. Gordon was struck on the right side of the head and body in the collision. His cheek and jawbone were bruised and swollen and his right arm and shoulder were jarred.

The impact stretched Gordon unconscious for five minutes. DiMaggio was out only temporarily.

No Fractures Found

X-ray pictures made tonight showed no fractures of any sort. Both Gordon and DiMaggio are being held at the hospital overnight and, unless something unforeseen develops, they will rejoin the Yankees at the Shoreham Hotel tomorrow.

The near-tragedy was as dramatic as it was unexpected. The Yanks were hugging a three-run lead entering the last half of the sixth, thanks to singles by Red Rolfe and DiMaggio, an error by Jonathan Stone and Bill Dickey's resounding double in the first, and Hoag's double, Gordon's long fly and another error in the second.

His knuckle ball working with mystifying success, Leonard turned back thirteen Yankees in a row from Rolfe, who ended the second, right through Dickey, who closed the sixth.

Spud Chandler gave the Senators three scattered hits in the first four innings and escaped the consequences of three clustered in the fifth through a double play. When Zeke Bonura doubled to start the sixth, the Yankee hurler was in trouble. Stone grounded out and Travis singled Bonura home. Buddy Myer skied out and, after Rick Ferrell walked, Wright was sent up to bat for Leonard.

Hoag Makes the Catch

His effort was a high, short fly, drawing Hoag and DiMaggio in from the deep outfield, and for which the eager Gordon dashed madly from his position at second. The three players arrived simultaneously as the ball descended. Hoag, victim of a crack-up with DiMaggio in Detroit early in 1936 which kept him out most of the season, stuck out his gloved hand and made the catch, skirting by DiMaggio and Gordon just before they crashed.

Players from both dugouts poured out on the field, umpires raced out to lend assistance. Doc Painter, Yankee trainer, and Dr. Larkin supervised first-aid ministrations while the crowd sat hushed in the stands.

After that sixth inning, Pete Appleton took up the pitching burden for the Senators and turned the McCarthymen back in order in the seventh. But the champions bunched six hits, including a triple and a single by Rolfe with a sacrifice and two passes, one of which forced in a run, to nick Appleton and Kendall Chase for five more runs in the eighth and ninth.

Chandler pitched steadily until the eighth, when, in a drenching rainstorm, he temporarily lost his grip. He gave a pass and two singles in the eighth, when the Senators fashioned a run, and in the ninth they rushed across two more on Goslin's single, Stone's double and Travis's single before Chandler disposed of them.

Misses Shoe-String Catch

DiMaggio, jeered when he first stepped to the plate, signalized his return to play with a fluke single which Stone kicked around the outfield after missing a shoe-string catch, and pulled down three flies before the crack-up. One of the plays was a glittering running catch on Stone to end the first inning.

Chandler gained the distinction of being the fourth Yankee pitcher to start and finish a game this year, a feat Red Ruffing has achieved twice. Monte Pearson and Joe Beggs are the others.

George Selkirk was on the sideline nursing an injured right wrist until the emergency brought him into action in the seventh. Manager McCarthy inserted him in left, sent Hoag to center and put Bill Knickerbocker at second.

In the confusion, Lou Gehrig again went hitless.

Frankie Crosetti shared this unenviable distinction. He has now gone hitless in nineteen trips to the plate.

The sixteenth Yankee double play of the campaign thrust back the Senators in the fifth, when they nicked Chandler for three blows.

Tomorrow Lefty Vernon Gomez will have a fling at the Griffmen.

The box score:

NEW YORK (A)	ab.	r.	h.	po.	a.	e.		WASHINGTON (A)	ab.	r.	h.	po.	a.	e.
Crosetti, ss.	3	1	0	1	1	0		Almada, cf.	4	1	0	3	0	0
Rolfe, 3b.	5	1	3	1	1	0		Lewis, 3b.	5	0	2	4	2	1
DiMaggio, cf.	1	1	1	3	0	0		Goslin, lf.	5	1	3	0	0	0
Selkirk, lf.	2	0	1	0	0	0		Bonura, 1b.	5	1	2	5	2	0
Gehrig, 1b.	5	0	0	9	0	0		Stone, rf.	4	1	2	2	0	1
Dickey, c.	4	0	1	3	0	0		Travis, ss.	5	1	2	0	0	0
Henrich, rf.	4	1	1	1	0	0		Myers, 2b.	4	0	0	1	3	0
Hoag, lf.-cf.	1	2	2	4	0	0		R. Ferrell, c.	3	0	2	6	0	1
Gordon, 2b.	2	0	0	0	3	0		Leonard, p.	2	0	0	1	0	0
Kn'k'b'r, 2b.	1	0	1	2	0	0		aWright	1	0	0	0	0	0
Chandler, p.	4	1	1	1	5	0		Appleton, p.	0	0	0	0	0	0
								bBurge	1	0	0	0	0	0
Total	37	8	10	27	12			Chase, p.	0	0	0	0	0	0
								Total	39	4	11	27	8	2

aBatted for Leonard in sixth.
bBatted for Appleton in eighth.

New York .... 2 1 0 0 0 0 0 1 4—8
Washington .... 0 0 0 0 0 1 0 1 2—4

Runs batted in—Dickey 2, Travis 2, Rolfe 3, R. Ferrell, Crosetti, Selkirk, Stone.

Two-base hits—Dickey, Hoag, Almada, Bonura, Stone, Three-base hit—Rolfe. Stolen bases—Myer, R. Ferrell. Sacrifice—Crosetti. Double play—Chandler, Crosetti and Gehrig. Left on bases—New York 5, Washington 11. Bases on balls—Off Chandler 3, Chase 2. Struck out—By Leonard 2, Chase 1, Chandler 1. Hits—Off Leonard 4 in 6 innings, Appleton 2 in 2, Chase 4 in 1. Losing pitcher—Leonard. Umpires—Kolls and Moriarty. Time of game—2:04.

Red Rolfe

Charley Keller

Spud Chandler & Joe DiMaggio
(Pitcher)   (CF)

Joe DiMaggio

Here's Postmaster Jim Farley presenting Joe McCarthy with a
watch at the Stadium for being voted the outstanding manager in
the major leagues last year by a poll taken by the St. Louis
Sporting News

A scrapbook look at Joe DiMaggio and friends.

Di Maggio's Bat Main Factor in Yank Victory

Two Homers Account For Five Tallies

By DANIEL,
Staff Correspondent.

ST. LOUIS, May 19.—Joe Di Maggio today once more was the superlative Giuseppe of 1937. Rid of the hoot owls of the Stadium, whose senseless vocalizations had got on his nerves, Joe opened the first Western tour of the Yankees with two home runs and a third hit, which lifted his batting average to an imperial .431.

Those five tallies which Di Maggio drove in with his blasts into the right and left field seats were quite important. For one thing, they beat the Browns, 11 to 7, and enabled the Bronx Bombers to get off on the right foot in this avowed effort to intimidate a Western contingent from which they won six out of seven in the Stadium recently. For another thing, those homers kept the Yankees only a game behind Boston's pace.

With his drive into the right center pavilion with one on in the fifth, Di Maggio tied Tommy Henrich for the club leadership in homer runs, at five. In the eighth, Giuseppe clouted one into the left center bleachers—the first Yankee four master of the season with two on base.

With that sixth home run, which brought the club total to 19, Di Maggio became the first member of the Bronx Bombers to achieve two circuit drives in one game this year.

Considering that Di Maggio missed eleven contests because of his holdout, and has appeared in just thirteen games, he seemed to be doing a fair to middling job. It won't be long before the Californian leaves Jimmy Foxx, Hank Greenberg and all the rest far behind.

Gomez meets Bobby Feller again on Sunday, in Cleveland Stadium. Bobby beat him in the Stadium last week, 3 to 2.

Newsom Fans Six Straight, But Di Maggio Jolts Him.

The conditions under which Di Maggio broke a 7 to 7 deadlock in the eighth inning truly were dramatic. By fanning Arndt Jorgens to end the sixth, Lou Gehrig, Twink Selkirk and Bill Knickerbocker in the seventh, and Johnny Murphy and Frankie Crosetti in the eighth, Buck Newsom had matched the American League record of six consecutive strikeouts.

Not since May 23, 1924, when Walter Johnson performed the feat, had the trick been turned in that circuit.

Red Rolfe's single, to break this skein, made Newsom just a trifle downcast. But Buck was riding high. He would show these Yankees by whiffing their slugging leader. Tommy Henrich walked, bringing up Di Maggio with two on and two out.

"Here goes sweet revenge for that wallop in the fifth," snickered Newsom, who had been spending a hot afternoon posing in all the ancient classic attitudes made famous by the late Bill Muldoon in his youth.

Buck really had something. He got two strikes on Di Maggio. Soon it was 3 and 2. Common sense dictated giving Joe nothing good and, if necessary, passing him to get at Jorgens.

Gomez Fails Once More, Needs Regular Turn.

But Newsom figured he could blow that ball by Giuseppe, who leaned on it with a vengeance. Jorgens singled, Gehrig doubled, and Newsom walked out of the box, blaming it all on Umpire Summers!

The victory was not without a little aloes for the Yankees. Making his seventh start, Lefty Gomez failed to go the route for the fifth time. He has won only two and lost 4. Yesterday's victory went to Johnny Murphy.

After Lefty had opened the fifth with passes to Bell and West, Joe McCarthy gave him the high sign. Gomez was fast enough, but his wildness forced him into a pack of trouble.

"What I need is regular work, every four days. I am stable worn," Gomez complained. "I certainly am not worried over any divorce suit now. Give me good weather and plenty of work and I'll get straightened out."

Medwick Catch Deciding Factor in National League All-Star Win; Strategy of McCarthy Criticized

Disappointed Supporters of Junior Major Believe Marse Joe Made Mistake Shifting Foxx to Third to Keep Batting Power in Line-up; Frick Loop's Pitchers Star

By DICK FARRINGTON

CINCINNATI, O. —T h e story of the 1938 "Dream Game," played at Crosley Field here, July 6, essentially is one of those "man bites dog" yarns— made so because the National League, following four years of futility out of five, came through to take its second triumph in the annual star spangled contest. It was in 1936 that the senior loop's luminaries put over their other win, the American leaguers having won three straight times, beginning with 1933, when the mid-season classic was introduced, and again in 1937. Thus, the standing is four to two with the A. L. on the up-side.

THE GAME IN DETAIL.
First Inning:
AMERICANS—Ott momentarily misjudged Kreevich's long fly, but took the ball near the embankment. Gehringer sent an easy roller to Vander Meer and was out at first. Averill was retired on his bounder, Herman to McCormick. No runs, no hits, no errors.

NATIONALS—Hack lined a single over Cronin's head. Herman hit to Cronin, who, with a double play in front of him, fumbled the ball and Hack went to third and Herman to first. Goodman was called out on strikes. Medwick hit a long fly to Averill and Hack easily scored after the catch. Ott was out on a short fly to Averill. One run, one hit, one error.

S. E. Post Luck

CINCINNATI, O.—While press box occupants were discussing the outcome of the All-Star game at Crosley Field and commenting upon the work of individual stars who made possible the victory for the Bill Terry aggregation, J. Roy Stockton of the St. Louis Post-Dispatch chipped in with the remark:

"Johnny Vander Meer and The Saturday Evening Post won the game for the National League."

Not only did the N. L. players go into the game with a spirit of "We won't let 'em beat us this time," recalling Tom Meany's Saturday Evening Post article, "New Minor League—the National?" but Stockton, who had prepared a story titled "The People's Choice—National League," for the same publication, had a hunch that the traditional Post luck would carry the N. L. through to victory.

Second Inning.
AMERICANS—Foxx went down swinging after Medwick pulled up on his high foul fly that fell near the stands. Vander Meer took DiMaggio's roller down the third base line and threw the runner out at first. Herman threw out Dickey. No runs, no hits, no errors.

NATIONALS—Lewis grabbed Lombardi's grounder with his gloved hand and tossed him out at first. McCormick popped to Gehringer. Durocher rolled to Cronin, who threw to Foxx for the putout. No runs, no hits, no errors.

Third Inning.

AMERICANS—Cronin got the first hit off Vander Meer, a line single over Hack's head. Lewis flied to Ott in deep center. Vander Meer took Gomez' high bounder and Lefty was out at first on a close play, Cronin advancing to second. Kreevich popped to Herman. No runs, one hit, no errors.

NATIONALS—Hank Leiber batted for Vander Meer and lined to Kreevich in deep left. Hack grounded out, Gehringer to Foxx. Herman singled between Lewis and Cronin. Dickey took Goodman's high foul. No runs, one hit, no errors.

Fourth Inning.

AMERICANS—Bill Lee went to the mound for the National leaguers. Medwick drew a base on balls. Medwick took Averill's fly in short left center. Durocher went back of Hack for Foxx' grounder and threw to Herman, forcing Gehringer at second. DiMaggio went down on a called third strike. No runs, no hits, no errors.

NATIONALS—Johnny Allen took over the pitching duties for the American leaguers. Medwick hit a high fly which Foxx took near the pitching mound. Ott got a triple on his drive to right center fence, which Averill played badly. Lombardi's single to left scored Ott. McCormick rolled to Gehringer and was out at first. Durocher struck out. One run, two hits, no errors.

Fifth Inning.

AMERICANS—Durocher lost Dickey's high fly back of third and the Yankee catcher got a double. Cronin flied to Ott. Lou Gehrig batted for Lewis and was thrown out by Herman, who made a nice stop far to his left, Dickey moving to third on the play. Hack made a brilliant stop of Allen's hard grounder and threw him out at first. No runs, one hit, no errors.

NATIONALS—Foxx moved to third base, replacing Lewis, and Gehrig went to first base for the Americans. Lee flied to Averill, who also gathered in Hack's looper to center. Herman was called out on a third strike. No runs, no hits, no errors.

Sixth Inning.

AMERICANS—Roger Cramer batted for Kreevich and was out, Herman to McCormick. Gehringer rolled to Durocher and was out at first. Averill struck out without taking his bat off his shoulder. No runs, no hits, no errors.

NATIONALS—Cramer went to left field for the Americans. A pitched ball grazed Goodman's shirt and he went to first. Medwick flied to DiMaggio. Goodman stole second and continued to third when Dickey's high throw went into center field. Ott struck out. Lombardi grounded out, Cronin to Gehrig. No runs, no hits, one error.

Seventh Inning.

AMERICANS—Mace Brown assumed the pitching duties for the Nationals. Foxx hit a hard smash off Durocher's glove for a single. DiMaggio forced Foxx, Durocher to Herman. Dickey popped to Hack. DiMaggio stole second. Cronin got a base on balls. Durocher juggled Gehrig's grounder and the Yankee first sacker was credited with a hit. Rudy York batted for Allen and went down swinging with the count three and two. No runs, two hits, no errors.

NATIONALS—Bob Grove was the third American League hurler. McCormick singled to center. Durocher laid down a bunt and when Gehringer failed to cover first Foxx' throw went into right field, McCormick scoring. Durocher also scored when DiMaggio, retrieving Foxx' throw, threw over Dickey's head. Durocher was credited with a hit and Foxx and DiMaggio drew errors on the play. Brown and Hack struck out, the third strikes being called. Herman was called out on a third strike. Two runs, two hits, two errors.

Eighth Inning.

AMERICANS—Hack made a great play on Cramer's badly bounding grounder and tossed to first for the out. Gehringer singled to right. Averill flied to Goodman. Brown took Foxx' tap and threw him out at first. No runs, one hit, no errors.

NATIONALS—DiMaggio gathered in Goodman's line drive. Medwick singled to left center. Averill took care of Ott's short fly. Lombardi dropped a Texas leaguer in right center, Medwick moving to third. McCormick forced Lombardi, Foxx to Gehringer. No runs, two hits, no errors.

Ninth Inning.

AMERICANS—DiMaggio hit a line single to left field. Medwick made a sensational one-handed catch of Dickey's drive near the scoreboard, falling down after making the catch. Cronin hit a line double to the fence in left center, scoring DiMaggio. Gehrig hit a terrific line drive which Goodman reached and snared near the right field stands, Cronin moving to third after the catch. Bob Johnson batted for Grove and took a called third strike. One run, two hits, no errors.

The Official Score

AMERICAN LEAGUE.

	AB.	R.	H.	TB.	O.	A.	E.
Kreevich, left field	2	0	0	0	1	0	0
Cramer, left field	2	0	0	0	0	0	0
Gehringer, second base	3	0	1	1	2	2	0
Averill, center field	4	0	0	5	0	0
Foxx, first-third base	4	0	1	1	5	1	1
DiMaggio, right field	4	1	1	2	0	1
Dickey, catcher	4	0	1	2	8	0	1
Cronin, shortstop	3	0	2	3	0	2	1
Lewis, third base	1	0	0	0	1	0
*Gehrig, first base	3	0	1	1	1	0	0
Gomez, pitcher	1	0	0	0	0	0	0
Allen, pitcher	1	0	0	0	0	0	0
Grove, pitcher	0	0	0	0	0	0	0
†York	1	0	0	0	0	0	0
‡Johnson	1	0	0	0	0	0	0
Totals	34	1	7	9	24	6	4

NATIONAL LEAGUE.

	AB.	R.	H.	TB.	O.	A.	E.
Hack, third base	4	1	1	1	1	2	0
Herman, second base	4	0	1	1	3	4	0
Goodman, right field	3	0	0	2	0	0
Medwick, left field	4	0	1	1	2	0	0
Ott, center field	4	1	1	3	3	0	0
Lombardi, catcher	4	0	2	2	5	0	0
McCormick, first base	4	1	1	1	11	0	0
Durocher, shortstop	3	1	1	1	0	3	0
Vander Meer, pitcher	0	0	0	0	0	3	0
Lee, pitcher	1	0	0	0	0	0	0
Brown, pitcher	1	0	0	0	0	1	0
§Leiber	1	0	0	0	0	0	0
Totals	33	4	8	10	27	13	0

*Batted for Lewis in fifth.
†Batted for Allen in seventh.
‡Batted for Grove in ninth.
§Batted for Vander Meer in third.

American	0 0 0 0 0 0 0 0 1—1
National	1 0 0 1 0 0 2 0 *—4

Runs batted in—Medwick, Lombardi, Cronin.

Two-base hits—Dickey, Cronin.

Three-base hit—Ott.

Stolen bases—Goodman, DiMaggio.

Pitching records—Vander Meer 0 runs, 1 hit in three innings; Lee 0 runs, 1 hit in three innings; Gomez 2 hits, 1 run in three innings; Allen 1 run, 2 hits in three innings; Brown 1 run, 5 hits in 3 innings; Grove 2 runs, 2 hits in 2 innings.

Struck out—By Gomez 1 (Goodman), by Allen 3 (Durocher, Herman, Ott), by Grove 3 (Brown, Hack, Herman), by Vander Meer 1 (Foxx), by Lee 2 (DiMaggio, Averill), by Brown 2 (York, Johnson).

Bases on balls—Off Lee 1 (Gehringer), off Brown 1 (Cronin).

Hit by pitcher—By Allen 1 (Goodman).

Earned runs—American League 1, National League 1.

Left on bases—American League 8, National League 6.

Winning pitcher—Vander Meer.

Losing pitcher—Gomez.

Umpires—Klem (N. L.) home plate; Geisel (A. L.) third base, for the first four and one-half innings; Ballanfant (N. L.) second base; Basil (A. L.) first base; Geisel (A. L.) home plate; Klem (N. L.) third base, for the remainder of the game. Official scorer—Tom Swope.

New York Gets 1939 Game.

The 1939 All-Star game is to be played at Yankee Stadium in New York as one of the sports features of the World's Fair to be held there. . . . In 1940, the contest will go to a National League city and in 1941 it will be played at Detroit. . . . Ford Frick, president of the National League, spiked a report that the two leagues would discontinue the annual mid-season classic after next year's contest. "We in the National League consider the game a fine show and one that peps up interest," said Frick. "The receipts also go to a worthy charity cause. I am sure Will Harridge (president of the American League) feels the same way I do about the game." . . . When Mace Brown got into the jam in the ninth inning, Bill Terry had Carl Hubbell warming up in the bullpen. . . . Following the game, Brown said he couldn't get his curve ball breaking where he wanted.

Friends of Vernon Gomez said the Yankee southpaw and his wife, the former June O'Dea, are near a complete reconciliation in their marital rift and that Lefty is in far better spirits than he had been. The Gomezes have been doing a lot of golfing together. . . . The Americans were held as high as 3 to 1 to win the game.

Star Light, Star Bright ∴ All Cannot Shine Same Night But Each Is Luminary in Own Right

YOUTH HAS ITS FLING, WITH AGE—Left to right, Bob Feller, Cleveland's 19-year-old strike-out sensation; Bob Grove of the Red Sox, 38-year-old graybeard of the classic, and Johnny Vander Meer, Cincinnati's sensational 23-year-old no-hit specialist. Feller did not have a chance to work, but Grove had his fling, as did Vander Meer, who retired nine of the ten batters to face him.

WHEN SCHNOZZOLA WAS ALL EARS —Ernie Lombardi of the Reds, who caught the entire game for the National Leaguers, and Manager Bill Terry (right), snapped in the conference which resulted in the stopping of the American League sluggers.

BOSS MAN—Joe McCarthy of the Americans, did a lot of looking as the Nats took their batting practice, but he didn't know his defense would crack wide open.

HOME RUN TWINS—Mel Ott (left) of the Giants, and Ival Goodman of the Reds, are fighting it out for the four-bagger championship in the National League, but neither found the range in the Dream Game, although Mel connected for a long triple in the fourth that was turned into a run. Goodman, hitless three times up, was robbed of a possible triple by DiMaggio.

TWO GOATS—Jimmy Foxx (left) of the Red Sox figured in the wild throwing outbreak that gave the Nationals two runs in the seventh inning, while Rudy York (right), Detroit Tiger bomber, suffered the ignominy of striking out with the bases filled when he was sent in as a pinch-hitter in the A. L. half of the same inning. To make matters worse for Rudy, the last pitch looked low to everybody in the park.

WORKING PRESS REALLY WORKED—This unusual view shows part of the newspaper and radio line-up atop the roof at Crosley Field, as well as a section of the crowd in the grandstand below.

LAUGH CLOWN—Al Schacht got the crowd in a good humor before play started. He went through a brand new repertoire of pantomime, then directed the orchestra, attired in bloomers, plug hat and swallow-tailed coat.

The Tail of The Comet

A SALUTE TO TOM SWOPE!

TOM SWOPE, Cincinnati Post scrivener, who had charge of press arrangements, was presented with a handsome watch, in behalf of THE SPORTING NEWS, by Arch Ward, sports editor of the Chicago Tribune, who originated the All-Star game in 1933, for his fine job in looking after the convenience and comfort of the typewriter athletes and radio men and for his able service as a baseball writer for 28 years. Swope was taken by surprise by the gift and displayed the timepiece to friends until his office inquired if he was going to write a running account of the contest. Swope established press headquarters at the Pavilion Caprice on the fourth floor of the Netherland Plaza, where telegraph facilities, typewriters, refreshments and food were provided in abundant quantity with the compliments of the National League and the Cincinnati club. Bill Cleary and Junior Sweeney were on the floor to see that only the wearers of press buttons were admitted. Plenty of press busses were provided between the hotel and Crosley Field before and after the game. There were 61 special wires in operation in the press box, the capacity of which was more than trebled to handle the 254 correspondents. Each writer was assigned to a definite numbered seat in the press box and all arrangements were handled smoothly.

Bill Slocum, General Mills (Wheaties) public relations man, looked a little like the "Man Without a Country" because he did not have a report to file, but made himself at home among the scribes. The former New York American baseball expert had 'covered' all previous Dream Games for his paper. He was in the Wheaties party that included C. S. Samuelson of General Mills and John H. Sarles and Brad Robinson of the Knox Reeves agency.

The umpires, by the way, receive no remuneration for their services in the game, but they are annually given a token by Commissioner Kenesaw M. Landis. This year, they were presented with valuable wrist watches.

One of the few active big-time players who thought enough of the game to be present, was Freddy Fitzsimmons, pitcher for the Brooklyn Dodgers. Unlike managers, coaches, etc., as members of the team, he was there on his own.

Thomas Jefferson Hickey, president emeritus of the American Association, who has been living in Los Angeles, was fanning as enthusiastically in the lobby of the Netherland Plaza and displaying as much pep as any of the younger visitors. Hickey, who is 67 years old, says his chief complaint is that he can't always buy THE SPORTING NEWS in the City of Angels "because they sell out too quickly."

Arriving at the Netherland Plaza, Pitcher Vernon Kennedy of the Detroit Tigers found that he had no room reservation, whereupon a bystander cracked, "Why didn't he bring along his trailer?" Kennedy occupies a trailer along the Detroit lake front during the summer.

Considerable color was added to the scene at Crosley Field by the uniforms of the vendors and ushers. The vendors wore all-blue uniforms, while the ushers were attired in red coats, blue caps and blue trousers piped in red. The price of each item hawked was indicated in large figures on the caps. After the game, the ushers surrounded the infield after the fashion of Andy (Chicago Cub) Frain's boys and prevented fans from walking across the infield—a regular routine at Crosley Field.

Al Schacht, the game's clown prince, drew salvo after salvo of applause before play started. In addition to his mimicry, Al took over the direction of the orchestra when it played "Alice Blue Gown" and "Blue Heaven." Just before the game started, Schacht was at his best. He took the mound and, following a regulation warm-up, gave his interpretation of a pitcher losing his stuff. Art Fletcher acted as his stooge and when Al imaginarily filled the bases, the Yankee coach went out and ordered him off the mound. Schacht refused to leave and when Fletcher decided to let him stay, Al kissed him on the forehead. Then, when an imaginary batter socked a home run, Fletch ran out and, with the aid of a noose, got the comical man out of there.

Although a capacity throng of 27,067 filled Crosley Field, the attendance was the second smallest in the history of the series. However, the receipts — $38,469.50 — were larger than at either of the two most recent games.

Johnny Vander Meer used 31 pitches for the ten men who faced him. He threw only 12 called balls.

Stanley Hack fouled off three straight pitches from Vernon Gomez before lining out his single to left in the opening round.

Joe Medwick hesitated because of the closeness of the fences and lost Jimmy Foxx's long foul down the left field line in the initial frame. Then Jimmy went down swinging on one of Vander Meer's fast curves, so Ducky Wucky was relieved of a lot of ignominy.

Ival Goodman's sleeve and cap were touched by Johnny Allen's pitch in the sixth and he went to first feeling that Allen had tried to dust him off. A moment later the hit-and-run play was flashed and Ott missed the ball. Bill Dickey threw high over second trying to catch Goodie, who went on to third. The Cincinnati outfielder was given credit for a stolen base and Dickey was charged with an error for the additional base taken by Goodman. He died there, however, when Joe Cronin made a long throw on Lombardi's grounder for the third out.

Bill Klem and Harry Geisel, the senior National and American League umpires who worked the plate, introduced a new quick change act when they switched positions at the end of the first half of the fifth inning, with Klem replacing Geisel at third base and Geisel succeeding Klem back of the catcher. In past years the umpires who carried out the plate assignment went to their dressing room, the starting chief to shed his chest protector and the second umpire-in-chief to put his on. Klem and Geisel, however, used one protector. Klem unbuckling it and handing it to Geisel, who strapped it on so quickly that a lot of fans missed seeing the two men switch positions. When Klem got to third base he was fumbling with his necktie. Manager Bill McKechnie of the Reds, a man who has had many a bitter argument with Klem during the heat of battle, was in the third base coacher's box at that time, so he stepped over and adjusted the Old, Old Arbiter's scarf.

Officials of the Hillerich & Bradsby Company, makers of Louisville Slugger bats, provided a treat for the players of both teams. Before they left their respective clubs, the company notified each "Star" that it would not be necessary for him to bring his favorite bat, because two "copies" of the war club of every performer had been especially turned for them in the Louisville Slugger plant, the bats being brought to Cincinnati. Headed by President J. A. (Bud) Hillerich and his sons, Ward and "Junior," the Hillerich & Bradsby delegation included John T. Rodgers, Henry Morrow, Stanley Held and Roscoe Hovatter.

Tom Swope, baseball writer of the Cincinnati Post, served as official scorer of the game, receiving his appointment from Commissioner K. M. Landis.

American League headquarters were represented by President and Mrs. Harridge and their son, Bill; Miss Dorothy Hummel, secretary to Harridge; Lew Fonseca, Ed Lehman, Tom Connolly, L. C. McEvoy, Henry P. Edwards and Miss Mary Ryan. Young Harridge planned to leave the following day with a friend on an auto trip to California.

The official National League delegation included President Ford Frick, with his son; Harvey Traband, secretary-treasurer; Bill Brandt, publicity chief, and Mrs. Stevens, Frick's secretary.

Bob Emslie, long since retired from the National League's staff of umpires, but still one of its scouts for umpire talent, was an interested spectator at the game.

Clark Griffith, president of the Washington Senators, and J. G. Taylor Spink, publisher of THE SPORTING NEWS, representing the advisory council of the Association of Professional Ball Players of America, the game's charity organization which benefits from the proceeds of the All-Star game, met with Win Clark, secretary of the association, and Eddie Collins, vice-president of the Boston Red Sox, at the Netherland Plaza the morning of July 6 to discuss the affairs of the organization.

Catcher Ernie Lombardi of the Reds, who worked the entire game, said he lost 14 pounds during his service behind the plate. Ernie expected to regain six or eight of the pounds, however, by tucking away a big steak and a few steins of beer, following the contest.

Among the visiting fans was J. W. (Gee) Bacon, Paris, Ky., who is personally acquainted with many of the players whom he has met during his annual winter sojourns in Florida. Bacon, a faithful rooter for the Reds, has attended the last 24 World's Series. He formerly served as president of the old Blue Grass League.

Both leagues had movie-takers on the job, getting pictures for winter use. Lew Fonseca, promotional director of the American League, was taking scenes of the crowd and also of performers demonstrating the right and wrong way of making various plays. Burton Holmes was in charge of the work for the National, which is now preparing an educational film for release this fall. President Ford Frick of the senior circuit was on the field before the game, taking colored movies for his own use.

Mrs. Clark Griffith was trying to talk her husband, president of the Washington Senators, into a winter vacation in Honolulu. But the Old Fox doesn't like the water, so it's likely to be Orlando, Fla., again.

Headed by Judge W. G. Bramham, president of the National Association, an impressive delegation of minor league officials were on hand for the All-Star game. Among those in attendance were President Frank J. Shaughnessy and Secretary William J. Manley of the International League, President George M. Trautman of the American Association, President Tommy Richardson of the Eastern League, President Ralph Daughton of the Piedmont League, President Ray Ryan of the Mountain State League, President Herman White of the Northern League, President Gene Lawing of the North Carolina State League and President Joe Bertig of the Northeast Arkansas League.

League President Ford Frick went into the Nationals' dressing room at Crosley Field, an hour before the game, and presented gold wrist watches, valued at $85 each, to every member of the National League squad.

Although all the All-Star players were besieged by autograph-hunters, Lefty Grove appeared to be the most-sought-after. He also was probably the most accommodating.

When Joe McCarthy asked Johnny Allen if he would like to pitch the second three-inning stretch for the American leaguers, Allen, who never hit it off with the Yankee pilot even before McCarthy traded him to the Indians, responded: "Aw, don't strain yourself, Joe." After taking the hill, Johnny shook off one of Bill Dickey's signals so long that Bill finally yelled, "All right, throw what you want to." Following the game, the Cleveland ace remarked: "From what I saw of those guys, I think I'll pitch a few more years in the American League and then round out my career as a hitter in the National."

The game furnished evidence that the American League ball is livelier than the National League ball. The first four and a half innings were played with the National League ball, in which the National leaguers made four hits and the American leaguers two. In the last four innings, played with the American League ball, the National leaguers made four hits and the American leaguers five, plus those two mighty drives by Dickey and Gehrig in the ninth, which Medwick and Goodman caught.

And the best crack of the day came from Vernon Gomez. The Yankee left-hander was taking a morning snack in the Frontier room of the Netherland Plaza with Charley Ruffing, his teammate and pal. Catcher Ike Danning of the New York Giants happened by and Ruffing and Gomez exchanged pleasantries with him. Danning was about to leave when Gomez chirped: "Ike, if you'll wait a minute you can walk out of here with a couple of real big leaguers."

SEE ALL, TELL ALL
AT ALL-STAR SCENE

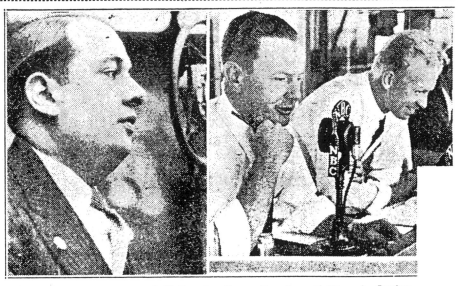

Harry Hartman, veteran of Station WCPO, Cincinnati, who regularly broadcasts the Reds' home games, looked after his own clientele through special permission from Commissioner Landis.

Tom Manning (left), of Station WTAM, Cleveland, and Red Barber of WLW, Cincinnati, collaborated in giving NBC network listeners an account of the game.

Bill Dyer, WCAU, Philadelphia, alternated with France Laux, KMOX, St. Louis, in sending a word picture of the contest over a nationwide hook-up for Columbia Broadcasting System.

Here is Laux, an All-Star in the broadcasting of the All-Star event. He has never failed to receive an assignment in the mid-summer game since its origin in 1933.

Joe DiMaggio slides home safely with the American League's only run in the 1938 All-Star game in Cincinnati. The American Leaguers lost that year 4–1. The catcher is Ernie Lombardi of the Cincinnati Reds, and the on-deck batter signaling DiMaggio safe is Rudy York of the Detroit Tigers.

A slew of sluggers: from the left, George Selkirk, Jake Powell, Tommy Henrich, Myril Hoag, and Joe DiMaggio.

Yanks Ahead Of '36 Pace In Home Runs

Champions on Way To Beat Own Record

By DANIEL,
Staff Correspondent.

CHICAGO, July 29.—Into the capital of the Midwest came the Yankees today with a lead of only one game over the Indians, and the Red Sox pressing hard, three lengths behind. Joe McCarthy's plan to sweep the series of four contests in St. Louis ran afoul of glittering pitching by the temperamental Oral Hildebrand, 4 to 3.

Though stopped after three straight victories, the Yankees were on a home run rampage reminiscent of their most truculent slugging spurts of 1936, when they set the all-time mark for circuit-drives at 182.

All three runs achieved off Hildebrand traced to homers. These pokes over the roof of the right field pavilion, by Joe Di Maggio, George Selkirk and Lou Gehrig, threw the contest for Yankee leadership into a Di Mag-Dickey tie at eighteen, with the Iron Horse only one behind.

What's more, the Yankees today boasted ninety-nine home runs and were well beyond their record pace of 1936.

Di Maggio's second homer of the St. Louis series, after a slump since July 13, and Selkirk's fourth of the season featured the fourth inning, when it looked as if Hildebrand would go the way of all St. Louis slingers.

Lou Gehrig's second four-master in two days opened the sixth, but there Hildebrand called a decided halt. He did not allow another hit.

Di Maggio got a single as well as his homer and came into Chicago batting .318. Giuseppe accumulated seven hits in St. Louis, and is tied for the club lead with Red Rolfe. Hoag is hitting .326, but Chink is only a part-time worker.

Speaker Says He Didn't Say It

By the Associated Press.

CLEVELAND, Aug. 2.—T r i s Speaker says it isn't so—that he didn't tell anyone he could name 15 better outfielders than Joe Di Maggio.

President Ed Barrow of the New York Yankees was quite amused at the statement attributed to the "Gray Eagle"—one of the best gardeners of all time. But Speaker wasn't.

"Fifteen better than Di Maggio?" He snorted today. "Why I don't know if there ever was even one.

"I never have discussed Di Maggio that way at all. Why, I would have a tough time naming even 15 great outfielders whom I've seen— I mean great outfielders.

"I've always considered Di Maggio one of the greatest and this year he's shown the hitting power everybody expected from him the first two years."

And pointing out that he hasn't had much chance to see the National Leaguers, Speaker said he thought Di Maggio the best of today's outfielders.

Joe's Catch Rated Tops In Stadium

The longer Joe DiMaggio plays center field, the more foolish Tris Speaker's statement about his defensive flaws seem.... Joe yesterday made what was undoubtedly the greatest catch in the history of Yankee Stadium, a gloved-hand stab of a long drive by Hank Greenberg, which traveled 450 feet on a line with the flag pole in left center.... Joe caught the ball within four or five yards of the fence, after taking his eyes off the drive three times to be sure he wouldn't crack up against the parapet. . . . He was slowing up to avoid a collision when he stuck out his gloved hand, with his back to the plate, and clutched the ball.

Joe Di Maggio.

Joe McCarthy stated afterward he never had seen a catch to equal it.... Nobody on the Yankees remembered a catch comparable with Joe's effort and Joe himself, grinning, said: "I couldn't make a better one, because this is the only park I could catch such a ball in." ... Earl Averill, who was on first when Hank connected, was halfway to third from first when the catch was made, but was able to get back safely because Joe didn't throw the ball for several seconds. . . . He was under the impression it was the third out.... Herb Kopf, Manhattan football coach, who was present, muttered, "I'd like to have him playing for me."

Spurgeon Chandler pitched the last four rounds for the Yanks and, although he was in frequent trouble, got by with only one run being scored off him.... Bobby Feller and his parents were in the stands. . . . The Tigers did considerable jawing with the umpires and really were on the short end of several close decisions.

NO-HIT, NO-RUN GAME HURLED BY PEARSON AS YANKS WIN TWO

Only 2 Reach Base on Walks, Monte Checking Indians, 13-0, Before 40,959

VICTORY HIS 10TH IN ROW

DiMaggio Gets 3 Successive Triples in Opener, Third in 9th Deciding, 8-7

By JOHN DREBINGER

Coming as a thrilling climax to an amazing demonstration of superiority over an already thoroughly beaten foe, Monte Pearson, slim right-hander of the Yankees, swept into baseball's Hall of Fame yesterday when, to the accompanying roars of 40,959 onlookers, he pitched a dazzling no-hit, no-run game against the Indians.

Two passes, coming in succession in the fourth inning, alone robbed the performance of being a perfect game. But in all other respects it was perfection itself, with not another member of Ossie Vitt's bewildered Tribe coming even close to getting a real hit or gaining first base by any other means.

The feat, the third in the major leagues this year—Johnny Vander Meer of the Reds pitched the first two in successive games—and the first in the American League since Bill Dietrich, hurling for the White Sox, held the Browns hitless and scoreless on June 1, 1937, was achieved in the nightcap of the third and final double-header with the Clevelanders at the Stadium.

A Drum-Fire of Hits

It was made amid a drum-fire of Yankee hits, including pairs of home runs for Tommy Henrich and Joe Gordon, which gave Marse Joe McCarthy's devastating machine a concluding triumph over Cleveland's crestfallen Tribe by a score of 13 to 0.

The first game also went to the Yanks. They won it, 8 to 7, on the wings of three successive triples by their peerless Joe DiMaggio. The third one, hit off Johnny Allen, tied a modern major league record and broke up the battle in the last of the ninth after the Indians seemingly had at least captured this one with a cluster of four in the upper half of the same inning.

As a result the Yanks, finishing up an exhausting string of five successive double-headers, sent what were once regarded as their "most formidable rivals" out of the arena too stunned to appreciate all that had happened. For the Indians won only one of the six contests of the series and are now sixteen full games behind the blazing pace-setters, who, in turn, maintained their margin of twelve lengths over the second-place Red Sox.

Five Runs in First

It was the great DiMage who was the hero of the afternoon as the teams trooped off the field for the intermission between the two games and, as the Yanks tore into Johnny Humphries, Vitt's pitching hope in the nightcap, for five runs in the first inning, that engagement certainly promised little further excitement.

Least of all did any one expect anything startling from Pearson, who, under pressure of the many double-headers of the past week, had to come back after only two days of rest. He had pitched and won the second game of Wednesday's twin bill against the White Sox.

But as the innings wore on, with the Indians going down like reeds before a high gale, the crowd began to sit up and take notice. Nine men went out in order in the first three rounds.

Lyn Lary and Bruce Campbell, however, led off the fourth with a pair of passes, though little attention was paid to this as the Yanks already were leading, 7—0, so the applause was merely perfunctory when Pearson, regaining his grip, struck out Jeff Heath, retired Earl Averill on an infield roller and also fanned Hal Trosky.

Gives Flawless Performance

And from then on Monte pitched with the flawless precision of an intricate piece of mechanism. Not another Indian got to first.

In desperation Vitt, striving to escape this last piece of ignominy, hurled two pinch-hitters into the ninth, Julius Solters and Frankie Pytlak. The former struck out and the latter sent a slow roller to Gordon, who pounced on the ball like a flash.

For those Yanks were really bearing down now, and while the crowd sat in breathless silence DiMaggio rushed in to provide himself with a better pair of sun glasses. He was the only player now on the field playing with the glaring light right in his eyes.

A moment later Campbell sent a low line drive to left, George Selkirk gobbled it up and the fans cut loose with an ear-splitting roar. They almost mobbed Monte before

---

Continued opposite

Pearson Pitches a No-Hit Game As Yankees Down Indians Twice

Continued From Page One

he had a chance to struggle to the dugout.

All told, twenty-nine men faced him. Two walked, seven struck out. It was his thirteenth victory of the year, and tenth in a row, against only five defeats. It was the first no-hitter for a Yankee pitcher since Sam Jones in 1923.

Opener Proves Thriller

After days of endless "big innings," which blast all semblance of competition out of the Yankees' daily fare for their constituents, the opener provided a thriller such as the Stadium has not seen in a long time. In fact, there were times during the closing rounds in which the crowd seemed to believe the pennant itself hung in the balance on every play as the Yanks twice overhauled their rivals before they finally won.

It started off as a pitching duel between Bump Hadley and the left-handed Al Milnar, with the Cleveland southpaw gaining a two-run jump in the fifth when Odell Hale banged a homer into the left-field stand behind Pytlak's single. In the sixth, the Tribe widened the margin by another tally on Averill's fourteenth homer of the year that landed in the right-field runway.

But in the same round the Yanks began to bestir themselves. With Red Rolfe on first, DiMaggio unfurled the first of his three triples, a tremendous clout in front of the left-field bleachers. That scored Rolfe and ended Milnar's dream of a shutout.

The next round saw Milnar handled even more roughly as the Yanks ripped off three runs on a trio of singles by Myril Hoag, Gordon and Red Ruffing, the latter pinch-hitting for Hadley, and a misplay by Hale. And in the eighth DiMaggio's second triple, with a little more distance to it than the first, ran the Yankee lead up to 5–3.

Two Errors by Gordon

But Johnny Murphy, who had replaced Hadley in the eighth, suddenly ran into an unexpected squall in the ninth. Two singles, two errors by Gordon and a pinch-hit triple by Solters sent four Indian runs across and it required the help of Ivy Paul Andrews to bring the uprising to an end with the Tribe again two in front.

Little did Andrews suspect that in the next few minutes he would be rewarded as the winning pitcher. With Dennis Galehouse now on the mound, Joe Glenn who, with Bill Dickey again nursing an ailing leg, did all the day's catching, singled. The fiery Allen replaced Galehouse at once and retired Dickey, who came up as a pinch hitter, and also Frankie Crosetti. But Rolfe and Henrich singled to push one run in.

Then, in almost story-book fash-

ion, DiMaggio sent another triple soaring over Averill's head in left center and the two runs this blow scored ended the struggle.

Aside from Pearson's pitching masterpiece, there was little else to the nightcap. Henrich's two home runs ran his total for the season to sixteen and Gordon's two brought the Flash's mark to nineteen. Joe also hit a triple between his homers and Henrich a single.

Exclusive of the 12,464 women who came in as guests of the management on Friday's Ladies' Day, the total attendance for the three twin bills with the Indians reached 116,336—a pretty fair "take" considering that, so far as making a pennant race out of the series, the Tribe might just as well have remained in Cleveland.

The Box Scores

FIRST GAME

CLEVELAND (A.)	ab.	r.	h.	po.	a.	e.
Lary, ss	4	0	0	3	3	0
Campbell, rf	5	0	0	1	0	0
Heath, lf	4	0	0	3	0	0
Averill, cf	4	1	2	4	1	0
Trosky, 1b	4	0	1	7	3	0
Pytlak, c	3	2	2	3	1	0
Keltner, 3b	4	1	1	0	4	0
Hale, 2b	3	2	1	4	3	1
Milnar, p	3	0	0	1	1	0
aSolters	1	1	1	0	0	0
Galehouse, p	0	0	0	0	0	0
Allen, p	0	0	0	0	0	0
Total	35	7	8	26	15	1

NEW YORK (A.)	ab.	r.	h.	po.	a.	e.
Crosetti, ss	5	0	1	3	3	1
Rolfe, 3b	5	1	3	1	3	0
Henrich, rf	5	1	3	0	1	0
DiMaggio, cf	4	1	3	4	0	0
Gehrig, 1b	4	0	1	11	1	0
Hoag, lf	4	1	1	3	0	0
Gordon, 2b	4	1	1	1	5	2
Glenn, c	4	0	1	1	0	1
ePowell	0	0	0	0	0	0
Hadley, p	1	0	0	0	0	0
bRuffing	1	0	1	0	0	0
cDahlgren	0	1	0	0	0	0
Murphy, p	0	0	1	1	0	0
Andrews, p	0	0	0	1	0	0
dDickey	1	0	0	0	0	0
fKnick'b'ker	0	1	0	0	0	0
Total	39	8	18	27	12	4

*Two out when winning run scored.
aBatted for Milnar in ninth.
bBatted for Hadley in seventh.
cRan for Ruffing in seventh.
dBatted for Andrews in ninth.
eRan for Glenn in ninth.
fRan for Dickey in ninth.

```
Cleveland ............... 0 0 0  0 1 1  0 0 4—7
New York ............... 0 0 0  0 0 1  3 1 3—8
```

Runs batted in—Hale 2, Averill, DiMaggio 3, Glenn, Ruffing, Hoag, Solters 2, Henrich. Two-base hits—Henrich, Trosky. Three-base hits—DiMaggio 3, Solters. Home runs—Hale, Averill. Stolen bases—Pytlak, Hale. Left on bases—New York 6, Cleveland 5. Bases on balls—Off Hadley 2, Milnar 3, Murphy 3. Struck out—By Milnar 2, Hadley 1. Hits—Off Hadley 5 in 7 innings, Murphy 3 in 1 (none out in 9th), Andrews 0 in 1, Milnar 9 in 8, Galehouse 1 in 0 (pitched to 1 batter), Allen 3 in 2-3. Winning pitcher—Andrews. Losing pitcher—Allen. Umpires—Rue, Kolls and Hubbard. Time of game—2:17.

SECOND GAME

CLEVELAND (A.)	ab.	r.	h.	po.	a.	e.
Lary, ss	2	0	0	3	3	2
bPytlak	1	0	0	0	0	0
Campbell, rf	3	0	0	2	0	0
Heath, lf	3	0	0	2	0	0
Averill, cf	2	0	0	1	0	0
W'therly, cf	1	0	0	0	0	0
Trosky, 1b	3	0	0	6	0	0
Hemsley, c	3	0	0	5	0	0
Keltner, 3b	3	0	0	0	3	0
Hale, 2b	3	0	0	1	2	0
Humph'rs, p	1	0	0	0	0	0
Galehouse, p	1	0	0	0	0	0
aSolters	1	0	0	0	0	0
Total	27	0	0	24	2	2

NEW YORK (A.)	ab.	r.	h.	po.	a.	e.
Crosetti, ss	4	1	0	1	2	0
Rolfe, 3b	5	2	2	2	3	0
Henrich, rf	4	2	3	1	0	0
DiMaggio, cf	5	2	3	0	0	0
Gehrig, 1b	4	2	3	6	1	0
Selkirk, lf	5	1	2	1	0	0
Gordon, 2b	4	4	2	1	6	0
Glenn, c	4	0	2	6	0	0
Pearson, p	3	0	0	0	0	0
Total	38	13	17	27	9	0

aBatted for Galehouse in ninth.
bBatted for Lary in ninth.

```
Cleveland ............... 0 0 0  0 0 0  0 0 0—0
New York ............... 6 0 2  3 0 2  1 0 —13
```

Runs batted in—Henrich 4, Gordon 6, Selkirk 2, Glenn. Three-base hit—Gordon. Home runs—Henrich 2, Gordon 2. Left on bases—New York 6, Cleveland 2. Bases on balls—Off Humphries 2, Pearson 2, Galehouse 1. Struck out—By Humphries 2, Pearson 7, Galehouse 5. Hits—Off Humphries 9 in 4 innings, Galehouse 4 in 4. Losing pitcher—Humphries. Umpires—Kolls, Hubbard and Rue. Time of game—1:54.
```
```

Di Mag's Race for Batting Title Holds Yank Interest

Indians Have Trio in Fight for Honor

By PAT McDONOUGH,
Staff Correspondent.

CLEVELAND, Sept. 13.—This is the third stop on the Yankees' present road trip, and at each city Joe Di Maggio finds at least one of his close rivals for the American League batting championship.

With the Yankees making a runaway of the race, American League fans are looking for other features to interest them, and they find in the struggle for batting honors a contest that has been closely fought all season.

Jimmy Foxx is the current pace setter with a mark of .347, but Earl Averill is just five points back, and Joe Di Maggio is at .338, one point ahead of Cecil Travis.

While the Yankees were splitting two games with Boston to start the trip, Di Maggio was able to collect only two hits and lost ground to Foxx, who gathered three blows.

Trosky and Heath
Also in Batting Race.

On reaching Washington the Yankees found Travis leading the pack. But Bump Hadley, Monte Pearson and Spurgeon Chandler took good care of Cecil, limiting him to one hit in thirteen official trips to the plate. Di Maggio collected three blows in the three games. Joe has dropped two points since leaving New York. But he has been looking forward to this trip, for it is in the West that Giuseppe does his best clouting.

Averill is not the only member of the Indians with a chance at the batting title. Hal Trosky is traveling at a .335 pace and Jeffrey Heath boasts a mark of .332.

It is a coincidence that Di Maggio and Averill should be engaged in a battle for the batting crown. In the popularity pool being conducted by a cereal company Di Maggio won the center field honors and a new automobile, while Averill gained the honor of being runner-up.

The Yankees today saw Averill in a new role, that of a right fielder. Earl was assigned his new post in a twin bill with the Browns on Sunday, with Roy Weatherly taking over the center field chores.

Averill's Lapse Cost
Harder Sixteenth Victory.

Averill's inexperience in his new field cost Cleveland a game. Left field in League Park here is short yet Averill permitted a ball to go over his head and hit the ground in front of the wall, the tying and winning runs meanwhile scoring.

The defect dropped the Vitt men half a game behind the Red Sox into third place and prevented Mel Harder from scoring his sixteenth victory of the season.

It seems Johnny Allen and Bob Feller have been getting the publicity and Harder has been winning the games for Cleveland. With Harder and Feller pitching Sunday the Yankees will not be called upon to face them in the two-game set here.

As matters stand now, the Yankees need not win 100 games to take the pennant, but they will undoubtedly pass the century mark with plenty to spare. An even split of the remaining twenty games would give them 102.

Since the Indians were dumped in five out of six games by the Yankees in New York two weeks ago they have picked up half a game, with eleven victories in sixteen games.

With the best pitcher in baseball, Bob Feller. They autographed this photograph to each other. DiMaggio to Feller: "The best pitcher I've hit against and without a doubt the best in the league. Continued success." Feller to DiMaggio: "— and *You* almost keep me out of Cooperstown with all your hits."

With the "Schnozz", Ernie Lombardi, catcher for the Cincinnati Reds.

DOWN IN FRONT

By Richards Vidmer

Copyright, 1938, New York Tribune Inc.

Short Cut to Fame

SOME of the greatest in the sphere of sports follow the long, long trail down the years before they find the laurel wreath of triumph. Some of the greatest never achieve the heights at all, but linger always on the fringe as the fates frown and force them back. But once in a while there comes a youngster who leaps into the championship class with such swiftness that he takes it as a matter of course and wonders why others look at him with envious eyes and a forgivable twinge of jealousy.

As the Yankees clinched their third successive American League pennant, I was thinking of Joe DiMaggio and how simple success must seem to him. And thinking of Joe DiMaggio I remembered some of the others who have struggled along the trail and found it hard and rough and never reached the end.

There was Mac Smith, one of the greatest golfers of his generation; always a threat, winner of many minor tournaments, but never the winner of any of the crowns he sought most—the national open, the British open, the P. G. A. For years he was rated one of the half dozen best in the game. And for years he was a close competitor when the highest honors were at stake. But he never caught up to one until age caught up to him and called a halt to his competitive efforts.

There is Harry Cooper of the current crop, accepted as one of the most consistent scorers through the years. But never a champion, always just a stroke or two back.

Richards Vidmer

There was Vinnie Richards, who could beat any tennis player in the world—except Tilden. He could beat even Tilden on occasion, but never in the national championships. Richards will go down as one of the greatest players ever to kill a lob or serve an ace, but he never was national champion.

Rapid Rise

AND in DiMaggio's own field there was, to mention one of many, Walter Johnson. He pitched through eighteen campaigns and his sun was setting before he knew the satisfaction of pitching for a winner. Yet even in those years when Washington finished last, Walter Johnson was recognized as one of the greatest pitchers in the game.

These are only a few of those who have found the trail long and hard, but how simple it must all seem to young Joe DiMaggio. He never has known anything less than triumph. He never has known the heartache and despair that belong to those who finish second. He has been on top from the very beginning and it probably will be a terrific shock when the day comes and he must look up to someone else.

From the beginning of his career, back with San Francisco in 1933, the way has been smooth and easy. Some players of major league abilities linger long in the minors before they are discovered by the scouts that bring them up and give them their chance. But Joe DiMaggio was noticed the first year he played professional baseball. He hit safely in sixty-one consecutive games and immediately the major leagues sat up and took notice of the Italian boy. From then on he was a marked man; marked for a major league trial.

The next year the Yankees bought him for future delivery and he knew he was going up. It was a rapid rise from the sandlots to the big show, but nothing compared to his rise since arriving in the American League.

All the Honors

WITH only three months' experience he was selected for the All-Star team in 1936. That fall the Yankees won the pennant. And the World Series. In 1937 he was again selected for the All-Star team, led the league in home runs, and again the Yankees won the pennant and the Series. This year for the third time he was named a member of the All-Star cast, and now once more the Yankees have won the pennant, with high prospects of capturing their third straight World Series, something no other team in baseball ever has done.

In short, Joe DiMaggio has never known anything less than the best since his arrival in the major leagues. Three years, three pennant winners, the prospect of three World Series winners, and three All-Star games. Others strive and struggle, hope and despair and never achieve any of those honors. But DiMaggio never has known anything else.

That is, he never has known anything else in the way of honors. This spring some of the applause was missing. He was offered a salary of $25,000 for his third season in the major leagues, a figure no other third-year player ever dreamed of. Yet he thought it wasn't enough. He wanted more and held out for a bigger increase, although he had been boosted $10,000 over his previous salary. The fans seemed to think he was asking a little too much and expressed their feelings with a barrage of Bronx cheers whenever he appeared at the plate.

How to Win Friends

WHETHER it was because of this unfriendly atmosphere or his lack of training or something else, Joe got off to an inauspicious start. But as the season progressed he struck his stride, rose into the select set of the league's five leading hitters, where he still remains, and changed the jeers to cheers so completely that he was voted the most popular center fielder in the game in the national poll conducted by the Kellogg Company. Last year, his second in the majors, he was selected as the most valuable player in the American League.

Offhand it's difficult to think of any honor that Joe DiMaggio hasn't received in his short, sensational career. The laurels that have been heaped upon him may seem too profuse when one remembers all that army of athletes who have struggled and still are struggling without ever reaching the World Series, the All-Star game, a most-valuable-player award or any of the things that Joe DiMaggio has achieved in three short seasons of competition.

But maybe Joe had something to do with earning those honors. It couldn't all be luck.

Barrow Spikes Report Of Di Maggio Trade

Reports that the Yankees are trying to trade Joe Di Maggio to the Tigers for Hank Greenberg are plain bunk.

Ed Barrow today told the World-Telegram that he had made no such offer to Detroit; that he would not make any such offer; and that he "would not trade Di Maggio for two Greenbergs."

"In the first place, Lou Gehrig still is a great first baseman and hitter," said Cousin Ed.

"In the second place, while Greenberg is a wonderful hitter, he would not go so well in the Stadium, with its long left field.

"Whoever dug up that deal for us did not stop to analyze the situation."

DiMaggio Wins in Poll

CHICAGO, Ill.—Polling more than 61 per cent of the votes cast for the center field berth in Kellogg's All-American baseball popularity contest, Joe DiMaggio of the New York Yankees qualified for the mythical team and will receive an automobile. Earl Averill of Cleveland, Roger Cramer of the Boston Red Sox and Lloyd Waner of Pittsburgh finished in that order behind DiMaggio.

DiMaggio is the second Yankee to win a place on the All-American Popularity team, the other being Lou Gehrig at first base. The Detroit Tigers also placed two players—Charley Gehringer at second and Pete Fox in right field. Joe Medwick of the Cardinals was the choice for left field, Joe Cronin, manager of the Boston Red Sox, won the shortstop position, and Mel Ott the hot corner berth.

The fans now are choosing the most popular catcher and will close the contest by selecting five pitchers. Gabby Hartnett of the Cubs and Bill Dickey of the Yankees were neck and neck in the catchers' poll early this week.

The Sporting News

THE BASE BALL PAPER OF THE WORLD

| VOLUME 106, NUMBER 8 | ST. LOUIS, OCTOBER 6, 1938 | TEN CENTS THE COPY 15c in Canada |

PRECEDENT BACKS CUBS IN SERIES WITH YANKS

ODDS-ON FAVORITES FACE NEVER-SCALED PEAK OF 3 STRAIGHT

POWERFUL GIANTS AND A'S OF PAST FAILED IN THIRD ATTEMPTS

Bruins, However, Lost to McCarthymen
In 1932 Clash and Enter Classic
Tired by Tense N. L. Race

By E. G. BRANDS.
Editor of The Sporting News.

NEW YORK and Chicago, the metropolises of the majors, whose representatives have appeared in the majority of fall classic games played and won the most pennants in the majors, again furnish the attraction in the thirty-fifth modern World's Series, as the Yankees of the American and the Cubs of the National League battle for the championship of the universe. The Yankees will be attempting what previous New York and Chicago teams in both leagues, besides Philadelphia and Detroit in the American circuit, have failed to do—win three successive World's Series, after capturing as many successive pennants. Only the Yankees, New York Giants and Philadelphia Athletics, however, faced the same opportunity as is presented the 1938 Yankees, for the previous Cubs, Yankees and Tigers lost the first of three successive fall classics in which they participated and, thus, were stymied at the start.

The Giants, first, had the chance offered them of winning three straight in 1923, after defeating the Yankees twice, but the Yanks pulled up with a victory in the third meeting and spoiled the record. The Athletics were in a similar position after defeating the Cubs and St. Louis Cardinals, but failed in 1931 against the Redbirds.

As a result, the chief question bandied about by the fans this week is not whether the Yankees can defeat the Cubs, but whether the Yankees can overcome the laws of chance and do what no other club in history has been able to accomplish—win three straight World's Series.

The Yankees and Cubs met in the fall classic once before, in 1932, and in that series the American League champions overwhelmed the National League pennant winners in four straight games. Will history repeat itself this year? If it does in one chapter, it will not in another, for, if the Yankees win, they will upset the precedent that no club can win three straight. If the Cubs are victors, then it will be the first time they have won a series at the expense of the Yankees.

Everything seems to be in favor of the Yankees—the odds, the ease with which they won the championship in the American, in comparison with the bitter battle the Cubs were forced to wage to come from behind and capture the flag, the slugging propensities of the American leaguers and, to many, at least, the superior pitching Joe McCarthy can muster. On the other side, in favor of the Cubs, it must be said they have the dash lacking in the Yankees; a wonderful inspiration in their new manager and veteran catcher, Gabby Hartnett; two exceptional pitchers in Bill Lee and Clay Bryant, with the possible addition of Dizzy Dean as the hurler who is capable of turning in a surprise victory; a closely-welded organization that is tight in the field, with few individual stars, but a cohesive team whose combined batting averages make up for the lack of high-percentage hitters.

SEEKING THEIR GREATEST RECORD--Third World's Title in Row

HAILED by some experienced observers as the "greatest club in the game's history—an assertion disputed by others—the New York Yankees, 1938 pennant-winners, are out to prove their right to that distinction by attempting to capture their third World's Series in a row, a feat no major league club has yet accomplished. Not even the league champion New York Giants of 1923, led by the astute John McGraw, nor the glamorous winning Philadelphia Athletics of 1931, directed by the wily Connie Mack, could emerge as victors in three successive series. The law of averages is heavily against the Yanks, but they have upset many traditions and may add one more to their belts this year.

Participating in winning the third American League pennant in succession were the following members of the Yankees, photographed together as a team, shortly before the season ended: First row, left to right—Joe Gordon, second baseman; Bill Knickerbocker, shortstop; John Schulte and Art Fletcher, coaches; Joe McCarthy, manager; Earle Combs, coach; Ellsworth Dahlgren, first base; Jake Powell, outfielder; Frank Crosetti, shortstop; Tim Sullivan, batboy. Second row—Tom Henrich, outfielder; Joe Glenn, catcher; Bump Hadley, pitcher; Spurgeon Chandler, pitcher; Paul Schreiber, batting practice pitcher; Bill Dickey, catcher; Robert Rolfe, third baseman; Lou Gehrig, first baseman; Earl Painter, trainer. Back row—George Selkirk, outfielder; John Murphy, pitcher; Ivy Andrews, pitcher; Joe DiMaggio, outfielder; Charley Ruffing, pitcher; Vernon Gomez, pitcher; Steve Sundra, pitcher; Arndt Jorgens, catcher; Myril Hoag, outfielder; Monte Pearson, pitcher.

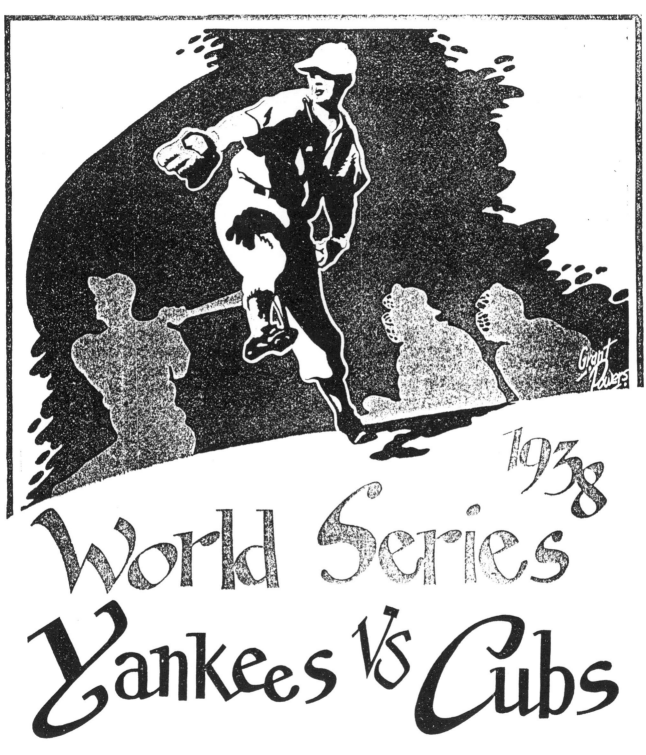

1938

World Series

Yankees Vs Cubs

official program 25¢

CHICAGO

	1	2	3	4	5	6	7	8	9	10	A.B.	R	1B	S.H	P.O.	A.	E.
6 HACK — Third Base																	
4 HERMAN — Second Base																	
9 DEMAREE L.F / 23 CAVARRETTA R.F																	
23 CAVARRETTA R.F / 7 GALAN L.F																	
43 REYNOLDS — Center Field																	
2 HARTNETT C.-Mgr / 12 O'DEA C																	
3 COLLINS — First Base																	
5 JURGES — Short Stop																	
Pitcher																	

8 Marty,OF
11 Lee,P
14 French,P
15 Lazzeri,IF
16 Carleton,P
17 Root,P
18 Bryant,P
22 J. Dean,P

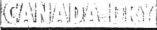
Ask the boy for a C-O-L-D CANADA DRY IT'S GINGERVATING

28 Russell,P
30 Asbell,OF
39 Garbark,C
41 Page,P
19 Corriden,Coach
20 Johnson,Coach

NEW YORK

	1	2	3	4	5	6	7	8	9	10	A.B.	R	1B	S.H	P.O.	A.	E.
1 CROSETTI — Short Stop																	
2 ROLFE — Third Base																	
17 HENRICH R.F / 9 HOAG R.F																	
5 DI MAGGIO — Center Field																	
4 GEHRIG — First Base																	
8 DICKEY — Catcher																	
3 SELKIRK L.F / 7 POWELL L.F																	
6 GORDON — Second Base																	
Pitcher																	

10 Knickerbocker,IF
11 Gomez,P
12 Dahlgren,IF
14 Hadley,P
15 Ruffing,P
16 Pearson,P
18 Jorgens,C
19 Murphy,P
21 Chandler,P
24 Andrews,P
25 Ferrell,P
26 Glenn,C
32 Sundra,P
29 Fletcher,Coach
30 Combs,Coach
McCarthy,Mgr.

PAY NO MORE

Beer, cans 20c	Peanuts 10c
Sandwiches 15c	Pop Corn 10c
Lemonade 20c	Red Hots 10c
Cigarettes 15c	Coffee 10c
Soft Drinks 10c	Ice Cream 10c

UMPIRES

National League	American League
1 Charles B. Moran	3 Louis Kolls
2 John W. Sears	4 Cal Hubbard

Joe DiMaggio receives the Babe Ruth All-America award in 1938 along with Yankee third baseman Red Rolfe. DiMaggio hit .324 that year, Rolfe .311, and the Yankees won the American League pennant and then the World Series in four straight games over the Chicago Cubs. The sweater, awarded along with the certificate, is today preserved in the Barry Halper collection of baseball memorabilia.

In the days before smoking was considered a health hazard, many baseball greats offered endorsements. Promoting ''The Baseball Man's Cigarette'' along with Joe DiMaggio are, clockwise from lower left, Yankee manager Bucky Harris, Bob Elliott of the Boston Braves, Ted Williams of the Boston Red Sox, Stan Musial of the St. Louis Cardinals, and Ewell Blackwell of the Cincinnati Reds.

NEW YORK YANKEES

WILLIAM KNICKERBOCKER
Utility Infielder

ROBERT ROLFE
Third Base

GEORGE SELKIRK
Outfielder

JAKE POWELL
Outfielder

TOM HENRICH
Outfielder

JOE DI MAGGIO
Outfielder

MYRIL HOAG
Outfielder

NEW YORK YANKEES

WESLEY FERRELL
Pitcher

LOU GEHRIG
First Base

ARNDT JORGENS
Catcher

BILL DICKEY
Catcher

JOE C. GLENN
Catcher

JOSEPH GORDON
Infielder

FRANK CROSETTI
Short Stop

ELLSWORTH DAHLGREN
Infielder

Game 1 October 5 at Chicago

NY Yankees	Pos	AB	R	H	RBI	PO	A	E
Crosetti	ss	4	0	1	0	4	6	0
Rolfe	3b	5	0	1	0	0	1	0
Henrich	rf	4	1	2	0	0	0	1
DiMaggio	cf	4	0	0	0	2	0	0
Gehrig	1b	3	1	1	0	10	0	0
Dickey	c	4	1	4	1	6	3	0
Selkirk	lf	4	0	1	1	1	0	0
Gordon	2b	4	0	2	1	4	2	0
Ruffing	p	3	0	0	0	0	1	0
Totals		35	3	12	3	27	13	1

Pitching	IP	H	R	ER	BB	SO
Yankees						
Ruffing (W)	9	9	1	1	0	5
Chicago						
Lee (L)	8	11	3	3	1	6
Russell	1	1	0	0	0	0

1st Inning

Yankees
1 Crosetti called out on strikes.
2 Rolfe grounded to Collins who made a great stop and threw to Lee covering first.
3 Henrich looked at a called third strike.

Chicago
Hack singled to left.
1 Hack caught stealing, Dickey to Crosetti.
2 Herman grounded to short.
3 Demaree fanned.

2nd Inning

Yankees
1 DiMaggio grounded to third.
Gehrig walked.
Dickey singled to right moving Gehrig to third, Dickey taking second on the throw to third.
Selkirk safe at first on Herman's bobble, scoring Gehrig with Dickey going to second.
Gordon singled to left, scoring Gehrig with Selkirk stopping at second.
2,3 Ruffing hit into a double play, Jurges to Herman to Collins.

Chicago
1 Cavarretta grounded to first.
2 Reynolds popped to second.
3 Hartnett fouled to Dickey.

3rd Inning

Yankees
1 Crosetti flied to center.
2 Rolfe flied to left.
Henrich beat out a grounder to first.
3 Henrich caught stealing, Hartnett to Herman.

Chicago
Collins singled to right.
1 Jurges fanned.
2 Lee tapped out in front of the plate, Dickey to Gehrig moving Collins to second (not a sacrifice hit).
Hack singled to right, scoring Collins and went to second on the throw to the plate.
Herman singled off Rolfe's glove and
3 Hack trying to score was out at the plate, Crosetti to Dickey.

4th Inning

Yankees
1 DiMaggio grounded out to short where Jurges made a sensational stop.
Gehrig singled to right but was out
2 trying for a double, Cavarretta to Herman to Jurges.
Dickey singled over second.
3 Selkirk popped to Hack.

Chicago
1 Demaree grounded back to the pitcher.
2 Cavarretta fanned.
3 Reynolds popped to first.

NY Y   020 001 000   3
Chi.   001 000 000   1

Chicago	Pos	AB	R	H	RBI	PO	A	E
Hack	3b	4	0	3	1	1	1	0
Herman	2b	4	0	1	0	2	5	1
Demaree	lf	4	0	0	0	2	0	0
Cavarretta	rf	4	0	2	0	1	1	0
Reynolds	cf	4	0	0	0	3	0	0
Hartnett	c	3	0	1	0	6	2	0
Collins	1b	3	1	1	0	10	1	0
Jurges	ss	3	0	1	0	1	3	0
Lee	p	2	0	0	0	1	0	0
a O'Dea		1	0	0	0	0	0	0
Russell	p	0	0	0	0	0	0	0
Totals		32	1	9	1	27	13	1

a Hit into force play for Lee in 8th.

Doubles—Crosetti, Gordon, Henrich.
Triple—Hartnett. Sacrifice Hit—Ruffing.
Stolen Base—Dickey.
Double Plays—Crosetti to Gehrig, Gordon to Crosetti to Gehrig, Jurges to Herman to Collins, Collins (unassisted).
Hit by Pitcher—Crosetti (by Lee).
Left on Bases—New York 8, Chicago 4.
Umpires—Moran (N), Kolls (A), Sears (N), Hubbard (A). Attendance—43,642.
Time of Game—1:53.

5th Inning

Yankees
Gordon doubled to left.
1 Ruffing sacrificed Gordon to third, Hartnett to Collins.
2 Crosetti fanned.
3 Rolfe grounded to second.

Chicago
1 Hartnett fanned, but Dickey dropped the third strike throwing Hack out.
2 Collins rolled out to second.
3 Jurges fanned.

6th Inning

Yankees
Henrich doubled to right.
1 DiMaggio flied to right.
2 Gehrig fanned.
Dickey singled to left, scoring Henrich. Selkirk beat out a hit down the first base line, Dickey stopping at second.
3 Gordon fanned.

Chicago
1 Lee flied to center.
Hack singled past third.
2 Herman forced Hack at second, Rolfe to Gordon.
3 Demaree popped to short.

7th Inning

Yankees
1 Ruffing flied to left.
Crosetti was hit by a pitched ball.
Rolfe singled to right, advancing Crosetti to third.
2,3 Henrich lined to Collins who made a great one-handed catch then stepped on first to double up Rolfe.

Chicago
Cavarretta singled to center.
1,2 Reynolds hit into a double play, Crosetti to Gehrig.
Hartnett tripled to right as the ball rolled to the wall after Henrich missed a shoe string catch.
3 Collins grounded to short.

8th Inning

Yankees
1 DiMaggio grounded to short.
2 Gehrig called out on strikes.
Dickey singled to right (his 4th hit). Dickey stole second.
3 Selkirk flied to center.

Chicago
Jurges popped a single to right.
1 O'Dea, batting for Lee, forced Jurges at second, Crosetti to Gordon.
2,3 Hack into a double play, Gordon to Crosetti to Gehrig.

9th Inning

Yankees
For Chicago—Russell pitching.
1 Gordon flied to center.
2 Ruffing grounded to second.
Crosetti doubled to right.
3 Rolfe grounded to second.

Chicago
1 Herman flied to center.
2 Demaree flied to left.
Cavarretta singled to right and took second on Henrich's fumble.
3 Reynolds popped to second.

YANKS CELEBRATE TRIUMPH IN SONG

Confident Air Bespeaks Aim to Sweep World Series in Four Straight Games

GOMEZ THANKS MANAGER

And Team-Mates, Too, for Help in Setting Record—Dean Bemoans Bitter Luck

By JAMES P. DAWSON
Special to The New York Times.

CHICAGO, Oct. 6.—The study in contrasts between victor and vanquished was more pronounced today than yesterday in the clubhouses of the world series combatants.

The Yankees, as might have been expected after the pounding they gave Dizzy Dean, were a singing, shouting, joyous, back-slapping band. Their emotions found expression in song, and principally in "East Side, West Side."

Echoing through the confined quarters as newspapermen trooped in after the game were shouts of "You said it" and "Right," a new catch-phrase they have acquired this season.

And in the Cubs' clubhouse the gloom was thick. They were a crestfallen lot, stunned by this second defeat and the cudgeling to which their hope, Dean, was subjected when the Yankee siege guns finally swung into action.

Little Hope for Chicagoans

The impression prevailed that the Yankees are looking forward to four straight, although none said so in so many words. The Cubs are wondering if they will salvage a game from the wreck of the series which impended tonight when the teams left for New York to transfer their base of operations. True, the Cubs, though down, are not altogether out. But there seems little hope for them.

Manager Joe McCarthy, nearing the realization of a feat that would place him on a managerial pedestal unchallenged—his third straight world series conquest—steered from this subject with sympathetic expression for Dean.

Lefty Vernon Gomez, now owner of a unique record, six straight world series triumphs, modestly thanked McCarthy for his confidence, reflected in leaving the southpaw in the box through seven innings, or until impending defeat dictated use of a pinch-hitter.

Frankie Crosetti, hero of the first game and trail-blazer in the home-run department in the second, smiled nervously as he modestly took the congratulations of his mates and tried to keep the voluble Joe Glenn from "poppin' off."

Smile Covers DiMaggio's Face

Partly in the background squatted the "iron man" of the club and the game, Lou Gehrig, smoking a cigarette. And Joe DiMaggio's face beamed. He had hit where the enemy couldn't pounce on the ball—over the left-field wall.

"Dean had plenty of heart in there, boys," said McCarthy. "You can't take that away from him. His arm may be gone, but he was a puzzle to us for seven innings, and he pitched a great game until the Yankee power finally caught up with him. It must have been quite a thrill seeing him out there giving everything he had until he could give no more.

"I'll start Monte Pearson in New York Saturday if he's feeling all right. He's been ailing with a cold and sinus trouble lately, you know, but he's come around fine during the last week, and if he's right he'll go. I'll tell you in New York."

Gomez came over, interrupting the conversation with an acknowledgment of gratitude for being allowed to pitch so long. "Go on, Lefty, you were great," was the way McCarthy dismissed him.

An Assist for the Record

"That's all right, but I'd feel better if I had more to say about getting that record," said Gomez. "The way I was pitching, I was lucky to be in there so long. Seems as if Frankie or Joe should get all the credit for that one."

The center of a gloomy picture, Dean was also the object of his mates' sympathy in the Cubs' dressing quarters. There was no noise here, no joy, just sadness. Larry French placed an arm around the shoulders of the humbled Dean. Neither spoke a word. The gesture spoke for itself.

"I just throwed myself out," said Dean. "I gave them all I had. I could do no more. They're the luckiest bunch of ball players I ever pitched against. It was my toughest defeat. Crosetti hit a fast ball after I thought I had him struck out at the two-and-two count. The pitch that was missed was a better one than the pitch he hit into the bleachers. But those things just happen. You can't help it. They were lucky to get those first two runs. That was an accident.

"They were lucky my arm gave 'way to. It went out on me in the sixth and pained me from then on. At times it felt as if the bone was sticking out through the flesh."

Gabby Hartnett congratulated Dean on a great pitching exhibition as he held the Yanks in check for seven innings. "He's there with nerve and heart," said the Cubs' skipper. "What a pitcher he'll make next year if his arm responds to treatment through the Winter.

"Say, DiMaggio really teed off on that one, didn't he? Boy, that was a blow! But never mind. We're not through yet. We'll get there. I'll start Clay Bryant Saturday in New York, and the line-up will be the same as today, with Joe Marty in center and hitting fourth."

YANKEES BEAT CUBS WITH HOMERS, 6 TO 3; LEAD, 2-0, IN SERIES

Game 2 October 6 at Chicago

NY Yankees	Pos	AB	R	H	RBI	PO	A	E
Crosetti	ss	4	1	1	2	5	3	0
Rolfe	3b	4	0	0	0	0	2	2
Henrich	rf	4	1	1	0	2	0	0
DiMaggio	cf	4	2	2	2	4	0	0
Gehrig	1b	3	1	1	0	6	0	0
Dickey	c	4	0	0	0	6	2	0
Selkirk	lf	3	0	1	0	0	0	0
Powell	lf	0	0	0	0	0	0	0
Gordon	2b	4	0	0	2	4	3	0
Gomez	p	2	0	1	0	0	1	0
a Hoag		1	1	0	0	0	0	0
Murphy	p	0	0	0	0	0	0	0
Totals		33	6	7	6	27	11	2

Pitching	IP	H	R	ER	BB	SO
Yankees						
Gomez (W)	7	9	3	3	1	5
Murphy (SV)	2	2	0	0	1	1
Chicago						
Dean (L)	*8	7	6	6	1	2
French	1	0	0	0	1	2

*Pitched to two batters in 9th.

NY Y	020	000	022						6
Chi.	102	000	000						3

Chicago	Pos	AB	R	H	RBI	PO	A	E
Hack	3b	5	2	2	0	0	3	0
Herman	2b	4	1	1	0	1	5	0
Demaree	rf	3	0	1	0	1	0	0
Marty	cf	4	0	3	3	2	0	0
Reynolds	lf	3	0	0	0	4	0	0
Hartnett	c	4	0	0	0	5	0	0
Collins	1b	4	0	1	0	10	0	0
Jurges	ss	3	0	0	0	4	1	0
Dean	p	3	0	2	0	0	2	0
French	p	0	0	0	0	0	0	0
b Cavarretta		1	0	1	0	0	0	0
Totals		34	3	11	3	27	11	0

a Hit into a force play for Gomez in 8th.
b Singled for French in 9th.

Doubles—Gordon, Marty.
Home Runs—Crosetti, DiMaggio.
Sacrifice Hit—Demaree.
Double Plays—Crosetti to Gordon to Gehrig, Gordon to Crosetti to Gehrig, Herman to Jurges to Collins.
Left on Bases—Yankees 2, Chicago 7.
Umpires—Kolls, Sears, Hubbard, Moran.
Attendance—42,108. Time of Game—1:53.

1st Inning
Yankees
1 Crosetti flied to deep left.
2 Rolfe bunted, thrown out by Dean.
3 Henrich popped to short.
Chicago
Hack singled to left.
1 Herman struck out.
Demaree singled to right sending Hack to third and when Rolfe fumbled the throw in Demaree got to second.
2 Marty flied to deep center, Hack scoring after the catch.
3 Reynolds struck out.

2nd Inning
Yankees
DiMaggio singled to left.
Gehrig walked.
1 Dickey popped to short.
2 Selkirk flied to center.
Gordon hit an easy roller but Herman and Hack collided, the ball going through for a double scoring DiMaggio and Gehrig.
3 Gomez flied to left.
Chicago
1 Hartnett flied to right.
Collins singled off Rolfe's glove.
2 Jurges forced Collins at second, Rolfe to Gordon.
3 Dean grounded to short.

3rd Inning
Yankees
1 Crosetti flied to left.
2 Rolfe grounded to second.
3 Henrich grounded to second.
Chicago
Hack beat out a bouncer to short.
Herman also beat out a hit behind second, Hack stopping at second.
1 Demaree sacrificed Hack to third and Herman to second, Dickey to Gehrig.
Marty doubled to deep center, scoring Hack and Herman.
Reynolds walked.
2 Hartnett flied to center.
3 Collins fanned.

4th Inning
Yankees
1 DiMaggio fouled to Hartnett.
Gehrig singled when Collins fell going for his grounder.
2,3 Dickey hit into a double play, Herman to Jurges to Collins.
Chicago
1 Jurges grounded to third.
Dean singled to left.
2,3 Hack grounded into a double play, Crosetti to Gordon to Gehrig.

5th Inning
Yankees
1 Selkirk fouled to Collins.
2 Gordon grounded to third.
3 Gomez grounded to second.
Chicago
1 Herman popped to second.
2 Demaree flied to center.
Marty singled to left.
3 Marty caught stealing Dickey to Crosetti.

6th Inning
Yankees
1 Crosetti flied to left.
2 Rolfe fanned.
3 Henrich grounded back to the pitcher.
Chicago
1 Reynolds popped to short.
2 Hartnett flied to deep center. Collins made it to first on Rolfe's wild throw.
3 Jurges forced Collins at second, Crosetti unassisted.

7th Inning
Yankees
1 DiMaggio grounded to third.
2 Gehrig flied to right.
3 Dickey flied to center.
Chicago
Dean singled to right.
1 Hack called out on strikes.
2 Herman fanned.
3 Dean trapped off first, Gomez to Gordon.

8th Inning
Yankees
Selkirk singled to right.
1 Gordon forced Selkirk at second, Hack to Herman.
2 Hoag, pinch-hitting for Gomez, forced Gordon at second, Herman to Jurges.
Crosetti hit a two-run homer into the left field bleachers.
3 Rolfe called out on strikes.
Chicago
For the Yankees—Murphy pitching.
1 Demaree fanned.
Marty singled to right.
2,3 Reynolds hit into a double play, Gordon to Crosetti to Gehrig.

9th Inning
Yankees
Henrich singled to right.
DiMaggio hit a two-run homer over the left field wall.
For Chicago—French pitching.
1 Gehrig fanned.
2 Dickey grounded to first.
Selkirk walked.
3 Gordon fanned.
Chicago
For the Yankees—Powell in left.
1 Hartnett flied to right.
2 Collins grounded to second.
Jurges walked.
Cavarretta, pinch hitting for French, singled past Gordon with Jurges stopping at second.
3 Hack lined to short.

Hits by Crosetti, DiMaggio in 8th and 9th, Each With Man On, Rout Dizzy Dean

PITCHING MARK BY GOMEZ

He Fails to Finish, but Gains 6th Straight World Series Triumph—42,108 Attend

By JOHN DREBINGER
Special to THE NEW YORK TIMES.

CHICAGO, Oct. 6.—Determined to capture their third successive world title in the shortest possible time, the Yankees today scored their second straight triumph over the Cubs, 6 to 3. Joe McCarthy's horde, for the first time in the series, put on display their famed home-run power and overcame Gabby Hartnett's heroically struggling forces with late-inning drives.

As a result, the combatants are now roaring Eastward with the American League pennant winners in possession of a near stranglehold on the world championship. For they now lead in games, 2 to 0, and with the series swinging to the Stadium in New York, where the third conflict will be staged on Saturday, scarcely any one concedes the National Leaguers a chance.

Two of baseball's most colorful pitchers—Vernon (Lefty) Gomez and Jerome Herman (Dizzy) Dean, were today's mound rivals before 42,108 chilled Chicagoans and Lefty gained the decision at the very moment he was retiring from the battlefield apparently worsted.

Goes Out in Eighth

Gomez went out for a pinch-hitter in the eighth and a moment later Frankie Crosetti, with the pinch-hitter, Myril Hoag, lurking on the basepaths, blazed a home run into the teeth of a stinging gale.

That shot transposed a 3-2 lead for the Cubs into a 4-3 margin for the Yankees, and in the ninth, again with a runner aboard the bases, Joe DiMaggio sent another mighty drive into that same gale and clear out of the park.

Those two towering smashes stunned the crowd, silenced Dean and, with Fordham Johnny Murphy contributing two closing innings of superb relief pitching, gave the Yankees their victory.

Named officially the winning pitcher, Gomez gained the distinction of becoming the first hurler in world series history to annex six straight triumphs. The Yankees' left-handed ace has yet to lose his first decision. He conquered the Cubs in his one start in the 1932 series and twice defeated the Giants in each of the 1936 and 1937 classics.

Crowd Cheers for Dean

His feat of conquering the Cubs today, in this sunny but still wind-blown contest, was a matter chiefly decided by the gods and for once in his own highly checkered and flamboyant career Dean left the field a vanquished fighter with the cheers of the crowd ringing in his ears. Usually they cheer the great mouthpiece only when he triumphs in spite of everything. It invariably has been jeers when he loses.

But today he really cut a heroic and tragic figure as he strove with all his cunning and with a $185,000 arm that through injury has lost all its one-time dazzling fire, to hold those Yankee sluggers in check.

And while the clinching shots of Crosetti and DiMaggio provided the dramatic touch at the finish, the game actually was lost by a strange piece of irony away back in the second inning.

At that moment, with the Cubs leading by 1 to 0, the flukiest of two baggers by Joe Gordon, the Flash, tossed two runs into the laps of the astonished Yanks.

Pressure Proves Too Much

And though in the following round the Cubs, riding with a new hero in Joe Marty, grabbed that lead back with a pair of tallies of their own, the pressure of holding a one-run margin instead of what might have been a three-run edge proved too much even for one who so abounds in self-assurance as this man Dean. In brief and in defeat, he was still the story even though his conqueror set a world series record.

There were practically no preliminary ceremonies to this game save those which normally attend any venture wherein the great man Dean is slated to play a stellar role. His first appearance on the field was the occasion for a grand rush by every one owning a camera and for more than forty minutes Dizzy, even if not quite his old jovial self, obliged with endless poses and extemporaneous speeches of rare wisdom.

Dean does all these things with ease, grace and tongue in check.

Actually the Cubs outhit the Yanks, 11 to 7. They collected nine off Gomez in seven innings and two off Murphy in the last two rounds. But when the chips were down and victory hung in the balance, it was the Yankees' long-range guns which toppled the enemy just as they have done so many times in the past.

After the game both clubs boarded their respective specials for New York and will arrive in the forenoon tomorrow for the third game, which will be played at the Stadium on Saturday, when Hartnett will stake his all on Clay Bryant, while Marse Joe will call on Monte Pearson.

Choosing a weapon.

Game 3 October 8 at New York

Chicago	Pos	AB	R	H	RBI	PO	A	E
Hack	3b	3	1	1	0	2	0	0
Herman	2b	3	0	0	0	1	1	1
Cavarretta	rf	4	0	1	0	2	0	0
Marty	cf	4	1	3	2	3	0	0
Reynolds	lf	4	0	0	0	0	0	0
Hartnett	c	4	0	0	0	3	1	0
Collins	1b	4	0	0	0	8	0	0
Jurges	ss	3	0	0	0	5	3	0
b Lazzeri		1	0	0	0	0	0	0
Bryant	p	2	0	0	0	0	0	0
Russell	p	0	0	0	0	0	0	0
a Galan		1	0	0	0	0	0	0
French	p	0	0	0	0	0	2	0
c O'Dea		1	0	0	0	0	0	0
Totals		34	2	5	2	24	7	1

a Popped out for Russell in 7th.

Double—Hack. Home Runs—Dickey, Gordon, Marty. Left on Bases—Chicago 7, Yankees 8. Umpires—Sears, Hubbard, Moran, Kolls. Attendance—55,236. Time of Game—1:57.

Chi	000	010	010					2
NY Y	000	022	01x					5

NY Yankees	Pos	AB	R	H	RBI	PO	A	E
Crosetti	ss	3	0	0	0	1	0	1
Rolfe	3b	4	0	1	1	0	1	0
Henrich	rf	4	0	0	0	3	0	0
DiMaggio	cf	3	1	1	0	1	0	0
Gehrig	1b	4	1	1	0	4	1	0
Dickey	c	3	1	1	1	12	0	0
Selkirk	lf	3	0	0	0	2	0	0
Gordon	2b	4	1	2	3	2	3	1
Pearson	p	3	1	1	0	2	0	0
Totals		31	5	7	5	27	5	2

Pitching	IP	H	R	ER	BB	SO
Chicago						
Bryant (L)	5⅓	6	4	4	5	3
Russell	⅓	0	0	0	1	0
French	2	1	1	1	0	0
Yankees						
Pearson (W)	9	5	2	1	2	9

1st Inning
Chicago
  Hack walked.
  Herman walked.
1 Cavarretta flied to center.
  Marty singled to deep short, loading the bases.
2 Reynolds struck out.
3 Hartnett struck out.
Yankees
1 Crosetti struck out.
2 Rolfe popped to short.
3 Henrich flied to center.

2nd Inning
Chicago
1 Collins struck out
2 Jurges struck out.
  Bryant got all the way to second on Crosetti's wide throw to first
3 Hack grounded to Pearson who made the putout.
Yankees
  DiMaggio walked.
1 Gehrig forced DiMaggio at second, Herman to Jurges.
  Dickey walked.
2 Selkirk struck out.
3 Gordon struck out.

3rd Inning
Chicago
1 Herman struck out.
  Cavarretta singled to right.
  Marty singled to center, sending Cavarretta to third.
2 Reynolds struck out.
3 Hartnett grounded to second.
Yankees
1 Pearson grounded to short.
  Crosetti walked.
2 Rolfe flied to center.
3 Crosetti caught stealing, Hartnett to Jurges.

4th Inning
Chicago
1 Collins flied to left.
2 Jurges lined to second.
3 Bryant called out on strikes.
Yankees
1 Henrich grounded to first.
2 DiMaggio grounded to short.
3 Gehrig popped to second.

5th Inning
Chicago
  Hack doubled to left.
1 Herman was called out on strikes.
  Cavarretta safe on Gordon's fumble, Hack going to third.
2 Marty forced Cavarretta at second, Rolfe to Gordon scoring Hack.
3 Reynolds fouled to Dickey

5th Inning (continued)
Yankees
1 Dickey flied to center.
2 Selkirk grounded to second.
  Gordon got the first hit off of Bryant a homer into the left field stands.
  Pearson singled to right.
  Crosetti walked.
  Rolfe singled to center, scoring Pearson and sending Crosetti to third.
3 Henrich fouled to Hack.

6th Inning
Chicago
1 Hartnett fouled to Gehrig.
2 Collins lined to right.
3 Jurges popped to Dickey in front of the plate.
Yankees
  DiMaggio singled past third.
  Gehrig singled to center, advancing DiMaggio to third.
1 Dickey fouled to Hack.
  Selkirk walked loading the bases.
  Gordon singled to left scoring DiMaggio and Gehrig, Selkirk stopping at second.
  For Chicago—Russell pitching.
  Pearson walked loading the bases.
2 Crosetti fouled to Jurges.
3 Rolfe popped to short.

7th Inning
Chicago
1 Galan, batting for Russell, popped to short
2 Hack called out on strikes.
3 Herman grounded to short.
Yankees
  For Chicago—French pitching.
1 Henrich flied to right.
2 DiMaggio grounded to short.
3 Gehrig flied to right.

8th Inning
Chicago
1 Cavarretta grounded out, Gehrig to Pearson.
  Marty homered into the left field seats.
2 Reynolds flied to left.
3 Hartnett flied to right.
Yankees
  Dickey hit a homer into the right field stands.
1 Selkirk grounded to the pitcher
2 Gordon grounded to first.
  Pearson safe on Herman's fumble.
3 Crosetti grounded to the pitcher

9th Inning
Chicago
1 Collins fouled to Gehrig.
2 Lazzeri, pinch-hitting for Jurges, grounded to second.
3 O'Dea, pinch-hitting for French, flied to right.

DiMaggio scores a run, albeit with an uncharacteristic lack of grace. It was in the sixth inning of game three of the 1938 World Series and came after a hit by Joe Gordon. The Yankees won that game 5-2 and took the Series in four straight from the Chicago Cubs.

Game 4 October 9 at New York

Chicago	Pos	AB	R	H	RBI	PO	A	E
Hack	3b	5	0	2	0	1	0	0
Herman	2b	5	0	1	0	1	3	0
Cavarretta	rf	4	1	2	0	1	0	0
Marty	cf	4	0	0	0	2	0	0
Demaree	lf	3	1	0	0	3	0	0
O'Dea	c	3	1	1	2	5	0	0
Collins	1b	4	0	0	0	10	0	0
Jurges	ss	4	0	2	0	1	0	1
Lee	p	1	0	0	0	0	0	0
a Galan		1	0	0	0	0	0	0
Root	p	0	0	0	0	0	0	0
b Lazzeri		1	0	0	0	0	0	0
Page	p	0	0	0	0	0	1	0
French	p	0	0	0	0	0	0	0
Carleton	p	0	0	0	0	0	0	0
Dean	p	0	0	0	0	0	0	0
c Reynolds		1	0	0	0	0	0	0
Totals		36	3	8	2	24	4	1

a Struck out for Lee in 4th.
b Struck out for Root in 7th.
c Flied out for Dean in 9th.

Doubles—Cavarretta, Crosetti, Hoag, Jurges. Triple—Crosetti. Home Runs—Henrich, O'Dea. Stolen Bases—Gordon, Rolfe. Wild pitches—Carleton 2. Left on Bases—Chicago 8, Yankees 6. Umpires—Hubbard, Moran, Kolls, Sears. Attendance—59,847. Time of Game—2:11.

Chi.	000 100 020	3
NY Y	030 001 04x	8

NY Yankees	Pos	AB	R	H	RBI	PO	A	E
Crosetti	ss	5	0	2	4	6	1	0
Rolfe	3b	5	0	1	0	0	0	0
Henrich	rf	4	1	1	1	1	0	0
DiMaggio	cf	4	1	1	0	3	0	0
Gehrig	1b	4	1	1	0	5	2	0
Dickey	c	4	0	1	0	7	0	0
Hoag	lf	4	2	2	1	1	0	0
Gordon	2b	3	2	1	0	2	4	1
Ruffing	p	3	1	1	1	2	3	0
Totals		36	8	11	7	27	10	1

Pitching	IP	H	R	ER	BB	SO
Chicago						
Lee (L)	3	4	3	0	0	2
Root	3	3	1	1	0	1
Page	1⅓	2	2	2	0	0
French	⅓	0	0	0	0	0
Carleton	*0	1	2	2	2	0
Dean	⅓	1	0	0	0	0
Yankees						
Ruffing (W)	9	8	3	2	2	6

*Pitched to three batters in 8th.

1st Inning
Chicago
Hack singled over second.
1 Herman forced Hack at second, Gordon to Crosetti.
2 Cavarretta forced Herman at second, Ruffing to Crosetti.
3 Marty fanned.
Yankees
1 Crosetti fanned.
Rolfe singled on a blooper to center. Rolfe stole second.
2 Henrich grounded to first, advancing Rolfe to third.
3 DiMaggio struck out.

2nd Inning
Chicago
1 Demaree fouled to Gehrig.
2 O'Dea lined to Dickey.
3 Collins grounded out, Gehrig to Ruffing.
Yankees
1 Gehrig popped to third.
2 Dickey grounded to first.
Hoag safe on first on Herman's throwing error.
Gordon singled into left, moving Hoag to third.
Ruffing singled to right, scoring Hoag and advancing Gordon to third.
Crosetti lined a triple to the left field corner, scoring Gordon and Ruffing.
3 Rolfe grounded to second.

3rd Inning
Chicago
1 Jurges grounded back to the pitcher.
2 Lee fanned.
Hack singled into left.
Herman blooped a single into short left-center, Hack stopping at second.
3 Cavarretta popped to second.
New York
1 Henrich grounded to first.
2 DiMaggio flew to Demaree at the 415-foot sign in left-center.
3 Gehrig grounded to second.

4th Inning
Chicago
1 Marty flied to deep right.
Demaree walked.
O'Dea walked.
2 Collins fanned.
Jurges grounded to Crosetti who tried for the force throwing to Gordon but Gordon lost the ball for an error. Demaree scoring and O'Dea going to third.
3 Galan, pinch-hitting for Lee, fanned.
Yankees
For Chicago—Root pitching.
1 Dickey hit a high fly to Marty in short right center.
2 Hoag lined to second.
3 Gordon flied to left.

5th Inning
Chicago
1 Hack flied to left.
2 Herman grounded to second.
Cavarretta beat out a bunt down the third-base line for a single.
3 Marty popped to short.

5th Inning (continued)
Yankees
1 Ruffing fouled to O'Dea.
2 Crosetti flied to right.
3 Rolfe struck out.

6th Inning
Chicago
1 Demaree flied to center.
2 O'Dea popped to second.
3 Collins rolled out Gehrig to Ruffing.
Yankees
Henrich homered into the right field stands.
1 DiMaggio fouled to O'Dea.
2 Gehrig fouled to Collins.
Dickey singled to right.
Hoag singled to right, Dickey stopping at second.
3 Gordon flied deep to Demaree who made a sensational leaping catch.

7th Inning
Chicago
Jurges got a ground-rule double as his hit bounced into the right field stands.
1 Lazzeri, pinch hitting for Root, fanned.
2 Hack popped to short.
3 Herman popped to short.
Yankees
For Chicago—Page pitching.
1 Ruffing grounded to second.
2 Crosetti bounced back to the pitcher.
3 Rolfe grounded to first.

8th Inning
Chicago
Cavarretta lined into the left field corner for a double.
1 Marty fanned.
2 Demaree grounded to second, moving Cavarretta to third.
O'Dea hit a two-run homer into the lower deck of the right field stands.
3 Collins flied to center.
Yankees
1 Henrich flied to center.
DiMaggio singled to left.
Gehrig singled to right, advancing DiMaggio to third.
For Chicago—French pitching.
2 Dickey popped to short.
For Chicago—Carleton pitching.
Carleton's second pitch went wild DiMaggio scoring and Gehrig going to second.
Hoag lined a double off the left field seats, scoring Gehrig.
Gordon intentionally walked.
Carleton uncorked his second wild pitch of the inning allowing Hoag to take third, Gordon held first.
Gordon stole second.
Ruffing walked to load the bases.
For Chicago—Dean pitching.
Crosetti hit a bloop double between Demaree, Marty and Jurges scoring Hoag and Gordon with Ruffing going to third.
3 Rolfe lined to first.

9th Inning
Chicago
Jurges singled into right center.
1 Reynolds, batting for Dean, flied to center.
2 Hack forced Jurges at second, Gordon to Crosetti.
3 Herman grounded back to the pitcher for the final out. **Yankees first team ever to capture 3 championships in a row.**

Each Yankee's Full Share in Pool Worth $5,815, Record for 4 Games

Losers to Get $4,674 Apiece, Also Above the Old Mark—Prize Comes Out of World Series Player Fund of $434,094

By The Associated Press.

The Yankees and Cubs sliced the largest financial melon ever received by players in a world series of four games when the returns were all in from the box office yesterday.

From a player pool of $434,094.66 the two pennant winners took as their share 70 per cent, or $303,866.26. The Yankees, as series conquerors, received 60 per cent of this latter total, or $182,319.76; the Cubs received $121,546.50.

After paying cash gifts amounting to $3,500 to such associates as bat boys and clubhouse attendants, the Yankees had arranged to split their prize into thirty and three-quarters shares. Thus, Manager Joe McCarthy, twenty-two players on the squad, the three coaches, the batting-practice pitcher and club trainer, each of whom was voted a full share, received $5,815.28 each.

Others Will Profit

Four other players or club officials received half a share each and Road Secretary Mark Roth three-quarters of a share.

Each of the Cubs, who split their pot only twenty-six ways—twenty-five full shares and one cut into portions—gets $4,674.87.

Previously the best pay per player for a four-game series was the $5,593.17 the Yankees received for winning in 1927 and the $4,244.60 the Cubs took in losing in 1932. The all-time record is $6,544, received by the Tigers, who defeated the Cubs in six games in 1935, and $4,656.40 collected by the Giants, who lost in six games in 1936.

Other Clubs Share

Each of the other first-division clubs in both leagues receives a share of the remainder of the players' pool. The Red Sox and Pirates, who finished second in the pennant races, each receive $32,557.10 to divide among themselves. The third-place finishers, the Indians and Giants, get $21,704.73 each, and the fourth-place Tigers and Reds $10,852.37 each.

The total gate for the four-game series was $851,166, of which the office of the Commissioner of Baseball receives $127,674.90. The owners of the two pennant-winning clubs and the two major leagues split $289,396.44 four ways.

The Final Statistics

Standing of the Teams

	W.	L.	P.C.
Yankees	4	0	1.000
Cubs	0	4	.000

Fourth-Game Statistics

Attendance (paid)	59,847
Gross receipts	$226,446.00
Commissioner's share	33,966.90
Players' share	115,487.46
Clubs' share	38,495.82
Leagues' share	38,495.82

Total for Four Games

Attendance (paid)	200,833
Gross receipts	$851,166.00
Commissioner's share	127,674.90
Players' share	434,094.66
Clubs' share	144,698.22
Leagues' share	144,698.23

The fourth game in the 1938 world series attracted more than 15,000 more persons and grossed nearly $40,000 more than did the fourth game of the 1937 series between the Yankees and Giants. The four-game total is also greater and, whereas the players last year shared $417,305.97, the 1938 athletes will divide $434,094.66.

YANKS WIN SERIES FROM CUBS BY 4-0; SCORE, 8-3, IN FINAL

Club First to Take 3 World Titles in a Row—McCarthy, Pilot, Shares Record

RUFFING AGAIN TRIUMPHS

Hurls 2d Victory as Losers Send Six to Box—Henrich, O'Dea Drive Home Runs

By JOHN DREBINGER

Baseball history was made yesterday as the Yankees again conquered the Cubs, 8 to 3, and captured the 1938 world series by 4 games to 0.

The triumph gave the New Yorkers the distinction of being the first club ever to annex three successive world championships. In addition, the Yankees' manager, Joseph V. McCarthy, who never played a game of major-league ball, became the first to direct a team which accomplished this magnificent feat.

What had happened to Bill Terry's Giants in 1936 and 1937 had come to pass again, with these latest National League champions as victims, and the final battle at the Stadium yesterday, viewed by 59,847 onlookers, seemed merely a repetition of what had gone before, only there was more emphasis to it.

Again Hurls Commendably

Burly Red Ruffing, victor in the series opener in Chicago last Wednesday, came back to spin another commendable performance on the mound, and behind him there again was that steady drumfire of long-range blows that tossed the Cubs into hopeless confusion whenever they made the slightest mistake. Perhaps their greatest mistake was in showing up at all.

Frankie Crosetti, concluding a brilliant stretch of four games with a grand flourish, drove in four of the Yankee runs, the first two with a triple in the second inning, which saw the Yanks score three times after a grievous misplay, with two out, had given them the necessary opening.

In the sixth Tommy Henrich sent a booming home run into the right-field stands and when, in the eighth, the Cubs had the temerity to whittle the score down to 4 to 3 on the wings of a homer by Kenneth O'Dea, the Yanks immediately lashed back in the same inning with a cluster of four. Crosetti fetched home the final pair with a double off Dizzy Dean, the celebrated hollow shell whom Frankie already had punctured once before in this series.

In desperation, a fighting Gabby Hartnett juggled his meager man power in every conceivable combination. He even benched himself, but unhappily he could not bench enough. The rules of the game still require that nine men must appear on the field at any given time.

Another Series Record

He hurled no fewer than six pitchers into the futile struggle, which in itself constitutes another world series record. Gabby started with Bill Lee, victim of the first game. The big right-hander faded out for a pinch hitter after three rounds on the mound, trailing, 3 to 0.

Then came an almost endless procession of hurlers, the veteran Charlie Root, the rookie Vance Page, the left-handed Larry French, Tex Carleton and finally, with a gesture more theatrical than effective, the great man Dean himself.

They called on Ol' Diz in that harrowing eighth with two runs already in, two out and the bags full and Crosetti, who had wrecked Dean's really heroic performance in that dramatic second game in Chicago, ruined this last show of bravado as well by deftly dropping a pop fly two-bagger in left field for the Yankees' final pair of runs.

And so Marse Joe, the square-jawed, affable manager whom only those behind the scenes ever see wielding an active hand, has achieved a feat which up to now had eluded the greatest of baseball leaders. The immortal John McGraw had his chance in 1923, but that Fall a Yankee team, which his Giants had walloped in 1921 and 1922, turned on the Little Napoleon. And in 1931 Connie Mack, after his Athletics had crushed the Cubs in 1929 and the Cardinals in 1930, missed his bid for a third straight world title when the Cards surged back to upset him.

The victory yesterday also marked the seventh world championship banner to be hauled in by these amazing Bronx Bombers, the fourth under McCarthy, who bagged his first in 1932.

It was also the fourth time the Yanks had recorded a grand slam of four straight. They first achieved this feat in 1927 at the expense of the Pirates, repeated the stunt with the Cardinals in 1928, and in 1932, their next world series appearance, bowled over the Cubs without losing a game. This, incidentally, gives the Chicagoans the unenviable record of having lost eight straight to the Yanks in world series warfare.

All told, over a span of twelve campaigns, this astounding New York club has brought to the American League six world championships by winning twenty-four games and losing only three. The Yanks dropped two in hammering the Giants into submission in 1936 and lost only one to the Terrymen last Fall.

Although the crowd again was far below capacity expectations, it exceeded Saturday's gathering by more than 4,000 and brought the highest single game receipts into the till, a total of $226,446. The total for the four games came to $851,166, thus marking the first time in five years that a world series harvest fell short of the $1,000,000 mark.

Highlights

- For the fourth time, the Yankees swept the World Series. In their six Series appearances during the span from 1927 through 1938, the Bronx Bombers won 24 of 27 Series games.
- Yankee pilot Joe McCarthy became the first manager ever to win three consecutive World Series.
- The 18 innings Red Ruffing pitched for the Yanks tied the record for a four-game Series.
- Bill Dickey rapped out four singles for the New Yorkers in Game 1.
- The Yankees clinched a victory in Game 2 with two-run homers in the eighth and ninth innings from the bats of Frank Crosetti and Joe DiMaggio.
- Joe Gordon drove in three Yankee runs in Game 3 with a homer and a single.
- Tommy Henrich homered in the sixth inning of Game 4 to provide what would be the game- and Series-winning tally.

Best Efforts

Batting

Average	Joe Marty	.500
Home Runs	(seven players)	1 each
Triples	Frank Crosetti	1
	Gabby Hartnett	1
Doubles	Joe Gordon	2
	Frank Crosetti	2
Hits	Stan Hack	8
Runs	Lou Gehrig	4
	Joe DiMaggio	4
RBIs	Joe Gordon	6
	Frank Crosetti	6

Pitching

Wins	Red Ruffing	2-0
ERA	Monte Pearson	1.00
Strikeouts	Red Ruffing	11
Innings Pitched	Red Ruffing	18

NEW YORK YANKEES ——1938

CHICAGO CUBS

Reprinted, with permission, from
The World Series, A Complete
Pictorial History, by John Devaney
and Burt Goldblatt (Rand McNally
and Company, Chicago, © 1972).

Again It's Dizzy Who Steals the Show

Joe McCarthy later called this Yankee team of 1938 his greatest. "We are the greatest ball club ever assembled, I believe," he said after the Yankees trampled the Cubs in four straight games. "We have the pitching, the power and the defensive play."

That kind of strength overpowered the Cubs, who had clinched the pennant on the last day of the season when Gabby Hartnett, their catcher-manager, hit a ninth-inning home run in the dusk at Wrigley Field. The man who gave this Series its drama, however, was Dizzy Dean. Dean had been obtained from the Cardinals in mid-season for $100,000, and though his arm ached, he'd won seven of eight games for the Cubs in their pennant drive.

Dizzy started the second game. His fastball a fat melon now, Dean mixed curves and off-speed pitches with cunning for seven innings. He went into the eighth with a 3-2 lead. George Selkirk singled, but Dean made Myril Hoag bounce into a force play. Now Frank Crosetti stepped into the batter's box. With the count two balls and two strikes Dean weaved a curve by Crosetti that Dizzy thought was strike three. The umpire called it a ball. On the next pitch Crosetti whacked a drive into the seats for a home run, and the Yankees, helped by another homer by DiMaggio in the ninth, won, 6-3.

Dean's pitching was called one of the most courageous performances in Series history. "My arm gave way," Dizzy said after the game. "It went out in the sixth inning and pained me from then on. At times it felt as if the bone was sticking

out of the flesh. . . ."

And then the old, defiant Dean surfaced. "They're the luckiest bunch of ballplayers I ever pitched against," he said.

Dizzy Dean:
". . . I was suffering out there, boy . . ."

Dizzy Dean, now living in Wiggins, Miss., remembered: *My arm was about to kill me. Gabby Hartnett, our catcher and manager, he came out to the mound in the seventh inning and he said, 'Diz, try to strike it through. If I take you out now with us ahead and something was to happen, they'd run me out of town.' 'I'll do all I can, Skip,' I said. Everytime I threw, it felt my arm was going to fall right off of me. I should have been leading 3-0 but Stanley Hack and Bill Jurges ran together on a little ground ball and it went through into leftfield. That scored a couple of runs. Gehrig scored all the way from first base on it and that made it 3-2 when Crosetti hit his home run. I had nothing on the ball. I couldn't have knocked a glass off a table. I was making a big motion, a big windmill motion, and then throwing off-speed balls. DiMaggio, Dickey, all those fellows, they was swinging off my motion, expecting more than I had, but I was suffering out there, boy. In the final game I relieved in the eighth and it was one of the biggest thrills I ever received in baseball. When they brought me in some 60,000 or 70,000 people in New York's Yankee Stadium, they roared.*

WRITERS HONOR DIMAGGIO

Player-of-Year Award Is Voted by New York Chapter

To the honors already showered upon Joe DiMaggio this Winter was added one more yesterday when the New York Chapter of the Baseball Writers Association announced it has chosen the Yankees' new home-run king to receive the Player-of-the-Year award at the chapter's fifteenth annual dinner at the Hotel Commodore on Jan. 30.

DiMaggio therefore becomes the eighth of a notable list of diamond celebrities whom the New York scribes have honored since the practice was instituted in 1931. That Winter the recipient was Bill Terry who the previous season had led the National League with a batting average of .401.

The following year Lou Gehrig received the plaque, followed by Herb Pennock in 1933, Carl Hubbell in 1934, Dizzy Dean in 1935 and Hank Greenberg in 1936. Last Winter the prize was awarded to Tony Lazzeri.

Out of uniform, but in 1938 style.

1939
A BATTING TITLE

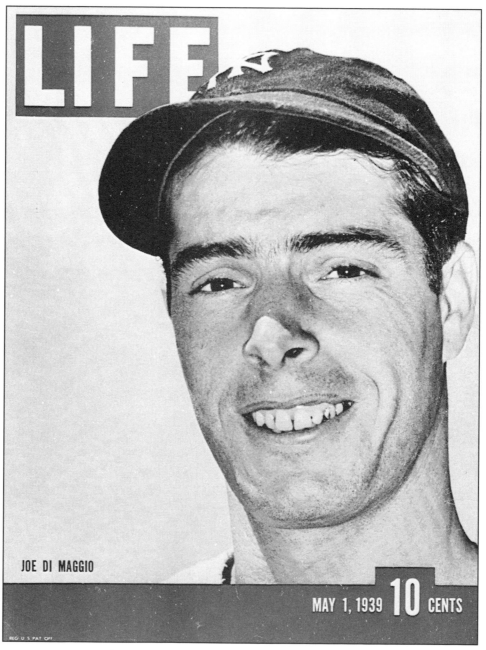

A special honor, making the cover of *Life* magazine.

A YEAR OF UPS AND DOWNS

In 1939, eight games into the season, I was chasing a fly ball in right center field in a game against the Washington Senators when the spikes in my right shoe caught in the ground. I felt something tear: it was the muscles of my right leg, torn away from the bone, just above the ankle.

It was the worst injury I had so far suffered as a Yankee. I finally got back into the lineup a little more than a month later. When I returned, the Yankees were surging and I joined right in on the march to the pennant. I got my first All-Star game home run that year. And it turned out to be my best year at the plate. I led the league in hitting with an average of .381, the tops of my career.

On the down side, it was the year that Colonel Jake Ruppert died: he was the Yankees' owner, and had brought me to New York. And, on a close personal level, it was the year Lou Gehrig had to leave the lineup after playing in an incredible 2,130 consecutive games; not too long after that he was diagnosed as having a fatal illness.

Joe DiMaggio

1939

JOE DiMAGGIO STATISTICS

Games	120
At Bats	462
Hits	176
Doubles	32
Triples	6
Home Runs	30
Runs Scored	108
Runs Batted In	126
Bases on Balls	52
Strike Outs	20
Stolen Bases	3
Slugging Average	.671
Batting Average	.381*

* Led the American League

STANDINGS

	Won	Lost	Percentage	Games Behind
New York Yankees	106	45	.702	
Boston Red Sox	89	62	.589	17
Cleveland Indians	87	67	.565	20.5
Chicago White Sox	85	69	.552	22.5
Detroit Tigers	81	73	.526	26.5
Washington Senators	65	87	.428	41.5
Philadelphia A's	55	97	.362	51.5
St. Louis Browns	43	111	.279	64.5

Five Yanks, Ott Named on All-Star Team

By the United Press.

ST. LOUIS, Jan. 10.—The New York Yankees, with five players named, dominated the 1938 all-star baseball team selected for the Sporting News, national baseball weekly, by members of the Baseball Writers' Assn. of America, it was announced today.

Eight players from the junior circuit were selected, as compared with three for the National League. In 1937 honors were evenly divided, only ten players being selected that year.

Two hundred and forty-nine baseball writers participated in the poll. Joe Di Maggio, of the Yankee outfield, led the list with 241 votes. Joe Medwick, St. Louis Cardinal outfielder, was second with 233 votes and Charles (Red) Ruffing, Yankee pitcher, third with 211.

Joe Cronin, manager and infielder for the Boston Red Sox, staged a comeback to win a place on the team for the sixth time, while Charles Gehringer, Detroit infielder, won a berth on the team for the sixth consecutive time.

The team:—

Player and Pos.	Team.
Joe Medwick, lf.	St. Louis Cardinals
Joe Di Maggio, cf.	New York Yankees
Mel Ott. rf.	New York Giants
Jimmy Foxx, 1b.	Boston Red Sox
Charles Gehringer, 2b.	Detroit Tigers
Joe Cronin, ss.	Boston Red Sox
Robert Rolfe, 3b.	New York Yankees
Bill Dickey, c.	New York Yankees
Charles Ruffing, p.	New York Yankees
Vernon Gomez, p.	New York Yankees
Johnny Vandermeer, p.	Cincinnati Reds

Yankee Chief Admits Offer Has Brought No Response

Star Warned Against Holding Out For Refund of Deducted 1938 Pay

By DANIEL.

Ed Barrow, president of the Yankees, today confessed he was at a loss to account for the failure of Joe Di Maggio to send in his signed contract. Giuseppe, who held out for $30,000 last year and got $25,000, with $1,850 deducted for the days he lost from league competition, some time ago promised not to put on another salary siege.

"That interview in which Joe was quoted as having said he would not sign until I sent him a check for $1,850 has been repudiated by his brother Tom," Barrow continued.

"But I will tell you this:—If Di Maggio makes the refund a condition, he is going to be mistaken. Quite definitely, he is not going to get it.

"I have had no word from the outfielder. He has not declared himself on the contract and he has not applied for the return of salary lost by his inactivity in 1938."

Di Maggio, who has received a duplicate of his 1938 agreement, may console himself with the fact that in Barrow's book that is an increase of at least $5,000. Cousin Ed is not an advocate of high salaries. The current standard for the Yankees was set by the late Colonel Jacob Ruppert, who felt that money squabbles with ball players demeaned him in the eyes of his friends. Barrow has no such psychology.

Efforts to get at the bottom of the Di Maggio mystery through inquiries in San Francisco have not been successful. The socking restaurateur is making no speeches this year. That the interview mentioning $1,850 was not based on some utterance by Joe is not given credence here.

Di Maggio Sees This His Big Season

By the Associated Press.

SAN FRANCISCO, Feb. 16.—Limited to a week and a half of actual training his first three years in the majors, Jolting Joe Di Maggio, the Yankees' outfield star, plans really to get in shape for the opening of the 1939 season.

Di Maggio will leave for the St. Petersburg (Fla.) camp of the world's champions on March 1, in time to arrive for the opening of training four days later.

Di Maggio denied and seemed annoyed at reports here that he would shortly sign a contract calling for $26,000. He reportedly received $25,000 last season.

Because he expects to be in excellent shape for the opening game Di Maggio predicted, "This is going to be my big year." This should be bad news for American League pitchers, whom Joe mauled for averages of .323, .346 and .324 in his three years in the big time.

"Do you know that in three spring training camps I haven't had over one and a half weeks of actual training?" Di Maggio asked.

"The first year my foot was burned and I was thrown out of training. The second year I had my tonsils removed and last year it was my own fault [he held out until after the season was under way], but the fact remains I have yet to open the season with the Yankees in first-class shape.

"For once I would like to start off feeling that I am fit for anything that comes along, and, barring accidents, I am going to be in that kind of condition this year.

"I feel that this is going to be my big year."

DIMAGGIO, RUFFING REACH YANKS' CAMP

Four Others Work Out First Time—No Word of Crosetti or Rolfe, Says McCarthy

By JAMES P. DAWSON
Special to THE NEW YORK TIMES.

ST. PETERSBURG. Fla., March 6.—Six more players arrived today and brought the number of Yankees in camp to thirty-three. Manager Joe McCarthy directed a three-hour workout, longest of the training period thus far, before a record gathering of 2,500 onlookers.

Charley Ruffing, who won twenty-one games and lost seven for the champions last year, arrived a week late. Joe DiMaggio, who disappointed himself with a .324 batting average last year, checked in, along with Babe Dahlgren, Lou Gehrig's understudy at first base, from San Francisco.

Bill Knickerbocker, utility infielder, and Walter Judnich and William Matheson, Kansas City rookies, in uniform for the first time, rounded out the sextet. All leaped into the thick of things as newsreel photographers recorded the occasion for posterity, and still camera men thought up new poses for the athletes.

No Word of Holdouts

Only Frankie Crosetti and Red Robert Rolfe of the Yankees were absent from camp. McCarthy said today he had had no word of them. He insisted that a long-distance phone call he received in the clubhouse during the workout had no reference to the club's only holdouts.

Ruffing said he weighed 208 pounds. He looked in great physical condition. "I have been working out for a month at Long Beach, Calif.," said the big pitcher. "I feel fine and should be ready with a day or two of drilling here. Did nothing much through the Winter but watch my diet and golf. I'm ready for another good season."

DiMaggio said he weighed 196, six pounds less than at the close of the last campaign. "I spent most of the Winter looking after my restaurant at Fisherman's Wharf," said DiMag. "Even if you don't ask me, business is booming. I spent a lot of money making improvements and expect there'll be some dividends from here on."

"Did you do any training on the Coast?" he was asked.

Big Season Predicted

"Naw," came the reply. "I did a little bit of throwing for a few days, but when I tried hitting I found my swinging bad and gave it up. I'll get plenty of work here for what I expect will be my big season."

Evidently suiting the action to the word, DiMaggio was the last off the field today. Even after the rest of the squad had gone to the showers and rubbing table, the San Francisco star was out fielding bunts.

Dahlgren, huskier and stronger than ever, had a good workout in the first regular infield drill. This found Gehrig at first base, Joe Gordon at second, Knickerbocker at short and Dahlgren and Matheson, who used to be an infielder, at third.

Even the "Iron Man," Gehrig, stuck to the last, giving Ziggy Sears little chance for work on relief.

Bill Dickey worked out for the first time this year in full catching paraphernalia—mask, chest protector and shinguards—though a hot sun flooded the field.

Baseball bargaining, as seen through the eyes and pen of cartoonist Gus Uhlmany. After all was said and done, Colonel Jake Ruppert truly got his money's worth from the likes of Joe DiMaggio, Lefty Gomez, Bill Dickey, and Tommy Henrich.

A classic DiMaggio: pensive, contemplative, waiting his turn.

Clowning it up with the "Clown Prince" of baseball, Al Schacht.

DiMaggio Sets Batting Title as Season's Goal

Yankees Return to Tackle Senators; Cold Prevents 2-Game Series in Boston

By Rud Rennie

Joe DiMaggio, the man on the magazine cover who is off to a good start on what may be his biggest year in baseball, was talking this afternoon about what he hopes to achieve. He wants to be the league's leading batsman, an honor he never has had.

For the second day in succession the game in Boston was called off because of cold weather. So the Yankees took a 2 o'clock train and were back in New York last night. They had a ride and a rest and are ready to take some exercise with the Washington Senators in the Stadium today. There will be two games here before the team goes West, not to return until May 16.

Eager to Lead League

"I want to make more base hits than anyone in the league," said DiMag. He was on the train, damp scenery sliding past the windows. "I want to win that batting crown."

He shook his head at the suggestion that he might hit sixty-one home runs for a record.

"That's a lot of home runs," he said. "I had a lot of luck when I hit forty-six in 1937. You have to have luck to have some of those fly balls drop into the stands for you. No, I'm not going for homers. I just want to hit that ball, get on base as often as I can and drive in runs."

The big, young Yankee slugger is encouraged as never before by his condition this early in the season.

Started Season in Stride

For the first time in his four years with the team, he has enjoyed a full measure of spring training without an ache or pain. He looked great down South. And he started the season at the top of his stride. It was the first time he ever was able to start right from scratch with the Yankees. The first year up he had a burned heel; the next year a lame arm and tonsil trouble and last year he was a holdout.

In the second week of the season he is hitting .409.

"The tip-off to me," he said, "on how I may go this year is my hitting against the Philadelphia pitchers. They've always been tough for me, but I hit good in the series with the A's. I figure if I can get hits where it was hard for me to get them before, I should be that much farther ahead."

Early Start Spurs Team

The team also benefits by DiMaggio's early start. Joe McCarthy pointed out while the team was in training that it should get away more successful with DiMaggio in the batting order for the first time so early in the season.

So Joe is willing to let Hank Greenberg and Jimmy Foxx battle each other for home-run honors. He has his heart set on winning the batting championship.

The Yankees have piled up six double-headers—one in Washington, two in Boston and three at home.

Dickey and Di Maggio Pace Yanks in Display of Power

Di Maggio Has Field Day; Lifts Average to .438.

Between them Dickey and Di Maggio made eight of the seventeen hits, which set a 1939 high for the New York run-making machine. It was the first exhibition of real power the Yankees had put on this spring.

With a triple, two doubles and a single, Joe brought his hit total for eight games to fourteen and lifted his average to a neat .438.

Joe's throwing could be a lot better. He has been putting more on the ball these last few days, but still is far from the thrower he was in 1936. However, Giuseppe's fielding is exemplary and that batting record speaks for itself.

His triple yesterday was the best-hit ball of a socking afternoon. Joe slammed it on a line to the scoreboard out in left field, some 435 feet from the plate. It rolled under the board and because of ground rules Giuseppe lost a homer.

This Di Maggio lad is a changed ball player. Last year he affected a scowl. He was being razzed by the fans and appeared to nurse a grievance against the whole world. Perhaps he did a lot of communing with one Joe Di Maggio over his chipino in his San Francisco restaurant this past winter. Or he may have been steered by some wise head. But the jolter is a new man.

Joe DiMaggio tries to stretch a double into a triple but gets foot-tied by Washington Senator third baseman, Buddy Lewis. The Yankees won anyway, 10–2.

YANKS OFF ON TOUR, STAR IN HOSPITAL

DiMaggio Undergoing Special Treatments—Shake-Up in Batting Order Looms

By JAMES P. DAWSON

Joe McCarthy led his Yankees out of town last night, on their first swing into the West, burdened with what might conservatively be called a dilemma.

Two week-end defeats at the hands of the Senators, the leg injury of last Saturday to his clouting star, Joe DiMaggio, and the torn shoulder muscle that overtook Charley (Red) Ruffing, the club's pitching ace, last Tuesday against the Athletics, gave the Yankee skipper plenty to think about as the train rolled out of Grand Central Station.

A shake-up in the batting order was forecast. Marse McCarthy would not announce his starting line-up for the first game in Detroit today, and this was accepted as an open admission that a change was contemplated.

DiMaggio was undergoing diathermic treatments in St. Elizabeth's Hospital when his mates departed. He entered the institution at noon yesterday accompanied by Dr. Robert Emmet Walsh, being taken in a wheel chair from his quarters in the Hotel New Yorker. Dr. Walsh said it would be at least ten days, perhaps two weeks, before the Yankee batting star could leave the hospital. It may be three weeks before DiMaggio is able to resume his post in center field. But President Ed Barrow of the Yankees yesterday said he hoped DiMaggio would be ready to play on May 13 in Philadelphia.

In the absence of DiMaggio, Jake Powell and Tommy Henrich will divide the duties in center, the former against left-handed pitching and Henrich against the right-handers.

At the same time the injury of DiMaggio definitely put a halt to negotiations between the Yankees and the Boston Red Sox involving the transfer of Powell. It was learned yesterday that Managers McCarthy and Joe Cronin discussed such a trade in Boston, although at the time denials were issued from both sides.

Times Wide World

JOE DIMAGGIO ON WAY TO HOSPITAL YESTERDAY

With Di Maggio Back, Yankees Present Power at the Gate as Well as Plate

By DANIEL.

Joe Di Maggio, greatest of the current crop of major league ball players and unquestionably destined for a niche at Cooperstown, today goes on display again in the Stadium. Once more the Yankees present an alluring player with box office magnetism as well as all the technical superlatives.

It will be recollected that in his seventh game of the season, in the Stadium on April 29, against Washington, Di Maggio made a sharp turn while fielding a liner and tore the muscles in his right foot.

After Giuseppe had missed thirty-five games, Joe McCarthy suddenly sent him back to the middle patrol in Detroit. The Yankees had gone into a lamentable tailspin and for the second time this season had lost two straight.

Up to that time Bill Dickey had been filling in nobly as the offensive bellwether. But with those two astonishing setbacks by Tommy Bridges and Buck Newsom, Dickey became mired in a batting slump. Out of the haze came Di Maggio, and then the Yankees proceeded to take two in a row in Chicago, and win the double-header to which the St. Louis series was reduced by Saturday's twister.

With his ambitions fastened on the American League batting championship, Di Maggio returns to action in the Stadium with an average of .487.

Against the Western teams, the Yankees have won twenty-four and lost only five. When the Bombers made their first tour of the back-country they won eight out of 10. In the Bronx, they took the hinterlanders by eight games to one. In their second junket through the sector of the Indians, Tigers, White Sox and Browns, McCarthy's maulers once more took eight out of 10.

Detroit has made the best showing, with three out of seven. Cleveland has collapsed against the Yankees, with only one out of eight. The White Sox have won one and lost six against the champions, and the Browns have contributed seven straight.

Never before was the West so futile against the New York club, and a lot of unfair charges have been made against the unsuccessful opposition.

One school of thought figures that the West started the season with a defeatist complex, and gave up before the starting bell had clanged.

Another coterie of deep thinkers holds that the Western teams have decided that the only available prize is second money, and that there is no sense in wasting good pitching against the Yanks.

The cold fact is that the league has thrown every punch it could summon at the Yankees, who have bobbed and weaved, and worn the other lads down.

The pitching situation on the Yankees perhaps is without parallel in the last thirty years of major league competition. Red Ruffing, Lefty Gomez and Monte Pearson, who lead the hurling corps, have been charged with four of the nine defeats suffered by the team.

But the second line of mound defense—Atley Donald, Bump Hadley, Steve Sundra and Johnny Murphy—has not lost a contest and has piled up 16 victories, as against 18 for the Big Three.

Donald has won six. Hadley, who also has taken half a dozen, got a new lease of life with that low-downer he discovered in St. Petersburg. Sundra has won three, and Murphy has answered alarms innumerable, without ever figuring in a losing game.

Hildebrand is one pitcher who doesn't seem to be able to adjust himself. He has lost two. Oral some time back suffered an attack of the flu and has yet to regain his strength. He is no Hercules even in his best form.

Di Maggio Now Hitting Puny .464

Special to the World-Telegram.

CHICAGO, June 9.—Joe Di Maggio today owned his second home run of the season. . . . It figured in his big day against the White Sox, which saw him get a double, a single and a pass in addition to his 410-foot wallop into the right-center pavilion. . . . Joe is batting a puny .464. . . . Di Maggio was a big factor in the defeat of Edgar Smith, the lefthander who baffled the Yankees on their first visit here. . . . The Bombers' record against southpaws is 15 won and 4 lost. . . . Di Maggio's circuit drive, hit off a 3-and-2 ball, was the first New York homer in five games and the forty-second of the season.

Freddy Lindstrom, now a radio commentator, says he has solved the mystery of the supremacy of the Yankees. . . . "They hit harder and play better than anybody else," said the former Giant. . . . Bill Dickey went to bat eighteen times without a hit until, in the seventh, he doubled. . . . He got another hit in the ninth. . . . Hack Wilson visited the Yankee bench. . . . Looking prosperous and rosy. . . . The Bombers even worked the squeeze on Pappy Dykes' feuders. . . . Dahlgren played a grand game.

THE DI MAGGIOS IN PICTURES.

THE metamorphosis of the DiMaggio family of San Francisco and of Joe, who brought it all about, is illustrated in pictures by Life magazine in its issue of May 1. which also carries the Yankee's face on the front cover. An eight-page spread begins with a close-up photograph of all the DiMaggios and follows with a picture of Joe in 1920, in contrast with his royal welcome to San Francisco in 1936; views of the home where he was reared and the handsome house he bought as a result of his baseball earnings; of his seafood restaurant; two strips of the Yankee outfielder in action, also several illustrations showing his popularity with girls, but, unhappily, the lay-out was prepared before he announced his engagement to Dorothy Arnold and the film actress is not shown.

Accompanying the pictures is a story of Joe, as written by Noel F. Busch, who states that the Yankee star became a baseball player because he was lazy, rebellious and endowed with a weak stomach and, thus, didn't follow the ancestral crab-fishing occupation. As much as he despises fishing, Joe also despises superstitions, the writer maintains. Busch evidently didn't know at the time the story was written of the young bomber's romance with Dorothy Arnold, for he declares: "Joe has not yet sublimated his appreciation of the opposite sex to the point of a courtship," although the attributed idolization of Lefty Gomez, whom DiMaggio "admires for his savoir-faire," and whose mannerisms he copies, may account for the fact that, like Gomez, he picked an actress for his helpmate.

Joe Di Maggio Lifts Yankees Out of Slump

Champions Now Lead By Nine Full Games

By DANIEL,
Staff Correspondent.

CHICAGO, June 8.—That magic influence and sovereign tonic, Joe Di Maggio, back in centerfield after an absence of thirty-five games since April 29, today had lifted the Yankees out of their serious and protracted slump of two consecutive defeats. With Giuseppe's triple driving in the first tally the world champions, who had eked out an anemic pair of runs on eight hits in eighteen innings in Detroit, ended the terrible suspense and defeated the White Sox by 5 to 2.

As the Red Sox had been rained out in St. Louis, the New York lead assumed the almost comfortable proportions of nine games. Joe McCarthy breathed much easier. Once more he could fare forth and face his fellow men without that sick feeling which only the leader of a club in a bad slump can experience.

Actually, the well-known siege of Lucknow, and the suspense of those Texas heroes of the Alamo, were only as mild toothaches compared with the sensations of Manager McCarthy as he saw the three-time world champions fail twice in the flivver capital. "This is the end," Joe must have said to himself as he moved over here.

The big decision to send Di Maggio back to earning his twenty-five grand was arrived at in Drawing Room A of the Pullman palace car St. Vitus, in the early hours of the morning. Only two days previous Marse Joe had informed inquirers that Giuseppe was not yet ready. But here was an emergency!

At it turned out Di Maggio was fully prepared to return to his labors. He showed complete recovery from the muscle tears in his right foot suffered in a game against Washington in the Stadium.

Di Maggio Hits Safely In Ninth Straight Game.

After having decided to take time by the forelock, as it were, and ask Di Maggio to do or die for dear old Yankee University, McCarthy did not tell a soul. Imagine the surprise of the newspapermen when they saw Giuseppe dash out, check in his glove with the umpires and take his place in the lineup. The scribes, especially those from the New York evening papers, clapped their hands for sheer joy.

Di Maggio certainly acted like a shot in the arm on his hitherto slumping teammates. For once they outhit the opposition, 9 to 7. Not only that. They sent Thornton Lee, once their Nemesis, to the hospital with a torn muscle in his left shoulder. Lee tried so hard he exploded.

As a matter of cold fact, Di Maggio wasn't so terribly hot even though it was over 100 on the field and 91 up in the cool press box. A better outfielder than Rip Radcliff might have caught that ball which went for Joe's triple in the first. Thereafter Di Mag was retired thrice, and was flattered with an intentional pass which figured in the scoring of three runs on one hit in the fifth inning.

However, Di Maggio did well enough. He emerged from the epoch-making battle with an average of .429 on twelve hits, including a homer, four doubles and a three-bagger.

The Di Maggio tonic even did Lefty Gomez some good. Though under the hot sun it wore off after seven innings and Fireman Murphy, answering his fifteenth alarm, turned in the usual high class climax.

For the first time this year Goofy made it two straight. He had beaten the Indians on June 1. 8 to 3. with seven hits. Gomez had failed to go the route in four of his previous seven starts, but yesterday's unfinished business really could not be set down to the discredit of the left-hander.

Gomez wanted to go on, but he was so wilted and bedraggled that McCarthy told him to go to the clubhouse and buy himself an ice cream cone.

DiMaggio, Back in Line-Up, Stars As Yankees Down White Sox, 5-2

Joe Triples in First Inning to Bat In Run ——Gomez Wins, but Retires After Seven Innings at Chicago Because of Heat

By JOHN DREBINGER
Special to The New York Times.

CHICAGO, June 7.—Galvanized into action by the return of Joe DiMaggio to the starting line-up, the Yankees today put a swift halt to that amazing losing streak which had reached the astonishing total of two.

Jolting Joe, back as a full-time performer for the first time since his leg injury on April 29, opened fire with a three-bagger. After that all the Yanks got hot, with the result that the world champions brought down the White Sox in the opening clash of a three-game series, 5 to 2.

Lefty Gomez, in fact, got hotter than any of the others under the broiling sun and was forced to withdraw and cool off after seven innings. But it was the weather, not the opposition, that forced Lefty to retire with a substantial three-run lead, and as Johnny Murphy, the famous relief specialist, saw to it that matters remained that way, the Yanks' merry senor received credit for the victory, his fourth against two defeats.

8,000 Attend Contest

Jimmy Dykes's starting hurler, Thorton Lee, also failed to go the distance, to the great chagrin of 8,000 onlookers, but it was more than the heat that drove him to cover. Victim of a bad fifth inning, which saw the Yanks break a two-all deadlock with a cluster of three runs on one hit, Lee suffered a severe pain in his left shoulder and withdrew after facing only one batter in the sixth.

The pain in the shoulder, however, doubtless was as nothing compared with the pain in the neck he must have suffered in that harrowing fifth.

A pass to Red Rolfe and a single to left by Tommy Henrich opened the fifth. When Gerald Walker played the Henrich hit none too well, the Yanks had runners on second and third.

After Lee had intentionally passed DiMaggio, Bill Dickey lifted a harmless looking fly to right field which Rip Radcliff dropped. One run counted on that. A wild pitch scored another and a long sacrifice fly to center by George Selkirk drove in the third.

The Box Score

NEW YORK (A)	ab	r	h	po	a	e
Crosetti, ss	5	0	0	2	4	0
Rolfe, 3b	4	1	1	0	0	0
Henrich, rf	5	2	2	1	0	0
DiMag'io, cf	4	1	1	3	0	0
Dickey, c	4	0	0	3	0	0
Gordon, 2b	4	1	2	1	1	0
Selkirk, lf	3	0	1	4	0	0
Da'lgren, 1b	4	0	0	13	0	0
Gomez, p	3	0	1	0	0	0
aRuffing	1	0	0	0	0	0
Murphy, p	0	0	0	0	0	0
Total	**36**	**5**	**9**	**27**	**13**	**0**

CHICAGO (A)	ab	r	h	po	a	e
Bejma, 2b	4	1	1	2	4	0
Kuhel, 1b	5	0	2	11	0	1
Walker, lf	4	1	0	2	0	0
Radcliff, rf	4	0	1	1	0	1
Appling, ss	2	0	0	1	3	0
Kreevich, cf	3	0	1	3	0	0
Owen, 3b	3	0	2	3	3	0
Rensa, c	3	0	0	4	0	1
bSteinbacher	0	0	0	0	0	0
Tresh, c	0	0	0	0	0	0
Lee, p	2	0	0	0	0	0
Frasier, p	1	0	0	0	0	0
cRosenthal	1	0	0	0	0	0
Brown, p	0	0	0	0	1	0
Total	**32**	**2**	**7**	**27**	**11**	**3**

aBatted for Gomez in eighth.
bBatted for Rensa in eighth.
cBatted for Frasier in eighth.

New York ....1 1 0 0 3 0 0 0 0—5
Chicago ....2 0 0 0 0 0 0 0 0—2

Runs batted in—DiMaggio, Selkirk, Gomez, Radcliff, Appling.

Three-base hit—DiMaggio. Sacrifice—Selkirk. Double plays—Crosetti, Gordon and Dahlgren; Gordon, Crosetti and Dahlgren. Left on bases—New York 9, Chicago 10. Bases on balls—Off Gomez 4, Murphy 3, Lee 3, Frasier 1. Struck out—By Gomez 2, Lee 3. Hits—Off Gomez 7 in 7 innings; Murphy 0 in 2; Lee 7 in 5 1-3; Frasier 2 in 2 2-3; Brown 0 in 1. Wild pitch—Lee. Winning pitcher—Gomez. Losing pitcher—Lee. Umpires—Ormsby, Summers, Basil and Bue. Time of game—2:08. Attendance—8,000.

Henrich First to Score

DiMaggio's influence manifested itself almost immediately when, with two out, Henrich singled in the first inning and the great DiMadge followed with a rousing clout to right center. Radcliff managed to get a glove on the ball but could not hold it, and before the sphere could be retrieved Henrich had counted and DiMaggio had pulled up at third for a triple.

The same inning saw the Sox pull ahead with a pair of tallies on two passes, Radcliff's single and an infield out, but the Yanks quickly drew even in the second. Joe Gordon outgalloped a bunt, swept around to third on Selkirk's single and tallied on Gomez's deft bunt.

Gomez allowed six more blows in his remaining six innings on the mound, but never appeared in serious difficulty, while Murphy in the last two gave no hits at all. Fordham Johnny, however, did fill the bases with passes, but that perhaps was done just to take Marse Joe McCarthy's mind off the intensive heat in the dugout.

Fine Catch by DiMaggio

It did not take DiMaggio long to find occasion for giving his dam-aged leg a thorough workout. His first inning triple saw him leg it every step of the way and in the fourth he came tearing in from center to make one of those effortless catches of Radcliff's short pop fly behind second.

Although it was blistering hot in the sun, there was a regular gale blowing that had the infielders and outfielders scurrying in all directions every time the ball took to the air.

The heat was so bad around the middle of the diamond that by the fifth inning even Gomez, who never appears to have more than an ounce or two of beef to spare, looked like something fished out of the lake.

Atley Donald, freshman star who has hung up five victories without losing a game, will start for the Yanks tomorrow, probably against Edgar Smith.

Man In The Next Seat: Joe DiMaggio

There, in the next seat on the airplane, was Joe DiMaggio and good company always makes the miles flash past with a measure of enjoyment.

DiMaggio was in a reflective mood, even though literally locked in by a sports writer on one side and a window with 30,000 feet of empty space on the other.

The Hall of Fame member, one of baseball's most illustrious figures, talked about the present and the past with an exacting recall for detail.

He was asked if he had any particular recollection of his debut with the New York Yankees, the day he broke in to start the 1936 season. That's almost 38 years ago but Joe said he most assuredly could remember it.

His start as a rookie had been delayed in the major leagues because of a burn suffered by a diathermy treatment machine in spring training. He was to miss the first 17 days of the schedule.

So he had to wait and wonder when he was going to be ready and what would happen when he went up to swing for the first time in competition.

The game was against the St. Louis Browns and a submarine pitcher named Elon (Chief) Hogsett, an Indian without head dress, was facing him.

"He always gave a lot of our good hitters, like Bill Dickey and Red Rolfe, some trouble, but I went 3-for-6 that day," said Joe. "We scored a lot of runs."

DiMaggio, only three years later, would be witnessing the demise of a man who was figured to be indestructible — Lou Gehrig, who had played 2,130 consecutive games for the Yankees and amassed the most astounding longevity streak in all of sports.

Gehrig was a notorious slow starter in the springtime so not too much concern was expressed when he didn't knock down the fences with line drives in exhibition games.

"It usually happened that he would go up in batting practice and miss seven or eight pitches without even coming close," commented DiMaggio. "We didn't think much about it.

"But there was an exhibition we played in Houston, on the barnstorming trip home, that made us all deeply concerned. Lou missed an easy foul pop and then, when he came back to the dugout, stumbled on all three steps on his way down to the bench.

"Lefty Gomez, trying to ease the situation, picked up a pebble and said, 'Look, fellows, this is what Lou just tripped over.' A couple days later, though, he went to a hospital for tests and found out the bad news. I guess he began to wonder about himself when he couldn't hit the ball with any power—not much more than a two-hopper to second base."

DiMaggio said Gehrig's courage was an inspirational thing to observe, considering he knew the spinal disease was fatal but he persevered to see if he couldn't somehow prevail.

A pair of Joes and a pair of Jims: U.S. Postmaster Jim Farley and Jim Farley, Jr. are flanked by Joe DiMaggio and manager Joe McCarthy.

ATHLETICS DOWNED BY 23-2 AND 10-0

Yanks Drive 8 Homers, New High, in Opener—13, for 2 Games Also a Record

TOTAL-BASE MARK FALLS

Dahlgren, DiMaggio, Gordon Have 3 Circuit Blows Each —Gomez Hurls 3-Hitter

By LOUIS EFFRAT
Special to The New York Times.

PHILADELPHIA, June 28.—A long-distance slugging spree, unparalleled in the 100-year history of the national pastime, carried the world champion Yankees to a pair of new major league records and one American League mark today as the New Yorkers punched the Athletics into submission twice, 23-2 and 10-0, at Shibe Park.

Blasting thirteen home runs, eight in the opening encounter, the McCarthymen shattered the homer standards for a single game and for two consecutive contests. And when in the seventh inning of the curtainer-raiser Babe Dahlgren propelled his second drive into the stands it meant that the Yankees had hit for a total of fifty-three bases, a new junior loop record and only two under the major league mark.

Dahlgren, Joe DiMaggio and Joe Gordon, each with three circuit smashes, paced the Yankees. Tommy Henrich, Bill Dickey, George Selkirk and Frankie Crosetti made one apiece as a banner crowd of 21,612 persons watched with amazement this mighty display of power, which threatened to go on indefinitely.

Gomez in Top Form

When the McCarthymen were not busy hitting four-baggers, they filled in the time with short-range blows that took effect just as well. They banged out twenty-seven in the opener and sixteen in the nightcap. All in all, it was quite a day and one that Monte Pearson and Vernon (Lefty) Gomez, who divided the twirling assignments, enjoyed themselves no end. Pearson yielded seven hits and then El Goofy came on to blank the Athletics with a brilliant three-hitter in the afterpiece.

When it was all over the experts rushed for the record books to determine how much damage the Yankees had done. They learned that the former record for home runs in one game was seven, credited to quite a few clubs, including the Yankees and most recently the Giants.

For most homers by one club in two consecutive games, the previous mark was eleven and belonged to the 1936 Yankees, while the former record for total bases, fifty, was achieved by the Yankees in 1932. The Reds of 1893 set the all-time high of fifty-five. There were one or two records that the champions barely missed, but they were content to rest on their newly won laurels and move on to Washington, where another double-header awaits them tomorrow.

Nine Runs in the Fourth

An inkling of how the Yankee power house mowed down the hapless A's may be gained from a description of the fourth inning of the opener, in which nine big runs crossed the plate.

Rolfe singled, advanced on a passed ball and scored on Henrich's single. DiMaggio then hit one over the left-field roof. Dickey's single was followed by Selkirk's grounder to second for the first out. Then Gordon homered. Dahlgren rolled to third, but Pearson walked and then successive singles by Crosetti and Rolfe and a double by Henrich accounted for the other tallies.

In the previous inning DiMaggio, Selkirk and Dahlgren had clouted homers to sew up the verdict. Thereafter the Yankees were after records and, like most of the things they set out for, they achieved them.

If any one thought that the New Yorkers had punched themselves weary in the first game he was wrong. For as soon as the nightcap started they picked up where they had left off.

Crosetti zoomed one into the left-field stands and before the inning had been completed Gordon had done likewise and the Yankees had five runs, more than enough. In the fifth DiMaggio and Gordon repeated and Dahlgren joined them in the ninth.

One More for the Book

A press-box statistician discovered at a late hour that the Yankees had made a fourth record, that of hitting three homers in one inning ten times. The former mark of nine also belonged to them.

For the sake of the records, the Philadelphia throwers were Lynn Nelson, Bill Beckman and Bob Joyce in the first and George Caster and Chubby Dean in the nightcap.

Unofficially, the Yankees certainly must have created no end of "double-header records." Recapitulation discloses that they scored thirty-three runs and made forty-three hits for eighty-seven bases.

After today's outburst, the season's high, by the way, Yankee homer totals are as follows: Selkirk 12, Gordon 11, Dickey 10, Henrich 7, Dahlgren 7, DiMaggio 6 and Crosetti 3.

ADDED HONOR FOR GEHRIG

1927 Yankee Flag to Be Hoisted Tuesday at the Stadium

The world's championship flag that the New York Yankees won in 1927 with a team hailed as one of baseball's greatest will be unfurled at the Stadium on Tuesday, it was announced yesterday by President Ed Barrow. This will be one of the extra features to "Lou Gehrig Appreciation Day" when the Iron Horse will be honored by club, players and fans.

Between the first and second games of the double-header with the Senators, Gehrig will lead the parade to the center-field flag pole. With him will be his old team mates—Babe Ruth, Bob Meusel, Earle Combs, Joe Dugan, Everett Scott, Mark Koenig, Wally Schang, Herb Pennock, Waite Hoyt, Tony Lazzeri and Benny Bengough.

OFFICIAL 5¢ SCORE CARD

1839 baseball 1939
Centennial

AMERICAN LEAGUE BASEBALL CLUB

THE YANKEES — OF NEW YORK — SEASON 1939

July 11, 1939

19 Murphy, p.
1 Crosetti, i.f.
2 Gehringer, i.f.
3 Foxx, i.f.

4 Appling, i.f.
5 McQuinn, i.f.
25 Keltner, i.f.
4 Hoag, o.f.

4 Johnson, o.f.
6 Case, o.f.
9 Williams, o.f.
24 Heath, o.f.

4 Gehrig, capt.
28 Bl'ckb'ne, coach
29 Fletcher, coach

UMPIRES
1 Goetz   3 Rommel
2 Magerkurth 4 Hubbard

AMERICAN	1	2	3	4	5	6	7	8	9	10	AB	R	IB	SH	P.O	A	E
8 Cramer — right field																	
2 Rolfe — third base																	
5 DiMaggio — center field																	
8 Dickey 8 Hayes / 9 Hemsley — catcher																	
5 Greenberg — first base																	
4 Cronin — shortstop																	
3 Selkirk — left field																	
6 Gordon — second base																	
11 Gomez 10 Grove / 16 Lyons 12 N'wsom / 10 Bridges 19 Feller / 15 Ruffing — pitcher																	

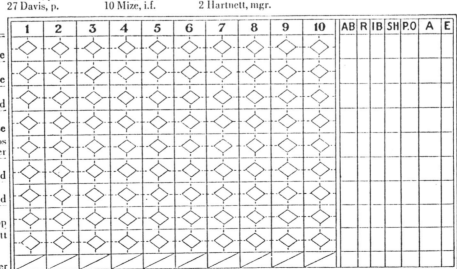

11 Lee, p.
33 Vander Meer, p.
17 Root, p.
27 Davis, p.

4 Herman, i.f.
4 Camilli, i.f.
5 Lavagetto, i.f.
10 Mize, i.f.

7 Jurges, i.f.
24 Arnovich, o.f.
8 Moore, o.f.
2 Hartnett, mgr.

19 Corriden, coach
30 Terry, coach

NATIONAL	1	2	3	4	5	6	7	8	9	10	AB	R	IB	SH	P.O	A	E
6 Hack — third base																	
11 Frey — second base																	
24 Goodman — right field																	
10 McCormick — first base																	
8 Danning 9 Phelps / 4 Lombardi — catcher																	
7 Medwick — left field																	
4 Ott — center field																	
21 Vaughan — shortstop																	
16 Fette 17 Wyatt / 21 Warneke / 30 Derringer / 31 Walters — pitcher																	

Before the 1939 All-Star game, Joe DiMaggio chats with Cincinnati Reds pitcher, Bucky Walters. Later that afternoon, DiMaggio hit a home run to help the American League to a 3–1 win over the National League.

SITE OF ALL-STAR CONTEST, NEW YORK YANKEE STADIUM

General View Showing Field and Crowds

Victory Gives American League
Five-to-Two Edge Over National
In "Dream Game" Competition

Feller Puts Down Threatened Uprising and Steals Pitching Show; Homer by DiMaggio Highlights Attack; Crowd of 62,892 Is Second Largest

By FREDERICK G. LIEB

NEW YORK, N. Y.—The American League, which dropped its second All-Star game to the National League in Cincinnati last year, again took the upper hand in this spirited mid-season competition at Yankee Stadium, July 11, defeating its historic rivals in a hard fought, well played contest, 3 to 1. It gave the Harridge circuit a margin of five to two in All-Star warfare and kept intact its record of never having lost such a contest in an American League park, previous victories having been scored in Comiskey Field, Chicago; Municipal Stadium, Cleveland, and Griffith Stadium, Washington.

New York was awarded this seventh classic ahead of schedule, as the second contest was played in the Polo Grounds in 1934. It was given to the great metropolis of the Atlantic Seaboard in recognition of the World's Fair and the big town did itself proud. With the exception of a few vacant spots in the extreme wings of the stands, the great Yankee Stadium was filled to the gunwales, the official paid attendance being 62,892 and the receipts $75,701.

It was the second greatest attendance at any of the seven All-Star games, being eclipsed only by that of the Cleveland Stadium in 1935, when 69,812 attended.

While Joe McCarthy used six Yankees in his starting lineup and five stuck out the game, the world's champions were not as invincible or impressive as they were in the fifth game in Washington two years ago when the rampaging Yanks, then paced by Lou Gehrig, rode rough-shod over the best pitching the National League had to offer.

As was the case in some of the earlier All-Star contests, it was a game dominated by the pitching, with a home run from the American League camp helping to decide the game in the junior circuit's favor. The pitching was gilt-edged on both sides, the American leaguers getting only six hits against seven for the losers.

Bad Leg Keeps Wyatt Out of It.

Red Ruffing, Tommy Bridges and Bob Feller did the mound work for McCar-thy's charges and Paul Derringer, Bill Lee and Lou Fette pitched for the National League. Fette was pressed into service, when Whitlow Wyatt, Brooklyn ace and American League discard, reported his leg was not in shape and he did not wish to pitch in such an important game unless he was at his best.

Gabby Hartnett's own pitching nomination, Bill Lee, proved the weakest link.

Derringer, strong Red righthander, who only recently settled his difficulty with the New York courts, making it possible for him to pitch in this jurisdiction, had a slight edge on Charley Ruffing, hefty Yankee twirling ace, in the first three innings. Paul yielded only two singles and escaped unscathed, while the Nationals picked up their only run on Ruffing in the third, an inning in which Big Red pitched magnificent ball to escape greater damage.

Ruffing had hurled brilliantly through the first two frames, when he got into difficulty in the third. However, the breaks were not in his favor. Vaughan scratched an infield hit to Cronin and then Ruffing fanned Camilli, batting for Derringer. Hack, a lefthanded hitter, caught the Yankees out of position when his fly to short left fell just inside the foul line. At that, Selkirk's throw just missed nipping Vaughan on a force play at second. Frey then drove a hot double past Greenberg, scoring Vaughan and sending Hack to third.

It was at this stage that McCarthy ordered an intentional pass for Ival Goodman, filling the bases. Ruffing then bore down and did a beautiful job. He struck out McCormick on three pitched balls, and shot two quick strikes over on Lombardi. The big Italian fouled one, which dribbled out of Dickey's glove and then lifted the next pitch to Cramer in short right.

Lee succeeded the effective Derringer in the fourth and almost immediately got into hot water. National League partisans let out a yell of triumph when Bill retired DiMaggio, but the big Cub righthander walked Dickey and Greenberg hit a sharp liner to left. Vaughan jumped for it, partly knocked it down and perhaps saved it from being a double.

Bill had enough stuff to fan Joe Cronin, but Selkirk hit a drive to right, which was disastrous to the National League. In trying for a shoestring catch on the ball Ival Goodman of the Reds injured his left shoulder, and was taken to nearby St. Elizabeth's Hospital.

X-ray photographs showed no break, but a fracture which will keep the Cincinnati slugger out of action for a fortnight.

Selkirk's hit scored Dickey with the tying run and Greenberg followed him when Vaughan failed to stop Gordon's sharp smash to left, a ball scored as an error.

With two down in the fifth. Joe DiMaggio, who has a difficult time connecting with all-star pitching, drove a real DiMaggio homer into the lower left field stands, increasing the American lead to two runs.

Bridges' pitching was much like that of Ruffing.

McCarthy, playing safe, derricked him in favor of young Bob Feller. With one out, Lombardi lashed out his second single and Medwick hit a hopper down to Cronin. Joe charged in fast, but in his haste to make a double play, he failed to come up with the ball. Ott then hammer-

The Official Score

NATIONAL LEAGUE.

	AB.	R.	H.	TB.	O.	A.	E.
Hack, third base	4	0	1	1	1	1	0
Frey, second base	4	0	1	2	0	4	0
Goodman, right field	1	0	0	0	0	0	0
†Herman	1	0	0	0	0	0	0
Moore, center field	1	0	0	0	0	0	0
McCormick, first base	4	0	0	0	7	1	0
Lombardi, catcher	4	0	2	2	6	0	0
Medwick, left field	4	0	0	0	1	0	0
Ott, center field-right field	4	0	2	2	4	0	0
Vaughan, shortstop	3	1	1	4	1	1	1
Derringer, pitcher	1	0	0	0	0	0	0
†Camilli	1	0	0	0	0	0	0
Lee, pitcher	0	0	0	0	0	0	0
§Phelps	1	0	0	0	0	0	0
Fette, pitcher	1	0	0	0	1	0	0
xMize	1	0	0	0	0	0	0
Totals	34	1	7	8	24	7	1

AMERICAN LEAGUE.

	AB.	R.	H.	TB.	O.	A.	E.
Cramer, right field	4	0	1	1	3	0	0
Rolfe, third base	4	0	1	1	1	0	0
DiMaggio, center field	4	1	1	4	1	0	0
Dickey, catcher	3	1	0	0	10	0	0
Greenberg, first base	3	1	1	1	7	1	0
Cronin, shortstop	4	0	1	1	2	3	1
Selkirk, left field	2	0	1	1	0	0	0
Gordon, second base	4	0	0	0	2	5	0
Ruffing, pitcher	0	0	0	0	0	0	0
*Hoag	1	0	0	0	0	0	0
Bridges, pitcher	1	0	0	0	1	0	0
Feller, pitcher	1	0	0	0	0	0	0
Totals	31	3	6	9	27	9	1

*Batted for Ruffing in third.
†Batted for Derringer in fourth.
‡Batted for Goodman in fifth.
§Batted for Lee in seventh.
xBatted for Fette in ninth.

Nationals ..... 0 0 1 0 0 0 0 0 0—1
Americans ..... 0 0 0 2 1 0 0 0 *—3

Runs batted in—Frey, Selkirk, DiMaggio.
Two-base hit—Frey.
Home run—DiMaggio.
Double play—Gordon, Cronin and Greenberg.
Pitching record—Ruffing 4 hits, 1 run in 3 innings; Derringer 2 hits, 0 runs in 3 innings; Bridges 2 hits, 0 run in 2 1-3 innings; Lee 3 hits 3 runs in 3 innings.
Struck out—By Ruffing 4 (Hack, Medwick, Derringer, McCormick); by Derringer 1 (Hoag); by Bridges 3 (Camilli Hack, Herman); by Lee 4 (Cronin, Bridges, Cramer, Feller); by Fette 1 (Gordon); by Feller 2 (Mize, Hack).
Bases on balls—Off Ruffing 1 (Goodman); off Bridges 1 (Vaughan); off Lee 3 (Dickey, Greenberg, Selkirk); off Feller 1 (Hack); off Fette 1 (Selkirk).
Left on bases—American League 8, National League 8.
Earned runs—American League 2, National League 1.
Winning pitcher—Bridges.
Losing pitcher—Lee.
Umpires—Hubbard (A. L.) at plate; Goetz (N. L.) first base; Rommel (A. L.) second base; Magerkurth (N. L.) third base.
Time of game—1:55.
Official scorer—Charles J. Doyle.

ed a single to Gordon's right, which the dexterous collegian did well to knock down, preventing Lombardi from scoring.

Feller Puts Out Fire in Hurry.

Bridges looked sad when McCarthy called him in and held his head low despite the applause of the crowd. Feller pitched only one ball to Vaughan and it retired the side. The nimble Gordon pounced on it and with the aid of Cronin and Greenberg converted it into a double play.

The sixth inning was the high tide, the Gettysburg of the National League hopes. Lou Fette, the Bees' leading winner, held back the Americans, but the Hartnett clan was helpless before the fast ball of young Feller, former Iowa farm lad. In Bob's three and two-thirds innings, the Nationals put only two men on base, Hack walking in the seventh and Ott opening the ninth with a single. Little Mel never left first, as Vaughan lifted to DiMaggio and Pinch-Hitter Mize and Hack both went down on strikes.

There was some confusion in the stands as to why Feller was permitted to pitch more than three innings. However, at a conference before the game it was decided that if either manager found it necessary to lift a pitcher, his third pitcher could go longer than the customary three-inning limit.

THE GAME IN DETAIL.

First Inning.

NATIONALS—Hack struck out. Gordon threw out Frey. Goodman flied to Cramer in deep right. No runs, no hits, no errors.

AMERICANS—Cramer dropped a single in short left field. Rolfe flied to Ott. Ott took DiMaggio's fly. Vaughan caught Dickey's short fly. No runs, one hit, no errors.

Second Inning.

NATIONALS — Cronin juggled McCormick's smash, but recovered and threw him out. Lombardi lined a single to left. Medwick was called out on strikes. Ott flied to Cramer. No runs, one hit, no errors.

AMERICANS — Vaughan took care of Greenberg's high fly. Cronin singled to right. Selkirk flied to Ott. Gordon also flied to Ott. No runs, one hit, no errors.

Third Inning.

NATIONALS—Vaughan singled off Cronin's glove. Derringer fanned. Hack singled to left, Vaughan pulling up at second. Frey doubled over Greenberg's head down the right field foul line, scoring Vaughan and sending Hack to third. Goodman was intentionally passed. McCormick was called out on strikes. Gordon ran out on the grass and took Lombardi's fly. One run, three hits, no errors.

AMERICANS—Hoag batted for Ruffing and fanned. Frey threw out Cramer. Rolfe lined to Vaughan. No runs, no hits, no errors.

Fourth Inning.

NATIONALS—Bridges went to the hill for the American leaguers. Medwick grounded to Cronin. Ott popped to Dickey. Vaughan drew a base on balls. Camilli batted for Derringer and struck out. No runs, no hits, no errors.

AMERICANS—Lee went in to pitch for the Nationals. Hack threw out DiMaggio. Dickey walked. Greenberg singled to left, Dickey stopping at second. Cronin went down swinging. Selkirk singled to right, scoring Dickey, Greenberg going to third. Vaughan erred on Gordon's grounder, Greenberg scoring. Bridges fanned. Two runs, two hits, one error.

Fifth Inning.

NATIONALS—Hack looked at a third strike. Frey was out. Greenberg to Bridges, who covered first. Bill Herman batted for Goodman and fanned. No runs, no hits, no errors.

AMERICANS—Terry Moore went to center field. Ott shifted to right for the National leaguers. Cramer struck out. Rolfe grounded to Frey. DiMaggio hit a home run into the left field grandstand. Dickey out to McCormick unassisted. One run, one hit, no errors.

Sixth Inning.

NATIONALS—Gordon threw out McCormick. Lombardi singled to left. Cronin fumbled Medwick's grounder. Ott singled off Gordon's glove, filling the bases. Feller went to the hill for the American leaguers. Vaughan hit into a double play, Gordon to Cronin to Greenberg. No runs, two hits, one error.

AMERICANS—Greenberg drew a base on balls. Frey fumbled Cronin's grounder but recovered in time to throw him out. Selkirk was purposely passed. Medwick made a running catch of Gordon's fly. Feller went down swinging. No runs, no hits, no errors.

Seventh Inning.

NATIONALS—Phelps batted for Lee and bounded to Gordon. Hack drew free transportation. Frey flied to Cramer. Moore popped to Rolfe. No runs, no hits, no errors.

AMERICANS—Fette went in to pitch for the Nationals. Frey whipped out Cramer. Rolfe singled over second base. DiMaggio fouled to Hack. Dickey out, McCormick to Fette on first. No runs, one hit, no errors.

Eighth Inning.

NATIONALS—Cronin took McCormick's fly. Gordon threw out Lombardi. Gordon made a sensational catch of Medwick's liner. No runs, no hits, no errors.

AMERICANS — Greenberg was out, Vaughan to McCormick. Cronin lined to Vaughan. Selkirk walked on four straight pitches. Gordon went down swinging. No runs, no hits, no errors.

Ninth Inning.

NATIONALS—Mel Ott bored a single to center field, the first hit off Feller. Vaughan hit a long liner to center but it sailed on a bee line to Joe DiMaggio. Big Johnny Mize batted for Fette and was the fourth pinch-hitter to strike out. Stanley Hack carried the count down to three balls and two strikes and then was called out on strikes by Magerkurth, Hack kicking at the decision as the umpire joined the crowd in rushing for the exits. No runs, one hit, no errors.

NOTES OF THE GAME.

TWO NEWCOMERS AT KEYSTONE.

THE two rival second basemen, Joe Gordon of the Yanks and Lonnie Frey of the Reds, were the only real newcomers in the starting lineups. Gordon won the post on this year's American League team, though Charley Gehringer, who had played sensationally and hit .500 in the previous six games, asked to be excused as he is nursing an injured leg. Billy Herman, who had been playing second base for the National League teams, ever since Frankie Frisch faded out, again was on Gabby Hartnett's squad, but the Cub chief preferred to take a chance on Frey, who has been playing brilliant ball for the Reds.

The Yankee management had the World's Series press room open before and after the game to cater to the "inner men" of the visiting scribes and dignitaries.

Myril Hoag struck out so strenuously while serving as Ruffing's pinch-hitter in the third that on the third strike the bat flew out of his hands and almost sailed into a box near the American League bench.

Clark Griffith and his old pitching ace and manager, Walter Johnson, talked of old times as they munched away at platters of chicken salad. "What a pitcher Walter would have made in an All-Star game around 1912 and 1913," said Griff.

When the starting lineups were read through the loud-speaker, an indignant Philadelphian yelled: "What does one have to do to make the All-Star team? All Morrie Arnovich is doing is hitting .372 and leading his league by 20 points."

A lot of Yankee fans booed their displeasure when Gabby Hartnett ordered an intentional pass for George Selkirk in the sixth. The strategy almost failed as Gordon hit a terrific thump, one of the longest drives of the game, that Medwick pulled down in front of the distant left field bleachers.

Derringer retired the first five Yankees to face him, Rolfe, DiMaggio, Dickey, Selkirk and Gordon. However, the two Red Sox, Cramer and Cronin, poked tall Paul for line singles. A press box wit remarked: "McCarthy should have played six Red Sox instead of six Yankees. The Red Sox are hot and the Yankees are cold."

When Tommy Bridges faced Joe Medwick in the fourth inning, it brought back recollections of the Tiger-Cardinal World's Series, when Tommy was one of Mickey Cochrane's pitching aces and Medwick the big powerhouse of the 'Gas-House attack. Tommy got rid of Ducky on a grounder to short.

Arky Vaughan leaped high for Red Rolfe's hot shot in the third inning and came down with the Dartmouth athlete's bid for a hit in his glove hand.

Stanley Hack proved why he is the National League's best third baseman when he went in back of third for Joe DiMaggio's hot shot in the fourth and with a great cross-diamond throw nailed the perplexed 'Frisco Joe at first.

Bill Lee pulled out of a menacing situation in the sixth. He lost Hank Greenberg, first up, on a pass. Joe Cronin then grounded to Linus Frey, who juggled what might have been a double play ball, but threw to first in time to get Cronin. With Greenberg on second, Lee purposely passed George Selkirk to create a double play setup. Joe Medwick then made a neat running catch of Joe Gordon's fly and Lee got Feller on strikes.

Despite the fact that New York has had its fill of early July baseball, a Lou Gehrig Appreciation Day, a red-hot interborough series between the Giants and Dodgers and two successive double-headers between the leading Yankees and the second-place Red Sox, the big city did itself proud for the game. The Stadium doors were thrown open at 9:30 and by game time only a little space in the extreme upper left field stands was unoccupied.

Joe DiMaggio's home run in the fifth inning off Bill Lee was a line drive into the left field seats. Lee had slipped over a strike on the American League's leading batter on his first pitch and DiMaggio caught hold of the next one.

Joe Cronin had difficulty in picking up ground balls for the American League side down at short. He fumbled momentarily on McCormick in the second, but recovered in time to get his man. He couldn't find the handle on Vaughan's grounder in the third and put Tommy Bridges in a hole by cuffing Medwick's double play ball in the sixth.

Among those who had to eat crow, and lots of it, were some of the pessimists who predicted Yankee Stadium would only be half full and estimated the crowd at a mere 40,000.

Cookie Lavagetto, brilliant Brooklyn third baseman, asked to be excused from all-star duty and ran down to Baltimore to consult the Johns Hopkins specialists on his troublesome leg. Cookie was a member of last year's victorious National League squad, but did no more than root for the Frick cause from the Redland bench in Cincinnati. As a result of his inability to play, Gabby Hartnett hastily added Eddie Miller, sensational freshman shortstop star of the Bees, to his roster. Oddly enough it left the two managers, Hartnett and McCarthy, with only two third basemen, Hack and Rolfe, and six shortstops, Vaughan, Jurges, Miller, Cronin, Appling and Crosetti.

Arky Vaughan let out quite a beef at Eddie Rommel when the former Athletic pitcher called him out on a quick-moving double play, Gordon to Cronin to Greenberg, in the sixth. It was the play on which Bob Feller retired the side on one pitched ball.

For the seventh straight time, the weatherman did his bit to make Arch Ward's

old "dream game" a success. Even the hot wave which prevailed in the east for several days lifted, making climatic conditions ideal for fans and players.

FELLER FINISHES WITH FLOURISH.

MEL OTT'S single opening the ninth inning was the first hit off Bob Feller, but Rapid Robert quickly put down the National leaguers. Arky Vaughan was retired on a liner to Joe DiMaggio and Feller then put his fireball to work. He fanned Johnny Mize, batting for Lou Fette, on three pitches, the third strike being called. Stanley Hack also looked at a third one to end the game.

Dutch Ruether, former crack southpaw of the Reds and Dodgers, who would have had no difficulty in making the All-Star line-ups had such a game been played in his day, stood in the New Yorker lobby the day before the game as a lot of unfamiliar faces, stars of today, passed the old gladiator. Then his face suddenly beamed. Gabby Hartnett hove into view. The National League All-Star chief extended his big paw and asked: "Say, do you want to pitch for my club? I can use a good lefthander."

On the eve of the game, the Baseball Writers' Association, with appropriate ceremonies, handed life memberships to Commissioner Landis and the major league presidents, Will Harridge and Ford Frick. Another similar card was made out to John Heydler, former National League president, but John did not leave his Van Buren Bay summer home for the game. "I guess this card should be worth something," said Landis. "I was 18 years in earning it."

Most of the big leaguers were quartered at the Hotel New Yorker, but a Detroit delegation, headed by Spike Briggs, son of the Tiger owner, and Jack Zeller, general manager of the Detroit baseball empire, held open house at the Belmont Plaza.

With the thousands of unreserved seats for sale at the Stadium, Broadway ticket brokers took an awful beating. On the morning of the game, they were selling the pasteboards below the figure charged at Yankee Stadium.

Charley Doyle of Pittsburgh did a good job as official scorer. He had several close ones to call, but there were few dissenting votes in the press stand.

Puffing on his pipe, Bill McKechnie, Redland manager, gave the National leaguers, especially his own red-legged athletes, all the moral encouragement he could muster. By another year the Wilkinsburg Scot hopes to direct the National League forces in St. Louis, inasmuch as the pennant-winning manager of the previous season looks after his league's fortunes in the All-Star game.

The Japanese beetles, which swarmed all over the field when the Yanks and Red Sox played their two week-end doubleheaders, were on hand to pester the athletes at the All-Star carnival. They were no respecters of persons. When Ford Frick and Gabby Hartnett posed for a picture, they were kept busy wiping the beetles off their necks.

Some of the Brooklyn fans in the stands gave Bill Terry, one of Hartnett's managerial assistants, a big generous boo when he took batting practice with the National leaguers.

Casey Stengel, manager of the Bees, had a ringside seat with Bob Quinn, his club president. "Here is where I can enjoy myself watching some other fellows doing the master-minding," said Stengel. But just as soon as the umpires cried "play ball," Casey was pulling as hard for his league as though he were directing things from the National League bench.

Lou Gehrig, captain of the Yankees, who was an honorary member of the Americans, was given a tremendous ovation by the crowd when he went to the plate with the lineup of the junior leaguers. The old Iron Horse, who was unsaddled by illness a short time ago, again was cheered when he returned to the dugout.

Bill Terry, manager of the Giants, coached at third base, and Red Cor-

riden, Cub wig-wagger, at first base for the Nationals, with Art Fletcher of the Yankees and Russell (Lena) Blackburne of the Athletics, handling the traffic at third and first, respectively for the Americans.

Arky Vaughan's hit in the third inning for the Nationals was a sharp grounder. Joe Cronin dashed far to his left, but the best he could do was knock down the ball. His throw was too late to nail Vaughan and it was ruled a hit.

The first walk of the game was Red Ruffing's intentional pass to Ival Goodman with one out in the third inning, after Linus Frey had doubled home Arky Vaughan and sent Stanley Hack to third. The pass filled the bases and the Americans' infield played back for a double play. But Ruffing fanned Frank McCormick for his fourth strike-out and got Lombardi on

a pop-up back of second.

There was some criticism of Joe McCarthy for using six Yankees in his starting line-up. "Why go through all the formality of trying to pick an All-Star club; why not let the Yankees play for the American League?" asked some of the objectors. However, the American League team was picked by the eight managers of the junior league, with Connie Mack passing final judgment on the selections. McCarthy, called upon to manage the club because of Mack's illness, took over the material Connie handed him and put what he considered his strongest lineup in the field. Joe said his greatest problem was not in regard to a Yankee, but who to start at first base, Hank Greenberg or Jimmy Foxx. "When you have to leave one of those two fellows sitting on the bench, it is tough," said Joe.

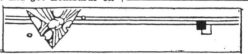

DiMaggio Makes 10 Outfield Putouts, One Shy of Record

The only thing that covered more ground in the Yankee Stadium outfield yesterday than Joe DiMaggio was the grass and, at that, it was a photo finish. Joe rolled up ten putouts and fell only one catch short of matching the American League record for the most putouts made by a center fielder in one contest. The mark is shared by three flychasers, Oscar Felsch and Johnny Mostil, who set it while performing for the White Sox, and Harry Rice, who was a busy gent in a Yankee uniform. Rice was the last center fielder to snare eleven flies in one game, performing the feat on June 12, 1930.

In coming close to the record DiMaggio made no fewer than five sensational catches. He sprinted toward the bleachers to pull down three drives, and his best catch of the afternoon was one which turned back Pete Fox in the fourth frame. In making that putout Joe dashed toward second base and made a shoestring catch of a low line drive.

DiMaggio also made a spectacular running catch in the third inning to rob Earl Averill of an extra base wallop. That was Joe's first putout of the afternoon.

Tommy Henrich made only one putout in right field. He took care of a drive off Hank Greenberg's bat, catching the ball deep in right field close to the foul line. E. T. M.

Historic Homer by DiMag

NEW YORK, N. Y.—Joe DiMaggio's homer against Howard Mills, Brown southpaw, at Yankee Stadium, July 25, takes its place among the real historic home runs of the great New York park, frequently dubbed "The House that Ruth Built."

DiMaggio's blow described an arc of 450 feet before it clattered among the benches in the left field bleachers, only the second homer in the 16-year history of the park to reach these distant seats.

Tiger First Baseman Hank Greenberg, the big boy from the Bronx, the borough in which the Stadium is located, was the first to reach these bleachers, doing it last year with one of the gentle thrusts which added up to the impressive total of 58 before the year was out. Hank's drive went even a little further toward left center than did Joe's great shot.

However, the banner clout of Stadium history generally is considered to be a home run which Jimmy Foxx hit deep into the upper left field grandstand several years ago. The ball had to have tremendous carry to reach the upper grandstand at that height. Lou Gehrig also had a historic drive against the screen in front of the center field stands, when this screen was 30 feet deeper than it is today. Babe Ruth also hit some prodiguous wallops to right field in the early years of the Stadium, but he never drove a ball over the fence back of the old right field bleachers, as frequently has been asserted. Once he hit well up on this fence, but the ball bounced back inside. Many spectators lost sight of the ball and thought he had cleared it.

Yanks Have Won 34, Lost 8 In West So Far This Season

.500 Ball From Now to Finish Would Give Champs 103 Victories

By DANIEL,
World-Telegram Staff Correspondent.

CLEVELAND, Aug. 30.—Joe Di Maggio is thriving splendidly on that diet of $15 telephone calls he has been making nightly to his fiancee of the flickers. Giuseppe's announced post-world series marriage to Dorothy Arnold appears to have provided the Yankee luminary with a new incentive and more urgent inspiration to deeds of derring do.

In the wake of the 7-to-6 Detroit victory which snapped the second best New York winning streak of the year at 10 straight, a checkup on Di Maggio's achievements today recommend Eros as a powerful aid to pennant winning. Only the god of love could have induced Giuseppe's 23rd home run, with two on bases, which tied the score for the Bombers in the ninth inning. With the Yankees in front by 12 lengths, the Tigers must not be begrudged their success. But the home victory was a sad anti-climax.

The picture into which Di Maggio crashed his fifth homer of this last Western trip was a dramatic and gale-driven one. Out of the south-west had come a twister. Buck Newsom had been stopping all rallies. He had struck out eight men. But Giuseppe walloped that ball into the teeth of the storm and into the lower left deck. A home run despite the fact that Di Maggio had broken his bat in propelling it.

As Joe already had made two singles off Buck, he raised his best-in-the-majors batting average to .408. He has hit safely in 15 straight contests, has driven in 104 runs, and is tied with Joe Gordon for the circuit leadership of the club. All this on a diet of long distance calls at $15 a coo.

Donald Once More
Loses Victory Formula.

As the Bombers need no more than half of their remaining 32 games to grab the pennant with 103 victories, a defeat more or less really is nothing serious. While the Yankees were running through those ten straight, the Red Sox blew their chance with five consecutive defeats.

However, there were two regrettable developments in yesterday's setback, and both had to do with the first break in McCarthy's pitching in six games. Marse Joe had had no trouble in that department since Monte Pearson was knocked out by the Browns on Aug. 24.

Johnny Murphy saved that one for Monte. But yesterday Grandma was not so effective. A double by Gehringer, an intentional pass to York and Higgins' single in the ninth inning gave the Bronx fireman his fourth defeat in 33 appearances. Murphy faced only four Tigers.

Trying for his fourteenth victory, Atley Donald once again lost the formula. With the score 5 to 1 against him after six innings, the Louisiana right hander was removed for a hitter. Then came Spud Chandler for two innings, and they got another run off him.

Thrice has Donald faced the Detroit club this year, and never has he gone more than six heats against it. The Tigers beat Atley after he had won 12 straight, and they seem quite definitely to have his number.

West Contributes Handsomely
To Yankee Success.

The world champions tonight encounter the Indians in the third game of the New York club's nocturnal experience. As they lost in Philadelphia and won in Chicago, McCarthy's lads have a chance to finish ahead in that league as well as in the sunshine race. With two contests under the arcs, this trip certainly has been an epoch-making one from that angle, as well as numerous other considerations.

Two meetings with the Indians will complete the New York club's schedule in the Middle West. It will leave here on Friday night for Boston with fond memories of one of the most remarkable seasons in this hinterland yet enjoyed by any team in the American League.

In the West the Bombers have won 34 and lost only eight.

Winning games is not the only thing the Yankees have been doing. They are going to fulfill McCarthy's prophecy that before they returned to the Stadium they would draw more than 250,000 paid admissions on this trip.

In three days in Detroit they attracted 73,674 customers. In 11 games in Briggs Stadium this season the Yankees played to 241,511 admissions. These figures are out of the books of the Detroit club.

DiMaggio Knows His Fences

Discussing Outfielding, Joe Tells Why He Never Has Fear of Collision.

By EDWARD T. MURPHY.

CLEVELAND, Sept. 1. The best defensive outfielder in baseball was sitting in the lobby of the Cleveland Hotel today. Not far away were other members of the Yankees, and they, like the best outfielder, were killing time because it was too early to go to the ball park.

A boy about fifteen shyly approached the best outfielder.

"Mr. DiMaggio, can I have your autograph?" asked the youngster timidly as he presented an open autograph book and fountain pen.

"Sure, sonny," said the outfielder taking the book and pen from the youngster's hands.

As DiMaggio inscribed his name on a page, the boy's face beamed with delight. Joe handed the book and pen back to the youngster.

"Gee, thanks a lot, Joe," said the youngster, as he eagerly inspected the latest and probably most highly prized autograph in his collection. The boy moved toward other members of the Yankees.

Now DiMaggio was asked, not for his autograph, but for information about the way he did the things which had made him such an outstanding fielder. First he was asked what he thought about when sprinting after a ball.

"Nothing but the catch," he said.

How Joe Avoids Fences.

Tommy Henrich, a first-rate outfielder himself, not so long ago, said that one of the things about DiMaggio's fielding which impressed him was that when Joe had to run after a ball he never showed fear of crashing into a wall. DiMaggio was asked if he realized how close he came to some of the American League fences this year in making many of his sensational running catches.

"When I'm in the outfield, I always know just about how far I am standing from a wall," he said. "When I have to run back and keep looking at the ball I always know when I have to start thinking about the fence. Sometimes I go far back and catch a ball without even thinking about the fence. Remember the ball I caught off Hank Greenberg this year? I knew I was pretty far from the concrete wall in dead center field when Greenberg came to bat, so when he hit that ball I just turned my back to the infield and ran as fast as I could. When I was still running I looked over my shoulder for the ball and kept on going. When I caught it I was about ten feet from the fence.

"I was fooled once this season by the flight of a ball. Heath of the Indians hit it in the Yankee Stadium. I was playing for him just about where I was when Greenberg hit his. Greenberg's ball came down when I was running after it, but Heath's didn't. It kept sailing, and I kept running. That's what fooled me. Heath's ball carried further than I thought it would, and just as I caught it I hit against the fence, not the concrete part but the wooden section. I think that ball was hit a little harder than Greenberg's. Anyhow, Hank's was easier to judge."

Hardest Ball to Catch.

"What is the most difficult ball for you to catch?" Joe was asked.

"Those low line drives hit directly at you that keep sinking rapidly," he said. "You have to tear in quick for them with your hands close to the ground and, as for the catch, you either do or you don't. Those babies are tough to handle."

Here the interview was interrupted. A hotel clerk came over to Joe and handed him a small parcel post package. Joe took it and gave the boy a tip.

"How long a stride do you take when you're running at top speed after a ball?" he was asked

"Gee, I don't know," he answered. "Do you think my stride is as much as six feet? Maybe it is around that. When I'm going after a long fly I know when I have to take a look at the fence. The most difficult playing field for me in our league? I'd say Fenway Park is. The playing field has a slope to it, and there is a corner in center field that has to be kept in mind all the time. Baseballs that carom off the fences in Boston take crazy bounds."

The subject of conversation was switched from fielding to batting. Joe is pretty good at that, too.

"You never can tell. I might be able to stay above .400 for the rest of the season," he observed. "I'll say it is tough to be a .400 hitter all year, but I'm going to try to make it. It would be nice to be the first Yankee player that ever hit .400. They've had some great hitters, Ruth and Gehrig and fellows like that."

Hitting at .500 Rate.

Joe was reminded that he has been hitting around the .500 mark most of this trip.

"Yeah, and I've had to do it to outbat Charley Keller on this trip," said he. "He's a real good hitter and, going to the plate right in front of me, he has been an inspiration for me. Next season that boy will give the others a battle for the batting championship."

DiMaggio's batting mark for the season is .405. In the eleven games played since this Western invasion started he compiled a percentage of .490. He has hit safely in sixteen games in a row, his mark for the string being .457. He can't afford to slow up, if he is to keep his season's average above .400.

POWER HITTER

.400 CLOUTER

HOME RUN KING

HIGH EXPLOSIVES—This trio of American League sluggers wants "plenty of bat" when they face a pitcher. Ted Williams, Red Sox; Joe DiMaggio, Yankees; and Jimmy Foxx, Red Sox, demonstrate their batting grips. Williams hits left-handed, DiMaggio and Foxx right-handed. But they all hit hard.

Joe Di Maggio Among Award Leaders

May Be Voted Most Valuable

By PAT McDONOUGH,
Staff Correspondent.

BOSTON, Sept. 7.—A leading candidate for designation as the most valuable player in the American League this year, as he was last, is Joseph Paul Di Maggio, center fielder of the Yankees.

Last year Di Maggio lost out to Charley Gehringer 78 votes to 74, and there is a feeling that sentimentality stuffed the ballot box for the second baseman who led the league in batting for the first time in his twelfth year as a regular. Whether that is true or not, Gehringer batted in 96 runs and Di Maggio 167.

The Yankee center fielder may not drive in that many runs this year, but he has a good chance to top the league in batting and an outside chance to lead the majors in runs batted in. With 122 tallies driven over the plate, he is the only one within a country mile of the pace-setting Jimmy Foxx of the Red Sox in that important department.

Joe goes into a series with Foxx's club today with a string of fifteen consecutive games in which he has hit safely. Over that span he has collected thirty hits for fifty-four bases and batted in 25 tallies. His batting average for the string is .484 and he's boosted his season mark from .321 to .340 in ten days.

Joe May Lead All Hitters This Season.

A continuation of this pace for a few more days would put Joe right on top in batting. Last year he hit .346 and was 25 points short of Gehringer's mark. This year it appears as if no one will hit better than .350.

In one department Joe will not match last year's effort. That is in home runs. He led with 46 last year but has only 28 to date. He's the Yankee's top man, however, boasting two more than Lou Gehrig and Bill Dickey.

Di Maggio will have rivalry from his own team mates in the balloting for the most valuable player award. There's reliable Frankie Crosetti, who's having a great year afield, and Bill Dickey, probably the most respected by opposing moundsmen.

Hank Greenberg and Jimmy Foxx, leaders in home runs and runs batted in, respectively, will probably have the best backing outside of the Yankee club.

In the Boston Red Sox, the Yankees are facing the best club in the league in tight ball games if the games won and lost by one run are any criterion. The Fenway Park club has won 19 and lost 10 by one run. The Yankees have taken fourteen games and dropped eleven by the narrowest of margins.

The Yankees have clinched the season series with every club in the league except the Red Sox. The standing with that club is eight triumphs for the Yankees and seven for the Bean-eaters.

The big story among the Yankees long has been Joe DiMaggio, who will get a terrific vote as the American League's most valuable player. We figured Joe deserved the honor over Charley Gehringer in 1937, but in 1938 there was no doubt that Jimmy Foxx was the head man. However, now Giuseppe demands the crown. He has been hitting over .400 and will win the major batting title. He has lifted himself into the fight for the runs-driven-in championship—that in spite of the fact that he was out of no fewer than 35 games with an injured foot.

He has made himself a neighbor of Foxx in the home-run standing. He matched his best previous hitting streak of the year when he batted safely in his seventeenth game in the Cleveland finale, which he won with two triples and a single, driving in six runs. He had done that in another game in the West. In a dozen games in the West he hit over .500. Nobody could get him out. He is the greatest player in baseball. Not alone as a hitter. His fielding has been marvelous, his throwing grand.

DiMaggio Hits 27th Homer as Yanks Triumph

YANKEES SET BACK RED SOX AGAIN, 5-2

Stretch Lead to 16½ Games —Pearson and Hildebrand Combine in Three-Hitter

---

OSTERMUELLER IS ROUTED

Crosetti Gets Two Doubles and Single to Star With DiMaggio at Plate

---

By JOHN DREBINGER

Feeling that the Red Sox still had a lot coming to them for certain earlier indignities they had heaped upon the world champions, the Yankees tossed a few more broadsides into Joe Cronin's men at the Stadium yesterday.

Joe DiMaggio touched off his twenty-seventh homer of the campaign in the first inning. Two rounds later the Yanks routed the left-handed Fritz Ostermueller, who had conquered the Bronx Bombers on three previous occasions this season, and with Monte Pearson and Oral Hildebrand collaborating in a three-hit performance, the thing added up to a 5-to-2 triumph that seemed wholly satisfactory to a crowd of 9,379.

That gave the McCarthy forces their second straight victory over the Sox and reduced the latter's lead over the champions in their season's series to ten games to seven. In the pennant race it widened the Yanks' margin over the fading Boston entry to sixteen and a half lengths, a distance so vast that for convenience it soon will have to be measured in light years.

Crosetti Reaching Stride

The early downfall of Ostermueller was perhaps the most gratifying event of the day, so far as the Yanks were concerned, with Frankie Crosetti joining DiMaggio in the general bombardment.

Frankie, who after a lame first half of the season, seems finally to have hit his world series batting stride. He uncorked two doubles and a single yesterday.

Crosetti's first two-bagger paved the way for the Yanks' initial tally in the first inning, a sacrifice fly driving Frankie home. A moment later DiMaggio fired his second homer in as many days into the lower left wing of the grand stand to make it two runs for the round.

Singles by Jake Powell, Babe Dahlgren and Pearson's sacrifice fly jolted Ostermueller for another run in the second, and in the third the Yanks finished Fritz with successive one-base blows by Keller, DiMaggio and Bill Dickey that drove in one run.

Pearson Hits Triple

Wilfrid Lefebvre, a rookie left hander, came on the scene to go down for another tally in the fourth on Pearson's triple and Crosetti's second two-bagger.

On the mound, Pearson's performance was not quite so satisfactory. Three-Card Monte finding it necessary to withdraw after five rounds with a lame arm. At that he allowed only one hit. Four successive passes gave the Sox their two runs in the fourth although this did not deprive Pearson of his eleventh victory against his five defeats. Hildebrand made certain of the triumph by blanking the Sox in the final four innings on only two blows.

DiMaggio Batting .408

DiMaggio, who drew a pass in one of his four trips to the plate and hit two blows in three official times up, boosted his batting mark to .408. The homer also gave him his 119th run driven in.

The Yanks announced that they would play a double-header with the Senators on Sunday. The twin bill was arranged by moving up Monday's single game.

If Pearson did not set a new record, he must have come close to tying one in the fourth when he tossed only one strike in the course of passing four batters in a row.

Ted Williams, the Boston freshman star slugger, was on the sidelines nursing a sore left wrist, the result of cracking into the right-field stands in Wednesday's game.

Great Catch by Cramer

The Yanks looked to have three and perhaps all of four runs all wrapped up in the sixth when Keller hit a tremendous drive right down the center of the fairway and high over Doc Cramer's head with two out and the bases full. But the Sox ball hawk, on the dead run, collared the ball in his gloved hand only a few strides from the flagpole.

As it was, the Yanks got some comfort out of the knowledge that in Cincinnati the Keller clout would have cleared the center-field fence with some thirty feet to spare.

After doubling to left in the first inning, Crosetti displayed his versatility by dropping a two-bagger just inside the right-field foul line in the fourth and stroking a fine single into that sector in the sixth.

Thwarted by the Red Sox in Boston last Saturday, Charlie Ruffing will make another attempt to bag his twenty-first victory of the year in the series final this afternoon.

The box score:

BOSTON (A.)	ab.	r.	h.	po.	a.	e.
Cramer, cf	2	1	0	4	0	0
Finney, rf	3	1	0	4	1	0
Foxx, 1b	3	0	0	5	0	0
Cronin, ss	3	0	1	0	0	0
Vosmik, lf	4	0	1	2	0	0
Tabor, 3b	4	0	1	0	3	0
Doerr, 2b	4	0	1	4	1	1
Peacock, c	3	0	0	4	1	0
Ost'm'ller, p	1	0	0	0	0	0
Lefebvre, p	2	0	0	0	2	0
Total	29	2	3	24	8	1

NEW YORK (A.)	ab.	r.	h.	po.	a.	e.
Crosetti, ss	4	1	3	1	3	2
Rolfe, 3b	3	0	0	1	2	1
Keller, rf	3	1	1	3	0	0
DiMaggio, cf	3	1	2	2	0	0
Dickey, c	3	0	1	4	0	0
Gordon, 2b	4	0	0	5	5	0
Powell, lf	4	1	1	1	0	0
D'hlgren,1b	4	0	2	10	0	0
Pearson, p	1	1	1	0	1	0
Hildebr'nd,p	2	0	0	0	0	0
Total	31	5	11	27	11	3

Boston .... 0 0 0   2 0 0   0 0 0—2
New York .... 2 1 1   1 0 0   0 0 ..—5

Runs batted in—Keller, DiMaggio, Dickey, Pearson, Cronin, Crosetti.

Two-base hits—Crosetti 2, Doerr. Three-base hit—Pearson. Home run—DiMaggio. Stolen base—Powell. Sacrifices—Keller, Pearson. Double plays—Pearson, Crosetti and Dahlgren; Crosetti, Gordon and Dahlgren; Gordon and Dahlgren; Finney, Peacock and Cronin; Rolfe, Gordon and Dahlgren; Tabor, Doerr and Foxx. Left on bases—New York 7, Boston 6. Bases on balls—Off Ostermueller 1, Pearson 5, Lefebvre 2, Hildebrand 1. Struck out—By Ostermueller 1, Pearson 1, Hildebrand 2, Lefebvre 2. Hits—Off Ostermueller 7 in 2 1-3 innings, Lefebvre 4 in 5 2-3, Pearson 1 in 5, Hildebrand 2 in 4. Winning pitcher—Pearson. Losing pitcher—Ostermueller. Umpires—Pipgras, Basil and Summers. Time of game—1:52. Attendance—9,379.

Setting the Pace

By FRANK GRAHAM

A Cup of Coffee Before the Game.

(The scene is the Yankees' clubhouse. The time, a half hour or so before yesterday's game with the Indians. The players are sitting or standing about, talking. Vernon Gomez, who is going to pitch, has just had a rub-down and is putting on his shirt. Joe DiMaggio is seated on a rubbing table, smoking a cigarette. A reporter enters.)

DiMaggio—Hello.

Reporter—Hello. How does it feel to be a .400 hitter?

DiMaggio—Swell.

Reporter—Feel any strain?

DiMaggio—Sure I do. It would be silly to say I didn't. I just hope I can bear up under it.

(A clubhouse boy comes in with a cup of black coffee and hands it to DiMaggio.)

DiMaggio—Thanks. . . . This is where I get my power.

Reporter—Do you drink much of it?

DiMaggio—Not too much. But I like to have a cup or two an hour before the ball game. This is my second cup. I don't eat any lunch, you see.

Reporter—What do you eat for breakfast—and what time do you have breakfast?

DiMaggio—I get up about 10:30 and have my breakfast about 11. I have two eggs . . . fried or scrambled . . . toast and coffee. Black coffee. I never put cream or sugar in my coffee.

Reporter—How about your dinner?

DiMaggio—A big steak, usually. Steak and vegetables.

(Monte Pearson, followed by Doc Painter, the trainer, comes over to the rubbing table.)

Pearson—Is that your coffee?

DiMaggio—Yes.

Pearson—Sorry to disturb you, but I'd like to use the table.

DiMaggio—Sure. Excuse me.

He Takes His Time Getting Dressed.

(DiMaggio and the reporter move away. DiMaggio sits on a stool in front of Joe Gordon's locker.)

Reporter—What time do you have dinner?

DiMaggio—Never less than an hour and a half after the ball game.

Reporter—What do you do meanwhile?

DiMaggio—I go down to the hotel and if I see anybody I know in the lobby I might stand around and talk for a while, or I go up to my room and listen to the radio.

Reporter—How are you about getting out of here after the ball game? Do you take your time or do you dress in a hurry?

DiMaggio—I'm the last one out every night. I come in and sit down and smoke a cigarette and wait around while the other fellows are taking their showers. Then I go in and take mine. I can take a good shower, and there's nobody to tell me to hurry up.

Reporter—Is there any particular reason why you take so much time?

DiMaggio—Yes. I'm lazy, anyway, and I don't like to hurry and, besides, it's good for me. Ty Cobb told me that. He told me he always took his time and never left the clubhouse till he was cooled off. I see these fellows rush in and take their showers and rush out and get dressed, and they're still perspiring when they leave the clubhouse. Cobb told me if I took my time and cooled out it would be better for me, because if I went out while I was still perspiring I might catch cold in my arm or my shoulder.

Getting in Shape in the Spring.

Reporter—Cobb has helped you considerably, hasn't he?

DiMaggio—You bet he has.

Reporter—What else did he tell you?

DiMaggio—He told me how to get in shape in the spring. He told me to run a lot and get my legs in shape. He said the first week I was at the training camp I should run and get my legs in shape and never mind my arm, because when I was in shape my arm would be in shape, too, and all I would have to do would be to throw a little and it would be ready for the season. He said: "When you go out with the other fellows and they run around the field a couple of times and stop, don't you stop. You keep on running. You keep doing that and you will be in shape." That's what I did this spring. I did a lot of running at St. Petersburg, and I didn't do much throwing until I had been there for a week or so and my arm never bothered me.

Reporter—Yes?

DiMaggio—He told me that if I got in shape in the spring I would be set for the year, and after that I could conserve my energy. He said that during the season I wouldn't have to do so much, and I found out that he was right. He said there was no sense staying out in the outfield practicing catching fly balls. He said: "You know how to catch a fly ball. Just catch a few and then come in. And on hot days come in the clubhouse where it is cool and rest for a half hour or so before the game." So I've been doing that.

Reporter—What do you do—lie down?

DiMaggio—No. I just sit around and have a cup of coffee.

Reporter—Do you drink any coffee right after the game?

DiMaggio—No. But I drink a lot of water. I drink a lot of water in the summer time anyway. But after a game I stop and take a big drink before I go in for my shower, and then I stop and take another on the way out.

A Lighter Bat in Hot Weather.

Reporter—Did he tell you anything else?

DiMaggio—Yes. I haven't done it yet, but I will. He told me to have a dozen bats soaked in oil and hung up during the winter, and I am going to have it done this winter. That may sound funny, but you know it does help a bat to have it oiled like that. It seems to have more spring to it or something, and you can hit better with it.

Reporter—How many bats do you use during a season?

DiMaggio—I use quite a few. I don't break many. I seldom break one. But I give them away. I have to give one to Joe Cronin every time we play the Red Sox. He comes in and says: "Where's my bat?" So, I give him one. He uses it in batting practice. The last time up he takes it up there and then when the game starts and he uses his own bat it feels lighter.

Reporter—You use a heavier bat, then.

DiMaggio—Yes. I use a heavier bat than Cronin.

Reporter—How heavy is it?

DiMaggio—I don't know exactly. I think it is 39 ounces. But I changed to a lighter bat this summer. Cobb told me to do that. He said: "When it gets hot, change to a bat about two ounces lighter." You'd be surprised how much difference it made. The lighter bat was like swinging a toothpick up there.

Reporter—Do you have any favorite bat—one that, if you broke it, it would break your heart?

DiMaggio—No. Once in a while I get a bat I like a lot, and I feel bad if I break it. I had one on this last Western trip that was very good. It was a good piece of wood. I could hit a ball on the handle with it and it wouldn't sting, like most bats will. And I was hitting good with it, too. I felt bad when I broke that bat. But I don't want to think too much about a bat. It might get like a superstition.

Reporter—Have you any superstitions?

DiMaggio—Ask Gomez. He'll tell you.

Reporter—You tell me.

DiMaggio—The reason I said that was that Gomez is the only one that noticed it. . . . Every time I go up to bat I knock the heel of my right shoe against the top step of the dugout.

Reporter—Any others?

DiMaggio—Only one. (He holds out his glove.) From the time I first come to the clubhouse until the game starts, this glove is never away from me. . . . I don't know how these things started. Just habits, I guess. . . . I'm not superstitious about anything else. . . . But when I do these things every day . . . I just . . . well . . . I feel right.

Champs' Third Baseman Stands Out in Majors

Triple Batting Crown Now Within Grasp of Di Maggio

By DANIEL.

As the Yankees today met the season's final invasion of the Stadium by the western clubs, Joe Di Maggio, with his .401 batting average, 120 runs driven in and 27 homers, stole the show and very properly got top billing. But behind the fanfare over Giuseppe there were other vital laborers in the dramatics of Joe McCarthy, without whose brilliant contributions Di Maggio would be a Hamlet misplaced in Love's Labor Lost.

Outstanding in the supporting cast of the greatest stock company in baseball was Robert Abial Rolfe, surnamed the Red. That the Blasters were 17 lengths in front of the Red Sox and only four games from their fourth straight pennant traced in no small degree to the varied activities of this true New Hampshire Yankee, son of Dartmouth College, and descendant of the man who married Pocahontas.

With 192 hits, Rolfe leads both leagues. Barney McCosky of the Tigers, with 174, and Frank McCormick, Reds, and Johnny Mize, Cardinals, with 172 each, are his only rivals for this title, and they never are going to catch him this year. Ruby Robert tops the American League in doubles, with 42, and is only one behind Enos Slaughter of the Cardinals for the major leadership.

Add the fact that Rolfe is hitting .332, better than ever before in his career at this late stage of a season; that he has driven in 66 runs, and with 14 homers already has set a new high for himself in that specialty and you have a pretty fair summation of the factors that once again have made Rolfe the All-America third baseman.

It is interesting to note that of all the Yankees, Rolfe last March was listed a dissatisfied ball player. Like others, Red held out. But, unlike others, he had to sign at the club's terms. Instead of sulking, Red tore right out and has piled up enough persuasion to make Ed Barrow correct his 1939 error when the 1940 contracts go out.

Foxx's Retirement Places Triple Crown Before Joe.

The Fates seem to be playing right into Di Maggio's hands. Only a few days ago the home run championship seemed to lie well beyond his reach. Jimmy Foxx, with 35, was eight in front of Giuseppe and apparently assured of the title which Hank Greenberg won last year with 58.

But on Saturday Foxx was rushed to a hospital for an appendectomy, and now Di Maggio discovers that the triple crown of all baseball may be his.

That he will win the batting title is certain. That he will overtake Ted Williams for the runs batted in laurels, with the Boston rookie only nine ahead of him, seems likely. That Joe will rally in the four-bagger industry and make up his deficit is another possibility.

Di Maggio is confronted with the glorious opportunity to revive the matchless triumphs recorded by Lou Gehrig in 1934 and since then not achieved by any other major leaguer. Five years ago the Iron Horse won the batting title with .363, the home-run championship with 49 and the runs-batted-in crown with 165. That was a ball player!

Barrow has said that in view of the easy time the Yankees have been having with that fourth pennant he is of a mind to stand pat for 1940 and challenge the strengthened field to knock the Bombers down.

However, the writer is in a position to divulge the fact that this week two men in whom Barrow is interested will be the subjects of final inspection by him. One is Hal Trosky, first baseman of the Indians, who is here for two games and is hitting .336, with 104 runs belted in.

The other is Greenberg, batting .311, and with 27 homers, tied with Di Maggio for the runner-up position in their league. Trosky is a left-handed hitter and as such is fashioned for the Stadium. But Hank is the greatest Jewish ball player of all time. He will be here beginning Thursday.

It is an open secret that Greenberg would welcome a shift to the Bronx.

DIMAGGIO HELD TO .267 MARK BY THE TIGERS

But Hits Seven of His Thirty Homers Off Their Pitching Staff.

By THE OLD SCOUT.

Lefty Gomez will easily recall the conversation because it took place about a month ago in the Yankees' clubhouse between him, Joe DiMaggio and a reporter. The subject was DiMaggio's batting percentage, at that time one or two points above .400, and his chances of keeping it that high for the remainder of the season.

"I want to see you finish with a .400 average, Joe," said Gomez. "I've got nine hits myself and I'll give them to you at the end of the season, if you need 'em for a .400 average."

"Thanks, Lefty," said Joe with a smile. "Your hits may be just what I'll need, but I won't be able to claim 'em."

"Don't take all of Gomez's at bats," advised the reporter. "If you do you won't be a .250 hitter."

"No at bats at all," said Gomez. "Just take my nine hits and add 'em to Joe's."

It turned out to be a case of true words having been spoken in jest. DiMaggio's stickwork fell off in the last two weeks of the season. He reached the end of the trail with an average of .381, having made 176 hits in 462 times at bat. He took over the American League batting crown for the first time, but was disappointed because his heart was set on being a .400 hitter.

Joe Needed Those Hits.

What DiMaggio needed was the nine hits Gomez was willing to surrender to him. With that many blows added to his total number of safeties Joltin' Joe would have hit .400 right on the nose. The mark would have been attained with 185 hits in 462 times at bat.

When Gomez was offering his base hits to DiMaggio, no one suspected things would turn out as they did.

In hammering his way to the championship DiMaggio was better than a .400 hitter against three teams, the Browns, Red Sox and White Sox. He mauled St. Louis pitchers for the sizzling percentage of .484 and against the Boston staff he compiled a mark of .475. He was a .414 batsman when pitted against the Chicago flippers.

The Tigers and the Indians were the most successful in dealing with the renowned slugger. Joe was held to mark of .291 by the Cleveland pitchers and batted a mere .267 in sixteen games against the Tigers. Mel Harder of the Indians tormented Joe with a steady diet of curves. The Yankee slugger admits Mel has been his consecutive hoodoo in the majors. Schoolboy Rowe and Buck Newsom of the Tigers had some successful days against Joe last season, but they still were victims of some of Joe's home run shots. Rowe stopped two of DiMaggio's batting streaks. One had lasted through seventeen games and the other twelve. A fifteen game streak was snapped by Newsom.

Squared Matters.

Although DiMaggio didn't hit better than .267 against the Detroit brand of pitching, he made more home runs against that staff than any other. He stung Detroit pitchers for seven of his thirty circuit drives. Six four-base blows were struck off Washington pitchers.

Against the Senators, DiMaggio batted .361 and featured extra base slugging. He gathered thirty hits against Washington pitchers for a total of fifty-six bases.

Here is DiMaggio's batting record compiled against each rival team:

	G.	A.B.	H.	1B.	2B.	3B.	H.R.	T.B.	P.C.
St.Louis.	17	64	31	21	8	1	1	44	.484
Boston ..	18	61	29	21	3	0	5	47	.475
Chicago .	15	70	29	20	3	2	4	48	.414
Phila. ..	19	69	25	14	6	0	5	46	.362
Wash't'n.	21	83	30	17	6	1	6	56	.361
Cleveland	14	55	16	9	3	2	2	29	.291
Detroit ..	16	60	16	7	2	0	7	39	.267
Totals	120	462	176	89	31	6	30	289	.381

The Umpire
By H.G. Salsinger

THEY ARE calling Joe DiMaggio the "greatest outfielder of all time," and the "greatest player of all time."

They are placing DiMaggio ahead of Ty Cobb, Babe Ruth, Tris Speaker, Joe Jackson, Honus Wagner, and the other immortals of the game.

After four seasons in the major leagues, during none of which he participated in every championship game, DiMaggio is being rated the No. 1 player of the game.

* * *

Best Today, But

DIMAGGIO is undoubtedly the best outfielder today, but if you call him the best ball player today you will have a number of disputes ahead of you. Several qualified judges are still not convinced that DiMaggio is a more valuable player than his team-mate, Bill Dickey. If the Yankees had to part with either DiMaggio or Dickey the chances are that DiMaggio would be the one to go, unless the Yankees would be playing the future, rather than the present.

DiMaggio has been a first-class outfielder for four years, but how many top-flight outfielders are there in the game? The best in the National League is Joe Medwick of the St. Louis Cardinals. In the American League DiMaggio has only two serious rivals, Charley Keller and Ted Williams. Keller of the Yankees is a first-cass hitter and slugger, and a good fielder. Williams of the Red Sox is probably the hardest hitter in base ball today, a player who in his first year led the major leagues in driving in runs, but who is no bargain as a fielder.

Comparison makes DiMaggio stand out above the modern field, but what would be his rank if he had Cobb, Speaker, Jackson and Ruth to compete with?

DIMAGGIO ANNEXED BATTING LAURELS

Yanks' Star Set .381 Pace for American League in 1939—Hit 30 Homers

FOXX 21 POINTS BEHIND

But Red Sox Clouter is on Top for Circuit Blows With 35— Williams High on List

By JOHN DREBINGER

Joe DiMaggio, spearhead of the world champion Yankees' devastating attack, won the batting championship of the American League for 1939 with a mark of .381, according to the official averages released for publication today.

Jolting Joe finished 21 points ahead of Jimmy Foxx, the renowned Red Sox clouter who had captured the title in 1938. Foxx topped his own 1938 title-winning percentage by 12 points, but the dazzling pace of DiMaggio, which until the final few weeks hovered above the .400 mark, proved too much for him.

In capturing the crown for the first time, DiMaggio embellished his performance with thirty home runs and a total of 310 bases for his 120 games, but neither of these accomplishments proved sufficient to lead the league.

Home-run honors were carried off by Foxx, who compiled a total of thirty-five circuit blows before suffering an attack of appendicitis after having taken part in 124 games. Hank Greenberg of the Tigers, who won the 1938 home-run derby with fifty-eight, finished second last season with thirty-three.

Williams Third On Homers

Ted Williams, sensational freshman star of the Red Sox, led the league in total bases with 344. Williams placed third in the home run race with 31.

Red Rolfe was another Yankee to figure prominently in the individual standings by recording the most hits, 213, and hitting the most doubles, 46. The champions' star third-sacker also scored the most runs, crossing the plate 139 times.

Johnny Lewis of the Senators was the leader in triples with 16 three-baggers, while his team-mate, George Washington Case, ran off with the base-stealing honors by pilfering 51 sacks, a remarkable increase over the top figures of recent years. In 1938 Frankie Crosetti led the base stealers with only 27 thefts.

Mike Kreevich of the White Sox led in sacrifice hits with 22.

New Marks for Yanks

Ken Keltner of the Indians equaled a record. He hit three homers in his last three times at bat in a game against the Red Sox on May 25. It marked the eleventh time that an American League batsman hit three successive homers in a single game.

Bill Dickey of the Yankees also hit three homers in a game which saw the American League champions tie a major league record by hitting and scoring in every inning against the Browns.

YANKEE OUTFIELDER GAINS HONOR AFTER MISSING 32 GAMES

BECOMES THIRD FLYHAWK IN LOOP TO JOIN SELECT GROUP

Jimmy Foxx, Selected in Three Previous Years, Finishes Second, Feller Third and Ted Williams Fourth

Joe's Seven-Year Batting Record

Year—Club,	League.	G.	AB.	R.	H.	TB.	HR.	RBI.	SB.	Pct.
1933—San Francisco	P. C. L.	187	762	129	259	414	28	169	10	.340
1934—San Francisco	P. C. L.	101	375	58	128	194	12	69	8	.341
1935—San Francisco	P. C. L.	172	679	173	270	456	34	154	24	.398
1936—New York	A. L.	138	637	132	206	367	29	125	4	.323
1937—New York	A. L.	151	621	151	215	418	46	167	3	.346
1938—New York	A. L.	145	599	129	194	348	32	140	6	.324
1939—New York	A. L.	120	462	107	176	310	30	126	3	.381
Major League Totals		554	2319	519	791	1443	137	558	16	.341

COMPLETING his fourth season in the majors by leading his league in batting, with a percentage of .381, Joe DiMaggio of the Yankees, also added the most valuable player award of 1939 for the American League to his laurels. The New York center fielder was voted the distinction by a committee for the Baseball Writers' Association of America, winning a place from every member and getting a total of 280 points out of a possible 336, and he will receive a Longines wrist watch as an award from THE SPORTING NEWS.

Joe drew 15 first-place votes of 14 points each, three second-place, three thirds, one fourth and two fifths for a long lead over Jimmy Foxx, Boston Red Sox first baseman, who finished second with 170 points, although having only one first-place vote. Two placed Jimmy second and 11 made him their third choice, only one of the 24 members of the committee failing to place him. Previously, Foxx had been voted the most valuable in the league three times.

Receiving three first-place ballots, Bob Feller, Cleveland pitcher, was third, with 155 points. Bob was placed on every ballot except two. Next came Ted Williams, freshman slugger of the Boston Red Sox, who led the league in runs batted in. He had a total of 126 points, although receiving no first-place vote. Charley Ruffing, Yankee pitcher, who won 21 games, also failed to receive a first-place selection, but piled up 116 points in the minor positions, to place him fifth, six points ahead of Bill Dickey, catcher of the Yankees, who was first choice of three members of the committee, but was unplaced by 11 others.

Two others received first-choice votes—Emil Leonard, pitcher of Washington, who won 20 games for a sixth-place club and beat the Yankees four times, and Mike Kreevich, Chicago White Sox center fielder. Leonard rolled up 71 points and Kreevich 38. Ranking ahead of Kreevich, however, were Bob Johnson, Philadelphia outfielder, with 52 points, and Joe Gordon, New York second baseman, with 43.

The following points were received by other players: Pitcher Clint Brown, Chicago, 34; Third Baseman Ken Keltner, Cleveland, 26; First Baseman George McQuinn, St. Louis, 24; Second Baseman Charley Gehringer, Detroit, 21; Pitcher Robert Grove, Boston, 17; Shortstop Joe Cronin, Boston, 15; Pitcher Ted Lyons, Chicago, 13; First Baseman Henry Greenberg, Detroit, 12; Pitcher Buck Newsom, Detroit, 11; Pitcher John Rigney, Chicago, 9; First Baseman Joe Kuhel, Chicago, 8; Outfielder Charlie Keller, New York, 7; Outfielder Geoffrey Heath, Cleveland, 7; Outfielder Gerald Walker, Chicago, 7; Catcher Frank Hayes, Philadelphia, 7; Pitcher Thomas Bridges, Detroit, 7; Third Baseman Robert Rolfe, New York, 6; Outfielder Barney McCosky, Detroit, 6; Infielder Eric McNair, Chicago, 5; First Baseman Hal Trosky, Cleveland, 4; Outfielder George Case, Washington, 3; Outfielder Myril Hoag, St. Louis, 3; Catcher Rudy York, Detroit, 1, and Shortstop Luke Appling, Chicago, 1.

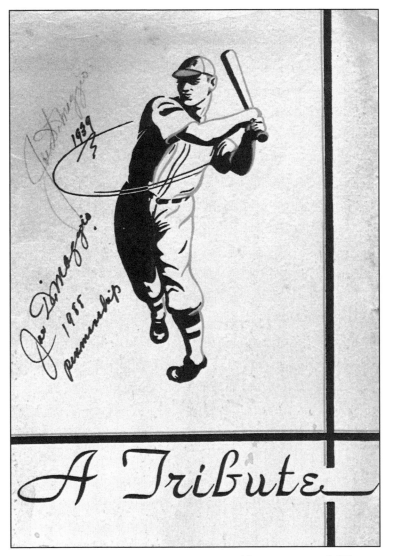

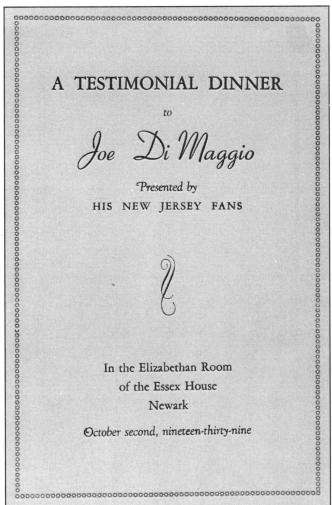

A TESTIMONIAL DINNER

to

Joe Di Maggio

Presented by

HIS NEW JERSEY FANS

In the Elizabethan Room
of the Essex House
Newark

October second, nineteen-thirty-nine

When you lead the league in batting with an average of .381, you can expect a lot of testimonials and tributes. "A Tribute" was signed by DiMaggio in October 1939 and almost five decades later in 1988, and is preserved in the baseball memorabilia collection of Barry Halper.
Earlier in the month he had been guest of honor at a dinner given by New Jersey fans.

Nation's Baseball Fans Eagerly Await Opening of World Series Wednesday

YANKEES FAVORED AT 1-3 OVER REDS

McCarthymen Hope to Become First Team to Take Four World Titles in Row

FIRST GAME AT STADIUM

65,000 Expected to Attend Wednesday—Scene Shifts to Cincinnati Saturday

By JOHN DREBINGER

The last Cincinnati fan having had his last good scare as his beloved Reds finally battered their way to a National League pennant, baseball moves swiftly into its final scenes this week with the staging of another world series, the thirty-sixth clash between the flag winners of the major loops. It promises to be a spectacular struggle even if it fails to hold the stage much longer than those of the past year or so.

For as the belligerents square off at the Yankee Stadium next Wednesday afternoon at 1:30 o'clock before an expected gathering of about 65,000, there will be in the one corner these same doughty Reds who have just brought to Cincinnati its second National League championship of all time and its first in twenty years.

And in the other corner there stalks in that mighty Yankee outfit which for four consecutive campaigns has demolished all opposition in the American League and which now stands poised to close in on its fourth straight world title, a feat without precedent.

Won in Both Leagues

Even the pilots in this impending conflict possess records that are most extraordinary. For not only is Marse Joe McCarthy, head man of the Yanks, the only manager to win three straight world series flags but the only skipper ever to win league pennants in both major loops. Prior to coming to the Yanks he won the National League pennant in 1929 with the Cubs.

And not to be outstripped, Bill McKechnie, the silent, canny Scot whom they affectionately call the Deacon, is the only pilot in baseball ever to win three major league titles with three different clubs. He first appeared at the top in the National League with the Pirates in 1925. He was back again in 1928 with the Cardinals and this year he has triumphantly brought home the Reds, a club that only two years ago was staggering home a bad last.

With the conflict again to be decided on a best four-out-of-seven basis, the first two games will be played at the Stadium, Wednesday and Thursday. Friday will be left open for traveling and on Saturday the scene will unfold itself for the third game in Cincinnati where only the 35,000 capacity of Crosley Field prevents perhaps the shattering of all known baseball attendance records.

Cincinnati Fans Excited

For there is no denying Cincinnati has worked itself into a terrific lather over this series. Its Reds scored a glorious pennant victory in 1919. They also won the ensuing world series only to learn with horror about a year later the thing had not been on the level. That was the notorious episode wherein certain members of the White Sox turned Black and for twenty years the Reds, unwitting victims of those harrowing events of 1919, have been waiting to blot out that last major scandal in baseball.

In accordance with the usual procedure, the fourth and fifth games also will be played in Cincinnati next Sunday and Monday. If the struggle still remains raging the fighting will return to the Stadium for the sixth and seventh games the following Wednesday and Thursday.

However, it seems to be almost the unanimous opinion of baseball's outstanding academic minds, as well as that vague group known as the betting fraternity, that those sixth and seventh games will never prove necessary and that by no later than the fifth game those Yanks will already have their fourth straight title tucked away.

The American Leaguers, in fact, enter the battle almost prohibitive favorites. They are the 1-to-3 choice to win the series and are quoted at 9 to 20 to win the first game.

Gomez May Not Play

This, mind, with their brilliant southpaw, Lefty Gomez, nursing a pulled muscle in his side that makes it extremely doubtful whether he will be able to appear in the series at all.

So profound, however, is the respect in which these mighty Yanks are held that even such a possible defection is scarcely seen as an obstacle. Not with burly Red Ruffing, Monte Pearson and a trio of brilliant youngsters, Steve Sundra, Atley Donald and Marius Russo, all primed to go at top speed.

In the main the Yanks look pretty much the same as they did a year ago when they crushed the Cubs in four straight.

The stricken Lou Gehrig, who, as a non-playing captain, must watch his first series in four years from the sidelines, has been replaced at first by the talented though less robust hitting Babe Dahlgren and in the outfield a new freshman sensation has been added to the cast in the hard-clouting Charlie Keller.

Keller's punch, added to an even greater Joe DiMaggio, who has just won the American League batting championship, along with the brilliant Joe Gordon, Red Rolfe, Frankie Crosetti and Bill Dickey, does make the Yanks loom as formidable as ever.

However, close observers do not consider the Reds quite as hopeless as expert opinion seems to make them. In the indefatigable Paul Derringer and Bucky Walters, McKechnie has one of the greatest two-man hurling staffs since the glamorous days of the two Deans in 1934. He also has a sparkling pitching youngster in the 22-year-old Gene Thompson, and the Reds also boast plenty of long-range power among such clouters as Ernie Lombardi, Frank McCormick, Wally Berger and Ival Goodman, along with a tight inner defense headed by Lonnie Frey.

In the event of rain, the teams will remain booked in the city where they happen to be until the game is played, with the remaining games of the schedule moved back accordingly.

Also, to avoid confusion should the weather look threatening on the morning of a game in New York, arrangements have been made whereby the public may find out whether there has been a postponement by phoning WEather 6-1212.

For the opener at the Stadium 34,000 unreserved seat tickets are to be placed on sale at 10 o'clock Wednesday morning. Twenty thousand upper grandstand tickets are priced at $3.30 each and 14,000 bleacher tickets are priced at $1.10 each.

Record of Past Series

Year	Winner	Loser	Games
1903—Boston (A.)	Pittsburg	5–3
1904—No series		
1905—New York (N.)	Philadelphia	4–1
1906—Chicago (A.)	Chicago	4–2
*1907—Chicago (N.)	Detroit	4–0
1908—Chicago (N.)	Detroit	4–1
1909—Pittsb'gh (N.)	Detroit	4–3
1910—Phil'phia (A.)	Chicago	4–1
1911—Phil'phia (A.)	New York	4–2
*1912—Boston (A.)	New York	4–3
1913—Phil'phia (A.)	New York	4–1
1914—Boston (N.)	Philadelphia	4–0
1915—Boston (A.)	Philadelphia	4–1
1916—Boston (A.)	Brooklyn	4–1
1917—Chicago (A.)	New York	4–2
1918—Boston (A.)	Chicago	4–2
1919—Cincinnati (N.)	Chicago	5–3
1920—Cleveland (A.)	Brooklyn	5–2
1921—New York (N.)	New York	5–3
*1922—New York (N.)	New York	4–0
1923—New York (A.)	New York	4–2
1924—Wash'ton (A.)	New York	4–3
1925—Pittsb'gh (N.)	Washington	4–3
1926—St. Louis (N.)	New York	4–3
1927—New York (A.)	Pittsburgh	4–0
1928—New York (A.)	St. Louis	4–0
1929—Phil'phia (A.)	Chicago	4–1
1930—Phil'phia (A.)	St. Louis	4–2
1931—St. Louis (N.)	Philadelphia	4–3
1932—New York (A.)	Chicago	4–0
1933—New York (N.)	Washington	4–1
1934—St. Louis (N.)	Detroit	4–3
1935—Detroit (A.)	Chicago	4–2
1936—New York (A.)	New York	4–2
1937—New York (A.)	New York	4–1
1938—New York (A.)	Chicago	4–0
*One tie game.		

SOME OF THE LEADING HITTERS ON THE YANKEES AND THE REDS

Bill Dickey, Joe DiMaggio, Charlie Keller and George Selkirk, who are all batting above the .300 mark for the McCarthymen

Facts on World Series

Contending Teams—New York Yankees, champions of American League, and Cincinnati Reds, champions of National League.

Managers—Joseph V. McCarthy, Yankees, and William B. Mc-Kechnie, Reds.

How Series Is Decided—Best four out of seven games.

Schedule—The first two games will be played on Wednesday and Thursday at the Yankee Stadium. Friday will be left open to allow the teams to travel and the third, fourth and fifth games are scheduled for Crosley Field, Cincinnati, on Saturday, Sunday and Monday. If sixth and seventh games are necessary they will be played at the Yankee Stadium the following Wednesday and Thursday.

In Case of Postponement—The teams will remain booked for the park in which they were scheduled until the game is played. The schedule for the remaining games is moved up accordingly. The same procedure will be followed if a game ends in a tie.

Time of Games—The games will start daily at 1:30 P. M., Eastern standard time, in New York and Cincinnati.

Seating Capacity of Parks—Yankee Stadium, 70,029, with additional room for 5,000 standees; Crosley Field, 36,000.

Radio—Broadcasting over Station WOR and Mutual network.

Information on Weather—If the weather appears doubtful on the mornings of the games in New York, information as to whether or not there has been a postponement ordered can be obtained by telephoning WEather 6-1212.

Betting Odds—Yankees favorites to win series, 1 to 3.

SERIES ELIGIBLES

Yankees—Spurgeon Chandler, Frank Crosetti, Ellsworth Dahlgren, William Dickey, Joseph DiMaggio, Atley Donald, Henry L. Gehrig, Vernon Gomez, Joseph Gordon, Irving Hadley, Thomas Henrich, Oral Hildebrand, Arndt Jorgens, Charles Keller, William Knickerbocker, John Murphy, Monte Pearson, Alvin J. Powell, Robert Rolfe, Warren Rosar, Charles Ruffing, Marius Russo, George Selkirk, Stephen Sundra. Coaches: Arthur Fletcher, Earle Combs.

Reds—Walter Berger, Anthony Bongiovanni, Stanley Bordagaray, Harry Craft, Paul Derringer, Linus Frey, Lee Gamble, Ival Goodman, Lee Grissom, Willard Hershberger, Henry Johnson, Edwin Joost, Ernest Lombardi, Frank McCormick, Lloyd Moore, William Myers, John Niggeling, Lewis Riggs, Leslie Scarsella, Milburn Shoffner, Al Simmons, Eugene Thompson, John Vander Meer, William Walters, William Werber. Coaches: Harry Gowdy, James Wilson.

The Sporting News

THE BASE BALL PAPER OF THE WORLD

VOLUME 108, NUMBER 8   ST. LOUIS, OCTOBER 5, 1939 ᴬ ᴺ

YANKEES MATCH POWER AGAINST PITCHING IN TITLE CLASH

PACED BY DI MAGGIO, BOMBERS HAVE ALL THEIR USUAL PUNCH

INFIELD, WITH DAHLGREN, IS RATED BY DANIEL AS BEST HE'S SEEN

Cincy Given Edge on Hill With Walters, Derringer; McCarthy Seeks Honors Achieved by No Other Pilot

NEW YORK, N. Y.—The Yankees went into the World's Series favorites over the Reds, 5 to 13. Around here, as the McCarthy clan strove to win a fourth world's championship and five titles in a row for the American League—achievements never previously recorded—we were disposed to see Cincinnati's pitching stronger, but New York's attack, backed by a fine outfield and the greatest infield in the game's history, winning in six games.

In the pre-series picture, we saw the Reds, frazzled and tired from a nerve-racking race, much too fatigued to beat the Yankees. We saw Joe DiMaggio soaring to socking heights, the home run power of the Bombers asserting itself once again.

We saw Joe McCarthy matching Connie Mack with a fifth world's championship, after having tied John McGraw with a fourth straight pennant.

However, before we go into too great detail about our World's Series visions, let us review what has happened. The Yankees won their pennant with 106 won and 45 lost, taking the flag by a margin of 17 games. In 1927, they set a league record with 110 victories and in 1936 they established another mark with a winning margin of 19½ lengths. However, until a better club comes along for the long haul of 154 games, this Yankee team will manage to do very nicely.

In the National League, New York did not fare so well. The collapse of the Giants, whom Terry had called the greatest team he yet had managed, was all the more poignant to Polo Grounds sufferers because Brooklyn finished in the first division, the Giants in fifth place.

Season of Grief for Memphis Bill.

Just what ails the Giants we leave for later discussions. In the meantime, we find Terry beset with myriad problems.

Terry suffered tremendous disappointment in Zeke Bonura, whom he found to be as poor a fielder as American leaguers had rated Zeke. It is possible Bonura will linger on, as McCarthy is going. Babe Young will receive a thorough trial next spring.

Terry also suffered intense anguish because Lohrman and Gumbert did not prove themselves the pitchers he figured they would be.

Terry received a blow when Burgess Whitehead went to pieces. He got a facer when Myatt proved no major leaguer. He got a stunner when Chiozza broke his leg. He got a shock when he discovered O'Dea was not the catcher Bill thought he was.

I think Terry was remiss when he did not make a more determined bid for help when Jurges was suspended. That was the turning point. The Giants went on to set a home record of nine straight defeats.

However, the milk has been spilt and there is no sense in recrimination. In

New York, if you aren't first you might as well be last, for all the fans care. They want a winner or they don't care a hoot.

Despite their flop, the Giants did pretty well at the box office, with something like 750,000 at home, and around 680,000 on the road.

The Yankees missed the million mark at home but passed it on the road, and altogether drew 2,000,000 paid admissions. The World's Fair hurt things around here until middle July. Radio hurt, too. Brooklyn night ball did not help the Yanks and the Giants. They must go for the lights, but it will not be in 1940.

The Yankees went into a fourth straight World's Series with another great club, which misses Lou Gehrig, whose career is finished. He was active in seven World's Series, six of them winning ones after the loss to the 1926 Cardinals.

What will Gehrig do in 1940? The tip is out that he will get his unconditional release and go into radio. There seems to be no job with the Yankees for him.

Still the Masters of Swat.

The Yankees entered the classic with the home run title, with the major league batting champion in Joe DiMaggio. Joe had to give up on that dream of hitting .400. He had to cut his ambitions to .390 and missed that, too. But he did very well, just the same, and established himself as the greatest player in the game.

Let us mass the various factors in the winning of this new pennant:

1—The all-round skill of DiMaggio, who not only hit well, but drove in 126 runs, and played a brilliant game in the field.

2—The pitching. Red Ruffing over 20 victories again; Sundra with his string which snapped at 11. Donald with 12 straight, Russo coming in from Newark to take up the lefthanded slack. Hildebrand, in his first season with the Bombers, making up for the letdown on the part of Murphy.

3—Old reliable Bill Dickey. Best catcher in baseball.

4—Charlie Keller coming through his freshman season with flying colors and sending Tom Henrich to the bench.

5—Babe Dahlgren, thrown into the breach with the tragic retirement of Gehrig, made himself the greatest fielding first baseman in the game and drove in an amazing lot of runs for his comparatively low batting average.

6—Joe Gordon's home run flair and continued drive for the heights at second.

7—The greatest infield it has been your correspondent's privilege to watch.

BLUE RIBBON ENTRIES FOR WORLD'S SERIES SWEEPSTAKES

 Joseph DiMaggio
 Charles Keller
 George Selkirk
 Thomas D. Henrich
 Alvin J. Powell
 Ellsworth Dahlgren
 Joseph Gordon

 William Dickey
 Warren Rosar
 Arndt Jorgens
 Charles Ruffing
 Vernon Gomez
 Monte Pearson
 Stephen R. Sundra

 Oral C. Hildebrand
 John J. Murphy
 Marius Russo
 Ival R. Goodman
 Harry Craft
 Walter Berger
 Anthony Bongiovanni

 Frank P. Crosetti
 Robert A. Rolfe
 Leslie Scarsella
 Linus R. Frey
 Edwin Joost
 William H. Myers
 William M. Werber

 Atley Donald
 Irving D. Hadley
 Stanley Bordagaray
 Ernest N. Lombardi
 Willard Hershberger
 William H. Walters
 Paul Derringer

Lee Grissom

Lloyd A. Moore

John Niggeling

Milburn Shoffner

John Vander Meer

Henry W. Johnson

Al Simmons

Lee Gamble

Wm. Knickerbocker

Lewis Riggs

Joseph V. McCarthy   William B. McKechnie

Spurgeon Chandler

Eugene Thompson

Frank McCormick

This was to become a typical scene: in 1939 Joe DiMaggio crosses home plate after belting a home run. Walking off is preceding scorer, Charlie "King Kong" Keller; waiting to congratulate DiMaggio is New York's next batter, catcher Bill Dickey, wearing number 8.

The Joe DiMaggio of 1939, by then a certified star. That was the year he won his first American League batting crown, hitting a hefty .381, and turning in a slugging average of .671.

CHARLES ERNEST KELLER

OUTFIELDER. Is playing his first year with the Yankees after having a sensational record with Newark in 1937 and 1938. This year, after being a bench warmer for half of the season, he was installed as the regular right fielder and made good at once. Is a graduate of the University of Maryland and jumped from the campus to the Newark club. A right-hand thrower but bats left-handed. Weighs 190 pounds although standing only 5 feet 10 inches. Was born October 12, 1916.

JOSEPH PAUL DI MAGGIO

CENTER FIELDER. One of the great players of all time, both on offense and defense, owning a great throwing arm and having the ability to go far and make almost impossible catches. Batted .331 in his first three years with the Yankees but his average of this year will boost that mark as he has been hitting around .400 all year. Di Maggio was born in Martinez, California, but now resides in San Francisco. Bats and throws right-handed. Weight 188 pounds; height 6 feet.

MARCELLUS MONTE PEARSON

PITCHER. Has been troubled somewhat by a sore arm this season but, nevertheless, has won two-thirds of his games. Has pitched and won three World Series games. Is a right-hand pitcher who was acquired by New York from Cleveland in a trade for Johnny Allen in December, 1935. Has won close to sixty games for the Yankees in four years, losing only twenty-three. Born in Oakland, Calif., September 2, 1909. Throws and bats right-handed. Pitched a no-hit game in 1938. Weight 180 pounds; height 5 feet 11 inches.

Game 1 October 4 at New York

Cincinnati	Pos	AB	R	H	RBI	PO	A	E
Werber	3b	4	0	0	0	0	1	0
Frey	2b	4	0	0	0	1	2	0
Goodman	rf	2	1	0	0	4	0	0
McCormick	1b	3	0	2	1	9	1	0
Lombardi	c	3	0	0	0	7	0	0
Craft	cf	3	0	1	0	2	0	0
Berger	lf	3	0	0	0	0	0	0
Myers	ss	3	0	1	0	0	1	0
Derringer	p	3	0	0	0	1	0	0
Totals		28	1	4	1	*25	5	0

One out when winning run was scored.

Double—Dahlgren. Triple—Keller.
Stolen Base—Goodman.
Double Plays—Rolfe to Gordon to Dahlgren,
Ruffing to Crosetti to Gordon to Dahlgren,
Gordon to Crosetti to Dahlgren.
Left on Bases—Cincinnati 1, New York 5.
Umpires—McGowan (A), Reardon (N), Summers (A),
Pinelli (N). Attendance—58,541.
Time of Game—1:33.

1st Inning
Cincinnati
1 Werber flied to left.
2 Frey flied to short-center.
3 Goodman fanned.
New York
1 Crosetti pooped to Goodman, in close.
2 Rolfe rolled out to second.
3 Keller flied to left.

2nd Inning
Cincinnati
  McCormick singled over Crosetti's head.
1,2 Lombardi rolled into a double play,
   Rolfe to Gordon to Dahlgren.
3 Craft fanned.
New York
1 DiMaggio flew out to right.
2 Dickey took a called third strike.
3 Selkirk struck out.

3rd Inning
Cincinnati
1 Berger struck out.
   Myers singled past second.
2,3 Derringer's grounder was deflected
   by Ruffing to Crosetti who threw to
   Gordon to force Myers and fired to
   Dahlgren to double up Derringer.
New York
1 Gordon fouled to McCormick.
2 Dahlgren rolled easily to second.
   Ruffing singled to left to be the
   Yankees first base runner.
3 Crosetti missed a third strike.

4th Inning
Cincinnati
1 Werber grounded to short.
2 Frey flied to deep right.
   Goodman walked.
   Goodman stole second.
   McCormick singled past third scoring
   Goodman.
3 Lombardi grounded back to the pitcher.
New York
1 Rolfe flew out to right.
2 Keller took a called third strike.
   DiMaggio singled by third, Werber
   let it go thinking it would turn foul.
3 Dickey grounded to first, McCormick
   making a brilliant stop.

5th Inning
Cincinnati
   Craft singled on a slow roller between
   Rolfe and Corsetti
1 Berger struck out.
2,3 Myers bounced into a double play,
   Gordon to Crosetti to Dahlgren.
New York
1 Selkirk grounded to first.
   Gordon singled past third.
   Dahlgren doubled down the left field
   line, Gordon scored when Berger threw
   to second.
2 Ruffing fouled to McCormick.
3 Crosetti flied to center.

6th Inning
Cincinnati
1 Derringer grounded to short.
2 Werber flied to left.
3 Frey flied to center.
New York
1 Rolfe flied to center.
2 Keller grounded out, McCormick to
   Derringer.
3 DiMaggio rolled out to short.

7th Inning
Cincinnati
1 Goodman grounded to third.
2 McCormick grounded to short.
3 Lombardi fouled to Dahlgren.
New York
1 Dickey pooped to second.
2 Selkirk lined to short right.
3 Gordon fanned.

8th Inning
Cincinnati
1 Craft pooped to third.
2 Berger grounded to second.
3 Myers grounded to short.
New York
1 Dahlgren struck out.
2 Ruffing struck out.
3 Crosetti grounded to third.

9th Inning
Cincinnati
1 Derringer tapped back to the pitcher.
2 Werber grounded to short.
3 Frey flew out to left.
New York
1 Rolfe grounded to first.
   Keller tripled to the right-center
   field bleachers.
   DiMaggio intentionally walked.
   Dickey singled over second, scoring
   Keller with the winning run.

Cin.	0 0 0	1 0 0	0 0 0									1
N.Y.	0 0 0	0 1 0	0 0 1									2

New York	Pos	AB	R	H	RBI	PO	A	E
Crosetti	ss	4	0	0	0	1	7	0
Rolfe	3b	4	0	0	0	1	2	0
Keller	rf	4	1	1	0	2	0	0
DiMaggio	cf	3	0	1	0	2	0	0
Dickey	c	4	0	1	1	4	0	0
Selkirk	lf	3	0	0	0	2	0	0
Gordon	2b	3	1	1	0	2	4	0
Dahlgren	1b	3	0	1	0	13	0	0
Ruffing	p	3	0	1	0	0	3	0
Totals		31	2	6	2	27	16	0

Pitching	IP	H	R	ER	BB	SO
New York						
Ruffing (W)	9	4	1	1	1	4
Cincinnati						
Derringer (L)	8⅓	6	2	2	1	7

YANKS' FIRE CHILLS RED-HOT RED FANS

Sun and Bombers Beat Down on Cincinnati Followers— Standees Pack Runways

NOTABLES IN THE THRONG

Bleacher Seats Sold Quickly for World Series Game— Traffic Moves Smoothly

From a Staff Correspondent.

CINCINNATI, Oct. 7 — Ideal weather combined with civic enthusiasm to fill Crosley Field today for the first World Series game Cincinnati has seen in twenty years.

The temperature hovered around 86, only slightly hotter than were the Reds' rooters before the Yankees got hot themselves and bagged their third straight victory. The crowd numbered 32,723, which means paid attendance, since there are no free passes to a World Series game. The receipts reached $150,027.27. The place could hold no more.

Every inch of space was filled with a shirt-sleeved sweltering, fanning assemblage. Bleacherites didn't bother to bring along their coats. Purchasers of higher priced tickets doffed theirs upon entering the park, particularly the fans who sat on the third-base side of the field, where the sun beat down from a blue sky and through fleecy clouds.

Jury Box in Outfield

Every seat in the plant save the bleachers is reserved for the series and every seat was crammed. Even a sort of jury-box arrangement flanking the outfield around the right and left field exits, was packed. Crosley Field has 30,255 permanent seats. Anything in excess of that represents standing room.

Fans were standing all over the stadium today. They packed the space back of the lower stand, jammed the ramps leading from the lower to the upper tiers, squatted on newspapers wherever there was a vantage point, and crowded into runways where policemen were not too strict in enforcing regulations.

Bleacher admissions were placed on sale at 8:30 o'clock, and it required less than two hours to exhaust the supply, so great was the crush awaiting the opening of box-office windows.

The upper tier filled next, then came the lower grandstand and box-seat ticket-holders. Not until noon did the management open the sale of standing-room tickets, which cost $3.45 each. And by that time the line almost circled the park.

La Guardia Sees Game

Fans came from all over the country. Mayor James G. Stewart was host to Mayor La Guardia of New York. Powell Crosley Jr., owner of the Reds, entertained a party.

Among the notables at the game were Judge K. M. Landis, Baseball Commissioner; President Will Harridge of the American League, President Ford C. Frick of the National League, George Ruppert, vice president, and Edward G. Barrow, president of the Yankees.

Game 2 October 5 at New York

Cincinnati	Pos	AB	R	H	RBI	PO	A	E
Werber	3b	3	0	1	0	0	1	0
Frey	2b	4	0	0	0	2	2	0
Goodman	rf	3	0	0	0	1	0	0
McCormick	1b	3	0	0	0	7	0	0
Lombardi	c	3	0	1	0	5	1	0
a Bordagaray		0	0	0	0	0	0	0
Hershberger	c	0	0	0	0	0	0	0
Craft	cf	3	0	0	0	3	1	0
Berger	lf	3	0	0	0	1	0	0
Myers	ss	3	0	0	0	5	3	0
Walters	p	2	0	0	0	0	3	0
b Gamble		1	0	0	0	0	0	0
Totals		28	0	2	0	24	11	0

a Ran for Lombardi in 8th.
b Fanned for Walters in 9th.

Doubles—Dahlgren, Keller. Home Run—Dahlgren. Sacrifice Hit—Pearson. Double Plays—Dickey to Crosetti, Walters to Myers to McCormick. Left on Bases—Cincinnati 2, New York 3. Umpires—Reardon, Summers, Pinelli, McGowan. Attendance—59,791. Time of Game—1:27.

Cin	000 000 000	0
N.Y.	003 100 00x	4

New York	Pos	AB	R	H	RBI	PO	A	E
Crosetti	ss	4	0	1	1	1	2	0
Rolfe	3b	4	0	0	0	0	0	0
Keller	rf	4	1	2	1	0	0	0
DiMaggio	cf	4	0	0	0	1	0	0
Dickey	c	3	0	1	1	8	1	0
Selkirk	lf	3	0	1	0	3	0	0
Gordon	2b	3	0	0	0	2	0	0
Dahlgren	1b	3	2	2	1	8	0	0
Pearson	p	2	0	0	0	5	0	0
Totals		30	4	9	4	27	9	0

Pitching	IP	H	R	ER	BB	SO
Cincinnati						
Walters (L)	8	9	4	4	0	5
New York						
Pearson (W)	9	2	0	0	1	8

1st Inning
Cincinnati
1 Werber popped to second
2 Frey flied to center
3 Goodman foul popped to Rolfe
New York
  Crosetti singled over Myer's head
1 Rolfe forced Crosetti at second, Walters to Myers
2 Keller forced Rolfe at second, Myers to Frey
3 DiMaggio flied out very deep to Berger in left-center.

2nd Inning
Cincinnati
1 McCormick flied to center
2 Lombardi flied to Selkirk in center
3 Craft struck out.
New York
1 Dickey struck out.
  Selkirk blooped a single into short
2 center but was out Craft to Myers trying to get to second
3 Gordon flied to center

3rd Inning
Cincinnati
1 Berger lined to deep left
2 Myers fanned
3 Walters grounded to Rolfe.
New York
  Dahlgren hit a ground rule double into the left field stands
1 Pearson sacrificed Dahlgren to third, Walters to Frey
2 Crosetti grounded to third, scoring Dahlgren
  Rolfe singled to right
  Keller doubled on a line drive down the left field line, scoring Rolfe
  DiMaggio beat out a slow roller down the third base line, Keller holding
  Dickey lined a single to right, scoring Keller and moving DiMaggio to third
3 Selkirk grounded to second.

4th Inning
Cincinnati
  Werber walked
1,2 Frey struck out and Werber was doubled up trying to steal second Dickey to Crosetti
3 Goodman fanned.
New York
1 Gordon grounded to third.
  Dahlgren homered into the lower left field stands.
2 Pearson struck out.
3 Crosetti tapped in front of the plate and was thrown out by Lombardi.

5th Inning
Cincinnati
1 McCormick fanned
2 Lombardi rolled out to the pitcher
3 Craft struck out
New York
1 Rolfe grounded to second.
  Keller singled to left.
2,3 DiMaggio grounded into a double play, Walters to Myers to McCormick.

6th Inning
Cincinnati
1 Berger tapped back to the pitcher
2 Myers grounded to short.
3 Walters tapped back to the pitcher.
New York
1 Dickey lined to the right field stands
2 Selkirk took a called third strike
3 Gordon struck out.

7th Inning
Cincinnati
1 Werber popped to short center.
2 Frey popped to third.
3 Goodman flied to DiMaggio with a nice running catch.
New York
1 Dahlgren struck out
2 Pearson popped to short.
3 Crosetti popped to Myers in short-left

8th Inning
Cincinnati
1 McCormick lined to deep left; Lombardi broke up **Pearson's no-hitter** with a single over second, Bordagaray ran for Lombardi
2 Craft struck out (third time)
3 Berger grounded out, Pearson to Dahlgren on a tap down the first base line
New York
  For Cincinnati—Hershberger catching
1 Rolfe flied to center
2 Keller flied to deep center
3 DiMaggio rolled out to short.

9th Inning
Cincinnati
1 Myers tapped back to the pitcher.
2 Gamble, pinch hitting for Walters, fanned; Werber singled to left for the Reds' second hit.
3 Frey forced Werber at second, Crosetti to Gordon.

Game 3 October 7 at Cincinnati

New York	Pos	AB	R	H	RBI	PO	A	E
Crosetti	ss	4	1	0	0	2	2	0
Rolfe	3b	4	1	1	0	2	2	0
Keller	rf	3	3	2	4	2	0	0
DiMaggio	cf	4	1	1	2	2	0	0
Dickey	c	3	1	1	1	5	1	0
Selkirk	lf	2	0	0	0	3	0	0
Gordon	2b	4	0	0	0	3	5	0
Dahlgren	1b	4	0	0	0	9	2	0
Gomez	p	1	0	0	0	0	0	0
Hadley	p	3	0	0	0	1	1	0
Totals		32	7	5	7	27	13	1

Pitching	IP	H	R	ER	BB	SO
New York						
Gomez	1	3	1	1	0	1
Hadley (W)	8	7	2	2	3	2
Cincinnati						
Thompson (L)	4⅔	5	7	7	4	3
Grissom	1⅓	0	0	0	1	0
Moore	3	0	0	0	0	2

1st Inning
New York
  Crosetti walked
1 Rolfe grounded to first moving Crosetti to second
  Keller hit a two-run homer into the right field stands at the 375 foot mark
2 DiMaggio struck out
  Dickey got all the way to third when he walked on a wild pitch with Lombardi having trouble retrieving the pitch
3 Selkirk was out on a great pick-up and throw by Werber on his bunt
Cincinnati
1 Werber grounded to second with Dahlgren making a great pick up of Gordon's throw which was in the dirt
2 Frey flied to center
  Goodman singled on a high bounder
  McCormick hit a Texas League single into right, moving Goodman to third
  Lombardi singled over second, scoring Goodman with McCormick stopping at second
3 Craft struck out.

2nd Inning
New York
1 Gordon fouled to Lombardi
2 Dahlgren popped to second
3 Gomez fanned
Cincinnati
  For New York—Hadley pitching
1 Berger fanned
  Myers singled past short
  Thompson singled on a Texas League just beyond Crosetti's reach, Myers stopping at second
  Werber singled to center, scoring Myers and advancing Thompson to third
2 Frey hit an easy grounder to Dahlgren who threw to Dickey getting Thompson at the plate, Werber to second
  Goodman singled to right, scoring Werber
3 McCormick popped to Gordon in short right

3rd Inning
New York
1 Crosetti fouled to Werber.
2 Rolfe fouled to right where Goodman made a sensational catch reaching into the stands for the ball.
  Keller walked
  DiMaggio hit a two-run homer over the fence in dead center.
3 Dickey rolled out to second.
Cincinnati
1 Lombardi flied to Selkirk in center.
2 Craft flied to center.
3 Berger popped to short.

4th Inning
New York
  Selkirk walked.
1 Gordon forced Selkirk at second, Myers to Frey.
2 Dahlgren fanned.
3 Hadley forced Gordon at second, Frey unassisted.
Cincinnati
  Myers singled over second.
1 Thompson sacrificed Myers to second, Dickey to Dahlgren
2 Werber grounded out, Dahlgren to Hadley.
3 Frey grounded to second

N.Y.	202 030 000	7
Cin	120 000 000	3

Cincinnati	Pos	AB	R	H	RBI	PO	A	E
Werber	3b	4	1	1	1	3	2	0
Frey	2b	4	0	0	0	2	2	0
Goodman	rf	5	1	3	1	2	0	0
McCormick	1b	5	0	2	0	9	0	0
Lombardi	c	3	0	1	1	5	0	0
b Bordagaray		0	0	0	0	0	0	0
Hershberger	c	1	0	0	0	1	0	0
Craft	cf	4	0	0	0	2	0	0
Berger	lf	4	0	0	0	2	0	0
Myers	ss	3	1	2	0	1	4	0
Thompson	p	1	0	1	0	0	2	0
Grissom	p	0	0	0	0	0	0	0
a Bongiovanni		1	0	0	0	0	0	0
Moore	p	1	0	0	0	0	2	0
Totals		36	3	10	3	27	10	0

a Grounded out for Grissom in 6th.
b Ran for Lombardi in 7th.

Home Runs—Dickey, DiMaggio, Keller 2. Sacrifice Hit—Thompson. Double Play—Rolfe to Gordon to Dahlgren. Hit by Pitcher—Lombardi (by Hadley). Wild Pitch—Thompson. Left on Bases—New York 3, Cincinnati 11. Umpires—Summers, Pinelli, McGowan, Reardon. Attendance—32,723. Time of Game—2:01.

5th Inning
New York
1 Crosetti grounded to short
  Rolfe singled between first and second.
  Keller hit his second two-run homer to the exact spot of his first homer
2 DiMaggio popped to third
  Dickey homered deep into the right field stands
  For Cincinnati—Grissom pitching
  Selkirk walked
3 Gordon flied to left in front of the scoreboard
Cincinnati
1 Goodman popped to short
2 McCormick fouled to Dickey in front of the Yankee dugout
  Lombardi was hit by a pitch
3 Craft flied to left.

6th Inning
New York
1 Dahlgren flied to very deep center
2 Hadley grounded to short.
3 Crosetti grounded to Werber who made a great stop
Cincinnati
1 Berger fanned
  Myers walked
2 Bongiovanni, pinch-hitting for Grissom, grounded back to Hadley, who threw wide to first but Dahlgren made a sensational one-handed stab for the out
  Werber walked
3 Frey grounded to second

7th Inning
New York
  For Cincinnati—Moore pitching
1 Rolfe grounded to short
2 Keller struck out swinging
3 DiMaggio tapped back to the mound
Cincinnati
1 Goodman flied to Selkirk in center
  McCormick singled between short and third
  Lombardi got to first on Hadley's throwing error to Gordon when the ball went into center, McCormick going to third
  Bordagaray ran for Lombardi
2,3 Craft hit into a double play, Rolfe to Gordon to Dahlgren

8th Inning
New York
  For Cincinnati—Hershberger catching
1 Dickey flied deep to center.
2 Selkirk flied to left.
3 Gordon popped to third.
Cincinnati
1 Berger grounded to short.
2 Myers grounded to short.
3 Moore grounded to third.

9th Inning
New York
1 Dahlgren flied to right.
2 Hadley tapped back to the mound.
3 Crosetti fanned.
Cincinnati
1 Werber grounded to second.
  Frey walked
  Goodman singled to right where Keller just missed a shoe-string catch at the foul line, Frey only to second fearing the possible catch
2 McCormick lined to right.
3 Hershberger flied out to right.

KELLER DRIVES TWO

Other Homers Smashed by DiMaggio, Dickey, Routing Thompson

YANKS GET 5 HITS, REDS 10

Hadley Victor After Injury Forces Gomez Out—32,723 at 3d World Series Game

By JOHN DREBINGER
Special to THE NEW YORK TIMES.

CINCINNATI, Oct. 7—With Charlie Keller firing two homers into a sweltering mass of noncombatants that sat packed in the right field bleachers, Joe DiMaggio exploding another high over the center field barrier and Bill Dickey dropping still a fourth into the laps of the stunned and crestfallen bleacherites, Yankee guns boomed today as Marse Joe McCarthy's Bronx Bombers, in an amazing exhibition of efficient shelling, leveled Cincinnati's homecoming Reds, 7 to 3, in the third game of the current world series.

The four homers, which comprised four-fifths of the entire Yankee attack and routed the rookie star, Gene Thompson, inside of five innings, gave the McCarthy invaders their third straight victory and brought them within a single game of their main objective—which is to bag their fourth straight world championship.

Those four devastating blows also stunned completely a gathering of 32,723 onlookers who for two hours had suffered through a misplaced July heat wave and then, mopping their brows, filed silently out, convinced the entire performance had been too incredible for belief.

Yanks Press Toward Goal

The Yankees had made only five hits against ten for Bill McKechnie's Reds, yet the American Leaguers, by reason of those four telling clouts, had won as decisively as though the Cincinnatians had struck no blows in self defense.

Not even the fact that Lefty Gomez, seeking his seventh individual triumph in world series competition, had to withdraw because of his injured side after working only a single round, sufficed to toss the Bronx Bombers out of their stride as they pushed relentlessly on toward their goal, which now seems likely to be attained within another twenty-four hours.

For as a somewhat disconsolate Gomez stepped off the field, Bump Hadley, a chunky, ever-smiling right-hander, moved in to take up the loose threads and fashion the way for another Yankee triumph.

For a few fleeting moments the crowd, which jammed every available inch of the stands, envisioned a possible turning of the tide. That was in the second inning when the Reds, already trailing, 2 to 1, rushed the somewhat unprepared Hadley for four hits and two runs to gain a 3-2 lead.

The Frugal McCarthy

But those hits, like all the other blows the Cincinnatians were to get, were all singles and their effect was like buckshot dropped on the Maginot Line. The Yankee howitzers completely flattened the foe and Commander McCarthy, being by nature a frugal man, used no more than were needed. Each of the Keller homers, one in the first and the other in the fifth, came with a runner aboard the bases, so that the Yanks' sensational rookie outfielder, just completing his first season in the big-time circuit, drove in four tallies. He also carried home a fifth, for he was on the base paths when DiMaggio unfurled his circuit blow in the third.

Only the Dickey blow came with the bases empty, though only for the reason that it came almost directly on the heels of the second Keller wallop in the fifth.

Dickey's shot finished Thompson and though Lee Grissom and Whitey Moore were to follow without allowing the Bombers another hit, all the damage for the afternoon had been thoroughly accomplished.

Injury Is Aggravated

Gomez made a heroic effort to add another victory to his unbeaten string and went to the mound with his side, which he injured a week ago last Sunday, encased in a polo belt. But the singular Castilian unhorsed himself almost at once. He aggravated the injury reaching for a bounder in the Reds' first inning, and, after giving up three hits and a run to the enemy, finished the inning, took his turn at bat in the second and then withdrew.

With the sky almost cloudless and the thermometer registering in the upper eighties, midsummer weather prevailed as the eager fans packed into the stands, the male portion of the audience losing no time divesting itself of its coats.

Climatically, at least, it was perhaps the hottest world series game ever played and certainly the first since St. Louis in 1931 which had for its setting a shirt-sleeved gathering.

In fact, under that broiling sun, everything in the arena seemed to be sizzling hot except the youthful Thompson, although it could scarcely be said he was the personification of coolness. For like ever so many other hapless rookies who had come to grief before him, Thompson soon was to learn that this world series warfare is nothing to the fluttering heart of a beardless youth who only a year ago was still looking forward to his first year in the majors.

Crosetti Draws a Pass

Thompson was palpably nervous as he faced Frankie Crosetti, the Yanks' lead-off man, and managed to get only one strike across before giving Crosetti a pass. The young right-hander was a trifle steadier against Red Rolfe, the latter getting himself rubbed out on a sharp grounder down the first base line. But this merely was to inspire a certain amount of confidence in Thompson, which almost immediately was to find itself sadly misplaced.

Quite fearlessly, Gene fired his next pitch squarely down the middle, and Keller just as squarely banged the ball into the distant right-field bleachers.

Even more trouble threatened to engulf the flustered Thompson immediately, for though he managed to slip a third strike over on DiMaggio for the second out he walked Dickey and then wild-pitched the Yankee catcher clear around to third. However, a snappy fielding play by Bill Werber and Frank McCormick effaced George Selkirk and the crowd breathed again.

Goodman Gets Aboard

A few minutes later the gathering started to whoop, for though the first two Reds, Werber and Lonnie Frey, were easily retired, Ival Goodman outgalloped a bounding ball to Gomez for an infield hit. It was in trying to hurry this play that Gomez damaged his right side again.

McCormick followed with a single to center, Ernie Lombardi hammered another one-base blow to center and the Reds had a run. The crowd nearly had a fit.

The fans implored Harry Craft to prolong the rally, but Gomez had enough left to fan Harry, and the round ended with the Yanks leading only 2 to 1.

In the second there was an even greater uproar as Hadley, after fanning Wally Berger, saw Billy Myers poke a single to right. Thompson, after two ineffectual attempts to sacrifice, singled to left and Werber also singled, driving in Myers to tie the score.

Frey's grounder to Babe Dahlgren resulted in Thompson getting himself tossed out at the plate, but Goodman followed with a sharp single to right, and as Werber crossed the plate the hills of Cincinnati echoed and re-echoed the frenzied cheers of that victory-hungry crowd.

Those cheers were to be the last to be raised for the Redlegs. With two runners still on the base paths, Hadley induced McCormick to pop to Joe Gordon for the third out, and the Cincinnatians never scored again.

In the meantime Thompson appeared to be getting along all right, but after retiring two in the third he stuck out his neck again—as have so many American League pitchers this year—and the inevitable result followed.

The youngster this time walked Keller and faced DiMaggio. Apparently Thompson hadn't heard that after the Yanks had finished their workout on Crosley Field yesterday the great DiMaggio had spent twenty minutes in a private session shelling those left and center field walls which in dead center measure only 383 feet from the plate.

Anyway, Jolting Joe quickly revealed he had utilized this extra time to good purpose, for he larruped the ball over the wall alongside the scoreboard and then trailed Keller around the bases. The Yanks up to now had struck only two blows, yet were leading, 4 to 3.

The next series of explosions came in the fifth, and that about made it unanimous. With one down, Rolfe singled for the only Yankee hit that wasn't good for four bases. Its purpose soon became clear, for a moment later Keller rammed his second circuit drive into the right field bleachers and the presence of Rolfe on the bases obviously again doubled the value of the homer.

Pluckily Thompson carried on. He retired DiMaggio on the end of a towering infield fly, but the Yanks had one shell left. Dickey dropped this one into the right field bleachers and the rout of Thompson was complete.

Game 4 October 8 at Cincinnati

New York	Pos	AB	R	H	RBI	PO	A	E
Crosetti	ss	4	1	0	0	2	3	0
Rolfe	3b	4	0	0	0	1	3	1
Keller	rf	5	3	2	1	2	0	0
DiMaggio	cf	5	2	2	1	3	0	0
Dickey	c	5	1	1	1	10	0	0
Selkirk	lf	4	0	1	0	1	0	0
Gordon	2b	4	0	1	1	0	3	0
Dahlgren	1b	4	0	0	0	11	0	0
Hildebrand	p	1	0	0	0	0	0	0
Sundra	p	0	0	0	0	0	0	0
Murphy	p	2	0	0	0	0	3	0
Totals		38	7	7	4	30	12	1

Pitching	IP	H	R	ER	BB	SO
New York						
Hildebrand	4	2	0	0	0	3
Sundra	2⅓	4	3	0	1	2
Murphy (W)	3⅓	5	1	1	0	2
Cincinnati						
Derringer	7	3	2	2	2	2
Walters (L)	3	4	5	2	1	1

Cincinnati	Pos	AB	R	H	RBI	PO	A	E
Werber	3b	5	0	2	1	0	1	0
Frey	2b	5	0	0	0	3	4	0
Goodman	rf	5	1	2	0	3	2	1
McCormick	1b	4	1	2	0	7	2	0
Lombardi	c	5	0	1	1	4	0	1
Craft	cf	4	0	0	0	3	0	0
Simmons	lf	4	1	1	0	3	0	0
Berger	lf-cf	5	0	1	0	4	0	0
Myers	ss	3	1	1	0	5	1	2
Derringer	p	2	0	1	0	1	0	0
a Hershberger		1	0	1	1	0	0	0
Walters	p	1	0	0	0	0	0	0
Totals		41	4	11	4	30	10	4

a Singled for Derringer in 7th.

N.Y.	000	000	202	3			7
Cin.	000	000	310	0			4

Doubles—Goodman, McCormick, Selkirk, Simmons. Triple—Myers. Home Runs—Dickey, Keller. Sacrifice Hits—McCormick, Rolfe. Left on Bases—New York 5, Cincinnati 9. Umpires—Pinelli, McGowan, Reardon, Summers. Attendance—32,794. Time of Game—2:04.

1st Inning
New York
1 Crosetti flied to right.
2 Rolfe fouled to Lombardi in front of the Reds' dugout.
3 Keller grounded to short.
Cincinnati
1 Werber grounded to short.
2 Frey grounded to second.
3 Goodman flied to left.

2nd Inning
New York
1 DiMaggio flied to right.
2 Dickey grounded out, McCormick to Derringer.
3 Selkirk grounded to second.
Cincinnati
McCormick doubled to right-center (The Reds' first extra-base hit of the Series).
1 Lombardi flied deep to center, McCormick going to third after the catch.
2 Craft fanned.
3 Berger grounded to second.

3rd Inning
New York
1 Gordon flied to deep left.
2 Dahlgren struck out.
3 Hildebrand struck out.
Cincinnati
1 Myers took a called third strike. Derringer singled to left.
2 Werber flied to center.
3 Frey fanned.

4th Inning
New York
1 Crosetti lined to short.
2 Rolfe grounded to first.
3 Keller fouled to Lombardi.
Cincinnati
1 Goodman grounded to second.
2 McCormick grounded to short.
3 Lombardi grounded to third.

5th Inning
New York
For Cincinnati—Berger moves to center, Simmonts to left (batting 6th).
1 DiMaggio grounded to third.
2 Dickey grounded to second. Selkirk doubled off the right field fence for the Yanks' first hit.
3 Gordon flied deep to center.
Cincinnati
For New York—Sundra pitching.
1 Simmons flied to right.
2 Berger grounded to Rolfe who threw high to Dahlgren who made a jumping catch for the out.
Myers tripled down the right field line.
3 Derringer fouled to Dickey.

6th Inning
New York
1 Dahlgren flied to Frey in short right. Sundra walked.
Crosetti sent a fly to Goodman who
2 dropped it but recovered to force Sundra at second (no error).
3 Rolfe lined to second.
Cincinnati
1 Werber fouled to Dickey
2 Frey called out on strikes.
3 Goodman grounded to third.

7th Inning
New York
Keller homered into the right field bleachers.
1 DiMaggio flied to Simmons at the fence. Dickey homered into the right-center stands.
Selkirk walked.
2 Gordon fouled to Simmons in front of the stands (good catch by Simmons).
3 Dahlgren forced Selkirk at second, Frey to Myers.
Cincinnati
McCormick got safely to first on Rolfe's fumble.
1 Lombardi fanned.
Simmons doubled to the center field scoreboard, advancing McCormick to third.
2 Berger grounded to second, scoring McCormick with Simmons holding second.
Myers walked.
Hershberger, pinch hitting for Derringer, singled on a blooper to short left, scoring Simmons with Myers racing to third.
Werber singled to right scoring Myers, Hershberger stopping at second.
For New York—Murphy pitching.
3 Frey struck out for the third time.

8th Inning
New York
For Cincinnati—Walters pitching.
1 Murphy popped to second.
2 Crosetti flied to center.
3 Rolfe flied to right.
Cincinnati
Goodman doubled to left-center.
1 McCormick sacrificed Goodman to third, Murphy to Dahlgren.
Lombardi singled to center, scoring Goodman.
2 Simmons forced Lombardi at second, Murphy to Crosetti.
3 Berger grounded back to the pitcher.

9th Inning
New York
Keller singled through the box.
DiMaggio singled to left, moving Keller to third.
Dickey hit a perfect double play ball to Frey but Myers dropped the ball with Keller scoring and DiMaggio safe at second and Dickey safe at first.
1 Selkirk flied to deep right, DiMaggio going to third after the catch.
Gordon grounded to Werber who threw to the plate but DiMaggio beat it (Gordon credited with a hit on the play).
2 Dahlgren popped to first.
3 Murphy fanned.
Cincinnati
1 Myers fanned.
2 Walters flied deep to center. Werber singled over short.
3 Frey fouled to Rolfe.

10th Inning
New York
Crosetti walked.
1 Rolfe sacrificed Crosetti to second, McCormick unassisted.
Keller was safe at first on Myers' fumble of his grounder, Crosetti going to third.
DiMaggio singled to right scoring Crosetti and when Goodman bobbled the ball Keller also scored, Lombardi dropped Goodman's throw to the plate and DiMaggio also scored (Goodman and Lombardi both got errors on the play).
2 Dickey flied deep to left.
3 Selkirk flied to center.
Cincinnati
Goodman singled to center.
McCormick singled off Crosetti's glove, moving Goodman to second.
1 Lombardi fouled to Dickey.
2 Simmons lined to right.
3 Berger lined to short, the **Yankees winning a fourth consecutive Series.**

YANKEES BEAT REDS BY 7-4 IN THE TENTH TO WIN SERIES, 4-0

Set Record by Annexing Their 4th Straight World Title— Sweep Second in Row

VICTORS AIDED BY ERRORS

Tie Score With 2 Runs in 9th and Put Over 3 in Next— Homers by Keller, Dickey

By JOHN DREBINGER
Special to THE NEW YORK TIMES.

CINCINNATI, Oct. 8—Marse Joe McCarthy's mighty Yankees, beyond question the most amazing club in the 100-year history of baseball, inscribed another brilliant page upon the records of the game today when they crushed the Cincinnati Reds in ten innings, 7 to 4, to close the 1939 world series in a whirl of statistics that attested still further to their greatness.

It gave the American League titleholders their fourth straight world championship, an achievement without precedent, as no other club had ever won more than two in a row, and it also marked the second successive time that these Bronx Bombers had vanquished National League rivals in the grand slam figures of four straight games. Today's victory was also the ninth in a row for the Yankees in series contests.

The end came in a bewildering flurry when Joe DiMaggio crashed a single to right in the tenth inning with two comrades, Frankie Crosetti and Charley Keller, on the base paths. Before the action of the play had been completed all three Yanks had swept across the plate as the Reds, crashing to earth with a terrible attack of jitters, committed two glaring errors.

Lombardi Drops Throw

Out in right field Ival Goodman allowed the hit to roll away from him for one misplay and after frantic relays had finally returned the ball to the plate Ernie Lombardi dropped the throw that was meant to stop the second run. And then, while the lumbering Cincinnati catcher still squatted on the ground, apparently brooding over the futility of it all, DiMaggio, wonder player of baseball's wonder team, streaked home with the third tally of a three-run rally that decisively snapped a 4-all tie.

That overwhelming mass of misfortune not only completely crushed Bill McKechnie's Reds but frayed beyond repair the nerves of a crowd of 32,794, which earlier had well nigh exhausted itself exhorting its favorites to win at least one game from this invincible McCarthy juggernaut.

And mighty close they came to winning it, too, for despite the fact that Keller, astonishing freshman star of the Yanks, hit his third homer in two days and Bill Dickey hit another to give the New Yorkers a 2-0 lead in the seventh, the Reds actually entered the ninth leading by 4—2.

Makes Grievous Misplay

Though McKechnie had fired both his pitching aces into the fray, first Paul Derringer and then Bucky Walters, a grievous misplay by Billy Myers in the wake of two blazing singles by DiMaggio and Keller enabled the Yanks to tie the score with two runs in the ninth.

It was a bizarre struggle, with virtually all the action crowding itself into the closing innings, beginning with the seventh, and it cannot be denied that the crowd, which had contributed $150,243 to the final series till, got its money's worth, although bitterly disappointed by the result.

As the struggle opened under another broiling, midsummer sun, Oral Hildebrand, tall right-hander of the Yankees, started on the mound against Derringer. Although Oral, making his first appearance in the series, blanked the Reds on two hits in the first four innings, he was forced to retire because of a pain in his side and Steve Sundra, one of McCarthy's star rookie moundsmen, took up the pitching in the fifth.

In the seventh the Keller and Dickey homers pushed the Yanks ahead, 2 to 0. Through this frame they had made only three hits off Derringer, but two of them sufficed to force the big Red right-hander out for a pinch-hitter in the Cincinnati half of the inning and Walters succeeded him.

Turns Upon Tormentor

But it was also in this round that the underdog finally bared his fangs and turned violently upon his tormentor as the Reds routed Sundra on three hits, one a damaging two-bagger by the veteran Al Simmons, who finally got into the series because Harry Craft was taken ill after four innings.

Three Cincinnati runs counted in this inning which started with Red Rolfe fumbling a grounder. Then followed Simmons's double, a pass, singles by pinch-hitter Bill Hershberger and Bill Werber, and out of the bullpen came Johnny Murphy, the noted Fordham relief specialist.

Johnny checked this drive, but in the eighth he went down for another run on Goodman's double and Lombardi's single and the sweltering crowd went into a frenzy as the Reds moved ahead, 4 to 2.

But in the ninth Keller, the husky, dark-haired Marylander who next Thursday will be 23, singled and so did DiMaggio. On the next play, Dickey slapped a grounder at Lonnie Frey and, had all gone well, the 1939 series might still be with us. However, with a simple double play before him, Myers, luckless shortstop of the Reds, dropped Frey's throw at second base. Keller scored and after a long fly to right by George Selkirk had moved DiMaggio to third, Joe Gordon drove Jolting Joe home with a single over third base. That tied it at 4—all.

Pass Starts the Drive

A pass to Crosetti started the final victory drive in the tenth. Rolfe sacrificed and then Myers succumbed again to the jitters by fumbling Keller's grounder.

It was too much for even so stouthearted a foeman as Walters to weather, and what followed must ever remain a positive nightmare to the National Leaguers who watched it.

DiMaggio ripped a single to right where Goodman fumbled it. Crosetti, of course, scored at once and Keller, coming all the way from first base, also counted as his slide knocked a futile throw-in to the plate right out of Lombardi's glove. And then, with Lombardi still on the ground beside the ball, DiMaggio winged across the plate from third base before the utterly befuddled Schnozzle could do a thing about it.

The victory marked the Yanks' eighth world championship and the fifth under McCarthy, who won his first in 1932.

In winning their last four straight world titles, the Bronx Bombers had actually dropped only three games, two to the Giants in 1936 and one to their city rivals in 1937.

DiMaggio's Base Running Is Praised

VICTORY SONGFEST LED BY M'CARTHY

Yanks' Pilot 'Tickled Beyond Words'—Plaudits for Keller, Dickey, DiMaggio, Murphy

M'KECHNIE PLANS CHANGES

Bill Declines to Elaborate, but Has No Criticism of Reds, Who Are Crushed

From a Staff Correspondent
CINCINNATI, Oct. 8—There was hoopla on all sides as the victorious Yankees trooped into their quarters today after their series sweep over the Reds.

"East Side, West Side," rang out in strident tones. "Roll Out the Barrel" followed, with Marse Joe McCarthy leading in a throaty baritone. Coaches Art Fletcher, Earle Combs and Johnny Schulte, slightly off key, lent lusty aid, for all that, and the players to a man joined in while shaking hands, slapping backs, playfully punching each other and generally giving themselves over to a wild celebration.

Everybody was glad the series was over. Everybody was tickled it had ended in four straight. The visitor felt somehow he was in the presence of a great ball club.

Noise Too Much for Harridge

President Will Harridge of the American League was drowned out by the shouting and singing. So were Warren Giles, Reds' general manager, and the crushed Paul Derringer, Cincinnati pitcher, who came in to present their felicitations.

The retired Lou Gehrig, missing active participation in a Yankee triumph for the first time in his long association with the club, joined in the hullabaloo and smilingly declared it "the greatest finish I have ever seen."

The plaudits were for the hammering Charley Keller, the quiet-spoken Bill Dickey with the noisy bat, the alert Joe DiMaggio for as fancy a bit of heads-up base running as has been seen in years, and for old reliable Johnny Murphy, the club's fireman, who has been putting out enemy flare-ups for so long he is entitled to enjoy the distinction of his first world series victory.

Manager McCarthy congratulated his boys. Keller was so enthusiastic he twice congratulated Mac, until the Yankee skipper said, "That's the second time you did that. Now I guess you want me to kiss you."

Pilot Praises Decision

"Don't forget it's nine straight world series victories, boys," yelled McCarthy to assembled writers. "And another thing, that decision by Pinelli in the tenth was one of the greatest I have ever seen. He called it right, exactly as it happened, on DiMaggio, in a tight situation. I guess it will be McCarthy pitching tomorrow. I'm tickled beyond words. It's great to have a ball club like this one winning the way it does. They proved themselves today, every one of them. Any time you beat Derringer and Walters in one day you've done something."

Coach Fletcher took time out from singing and shouting to praise DiMaggio. "I told him nothing but watch the ball," said Fletcher. "And boy, he watched it. He gave us one of the greatest pieces of sliding I've ever seen. He had to slide over Lombardi's hand and then dig down and touch the plate, and he did it to perfection. Lombardi found out you can't sit down with those Yankees on the base paths, hey?"

DiMaggio was tickled and proudly showed his scars of battle. His legs and hips are covered with sliding bruises.

Keller and Dickey congratulated each other on their homers and Keller wise-cracked: "It's great to hit a homer in a world series, until Dickey comes up and hits one fifty feet farther."

Di Maggio Standout In Series

He's Successor To Ruth, Gehrig

The standout ball player of the world series of 1939 is Joe Di Maggio, who in his fourth season with the Yankees has won the batting championship of the major leagues. Once the Bombers had a Babe Ruth. They also had a Lou Gehrig. But the old order changed. Now it's Di Mag, with Joe Gordon coming right behind him in the home run potentialities column. Giuseppe has hit 30, Flash 28.

With Gehrig on the sidelines, unable to act even as a pitch hitter, the Yankees haven't a single active player who has figured in a losing world series. The Bombers have not been beaten by the National League entry since 1926, when Rogers Hornsby's Cardinals called in Grover Alexander to fan Tony Lazzeri with the bags loaded in the seventh inning of the seventh game.

After the 1926 defeat the Yankees tore off on three consecutive four-straight exploits, against the 1927 Pirates, 1928 Cardinals and 1932 Cubs. The 1927 and 1928 triumphs were under the managership of Miller Huggins. The 1932 victory began a run of four straight classic successes under the leadership of Joe McCarthy.

Marse Joe was not able to win a series while he piloted the Cubs. He was foiled by Connie Mack in 1929. But as manager of the Yankees McCarthy has won 16 world series games and lost only three.

The Giants were beaten 4 to 2 in 1936, and 4 to 1 in 1937. Last October the Cubs were trounced four in a row. In winning a third straight world championship, McCarthy accomplished a trick which no other leader had been able to achieve. Now he goes for the super-record—four in a row.

Lefty Gomez Unbeaten In World Series Play.

Gehrig has been in seven series, only one of which was lost by the Yankees. Bill Dickey has played in four classics, all New York victories. Lefty Gomez has a similar record with six games won and none lost. Di Maggio is one of the younger school who have been in three straight winning series.

On the Cincinnati Reds we find a small army of players to whom a world series is a new sensation. Just how they will react to this, against a club as experienced in inter-league competition, is something to consider. Along with the possibility that the Reds are very tired and may suffer a reaction, Bucky Walters is 10 pounds under weight, Paul Derringer is under par, too. Lon Frey and Billy Myers have bad legs, Ival Goodman has been bothered with a crick in the neck.

Bill McKechnie will take to the field with only three men who have had series experience. They are Derringer, Al Simmons and Wallie Berger.

Derringer as a freshman with the Cardinals in 1931, lost both of his starts. And on each occasion, to Lefty Grove.

Simmons played for the Athletics in three successive series, starting in 1929. That year the Macks beat the Cubs. In 1930 they won from the Cards. But in 1931 the A's lost to the Cardinals.

Wallie Berger was with the Giants in the 1937 series, which the Yankees won by four games to one.

Thus, against the array of unbeaten world series heroes of the Yankees the Reds haven't a single player with a clean classic record.

Highlights

- The Yankees increased their record of World Series sweeps to five (no other team in history has swept more than one).
- The Yanks set a Series standard by winning their fourth straight world title.
- Charlie "King Kong" Keller set an all-time Series record for a rookie by belting three home runs.
- As a team, the Yankees batted only .206, three percentage points better than the Reds.
- With the score tied, 1–1, in the bottom of the ninth of Game 1, King Kong Keller tripled and then scored the game-winning run when Bill Dickey singled.
- Monte Pearson pitched the Yankees to a two-hit shutout in Game 2, and had a no-hitter into the eighth inning where it was spoiled by an Ernie Lombardi single.
- Yankee sluggers hit four home runs in Game 3, two by Keller and one each from DiMaggio and Dickey. Keller drove in four runs that game.
- The Reds committed three errors in the top of the tenth inning of Game 4, which enabled the Yankees to score three runs and win the Series. A double error on a single by DiMaggio—fumbled first by outfielder Ival Goodman, then his throw to the plate was dropped by Ernie Lombardi—allowed both Keller and DiMaggio to score.

Best Efforts

Batting

Average	King Kong Keller	.438
Home Runs	King Kong Keller	3
Triples	King Kong Keller	1
	Billy Myers	1
Doubles	Babe Dahlgren	2
Hits	King Kong Keller	7
Runs	King Kong Keller	8
RBIs	King Kong Keller	6

Pitching

Wins	(four players)	1 each
ERA	Monte Pearson	0.00
Strikeouts	Paul Derringer	9
Innings Pitched	Paul Derringer	15⅓

NEW YORK YANKEES ——————1939
CINCINNATI REDS

Reprinted, with permission, from
The World Series, A Complete
Pictorial History, by John Devaney
and Burt Goldblatt (Rand McNally
and Company, Chicago, © 1972).

Break Up the Yankees

The Yankees were ruining baseball. They were ruining the World Series. They won all the time. Those were the complaints—in New York and elsewhere—as the Yankees easily won their fourth straight pennant, then swept by the Reds in four straight games, their fifth sweep in 13 years. It was the Yank's fourth straight world championship, their eighth in 17 years. Fans, writers, and baseball people offered all sorts of remedies for the same solution: Break up the Yankees.

No one would break up the Yankees until the big league draft of 20-odd years later, which allowed the teams with thin pocketbooks to bid equally with the richer clubs for young talent. But despite the flow of young talent from their farm clubs—King Kong Charlie Keller was their newest addition—the Yankees had to struggle to win two of the four games. And at least two games were ones to relish in the replaying in years to come.

In the second game the Yanks' Monte Pearson, like Herb Pennock in 1927, came within five outs of the first no-hit Series game. In the eighth Ernie Lombardi slapped a single to dash Pearson's hopes. In the ninth Bill Werber cracked another hit. But Pearson let neither man score and won his fourth Series game, a 4-0 shutout.

Those who saw the fourth and final game can still see the Reds' mammoth catcher, Ernie (Schnoz) Lombardi, sprawled helplessly near the plate, the ball nearby as Joe DiMaggio galloped home untouched. With the Yankees ahead, 5-4, in the top of the tenth, DiMaggio hit a sharp drive into left that bounced in front of Ival Goodman. When Goodman bobbled the ball, Charlie Keller tried to score all the way from first. The throw bounced in front of Lombardi as Keller slid home underneath him. The ball rolled a few feet away as Lombardi collapsed into a kneeling position. DiMaggio, who never stopped running, circled the bases and sped across the plate while

Lombardi flopped helplessly next to the ball in what writers called "Ernie's Swoon" or "Ernie's Snooze."

The Yankees rode home jubilant, horseplaying in their special railroad cars. Watching over a game of bridge, a bemused smile on his face, was the Iron Horse, Yankee captain Lou Gehrig. His streak of 2,130 games had ended when he took himself out of the lineup earlier in the season. He was suffering from a terminal illness and had not played in the Series, watching in uniform from the bench. When the Yankees won that last game, 7-4, he took off for the last time the only uniform he'd ever worn on a big league baseball field.

Johnny Vander Meer:
The real story of Lombardi's "snooze"

The man who pitched two successive no-hitters for the Reds in 1938, Johnny Vander Meer, watched the 1939 Series from the bench after hurting his arm during the season. In St. Petersburg, Fla., he said: *The story has never been told of what happened when Lom collapsed. Lom was a very honest man and he had the reputation for telling the truth, but no one saw any reason for telling what happened because we'd lost the game whether DiMaggio scored or whether he didn't. His run made no difference. And Keller scored well ahead of the throw, so that was no fault of Lom's. What happened was that the throw bounced in late and it hit him in the [protective] cup. He wasn't able to move. It was ridiculous to blame Lom. They would have gotten DiMaggio if the pitcher [Bucky Walters] had been backing up the catcher, like he should, but he was on the mound. If anyone took a snooze, like they said Lom did, it was Bucky standing on the mound instead of backing up the throw.*

AMERICAN LEAGUE ALL☆STAR☆TEAM

Bill Dickey | Red Rolfe | George Selkirk | Myril Hoag | Joe DiMaggio | Joe Gordon | Lefty Gomez

Hank Greenberg | Bob Feller | Frank Crosetti | Tommy Bridges | Charley Ruffing

The All-Star Teams

NATIONAL LEAGUE

Pos., Name and Club	B.A.
1B.: Frank McCormick, Reds	.338
1B.: Johnny Mize, Cardinals	.326
1B.: Dolf Camilli, Dodgers	.279
2B.: Linus Frey, Reds	.292
2B.: Billy Herman, Cubs	.266
3B.: Stanley Hack, Cubs	.301
3B.: Cooky Lavagetto, Dodgers	.292
SS.: Arky Vaughan, Pirates	.289
SS.: Billy Jurges, Giants	.264
O.F.: Morris Arnovich, Phillies	.302
O.F.: Mel Ott, Giants	.321
O.F.: Joe Medwick, Cardinals	.328
O.F.: Ival Goodman, Reds	.297
O.F.: Terry Moore, Cardinals	.288
C.: Ernie Lombardi, Reds	.308
C.: Harry Danning, Giants	.301
C.: Babe Phelps, Dodgers	.293
Grand Average	.315

AMERICAN LEAGUE

Pos., Name and Club	B.A.
1B.: Hank Greenberg, Tigers	.299
1B.: Jimmy Foxx, Red Sox	.353
1B.: George McQuinn, Browns	.350
2B.: Joe Gordon, Yankees	.325
3B.: Red Rolfe, Yankees	.316
SS.: Joe Cronin, Red Sox	.286
SS.: Frank Crosetti, Yankees	.230
SS.: Luke Appling, White Sox	.300
O.F.: Joe DiMaggio, Yankees	.406
O.F.: George Selkirk, Yankees	.295
O.F.: Doc Cramer, Red Sox	.331
O.F.: Bob Johnson, Athletics	.319
O.F.: Myril Hoag, Browns	.325
O.F.: George Case, Senators	.322
C.: Bill Dickey, Yankees	.338
C.: Rollie Hemsley, Indians	.285
C.: Frank Hayes, Athletics	.281
Grand Average	.311

NATIONAL LEAGUE

Name and Club	Won	Lost
Paul Derringer, Reds (R)	9	3
John Vander Meer (Reds) (L)	4	5
Bucky Walters, Reds (R)	16	5
Lou Fette, Bees (R)	8	3
Lon Warneke, Cardinals (R)	9	2
Whitlow Wyatt, Dodgers (R)	7	0
Bill Lee, Cubs (R)	8	8
Curt Davis, Cardinals (R)	9	5
Grand Totals	64	31

AMERICAN LEAGUE

Name and Club	Won	Lost
Lefty Gomez, Yankees (L)	6	2
Red Ruffing, Yankees (R)	11	2
Tom Bridges, Tigers (R)	10	1
Bob Feller, Indians (R)	12	3
Lefty Grove, Red Sox (L)	7	2
Buck Newsom, Tigers (R)	8	5
Ted Lyons, White Sox (R)	8	1
John Murphy, Yankees (R)	1	2
Grand Totals	63	18

Jovial Gabby Hartnett will forget the Cubs' troubles for a day and pilot the NL stars.

Joe McCarthy, Yankee and All-Star manager, hopes he can pick a winner.

A scrapbook All-Star team.

More Gehrigs and DiMaggios Are Needed To Help Fight Crime, Alcatraz Head Says

Greater educational activity in behalf of the youth of America, more clubs for growing children and the development of more Lou Gehrigs and Joe DiMaggios were urged yesterday as ways to cut crime in the bud by James A. Johnston, warden of Alcatraz Prison, the "Big House on the Rock" in San Francisco Bay. He spoke at a luncheon meeting of more than 200 persons at the Advertising Club, 28 Park Avenue.

Lou Gehrig, recently named to the Municipal Parole Commission by Mayor La Guardia, was among the guests.

"Youth is the time of lawlessness," Mr. Johnston said. "Don't wait until they get to Alcatraz. I feel sorry for them and I wish I could turn back the clock when I interview them. For I don't like to see them come to Alcatraz, where we have the 'escape artists.' It's the end of the trail."

He said that while they treated prisoners on the "Rock" humanely and provided the proper amount of work and recreation, he regretted the fact that they had to "keep" them. Praising the prison systems in the various States, he said they should not be criticized because some of the men released from prisons eventually came back.

He emphasized that the prison wardens get "damaged, second-hand material" to start with and that with such material they find it difficult in some cases to turn back to society a "white-winged angel."

Mr. Johnston said the best work the members of the Advertising Club and others in society could do was to encourage school work, to give the children more models like "Lou Gehrig and Joe DiMaggio to emulate."

"The children want them," he declared; "they really do. They do them good. So why not give them more Gehrigs and more DiMaggios?"

The veteran warden admitted, however, that he had no magic formula for the solution of crime, despite the fact that he and other prison heads frequently got together to swap ideas and history cases in the hope of bobbing up with a new idea. Many times the conferences echoed with new words for old ideas, he said. The best way to nip crime is to get it in the bud, he declared.

Presiding at the luncheon was G. Lynn Sumner, president of the Advertising Club of New York. William B. Cox, executive secretary of the Osborne Association of New York, 114 East Thirtieth Street, thanked Mr. Johnston for appearing before the group, which included many persons interested in correction.

By Joe Williams

Di Maggio Showed Grit in Winning Fans' Support

One paragraph in the sports page disclosed the details of Joe Di Maggio's impending marriage. Another paragraph revealed the Yankee star had picked up a check of $5,541.89, his share of the world series swag.

All of which reminds us that Mr. Di Maggio had quite a large and satisfactory year for himself last season. He was the ball player of the year, a stand out comparable to the Cobbs, the Ruths and the Hornsbys of yesteryear.

From the beginning it had been predicted the San Francisco Italian would one day reach the pinnacle of baseball greatness. It was just a question of how long it would take him to adjust himself to major league conditions. At no time was there any question of his natural abilities.

But Mr. Di Maggio had a harder fight clinching his position as the No. 1 man of baseball than was necessary. He went through a tough season last year, a season that was tough on his nerves, morale and spirit. All of a sudden he found he had lost his popularity. Fans booed him all over the circuit, and on his home grounds the booing was loudest and longest.

Fans Sided with Ruppert.

This was peculiar treatment for a young man who admittedly was destined to be a baseball idol. And it has a peculiar background. Mr. Di Maggio had arrayed himself against a club owner, and for one of the few times in history the fans sided with the club owner.

You may recall the circumstances. Mr. Di Maggio was offered a handsome up in pay by the late Jacob Ruppert and spurned it. Not only that, he refused to join the club in the South.

When finally he signed the fans had made up their minds the young man had developed an inflated bean, and every time he walked out on the field they let him know about it.

It is difficult for all young men to remain untouched by sudden fame, and this son of a waterfront fisherman would have been something less than human if he hadn't experienced a certain feeling of added importance. They said his unwise salary row with Ruppert was inspired by outsiders and very likely it was.

Anyway, it was a blunder, for Ruppert, notable for his generous policies, had been more than fair. The fans sensed this, and that's why they turned against the young ball player. But as the philosopher says, out of every evil comes some good, and Mr. Di Maggio's distressing adventures last year made him a better man and a better ball player.

How It Feels To Be Boo-ed.

We had a long talk with him about the situation in the South last spring, and he frankly admitted he had been a "damn fool."

"I really believed I was entitled to the kind of money I was asking," he said. "But I was stubborn, I wouldn't concede there were two sides to the controversy, and, worst of all, I didn't take into consideration what I was doing to the team by not reporting."

How did all that booing affect him?

The good-looking, black-haired youth with the small, quick grin, grimaced elaborately. . . . "Boy, you can never appreciate what that can do to you until you have gone through it. Makes your whole insides turn over. Even makes you afraid to pick up your glove and start for the outfield.

"It keeps on going from town to town and you say to yourself, 'Pretty soon I'll get used to it.' But you never do. In fact, the more you try to ignore it the more piercing it becomes. I finally started stuffing my ears with cotton, but that didn't do any good either. Even if I couldn't hear the yells, I knew they were there just the same."

The abuse didn't stop on the field. For months the young man's fan mail was all pan mail. . . . "And some of those letters were beauts, too," he smiled wryly. "I don't think any ball player was ever told off in so many different ways and in so many different languages."

New Contract Coming Up.

It was a high tribute to the young man's grit and determination that he played as well as he did last year. He's sensitive and bruises easily. To be called a bum in spades day in and day out, in one city after another, is an ordeal calculated to get even an iron man down.

"It got so I couldn't sleep at night," Mr. Di Maggio told us. "I'd wake up with a start, with the boos dinning in my ears. I wouldn't be able to go back to sleep, so I'd get up, light a cigaret and walk the floor, sometimes till dawn. I can guarantee you I had plenty of time to think about life and its problems."

It was a trying experience, but the fine, sensible qualities in the young man's makeup enabled him to turn it to a personal, lasting profit. He fought back, won the fans over and the end of the 1939 season found him established as the player of the year. More important than that, it found him with both feet squarely fixed in the ground.

Pretty soon the Yankee office will be busying itself with new contracts. Mr. Di Maggio is among those who have new ones coming. He may be easy to sign and he may not. We don't blame ball players for trying to do the best they can. But one thing we're certain of: Mr. Di Maggio isn't going to let outsiders do his thinking for him any more, because, as he says: "You know there are times even now when I can still hear those boos."

Joe DiMaggio Star, Dominic Goat, in Coast Charity Game

OAKLAND, Cal.—It took the sake of charity to bring together here, on October 21, most of the major and Coast league stars in the eleventh annual Alameda Elks charity game, as Joe DiMaggio led the team from the big circuit to a 15 to 6 victory.

DiMaggio opened up in the first inning against the pitching of Ken Sheehan of Oakland with a 400-foot triple into deep center field to score two runs ahead of him.

He came back in the second inning with a single, and hit again in the fourth for a double.

The game, however, was one of those listless affairs, with no support in the field for either Sheehan or Major Hurler Lee Grissom.

Dominic DiMaggio, San Francisco center fielder who was one of the most consistent fielders in the Coast League this year, and finished second behind Dallessandro in batting, booted two ground chances and dropped a fly ball.

Joe Cronin, Boston Red Sox manager, and Sam Chapman of the Athletics, did a little booting of their own behind Grissom, and in general, most of the players showed what being away from practice for a few weeks will do to a ball player.

Over 5,000 watched the contest.

Batteries—Majors: Grissom, Posedel, Ardizoia and Lombardi; Minors: Sheehan, Lieber and Monzo, Raimondi, Fernandes.

EMMET BRITTON, JR.

TODAY'S PROFILE
By UNITED PRESS

LEAN, swarthy Joe Di Maggio, the greatest batter in the major leagues today, may well be termed the "man who made the Yankees."

Before the arrival of Di Maggio, the Yankees, despite a fairly well-balanced club and an array of good hitters, were unable to get much further than second place in the American League. Since Di Maggio became a centerfield fixture, the Yankees have won four straight pennants, a record achievement.

Di Maggio is presently everything a good young ball-player should be. He's not the swashbuckling type of the Babe Ruth-Miller Huggins era. What money he doesn't save he has invested in a prosperous restaurant in his home state. His elder brother, Tom, is his trusted financial adviser while two other brothers, Dominic and Vince, are also in baseball, as outfielders.

Di Maggio was born in Martinez, Cal., Nov. 25, 1914. He weighs close to 200 pounds and stands half an inch over six feet in height. He hits right-handed and throws right.

The Sporting News
Baseball Questionnaire

Name (In Full) *Joseph Paul DiMaggio Jr.* Date _____

Born in *Martinez* of *California*
City, Town or Township — State

on *November 25, 1914* Present Height *6 feet 2 inches*
Month, Day, Year

Present Weight *200* Married/or Single *Married*

If Married, Give Date and wife's former name *Dorothy Arnold — Nov 19, 1939*

Color of Eyes *Brown* Color of Hair *Black*

Nickname *Many of them* How did you acquire the nickname

newspaper men

Hobby or Hobbies *Fishing*

Nationality *Italian* Name Pronounced _____

If a graduate of preparatory school, junior college or college, list name of institution, the years attended or when graduated and degree received _____

Address during off-season *2150 Beach San Francisco Calif.*
Street — City — State

How do you bat and throw: Bats *right* Throws *right*

What do you consider the outstanding performance of your big league career? *Getting 5 for 5 in a game against Washington — two home runs, a triple, double and a single with a walk*

To whom do you owe your chance in the major leagues? *Bill Essick*

Do you have any brothers in Organized Ball? List them by name and their present clubs *Vince — Cincinnati (Reds) — Dominic — Boston (Red Sox)*

He has been insured for $100,000 by the Yankees and has had yet to play a full season with the club, due to injuries and salary trouble.

A contender for the Most Valuable Player award in the American League ever since he began to play with the Yankees, Joe finally gained undisputed recognition this year when he won 15 of 24 first place ballots. A big factor was the lusty Di Maggio final batting average for the 1939 season — .381 and some of the most brilliant catches and throws ever made by an American League fly-chaser.

Joe likes movies and spaghetti but hasn't much use for books. Although he regards Joe Cronin, another Californian, as his baseball hero, he credits Frank O'Doul, his manager at San Francisco when he was with the Seals, with giving him his greatest help in the game.

In four seasons with the Yankees, Joe has never hit below .320. Until he fell into a slump during the last few weeks of the 1939 season, his average was above .400. He drove in 126 runs and hit 30 homers.

Joe staged a one-man holdout war against the Yankees last year. He received $15,000 in 1937 and turned down a $10,000 jump for 1938. He held out and was docked some salary but he finally signed for $25,000.

Di Maggio is single but reports are that he plans soon to marry Dorothy Arnold, an actress.

1940
A SECOND BATTING
TITLE

MVP of 1939, DiMaggio was a league-leading batter, in the process of establishing a legendary presence in the baseball world.

A YEAR WITHOUT A PENNANT

As a member of the Yankees in 1940, I had no idea what it was like to end the baseball year without a trip to the World Series. Since 1936, we had won the American League pennant every year I had been with the team — four straight — and we had also triumphed in each of those World Series.

I was, however, about to be brought back to the reality that the Yankees were, in truth, mortal. For me, everything was going well in spring training until the last game before the regular season, an exhibition against the Dodgers at Ebbets Field. Sliding into second, I injured my right knee, and so for the fourth time in five years I had to sit out opening day.

I came back in mid-May. Later that year we were in a horse race for the pennant, but for a change we wound up being the also-ran. At season's end we trailed the Detroit Tigers by two games and the Cleveland Indians by a game. The only consolation I had was in winning the batting crown that year, hitting .352.

Joe DiMaggio

1940

JOE DiMAGGIO STATISTICS

Games	132
At Bats	508
Hits	179
Doubles	28
Triples	9
Home Runs	31
Runs Scored	93
Runs Batted In	133
Bases on Balls	61
Strike Outs	30
Stolen Bases	1
Slugging Average	.626
Batting Average	.352*

* Led the American League

STANDINGS

	Won	Lost	Percentage	Games Behind
Detroit Tigers	90	64	.585	
Cleveland Indians	89	65	.578	1
New York Yankees	88	66	.571	2
Boston Red Sox	82	72	.532	8
Chicago White Sox	82	72	.532	8
St. Louis Browns	67	87	.435	23
Washington Senators	64	90	.416	26
Philadelphia A's	54	100	.351	36

By Daniel

Di Maggio's Best-Dressed Ranking Far Cry from Cap-Wearing Players

In 1914, when Buck Herzog became manager of the Cincinnati Reds, he horrified the baseball world with a peremptory order barring the wearing of caps off the field. For many years that rakish type of headgear had been the distinguishing mark of major leaguers in their hours of relaxation. But the revolutionary Herzog produced a ball club in derbies and black pork-pies, and made men wonder where America was heading. The cap manufacturers ranted, and when the Cincinnati team finished a rousing last they burned Herzog in effigy and a high hat.

When the effulgent Babe Ruth came to the Yankees in 1920 he revived the cap as the trademark of the diamond. In fact, he still wears that brown contraption. But it wasn't long before the Bam discovered himself among a withering minority. With the greater influx of college men into baseball, and the lifting of salaries, sartorial standards achieved a shrieking pitch. The ballplayer sprouted into the tailor's delight, a favor to the eye.

With the designation of Joseph Paul Di Maggio, Jr., of San Francisco and the world champion Yankees, as the eighth best-dressed man in America, the development of the diamond gallant into an aesthetic thrill nears its climax. From eighth to first is only a matter of a few morning coats and afternoon ensembles. The time is not far distant when men's suits, and not baseball bats, will bear the legend, Di Maggio Model, and ballplayers will be pursued not for their autographs but for glimpses of their sartorial splendors.

Yea, verily, the year may be approaching when the club owners will award a prize for the best togged-out player, and the most-valuable designation will be lost with Buck Ewing's mustache and Dizzy Dean's arm.

* * *

An original watercolor portrait of Joe DiMaggio, painted by one of America's most famous artists, Norman Rockwell. The painting is now part of the collection of Barry Halper.

The youthful Joe DiMaggio had a lot to smile about at the dawn of the 1940s: with his league-leading 46 home runs in 1937, a batting crown won with a .381 average in 1939, and the established presence as a superstar.

A not uncommon sight: DiMaggio scoring, this time sliding in with a cloud of dust and a foot sweeping across the plate.

Di Maggio Wants $40,000

Yankees Believed Offering $30,000 Which May Result in Long Dispute

By DANIEL.

Just what salary the Yankees will offer to Joseph Paul Di Maggio Jr., the big restaurant man from San Francisco, today had been communicated by Edward G. Barrow to his fellow directors. They held a meeting preliminary to the session in which Barrow, George M. Weiss and Joe McCarthy will exchange ideas in the club offices on Monday. The bid to Di Maggio is quite likely to read $30,000. And it is almost certain that the first reaction will be indignation. Private advices from San Francisco place the outfielder's estimate of his services at $40,000.

From this corner of the ring it looks as if Barrow and Di Mag might lock horns in a somewhat prolonged salary dispute. However, Cousin Ed never has been anything but tough in such matters, and he appears to have a lot of arguments in his favor this time. Barrow is almost certain to ask Di Maggio to play through an entire season for the first time in his New York career before making any squawk about salary.

Last season, when Di Maggio won the batting championship of the major leagues, he missed 32 games with a foot injury. It will be recollected that after a holdout session Joe signed for $25,000 and reported on time at St. Petersburg.

Di Maggio last spring recognized that he was in a poor strategic position. Fooling around on a lot behind his San Francisco seafoodery, he injured the foot which later was to be hurt anew and send him to the sidelines for 38 days. On April 29 he hurt an ankle when his spikes caught as he lunged for a drive from Roberto Estalella's bat. Joe did not return to action until June 7. When he was hurt he was hitting .435.

Di Mag Will Cite Gehrig's Retirement.

Those who advise Di Maggio believe that among the numerous arguments in his favor is a slight easing of the financial situation on the New York club. They believe Joe is entitled to some of the dough the world champions are going to save through the retirement of Lou Gehrig, who last season received $34,000. It wasn't until the highly paid Babe Ruth had quit the New Yorks that Lou began to get what he really was worth.

In the minds of those who run the Yankees, the Di Maggio situation presents no analogy. They point out that in 1939, with a club winning its fourth straight pennant, a team hailed as the all-time miracle of the game, the Yankees failed to draw 1,000,000 customers in the Stadium. They were outdone by the third-place Dodgers, with a club hardly as opulently paid as were the Bombers.

Once again the payroll of the New York club will go over the $300,000 level, and that means a heavy hand in dealing with holdouts who may prove somewhat numerous and perhaps insistent.

The one player whom Barrow recognizes as being worth an increase is Babe Dahlgren, who stepped into Gehrig's spot at first base and gave the most polished defensive demonstration in the majors. Dahlgren also drove in 88 runs.

Giants Resigned to Stewart at Third.

Horace Stoneham's belief that there is little chance for the Giants to make a deal before the training season envelopes a resignation to Gabby Stewart as the regular third baseman. George Myatt will be around with a knee mending from an operation, and Lou Chiozza will be on hand with a leg that was badly shattered last season. Tom Hafey, of course, is gone to Atlanta. There is no opposition for Stewart, who never has played in the Big Time.

Last season Stewart played all over the Jersey City infield. He operated in 133 games, for a batting average of .291. That would be a passing mark. But he drove in only 49 runs with 419 at-bats. Not so hot.

However, it is silly to draw up an estimate of a young player with finality on the basis of minor league performance. Now and then a lad will do far better in the majors than he had done in the minors.

With Babe Young at first, Nick Witek at second and Stewart at the far turn, the Giants will have three novices in their starting infield. Witek last season hit .331 for Newark and belted in 101 tallies.

OUTFIELDER GETS REPORTED $30,000

DiMaggio Reaches Compromise With Yanks and Will Arrive at Florida Camp Friday

ROLFE ENTICED BY $17,000

Third Baseman Will Report on Saturday, but Blair Likely Will Play Exhibitions

By JAMES P. DAWSON
Special to THE NEW YORK TIMES.

ST. PETERSBURG. Fla., March 5—The holdout problem for the Yankees came to a sudden end today. Red Robert Rolfe and Joe DiMaggio fell into line in that order, making it possible for Manager Joe McCarthy henceforth to give his undivided attention to the conditioning of his regulars and the schooling of the rookies he has assembled at Huggins Field.

Word came over the telephone early from President Ed Barrow in New York that Red Robert had struck an accord. It is understood the Penacook scooter compromised on $17,000.

DiMaggio's acceptance of terms was announced by Road Secretary Mark Roth at dusk after another call from President Barrow. The game's greatest figure had been reported holding out for $35,000. Speculation placed his compromise figure at $30,000, an increase of $2,500 over the $27,500 he collected in 1939.

DiMaggio Tells Plans

DiMaggio notified President Barrow he would start from San Francisco on the first train and would arrive here in time to don a uniform Friday before the first exhibition game against the Cardinals on Saturday. It is suspected DiMaggio will be accompanied by his bride.

Whether Rolfe will get into the Cardinal game is doubted. A notoriously slow starter, Red Robert will have lost practically an entire week of training. As a consequence, the Yanks may be well on the way back to New York before the flame-haired infielder starts guarding third base.

In the meantime Lou (Buddy) Blair will get a chance. McCarthy carefully stationed himself back of third base again, coaching the Newark graduate in the art of covering the hot corner.

In advance of the first scrub game, scheduled for tomorrow, the Yankee skipper sent his athletes through their longest drill of the campaign. They started shortly before 11 A. M. and it was 1:45 P. M. before the "all-off" sounded. By that time everybody was thoroughly exercised, including Marse Joe.

Tommy Henrich and Bill Matheson were the hardest worked of the group. Henrich was stationed at second base for an infield workout, while Matheson was at third until Coach Art Fletcher tired of hitting grounders.

.400 Mark Seen for Di Mag

McCarthy Feels Experience Will Lead Joe to His Greatest Season

By DANIEL,
World-Telegram Staff Correspondent.

ST. PETERSBURG, Fla., March 6.—With Joe Di Maggio, last of the Yankee holdouts, signed to a $32,000 contract, Joe McCarthy finally got straightened away in his drive for a fifth consecutive pennant.

Di Maggio and Red Ruffing, both coming from California, are scheduled for their first workouts here on Friday morning. Red Rolfe, who also accepted terms yesterday, is on his way from Penacook. N. H., and due at Miller Huggins Field tomorrow. Rolfe, who received $15,000 last season, took a $1,500 increase. He got tired of looking at snow.

Ten days ago, on his arrival here, McCarthy was confronted with ten unsigned ball players. Most of them, he was confident, would surrender quickly. But from Di Maggio, Ruffing and Rolfe, the manager looked for a hard fight. Particularly did he fear the prospect of a Di Maggio siege, as Giuseppe was shouting for $40,000, and getting plenty of advice from San Francisco financial geniuses.

McCarthy's hands were tied. In the case of Di Maggio he was confronted with the greatest player in the game, who had won the 1939 batting championship of the majors with .381. Against any of his holdouts, McCarthy was without the customary weapon of a world championship club against a disgruntled player—the threat of a trade—under a new rule. McCarthy could not get rid of a player for anything more than the waiver price of $7500.

Last season Di Maggio received $25,000, under his contract, and an additional $2500, which was a refund of salary deducted while he was holding out in 1938. Giuseppe insisted his 1939 salary was $27,500, and that the proffered $30,000 contract was an insult to the whole Di Maggio clan. Ed Barrow held that with his offer of $30,000 he was tendering an increase of $5000. Last evening they fought it out for the last time over the telephone, and Di Maggio accepted terms with him. He is bringing his bride with him.

"Now I can open up," smiled McCarthy, as he prepared for the opening exhibition games, with the Cardinals, this week end. "While Di Maggio was holding out it was impolitic for me to discuss his chances this year. I am convinced that if there is a .400 hitter in the current generation of major leaguers, Di Maggio is the man.

"Mechanically, physically, Di Maggio is perfection at the plate, and in the outfield. This season he will begin to cash in seriously on his experience."

Joe Now Wise to Pitchers, Says McCarthy.

"In the past, pitchers who had no business stopping Joe did so not with their arms, but by outwitting him. Those birds are not going to get away with it any longer. Di Maggio has had enough time to study them, and the job of hitting, and he's on his way to bigger things."

In so far as is known, Di Maggio is coming here without previous baseball work this spring. Even if he had been inclined to work in San Francisco, recent rains have prevented him.

In 1938, when Di Maggio held out long enough to miss two weeks of play, he was subjected to a terrific razzing by the fans. This certainly did not help his hitting. He confessed he had learned a lesson.

Last spring he was here with the early birds, and got off to a flying start, hitting around .400 for better than half the season. This in spite of a foot injury which kept him out of the lineup for some 30 contests.

Scrapbook notes.

Di Mag Says He'll Be Ready To Play in All-Star Game

But Ruffing May Miss Classic; Yankees Resume Mauling Reds

By DANIEL.
World-Telegram Staff Correspondent.

ST. PETERSBURG, Fla., March 12.—For the first time since the world series last October, all the Yankees were assembled here today, and in action. Joe McCarthy's happy family was completed by the arrival from California of Joe Di Maggio and Charley Ruffing, who went into serious action at Miller Huggins Field this morning.

Di Maggio, who drove all the way from San Francisco through rains and washouts, had a light workout here yesterday, while the Bombers were beating the Reds in Tampa, 8 to 7. Ruffing and Pauline, who made the trip from Long Beach, Cal., by rail, checked in late yesterday. They are living at the Yankee hotel, but the Di Maggio honeymooners are some dozen miles from town, at Lido Beach.

When Giuseppe arrived he announced it would take him 10 days to get into shape for his 1940 unveiling. He confessed he had not thrown a ball or swung a bat since the world series. What with a rainy winter at home, and his wedding, he had had no opportunity for training, he explained.

But when Joe McCarthy asked Di Maggio if he wanted his name erased from the American League All-Star team for Sunday's game the outfielder exclaimed: "No! I certainly want to be in that one. I don't know how many innings I will last, but you can put me down to start in center field."

Di Maggio came in weighing 194 pounds, which is just about what he scaled here last March. In 1938 he reported at 203.

Di Maggio Sees Keller Rival for Batting Title.

After telling of a narrow escape from a washed-out bridge and floods in a California canyon, Di Maggio talked about the job at hand. "Is this my .400 year? Well, that's a lot of hitting and any man who announces he is going to give that mark a battle is a sucker. I figured I did very well last season, with .381.

"As for retaining the batting championship of the American League, what about this boy Keller of ours? I want to make the prediction that Charley will give me a fight. He's a fast, powerful kid, while I am an old married man." Giuseppe smiled as he went over his collection of bats.

Then Di Maggio reached into the bag of formal statements and came out with B 105—"I will be in there swinging."

Ruffing said he had done a little throwing around Long Beach in between rains and had felt no twinges on his soupbone. Last season Red injured his flipper as early as April and flashed through a 21-victory campaign despite inability to pitch a curve.

Red performed a miracle in the world series. But if he had been called on for a second start he could not have made it.

"In so far as I know, the arm has recovered, but I am not going to throw too much pressure on it too soon," he added. It looks as if Red will have to bow out of the All-Star contest, for which he was chosen along with Lefty Gomez.

Joe Gordon, whose home run sank the Cardinals in the ninth on Sunday, beat the Reds in the eighth yesterday with a single. For this fifth straight triumph over Cincinnati pitching credit went to Steve Sundra, who in the last three rounds blanked the National League champions with one hit.

Joe McCarthy was especially jubilant over Steve's form, as he looks to the Cleveland Slovak to give him plenty of pitching insurance. Last year Sundra won 11 and lost only 1, with an earned-run mark of 2.75.

DIMAGGIO TO MISS FIRST GAME AGAIN

Jinx to Keep Him From Fourth Opener of Five During His Service With Yankees

---

NOT TO ACCOMPANY CLUB

Star Is Advised to Rest Knee —Athletes Drill at Polo Grounds and Stadium

---

By JAMES P. DAWSON

Joe DiMaggio, whose habitual absence from the Yankees' line-up on opening day has marked his baseball career as indelibly as have his batting feats, will be following custom today when the Yankees open the American League season against the Athletics at Shibe Park. The great outfielder will not even accompany the world champions to Philadelphia.

Dr. Robert Emmet Walsh, Yankee physician, made a thorough examination of DiMag's right knee yesterday and announced Joe would be out of action three or four days. He strained a tendon in the knee after hitting a double with two out in the ninth inning of Sunday's exhibition game against the Dodgers in Flatbush.

At the time DiMaggio's injury was minimized, although Tommy Henrich had to replace him in centerfield. The knee was swollen yesterday, however, and Dr. Walsh recommended that DiMaggio remain here for rest and treatment. If the injury responds as is expected, Dr. Walsh said, DiMaggio would be ready for the first Stadium game of the season on Friday, when the champions tackle the Senators.

DiMaggio missed three of the four previous openings the Yankees have had during his association with the club. In 1936 X-ray burns on his right instep kept him out. The following year he had a shoulder ailment. Last year, although he started, an early season injury overtook him and forced him to the sidelines.

DiMaggio was the only idler in an army of ball players that disturbed yesterday's peace and quiet in the lower Bronx and Harlem. The Yankees worked out at the Stadium, while across the Harlem, at the Polo Grounds, most of the Giant regulars drilled.

Ruffing Real Job of Yanks

Lady Luck Continues to Frown On Red—DiMaggio in Game

By DANIEL.

For the second time in the process of playing 15 American League games and dropping nine of them, the Yankees today had lost three in succession. They had done all that muddling around minus the services of Joe Di Maggio, and Giuseppe was even sadder about it than were his downcast and puzzled companions.

"We can't afford to keep falling back," moaned Di Maggio. "And I think I'll do something about it."

Di Maggio did. He started in centerfield this afternoon against the Tigers and batted in his old clean-up spot.

Off in a corner of the clubhouse sat the real Job of the New York clubhouse—Charles Herbert Red Ruffing. The big right hander just kept shaking his head. Last year at this stage of the race he had won four in a row, and was to go on to seven straight before being stopped. In 1938, he scored his fourth victory on May 8.

But today Ruffing looking like a man who had read the handwriting on the wall. He had won only one game and lost two, and had suffered a second triumph to be crashed from his grasp in the eighth inning of the Bombers' second setback by the Tigers, 6 to 4. A home run by Hank Greenberg, a double by Pinkie Higgins, a pinch homer for Billy Sullivan, and Ruffing had trudged the long mile to the showers, with Johnny Murphy coming in to take the official rap for the trouncing.

For four straight years, Ruffing achieved the distinction of winning 20 or more games. In hurling the world champions to their four consecutive pennants, Big Red gathered 82 victories. Now the Fates hint that the 36-year-old right hander has come to the end of that glorious string. And he sits sullen, determined to fight back. But, like the rest of the New York club, Red is not quite clear as to how to go about it. Everything the Bombers do these days curdles like milk in an electric storm.

Joe Di Maggio. Red Ruffing.

McCarthy Scrambles Batting Order Without Success.

For the second meeting with the Tigers, Joe McCarthy scrambled the batting order. He lifted Bill Dickey into the clean-up spot and the catcher responded with a wasted single and two strikeouts. Ditto for Carlo Keller, who was moved up to third.

In the No. 3 niche Twink Selkirk had made eight hits in his most recent 16 times at bat, and had appeared in all the glad raiment of a .353 average. But in his new location, batting fifth, Twink fizzled after having hit safely in four straight contests. The Bombers left nine on bases, making their ten-game total 78.

That same old southpaw jinx rose up to smack the Yankees for the seventh time. They have lost to only two right handers—Emil Leonard of the Senators and Emerson Dickman of the Red Sox.

While Tommy Bridges was pitching for Detroit, the Yankees were all smiles, with Tommy Henrich's two doubles pacing their attack. But in the seventh Bridges was supplanted by Tom Seats, a left handed rookie drafted from the Cardinal farm at Sacramento.

As soon as they glimpsed the crooked arm, the Bombers blanched. He was the twelfth left hander they had been forced to contend with this season, and they sensed what was coming. Seats allowed one hit and finished the game with Dickey standing at the plate with his bat on his shoulder.

On this date last year the Yankees took first place, and had won 10 and lost 4. On May 7, 1938, the Bombers had won 12 and lost 7. This morning the standing showed this entry: New York, won 6, lost 9. Obviously this is a different year and something is loose. What's the answer?

DIMAGGIO DENIES LINK WITH GOULD

Tells Landis He Never Has Shared Baseball Pay With an Agent or Manager

INQUIRY BEING PRESSED

Club Not Interested in Star's Business Ventures—Yanks Halted by Chicago Cold

By JAMES P. DAWSON
Special to THE NEW YORK TIMES.

CHICAGO, May 16.—That his baseball salary is now, ever has been or ever will be shared on a percentage basis with a manager or agent was emphatically denied today by Joe DiMaggio.

The denial was made to K. M. Landis. The baseball commissioner summoned the game's outstanding player along with Joe McCarthy, manager of the Yankees, to a conference in his office for interrogation on reports that DiMaggio's salary was being shared by a manager.

Reports published here were to the effect that Joe Gould, boxing manager, and James J. Braddock, former heavyweight champion of the world, were secretly managing DiMaggio in an arrangement whereby the player paid Gould 12 per cent of his gross earnings, including his baseball club salary. The reports stated 2 per cent of this amount went to Braddock.

Statement by McCarthy

After the session with Judge Landis, McCarthy issued the following statement:

"Judge Landis summoned DiMaggio and myself by wire yesterday to question Joe on reports that he is paying part of his baseball club salary to a manager. Joe assured the judge there was nothing to the report. I advised Mr. Barrow [Ed Barrow, president of the Yanks] of the denial over the long-distance telephone this morning. The club is interested only in whether DiMaggio shares his baseball salary with a manager. We are satisfied with his denial. What moneys he makes from outside sources, such as testimonials, picture or radio work, is his own business. We are not concerned with that."

DiMaggio declined to discuss the matter. Beyond admitting the summons to Manager McCarthy and DiMaggio, Landis withheld comment.

From another source it was learned Landis had questioned DiMaggio specifically about the existence of any managerial or agent's relations between himself and Gould or Braddock or both. The player's response was a flat denial and the added information that no one ever has been authorized to act as his agent.

Landis, it is understood, plans further to press his investigation.

This was not the first time official cognizance has been taken of the association of Gould's name with that of DiMaggio. Last year the Yankee star was summoned before Landis and questioned about the matter, it became known today.

In 1938 DiMaggio was advised by Barrow that the Yankee club was against his engaging Gould as manager when reports to this effect were in circulation. On that occasion Gould told Barrow and McCarthy that he was not associated in any way with DiMaggio's baseball business affairs, McCarthy said today.

Testimonials Banned

Baseball authorities are resolutely opposed to even indirect mingling of baseball with boxing or horse racing. Similarly the game's authorities are exercising stricter regulation over the use of players' names in testimonial advertising. On the bulletin board of the Yankee clubhouse in New York is a letter signed by Barrow notifying the players they no longer are to pose in their baseball uniforms for pictures endorsing products.

The DiMaggio development enlivened what was otherwise a dull day in the Yankee camp. For the third day in a row unfavorable weather kept the team idle. Today's scheduled opener with the White Sox was postponed early because of wet grounds and cold. McCarthy said he would pitch Marvin Breuer tomorrow. Manager Jimmy Dykes is expected to start the left-handed Edgar Smith for the Sox.

Joe Di Maggio In Only One Opener

In five years with the Yankees, Joe Di Maggio has been in the opening game only once, and has missed 82 contests. He was out of 15 this season. Here is his record up to 1940:

Year.	Missed	Hit.	R.B.I.	H.R.
1939	32	.381	126	30
1938	12	.324	140	32
1937	6	.346	167	46
1936	17	.323	125	29

Joe DiMaggio Named Winner Of Academy Award for Sports

Yankee Outfielder Selected in Poll of 145 Men in Athletics

By the Associated Press

New York, May 26.—Joe Di-Maggio, New York Yankees' outfielder, has been selected as winner of the Golden Laurel Award of the American Academy of Sport as the outstanding performer in the sport world during 1939. He will receive the prize, a gold medallion, at the World's Fair tomorrow.

DiMaggio was chosen by a poll of 145 outstanding figures in various branches of sport. He received 27 first-place votes to 19 for Joe Burk, of Bridgeville, N. J., national sculling champion. Third place went to Bucky Walters, Cincinnati Reds' pitcher, with 16 votes. Heavyweight Champion Joe Louis and Joe McCarthy, manager of the Yankees, received 12 votes each, and Tennis Champion Alice Marble 11.

Selectors were asked to name first, second and third choices in case of possible deadlock, and 64 sports figures were mentioned. Professional baseball was first

JOE DIMAGGIO

with 16 names listed, and football was second with 10.

Don Budge won last year's Golden Laurel by an overwhelming margin, but received only one vote this year.

Joe Di Maggio At Gimbels

Joe Di Maggio, wearing the Laurel of Gold awarded to him at the World's Fair, will greet admiring young fans Saturday morning from 10:30 to 11:30 at Gimbels' University Shop.

The affair will be a sort of "Baseball Information, Please," for the youngsters will fire questions about the diamond and players at Joe and he is expecting to answer them.

Next to Babe Ruth, Di Maggio probably is the most popular baseball idol of this generation and it will therefore be a keen pleasure for the youthful fans to be able to greet him personally and shake hands with their Yankee hero.

DiMaggio Trophy Stolen

Some one with a fondness for Joe DiMaggio and sports cartoons broke into the trophy room of the Academy of Sports at the World's Fair last night, took a gold laurel wreath belonging to the baseball player from a showcase, and fifty original cartoons which were on display. The theft was discovered by an attendant during a dinner given by the academy to 200 young men who had been receiving instructions in sports at the Fair during the Summer. The laurel wreath had been given to DiMaggio at the opening of the academy this year.

Golden Laurel of Sport
Presented to DiMaggio

YANKS' OUTFIELDER HONORED AT FAIR

Joe DiMaggio, No. 1 Athlete of 1939, Receives Award in Court of Sport

MANY NOTABLES ATTEND

Curtiss, Yale Old Blue, Makes Presentation—Mural by Jenkins Is Unveiled

By ALLISON DANZIG

In the presence of a group of notables representative of many fields of sport, Joe DiMaggio received the Golden Laurel as the outstanding athlete in the United States in 1939 at the World's Fair yesterday.

The presentation was made by Julian W. Curtiss in outdoor ceremonies in the Court of Sport, following a luncheon and brief exercises in the Academy of Sport. The famous Yankee outfielder was selected for the award, won last year by J. Donald Budge, the world's champion tennis player, by the vote of the Sport Academy membership.

DiMaggio received 27 first-place votes of a total of 145 cast. Joe Burk, the sculling champion, was second with 19, followed by Bucky Walters, Joe McCarthy, Joe Louis and Miss Alice Marble.

Joe Speaks Briefly

In accepting the award, DiMaggio stated that he never dreamed when he started his big league career with the Yankees that such an honor would come to him. He spoke briefly, saying that he was worried about getting back to the ball park in time for the game.

Christy Walsh, director of the Academy of Sport, welcomed the guests, and after Commander Howard A. Flanigan, vice president in charge of operations at the Fair, had delivered the official greeting, Mr. Curtiss, perennial referee of the Poughkeepsie rowing regatta and one of Yale's most distinguished Old Blues, took over.

A GREAT OUTFIELDER BEING HONORED AT THE WORLD'S FAIR

Joe DiMaggio of the Yankees receiving Golden Laurel from Christy Walsh (left) and Julian W. Curtiss yesterday. The figure in the background is an enlarged photograph of DiMaggio in the Academy of Sport.

Times Wide World

Mr. Curtiss, who was in college competition in 1878, spoke of the comfort of sport and its companionships, his recipe for a long life.

Cartoon Mural Unveiled

Immediately before the award of the Golden Laurel in the outdoor court, the cartoon mural by Burris Jenkins Jr. was unveiled. The mural, a sports panorama, measures 80 by 18 feet.

Among those present were Tad Wieman, Major Biff Jones, Captain F. A. (Andy) March 3d, Big Bill Edwards, Arthur (Doc) Hillebrand, Ken Strong, Charles Brickley, Earl Sande, Nat Holman, Joe McCluskey, Frank Shields, Colonel John Reed Kilpatrick, Arthur Donovan, Artie McGovern, Moose McCormick, Mrs. Lou Gehrig, Mrs. John McGraw, Mrs. James J. Corbett and Mrs. Ed Barrow.

Joe Hitting Consistently Despite Handicap of Injury

Expected To Be Back in Full Stride by Middle of Season

By DANIEL.

Though, with an average of .327, Joe Di Maggio today still was quite a distance behind the pace in the fight for the batting championship of the American League, which he won last year with .381, the center-fielder of the Yankees had strong support that he would repeat.

Giuseppe was keeping himself in the running despite the handicap of his bad knee. Nearly two months have passed since Joe injured it in an exhibition game in Brooklyn, but he is perhaps the slowest healer in the majors, and it may be July 4 before he is as good as new.

Running straightaway, Di Maggio betrays no handicap. But when he has to make a quick turn he suffers. This explains the fact that he has not been quite so adroit in the field. And it also helps to explain his having hit into four double plays. Last season it was quite a feat to make Giuseppe the second out.

While Joe has not been getting hits in clusters reminiscent of last season, and has accounted for only half a dozen homers in 28 games, he is even more consistent than he was in 1939. He has been stopped in only two games—strangely enough, by a left hander on each occasion. Al Smith of the Indians and Thornton Lee of the White Sox turned the trick.

Before long, a lot of the lads who are close to the top of the league's batting roster will move down where they belong. This list includes Lou Finney, Rip Radcliff, Earl Averill, Doc Cramer, Taft Wright, Frank Hayes, Luke Appling, and Ray Mack.

Ted Williams and Jimmy Foxx are going to be tough all the way, though the Boston outfielder has been somewhat erratic. While hitting around .350, Ted has accounted for only four home runs and is being bothered by slow stuff.

On the Yankees, Di Maggio today was headed by George Selkirk, by a single point. Twink held his lead with two for four in the 4-to-3 defeat, which ended the series with the White Sox.

With two victories in Boston and another pair here, the White Sox certainly cannot be classed as pushovers. However, they should have been beaten in their farewell in the Stadium until July 14. Spud Chandler, who set out to pass the .500 mark with a fourth victory, failed to cover the plate in the fatal sixth and, it is hoped, learned a lesson in his fourth defeat.

McNair started the inning with a single to center. Tresh was hit by a pitched ball, and it was obvious

Geo. Selkirk.   Joe Di Maggio.

Rigney would bunt. He cased a roller down toward first, and Dickey dashed to field the ball. So did Dahlgren. And so did Chandler. With Rolfe covering third, the plate was left unprotected.

Mule Haas took it all in at a glance, and sent McNair in. Dahlgren, who had retired Rigney, made a wild throw and Tresh also scored. The Bombers went to the fore with two in the eighth, but the lapse in the sixth was the ball game. Hits by Kreevich and Wright off Murphy, after Spud had retired with one out in the ninth, prevented the Yanks from hanging only three and a half lengths behind the pace of the Red Sox, who on Foxx's three-run homer in the ninth finally beat the Browns.

For the next three days the champions will encounter the Indians, who have beaten them four out of five, and who think they can win the pennant. Through Sunday, New York fans will get an opportunity to see Vitt's great middle combination—Boudreau and Mack—in action.

Friday, when the Yankees are scheduled to play the second game of their series with the Indians, has been designated as Joe Di Maggio Day. That afternoon, at 3 o'clock, Di Maggio will receive the Baseball Writers' Assn. Sporting News award as the American League's outstanding player for 1939.

Mayor Fiorello H. La Guardia will make the presentation, and Jim Earley is to give his benediction to the player who in 1941 will head the pay roll of President Jim of the Yankees.

Di Maggio clinched the 1939 award with a batting average of .381, the best in the majors; 30 homers; and 126 runs driven in.

22,051 on Hand to Honor Di Maggio

Joe Di Maggio Day in the Stadium found 22,051 persons in attendance.... Not counting Mayor Fiorello H. La Guardia, who presented to Joe the watch and scroll that went with the Baseball Writers' Assn.—Sporting News award as the most valuable player of his league for last season.... Flanked by Sid Mercer, president of the national association of writers, and John Throckmorton Drebinger, chairman of the New York chapter, the Little Flower said a very few well-chosen words to Giuseppe.... The goat of the Cleveland defeat for a time was his team's hero.... In the fourth inning Jeff Heath poked a two-run homer into the right field stands, to put the Indians in front.... But in the seventh, Heath converted a liner from Crosetti's bat, which should have been the third out, into a double that helped to blow the game.... Heath replaced Beau Bell, despite the fact that Jeff was hitting only .218.... That Sundra still has the gopher ball knack was stressed in the ninth, when Weatherly led off with a homer. ... Then came the best fielding stunt of the contest.... Tommy Henrich dashed long and far to grab Boudreau's fly in right center.... As Trosky followed with a single, that was a very important catch.... In fact, it kept Sundra from being relieved by Bump Hadley, who was waiting for the nod.... It was Ladies Day, with 7880 of the fair guests in view.... In the first, Trosky and Mack stood around while Rolfe's easy foul dropped to the ground.... Then Red singled, sending Gordon, who had singled before him, to third.... Henrich's fly scored the run.

Di Maggio Takes Over

Joe Grabs Batting Lead Among Yankees

Joe Di Maggio.

The Red Sox leave here this evening and the Browns come into the Stadium. . . . There will be a double-header on Sunday. . . . The Red Sox lead the Yankees four games to three. . . . Joe Di Maggio regained the club batting leadership, with .315. . . . George Selkirk, with .305 comes next but Charley Keller has dropped to .293. . . . After having hit in eight straight games Keller was halted in the first half of the holiday double-header. . . . He got an infield hit in the afterpiece. . . . Boston's run in the first inning of the nightcap broke a string of 18 scoreless rounds in the Yankee park. . . . Things are looking up for the Red Sox pitching staff. . . . Herb Hash, who held the Yanks to six hits in the second game, was the third Cronin starter to go the route in the last of four games. Galehouse and Butland had preceded Hash. . . . Sundra, who last season won 11 straight, has yet to score his first victory and has lost three. . . . The Yanks won the first game in the second inning, with three runs. . . . Dickey's homer, No. 3 for William, opened the onslaught, and Selkirk, Gordon and Crosetti kept it going with singles. . . . With Gordon scoring and Crosetti bunting, the Bombers pulled the squeeze. . . . Tabor heaved the ball to the stand and Crosetti was nipped trying to reach second. . . . Knickerbocker, who got two doubles and a single in the twin bill, initiated the fourth run off Grove with a two-bagger.

* * *

The 20,000 fans who were turned away at the Ebbets Field gates yesterday felt at least they were spared a sad afternoon watching their club blow two to the Giants. . . . The paid count of 34,548 was actually less than the average number of fans who have seen the two teams clash in five playing days this year. . . . They have drawn 175,678 with 51,659 at one Polo Grounds game. . . . Joe Gallagher made his debut in right field and failed to impress. . . . He didn't get a ball out of the infield in four trips to the plate in two games and lost a ball in the sun. . . . The Brooklyn attack was crippled by the inability of Joe Vosmik to land one safe in nine trips to plate, dropping from .304 to .262. . . . Leo Durocher made his second appearance at second base, finishing for Johnny Hudson who was lifted for a pinch-hitter. . . . The base hit that started the eight run 12th inning rally for the Giants, was a ball that skidded off Leo's glove. . . . Pete Coscarart, still recuperating on the sidelines, would have fielded it and Hudson might have. . . . Another critical blow in this frame was Bill Jurges' safe bunt, which Wyatt circled before fumbling. . . . It actually allowed the winning run. . . . Ernie Koy's homer in the last half of the 12th was his first of the year and drew cries of derision.

Joe Vosmik.

9 RUNS IN SECOND MARK 15-2 VICTORY

DiMaggio Homer With Bases Full Features Big Yankee Drive Against Indians

RUSSO WINS FROM MILNAR

Umpires Keep Coaches From Fighting—Triumph Fourth in Row for McCarthymen

By ARTHUR J. DALEY

There is an adage to the effect that whoever plays with fire is certain to get burned. Since the Yankees are the hottest team in baseball at the moment, they scorched the league-leading Cleveland Indians before 12,732 fans at the Stadium yesterday, parboiling them with a nine-run inning and triumphing, 15 to 2.

This victory, fourth in a row for the revitalized Bronx Bombers and their eleventh in their last thirteen starts, rocketed them into third place, one percentage point ahead of the Red Sox. It also contrived to shave the Indian lead over them to eight games and over Detroit to four and a half.

After this débâcle Ossie Vitt's erstwhile rebels must be on the verge of another uprising. They were a bad team that played bad ball half-heartedly. Rusty Russo throttled them with six scattered hits, two of them homers by Roy Weatherly and Beau Bell. But they fielded indifferently and seemed at any moment ready to sit down and have a good cry.

The nine-run second inning, the biggest single frame the Yanks have had this season, was begun by slipshod Indian play. Then Joe McCarthy's operatives got into the spirit of the thing and really took over. The high spot was Joe DiMaggio's twenty-sixth home run, hit with the bases full.

Two Homers in First

This frame really deserves to be described in detail. Weatherly and Tommy Henrich had matched homers in the first and George Selkirk opened the second by getting a walk from Lefty Al Milnar, the No. 2 Cleveland ace. Bill Dickey singled him to third and Babe Dahlgren popped out.

Frankie Crosetti topped weakly to Milnar. He started to throw home, then to first. Finally it dawned on him that the proper play was a twin killing via second. So Milnar heaved one to center field, Selkirk scoring, Dickey reaching third and Crosetti second.

Russo's single to right sent in the second run. Gordon, like Crosetti before him, rolled to Milnar, who attempted the identical double-play manoeuvre he had mangled previously. This time Ray Mack dropped the ball. Rolfe singled to left, Henrich forced Russo at the plate and the stage was set for the DiMaggio jackpot shot.

With the bases finally emptied, Milnar started filling them again by walking Selkirk once more. Thereupon Dickey lined his seventh homer into the right field stands, and that finished the Cleveland pitcher. Harry Eisenstat came in to take care of the last out, and Bill Zuber staggered through the last six frames. But nothing mattered any more.

Sewell Wants to Fight

As Milnar was making his exit Coach Combs tossed a barbed query into the Cleveland bench. Possibly it was, "Why not blame Vitt for that?" At any rate Coach Luke Sewell wanted to fight him, and players from both dugouts swarmed onto the field. The umpires quelled the disturbance without extra aid. It was the only fight that the Indians showed all afternoon.

Even the fans are riding the Rebels. A raucous "Cry Babies!" could be heard distinctly all throughout the game. Faint booing greeted every substitution that Vitt made as the Indians wound up the game with their junior varsity on the field.

DiMaggio today will receive the 1939 trophy for being the most valuable American League player. Mayor La Guardia will present it. The Great Man celebrated in advance with a single, a double and a homer.

It will be Al Smith against Steve Sundra today and Bobby Feller against Red Ruffing tomorrow.

The box score:

CLEVELAND (A.)	ab.r.h.po.a e.	NEW YORK (A.)	ab.r.h.po.a e.
Chapman, lf.	4 0 0 1 0 1	Gordon, 2b..	5 2 1 1 2 0
Weatherly, cf.	4 1 1 4 0 0	Rolfe, 3b....	4 2 2 1 2 0
Boudreau, ss.	3 0 1 1 1 0	Henrich, rf..	4 3 3 2 0 0
Peters, ss....	1 0 1 0 0 0	DiMaggio, cf.	5 2 3 4 0 0
Trosky, 1b..	2 0 0 4 1 0	Selkirk, lf	.3 2 1 1 0 0
Grimes, 1b..	2 0 0 5 0 0	Dickey, c....	5 2 2 2 1 0
Bell, rf.....	3 1 1 0 0 0	Dahlgren, 1b.	4 0 0 12 1 0
Campbell, rf.	1 0 0 0 0 0	Crosetti, ss..	4 2 1 4 4 0
Keltner, 3b.	3 0 1 0 1 0	Russo, p....	3 0 1 0 2 0
Hale, 3b....	1 0 0 0 1 0		
Mack, 2b....	2 0 1 2 1 1	Total .	37 15 12 27 12 0
Hensley, c...	1 0 0 2 1 0		
Petlak, c....	2 0 0 5 0 0		
Milnar, p...	1 0 0 0 1 1		
Eisenstat, p.	0 0 0 0 1 0		
Zuber, p....	2 0 0 0 1 0		
Total ...	32 2 6 24 9 3		

Cleveland ....1 0 0 1 0 0 0 0 0— 2
New York ....1 9 1 0 0 4 0 0.—15

Runs batted in—Weatherly, Henrich, Crosetti, Russo, Gordon 2, DiMaggio 6, Dickey 3, Bell, Selkirk. Two-base hits—Crosetti, DiMaggio, Bell. Home runs—Weatherly, Henrich, DiMaggio, Dickey, Bell. Sacrifice—Russo. Double play—Crosetti and Dahlgren. Left on bases—New York 8, Cleveland 4. Bases on balls—Off Milnar 2, Zuber 2, Russo 1. Struck out—By Russo 3, Zuber 4. Hits—Off Milnar 6 in 1 2-3 innings, Eisenstat 0 in 1-3, Zuber 6 in 6. Losing pitcher—Milnar. Umpires—Summers, Basil, Grieve and Rommell. Time of game—1:50. Attendance—12,732.

It's Joe vs. Dominic Now When Yanks Meet Red Sox

Di Maggios in Latest Brother Act

By PAT McDONOUGH.

Fans who take in the series between the Yankees and Red Sox, which opened with a double-header today, will see a brother combination which may very well rival the Meusels, Waners, Ferrells, Sewells, Johnsons, Barneses and others.

Playing center field for each club is a member of the talented Di Maggio family of San Francisco. Joe of the Yankees has established himself as one of the greatest players in the game. But Dom, in his freshman year in the big time, has come with a rush.

The two were rivals as regulars for the first time last week, as the Red Sox were host to the Yankees at Fenway Park. When the series was over it was Dom who won the honors over his brother, belting 11 hits in the five games for a .611 average, while Joe hit .429, with nine hits.

In addition, Dom made one of the greatest catches of the season on Tommy Henrich, taking a drive against the right-center field fence. Frank Shellenback, now coach of the Red Sox and former Coast League pitcher, has high praise for the 22-year-old Dominic.

"If I had the three brothers in one outfield I would play Dom in center," said Frank. Dom has a more accurate arm than Joe and can go farther for a fly ball. The kid is a better base runner than Joe, even though he hasn't the Yankee's speed in getting down to first base. Dom takes the longest lead I've ever seen anyone take, but he rarely gets caught off base."

A strange thing about the Di

Dominic   Giuseppe

Maggio brothers is that Joe was passed up by the Red Sox and Dom got the go-by from the Yankees. Boston was afraid Joe had a bad knee and New York thought Dom wouldn't do with glasses.

Dominic's great play against the Yankees enabled him to lift his season mark from below .300 to .316. He's still some 18 points behind his brother.

The series with the Sox also gives New York fans a chance to see Jimmy Foxx as a catcher. Jimmy was moved behind the plate to bolster the club's attack and defensive strength in one of the team's weak spots. That he has succeeded on all counts is evidenced by the fact the Boston team has won six out of eight games Jimmy has received.

Foxx caught a double-header against the Yankees while suffering from a bruised leg and a sore arm. The activity behind the plate has not seemed to affect Jimmy's home-run proclivities. He still continues to top the league with 26 circuit drives.

The Yankees entered the series with a budding string of three straight victories, hung up at the expense of the tail-end Athletics. The team played headsup baseball and may again make a determined bid for one of the highest first division positions.

The DiMaggio brothers, Joe and Dom, are embraced by the "Splendid Splinter", Ted Williams

★ OFFICIAL · PROGRAM ★

MAJOR LEAGUE ALL STAR GAME

SPORTSMANS
PARK
SAINT
LOUIS

Price 25 Cents

TUESDAY
JULY 9,
1940
1:30 P.M.

Ken Keltner, 3B
Indians

Robert Rolfe, 3B
Yankees

★★★★★★★★★★

1940

AMERICAN

LEAGUE

STARS

★★★★★★★★★★

Joe DiMaggio, OF
Yankees

Al Milnar, P
Indians

ALL-STAR NOTES

The American League has outbatted the senior circuit as a team in previous All-Star games with a mark of .271 against .238. However, the National League stars have been stronger defensively, making only 3 errors while the Americans have miscued 10 times.

• • •

Four players will represent the National League champion Reds in this season's classic and only First Baseman Frank McCormick has never played with another National League team. Derringer, Walters, and Lombardi all came to Cincinnati in trades with other National League clubs.

The Red Sox first string outfield composed of Williams, Cramer, and Finney, which has been giving opposing American League hurlers so much trouble this season, has been chosen in its entirety for the All-Star game.

• • •

Old favorites who will not be around in this year's game include Lou Gehrig, Charley Gehringer, Gabby Hartnett, Paul Waner, Vernon Gomez, Earl Averill and Dizzy Dean. Gehringer's All-Star record is of particular interest. Playing in 6 classics from 1933 through 1938, Charley made 10 hits in 20 trips to the plate for a .500 percentage.

Harry Lavagetto, IF
Dodgers

Hank Leiber. OF
Cubs

★★★★★★★★★★

1940

NATIONAL

LEAGUE

STARS

★★★★★★★★★★

Merrill May. 3B
Phillies

Whitlow Wyatt. P
Dodgers

ALL-STAR NOTES

Vernon "Lefty" Gomez, New York Yankee hurler, has an enviable record in All-Star competition. Gomez has been credited with 3 victories as against 1 loss while giving up 11 hits in 18 innings.

•   •   •

Joe Medwick, now wearing a Brooklyn uniform, is participating in his seventh All-Star game. Joe was chosen from 1934 through 1939 while playing with the Cardinals.

•   •   •

Six National League players are making their debut in All-Star competition this year while 9 American Leaguers will be making their first appearance. The 6 National Leaguers are Coscarart, French, Higbe, May, Mulcahy, and West. The group from the junior circuit includes Boudreau, Finney, Keller, Keltner, Leonard, Mack, Milnar, Pearson, and Williams.

•   •   •

Joe Cronin will manage the American League team from the bench this year but he does so with a noteworthy playing record behind him in All-Star games. In 6 contests, Cronin has batted .305, gathering 7 hits in 23 trips to the plate.

•   •   •

Bill Jurges and Billy Herman, second base combination for the Cubs for many years before the trade that sent the shortstop to New York, may be reunited in this season's All-Star game, both players having been selected on the National League squad.

ALL-STAR TILT TRIUMPH CONTINUES NATIONAL LEAGUE'S 'GLORY YEAR'

Senior Circuit Pitchers Make American Sluggers Say 'Uncle,' in Yielding Only Three Hits, and Rub Some of Glamour Off Yankees; Cronin's Tactics Meet Criticism

By FREDERICK G. LIEB

THE year of 1940 bodes well for the National League. Things started to look up in Tampa, Fla., last St. Patrick's Day, when the Nationals, still groggy from World's Series pastings in eight straight games in 1938 and 1939, won a rather surprising 2 to 1 exhibition All-Star victory for Finnish Relief from an American League club which supposedly had heavier artillery and stronger armament. American League supporters said their pitchers were not yet ready and their big hitters had not located the range, and to wait for the real All-Star game in Sportsman's Park in St. Louis, July 9. That day arrived and with it came fresh laurels for Bill McKechnie and the National League. As in the Florida combat in the spring, the American leaguers looked stronger on paper, but when the final score was hung up at Sportsman's Park, the legions of Frick had four runs and the men of Harridge none. A crowd of 32,373 paid $42,420.79 to see the fun.

With the exception of the Washington game in 1937, which the Americans won, 8 to 3, the eighth All-Star game was the most one-sided of the series. Not only was it the first shutout, but the total of three hits for the losers was the weakest batting seen in the event so far. Certainly, it was the most impressive victory scored by a National League team in an interleague game in a long time, perhaps since the Cardinals, with Dizzy Dean pitching, won the seventh and deciding game of the 1934 World's Series from the Detroit Tigers by an 11 to 0 score.

While the American League still has a five to three edge on the Nationals in All-Star play, the victory in St. Louis, July 9, was the third won by the National in the last five years. Beginning with Bees Field in Boston in 1936, the National League has acquired the knack of winning in even years in their own parks. They won their second game in Crosley Field, Cincinnati, in 1938 and then made it No. 3 in St. Louis in 1940. Sportsman's Park, of course, is used by the clubs of both leagues, and for the recent game in St. Louis, the National League club was the host.

West and N. L. Pitchers Star

While the three-run homer by Max West, a boy born in the Show-Me State of Missouri, was the real drama of the game, the outstanding feature of the St. Louis

346,634 at Eight Star Tilts

The St. Louis attendance of 32,373 for the 1940 All-Star game was the fifth highest in the eight-year history of the event and brought to 346,634 the total paid admissions at the eight contests, with aggregate receipts of $407,128.59.

The record for attendance and receipts was set at the 1935 game in Cleveland, when a crowd of 69,812 paid $93,692.80 to see the stellar contest.

Following are the figures on attendance and receipts for each year:

Year—City	Attend.	Receipts
1933—Chicago	49,200	$51,000.00
1934—Polo Grounds	48,363	52,982.00
1935—Cleveland	69,812	93,692.80
1936—Boston	25,534	24,388.00
1937—Washington	31,391	28,475.00
1938—Cincinnati	27,069	38,469.00
1939—Yankee Stad.	62,892	75,701.00
1940—St. Louis	32,373	42,420.79
Totals	364,634	$407,128.59

contest was the impotence of the famous American League clubbers against Bill McKechnie's extensive parade of pitchers. After the Wilkinsburg Scot had pitched his two Red aces, Paul Derringer and Bucky Walters, at the start of the game, several American leaguers remarked: "Well, Bill has used up his two big boys. Wait until our sluggers get at some of his other pitchers." They still are waiting. Whitlow Wyatt, discarded by three American League clubs; Larry French, Cub southpaw veteran, and faithful old Carl Hubbell all were as effective as the two pitching princes of the Redland stable. Against the quintette, the American leaguers put only five men on bases, and Luke Appling, Chicago White Sox shortstop, who made two of his team's hits, was the only player to get past first base.

After Charley Ruffing of the Yankees got off to a rocky start, three runs scoring before he put a man out, the American League pitching also was good, but with the exception of their middle man, Buck Newsom of the Tigers, it lacked the general excellency of the National League staff. Bobby Feller, who closed for the American League, pitched the same kind of ball he did in the Tampa contest in the

spring, when his wildness gave the Nationals their winning run in the ninth. The Cleveland fireballer was fast, but he also was wild. In his two innings, he fanned three, but also walked two and hit another, and Harry Danning, Giants' hard-hitting catcher, singled home a run just as did Pete Coscarart off Bobby in Tampa. In Buck Newsom's three innings, he yielded one hit and a walk, but was never threatened. Buck also made one of the three American League hits, only to be wiped off the bases in a double-play.

The Nationals made only seven hits themselves, with young Max West of the Bees and Billy Herman of the Cubs as the clouting heroes. Ott was named in McKechnie's starting lineup, but Bill made a last-minute shift and put West into right field as the National players took the field for the first inning. Arky Vaughan of the Pirates opened with a lucky single to Joe Gordon, a ball which hit a hard spot in the infield and took a high bounce just as Joe was set for it. On a hit-and-run play, Herman whistled a single past Third Baseman Travis, sending Vaughan to third. West, making his first appearance as a mid-summer All-Star hitter, swung and missed a first strike, but connected with the second pitch Ruffing threw to him and sent it into the unscreened section of the right center stands for a home run, giving the Nationals a quick block of three runs. It was the most scoring for the National League in any one inning since the second game at the Polo Grounds, New York, in 1934, when it had two clusters of three runs.

Hero One Minute, Casualty the Next.

Unfortunately, an injury forced West to hobble off the field an inning later. Max leaped against the concrete wall in right field for Appling's high line drive. He crumpled in front of the wall in right field, and after getting first aid treatment, he hobbled off the field with a bruised hip, to the cheers of the St. Louis fans. The injury was not serious. Curiously, it was the fourth straight All-Star game in which one of the stars met an injury. In 1937, in Washington, Dizzy Dean had a toe broken when a line drive from Earl Averill's bat hit his foot. In 1938, Johnny Allen, Cleveland hurler, damaged his pitching arm in Cincinnati, while a year ago Ival Goodman, Red outfielder, injured his shoulder while trying to make a diving catch at the Yankee Stadium.

Billy Herman, fast second sacker of the Cubs, who has shown a return to his former stride this year, matched the three American League hits himself, getting three singles in as many times up before McKechnie replaced him with Pete Coscarart of Brooklyn in the sixth.

McKechnie, incidentally, proved he could show the public practically his entire squad, and still keep a high-class club in the field at all times. Center Fielder Terry Moore, who knows the Sportsman's Park terrain, was the only player McKechnie kept in the lineup for the entire contest. Bill used 22 of his 25 players, and at the finish he had only three left on the bench—Leo Durocher, playing manager of the Dodgers, and the two Philly hurlers, Kirby Higbe and Hugh Mulcahy. McKechnie used one team for the first five innings and almost an entirely different club for the last four.

Joe Cronin also ran more men into the box-score than Joe McCarthy, American

League manager for the past four games, has been in the habit of doing. However, most of Joe's changes came late in the game, and Lou Boudreau and Ray Mack the sensational Cleveland infield pair, played only the last inning. Cronin used 18 of his players, and might have employed two more, Bob Johnson of the Athletics and George McQuinn, but both players were on the casualty list Only Foxx and DiMaggio played the entire game for the American League All-Stars.

The major league owners have decided to give the All-Star game back to the fans, and there is no use in harping on an old issue. However, the weak showing of the American League team at bat was pretty good proof that a new means of picking the players was in order. Cronin started the game with five Yankees in his lineup; in fact, player for player, with the exception of Travis instead of Rolfe at third and Appling instead of Crosetti, Boston Joe opened hostilities with exactly the same club which McCarthy put into the field against McKechnie's training camp All-National Stars in Florida. If Rolfe had not become ill a few days before the game, necessitating a last-minute shift to Travis, it would have been virtually the same club. In the March game, the American League team was picked from five squads, when the Yankees still were regarded as the unbeatable team of baseball. In the St. Louis game, the players of the entire league were available, and the Yanks were a poor fourth.

On the day of the All-Star game, Detroit led in the American League, and Cleveland was trailing by a scant margin. They were the two standout clubs of the league, yet in the opening line-up, neither of these clubs had a single representative. The starting lineup and the team which played most of the game was made up of five Yankees, two Red Sox, one White Sox and one Washington Senator, and the last-named was an added starter for a Yankee regular.

No one should begrudge the National League a clean and brilliantly won victory. Tight, keen competition is the life blood of baseball, and a better showing for the National League in All-Star and World's Series competition not only is desirable, but necessary to keep these events in their proper spots on the nation's sports calendar. The National League pitching was so good that it might have stopped any kind of hitting, but certainly players like McCosky, Gehringer and Radcliff, to mention a few, deserved a chance to swing against it.

Yank Glamour Slightly Tarnished

Cronin also managed his club as though he still were hypnotized by the glamour of the Yankees who were world's champions for four consecutive years. For several years, especially in the All-Star game in Washington, the great McCarthy players rode roughshod over National League opponents, just as they have done in World's Series play. Their praises were sung to the skies. Therefore, it is no more than fair to say that the failure of the 1940 American League team was due in a large measure to the shortcomings of these same Yankees.

The five Yankees appeared officially at bat ten times, without getting as much as a base on balls, and with only Di-Maggio hitting a ball past the infield. Gordon made the best fielding play of the game, a stop on Herman behind second base, but his acrobatic throw failed to get his man. It had been said that Joe didn't earn a place on this year's club, and he proved it with two strikeouts in as many times up. Keller fanned once and rolled out weakly in his next attempt. DiMaggio broke into the All-Star game in his freshman year in 1936 and has played every inning of the five games since then. But he never has glistened as an All-Star batsman and four futile times at bat brought his average for the five games down to .142. In short, the Yankee slump, which has kept a top-heavy spring favorite in fourth place and last in team batting and scoring, was carried into the All-Star game.

One also must question Cronin's judgment for starting Ruffing. This is not exactly second guessing. There was an arching of eyebrows and the asking of numerous "Whys?" on the eve of the game when Joe announced he would start with Ruffing. With an abundance of pitchers, including Milnar, one of the standouts of the first half of the season, Cronin led off with a hurler who has had difficulty in winning half of his games and who was badly battered by the lowly Athletics a few days before the All-Star game. Bridges, on the other hand, had pitched one of his best efforts of the season shortly before the St. Louis dream game.

With the Nationals getting a three-run jump at the very outset, it was necessary for the American leaguers to swing from their bootstraps and try for a mess of runs. However, inning after inning swept by, without the big A. L. scoring thrust. At no time were the Harridge leaguers in a position to play for only one run.

An unusual feature of the game was that First Baseman Jimmy Foxx, the only player who was eligible for all eight games, had only four putouts. The 18 American leaguers made only four assists among them, Foxx getting two of them. Gordon and Keltner each ferried only one ball to first and neither of the shortstops, Appling and Boudreau, had a fielding chance. Incidentally, Foxx brought down his All-Star batting average with three futile times at bat.

Ernie Lombardi, big Cincinnati catcher, who caught the entire game for the National League in both 1938 and 1939, getting two hits in four times at bat in each game, kept his .500 average intact with one hit in two attempts. Herman's three hits in as many times up in the seventh series in which he has been an active participant, boosted his average from .333 to .450. It was the seventh All-Star game for the popular Cub.

The game just missed being the first errorless contest in the eight-year All-Star history. Rollie Hemsley failed to stop Finney's throw to cut off Ott in the eighth, permitting Danning to advance to second for the lone boot. The fielding was good, but the pitching, on the whole, was so excellent, especially on the National League side, that fielding gems were exceedingly rare.

THE GAME IN DETAIL

First Inning

AMERICAN—Travis flied to T. Moore. Williams walked. Keller struck out. Di-Maggio grounded out to Derringer. No runs, no hits, no errors.

NATIONAL—Vaughan singled. Herman singled, Vaughan going to third. West hit a home run into the stands in right center, scoring behind Vaughan and Herman. Mize flied to Williams. Lombardi singled to center. Medwick fouled to Foxx. Lavagetto popped to Gordon. Three runs, four hits, no errors.

Second Inning

AMERICAN—Foxx was called out on strikes. Appling doubled off the wall in right field. West fell against the wall trying to make a leaping catch of Appling's drive and had to leave the game, Nicholson replacing him. Dickey grounded out, Herman to Mize, Appling taking third. Gordon struck out. No runs, one hit, no errors.

NATIONAL—T. Moore fouled to Foxx. Derringer struck out. Vaughan struck out. No runs, no hits, no errors.

Third Inning

AMERICAN—Walters went in to pitch for the National League. Walters threw out Ruffing. Travis flied to Medwick. Williams grounded out to Herman. No runs, no hits, no errors.

NATIONAL—Herman singled to center. Nicholson fouled to Keller, Herman going to second after the catch. Mize grounded to Gordon, Herman going to third. Lombardi flied to Keller. No runs, one hit, no errors.

Fourth Inning

AMERICAN—Phelps went in to catch for the Nationals. Keller grounded to Herman. DiMaggio flied to Nicholson. Foxx grounded out to Vaughan. No runs, no hits, no errors.

NATIONAL—Newsom went in to pitch and Hayes to catch for the Americans. Medwick lined to Gordon. Lavagetto flied to Keller. T. Moore flied to Williams. No runs, no hits, no errors.

Fifth Inning

AMERICAN—Wyatt went in to pitch for the Nationals. Appling grounded to Mize. Hayes grounded out, Lavagetto to Mize. Gordon struck out. No runs, no hits, no errors.

NATIONAL—Wyatt was called out on strikes. Vaughan flied to Williams. Herman singled to right. Nicholson flied to Keller. No runs, one hit, no errors.

Sixth Inning

AMERICAN—Miller went to short, May to third, Coscarart to second, McCormick to first, Ott to right field and J. Moore to left for the Nationals. Newsom singled to right for the second American League hit. Travis hit into a double play, Coscarart to Miller to McCormick. Williams grounded to Coscarart. No runs, one hit, no errors.

NATIONAL—Keltner went to third base, Greenberg to left field and Finney to right for the Americans. McCormick fouled to Keltner. Phelps walked. J. Moore fouled to Keltner. May flied to DiMaggio. No runs, no hits, no errors.

Seventh Inning

AMERICAN—French went in to pitch and Danning to catch for the Nationals. Greenberg fouled to Danning. DiMaggio popped to Miller. Foxx lined to T. Moore. No runs, no hits, no errors.

NATIONAL—Feller and Hemsley formed the new American League battery. T. Moore walked. French sacrificed, Foxx to Gordon, who covered first. Miller struck out. Coscarart was called out on strikes. No runs, no hits, no errors.

Eighth Inning

AMERICAN—Appling singled to right. Hemsley fouled to Danning. Mack batted for Gordon and struck out. Feller struck out. No runs, one hit, no errors.

NATIONAL—Mack went to second base and Boudreau to short for the Americans. Ott walked. McCormick sacrificed, Keltner to Foxx. Danning singled to right, scoring Ott and went to second when Hemsley let Finney's throw roll through him. J. Moore grounded out, Foxx to Feller, who covered first, Danning moving over to third. May was hit by Feller's first pitch. Terry Moore struck out. One run, one hit, one error.

Ninth Inning

AMERICAN—Hubbell went in to pitch for the Nationals. Keltner struck out. Finney walked. Greenberg fouled to Danning. DiMaggio flied to J. Moore. No runs, no hits, no errors.

The Official Score

NATIONAL LEAGUE

Player—Position	AB.	R.	H.	TB.	O.	A.	E.
Vaughan, shortstop	3	1	1	1	0	1	0
Miller, shortstop	1	0	0	0	2	1	0
Herman, second base	3	1	3	3	0	3	0
Coscarart, second base	1	0	0	0	0	2	0
West, right field	1	1	1	4	0	0	0
Nicholson, right field	2	0	0	0	1	0	0
Ott, right field	0	1	0	0	0	0	0
Mize, first base	2	0	0	0	8	0	0
McCormick, first base	1	0	0	0	2	0	0
Lombardi, catcher	2	0	1	1	3	0	0
Phelps, catcher	0	0	0	0	1	0	0
Danning, catcher	1	0	1	1	6	0	0
Medwick, left field	2	0	0	0	1	0	0
J. Moore, left field	2	0	0	0	1	0	0
Lavagetto, third base	2	0	0	0	0	1	0
May, third base	1	0	0	0	0	0	0
T. Moore, center field	3	0	0	0	2	0	0
Derringer, pitcher	1	0	0	0	0	1	0
Walters, pitcher	0	0	0	0	0	1	0
Wyatt, pitcher	1	0	0	0	0	0	0
French, pitcher	0	0	0	0	0	0	0
Hubbell, pitcher	0	0	0	0	0	0	0
Totals	29	4	7	10	27	10	0

AMERICAN LEAGUE

Player—Position	AB.	R.	H.	TB.	O.	A.	E.
Travis, third base	3	0	0	0	0	2	0
Keltner, third base	1	0	0	0	2	1	0
Williams, left field	2	0	0	0	3	0	0
Finney, right field	0	0	0	0	0	0	0
Keller, right field	2	0	0	0	4	0	0
Greenberg, left field	2	0	0	0	0	0	0
DiMaggio, center field	4	0	0	0	1	0	0
Foxx, first base	3	0	0	0	4	2	0
Appling, shortstop	3	0	2	3	0	0	0
Boudreau, shortstop	0	0	0	0	0	0	0
Dickey, catcher	1	0	0	0	2	0	0
Hayes, catcher	1	0	0	0	1	0	0
Hemsley, catcher	1	0	0	0	3	0	1
Gordon, second base	2	0	0	0	3	1	0
Mack, second base	1	0	0	0	0	0	0
Ruffing, pitcher	1	0	0	0	0	0	0
Newsom, pitcher	1	0	1	1	0	0	0
Feller, pitcher	1	0	0	0	1	0	0
Totals	29	0	3	4	24	4	1

Americans	0	0	0	0	0	0	0	0	0—0
Nationals	3	0	0	0	0	0	1	*	—4

AMERICAN LEAGUE

(Including games of July 11.)
Compiled by Howe News Bureau.

Batting.	G.	AB.	R.	H.	RBI.	Pct.
Gelbert, Washington	18	49	7	20	7	.408
B. Mills, New York	18	33	5	13	7	.394
Carey, Boston	12	23	1	9	1	.391
Heusser, Philadelphia	23	11	4	4	4	.364
Wright, Chicago	69	275	44	98	41	.356
Appling, Chicago	66	253	38	90	37	.356
Finney, Boston	68	307	49	109	38	.355
Radcliff, St. Louis	73	277	40	98	38	.354
Simmons, Philadelphia	24	51	7	18	12	.353
McCosky, Detroit	66	273	62	95	23	.348
Travis, Washington	64	251	32	87	31	.347
Hayes, Philadelphia	64	224	38	77	44	.344
Peacock, Boston	33	59	12	20	9	.339
Greenberg, Detroit	68	266	53	90	71	.338
Williams, Boston	69	272	63	92	54	.338
Rosar, New York	24	71	7	24	8	.338
Silvestri, Chicago	12	9	3	3	3	.333
Solters, Chicago	45	152	21	50	30	.329
Mack, Cleveland	75	269	35	86	41	.320
Dietrich, Chicago	10	22	3	7	5	.318
J. DiMaggio, New York	58	221	34	70	48	.317
Sullivan, Detroit	37	101	18	32	24	.317
Rosenthal, Chicago	57	149	24	47	25	.315
Weatherly, Cleveland	58	245	35	77	22	.314
Moses, Philadelphia	72	281	53	88	25	.313
Lewis, Washington	75	305	51	95	31	.311
Higgins, Detroit	58	212	36	66	33	.311
D. DiMaggio, Boston	27	61	11	19	4	.311
Tresh, Chicago	65	220	31	68	36	.309
Spence, Boston	12	13	1	4	3	.308
Ostermueller, Boston	13	13	1	4	0	.308
Walker, Washington	76	323	49	98	55	.307
Cramer, Boston	72	319	46	98	27	.307
Selkirk, New York	67	229	38	70	37	.306
Myer, Washington	26	72	11	22	8	.306
Trosky, Cleveland	70	259	45	79	50	.305
Siebert, Philadelphia	73	295	39	80	42	.305
Foxx, Boston	73	278	55	84	68	.302
Johnson, Philadelphia	68	252	50	76	52	.302
Boudreau, Cleveland	75	310	53	93	40	.300
York, Detroit	73	267	42	80	52	.300
Case, Washington	77	327	61	98	33	.300

Pitching.	G.	IP.	W.	L.	Pct.
Trotter, St. Louis	16	29	3	0	1.000
Appleton, Chicago	13	29	2	0	1.000
McKain, Detroit	10	19	2	0	1.000
Wagner, Boston	8	19	1	0	1.000
Newsom, Detroit	17	134	12	1	.923
Rowe, Detroit	11	65	6	1	.857
A. Smith, Cleveland	15	92	9	2	.818
Milnar, Cleveland	19	134	12	3	.800
Ross, Philadelphia	12	73	4	1	.800
Wilson, Boston	18	66	4	1	.800
Heving, Boston	16	30	4	1	.800
Feller, Cleveland	20	154	13	5	.722
Grove, Boston	12	85	5	2	.714
Breuer, New York	13	100	7	3	.700
Russo, New York	15	85	6	3	.667
Dietrich, Chicago	10	57	4	2	.667
Gomez, New York	3	17	2	1	.667
Allen, Cleveland	15	76	5	3	.625
Bridges, Detroit	14	104	6	4	.600
Lawson, St. Louis	15	39	3	2	.600
Hash, Boston	24	94	7	5	.583
Gorsica, Detroit	13	71	4	3	.571
Galehouse, Boston	14	94	5	4	.556
Lyons, Chicago	11	87	5	4	.556
Dickman, Boston	16	61	5	4	.556
Ruffing, New York	15	118	7	6	.538
Babich, Philadelphia	15	107	7	6	.538
Leonard, Washington	17	146	9	8	.529
Potter, Philadelphia	16	105	6	6	.500
Pearson, New York	13	93	6	6	.500
E. Smith, Chicago	15	92	6	6	.500
Bagby, Boston	17	77	6	6	.500
Chandler, New York	13	82	4	4	.500
Benton, Detroit	21	45	4	4	.500
Hudlin, Washington	12	61	3	3	.500
Coffman, St. Louis	15	53	2	2	.500
Hadley, New York	13	43	2	2	.500
Donald, New York	9	38	2	2	.500
Beckman, Philadelphia	15	35	1	1	.500
Seats, Detroit	9	24	1	1	.500
Carrasquel, Washington	8	9	1	1	.500

NATIONAL LEAGUE

(Including games of July 11.)
Compiled by Elias Baseball Bureau.

Batting.	G.	AB.	R.	H.	RBI.	Pct.
Butcher, Pittsburgh	17	23	4	9	4	.391
J. Martin, St. Louis	43	113	12	39	21	.345
Danning, New York	65	251	40	86	58	.343
Walker, Brooklyn	60	235	34	79	29	.336
Riggs, Cincinnati	15	27	3	9	2	.333
May, Philadelphia	61	214	30	71	28	.332
V. Davis, Pittsburgh	44	121	15	40	14	.331
Nicholson, Chicago	65	232	38	75	53	.323
Gleeson, Chicago	59	222	39	71	37	.320
Herman, Chicago	75	310	50	99	38	.319
Hershberger, Cin'ti	31	66	3	21	16	.318
Gustine, Pittsburgh	58	224	26	71	24	.317
Demaree, New York	43	168	33	52	27	.310
Orengo, St. Louis	55	162	32	50	25	.309
Garms, Pittsburgh	31	68	14	21	14	.309
Ross, Boston	67	256	42	78	39	.305
Leiber, Chicago	51	187	23	57	36	.305
Phelps, Brooklyn	55	177	27	54	32	.305
Rowell, Boston	48	151	14	46	19	.305
Joe Moore, N. York	65	264	46	80	26	.303
Lombardi, Cincinnati	60	223	30	67	42	.300

Pitching.	G.	IP.	W.	L.	Pct.
Fitzsimmons, Brooklyn	9	58	7	1	.875
Sewell, Pittsburgh	15	56	5	1	.833
Mooty, Chicago	11	55	5	1	.833
Tamulis, Brooklyn	17	68	5	1	.833
Melton, New York	17	84	8	2	.800
Salvo, Boston	5	39	3	1	.750
Blanton, Philadelphia	8	45	3	1	.750
Lanning, Pittsburgh	17	41	3	1	.750
Kimball, Brooklyn	18	27	3	1	.750
Walters, Cincinnati	17	145	11	4	.733
Beggs, Cincinnati	14	37	5	2	.714
Pressnell, Brooklyn	16	54	5	2	.714
Thompson, Cincinnati	17	122	10	5	.688
Errickson, Boston	17	108	6	3	.667
Carleton, Brooklyn	14	92	4	2	.667
Lohrman, New York	14	82	7	4	.636
Turner, Cincinnati	11	86	5	3	.625
Raffensberger, Chicago	20	56	3	2	.600
Derringer, Cincinnati	18	150	10	7	.588
Gumbert, New York	16	106	7	5	.583
French, Chicago	21	132	9	7	.563
Hubbell, New York	13	98	5	4	.556
Hamlin, Brooklyn	15	88	5	4	.556
Casey, Brooklyn	16	73	5	4	.556
McGee, St. Louis	19	101	6	5	.545
Passeau, Chicago	23	146	9	8	.529
Wyatt, Brooklyn	19	117	7	7	.500
Brown, Pittsburgh	23	94	6	6	.500
Shoun, St. Louis	30	78	4	4	.500
Russell, St. Louis	23	46	3	3	.500
Moore, Cincinnati	10	30	2	2	.500

Poolside with roommate and ace pitcher, Lefty Gomez, who seems to object to a little friendly toweling down.

With fellow slugger, Charlie "King Kong" Keller.

DiMaggio Bats Across Nine Tallies
As Yanks Check Browns, 10-4, 12-6

Joe Smashes Three Homers and Two Singles
—Keller Gets a 4-Run Circuit Drive—
St. Louis Losing Streak Now 10

By JAMES P. DAWSON

With an old-fashioned demonstration of home-run hitting that thrilled 17,045, the Yankees twice submerged the Browns at the Stadium yesterday to creep within a game and a half of the third-place Red Sox.

The McCarthymen started by hitting for the cycle—a single, a double, a triple and a homer—in the first inning of the opener, which they captured, 10 to 4.

They finished with Charley Keller hitting a homer with the bases filled in the eighth inning of the nightcap to clinch victory by 12 to 6 and send fans home to late dinners that were more enjoyable because of the day's festivities.

Walloping Joe DiMaggio's mighty bat spoke the vital victory message in this day of heavy clouting. Three times he hit for the circuit and twice he walloped singles, driving in nine runs.

Two of Joe's homers came in the opener, when, with two singles to boot, he enjoyed his greatest day of the year with a perfect batting average as he hammered in seven runs.

Coming back in the nightcap with the Browns in front by a single run, it was DiMaggio's third homer of the day, his sixteenth of the campaign, in the seventh inning, that hurtled the Yanks to the fore, sent the crowd into a frenzy and set the fashion for the masterpiece Keller stroked later.

Four of Fred Haney's hurlers were the victims in the first skirmish as husky young Spud Chandler notched his fifth triumph of the campaign. Three St. Louis flingers were pounded in the nightcap, one of them, George Coffman, back on a repeat performance. With Monte Pearson hammered to cover under a five-run attack in the fourth inning, Bump Hadley came through with a relief turn that meshed smoothly with the late Yankee hitting and an amazing defensive collapse that held five St. Louis errors.

Outlook Is Brighter

While all this was going on at the Stadium, the White Sox were treating the Red Sox to the kalsomine brush in Boston, twice shutting out the Yawkey clan and making the immediate outlook for the Yankees just a bit more attractive.

Emil Bildilli started the nightcap, seeking to stave off the Browns' tenth straight reverse. Five runs routed him in the third, when Bill Trotter came on the scene. DiMaggio's homer which pushed the Yanks to the fore in the seventh influenced Trotter's extraction for a pinch-hitter in the eighth, bringing Coffman back to be the victim of Keller's four-run homer in a five-run eighth inning with which the Yanks closed a perfect day.

A five-run cluster in the third inning gave the Yanks a rosy outlook early in the nightcap. This came as a consequence of an error by Harlond Clift, another by Johnny Berardino and still a third by Don Heffner, Frankie Crosetti's double and Joe Gordon's triple with two on, which also moved Bildilli out of the picture.

But the edge was only temporary. In the fourth Pearson went to pieces and the score was tied. Then Hadley got by until the sixth when Radcliff scratched a single, McQuinn walked, Clift sacrificed and Radcliff slid home under Rolfe's throw on Heffner's grounder.

Connects for No. 16

That one-run margin plagued the Yanks until the seventh. Rolfe singled, took second as Keller went out, and was wafted home on the wings of DiMaggio's No. 16.

In the eighth Crosetti's third hit of the game, a single, scored Dahlgren from second and Keller came up with the bases loaded to deposit his seventeenth homer in the lower rightfield stand.

DiMaggio was all over the place in the opener. He played no favorites, slugging robustly against all four of Haney's hurlers, Johnny Niggeling, Howard Mills, George Coffman and Bill Cox.

Of course, some other Yanks contributed to the St. Louis downfall. Gordon exploded a triple, Will Dickey bashed a double, Crosetti laid down two surprise bunts in succession and, scurrying like a scared jack-rabbit, made the stabs good. But it was the hitting of DiMaggio that told the tale and insured for Chandler his fifth victory of the campaign.

The Box Scores

FIRST GAME

ST. LOUIS (A.)	ab.	r.	h.	po.	a.	e.
Cullenbine, lf	5	0	0	2	0	0
Radcliff, rf	4	0	1	2	0	0
McQuinn, 1b	5	0	1	8	0	0
Clift, 3b	4	0	1	3	3	0
Judnich, cf	4	1	3	0	0	0
Berardino, ss	4	1	1	1	3	0
Heffner, 2b	4	2	2	3	1	0
Susce, c	2	0	1	3	0	0
Coffman, p	0	0	0	0	1	0
aHoag	1	0	0	0	0	0
Cox, p	0	0	0	0	0	0
bStrange	1	0	1	0	0	0
Niggeling, p	0	0	0	0	0	0
H. Mills, p	1	0	0	0	1	0
Grace, c	3	0	0	2	0	0
Total	38	4	11	24	9	0

aBatted for Coffman in seventh.
bBatted for Cox in ninth.

NEW YORK (A.)	ab.	r.	h.	po.	a.	e.
Crosetti, ss	4	2	2	2	0	1
Rolfe, 3b	3	2	1	0	1	0
Keller, rf	1	3	1	1	0	1
DiMaggio, cf	4	3	4	2	0	0
Selkirk, lf	5	0	0	3	0	0
Dickey, c	5	1	1	4	0	0
Gordon, 2b	4	0	1	2	5	0
Dahlgren, 1b	4	0	0	11	2	0
Chandler, p	3	0	0	2	3	0
Total	33	10	10	27	14	2

St. Louis .... 0 2 0 0 4 0 0 0 2—4
New York .... 4 0 0 3 0 0 0 3 .—10

Runs batted in—Keller, DiMaggio 7, Gordon, Heffner, Susce, Selkirk, Strange, Berardino.
Two-base hits—Dickey, Heffner 2, Judnich. Three-base hit—Gordon. Home runs—DiMaggio 2, Berardino. Stolen base—Crosetti. Double plays—H. Mills, Heffner and McQuinn; Rolfe, Gordon and Dahlgren. Left on bases—New York 8, St. Louis 8. Bases on balls—Off H. Mills 6, Coffman 1, Cox 1, Chandler 1. Struck out—By Niggeling 1, Chandler 4, H. Mills 1, Coffman 1, Cox 1. Hits—Off Niggeling 4 in 2-3 inning, H. Mills 2 in 3 1-3, Coffman 2 in 2, Cox 2 in 2. Hit by pitcher—By Niggeling (Crosetti). Wild pitch—H. Mills. Passed ball—Susce. Losing pitcher—Niggeling. Umpires—McGowan, Pipgras and Ormsby. Time of game—2:06.

SECOND GAME

ST. LOUIS (A.)	ab.	r.	h.	po.	a.	e.
Grace, lf	4	1	0	2	0	0
Bern'dino, ss	5	1	1	3	5	1
Judnich, cf	3	1	2	0	0	0
Radcliff, rf	5	2	2	0	0	0
McQuinn, 1b	2	0	1	12	0	0
Clift, 3b	3	1	1	3	4	2
Heffner, 2b	4	0	0	2	5	2
Swift, c	4	0	2	1	0	0
bHany	0	0	0	0	0	0
Susce, c	0	0	0	0	0	0
Bildilli, p	1	0	0	0	0	0
Trotter, p	1	0	0	0	2	0
aCullenbine	1	0	0	0	0	0
Coffman, p	0	0	0	0	0	0
Total	38	6	7	24	17	5

aBatted for Trotter in eighth.
bRan for Swift in eighth.

NEW YORK (A.)	ab.	r.	h.	po.	a.	e.
Crosetti, ss	4	2	3	2	1	0
Rolfe, 3b	3	3	1	0	2	1
Keller, rf	5	2	1	1	0	0
DiMaggio, cf	4	1	1	4	1	0
Selkirk, lf	3	1	0	0	0	0
Gordon, 2b	5	0	1	3	4	0
Rosar, c	4	0	0	6	6	0
Dahlgren, 1b	3	1	0	11	0	0
Pearson, p	1	1	0	0	0	0
Hadley, p	3	1	0	0	1	0
Total	35	12	7	27	11	1

St. Louis .... 0 0 0 5 0 1 0 0 0—6
New York .... 0 0 5 3 0 0 2 5 .—12

Runs batted in—Keller 5, Selkirk, Gordon 2, Radcliff 3, Clift, Heffner, DiMaggio 2, Crosetti, McQuinn.
Two-base hits—Crosetti 2, Berardino. Three-base hits—Gordon, Radcliff. Home runs—Clift, DiMaggio, Keller. Sacrifice—Clift. Double plays—Rosar and Gordon; Berardino, Heffner and McQuinn. Left on bases—New York 6, St. Louis 7. Bases on balls—Off Bildilli 4, Trotter 2, Coffman 1, Pearson 2, Hadley 4. Struck out—By Pearson 1, Hadley 3, Trotter 1. Hits—Off Bildilli 2 in 2 2-3 innings, Trotter 3 in 4 1-3. Coffman 2 in 1, Pearson 4 in 3 1-3, Hadley 3 in 5 2-3. Wild pitch—Hadley. Winning pitcher—Hadley. Losing pitcher—Trotter. Umpires—Pipgras, Ormsby and McGowan. Time of game—2:15. Attendance—17,045.

Among other things, DiMaggio's nightcap homer tied him with Keller for the Yankee circuit-hitting honors, each with sixteen. But Charley's jackpot homer later in the game gave him a margin of one before the day was done.

Yanks Down Indians for 5th Straight

SUNDRA HURLS, BATS WAY TO 5-3 VICTORY

Single in 7th Scoring Two Breaks Deadlock as Yanks Down Indians Again

DiMAGGIO SMASHES NO. 27

Honored With Award, He Ties Count in Fourth—Winners 7 Games From 1st Place

By JOHN DREBINGER

The spectacular dash of the Yankees that may yet bring that elusive fifth straight American League pennant to New York is still moving irresistibly onward.

It swept the Indians down to defeat for the second successive afternoon at the Stadium yesterday and sent a ladies' day crowd of 22,051 shrieking jubilantly out of the arena as the now fully aroused Bronx Bombers, inspired by Joe DiMaggio's twenty-seventh home run of the campaign, flattened Ossie Vitt's faltering front runners, 5 to 3.

As a consequence, Marse Joe McCarthy's thundering juggernaut scored its twelfth victory in the last fourteen games, extended its winning streak to five triumphs in a row and whittled the once almost unsurmountable lead of the Indians to a matter of seven lengths. The Indians are four games in front of the second-place Tigers.

As an eye-filling spectacle, the DiMaggio circuit blow perhaps was the feature event of the afternoon. But the real batting hero of this crucial struggle was one Steve Sundra, who not only pitched the entire battle for the world champions but practically won it with a surprise single in the seventh.

Sixth Defeat for Al Smith

The Jolting Joe clout had merely tied the score in the fourth after a Jeff Heath homer in the same round had given the Tribe a 2-1 margin. But the Sundra single dramatically untied it and tallied two, to send the left-handed Al Smith, who was seeking his fourteenth victory, plunging down to his sixth defeat instead.

Unlike Thursday's débâcle, the Indians on this occasion really fought back with considerable stubbornness. Not only did Heath hit for the circuit, but Roy Weatherly opened the ninth with another circuit smash.

But the Yanks somehow looked to have the jump on their rivals practically from the beginning, hopping on Smith for a run in the first inning when Joe Gordon singled to left, swept around to third on Red Rolfe's single to right and over the plate on Tommy Henrich's fly to Weatherly in center.

That lead Sundra held until the fourth, when Heath, after Hal Trosky had singled, lifted his No. 11 of the season into the lower right stand.

Indians' Lead Wiped Away

But the Indians' margin was short lived. Earlier in the afternoon they had presented DiMaggio with his most valuable player award for 1939 and in the last of the fourth Jolting Joe lost no time demonstrating that he is quite apt to prove as valuable this year to the world champions as last. In brief, he belted the ball deep into the lower left stand and the score was deadlocked.

Two were out when the Yanks put on their victory drive in the seventh. It opened with Babe Dahlgren firing a single into right and Frankie Crosetti sweeping a low drive to left which Heath almost caught at his shoe laces. But Jeff caught only his laces and as the ball rolled away, Crosetti receiving credit for a double.

Then, to the consternation of one and all, Sundra sliced a single to right, Dahlgren and Crosetti scored and that was the ball game.

Off Johnny Allen the Yanks picked up one more tally in the eighth on a pass and singles by DiMaggio and George Selkirk. That clinched it quite definitely despite Weatherly's eleventh homer of the year in the ninth.

Just before the game Mayor La Guardia presented DiMaggio with a gold watch. The Sporting News award for having been voted the most valuable player in the American League by the Baseball Writers Association last year.

Sundra on Victory Streak

The victory was Sundra's third of the year and also third in a row. Steve hadn't won a game until Aug. 9.

Following Weatherly's homer the Indians threatened more trouble when Lou Boudreau hammered a drive into right center. But Henrich dashed their hopes immediately with a dazzling catch.

And today the Yanks have nothing more serious to hurdle than Bob Feller, who, beaten only six times this year, will be seeking his twenty-third victory of the season in the series final.

Joe DiMaggio receiving award as most valuable player of the American League in 1939 from Mayor La Guardia. In the center is John Drebinger, chairman of the New York chapter of the Baseball Writers Association.

Times Wide World

The box score:

CLEVELAND (A.)	ab.	r.	h.	po.	a.	e.		NEW YORK (A.)	ab.	r.	h.	po.	a.	e.
Chapman, rf.	4	0	0	2	0	0		Gordon, 2b.	4	1	1	2	5	0
Weatherly, cf.	4	1	2	1	0	1		Rolfe, 3b.	4	0	1	1	3	0
Boudreau, ss	4	0	0	2	1	0		Henrich, rf.	3	1	0	3	0	0
Trosky, 1b.	2	1	2	9	0	1		D'Maggio, cf	4	1	2	2	0	0
Heath, lf.	4	1	1	3	0	1		Selkirk, lf.	4	0	1	0	0	0
Keltner, 3b.	4	0	1	1	3	0		Dickey, c.	4	0	0	2	1	0
Mack, 2b.	2	0	0	3	4	0		Dahlgren, 1b	3	1	2	12	0	0
Hemsley, c.	3	0	0	3	1	0		Crosetti, ss	3	1	1	5	1	0
Smith, p.	2	0	0	0	1	0		Sundra, p.	3	0	1	0	5	0
aCampbell	1	0	0	0	0	0								
Allen, p.	0	0	0	0	0	0		Total	32	5	9	27	15	0
Total	31	3	6	24	10	2								

a Batted for Smith in eighth.

Cleveland	0	0	0	2	0	0	0	0	1—3
New York	1	0	0	1	0	0	2	1	.—5

Runs batted in—Henrich, Heath 2, DiMaggio, Sundra 2, Selkirk, Weatherly. Two-base hit—Crosetti. Home runs—Heath, DiMaggio, Weatherly. Double plays—Gordon and Dahlgren; Dickey and Crosetti; Mack, Boudreau and Trosky. Left on bases—New York 4, Cleveland 3. Bases on balls—Off Sundra 2, Allen 1. Struck out—By Sundra 2, Smith 2. Hits—Off Smith 7 in 7 innings, Allen 2 in 1. Losing pitcher—Smith. Umpires—Basil, Grieve, Rommel and Summers. Time of game—1:50. Attendance—14,171 paid; 7,880 ladies.

Late Surge Won Di Maggio Hitting Title

His 179 Safeties Included 31 Homers

By DANIEL.

Though the vast majority of the Yankees, who in 1940 dropped from the heights of four straight world championships to third place in the American League, are due for salary slashes, it looks as if Joseph Paul Di Maggio, Jr., might be quite safe with his $25,000 stipend. Official averages of the Harridge circuit, issued today, confirmed the impression that Giuseppe had retained his batting championship, with .352.

This was a 29 point drop from Joe's winning record of 1939, but it was good enough to beat out Luke Appling of the White Sox with his .348; Ted Williams, Red Sox, who hit .344; Rip Radcliff of the Browns, with .342, and Barney McCosky and Hank Greenberg of the Tigers, who landed right on the .340 target.

It is conceivable that Di Maggio would have done better if he had not been handicapped by a bad knee, which kept him out of 22 contests. He appeared in 132 games, for 318 bases on 179 hits. Joe walloped 28 doubles, nine triples and 31 homers. He stole only one base. In compiling his .381 average last year, Di Maggio hit for only 310 bases, with 30 homers.

Giuseppe's rise to the title was a game one. In July, he had the league's longest batting streak of the campaign, with 23 games. In past years, Di Maggio ran into a slump in September. But in 1940 he staged a late rally, and passed Appling and Radcliff.

Red Rolfe, who piled up the greatest hit total in 1939, with 213, suffered a startling reversal, with 147 blows for nothing better than .250. This and other individual declines dropped the Yankees to last place in team batting, with a harrowing .259, as against .286 for the Red Sox and the Tigers. However, the Bombers retained the home run laurels, with 155, beating the Red Sox by 11.

The New York club lost the runs-batted-in lead, with 757 as against 829 for the Tigers. Joe McCarthy's men also collapsed in total runs, hits and bases. But they finished second in defense, allowing 671 runs, while the Indians kept the opposition to 637.

Hank's 41 Homers and 384 Bases Best.

Hank Greenberg, voted the league's most valuable player for 1940, led the majors in homers, with 41. He hit 15 of those in the September pennant drive. Jimmy Foxx was second in the circuit derby, with 36, and Rudy York third, with 33. In 1939, Jimmy won with 35.

Foxx lifted his major home run total to an even 500 for 14 years, and stands second only to Babe Ruth, with Lou Gehrig dropping to third, with 494. Foxx hit homers with the bases loaded in two successive games against the Tigers in May, matching Bill Dickey's feat of 1937.

As for Dickey, he dropped to only 9 homers, and an average of .247 in 1940.

Greenberg wound up with the best base total—384, on 50 doubles, 8 triples and 41 homers. He topped the circuit in two baggers. McCosky led in triples, with 19. At 200, McCosky, Radcliff and Doc Cramer, just traded by Boston to Washington, tied for the leadership in hits.

In total bases, the garrulous Mr. Williams of Boston was second, with 333. George Case of Washington led in base stealing, with 35, and had no competition in that specialty. Pinkie Higgins got three homers in one game.

Only One Yankee On Ruth's Team

Babe Ruth today announced the following selections for his 1940 All-America baseball team, with Joe Di Maggio the only Yankee named.

Stanley Hack, 3b, Cubs.
Charley Gehringer, 2b, Tigers.
Hank Greenberg, lf, Tigers.
Joe Di Maggio, cf, Yankees.
Johnny Mize, 1b, Cardinals.
Ted Williams, rf, Red Sox.
Harry Danning, c, Giants.
Luke Appling, ss, White Sox.
Bob Feller, p, Indians.
Buck Newsom, p, Tigers.

Fans come in all sizes and shapes, young and old.

Captured in the field: pictures from a boy's scrapbook, now in the Barry Halper collection.

1941
THE HITTING STREAK

With this swing Joe DiMaggio drives a single to center, to run his consecutive game hitting streak of 1941 to 44 games, and tie the major league record set by Wee Willie Keeler back in 1897.

FIFTY-SIX GREAT GAMES

I have said many times that you have to be lucky to keep a hitting streak going. I was lucky out in the Pacific Coast League to go 61 games in 1933, and I had the same good fortune in New York in 1941, getting a hit in 56 consecutive games.

There was, of course, a lot of pressure that built up along the way, especially during the streak with the Yankees in '41. Our manager, Joe McCarthy, was a great help. He never gave me the "take" sign once. In fact, at times, he even gave me the hit sign in situations where the count was three balls and no strikes, something a manager would normally never do at that time under any other circumstances.

When my streak came to an end after 56 games in Cleveland against the Indians, it was again a matter of luck — this time bad luck. The two pitchers that day, Al Smith and Jim Bagby, got the credit, but it was really third baseman Ken Keltner who deserved it. I hit the ball hard in that game but mother luck wasn't smiling on me that day. Keltner was there twice to turn hits into outs.

Joe DiMaggio

1941

JOE DiMAGGIO STATISTICS

Games	139
At Bats	541
Hits	193
Doubles	43
Triples	11
Home Runs	30
Runs Scored	122
Runs Batted In	125*
Bases on Balls	76
Strike Outs	13
Stolen Bases	4
Slugging Average	.643
Batting Average	.357

* Led the American League

STANDINGS

	Won	Lost	Percentage	Games Behind
New York Yankees	101	53	.656	
Boston Red Sox	84	70	.545	17
Chicago White Sox	77	77	.500	24
Cleveland Indians	75	79	.487	26
Detroit Tigers	75	79	.487	26
St. Louis Browns	70	84	.455	31
Washington Senators	70	84	.455	31
Philadelphia A's	64	90	.416	37

Barrow Refuses to Meet Demands of Other Yanks

Giants and Dodgers Also Beset By Salary-Striking of Stars

By DANIEL.

Before another week end rolls around the Giants will be training at Miami and the Dodgers will be working in Havana. On Feb. 24 the Yankees open their preliminary season at St. Petersburg. But despite the imminence of conditioning gestures, all three local clubs today were beset with salary strikers, some of whom may prove difficult to placate.

The New York teams are not the only ones having holdout trouble. But as the years pass there is a growing tendency among the players to keep their financial grievances to themselves until they are certain amicable negotiations no longer can be effective. For example, the Tigers have yet to sign Hank Greenberg, most valuable player of the majors in 1940, for which season he received $34,000 under his contract and $10,000 in bonuses. It is understood that Buck Newsom also has yet to be signed.

The Cardinals are having grief with Johnny Mize, who hit 43 homers last season and demands a lot more than the $15,000 he received in 1940. It is apparent that the St. Louis club is going to be forced into the Medwick pattern with Big Johnny and that it won't be long before Mize, too, will have to be sold.

Red Ruffing.   Bill Dickey.

Around here the chief recalcitrant is Joe DiMaggio of the Yankees, who last year retained the American League batting championship with .352 as against .381 for 1939. The dope is that Giuseppe received $32,500 last season. Ed Barrow has hinted that this guess may be a bit too high.

Barrow refuses to discuss the DiMaggio case or even to admit that Joe's unsigned contract has been seen around 55 W. 42nd St. However, Cousin Ed has some interesting views on the holdout. Barrow insists that DiMaggio does not run enough, that his legs are not in first-class condition, and these reasons explain the injuries which Giuseppe suffers each season. Ed has told DiMaggio that before he can be in a good strategic position he must play through a 154-game schedule. Last year DiMaggio missed 30 games in center field with a bad knee.

While DiMaggio was out, a lot of humpty-dumpty lefthanders knocked the Yankees over, and took the pennant from them, then and there.

Ruffing and Dickey Resist Salary Cuts.

DiMaggio had turned down a duplicate of his 1940 contract. But Red Ruffing, Bill Dickey, George Selkirk, Johnny Murphy, Frankie Crosetti and Red Rolfe are among the Yanks who are resisting salary slashes.

Ruffing, who for four straight years was good for at least 20 victories a season, dropped to 15 in 1940. Dickey fell to .246 in the batting averages, Crosetti to .193, Rolfe to .245 and Selkirk to .269. Murphy won eight and lost four.

Ruffing and Dickey were in the $20,000 bracket, Crosetti and Rolfe got $18,000 each. They admit they had tough years. They confess the Yankees fell into third place. But they insist the dethroned Bombers made more money than the four-time world champions of 1939.

The Barrow fight with Rolfe and Crosetti is complicated by the prospect of seeing the two infield veterans reduced to bench-warmers by Priddy and Rizzuto. This possibility Red and Frankie refuse to concede.

Di Maggio Signs, $35,000

Special to the World-Telegram.

ST. PETERSBURG, Fla., March 6.—Joe Di Maggio's two-month salary battle with Ed. Barrow came to an end today. The Yankee centerfielder and American League batting champion of 1940 and 1939 accepted terms and said he would leave San Francisco tomorrow. He is expected in uniform on Miller Huggins Field next Tuesday. He will have missed the first four exhibition games.

Di Maggio's salary for 1941 will be $35,000, an increase of $2500 over his return for last year. In January Giuseppe received a contract calling for $30,000 and in high indignation rushed it back to the New York office.

Later Barrow lifted his offer to $32,000, then to $34,000, and on Monday to $35,000. With this last tender went an ultimatum and a warning that not only was Joe hurting himself by missing a lot of training but jeopardizing the comeback campaign of the Yankees.

Early this afternoon Di Maggio telegraphed to Barrow in the New York office that he was ready to sign.

Di Maggio remains the second highest paid ball player in the major leagues. Hank Greenberg still tops Giuseppe. Last year Hank signed for $40,000 and received bonuses totaling $10,000. Recently it was divulged that Greenberg, slated for a call to the army in July, would get a salary rise. It was said he had signed for $42,000.

This is Di Maggio's sixth season with the Yankees, and it is hoped it will be his first complete one. He has been hounded by trouble ever since he came to the New York club.

DIMAGGIO GETS A TICKET

Joe, En Route to Yanks' Camp at 70 M.P.H., Loses 30 Minutes

MERCED, Calif., March 7 (.P)—A ticket for speeding seventy miles an hour delayed Outfielder Joe Di-Maggio another thirty minutes today in his hurry-up auto trip to the New York Yankees' training camp at St. Petersburg, Fla.

He was arrested by State Highway Patrolman Wayne Langston just north of Merced. The ball player was accompanied by his wife, Dorothy.

Police Officer James Turner, to whom DiMaggio was brought by Langston, took the ticket and told Joe he would appear in court for him. He did not have to put up bail.

DiMaggio already was late for his St. Petersburg appointment, due to contract troubles. They've been ironed out, however, to the tune of a sum in the neighborhood of $35,000.

Outfielder Encouraged As Arm Regains Strength

Joe Handicapped in Past Campaigns by Injury Jinx

By DANIEL,
World-Telegram Staff Correspondent.

FORT WORTH, April 1.—Joe Di Maggio, at least, was on his way today. With a big afternoon in the 16 to 4 victory at San Antonio, the center fielder of the Yankees headed for what he hoped would be his third consecutive batting championship of the major leagues. He won with .381 in 1939, dropped to .352 last season, and now plans a resurgence to the more impressive brackets.

For some time Giuseppe has been kept rather low in spirit from trouble with his arm. He had most disturbing visions and his hitting suffered. But now that the throwing equipment has responded to treatment, a more resilient and eager Di Maggio is in circulation.

Under a hot sun in the city of the Alamo, Joe achieved not only his first home run of the year but three doubles as well, and fattened his average to a more opulent .429. His four bagger left the park at the 360-foot mark in left center and scored Phil Rizzuto and Buddy Blair ahead of him.

Lefty Gomez. Joe Di Maggio.

In 1940 Di Maggio's 31 home runs left him far behind Hank Greenberg with his 41. In his quest of the runs-driven-in championship Giuseppe again was balked by Hank, 133 to 150. But this time Joe hopes to be in there for the full schedule. Last year a bad knee, injured at the close of the training season, and later a charley horse, kept him out of 22 games. Playing in 154, the star of the Yankees would be terrific competition for anyone.

With Joe in Class 3 and safe from the draft and Greenberg likely to be called to the army by June, there is another angle which promises to help Di Maggio

succeed in his ambition to gain that triple crown which has eluded him.

As Di Maggio moved his heavy artillery into fighting range he finds Charley Keller, who got his sixth homer yesterday, leading the Yankees in their old specialty. King Kong also tops the runs-driven-in column with 24 and is batting an impressive .375.

There was just one untoward development in the carnival at San Antonio. Making his fourth appearance of the month Lefty Gomez was not quite the dashing caballero he had been against Louisville, Brooklyn and Kansas City. In 13 innings against these clubs Vernon had given only nine hits and two runs.

But the Missions got to Lefty for a half-dozen blows and a pair of tallies. Not exactly bad. But he issued six passes and fanned only four. Gomez wasn't as fast as he had been. But more noticeable was the ineffectiveness of his curve. He couldn't get it over, and when he let down the minor leaguers got to him pretty lustily.

For Gomez, every outing is a thing of desperation. As a matter of fact, he is fairly safe. Joe McCarthy says: "This man did wonders for the Yankees. It would be rank ingratitude to cast him off like an old pair of shoes, or a broken bat."

However, Lefty thinks every appearance means the difference between "stay" and "go" and under his gay exterior he is the most harassed man on the New York club.

"Here's a strange thing," Gomez remarked on the move into Fort Worth. "I don't believe I felt better any day of the training season than I did yesterday. I thought I had everything. But the box score hollers 'liar,' so what is a guy to do?"

Di Maggio Still in Slump

Yankees' Second String Pitchers
Proving Cousins to Westerners

By DANIEL,
World-Telegram Staff Correspondent.

DETROIT, Mich., May 5.—Joe Di Maggio, batting champion of the American League for the last two years, isn't hitting his weight. Add the failure of Joe McCarthy's second line of pitching defense, and you have a fairly comprehensive explanation why this first Western trip of the Yankees, planned to strike terror into the hearts of the Indians, has produced only three victories in six starts.

The tour was beaten down to a .500 level in a 10-to-1 trouncing by the Tigers. With Showboat Newsom pitching five-hit ball before 43,741 customers, the Bengals for once this year really looked like champions, and forgot all about the impending loss of Hank Greenberg to the Army.

Di Maggio's slump, which he forgot to leave behind him in Yankee Stadium, has been even more amazing than the .528 pace at which he slugged through the first eight games of the pennant race. As Giuseppe had hit safely in all 19 exhibitions in which he had played, his powerful start against American League pitching was rather expected.

But on April 22, in Philadelphia, something happened to Di Maggio. A busher by the name of Lester McCrabb not only stopped Joe but did not let him push a ball out of the infield. Since then, in a dozen contests, Di Maggio hasn't hit any better than Gerald Priddy. Joe has been held to seven hits in 43 times at bat, for a resounding .169. He has dropped 195 points, to .333.

In the six games of this trip, Di Maggio has fashioned exactly four blows—three of them doubles, to be sure — in 21 tries, for a measly .190.

Giuseppe headed for the West with designs on the homer and runs-driven-in titles, as well as the batting leadership. But out here he hasn't found the four-base range. While he has remained static with five circuit drives, Joe Gordon and Charley Keller have caught up with him.

Trigger belted his fifth in Chicago

N. Y. Batting

GIANTS.

Demaree	.400	Arnovich	.273
Jurges	.375	Danning	.270
Hartnett	.333	Orengo	.251
Young	.310	Moore	.211
Ott	.292	Rucker	.200
Whitehead	.280		

DODGERS.

Vosmik	.414	Owen	.282
Lavagetto	.370	Reese	.280
Wasdell	.370	Walker	.276
Reiser	.341	Phelps	.250
Kampouris	.320	Coscarart	.227
Camilli	.309	Riggs	.200
Medwick	.291	Waner	.176

YANKEES.

Rosar	.476	Keller	.268
Dickey	.371	Rolfe	.247
Di Maggio	.333	Selkirk	.238
Gorgon	.299	Henrich	.227
Bordagaray	.273	Priddy	.180
Rizzuto	.272	Sturm	.100

on Saturday. King Kong got his off Bobo. It hit the center field screen on the fly, and winged 450 feet. Had there been no impediment, it would have been one of the most remarkable homers hit on a club rich in circuit distinctions. As it was, Keller had to beat it out. He was past third before Frank Croucher got the relay.

———

**Di Maggio Enjoys First
Three-Hit Day in Weeks.**

There is one Yankee who hopes the opposition, which has thrown three straight left handers at Mc-Carthy's team, keeps right on showing that type of slinging. He is Joe Di Maggio, whom south-paws have pulled out of his slump. He was hitting .320 today.

With two blows in the finale in Cleveland and three off Johnson, Giuseppe has had two good games in succession for the first time since the eighth contest of the season. In the ninth, McCrabb, of the Athletics, stopped him and only now is he getting his breath back.

Di Maggio yesterday collected as many as three hits for the first time in 17 games. With a little more leniency in scoring, Joe would have had a fourth blow. He almost knocked Jim Tabor down with a drive. The third baseman stifled it, and then made three futile efforts to find the handle on the ball. Finally Jim heaved his glove into the air and quit.

**Chandler Has
McCarthy Worried.**

Perhaps the incentive of brotherly rivalry with bespec-tacled Dominic had something to do with rousing Joe. But even with his three singles the Yankee Di Maggio was outdone by the Boston edition. Dom opened with a triple, then beat out a bunt to an unready Rolfe, and finally crashed a double off the left field wall.

Just what to do about Spud Chandler, who for a third time failed to finish, is giving Mc-Carthy some worry. A double-play helped the Georgian in the first round after he had been walloped for two runs on three hits. In the second he was knocked silly with five more drives.

In came Steve Peek and his knuckler, and they were poked for a three-run homer by Tabor. Charley Stanceau got a three-run pasting in his one inning, and Norman Branch kept the Red Sox scoreless in the eighth.

Yankee Stars Rent West Side Suites

Joe Di Maggio and Vernon (Lefty) Gomez of the Yankee baseball team have rented apartments on the upper West Side. Di Maggio will live in 400 West End Ave. and Gomez in 825 West End Ave. Apartment Leasing Service, Inc., negotiated the leases.

E. Eugene Grossman, managing director of 300 Central Park W., leased a seven-room apartment in the building to H. L. Kreielsheimer through Francis R. Jaffin, broker.

Arthur S. Lukath, Inc. has rented two adjacent apartments in the buildings under construction at 40 Central Park S. to Mary Hyman, attorney, for Culver, Hollyday & Co., Inc., agents.

Nehring Bros., agents, leased apartments in 180 Cabrini Blvd., Castle Village, Manhattan, to Chester W. Craig, auditor of the Gulf Oil Co. and to Jack Winters, a teacher in P. S. 19, Manhattan.

Wm. A. White & Sons have leased at London Terrace to Arthur L. Finn, Randall Gould, Raymond R. Taylor, Redney S. Pullen. Jr., Charles Campbell, Mary G. Yerkes and Edis Hatch, Clara F. Butler, Lorraine Owens and Winifred Edwards, Glenda R. McHugh, Maria Burris and to Julie Rogers.

Di Mag Off to Fine Start

Two Losses Don't Worry McCarthy, With Yanks Flashing Power, Pep

By DANIEL.

Though the Yankee drive had been stalled by two straight defeats by the Athletics, Joe McCarthy today refused to regard the stoppage as anything more than a passing inconvenience. "We lost another one, 10 to 7, because our pitching did not stand up," Joe said, as he reviewed the 13-hit attack, including three homers, with which the Mackmen punished Marvin Breuer, Johnny Murphy and Steve Peck, in his major league debut.

"However, it isn't hurling or any other feature of defense which worries me. We hit only .257 as a club last year. If we can keep our attack going as we did against Nelson Potter I won't complain. Any disappointments I have suffered in the last two days have been discounted by the fine work of Joe Di Maggio and Phil Rizzuto. Di Maggio looks better than ever."

It was a pity that a gorgeous demonstration of hitting such as Di Maggio staged against Potter had to be wasted in a defeat. Batting brilliantly in his third straight league game and, 19 exhibitions included, his 22nd consecutive contest, Giuseppe belted one of the longest homers yet seen in the Stadium, as well as two doubles and a single.

Phil Rizzuto, the Flea who has taken over at short for New York, made his first hits in the American League and tried resolutely to steal the headline from Big Wop. Phil got a double, two singles and a pass and continued his superlative work in the field.

But Di Maggio, with eight hits and a league batting average of .615, took charge with a two-bagger that sparked a two-run-assault in the opening inning, and remained the head man through the ninth, in which he crashed that titanic homer.

Giuseppe lined the ball some 430 feet into the Yankee bullpen in the alley between the left-field stands and the bleachers. Last season, when Di Mag got 31 homers, he did not achieve his first until May 17, against Lefty Smith of the White Sox. Joe had lost a whole month with a bad knee. With this early start he is tough competition even for Hank Greenberg.

Selkirk Drives Homer
In Fight for Job.

After having been quiescent for two days, the home-run power of the Bombers broke out not only in Giuseppe's wallop, but in a Twink Selkirk poke into the right-field stands. This was none of your run-of-the-mine loopers. George whaled it into the upper deck, a very manly blow.

However, the Yankees showed a 2-to-4 deficit in the four-base department, Dick Siebert having hit two and Bob Johnson one yesterday, and Sam Chapman one in the Stadium opener. The gopher ball habit that ruined Yankee pitching in 1940 has not been throttled. It will have to be killed or there won't be any 1941 pennant for Mr. McCarthy's nobles.

The Selkirk homer was made by Twink in the role of a pinch-hitter and carried with it a tremendous dramatic kick. That blow was Twink's fight for his old job.

For some 10 days before the season opened Selkirk was billed as the starting right fielder. Tom Henrich had been benched with a sore arm and a .200 average and George looked safe for a spell. But when the Bombers went into action in Washington Henrich had the post and Selkirk the chagrin.

Twink's homer is sharp warning to Tommy, who in 11 minutes at bat, has produced just two hits, one a double. Yesterday he opened with the two-bagger and then got two walks, a steal, a strikeout and an infield out.

Rather startling is the slump of Charley Keller, who tore through the training season like a batting tycoon, but in three league battles has fathered one measly single in a dozen tries.

MAY 15,1941...JOE DiMAGGIO BEGAN THE *LONGEST HITTING STREAK* IN THE HISTORY OF BASEBALL ...56 STRAIGHT GAMES WITH A SINGLE AGAINST EDSMITH... CHICAGO...

STOPPED BY AL SMITH & JIM BAGBY CLEVELAND... 2 MONTHS 2 DAYS LATER

Jo Hochmann

Joe's Homer in 4th Keeps 3 Bomber Streaks Intact

McCarthy's Hopefuls at Top For First Time in Two Months

By DANIEL.

For the first time in exactly two months, the Yankees today were in first place in the American League race. Beating the Browns again, 7 to 5, while the Indians were dropping a second decision to the Red Sox, the Bombers moved up with .603, as against .597 for the Tribe. In the games won column Cleveland had the edge over New York, 40 to 38. But in the losing side of the ledger the Yankees were a pair to the good, 25 to 27.

It was on April 25, when Tiny Bonham shut out the Senators, 6 to 0, that the Bombers first visited the top of the 1941 standing. The next afternoon Red Ruffing got an 8-to-3 decision over Washington, and the Yanks remained in the lead. But two defeats followed, and the McCarthy Clouting Circus became the pursuer.

The surge back into the pace-making position was accomplished with 13 out of 16, capped by three in a row after a recent winning streak of eight straight. While all this was going on, the Indians were losing seven out of 16. In fact, Bob Feller & Co. have dropped seven out of 11.

For the past fortnight baseball fans have been having a lot of fun discussing a new form of an old question: "If you were managing the Yankees or the Indians, would you choose Joe Di Maggio in preference to Bob Feller, or would you take the pitcher?"

The situation today appeared to make a preference for Di Maggio rather emphatic. That the Bombers once again were on top was due in large measure to the day-after-day leadership and unwavering power and skill of the center fielder.

The battle yesterday furnished striking testimony of the tremendous value of Giuseppe the Jolter.

The two-run winning margin of the Bombers was furnished by Di Maggio's 16th homer, which came off Dinty Galehouse in the fourth inning, with Tommy Henrich on base.

The Yankees needed a homer to keep their circuit spree going and Giuseppe was the man who stretched that incredible record to 34 jackpotters in 20 consecutive games.

That four-bagger was the only hit made by Di Maggio in four trips to the plate. It sent his batting streak into its 37th straight contest, only four behind the American League mark established by George Sisler in 1922.

Ordinarily a socking saturnalia such as the one the Bombers have been enjoying since June 1 would earn flamboyant notice. But the customers have come to take those daily homers for granted. Now the spotlight is trained on Di Maggio, whose unbroken skein has intrigued the fans more than they have been thrilled by any individual feat here since Babe Ruth bettered the home run record with 60 in 1927.

Di Maggio Now Contender For All Three Titles.

With his poke into the left field stands, Di Maggio passed Rudy York in the struggle for the home run championship of the American League. Joe took that title in 1937, with 46, and is confident he can do it again. York has slumped badly in the last month and those who predicted Rudy would lag behind without Hank Greenberg as a bellwether believe they had the correct dope.

With 53 runs driven in, Giuseppe found himself in the thick of still another title struggle. Both York and Charley Keller were a bit in front of Joe in that race. But the way Di Mag has been going nothing lies beyond his powers.

In fact, Joe is quite likely to make vigorous gestures in the direction of the batting championship, too. Just now Ted Williams does not seem to be within hailing distance. But Giuseppe looked beaten at this stage of the 1940 race and even on a bogged-down club, eventually came through for his second straight title with .352. It will take closer to his 1939 average of .381 to win this one. But Jolting Joseph from Fisherman's Wharf can do it.

For his streak of 37 straight games, Di Maggio's record is 56 hits in 146 times at bat, for a healthy .384.

Joe McCarthy is of the opinion that Di Maggio's anxiety over his spree is not helping his general average. However, the manager is quite satisfied with his star's contributions, and is pulling as hard as Tim Sullivan, the bat boy, to see Di Mag pass the Sisler record, and go after Willie Keeler's 44.

The home stay of the Yanks will be broken into tomorrow when they go to Philadelphia. Two days there, Sunday's double-header in Washington, and then they will return for a Tuesday bargain bill in the Stadium with Boston.

A happy Joe DiMaggio.

GEORGE SISLER.

When he singled to center in the first inning of the Yankees-Athletics game in Philadelphia yesterday, Joe Di Maggio was close on the heels of two great records. He had hit safely in 39 consecutive games and was gunning for the American League mark of 41 set by George Sisler and the all-time major league record of 44 made by Wee Willie Keeler. In these 39 games, Di Maggio has made 59 hits.

Sisler's record was made in 1922 and during that run the St. Louis first sacker hammered out 78 hits. He was finally stopped by Bullet Joe Bush of the Yankees. Sisler finished that season with a batting average of .420.

Before that American League mark was made the record was held by Ty Cobb, who batted safely in 40 games in a row during the season of 1911. Cobb made 77 hits during his streak, and finally was stopped by Ed Walsh of the White Sox and his famous spitball.

Keeler's record of 44 games in which he hit safely was made in 1897 when he was with the Baltimore Orioles of the old National League. He poked out 82 hits during his streak.

Another great consecutive hitting record was made by Bill Dahlen of the Chicago Cubs in 1894. He ran his string to 42, was stopped one day, then went 28 more games without failing to get a hit. This gave him a remarkable mark of hitting safely in 70 out of 71 games.

It must be said, however, that both Keeler and Dahlen had an easier time of it than present-day batters because when they made their records the foul-strike rule was not in vogue.

Fans Come from Miles Around to See DiMaggio Make History

Washington, D. C., June 29 [Special].—Outside the dressing room door, hundreds of fans howled for Joe DiMaggio. Inside, the record breaking Yankee outfielder grinned thru the streams of perspiration that poured from his black hair, down his face. Teammates slapped him on the back and yelled congratulations as they hurried thru their showers and dressing to catch the train back home.

What did DiMaggio say? How did he feel? "What can I say? How would you feel? Great. Tickled silly. Terrific. Anything you want," he answered.

Joe tugged off his socks, grabbed a towel and headed for the hissing showers. "Don't forget one thing," he yelled back. "I was up there a lot of times when Joe McCarthy could have given me the take sign. He didn't tho. He let me hit whenever I wanted to. Don't ever think that didn't help."

Joe Gets a Reception.

Fans came from New York, Philadelphia, Baltimore, and points south and west to watch DiMaggio crack George Sisler's 19 year old consecutive games batting record of 41 straight by hitting safely in both games of today's double header. Spectators were lined up outside the park when Joe arrived before the game.

When he stepped onto the field, they swarmed from the stands, pulling and tugging at him, pleading for autographs. All thru batting practice, kids and oldsters alike were hopping from their seats and flocking around the batting cage. After the game they were still waiting for him. He had to struggle thru the crowd.

It was no soft touch for the slugger. Dutch Leonard has always been a tough nut for him, and the Yanks. And Dutch had his stuff. Umpire Johnny Quinn, who called balls and strikes, said, "Dutch had as much stuff as I've ever seen him have. He was pitching out of a background of white shirts, too. That pitch he made to Dimag in the sixth was a perfect one. But Dimag hit."

Hit a Low, Fast One.

"The pitch was a fast ball, low and over the outside corner," Joe said. "It looked good to me, so I swung at it." Leonard explained: "I was behind him most of the time, so I couldn't throw knucklers. If that fast ball had gotten by him I could have tossed him one. That's what I was trying to set him up for."

The pitch Joe hit in the seventh inning of the second game off Walt Masterson to break the record was an ordinary fast ball, waist high, and a little to the outside of the plate. "I was trying for the outside corner and maybe I made it too good," Masterson said. "I wouldn't have minded except that if I had gotten him out, the score would still have been tied."

In six of the 42 games DiMaggio failed to make a hit until the last time at bat.

It is the seventh inning of the second game of a double-header with the Washington Senators in 1941, and Joe DiMaggio lines a single to center to set a new American League record by hitting safely in 42 consecutive games. The Washington catcher is Jake Early.

Di Maggio Set Record On Pledge to Dying Boy

By the Associated Press.

PHILADELPHIA, July 1.—Only Joe Di Maggio and a few of his fellow Yankee players knew when he stepped up to the plate in Washington's egg-frying heat he had a special and particular reason for wanting to hit safely in both ends of the double-header.

Other than breaking George Sisler's 19-year-old record of hitting safely in 41 consecutive games he had made a promise to wan, wasted 10-year-old Tony Norella—a million-to-one chance that the joy of his feat would give a few more hours, a few more days of life to the doomed Carbondale (Pa.) youngster.

Tony followed the Yanks devotedly despite his suffering from an incurable spleen disease. His physician got Joe to visit the lad last Saturday and Tony's dark eyes shone in sheer ecstasy.

Said Joe on departing:

"You be listening in on your radio tomorrow, Tony, and hear me break that hitting record for you. That's a promise, kid."

Little Tony Norella died before the umpire announced the batteries Sunday, but he never doubted his friend Joe would be a man of his word.

And down in Washington, Di Maggio redeemed his pledge without knowing there'd be no Tony at the radio.

DiMaggio Aims To Set Record That'll Stand

McCarthy Sees Joe Going on Indefinitely

Already ranked among the greatest hitters in baseball annals, Joe Di Maggio resolved today to stretch his consecutive game clouting streak so far that it will stand even longer than the 19-year-old record he just shattered, says the Associated Press.

Joe connected in his 41st and 42nd straight contests to equal and surpass George Sisler's 1922 mark while the league-leading Yankees were taking a double-header from the Senators in Washington yesterday.

"Here's where the big test comes," Di Maggio said after receiving the congratulations of his Yankee teammates in the clubhouse. "It's going to be even tougher from now on, but I'd sure like to make it last a while."

"How about making it 50, Joe?" Catcher Bill Dickey yelled.

"Fifty nothing," Manager Joe McCarthy retorted. "Joe's liable to stretch it indefinitely."

Di Maggio, jubilant over a feat he's been aiming at ever since he entered the majors, said the "big test" meant that every pitcher in the league would be "trying double" to stop the streak.

"It's that way after setting a record in every sport," he said. "Everybody tries to beat the guy who set it."

Joe admitted he thought for a time he wasn't going to make the grade in the first game yesterday. He sent a booming fly to the outfield and popped weakly to third before lashing out a double in the sixth. His record-setting smash, a single, came in the seventh frame of the nightcap after he had sent two flies to the outfield and hoisted to short in his first three appearances.

JOE DI MAG BAGS 'PLAYER OF MONTH' TAG ALONG WITH HITTING STREAK MARK

19-Year-Old Record of Sisler

Falls Before Relentless Drive

Of Yankees' Great Outfielder

Starting May 15, Coast Italian Hits in 41st and 42nd Games,

June 29, to Surpass Standard for Sustained Hitting;

Work Makes Him Standout for Month of Brides

By DANIEL M. DANIEL
Of the New York World-Telegram

FOR THE last few weeks there has been considerable public discussion of the question whether, given a chance to choose between Joe DiMaggio and Bob Feller, a major league manager would pick the outfielder or the pitcher. It seems to me that recent developments have furnished an ample answer. I have seen Feller pitch and he is the current No. 1. I also have seen this man DiMaggio in action day after day, in the vast majority of games in which he has competed since he joined the Yankees. And I would choose Giuseppe.

DiMaggio's great batting streak, which has beaten the modern record of 41 straight games set by George Sisler of the St. Louis Browns in their near-pennant season of 1922, merely calls attention to the superlatives of this young man from San Francisco. Most emphatically, he is THE SPORTING NEWS' "Player of the Month." Make it "Player of the Year." Yes, I know all about the recent achievements of Ted Williams, who threatens to remain up there right through the campaign.

DiMaggio started his batting spree on May 15, against the lefthanded Edgar Smith of the White Sox. He got one hit that afternoon. On May 14, Joe had been shut out by Mel Harder, the most difficult pitcher in the league for him. Harder has had Joe's number ever since the outfielder came to the Yanks in 1936.

However, DiMaggio ran into Mel again during the streak in the nightcap of a double-header on June 1, and hurdled the eighteenth successive game. It was touch-and-go in the finale that afternoon, but Di-Mag went, banging a hit through Ken Keltner.

At times in that streak, DiMaggio cut it much too fine to suit the customers. On six occasions he did no get his hit until his last time at bat. The most dramatic of these came June 26, against Elden Auker of the Browns. Auker set out to stop Di-Maggio and in Joe's first three efforts he certainly was stopped.

Chance for Gift Hit. Not Awarded.

In the second inning, DiMaggio flied out to Roy Cullenbine. In the fourth, Joe crashed a hot grounder right at Johnny Berardino, who booted it. The scorer could have made it a hit, but the scorer was going to let Joe make his own hits, the way Joe wanted to make them. So the error sign was hung up. In his third effort, DiMag grounded out to Harlond Clift.

Came the eighth inning, with the Yankees and the crowd—and the press box, too—all excited. Would he be stopped?

DiMaggio was the fourth man on the list before Auker. The underhanded slinger was determined not to be forced to face Joe again. But he was too anxious. Johnny Sturm was retired and Red Rolfe wangled a pass on four bad ones.

Now came Tom Henrich. Joe McCarthy wasn't going to risk a double-play, so he ordered Thomas to bunt. This was done, and DiMaggio came up with a runner on second and two out. Joe swung on the first pitch and lined it viciously into left for a double. Game No. 38.

You should have heard the roar of that crowd! You should have witnessed the scene in front of the Yankee dugout! It was more exciting even than Babe Ruth's sixtieth home run when he set the all-time record in 1927.

Joe put the clincher on the record in the double-header in Washington, June 29, doubling in the first game to tie Sisler's modern mark and moving his own record to 42 with a clean single in the second tilt.

DiMaggio's batting streak certainly captured the fans and fired their imaginations. Joe always is skillful and colorful. Dramatize a player like that with a streak like his and you have the superb, turnstile-clicking, electrifying situation.

The day DiMaggio hit Auker belatedly, Marius Russo was pitching a one-hitter.

Congratulations by Sisler

Among those following Joe Di-Maggio's hitting streak with the keenest interest was George Sisler, who set the previous mark by connecting safely in 41 consecutive games while with the Browns, 19 years ago.

Upon learning that DiMaggio had set a new record by hitting in his forty-second straight game, Sisler, now a sporting goods dealer in St. Louis, promptly wired the Yankee slugger: "Congratulations. I'm glad a real hitter broke it. Keep going."

Tom Henrich's home run had stretched the club's circuit spree to 35 in 21 straight games—a feat undreamed of even in the Ruth and Gehrig heyday. But the crowd virtually ignored the Russo feat, and took the Henrich homer for granted. The hero was DiMaggio.

Batting streaks always have intrigued the customers. They first became conscious of such feats in 1894, when Bill Dahlen, shortstop with the Chicago Nationals, hung up a record of 42 straight games.

This was not touched until 1897, when Wee Willie Keeler—the master scientist who hit them where they weren't—established the present major league record of 44 games.

From July 27 through September 17, 1922, Sisler made the American League mark of 41 games. That same year, Rogers Hornsby, then with the Cardinals, turned in the best streak of the National League, 33 games.

Until DiMaggio came along this season, Hornsby's record was tops for a right-handed hitter.

Hit in 61 Straight With Seals

Batting streaks are old business with DiMaggio. When he was with San Francisco in the Pacific Coast League, in 1933, only 18 years old. Giuseppe established a loop mark by hitting in no fewer than 61 consecutive games, from the second contest of May 28 through the game of July 25.

"I never will forget the day I was stopped," DiMaggio told me. "It was against Oakland and Ed Walsh, Jr., was pitching. He sure stopped me. But I got my revenge. In the ninth inning I drove out a long fly which won the battle for us."

Until DiMaggio set out on his 1941 spree, the Yankee club record for a batting streak was 29. Roger Peckinpaugh, then shortstop for the New York club, set the mark in 1919. Earle Combs matched it in 1931, Lloyd Brown, Washington southpaw, stopping him.

The streak of all streaks in Organized Ball stands to the credit of Joe Wilhoit, who hit in 69 straight games in the old Western League.

Wilhoit made his record in 1919, playing with the Wichita team. He started the streak June 14 and carried on continuously

Yankee Bomber Ready for Takeoff   Signs Don't Bother Him

until August 20. During that period, Wilhoit, an outfielder, averaged .505. On the strength of his remarkable hitting, the Red Sox bought him, but he did not stick. He previously was with the Braves, Giants and Pirates.

For details of the DiMaggio streak, for the game-by-game story of his remarkable skein, I refer you to the accompanying table. So much for Joe and his socking string.

In my book, Joe is the greatest player now in the major leagues. He has a grand chance to win the homer and runs-batted-in championships, and though Ted Williams is far in front of him in the averages, it would not surprise me if Giuseppe took the American League batting title for the third straight year.

DiMaggio is a big fellow. He is powerful, with amazing wrists. His batting style, as analyzed in the American League motion picture this year, is sui generis. He strides not at all. His feet are about 16 inches apart and as he drives into the ball, there is no step. Just sheer power from the wrists and arms.

In the field, his virtuosity is not generally appreciated. That is because he makes the tough ones look so soft. He has an easy, loping stride, and he does everything out there with the classic touch of grace.

That arm of Joe's is deadly, too. Last season the wing hurt, and he dropped to an incredible low of only five assists. But this year he already has made eight, and the whip is as strong as ever. They don't dare run on Giuseppe.

This man is the fans' player, the players' player, the managers' player. And the player of the press box, as well. Lucky the New York club, which can keep getting these superlative players in a dramatic sequence. Imagine Hal Chase, Babe Ruth, Lou Gehrig, Bill Dickey and Joe DiMaggio, all in the uniform of the Yankees down through the years. Most clubs would be content with just one of those star performers.

Off the field, DiMaggio is well groomed. He goes for dark suits, dark ties. His hair is slicked down. He is affable, easy of approach, with a keen sense of humor. On the field, he rarely smiles. Off the diamond, he is playing jokes. He is closer to Lefty Gomez than any other player on the club. That may be due, in part, to the fact that Mrs. Gomez, who was June O'Dea of the musical comedy stage, and the DiMaggio bride, who was Dorothy Arnold of the movies, are pals. Before DiMaggio was married, his constant companion was John Schulte, the coach. John was delegated, it seems, to be the DiMaggio bodyguard by Joe McCarthy.

DiMaggio last season appeared to have hit his peak. Now it is apparent that this son of an Italian fisherman has yet to achieve his zenith as a ball player.

Most emphatically, the Player of the Month!

Sisler Outbatted DiMaggio in String

GEORGE SISLER'S American League record of hitting safely in 41 games went by the boards, June 29, when Joe DiMaggio ran his string to 42 in the second game of a double-header, after tying the mark in the opening contest. On July 1, DiMaggio hit safely in both games of a twin-bill, tying Willie Keeler's major league record of 44.

While the St. Louis Browns' former first baseman did not have a home run during his run from July 27 to September 17, 1922, Sisler had a much better batting average than the new modern-day title-holder, hitting .454 against .377 for DiMaggio, since the latter started his string on May 15.

Figures comparing the performances of the two consecutive-game leaders during their batting streaks follow:

DIMAGGIO'S CONSECUTIVE GAME RECORD	AB.	H.	2B.	3B.	HR.	SISLER'S CONSECUTIVE GAME RECORD—1922	AB.	H.	2B.	3B.	HR.
May 15—Chicago	4	1	0	0	0	July 27—New York	5	1	1	0	0
May 16—Chicago	4	2	0	1	1	July 28—New York	3	1	0	0	0
May 17—Chicago	3	1	0	0	0	July 29—Boston	2	1	0	0	0
May 18—St. Louis	3	3	1	0	0	Aug. 5—Philadelphia	4	2	0	1	0
May 19—St. Louis	3	1	1	0	0	Aug. 6—Washington	4	3	0	0	0
May 20—St. Louis	5	1	0	0	0	Aug. 7—Washington	3	2	0	0	0
May 21—Detroit	5	2	0	0	0	Aug. 8—Washington	4	2	1	0	0
May 22—Detroit	4	1	0	0	0	Aug. 9—Washington	5	1	0	0	0
May 23—Boston	5	1	0	0	0	Aug. 12—Chicago	4	3	2	0	0
May 24—Boston	4	1	0	0	0	Aug. 13—Chicago	4	1	1	0	0
May 25—Boston	4	1	0	0	0	Aug. 15—Washington	4	3	1	0	0
May 27—Washington	5	4	0	0	1	Aug. 15—Washington	5	2	0	1	0
May 28—Washington	4	1	0	1	0	Aug. 16—Washington	4	1	0	0	0
May 29—Washington	3	1	0	0	0	Aug. 16—Washington	5	1	0	0	0
May 30—Boston	2	1	0	0	0	Aug. 17—Washington	5	1	0	0	0
May 30—Boston	3	1	1	0	0	Aug. 18—Philadelphia	5	1	0	0	0
June 1—Cleveland	4	1	0	0	0	Aug. 19—Philadelphia	4	3	0	1	0
June 1—Cleveland	4	1	0	0	0	Aug. 19—Philadelphia	3	1	0	0	0
June 2—Cleveland	4	2	1	0	0	Aug. 21—Philadelphia	5	2	0	0	0
June 3—Detroit	4	1	0	0	1	Aug. 22—Boston	5	3	0	0	0
June 5—Detroit	5	1	0	0	0	Aug. 23—Boston	4	3	1	0	0
June 7—St. Louis	5	3	0	0	0	Aug. 24—Boston	6	4	1	0	0
June 8—St. Louis	4	2	0	0	2	Aug. 25—New York	3	2	0	0	0
June 8—St. Louis	4	2	1	0	0	Aug. 25—New York	5	1	0	0	0
June 10—Chicago	5	1	0	0	0	Aug. 26—New York	4	1	0	0	0
June 12—Chicago	4	2	0	0	1	Aug. 28—New York	5	1	0	0	0
June 14—Cleveland	2	1	1	0	0	Aug. 29—Cleveland	4	1	0	0	0
June 15—Cleveland	3	1	0	0	1	Aug. 30—Cleveland	4	3	0	1	0
June 16—Cleveland	5	1	0	0	0	Aug. 31—St. Louis	5	3	2	0	0
June 17—Chicago	4	1	0	0	0	Sept. 1—Detroit	4	2	0	0	0
June 18—Chicago	3	1	0	0	0	Sept. 2—Detroit	4	2	0	0	0
June 19—Chicago	3	3	0	0	1	Sept. 3—Detroit	5	1	0	0	0
June 20—Detroit	5	4	0	0	0	Sept. 4—Cleveland	4	4	2	1	0
June 21—Detroit	4	1	0	0	0	Sept. 4—Cleveland	3	3	1	0	0
June 22—Detroit	5	2	1	0	1	Sept. 5—Cleveland	4	2	0	0	0
June 24—St. Louis	4	1	0	0	0	Sept. 6—Cleveland	5	2	0	0	0
June 25—St. Louis	4	1	0	0	1	Sept. 8—Detroit	3	2	0	0	0
June 26—St. Louis	4	1	1	0	0	Sept. 9—Detroit	5	3	0	1	0
June 27—Philadelphia	3	2	0	0	1	Sept. 11—Detroit	5	2	0	1	0
June 28—Philadelphia	5	2	1	0	0	Sept. 16—New York	4	1	1	0	0
June 29—Washington	4	1	1	0	0	Sept. 17—New York	3	1	0	0	0
June 29—Washington	5	1	0	0	0						
Totals	167	63	11	2	11	Totals	171	79	14	7	0
Average for string .377.						Average for string .454.					

Joe in Jovial Mood

DiMaggio Ties Record as Yanks Take Two Before 52,832

YANKEE STAR HITS 44TH GAME IN ROW

DiMaggio Bats Safely in Two Contests to Equal Keeler's All-Time Major Mark

RED SOX ROUTED, 7-2, 9-2

New Yorkers Add to Lead, but Their Record Homer Streak Ends After 25 Games

By ARTHUR DALEY

The greatest of the present-day ball players drew even with one of the legendary figures of the past yesterday when Joe DiMaggio equaled Wee Willie Keeler's all-time major league record of hitting safely in forty-four consecutive games.

A double-header at the Stadium with the Red Sox gave Jolting Joe the opportunity of overhauling the old Oriole batting artist. And a vast crowd of 52,832, a record for the Stadium this season, wheeled through the turnstiles to see him do it.

This was the Great Man's personal show. No one seemed to care who won the games. The spectators merely wanted to see DiMaggio hit.

Ovation Greets Solid Hit

Twice in the first fray he went out while a pall settled over the stands. In the third trip he scratched a hit that half in the crowd suspected was an error. So when he lined a ringing single to left in his next try roars of delight filled the humid air.

With those hits DiMaggio boosted his modern mark to forty-three straight games. But could he equal Keeler's record of 1897? That was the question uppermost in every one's mind during the intermission.

The crowd did not have long to wait. On his first trip Jolting Joe

YANKEE SLUGGER CONNECTING TO EQUAL 44-YEAR-OLD MARK

Joe DiMaggio driving a single to center field in the first inning of the nightcap at the Stadium yesterday. The blow ran his consecutive hitting streak to 44, tying Willie Keeler's record, made in 1897. Johnny Peacock is the Red Sox catcher and Joe Rue the umpire.

lined a screaming single to center. He had done it.

Oh, yes. The double-header. The Yankees won both ends with a tremendous display of batting power, cracking out twenty-five hits for 7-to-2 and 9-to-2 victories. By way of lending emphasis to the Bomber clouting the second fray went only five innings before storm clouds and the resultant darkness and rain caused a cessation of play.

For all of the robust slamming of Boston pitchers, the Yankees failed to get a home run in the first game, although Bill Dickey blasted for the circuit in the second one. So the New York record of hitting homers in successive games was halted at 25 contests, in which 40 were hit. Since the old figures, set by the Tigers last

year, were 26 four-masters in 17 games, the McCarthymen didn't do a bad job.

Red Sox Appear Lethargic

The Sox looked feeble all afternoon, a dull lethargic club that could not compare with the alert, dashing Yankees who, incidentally, dashed even farther ahead of the second-place Indians, whom they now lead by two and a half games. The issue was not in doubt long. In the opener five straight hits in the fourth drove Mickey Harris to cover and the score mounted after that. Marius Russo pitched steadily and yielded only six hits in six innings before the heat forced him to retire. Spud Chandler gave only one the rest of the way.

Russo was weakening in the sixth. This was the inning when

DiMaggio hit a home run. Unfortunately, however, it was the wrong DiMaggio, Dom instead of Joe. A walk and two more singles drove in another tally, so Joe McCarthy played safe, retiring his left-hander by the pinch-hitter route.

The second game saw Tiny Bonham pitch four-hit ball. A single by Ted Williams and a home run by Manager Joe Cronin provided the Boston tallies, but these came in the fourth after the Yankees had the game tucked away.

They pounced on Jack Wilson in the first, when an error, singles by DiMaggio and Charlie Keller and a double by Dickey provided three tallies. Wilson went out in the third under a four-hit onslaught featured by Dickey's homer into the right field bleachers.

Bonham a Good Omen

It was odd that Bonham was pitching when DiMaggio equaled Keeler's record because the last time Tiny had started was May 15, the very day when Jolting Joe started his streak.

With Buddy Rosar still hobbling around on an injured ankle, Ken Silvestri caught his first game as a Yankee at the Stadium. And he made his first New York hit, a double while batting right-handed against Harris. Then he doubled again, batting left-handed against Mike Ryba.

Tommy Henrich visited some fans in the right-field stands in the sixth inning of the opener when he landed head-first in the box while making a gorgeous gloved-hand catch of Ryba's towering foul.

Nelson Potter, secured from the Athletics on waivers, reported to the Red Sox and promptly saw action as relief pitcher in the opener.

The Yanks are so much on their toes these days that Johnny Sturm raced from first to third on a bunt by Red Rolfe. The Sox neglected to cover the bag.

Lefty Grove, Red Sox veteran seeking his 299th victory, will oppose Lefty Gomez today.

Yanks' Homer Streak

Date. June - Player.	Pitcher.	Opposing Club.
1—Sturm	Harder, Cleveland	
1—Selkirk	Harder, Cleveland	
2—Henrich	Feller, Cleveland	
2—Henrich	Feller, Cleveland	
3—DiMaggio	Trout, Detroit	
5—Henrich	Newhouser, Detroit	
7—Keller	Muncrief, St. Louis	
8—DiMaggio	Auker, St. Louis	
8—DiMaggio	Auker, St. Louis	
8—Henrich	Auker, St. Louis	
8—Rolfe	Auker, St. Louis	
8—Keller	Bob Harris, St. Louis	
8—Gordon	Bob Harris, St. Louis	
8—DiMaggio	Kramer, St. Louis	
10—Crosetti	Rigney, Chicago	
10—Keller	Rigney, Chicago	
12—Gordon	Lee, Chicago	
12—DiMaggio	Lee, Chicago	
14—Henrich	Feller, Cleveland	
15—DiMaggio	Bagby, Cleveland	
16—Gordon	Milnar, Cleveland	
17—Keller	Rigney, Chicago	
18—Keller	Lee, Chicago	
19—Keller	Edgar Smith, Chicago	
19—DiMaggio	Ross, Chicago	
20—Henrich	Newsom, Detroit	
20—Keller	Newsom, Detroit	
21—Rizzuto	Trout, Detroit	
22—DiMaggio	Newhouser, Detroit	
22—Rolfe	Newsom, Detroit	
24—Rolfe	Muncrief, St. Louis	
24—Henrich	Muncrief, St. Louis	
24—Gordon	Muncrief, St. Louis	
25—DiMaggio	Galehouse, St. Louis	
26—Henrich	Auker, St. Louis	
27—DiMaggio	Dean, Philadelphia	
28—Keller	L. Harris, Philadel.	
29—Henrich	Carrasquel, Wash.	
29—Gordon	Hudson, Washington	
29—Keller	Hudson, Washington	

Manager Joe McCarthy congratulating DiMaggio in the clubhouse after the double-header.

Times Wide World

44-YEAR-OLD RECORD TIED

DiMaggio an Opposite of Keeler, Whose Mark He Equaled

Forty-four years passed between the forty-four-game batting streaks of Jolting Joe DiMaggio of the Yankees and Wee Willie Keeler of the Baltimore Orioles. In physical appearance they were marked contrasts—Keeler, 5 feet 4½ inches in height and 138 pounds in weight, who placed his hits; DiMaggio, 6 feet 2 inches tall and a solid 200 pounds, who powders the ball.

Keeler, a left-handed batter, was stopped by Frank Killen, a left-handed pitcher, on June 17, 1897. DiMaggio, a right-handed batter, has a chance to break the old record today.

Here is a comparison of the two forty-four-game hitting streaks:

	AB.	H.	2b.	3b.	HR.	P.C.
Keeler	201	82	11	10	0	.408
DiMaggio	174	66	12	3	12	.379

The box scores:

FIRST GAME

BOSTON (A.)	ab.r.h.po.a.e.	NEW YORK (A.)	ab.r.h.po.a.e.
D.DiMag.,cf	4 1 3 0 0 0	Sturm, 1b	4 0 2 12 0 0
Finney, 1b	3 1 0 5 2 0	Rolfe, 3b	5 2 2 2 2 0
Williams, lf	4 0 1 1 0 0	Henrich, rf	5 0 2 3 1 0
Cronin, ss	4 0 1 1 1 0	J.DiMag., cf	4 0 2 2 0 0
Spence, rf	4 0 1 4 1 0	Gordon, 2b	4 0 0 3 3 1
Tabor, 3b	4 0 1 2 2 1	Keller, lf	5 1 1 0 0 0
Doerr, 2b	4 0 1 0 0 0	Rizzuto, ss	4 1 3 2 7 0
Pytlak, c	2 0 1 7 1 0	Silvestri, c	2 2 2 5 1 0
Harris, p	1 0 0 0 0 0	Russo, p	2 1 1 0 3 0
Ryba, p	1 0 0 1 0 0	aSelkirk	1 0 0 0 0 0
bPeacock	1 0 0 0 0 0	Chandler, p	1 0 0 0 0 0
Potter, p	0 0 0 1 0 0		
		Total	37 7 15 27 15 1
Total	33 2 7 24 8 1		

aBatted for Russo in sixth.
bBatted for Ryba in eighth.

Boston	0 0 0	0 0 2	0 0 0—2
New York	0 0 0	4 0 2	0 1 .—7

Runs batted in—Silvestri 2, Russo, Sturm, D. DiMaggio, Spence, Rolfe, J. DiMaggio, Gordon. Two-base hits—Silvestri 2, Russo. Three-base hit—Rizzuto. Home run—D. DiMaggio. Sacrifice—Gordon. Double play—Spence and Pytlak. Left on bases—New York 11, Boston 5. Bases on balls—Off Harris 1, Russo 1, Ryba 1, Potter 2. Struck out—By Russo 4, Ryba 5, Chandler 1. Hits —Off Harris 8 in 3 1-3 innings, Ryba 6 in 3 2-3, Potter 1 in 1, Russo 6 in 6, Chandler 1 in 3. Wild pitch—Potter. Winning pitcher—Russo. Losing pitcher—Harris. Umpires—Summers, Rue, Rommeli and Stewart. Time of game—2:32.

SECOND GAME

BOSTON (A.)	ab.r.h.po.a.e.	NEW YORK (A.)	ab.r.h.po.a.e.
D.DiMag.,cf	2 0 0 1 0 0	Sturm, 1b	3 1 0 5 1 0
Finney, 1b	2 0 1 7 1 1	Rolfe, 3b	3 2 2 0 2 0
Williams, lf	2 1 1 1 0 2	Henrich, rf	3 0 0 0 0 0
Cronin, ss	2 1 2 0 4 0	J.DiMag., cf	3 1 1 2 0 0
Spence, rf	2 0 0 0 0 0	Keller, lf	3 2 3 1 0 0
Tabor, 3b	2 0 0 0 1 1	Dickey, c	2 1 2 4 0 0
Doerr, 2b	2 0 0 1 0 0	Gordon, 2b	3 1 1 2 1 0
Peacock, c	2 0 0 4 0 0	Rizzuto, ss	3 0 1 1 1 0
J.Wilson, p	1 0 0 1 1 0	Bonham, p	3 0 0 0 1 0
Dobson, p	1 0 0 0 0 0		
		Total	26 9 10 15 6 0
Total	18 2 4 15 7 3		

*Game called at end of fifth, rain and darkness.

Boston	0 0 0	2 0—2
New York	3 0 4	2 0—9

Runs batted in—Keller 2, Dickey 3, Rizzuto, Cronin 2, Henrich, J. DiMaggio. Two-base hits—Keller, Dickey, Rolfe. Home runs—Dickey, Cronin. Double play—Sturm and Rizzuto. Left on bases—New York 4, Boston 1. Struck out—By Bonham 3, Wilson 2, Dobson 1. Hits—Off Wilson 7 in 2 2-3 innings, Dobson 3 in 2 1-3. Wild pitch—Dobson. Losing pitcher—Wilson. Umpires—Rue, Rommel, Stewart and Summers. Time of game—1:05. Attendance—52,832.

DiMaggio's Record-Tying Hit Acclaimed by Stadium Throng

By Everett B. Morris

THE Yankee home-run hitting steark, twenty-five games and forty homers long, was terminated by the Red Sox in the first half of yesterday's double-header at Yankee Stadium, but the assembled multitude did not go into mourning. It was too busy and too happy celebrating the exploits of Joe DiMaggio to cry over the failure of their hero, or one of his mates, to belt the ball out of the park.

It was obvious that the customers were only mildly interested in the Yankees' efforts to dispose of the Bostonese as challengers to their eminence in the American League, anly only slightly more so in the team's desire to improve upon its sluggin record.

That vast mob, packed in steamy, perspiring proximity to a field covered with a blueish heat haze, had come to cheer DiMaggio and lend moral support to his spectacular quest for an all-time consecutive game-hitting record. The great Di-Mag, idol of those packer center field bleachers, where the sun beat unmercifully on his worshipers, began the day with a modern record of forty-two straight games in which he had made at least one hit.

All-Time Record Tied

Before the second game was an inning old DiMaggio had equaled the all-time high of forty-four games, established long before he was born by a little fellow named Willie Keeler, whose motto was "hit 'em where they ain't."

DiMaggio has been hitting them "where they ain't" since May 15. His blows in the fifth and sixth innings of the first game brought his total up to sixty-five, and when he tied Keeler's mark by lining a single off Jack Wilson in the first inning of the second contest, the flood of hits reached the sixty-sixth notch on the counter.

Every time DiMaggio walked up to the plate with that club in his hand the crowd applauded. It murmured its disappointment when he hoisted a harmless foul fly to Lou Finney the first time up with two men on base, and it yelped expectantly when he smacked a hard one at Jim Tabor in the third. But Tabor made a good stop and throw and Joe was out.

Joe had no part in the Yankee up-

rising in the fourth which disposed of Mickey Harris as a pitcher, but he had fun from there on. Facing the ancient Mike Ryba, the relief flinger who works almost every day for Boston, DiMaggio carried the count to three and two and then splashed a high bounder toward third. Tabor had to make a quick throw, but he made a bad one, too; so bad that before the ball was retrieved DiMaggio was on second.

Writers Look to Scorer

In the press box every one craned his head toward Dan Daniel, the official scorer. He smiled a little and held up one finger, indicating that in his judgment—which is final—DiMaggio had made a hit. The crowd had no way of knowing the scorer's decision on a play which might have been scored an error for Tabor because the public address system in the stadium is used only for announcing battery changes and pinch hitters and there is no hit or error signal on the scoreboard.

Hence there was no great jubilation over this vital hit. But joy knew no bounds when, in the next inning, DiMaggio rifled a screaming single to left field with two on base. The cheers were deafening and continuous and they broke out again when the grinning centerfielder trotted out to his post at the end of the inning. Somehow—and it seemed incredible that it could do so—the throng outdid itself in vocal demonstrativeness when DiMaggio smacked his record-equaling hit off Wilson in the second game.

One more game and one more hit and DiMaggio, already a modern immortal by reason of surpassing George Sisler's mark of forty-one straight hitting games, will move past the ghost of Wee Willie Keeler to the throne as the king of consistent hitters.

By Joe Williams

Di Maggio Goes
Ahead of Feller
As Turnstile Lure

The Ruthian days are gone, but the potent mace is still the most vibrant turnstile tonic in baseball.

Late last winter Will Harridge, president of the American League, who keeps precise tabs on such things in his office, told us Bob Feller, the Cleveland fireball pitcher, was the only individual box-office attraction left in the game.

"Whenever he appears the attendance goes up," revealed Mr. Harridge. "That isn't true of any other individual in the game. It hasn't been true of anybody since Ruth's time."

Obviously these comments were made before Joe Di Maggio started his spectacular streak. For the time being at least the $37,500 outfielder is the outstanding draw in baseball. The Yankees drew 220,860 paid admissions for the 12 games of their last home stay. The turnouts ranged from 8692 to 44,000. There was an epochal Monday crowd of 12,552. Feller was part of the lure for the 44,000 attendance—but the very next day with Feller in the dugout the attendance was 43,000. By that time Di Maggio was in the middle of his streak. It has been the same on the road. No crowd, even on weekdays, has dipped below 8000. The sensational hitter will always be more important at the gate than the best pitcher, because he's in the game every day. You get to see the Fellers only once in four days.

* * *

Di Maggio Must Have Color.

We were traveling with the ball clubs when George Sisler made the record which Di Maggio bettered. It excited no such widespread interest or excitement. Sisler wasn't a very colorful player; he was brilliant without being electrifying. Di Maggio isn't supposed to have much color, either. But perhaps he has more of this hard-to-identify quality than is generally suspected. There must be some reason why his streak, noteworthy as a consistent performance but otherwise scarcely world-rocking, struck such a responsive cord. The Yankee background, with its rich hitting tradition, may have had something to do with it. Because of these traditions a Yankee hitter seems to stand out more conspicuously than any other hitter. It may not make sense, but the supporting evidence isn't negligible. As we've pointed out before, there is the case of Ted Williams who has been hitting over .400 for a month—a truly remarkable performance for consistency, yet unless you happened to be reading the Boston papers you'd hardly know he was in the league. Certainly the Di Maggio streak almost completely submerged him, and we haven't heard that the customers were tearing down fences to see him hit .400.

Ty Cobb says there is no telling how great Di Maggio could be if he took the dreary matter of condition—off-season condition—more seriously. Di Maggio is no good-time Charley, but he isn't enthusiastic about working on condition during the winter months. He prefers a pleasant sedentary life to long hours on the road and in the hunting fields. This is the first season he's been in every game going into July. He engaged in one of his usual salary debates last winter, and the front office told him sharply to get in shape so he could play a full year and then talk contract. This is a sensitive point with Di Maggio. He insists he is never far out of condition, even in the winter, and that a series of circumstances over which he had no control kept him out of the lineup. Which is more or less true. Just the same Di Maggio hasn't the Cobb or the Hornsby intensity about condition, about working to build up leg strength and energy, about taking the long-range point of view as to his future. It may be that he doesn't need to, having so many natural gifts. It does not seem an exaggeration, however, to suggest he is doing pretty fair in his own way. Whether he could do better is something else.

* * *

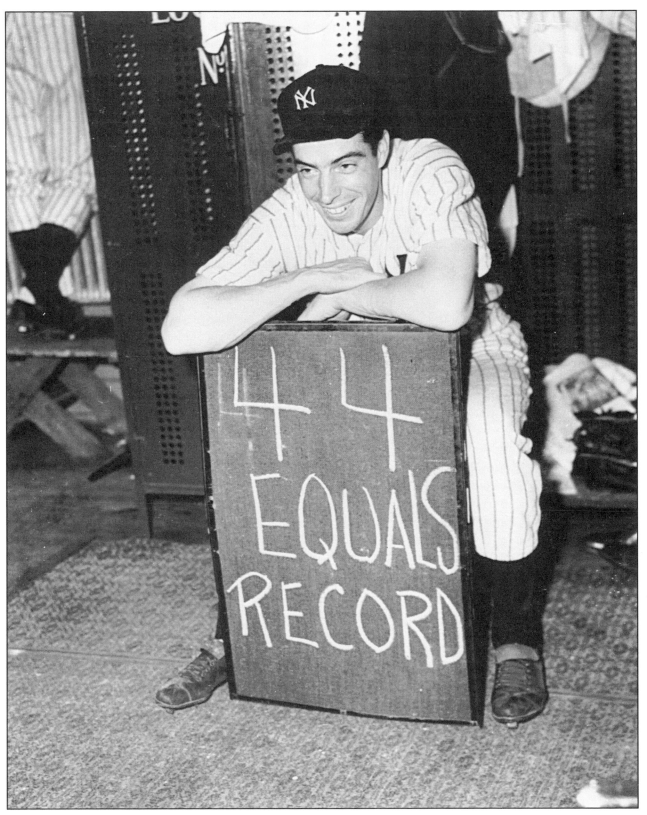

A happy Joe DiMaggio makes the record books, hitting safely in 44 consecutive games.

9th ANNUAL ALL-STAR GAME

Official SOUVENIR Program 25c

AMERICAN LEAGUE vs NATIONAL LEAGUE
JULY 8th 1941 — AT DETROIT

Briggs Stadium

HOME OF THE AMERICAN LEAGUE CHAMPIONS

JAMES EMORY FOXX, chosen in seven All-Star contests, has a batting average in six of .333. He is a dangerous long distance hitter and holds numerous batting records. Was selected as the most valuable player in the American League on three occasions.

JOSEPH DI MAGGIO is adding new honors to a career that has had more than its quota. One of the greatest players in the Game's history. On July 2 of this year he set a new all-time Major League record by hitting safely in 45 consecutive games.

CECIL H. TRAVIS, veteran Washington infielder, is among the ten leading 1941 batsmen in the American League. He is also a versatile defensive player. In 1940 he was also in the distinguished class, with an average of .322.

AMERICAN LEAGUE STARS

THEODORE TED F. WILLIAMS, rangy Red Sox outfielder is currently leading the American League with an average of better than .400. In 1940 he was also among the top-notchers and hit better than .300 in 1939, his first year in the Majors. Only twenty-two, he is unquestionably one of the American League's greatest performers.

ROBERT P. DOERR, since Charlie Gehringer's decline considered by many to be the League's leading second baseman. He came to the Red Sox from the Pacific Coast League in 1937 and is a finished performer in the infield, as well as a capable batsman.

JOHN GEOFFREY HEATH, one of the more important reasons why the Cleveland Indians have been setting the pace. Near the top of the A. L. batting list, Heath is also a capable defensive player. He joined the club in 1936 for a brief stay, was with Milwaukee for a while and rejoined the Indians late in 1937.

CHARLES E. KELLER, another graduate from the Yankee Newark farm, has been with the New York club since 1939. He is a university graduate who led the International League in batting in 1937. He hit for .286 in 1940 and is a leader this year in home runs and runs batted in.

ROY CULLEN-BINE, former Tiger, who after having been declared a free agent, signed with Brooklyn, for a $25,000 bonus, in 1940. Traded soon after to the St. Louis Browns, Roy failed to show much more than he did at Brooklyn. However, this year he has been hitting with the top-notchers and fielding acceptably.

DOMINIC DI MAGGIO, brother of Joe, is a star in his own right, being able to hit, field and throw with unerring accuracy. Like Joe a product of the Pacific Coast League. Dominic joined the Red Sox in 1940 and finished the season with a batting average of .301.

American League Favored to Score Sixth All-Star Victory in Detroit Today

57,000 TO SEE WYATT START WITH FELLER

American Leaguers Marshal Heaviest Hitters, Headed by Williams, DiMaggio

APPLING, HURT, OFF TEAM

Baker Picks Leonard in His Place—Game With National Circuit to Benefit USO

By JOHN DREBINGER
Special to THE NEW YORK TIMES.

DETROIT, July 7—For the second time in nine months this industrial metropolis of the Midwest tonight found itself playing host to baseball's outstanding figures.

Tomorrow the Motor City, which last Fall provided the setting for part of the world series, will see the pick of the National and American League players clash in the ninth edition of the charity All-Star game. The battle at Briggs Stadium will be played this year for the benefit of the United Service Organizations, and with reasonable weather prevailing, a capacity crowd of 57,000 is expected to be on hand.

Although the American Leaguers, who will have their renowned Bob Feller on the mound for the first three innings, plus the record-wrecking Joe DiMaggio and the .405 hitting Ted Williams, have been installed favorites at 5 to 9, to score their sixth victory in the fixture, betting is reported light because of the uncertainty of the final make-up of the two battle-fronts.

Of course, this being strictly an American League city, the sympathies of the crowd tomorrow will be with the forces that Del Baker, Tiger pilot, will direct against the wily Bill McKechnie, head man of the world champions Reds.

SOME OF THE PLAYERS WHO WILL APPEAR IN ALL-STAR GAME

Red Ruffing, Joe Gordon, Bill Dickey, Charlie Keller and Joe DiMaggio of the Yankees

Weather Is Main Concern

As the fifty chosen diamond stars, Commissioner K. M. Landis, the two league presidents and their club owners converged on the city today, the chief concern of all seemed to be the weather. Showers fell intermittently all day, causing anxiety for the morrow.

Up to now the midsummer classic has fared miraculously well, as none of the eight preceding games ever suffered a postponement. Should there be one tomorrow, the conflict will be set for 10 o'clock, Eastern standard time, Wednesday morning. The starting time for tomorrow is 1:30 P. M. (2:30 New York time).

Forecasts tonight gave rise to some optimism. The weather man predicts it will be fair and warmer, and while some cloudiness will continue, he gave assurances no heavy rainfall is in prospect.

Following a meeting of the rival skippers with Commissioner Landis this afternoon, McKechnie and Baker announced their tentative starting line-ups, though each gave it reluctantly and with caution. Confronted with the difficult task of naming nine from a list of twenty-five of the best in his league, each manager seemed eager to guard his hand until the hour of play arrives.

American Shut Out in 1940

McKechnie said he would start Whitlow Wyatt, the Dodgers' ace right-hander, but whether he would continue with the startling tactics he employed in giving the National Leaguers a spectacular 4-to-0 shut-out last year was a matter he left to conjecture.

Last year McKechnie fired Bucky Walters, Paul Derringer, Wyatt, Larry French and Carl Hubbell at the vaunted American League power to record the first shut-out in All-Star history.

Indications tonight were that McKechnie would follow with Walters and then possibly Lon Warneke of the Cardinals and Derringer. The fact that two of his seven picked hurlers, Claude Passeau of the Cubs and Hubbell, had pitched complete league games Sunday served to scramble McKechnie's plans further.

Last-minute injuries added to the problems confronting the pilots. Luke Appling, clouting White Sox shortstop, went out of action with a damaged knee yesterday and was taken off the list. As the American Leaguers had named three other shortstops in their original selections, Baker decided to fill the vacancy with another pitcher, naming Dutch Leonard, knuckleball specialist of the Senators.

Harris Is in Line

Marius Russo is on the uncertain

Whitlow Wyatt of Brooklyn, National League starting pitcher.

Bob Feller of Cleveland, the American League's opening choice.

Times Wide World

list with a slightly pulled tendon, and should the Yankee left-hander be withdrawn tomorrow, Mickey Harris of the Red Sox will be named in his place.

The National Leaguers also had two uncertain starters. Arky Vaughan, Pirate shortstop, is suffering from a stone bruise, and Mickey Owen, Dodger catcher, is recovering from a cut over his left eye.

McKechnie announced Owen as his probable starting catcher, but report had it that this selection will be recalled when Leo Durocher, the Dodger manager and one of McKechnie's coaches, arrives tomorrow morning. Durocher is understood to be dead set against Owen's going behind the plate, in which case McKechnie probably will call on Harry Danning, the Giant backstop.

The National League infield will consist of Johnny Mize of the Cards, Lonnie Frey of the Reds, Eddie Miller of the Braves and Stanley Hack of the Cubs. Mel Ott of the Giants, the circuit's leading home-run clouter; Pete Reiser, the sensational Brooklyn rookie, and Bob Elliott of the Pirates will patrol the outer defenses.

Baker, while he quickly named

Feller as his starting hurler, seemed in a quandary when it came to naming the pitchers who will follow the Indian ace. He intimated, however, that he probably would follow with the White Sox left-hander Thornton Lee and then possibly Sid Hudson of the Senators should Russo be unavailable.

Under the rules no pitcher is allowed to toil more than three innings unless he is the last to go to the mound and the game goes into extra innings.

The Yankees, as usual, will dominate the American League's opening battlefront. In addition to the mighty DiMaggio, who has a forty-eight-game record hitting streak running, the Bronx Bombers will have Joe Gordon on second and the veteran Bill Dickey behind the plate.

DiMaggio, whose hitting streak will not be at stake in this contest, will be flanked by the clouting Red Sox gardener, Williams, and Jeff Heath of the Indians. Rudy York, Detroit's popular first sacker; Joe Cronin, Boston's player-manager, and Cecil Travis of the Senators will round out the infield.

Despite their defeat last year in St. Louis, the American Leaguers hold the upper hand in all-star competition with five victories against three.

Line-up and Facts on Game

NATIONAL LEAGUE

	Bat. Avge.
Hack, Cubs, 3b	.310
Frey, Reds, 2b	.238
Reiser, Dodgers, cf	.360
Mize, Cardinals, 1b	.348
Ott, Giants, rf	.292
Elliott, Pirates, lf	.289
Miller, Braves, ss	.241
Danning, Giants, c	.260
Owen, Dodgers, c	.257

AMERICAN LEAGUE

	Bat. Avge.
Gordon, Yankees, 2b	.260
Travis, Senators, 3b	.361
J. DiMaggio, Yankees, cf	.357
Williams, Red Sox, lf	.405
Heath, Indians, rf	.371
Cronin, Red Sox, ss	.338
York, Tigers, 1b	.293
Dickey, Yankees, c	.330

RESERVES

National	Avge.	American	Avge.
F. McCormick, Reds, 1b	.262	Foxx, Red Sox, 1b	.290
Herman, Dodgers, 2b	.296	Doerr, Red Sox, 2b	.258
Vaughan, Pirates, ss	.300	Boudreau, Indians, ss	.273
Lavagetto, Dodgers, 3b	.314	Keltner, Indians, 3b	.281
Slaughter, Cardinals, of	.323	D. DiMaggio, Red Sox, of	.309
Medwick, Dodgers, of	.292	Keller, Yankees, of	.283
Nicholson, Cubs, of	.256	Cullenbine, Browns, of	.367
T. Moore, Cardinals, of	.317	Hayes, Athletics, c	.316
Lopez, Pirates, c	.276	Tebbetts, Tigers, c	.286

PITCHERS

	W.	L.		W.	L.
Wyatt, Dodgers	13	4	Feller, Indians	16	4
Walters, Reds	10	6	T. Lee, White Sox	10	5
Derringer, Reds	7	10	Benton, Tigers	6	1
Warneke, Cardinals	9	4	Hudson, Senators	5	8
Hubbell, Giants	6	3	Smith, White Sox	7	9
Passeau, Cubs	8	7	Russo, Yankees	7	5
Blanton, Phillies	5	4	Leonard, Senators	6	10
			Ruffing, Yankees	9	3

Managers—National League: Bill McKechnie, Reds. American League: Del Baker, Tigers.

Coaches—National League: Leo Durocher, Dodgers, and Jimmy Wilson, Cubs. American League: Art Fletcher, Yankees, and Mervyn Shea, Tigers.

Umpires—(First 4½ Innings): William R. Summers (A. L.), plate; Ralph Pinelli (N. L.), first base; William T. Grieve (A. L.), second base; Louis Jorda (N. L.), third base.

Place—Briggs Stadium, Detroit.

Starting Time—1:30 P. M. Eastern standard time (2:30 P. M., New York).

Weather Forecast—Fair and warm.

Probable Attendance—57,000 (capacity).

Probable Betting Odds—American League favored, 5 to 9.

Beneficiary—Net proceeds will go to the United Service Organizations.

Radio Broadcasts—Columbia Broadcasting System (WABC) and Mutual Broadcasting System (WOR) will give accounts of contest.

In the event of a postponement today, the game will be played at 11 A. M. (Eastern daylight time) tomorrow. If it is impossible to play the game then, it will be canceled.

NATIONALS' BIG ALL-STAR ERROR WAS IN NOT GETTING WILLIAMS OUT

But Had McKechnie Ordered Bosox Slugger Passed, Winning Run Would Have Been on Second Base; Vaughan's Two Homers a Record; Wyatt, Feller Stand Outs

By FREDERICK G. LIEB

IN THE ninth All-Star game, played at Briggs Stadium, Detroit, July 8, before a frenzied crowd of 54,674 fans, the National League team was within one put-out of victory, a victory which would have been its second in succession and closed the gap of American League triumphs to five to four. But, as Bill McKechnie, the National League pilot, ruefully said in the Detroit clubhouse after it was over: "You've got to get them all out." One master home run by the tall, lithe Red Sox youngster, Ted Williams, undid the heroic efforts of Arky Vaughan, Pirate shortstop, and his National League mates in the previous eight and two-thirds innings, for the final victory perched on the banner of the American League, 7 to 5, while the margin of the junior league's supremacy was restored to its former high of three games. The Americans now lead in this interesting mid-summer competition, six victories to three.

The attendance at Briggs Stadium was the third greatest in the All-Star series and was exceeded only by the 69,812 crowd for the third game in Cleveland in 1935 and the 62,892 throng at Yankee Stadium for the seventh game in 1939. The receipts were $63,267.08, which this year went to the United Service Organizations after deducting expenses of conducting the game.

A press box wag said after the game: "The National League must feel the same way Billy Conn felt when Joe Louis knocked him out, just as he had the world's heavyweight championship within his grasp." Two incidents in the final chapter, a bad hop of Pinch-Hitter Ken Keltner's grounder to Eddie Miller, the Nationals' ninth-inning shortstop, and Cecil Travis' art in breaking up a double play made it possible for Ted Williams to come up for his last time at bat. He was the man Bill McKechnie and his fourth pitcher, Claude Passeau, had to reckon with before the ball game could be entered in the records. Perhaps Long Ted was due. He hadn't been a ball of fire in his previous efforts to wreck National League pitching in All-Star competition. In five times at bat in the Tampa and St. Louis games of 1940, he had failed to get a hit. In his four previous times up in the Detroit affair, he had drawn a walk and was credited with a gift double in the fourth when Bob Elliott skidded and fell on the wet turf trying to field his line drive. In the eighth, Passeau had struck him out, right

12 All-Star Marks Set

An even dozen records were set in the 1941 All-Star game, with Arky Vaughan of the Pirates accounting for four of the marks and Billy Herman of the Dodgers registering three.

Following are the new records:

Most home runs, one game, two—Vaughan.

Most runs batted in, one game, four—Vaughan, and Ted Williams, Red Sox.

Home runs, consecutive innings and times at bat, two—Vaughan (in seventh and eighth innings).

Most putouts, outfielder, game, six—Pete Reiser, Dodgers.

Most errors, outfielder, game, two—Reiser.

Most consecutive hits, five—Herman, three in 1940, two in 1941.

Total All-Star hits—Herman, 11 in eight games.

Most games played in, eight—Herman; Mel Ott, Giants; Joe Medwick, Dodgers.

Most errors, game, both teams, five—Americans three, Nationals two.

Most outfield errors, game, both teams, four—Nationals two, Americans two.

Most games won on home diamond, five—Americans.

after Joe DiMaggio had doubled. But any hitter with a batting average of .405 is a peck of trouble.

Should Passeau Have Given Him Pass?

The National League could have passed up the menace. McKechnie and his aides, Durocher and Wilson, and Danning, Herman and McCormick, had a conference in the middle of the diamond with Passeau. They could have walked Williams, filling the bases, and taken a chance on Dom DiMaggio, a righthanded hitter. However, the Nationals were still one run to the good with two out, and runners on third base and first. By walking Williams, the National League would have put the "winning run" on second base. Some argued shrewd, cagey Carl Hubbell, with his deceptive lefthanded screwball, should have been called in to face Williams, a lefthanded hitter. But the pitcher then in the bullpen was Lon Warneke, as right-handed as Passeau.

There was criticism of both managers on the manner in which they played their cards. Some of it may have been justified. It seems to me that both McKechnie and Del Baker should have jockeyed their material so that such robust sluggers as Mel Ott and Charlie Keller would have seen more service than brief appearances as pinch-hitters. Yet, I do not think McKechnie justly can be criticized for his ninth-inning tactics. It was a gamble if he let Williams hit; it was just as much of a gamble to walk the young slugger, and an axiom of the late John McGraw was: "Never put the winning run on second base unless you cannot help it."

So, it was a proper match of wits between Williams, who had only one fluke hit for eight All-Star times at bat, and Passeau, famous as a fast ball pitcher. Passeau worked rapidly. In the eighth he had fanned powerful Jimmie Foxx with three straight pitches, leaving runners on third and second. Just before facing Williams, he had subdued the elder DiMaggio on three pitches, two strikes and the near double-play ball. Pitching more gingerly to Williams, the count was two balls and one strike when Ted rammed deep into the upper right field seats, scoring the Yankees' Gordon and Joe DiMaggio ahead of him. There was no doubt of the drive's destination from the moment it left Williams' long bat.

Two-Homer Vaughan in the Shade

If Williams hadn't hit that ball, all the hero's laurels would have gone to Floyd Ellis Vaughan, veteran shortstop of the Pirates, a former National League batting champ and a veteran All-Star performer. Arky recently has been on the sidelines with a stone bruise on his right heel and because Frisch, his manager, has not wished to break up a winning combination, but Vaughan was hot in this game. Starting with a modest single in the fifth, Arky hit a two-run homer off the young Washington righthander, Sid Hudson, in the seventh, and duplicated the feat at the expense of Edgar Smith, White Sox southpaw, in the eighth. Vaughan and Williams set a new record for driving in four runs in an All-Star contest; Arky became the first All-Star player to hit two homers in one game, while the three hits in four times at bat boosted his All-Star batting average for six games to the healthy mark of .400.

The ninth All-Star game was hardly an exhibition of baseball at its best; there were muffs, fumbles, misjudged line drives and other mistakes which did not get into the box score. Even so, there were more actual errors in the game than in any of the eight which preceded it. Pete Reiser, young Brooklyn outfielder, one of the two National leaguers to go the entire nine innings, let two ground balls roll through him and misjudged Joe DiMaggio's eighth-inning double. Yet, from the fans' standpoint, these human frailities made it the best of all the All-Star games. It wasn't a game between perfect robots, but between flesh and blood ball players, and it was chock-full of drama, thrills and excitement. The tension in the last three innings was so acute one could feel it in the very air. One felt the ball game hung on every pitch, and eventually it fluttered to the American League on the last delivery of the game, the fast ball which Passeau served to Williams.

The game started much as did those of

recent years, a pitching duel with a minimum of hits. In fact, the American League club, which was blanked with three hits in St. Louis in 1940, had to go to the fourth inning before it could register its first blow. Then there were some uncomplimentary remarks about the American's alleged power, but later it got going.

Bobby Feller, fireball ace of the Indians, and Whit Wyatt, Brooklyn sharpshooter who was discarded by three American League clubs, were the starting hurlers and did the best pitching for their respective sides. Feller gave up one hit in his three innings, but only nine men faced him, as Frey, the man who plastered Bobby for a single, was picked off base. Feller gave no walks and fanned four. Wyatt walked one man, Williams, in his two innings, but Ted was wiped off the base paths in a double play.

McKechnie started with the same tactics he employed so successfully in 1940, when he used Derringer, Walters, Wyatt and French in two innings each and pitched Carl Hubbell in the ninth. Had he followed the system and used Hubbell in the ninth, he might have duplicated last summer's victory. However, after three of the 1940 hurlers, Wyatt, Derringer and Walters, each worked two innings, Passeau was permitted to go three rounds. Derringer was hardly responsible for giving up the first Baker run, as it came in on the double by Williams on which Elliott fell on the wet grass. Walters, who succeeded big Oom Paul, was lucky to get by with one run, giving up three hits and two walks in his two rounds. After retiring the side in order in the seventh, Passeau yielded six hits in the last two frames. That's as many as the Americans made in New York in winning, 3 to 1, in 1939, and twice as many as they made in St. Louis in 1940.

On the American League side, Baker succeeded Feller with Thornton Lee, the White Sox southpaw; Sid Hudson, the Washington sophomore, and wound up with Dykes' second lefthanded star, Edgar Smith. Lee gave up four hits and one run in his three innings, and there was considerable surprise when young Hudson, a Class D pitcher two years ago, was sent to the mound in the seventh with his team enjoying a slender, 2 to 1 edge. Had Baker lost the game, this pitching choice would have come in for a lot of criticism, as the experienced Ruffing seemed a far better bet under the circumstances. The first three hitters to face Sid stung him for ringing hits, a single by Slaughter, Arky Vaughan's first homer and Billy Herman's double. Billy was sacrificed to third, another questionable play against a wobbly pitcher, where he was left. Ed Smith pitched the last two frames for the junior leaguers; he fanned Reiser and Slaughter in the eighth, but in with these strikeouts were Mize's double and Arky's second four-bagger. Smith got rid of the side in order in the ninth.

Conspicuous among the players, in addition to Williams, Vaughan, Feller and Wyatt, were Lou Boudreau, second American League shortstop; Billy Herman, second National second sacker, and Stanley Hack, McKechnie's third baseman. Boudreau hit safely in both his times up; Herman smacked a double and a single and reached base on an error, bringing his All-Star average for three games up to .300, while Hack had a single, a walk and a sacrifice and played brilliantly in the field,

his catch of a line drive by Bill Dickey being the best play of the game.

After hitting safely in 48 American League games, Joe DiMaggio doubled in the eighth, to keep the streak alive against National All-Star pitching, though the game does not go into the records. Some say the hero of the American League should be Cecil Travis for breaking up the double play in the ninth, whereby Herman was forced to throw wide to first in his effort to retire DiMaggio.

The Game in Detail

First Inning
NATIONAL—Hack struck out. Moore popped to Cronin. Reiser struck out. No runs, no hits, no errors.

AMERICAN—Doerr popped to Frey. Travis flied to Reiser. Joe DiMaggio fouled to Hack. No runs, no hits, no errors.

Second Inning
NATIONAL—Mize flied to Joe DiMaggio. Nicholson was called out on strikes. Vaughan flied to Williams. No runs, no hits, no errors.

AMERICAN—Williams walked. Heath hit into a double play, Frey to Vaughan to Mize. Cronin flied to Nicholson. No runs, no hits, no errors.

Third Inning
NATIONAL—Frey singled to right for the first hit of the game, but was caught off first and retired, Feller to York to Cronin. Owen flied to Williams. Ott batted for Wyatt and fanned, but Dickey had to throw him out. No runs, one hit, no errors.

AMERICAN—Paul Derringer and Al Lopez became the National League battery. York flied to Reiser. Frey threw out Dickey. Cullenbine batted for Feller and grounded out, Derringer to Mize. No runs, no hits, no errors.

Fourth Inning
NATIONAL—Thornton Lee went in to pitch for the American League. Hack singled past Cronin. Moore flied to Heath. Reiser hit into a double play, York to Cronin. No runs, one hit, no errors.

AMERICAN—Elliott went to right field for the National League. Frey threw out Doerr. Travis doubled to center for the first American League hit. Reiser made a running catch of Joe DiMaggio's long fly, Travis taking third after the capture. Elliott fell in fielding Williams' liner and it went for a double, scoring Travis. Heath was called out on strikes. One run, two hits, no errors.

Fifth Inning
NATIONAL—Mize grounded to York. Travis threw out Elliott. Vaughan beat out a slow roller to Doerr. Herman batted for Frey and singled to center, Vaughan stopping at second. Lopez forced Vaughan, Travis, unassisted. No runs, two hits, no errors.

AMERICAN—Walters became the third National League pitcher and Herman went to second base. Cronin was called out on strikes. York singled to left. Dickey singled down the third base line, York stopping at second. Lee lined to Reiser and York took third, Dickey holding first. Doerr struck out. No runs, two hits, no errors.

Sixth Inning
NATIONAL—Gordon went to second base and Boudreau to short for the American League. Walters doubled down the third base line. Hack sacrificed, Lee to York. Moore flied to Williams and Walters scored, tying the count at one-all. Heath muffed Reiser's fly and the runner reached second. Travis threw out Mize. One run, one hit, one error.

AMERICAN—Slaughter went to right field for the National League. Travis lined to Herman. Joe DiMaggio walked. Williams flied to Reiser. Heath walked. Boudreau singled to center, scoring J. DiMaggio and sending Heath to third. When Reiser fumbled the ball, Boudreau went to second. York flied to Reiser. One run, one hit, one error.

The Official Score

NATIONAL LEAGUE

Player—Position.	AB.	R.	H.	TB.	O.	A.	E.
Hack, third base	2	0	1	1	3	0	0
Lavagetto, third base	1	0	0	0	0	0	0
T. Moore, left field	5	0	0	0	1	0	0
Reiser, center field	4	0	0	5	0	2
Mize, first base	4	1	1	2	5	0	0
F. McCormick, first base	0	0	0	0	0	0	0
Nicholson, right field	1	0	0	0	1	0	0
Elliott, right field	1	0	0	0	1	0	0
Slaughter, right field	2	1	1	1	0	0	0
Vaughan, shortstop	4	2	3	9	1	2	0
Miller, shortstop	0	0	0	0	0	0	0
Frey, second base	1	0	1	1	1	3	0
Herman, second base	3	0	2	3	3	0	0
Owen, catcher	1	0	0	0	0	0	0
Lopez, catcher	1	0	0	0	3	0	0
Danning, catcher	1	0	0	0	3	0	0
Wyatt, pitcher	0	0	0	0	0	0	0
*Ott	1	0	0	0	0	0	0
Derringer, pitcher	0	0	0	0	0	1	0
Walters, pitcher	1	1	1	2	0	0	0
‡Medwick	1	0	0	0	0	0	0
Passeau, pitcher	1	0	0	0	0	0	0
Totals	35	5	10	19y	26	7	2

AMERICAN LEAGUE

Player—Position.	AB.	R.	H.	TB.	O.	A.	E.
Doerr, second base	3	0	0	0	0	0	0
Gordon, second base	2	1	1	1	2	0	0
Travis, third base	4	1	1	2	1	2	0
J. DiMaggio, center field	4	3	1	2	1	0	0
Williams, left field	4	1	2	6	3	0	1
Heath, right field	2	0	0	1	0	1
D. DiMaggio, right field	1	0	1	1	1	0	0
Cronin, shortstop	2	0	0	3	0	0
Boudreau, shortstop	2	0	2	2	0	1	0
York, first base	3	0	1	1	6	2	0
Foxx, first base	1	0	0	2	2	0
W. Dickey, catcher	3	0	1	1	4	2	0
Hayes, catcher	1	0	0	2	0	0
Feller, pitcher	0	0	0	0	1	0
†Cullenbine	1	0	0	0	0	0	0
Lee, pitcher	1	0	0	0	1	0
Hudson, pitcher	0	0	0	0	0	0	0
§Keller	1	0	0	0	0	0	0
E. Smith, pitcher	0	0	0	0	1	0	1
xKeltner	1	1	1	1	0	0	0
Totals	36	7	11	17	27	11	3

*Batted for Wyatt in third.
†Batted for Feller in third.
‡Batted for Walters in seventh.
§Batted for Hudson in seventh.
xBatted for Smith in ninth.
yTwo out when winning run scored.

Nationals .... 0 0 0 0 0 1 2 2 0—5
Americans .... 0 0 0 1 0 1 0 1 4—7

Runs batted in—Williams 4, Moore, Boudreau, Vaughan 4, D. DiMaggio, J. DiMaggio.
Two-base hits—Travis, Williams, Walters, Herman, Mize, J. DiMaggio.
Home runs—Vaughan 2, Williams.
Sacrifice hits—Hack, Lopez.
Double plays—Frey, Vaughan and Mize; York and Cronin.
Pitching record—Feller 1 hit, no runs in 3 innings; Lee 4 hits, 1 run in 3 innings; Hudson 3 hits, 2 runs in 1 inning; Smith 2 hits, 2 runs in 2 innings; Wyatt 0 hits, 0 runs in 2 innings; Derringer 2 hits, 1 run in 2 innings; Walters 3 hits, 1 run in 2 innings; Passeau 6 hits, 5 runs in 2 2-3 innings.
Struck out—By Feller 4 (Hack, Reiser, Nicholson, Ott); by Hudson 1 (Moore); by Smith 2 (Reiser, Slaughter); by Derringer 1 (Heath); by Walters 2 (Cronin, Doerr); by Passeau 3 (Keller, Williams, Foxx).
Bases on balls—Off Wyatt 1 (Williams); off Walters 2 (J. DiMaggio, Heath); off Passeau 1 (Travis); off Hudson 1 (Hack).
Left on bases—American League 7, National League 6.
Earned runs—American League 6, National League 5.
Winning pitcher—Smith.
Losing pitcher—Passeau.
Official Scorer—Tom Swope, Cincinnati Post.
Umpires—Summers (A. L.) at plate; Jorda (N. L.) first base; Grieve (A. L.) second base; Pinelli (N. L.) third base (for first 4½ innings); Pinelli (N. L.) at plate; Summers (A. L.) third base; Jorda (N. L.) second base; Grieve (N. L.) second base (last 4½ innings).
Time of game—2:23.
Attendance—54,674.

Seventh Inning

NATIONAL—Sid Hudson went to the mound, Jimmie Foxx to first base and Dominic DiMaggio to right field for the American League. Slaughter singled to left and took second on Williams' fumble. Vaughan lined a home run into the upper right field stands, scoring behind Slaughter. Herman doubled to left. Lopez sacrificed, Dickey to Gordon. Medwick batted for Walters and Boudreau threw him out, Herman remaining on third. Hack walked. Moore struck out. Two runs, three hits, one error.

AMERICAN—Claude Passeau and Hank Danning formed the new National League battery. Hack made a one-handed stab of Dickey's liner. Charlie Keller batted for Hudson and struck out. Vaughan threw out Gordon. No runs, no hits, no errors.

Eighth Inning

NATIONAL—Edgar Smith went to the mound and Frank Hayes behind the bat for the American League. Reiser was called out on strikes. Mize doubled off the right field screen. Slaughter was called out on strikes. Vaughan hit his second home run into the upper stands in right field and trotted home behind Mize. Herman was safe when Smith, covering first base, fumbled Foxx' toss of his grounder. Danning popped to Gordon. Two runs, two hits, one error.

AMERICAN—McCormick went to first base for the National League. Travis fouled to Hack. Joe DiMaggio doubled to center. Williams was called out on strikes. Dominic DiMaggio singled to right-center, scoring brother Joe. Boudreau singled to center, sending D. DiMaggio to third, and took second on Reiser's fumble. Foxx struck out. One run, three hits, one error.

Ninth Inning

NATIONAL—Passeau flied to Dominic DiMaggio. Lavagetto batted for Hack and grounded out, Foxx to Smith. Moore fouled to Foxx. No runs, no hits, no errors.

AMERICAN—Lavagetto went to third and Miller to short for the Nationals. Hayes popped to Herman. Keltner batted for Smith and scratched a hit to Miller. Gordon singled to right, Keltner stopping at second. Travis walked, filling the bases. Joe DiMaggio forced Travis, Miller to Herman, Keltner scoring and Gordon going to third. Williams hit a home run into the upper right field stands and scored behind Gordon and DiMaggio. Four runs, three hits, no errors.

All-Star Twinklings

After watching Bobby Feller mow down the Nationals in his three-inning term, striking out four men, Wally Pipp, first baseman of Miller Huggins' early Yankee champions, remarked that he thought Feller may be even a better pitcher than was Walter Johnson. "Walter Johnson had terrific speed," said Wally, "but when he was at his top form, his curve was more or less of a joke to us. It only broke a few inches. Feller, on the other hand, not only has that blinding speed, but he has developed the best curve I ever have seen possessed by a pitcher whose leading forte is a fast ball."

There was only one Tiger player, Rudy York, in action, but Detroit, which has had American League ball since the league's inception, rooted as hard for the loop's All-Stars as it did for the Tigers in the dramatic World's Series of 1940. . . . Ted Williams said the ball he hit was waist high, and that after he fanned in the eighth, he had a hunch he might hit a homer if he came up again in the ninth. "I just shut my eyes, and swung with all I had," said Ted. "Then, when I looked up I heard the yell of the crowd and saw the ball headed for the stands."

As pinch-hitter, Mel Ott fanned in the third inning, the bat of the little Giant slipping out of his hands and flying all the way down to York at first. Bill Dickey dropped the third strike, so he had to throw Mel out at first. It seemed that the bat, the ball and the runner were all in a race to see which would reach York's bag first. . . . Someone asked Tris Speaker, usually considered the greatest of all center fielders, what he thought of Pete Reiser's antics in center field. "Don't be too hard on the young fellow," said Tris. "Everybody has to learn, and they tell me Reiser is a mighty sweet hitter."

After seeing Cubs Jimmie Wilson, Stan Hack, Bill Nicholson and Claude Passeau in their satin uniforms of baby blue, with white shields, Clark Griffith, president of the Washington club and a Chicago National player of the nineties, said: "Now, I have seen everything."

Two old San Francisco sand-lotters, Joe Cronin and Umpire Babe Pinelli, squared jaws at each other in the fifth, when Babe ruled that Bucky Walters had buzzed a third strike over on Cronin. It was the most vigorous beef of the game. The next hitter, Rudy York, also lodged verbal disapproval with Pinelli on another called strike, but all was forgotten when the Tiger singled.

While Joe DiMaggio hit one double and scored three runs in the All-Star game, the Yankees' wonder clouter wasn't exactly pleased with his showing. Joe has been a little vexed at his failure to do better against National All-Star pitching and was just a little ashamed of his average of only .143, three hits in 21 times at bat in his first five games. In the midst of his greatest hitting streak, he had hoped to boost that considerably this year. But, by getting one for four in Detroit, DiMag only raised his average to .160 for six games.

Mickey Cochrane, former top-ranking catcher, who managed the Americans in the game at Cleveland in 1935, was shaking hands with old cronies. Mickey is doing well in business, but some of his friends say he still has the baseball "itch" at World's Series and All-Star game time.

When Al Lopez took up the National League's catching chores in the third inning, the Detroit announcer, not so well posted on the Frick league's doings, introduced him as "Al Lopez of Brooklyn." It has been six years since the peppery Tampa Cuban caught for the Dodgers, but with Brooklyn having its first real chance to get into a World's Series in 21 years, Al wishes the announcer's words were true. This is Al's twelfth year in the league, in nine of which he caught more than 100 games, but he still is without a taste of World's Series gravy.

Arch Ward, Chicago Tribune sports editor, who first sold the idea of the All-Star game to the major leagues, suggests that League Presidents Will Harridge and Ford Frick should do something to help patrons identify the All-Star players in future games. He thinks special uniforms with designated numbers might help. In the first All-Star contest, played in Chicago in 1933, John Heydler, then National League president, had special uniforms made for his players, with the words, "National League," lettered across their blouses. He abandoned this uniform after one trial, saying the fans preferred to see the players in their individual uniforms, contending it gave the game more of an All-Star flavor.

Joe DiMaggio, in the familiar Yankee pin stripes, congratulates Ted Williams, who has just hit a three-run homer to win the 1941 All-Star game for the American League, 7–5, at Briggs Stadium in Detroit. DiMaggio scored just ahead of him. Number 30 is American League coach Marv Shea.

On the way: Joe DiMaggio hits safely in 21 straight games and approaches the historic marks of consecutive-game hitting, set by Rogers Hornsby, George Sisler, and Wee Willie Keeler.

Joe DiMaggio's 56-game hitting streak inspired sportswriters to poetry, and even provoked a melody. "Joltin' Joe DiMaggio" was introduced by Les Brown and his Band of Renown in 1941. The song, with music by Ben Homer and words by Alan Courtney.

Joe DiMaggio posed for this poster to promote Hillerich & Bradsby's famous Louisville Slugger bats. He was paid $100 for the endorsement.

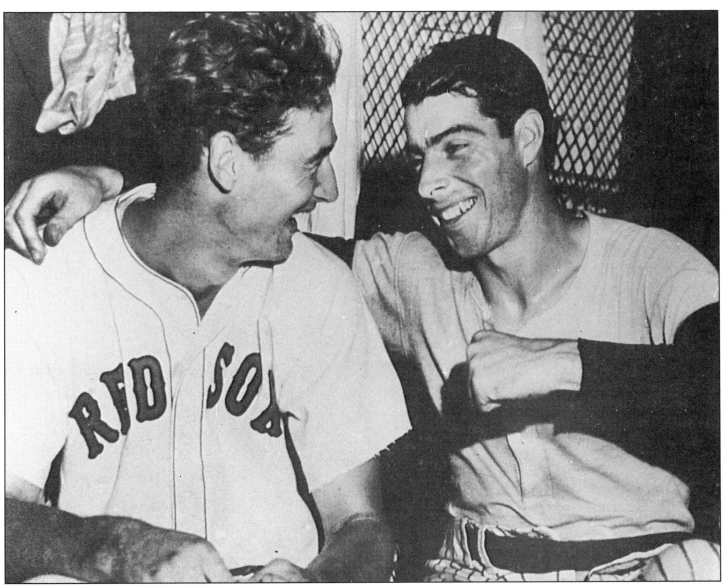

Certified sluggers, Joe DiMaggio and Ted Williams, share the joy of triumph in the locker room after the 1941 All-Star game.

Sensational
JOE DIMAGGIO

Will Seek To Hit Safely In His
49th
Consecutive Game.

Thur. Nite, July 10
AT ST. LOUIS

Browns vs. Yankees
Sportsman's Park--8:30 P. M.

Tickets Now on Sale at Browns Arcade Ticket Office--Phone, CHestnut 7900.

★ Joe DiMaggio ★

By the Sports Editor

Loss of a job as a newsboy brought Joe Di Maggio, great Yankee slugger, into professional baseball, he disclosed yesterday as he lolled about in his hotel room, relaxing after the All-Star game Tuesday and awaiting, with the other New York players, the opening game of the series with the Browns at Sportsmans Park tonight.

"Yes," laughed the big black-haired outfielder who has broken all records for safe hitting in consecutive games, and who obviously was highly amused by the recollection of the newsboy incident, "yes, it was losing that job that led me into professional baseball.

MADE GOOD ON CORNER

"When I started selling papers as a kid on the busy corner of Sansome and Market in San Francisco, I had a tough time peddling 60 papers a day, but I gradually worked the sales up to from 150 to 175 a day and was making pretty good money for a youngster.

"But just as I thought I was all set with a steady income, the route boss that had given me the job was promoted, and when the new boss found out how high my sales were each day he decided his cousin was going to have a better future on that corner than myself, so I was fired.

"Out of work, I decided to practice at the San Francisco Coast League ball park. I had been playing baseball, semiprofessionally, but had not thought about taking up the game seriously until I lost that job selling papers."

VINCE GOOD TALKER

At that time Di Maggio was a shortstop, and, as he points out himself, a poor one. However, his brother Vince, now with Pittsburgh and then playing the outfield for San Francisco, induced Charley Graham, head of the San Francisco club, to give Joe a tryout at shortstop.

The Pacific Coast League season was on the threshold of its final games that year, 1932, and it so happened that the present Chicago Cub veteran, Augie Galan, who was the San Francisco shortstop in 1932, was to leave the team for a trip to Honolulu.

"Vince must have had great perasuasive power," Joe commented yesterday as he unfolded the story. "Galan left and Mr. Graham gave me the chance at shortstop. The Coast League season then had two days to run, a single game on a Saturday and a double-header Sunday, and I was the San Francisco shortstop.

"Incidentally, I received nothing for that tryout, being glad of the chance to show what ability I had."

Vince Di Maggio. How did Joe become and outfielder?

"That's easy to explain," continued the powerful batter who, in less than a half decade with the Yankees, has developed into one of the game's greatest ballplayers, as well as one of the highest paid, his salary at the current writing being reported as somewhere between $32,000 and $42,000 a year.

"During the training season of 1933 with the San Francisco club," Joe added, "I was still working at shortstop, and one day I made as high as 11 errors."

MAKES GOOD CATCH

"The season opened and I was on the bench, but in an early game Jimmy Caveney, then manager of San Francisco, sent me up as a pinch batter. I drew a walk and after the inning was over, I figured I was through for the day, but Caveney told me to finish out the game in right field.

"That's the first time I ever played the outfield. Luckily, I made one pretty good catch, staggering into a ball somehow and grabbing it backhanded. I also went to bat once more during the game and hit a long fly ball. From then on I've been in the outfield."

Di Maggio did not mention that he batted .340 for San Francisco in 1933, his first full season as a professional. Nor that he followed up with .341 in 1934, then crashed the leather for a .398 average in 1935 before the Yankees bought him for $25,000, along with a $5000 bonus to the San Francisco club and five players.

KEEP EYE ON BALL

To what does Di Maggio attribute his success as a batter?

"Well, I know of nothing special," the 26-year-old super star remarked, "except that I believe I am able to keep my eye focused squarely on the ball because of the way I stand."

Di Maggio stands at the plate with his feet well apart and when he swings into a ball, his left or front foot moves only very slightly forward.

"With that stance I keep my head rigid and therefore my eyes remain fixed on the ball," Joe pointed out. "I get power in the swing from my arms and shoulders, the lower body helping very little, except as a firm brace."

FAVORITE PITCH

Joe says he'd rather have a fast ball right down the middle, belt high, than any other pitch.

"Of course," he smiled, "I seldom get that pitch, but when I do I certainly like to tear into it. The pitchers have no set way to pitch to me. They all just mix up their different pitches, and I'll get one here, there and some place else."

Mel Harder, right-hander of the Cleveland Indians, has been the hardest pitcher Di Maggio has faced in the American League, he admits.

"Yes, he's been a tough one, and he almost stopped me during the streak, but I finally beat out a hit on him."

It is worthy of note that the bat Di Maggio used during most of his current batting success was not the one he set the new record with recently.

BAT DISAPPEARED

"The one I had been using disappeared between games of a double-header. It was my pet, 36 ounces in weight and 36 inches long, and perfectly balanced. I then had to use another of my bats in the next game, but I got a hit for the record, and that's the bat I sent to San Francisco to be auctioned off for the United Service Organizations."

Di Maggio relates that a week later, his favorite bat was returned to him by a friend who turned sleuth and tracked it down.

As Joe spoke, a fresh batch of fan mail was delivered.

"I read them all," Joe answered a query. "Not only that, but I acknowledge every letter I receive, sending a card in reply. It's part of the game."

Di Mag Held Hitless in 11 Games This Season

Joe Di Maggio, whose consecutive games hitting streak is baseball's greatest sideshow, brought his big tent and big bat to Cleveland today.

The Yankees' great centerfielder started his now sensational 55-game streak on May 15, after he had failed to hit in 11 of the 27 games the Bombers had played up to that time.

On June 29, against the Senators in Washington, he hit in his 42d consecutive game to break George Sisler's modern major league record of 41. Willie Keeler's all-time major league record of 44 straight games was the next to fall, in New York against the Red Sox on July 2.

Now, as Di Maggio rolls along toward the all-time organized baseball mark of hitting in 69 straight games, set by Joe Wilhoit of the Wichita Western League Club in 1919, the interest in his feats as an individual surpasses that in the doings of the Yankees as a team.

Joe has collected 88 hits in the 55 games—54 singles, 16 doubles, four triples and 14 home runs—for 154 total bases.

The day-by-day record of his 55-game streak:

May 15: One single.
May 16: One triple, one homer.
May 17: One single.
May 18: One double, two singles.
May 19: One double.
May 20: One single.
May 21: Two singles.
May 22: One single.
May 23: One single.
May 24: One triple.
May 25: One double.
May 26: Unscheduled.
May 27: One homer, three singles.
May 28: One triple.
May 29: One single.
May 30: (1st game) One single; (2d game) One double.
May 31: Rained out.
June 1: (1st game) One single; (2d game) One single.
June 2: One single, one double.
June 3: One homer.
June 4: Rained out.
June 5: One single.
June 6: Open date.
June 7: Three singles.
June 8: (1st game) Two homers; (2d game) One single, one double.
June 9: Open date.
June 10: One single.
June 11: Rained out.
June 12: One homer, one single.
June 13: Open date.
June 14: One double.
June 15: One homer.
June 16: One double.
June 17: One single.
June 18: One single.
June 19: One homer, two singles.
June 20: One double, three singles.
June 21: One single.
June 22: One homer, one double.
June 23: Open date.
June 24: One single.
June 25: One homer.
June 26: One double.
June 27: One homer, one single.
June 28: One single, one double.
June 29: (1st game) One double; (2d game) One single.
June 30: Open date.
July 1: (1st game) Two singles; (2d game) One single.
July 2: One homer.
July 3: Open date.
July 4: Rained out.
July 5: One homer.
July 6: (1st game) Three singles, one double; (2d game) One triple, one single.
July 7: Open date.
July 8: Open date. (All-Star game.)
July 9: Open date.
July 10: One single.
July 11: Three singles, one homer.
July 12: One single, one double.
July 13: (1st game) Three singles; (2d game) One single.
July 14: One single.
July 15: One single, one double.

RECAPITULATION

Singles, 54. Doubles, 16. Triples, 4. Home runs, 14. Total bases, 154.

Joe DiMaggio rewrites the record books with this hit — the 56th consecutive game in which he hit safely.

DiMaggio's Streak Ended at 56 Games, but Yanks Down Indians Before 67,468

SMITH AND BAGBY STOP YANKEE STAR

DiMaggio, Up for Last Time in Eighth, Hits Into a Double Play With Bases Full

M'CARTHYMEN WIN BY 4-3

Stretch Lead Over Indians to 7 Lengths Before Biggest Crowd for Night Game

By JOHN DREBINGER

Special to THE NEW YORK TIMES.

CLEVELAND, July 17 — In a brilliant setting of lights and before 67,468 fans, the largest crowd ever to see a game of night baseball in the major leagues, the Yankees tonight vanquished the Indians, 4 to 3, but the famous hitting streak of Joe DiMaggio finally came to an end.

Officially it will go into the records as fifty-six consecutive games, the total he reached yesterday. Tonight in Cleveland's municipal stadium the great DiMag was held hitless for the first time in more than two months.

Al Smith, veteran Cleveland left-hander and a Giant cast-off, and Jim Bagby, a young right-hander, collaborated in bringing the DiMaggio string to a close.

Jolting Joe faced Smith three times. Twice he smashed the ball down the third-base line, but each time Ken Keltner, Tribe third sacker, collared the ball and hurled it across the diamond for a put-out at first. In between these two tries, DiMaggio drew a pass from Smith.

Then, in the eighth, amid a deafening uproar, the streak dramatically ended, though the Yanks routed Smith with a flurry of four hits and two runs that eventually won the game.

Double Play Seals Record

With the bases full and only one out Bagby faced DiMaggio and, with the count at one ball and one strike, induced the renowned slugger to crash into a double play. It was a grounder to the shortstop, and as the ball flitted from Lou Boudreau to Ray Mack to Oscar Grimes, who played first base for the Tribe, the crowd knew the streak was over.

However, there were still a few thrills to come, for in the ninth, with the Yanks leading, 4 to 1, the Indians suddenly broke loose with an attack that for a few moments threatened to send the game into extra innings and thus give DiMaggio another chance.

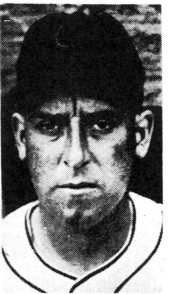 

PITCHERS WHO HALTED YANKEE SLUGGER

Al Smith   Jim Bagby Jr.

Times Wide World

DiMaggio's Record Streak

Date	Opponent	ab.	r.	h.	2b.	3b.	hr.	Date	Opponent	ab.	r.	h.	2b.	3b.	hr.
May 15	White Sox	4	0	1	0	0	0	June 17	White Sox	4	1	1	0	0	0
May 16	White Sox	4	2	2	0	1	1	June 18	White Sox	3	0	1	0	0	0
May 17	White Sox	3	1	1	0	0	0	June 19	White Sox	3	2	3	0	0	1
May 18	Browns	3	3	3	1	0	0	June 20	Tigers	5	3	4	1	0	0
May 19	Browns	3	0	1	1	0	0	June 21	Tigers	4	0	1	0	0	0
May 20	Browns	5	1	1	0	0	0	June 22	Tigers	5	1	2	1	0	1
May 21	Tigers	5	0	2	0	0	0	June 24	Browns	4	1	1	0	0	0
May 22	Tigers	4	0	1	0	0	0	June 25	Browns	4	1	1	0	0	1
May 23	Red Sox	5	0	1	0	0	0	June 26	Browns	4	0	1	1	0	0
May 24	Red Sox	4	2	1	0	0	0	June 27	Athletics	3	1	2	0	0	1
May 25	Red Sox	4	0	1	0	0	0	June 28	Athletics	5	1	2	1	0	0
May 27	Senators	5	3	4	0	0	1	June 29	Senators	4	1	1	1	0	0
May 28	Senators	4	1	1	0	1	0	June 29	Senators	5	1	1	0	0	0
May 29	Senators	3	1	1	0	0	0	July 1	Red Sox	4	0	2	0	0	0
May 30	Red Sox	2	1	1	0	0	0	July 1	Red Sox	3	1	1	0	0	0
May 30	Red Sox	3	0	1	1	0	0	July 2	Red Sox	5	1	1	0	0	1
June 1	Indians	4	1	1	0	0	0	July 5	Athletics	4	2	1	0	0	1
June 1	Indians	4	0	1	0	0	0	July 6	Athletics	5	2	4	1	0	0
June 2	Indians	4	2	2	1	0	0	July 6	Athletics	4	0	2	0	1	0
June 3	Tigers	4	1	1	0	0	1	July 10	Browns	2	0	1	0	0	0
June 5	Tigers	5	1	1	0	1	0	July 11	Browns	5	1	4	0	0	1
June 7	Browns	5	2	3	0	0	0	July 12	Browns	5	1	2	1	0	0
June 8	Browns	4	3	2	0	0	2	July 13	White Sox	4	2	3	0	0	0
June 8	Browns	4	1	2	1	0	1	July 13	White Sox	4	0	1	0	0	0
June 10	White Sox	5	1	1	0	0	0	July 14	White Sox	3	0	1	0	0	0
June 12	White Sox	4	1	2	0	0	1	July 15	White Sox	4	1	2	1	0	0
June 14	Indians	2	0	1	1	0	0	July 16	Indians	4	3	3	1	0	0
June 15	Indians	3	1	1	0	0	1								
June 16	Indians	5	0	1	1	0	0	Total		223	56	91	16	4	15

Gerald Walker and Grimes singled, and, though Johnny Murphy here replaced Gomez, Larry Rosenthal tripled to score his two colleagues. But with the tying run on third and nobody out the Cleveland attack bogged down in a mess of bad base-running and the Yanks' remaining one-run lead held, though it meant the end of the streak for DiMaggio, who might have come up fourth had there been a tenth inning.

Started May 15

It was on May 15 against the White Sox at the Yankee Stadium that DiMaggio began his string, which in time was to gain nation-wide attention. As the great DiMag kept clicking in game after game, going into the twenties, then the thirties, he became the central figure of the baseball world.

On June 29, in a double-header with the Senators in Washington, he tied, then surpassed the American League and modern record of forty-one games set by George Sisler of the Browns in 1922. The next target was the all-time major league high of forty-four contests set by Willie Keeler, famous Oriole star, forty-four years ago under conditions much easier then for a batsman than they are today. Then there was no foul-strike rule hampering the batter.

But nothing hampered DiMaggio as he kept getting his daily hits, and on July 1 he tied the Keeler mark. The following day he soared past it for game No. 45, and he kept on soaring until tonight. In seeking his fifty-seventh game, he finally was brought to a halt.

Actually, DiMaggio hit in fifty-seven consecutive games, for on July 8 he connected safely in the All-Star game in Detroit. But that contest did not count in the official league records.

Did Better on Coast

DiMaggio's mark ends five short of his own Pacific Coast League record of sixty-one consecutive games, which he set while with San Francisco in 1933. The all-time minor league high is sixty-seven, set by Joe Wilhoit of Wichita in the Western League in 1919.

The contest tonight was a blistering left-handed mound duel between Gomez and Smith, with Gomez going ahead one run in the first on Red Rolfe's single and Tommy Henrich's double.

A tremendous home run inside the park, which Walker outgalloped, tied the score in the fourth and the battle remained deadlocked until Joe Gordon untied it with his fifteenth homer of the year into the left-field stand in the seventh.

In the eighth the Yanks seemingly clinched victory when Charlie Keller rifled a triple to center past Roy Weatherly, who played the ball badly, needlessly charging in when he might just as well have played it safe for a single.

In its wake came singles by Gomez and Johnny Sturm. A double by Rolfe and two runs were in. Smith walked Henrich to fill the bases, and in this setting, with one out, the result of a harmless grounder by Phil Rizzuto, Bagby stepped in to face the great DiMag. A moment later the streak was over.

Traffic Snarl on Bases

The Indians were guilty of atrocious work on the bases in the ninth after Rosenthal had cracked Murphy for a triple to drive in two. Hal Trosky, pinch hitting, grounded out to first. Then Soup Campbell, batting for Bagby, splashed a grounder to Murphy. Rosenthal tried to score, was run down between third and home.

Yankee Box Score

NEW YORK (A.)								CLEVELAND (A.)						
	ab.	r.	h.	po.	a.	e.			ab.	r.	h.	po.	a.	e.
Sturm, 1b..	4	0	1	10	2	0		Weatherly, cf.	5	0	1	4	0	0
Rolfe, 3b...	4	1	2	2	3	0		Keltner, 3b..	3	0	1	1	4	0
Henrich, rf.	3	0	1	4	0	0		Boudreau, ss.	3	0	0	0	2	0
DiMaggio,cf.	3	0	0	2	0	0		Heath, rf..	4	0	0	0	0	0
Gordon, 2b..	4	1	2	0	1	0		Walker, lf..	3	2	2	1	0	0
Rosar, c..	4	0	0	5	1	0		Grimes, 1b..	3	1	1	12	0	0
Keller, lf...	3	1	1	0	0	0		Mack, 2b..	3	0	0	4	7	0
Rizzuto, ss..	4	0	0	2	1	0		aRosenthal...	1	0	1	0	0	0
Gomez, p....	4	1	1	2	1	0		Hemsley, c..	3	0	1	5	1	0
Murphy, p...	0	0	0	0	1	0		bTrosky	1	0	0	0	0	0
								Smith, p....	3	0	0	0	0	0
Total....	33	4	8	27	10	0		Bagby, p....	0	0	0	0	0	0
								cCampbell ..	1	0	0	0	0	0
								·Total....	33	3	7	27	14	0

aBatted for Mack in ninth.
bBatted for Hemsley in ninth.
cBatted for Bagby in ninth.

New York ....1 0 0 0 0 0 1 2 0—4
Cleveland ....0 0 0 1 0 0 0 0 2—3

Runs batted in—Henrich, Walker, Gomez, Gordon, Rolfe, Rosenthal 2.
Two-base hits—Henrich, Rolfe. Three-base hits—Keller, Rosenthal. Home runs—Walker, Gordon. Sacrifice — Boudreau. Double play — Boudreau, Mack and Grimes. Left on bases—New York 5, Cleveland 7. Bases on balls—Off Smith 2, Bagby 1, Gomez 3. Struck out—By Gomez 5, Smith 4, Bagby 1. Hits—Off Smith 7 in 7 1-3 innings, Bagby 1 in 1 2-3, Gomez 6 in 8 (none out in ninth), Murphy 1 in 1. Passed ball—Hemsley. Winning pitcher—Gomez. Losing pitcher—Smith. Umpires—Summers, Rue and Stewart. Time of game—2:03. Attendance—67,468.

To make matters worse, Campbell, dashing past first base, never looked to see what was going on and so made no attempt to grab second during the run-up. Weatherly, amid no end of hoots and jeers, grounded out for the final play.

The victory was Gomez's eighth, his sixth in a row. It was the Yanks' seventeenth in their last eighteen games and thirty-first in their last thirty-six contests. Their lead over the thoroughly demoralized Tribe was stretched to seven games.

With 40,000 reserved-seat tickets disposed of in the advance sale, a banner crowd was assured before a fan showed up, and with ideal weather conditions prevailing, the unreserved sections lost no time clinching the matter.

A swing band, barricaded behind a wire screening just to the rear of home plate, provided entertainment for the early arrivals. And just to match the southpaw efforts of Gomez and Smith the band leader also was left handed.

Although Bill Dickey has fully recovered from the charley horse which has kept him on the sidelines the past few days, Manager McCarthy decided to give his veteran backstop an additional day of rest inasmuch as Rosar has been thumping the ball at a merry clip.

Just before the game, Manager Peckinpaugh received an electric refrigerator, a gift from his admirers.

D'MAGGIO SORRY IT'S OVER

Wanted to Go On Improving His Streak as Long as He Could

CLEVELAND, July 17 (AP)—Joe DiMaggio, whose hitting streak of fifty-six games was ended tonight, expressed regret that he had failed to extend the record.

After the game DiMaggio said:

"I can't say that I'm glad it's over. Of course, I wanted to go on as long as I could.

"Now that the streak is over, I just want to get out there and keep helping to win ball games."

A CABBIE, A JINX,
AND DiMAGGIO

by Russell Schneider of *The Cleveland Plain Dealer*

The phone rang and it was evident that the voice belonged to a man who was upset.

"I read your article about Joe DiMaggio this morning, when he talked about his 56-game hitting streak being stopped, and I had to call you," he said.

In his next breath, I knew why.

"I was the cab driver who picked up DiMaggio and Lefty Gomez that night . . . the one Joe thinks might have jinxed him; and jeez I'm sorry he feels that way."

The man identified himself as William Kaval of Parma (Ohio).

DiMaggio had told *The Plain Dealer*, "Right away the cab driver recognized me. He said, 'Joe, I got a strange feeling in my bones that you're going to get stopped tonight.'"

Confirmed Kaval, "Well, that's something the way it happened. I remember making a lot of stupid small talk with DiMag, and he was very nice.

"I never liked the Yankees — I really hated them like everybody else did in Cleveland those days — but I always liked DiMaggio. He was somebody special to me.

"So just before we got to the stadium, I said to him, 'Joe, I hope you keep the streak going for a hundred games, but I feel like you're not going to get a hit tonight. I hope you do, but I don't think you will.'

"He smiled and said, 'Well, if I don't, I just don't.' But he wasn't mad. In fact, he was just as pleasant when he got out as when he got in my cab.

"Joe gave me a real good tip, too, and if Gomez was mad, like DiMag claimed he was, he didn't say anything to me.

"Maybe Gomez did cuss me out, but if he did, he didn't do it until after I let them out at the players' entrance," continued Kaval . . . who stopped driving cabs in 1942.

How much was DiMaggio's tip?

"Thirty cents," replied Kaval. "But you've got to remember, in those days the meter began at 15 cents and it clicked only once, for a nickel, from the Sheraton to the stadium. That means he owed me 20 cents and he gave me a half-dollar.

"That's 150 percent, isn't it?" asked Kaval.

"I'd heard that story about Gomez being mad, but I never said much about it," continued Kaval. "Not after awhile, anyway, because most of my friends were skeptical. They didn't really believe me when I told them about driving DiMaggio to the stadium that night.

"But I read your story this morning and I said to myself, 'Darn it, I'm going to call Schneider and ask him to do me a favor.'

"The next time you see DiMaggio, would you tell him for me that I'm sorry if he thinks I put the evil eye on him? I sure didn't mean it that way.

"Like I said, I always hated the Yankees, but I liked DiMaggio.

"One more thing," added the ex-cabbie. "Would you ask Joe if he'd autograph a baseball for me? I'd sure like that."

Then Kaval's wife's voice was heard in the background.

"After what you said to him, he'll probably want to *throw* an autographed baseball *at* you."

But I don't think so.

It had to end sometime. After 56 consecutive games, Joe DiMaggio finally came up, as he signals, hitless. It is a record that most baseball observers feel will never be broken.

Joe D streak halted at 56

July 17, 1941
Yanks 4, Indians 3

The classic game for today features New York's classic ballplayer: Joe DiMaggio. Why would 67,468 Cleveland fans pour into Cleveland's Municipal Stadium for a mid-summer game against the Yankees? Because it was a chance to see the great DiMaggio, who had hit safely in 56 consecutive games. This was the day the streak ended. His record still stands.

By JACK SMITH

CLEVELAND, July 17 — One of the greatest feats in the history of baseball — Joe DiMaggio's 56-game hitting streak — ended under the gleaming arclights of huge Municipal Stadium here tonight. The largest crowd ever to see a night game, 67,468 roaring fans, sat tensely through nine spectacular innings which ended with the Yankees beating the second-place Indians, 4-3.

In four trips to the plate, the great Yankee outfielder failed to get the ball out of the infield, drawing one walk and slapping three infield grounders. It was the end of the streak that surpassed by 12 games the previous all-time high for the major leagues and was the driving force in a Yankee surge that carried them from fourth place into the seven-game lead they now hold.

There was nothing glum or crestfallen about DiMag afterward. Joe wore a smile as broad as his shoulders and shouted from the steam of the shower room to his Yank teammates, "I'm tickled to death it's all over. I'm sure proud of the record, but I might as well admit it was quite trying. Naturally I wanted to keep it going. But as long as I didn't, I'm happy about the whole thing."

Joe's streak started more than two months ago, on May 15, when he punched a single into right field off southpaw Ed Smith of the White Sox. During that time he faced every team in the league at least once and teed off on every kind of hurling until the combined work of lefty Al Smith and righthander Jim Bagby stopped him tonight.

DiMaggio was robbed the first time up when he smashed a sizzling grounder toward third. Ken Keltner speared it close to the foul line with a great backhand stab and threw him out at first by two steps.

Joe walked on a 3-2 pitch in the fourth and, in the seventh, whacked the first pitch back to Keltner again. Against Bagby he slapped an easy grounder to Lou Boudreau for an inning-ending double play.

Smith had allowed only two hits as he started the seventh. Henrich and DiMag were infield outs. The third out was not so easy. It didn't come until after Joe Gordon wafted his 15th homer over Walker's lunging hands into the left-field stands 335 feet from the plate.

That should have been the tipoff that Smitty was tiring. He couldn't get past the eighth. Charley Keller led with a liner to center that Roy Weatherly played into a triple. After Keltner threw out Phil Rizzuto, Gomez lined a 3-2 pitch to left, scoring Keller. Johnny Sturm dropped a single into center and Rolfe banged a double to right, scoring Gomez. A walk to Henrich filled the bases, finished Smith and brought DiMaggio to the plate to face Bagby.

It was not Joe's night. He sent an easy grounder to Boudreau, who flipped to Ray Mack for the force on Henrich. Mack pivoted and fired to Grimes for the double play.

YANKEES	ab	r	h	bi	INDIANS	ab	r	h	bi
Sturm 1b	4	0	1	0	Weatherly cf	5	0	1	0
Rolfe 3b	4	1	2	1	Keltner 3b	3	0	1	0
Henrich rf	3	0	1	1	Boudreau ss	3	0	0	0
DiMaggio cf	3	0	0	0	Heath rf	4	0	0	0
Gordon 3b	4	1	2	1	Walker lf	3	2	2	1
Rosar c	4	0	0	0	Mack 2b	3	0	0	0
Keller lf	3	1	1	0	Rosenthal ph	1	0	1	2
Rizzuto ss	4	0	0	0	Hemsley c	3	0	1	0
Gomez p	4	1	1	1	Trotsky ph	1	0	0	0
Murphy p	0	0	0	0	Smith p	3	0	0	0
					Bagby p	0	0	0	0
					Campbell rh	1	0	0	0
Totals	33	4	8	4	Totals	33	3	7	3

Yankees	100	000	120—	4
Indians	000	100	002—	3

LOB—Yankees 5, Indians 7. 2B—Henrich, Rolfe. 3B—Keller, Rosenthal. HR—Walker, Gordon. DP—Indians 1.

	IP	H	R	ER	BB	SO
Gomez (W, 8-3)	8	6	3	3	3	5
Murphy	1	1	0	0	0	0
Smith (L, 6-7)	7⅓	7	4	4	2	1
Bagby	1⅔	1	0	0	1	1

As he looks now

Joe DiMaggio Talks about His Streak

Hit in 56 Straight Games 28 years Ago

by HERB GOREN
Christian Science Monitor

TWENTY-EIGHT YEARS have passed since Joe DiMaggio compiled the greatest achievement in any baseball season — his 56-game hitting streak in 1941.

It is an achievement that has been n o m i n a t e d as baseball's greatest accomplishment, topping Babe Ruth's 60 home runs and Johnny Vander Meer's consecutive no-hit games.

Nowadays, J o e DiMaggio is something of a maverick in baseball, a coach-vice-president of the Oakland Athletics. That's like working in the mail room and doubling in an executive suite. And when I called to re-live the memories o f that streak, Joe seemed surprised.

"Why talk about that now?" he said.

"Because," I said, "it might just be the greatest record any ballplayer ever made."

"I'll leave that for the historians," he replied. "But I'll tell you this: it was an honest record. You saw it. Every base hit was an honest base hit."

I saw it for the *New York Sun* It started out modestly, a single by Joe against a left-hander named Edgar Smith the middle of May, a year in which the Yankees started out in trouble. They were fourth when the streak started. It lasted for two months and two days. When it ended, the Yankees had a grip on first place, and they wrapped up the pennant on Sept. 4, the earliest clinching in history.

And in a very real sense, Di-Maggio carried the Yankees on his broad back. They came alive when the streak became a day-to-day headline and they never stopped winning.

Baseball statistics in 1941 were not provided for by the ball clubs as they are today. Each writer kept his own book. And none got excited about Joe's streak until it had reached 33. That's when he tied the National League record held by Rogers Hornsby, who at the time was universally acclaimed as the greatest right-handed hitter in the game.

That was on June 20 against the Tigers. Joe had four hits that day, the first two against Bobo Newsom. Eight days later, Joe came up against a pitcher who had vowed to stop him.

"Johnny Babich," Joe remembered. "He'd had a tryout with us, and the club sent him out. Then in 1940, he caught on with the A's and he beat us five times. It cost us a pennant. Well, he was still sore, and he seemed to think that if he stopped me, even if he walked me four times, he'd be rubbing it in.

"Well, the first time, the first three pitches were high and wide. They gave me the hit sign, but I couldn't reach that fourth pitch with a ten-foot pole. The second time, ball one, ball two, ball three. But now he gave me one I could get to, and I knocked him on the seat of his pants." It went for a double.

The next day, in Washington, there was a doubleheader and Di-Maggio tied and broke the American League record of 41 held by George Sisler. But not without a slightly traumatic experience.

"I was on the bench," he said.

And, in younger days

"Tommy Henrich hit ahead of me and when he got to the bat rack, he noticed that my bat wasn't there. Mine always rested next to Tommy's. I treasured that bat. And just about then, an usher came down and called over to me. He said he saw somebody poking around there during batting practice. I never used that bat before games. It was stolen."

So DiMaggio had to go with Bat No. 2, and it wasn't quite the same. Joe explained it this way:

"I would order a dozen bats. They would all look alike, same size, same weight. But there's always one that feels different. That's the one I'd work on. I would dip it in olive oil. I'd sprinkle it with resin. I'd put a small flame to it. And when it was good and dry, I'd file it down with sand paper. It would be hard and smooth and black. This was my bread-and-butter bat."

For two days, DiMaggio stayed with Bat No. 2. Meanwhile, there were appeals on the radio and in the press for the return of DiMaggio's bat. Joe put some friends to work. They found the culprit in Newark, N.J., and returned the bat to its rightful owner.

So DiMaggio went back to his first bat, and No. 2 was auctioned off in San Francisco for the benefit of the United Service Organization. It brought $1,600. The all-time streak was 44, by Wee Willie Keeler, the man who immortalized, "I hit 'em where they ain't." DiMaggio passed Willie against Dick Newsom of the Red Sox.

By now, DiMaggio felt a release from the tension of a record he already held, and he got even hotter. He also broke Bat No. 1, and was on a third when the Yankees played a night game in Cleveland's Municipal Stadium before a record crowd under the lights, 67,000 fans.

The streak was 56 games long. Cleveland started a left-hander named Al Smith, and the first two times, Joe drilled hot shots over third base. Somehow, Ken Keltner backhanded both drives and threw him out. The third time, Joe walked.

On his fourth trip, the bases were loaded with one out. Cleveland brought in Jim Bagby, and this time Joe ripped a hot one to the right of Lou Boudreau at short. Lou set himself for it. The ball took a savage hop and Boudreau grabbed it bare-handed.

"No," said DiMaggio. "He smothered it with his chest."

"No," said Boudreau the other day. "I got it with my bare hand. I know. The hand was stinging for an hour after the game was over."

So was DiMaggio. In the dressing room that night he told me he was glad, really. He said the pressure was off.

Ken Keltner had a strange experience too. He was in the clubhouse congratulating himself on his plays when a special cop came in. Ken lives in Milwaukee these days, and thinking back, he said: "The cop told me there were some guys outside gunning for me. He said I'd better get a police escort to the parking lot, just to be on the safe side."

The end of the streak did nothing to satiate DiMaggio's appetite for base hits. He went off on another tear of 16 straight games. The pennant came easily. ∎

LAST CHANCE: A pensive Joe DiMaggio waits for final turn at bat in eighth inning. With bases loaded, DiMag bounced into DP.

Jolting Joe Glad It's Over

Setting Is Dramatic as Final Out Ends Strain of Hitting in Fifty-six Games.

By HERBERT GOREN.

Cleveland, July 18.—Joe DiMaggio's monumental hitting streak, fifty-six games long and more than two months old, is dead. It came to an end in vast Municipal Stadium last night as the Yankees rolled over the Cleveland Indians 4 to 3, before 67,458 fans, and the regret that Joe felt over its passing was more than offset by relief from the heavy pressure that attended his amazing achievement.

For, while DiMaggio kept saying he felt no pressure, once he had passed George Sisler's modern record of forty-one straight games, there was a certain amount of anxiety that stirred within him every afternoon and it grew as the innings passed and he was still hitless.

Joe was stopped in three official trips to the plate last night. The second time he came to bat he walked. The left-handed Al Smith, who used to toil for the Giants, horse-collared him twice, and Jim Bagby came in out of the bull pen in the eighth inning to eliminate DiMaggio's last chance.

There was a dramatic backdrop for DiMaggio's final time at bat. The Yanks were ahead, 4 to 1, and the bases were filled with one out. Two runs already had been scored in the inning. Charley Keller had tripled, Lefty Gomez and Johnny Sturm had singled, Red Rolfe had doubled, and Tommy Henrich, with first base open, drew a pass.

DiMaggio's Final Out.

That prompted Manager Roger Peckinpaugh to yank Smith. Bagby walked in, and the immense throng roared for and against DiMaggio. Everybody on the Yankee bench was standing. This was like old times, like those days when Joe was bearing down on the record and had not reached it.

Bagby's first pitch was too low. Joe let it go by. The next was down around his knees and Joe foul-tipped it. DiMaggio let a second ball go by. Then he came around on Bagby's fourth pitch and bounced a grounder at Shortstop Lou Boudreau. The ball took a nasty hop and almost skipped over Boudreau's shoulder, but Lou got his glove up in time and started a double play, Boudreau to Ray Mack to Oscar Grimes, who was on first base.

DiMaggio betrayed no emotion. He rounded first base, jogged into center, picked up his glove and was ready for the inning to start. There was no kicking of the dirt, no shaking of his head. He had gone a long, long way, as far as he could.

DiMaggio's streak carried the Yankees from second place into the league lead by six full games. The night it ended the Bombers grabbed another game on the Indians. The record drive was started on May 15 in Chicago and during its existence DiMaggio hit at a .408 pace. Today he leads the American League in runs batted in, runs and hits, is tied for the top in homers and is on his way toward overtaking Ted Williams for the batting crown.

DiMaggio's numbers

Some little known facts about Joe DiMaggio's record 56-game hitting streak:

• It started against a pitcher named Smith (Edgar) of the Chicago White Sox on May 15 and it ended against a pitcher named Smith (Al) in Cleveland two months and two days later.

• In the 56 games, DiMaggio had just one hit 34 times.

• A crowd of 67,468 attended the game the night DiMaggio was stopped.

• In the 56 games, DiMaggio hit safely against 43 different pitchers with Elden Auker and Bob Harris of the St. Louis Browns serving as his favorite patsies by contributing five hits each.

• During the streak, DiMaggio had 91 hits, including 16 doubles, four triples and 15 homers, for a .408 average. He also scored 56 runs and drove in 55 and struck out seven times in the 56 games. For the season, DiMaggio struck out 13 times in 541 at bats.

• For the season, DiMaggio batted .357 and finished third in the American League. Ted Williams won the batting title with a .406 mark. Cecil Travis of the Senators was second, two points ahead of Joe D.　　**—Pepe**

DIMAGGIO'S 56-GAME STREAK CAPTIVATED A NATION

In 1941, Joltin' Joe's heroic effort was spread out over two months and dominated the news

BY RICK TALLEY
The Chicago Tribune

IT has been called the greatest individual achievement in the history of baseball. The most inviolate record in baseball. An imperishable mark.

Joe DiMaggio's 56-game hitting streak.

The year, 1941. Whirlaway was to win racing's Triple Crown. Joe Louis would knock out Billy Conn. Bobby Riggs was the U.S. singles tennis champ. Sid Luckman quarterbacked the Bears. Frankie Albert was All-America at Stanford. Ted Williams hit .406.

Joe DiMaggio was the symbol of the time. Life wasn't complicated during the summer of '41. It was understandable.

"Everybody knew Joe DiMaggio," wrote Jimmy Breslin years later, "and could depend on him, and there was never any trouble when Joe DiMaggio played center field.

"Our wars had enemies to hate and heroes to glorify, and the summers were soft and the music was slow and the kids went to school and the questions could be answered."

It was the year actor Mickey Rooney would become engaged to Hollywood newcomer Ava Gardner. People listened to Dr. IQ, Major Bowes, and Henry Aldrich on the radio. "Sergeant York" was a hit movie. So was "Citizen Kane."

Ballplayers had draft numbers. Whole boiled live lobster cost $1.10.

Americans were aware of a shadow of a war, even though the bombs wouldn't fall on Pearl Harbor for another seven months. It was the summer of Lou Gehrig's death, and people sang a No. 1 hit song they didn't understand: "Hut-sut rawlson on the rillerah and a brawla, brawla soo-it."

And Joe DiMaggio was to hit safely in 56 consecutive games.

It started on May 15 against the White Sox, with the 26-year-old DiMaggio, in his sixth pro season, fighting a slump.

"I'm lunging and hitting some on the handle," DiMaggio told reporters. Two months later, after the streak had been ended in Cleveland, DiMaggio would say: "I wanted it to go on forever."

The peculiarity of a hitting streak, and the beauty, is that it builds so slowly. Nobody noticed DiMaggio's streak until the 18th game. He had been fighting a swollen neck, and the Yankees were fighting a slow start. But he kept getting his hits. Then, by the time the streak had reached 24, Joe recalled "for the first time that year I really knew I was hitting the ball well."

His first goal was to break the Yankee mark of 29, shared by Roger Peckinpaugh and Earle Combs.

Once that was accomplished, he swept toward marks held by Ty Cobb and George Sisler. This wasn't new to Joe. When he was 18, he had hit safely in 61 consecutive Pacific Coast League games.

Now, though, as DiMaggio's streak drew more and more attention, the pressure became massive. He couldn't stop in restaurants because fans would tear at his clothes for souvenirs. He quit going out in public altogether.

"Some days I would open my hotel door," DiMaggio would say later, "and there'd be 50 kids waiting outside my room for autographs. I got to know more back exits from hotels than any man in the world."

To this day, Joe DiMaggio remains one of baseball's most popular folk heroes

During the streak, DiMaggio never bunted once (Pete Rose bunted safely six times during his 44-game streak).

"I don't know if Joe can bunt," said his manager, Joe McCarthy. "And I'll never find out."

The closest scorer's call during his streak came in game No. 30, when he established the Yankee record.

It was a routine, seventh-inning ground ball to shortstop Luke Appling of the White Sox — but as Appling reached for the ball, it took a bad hop and caromed off his shoulder. Appling grabbed for the ball, dropped it, picked it up and fired late to first.

In those days, the Yankee Stadium scoreboard did not register hits and errors, so everybody looked quickly toward the press box for a signal. The official scorer, Dan Daniel, hesitated — then leaned over the railing and held up a finger to indicate a hit.

It was the only hit in the streak that DiMaggio felt wasn't clean. The rest of the time, he was remarkable. In 223 at bats, he got 91 hits (.408), including 16 doubles, four triples, and 15 home runs. He also had 55 RBI and only seven strikeouts during the amazing two-month span.

The whole nation was swept up in DiMaggio's quest to topple the marks of Sisler (41) and Willie Keeler (44).

In every radio newcast, the announcer would begin: "Before we give you the news — yes, Joe DiMaggio did hit in his 33rd straight game." Or: "Germany invades Russia. Details in a moment. First, Joe DiMaggio got his hit today to extend . . . "

In game No. 36, it almost ended. Bob Muncrief, 25-year-old rookie for the St. Louis Browns, had stopped him three straight times. Then, in the bottom of the eighth, DiMaggio lined a single to left.

"Why didn't you walk DiMaggio the last time up to stop him?" manager Luke Sewell asked Muncrief afterward.

"That wouldn't have been fair," said Muncrief. "To him or me. Hell, he's the greatest ballplayer I've ever seen."

By now, though, everybody was out to stop DiMaggio. Newspapers heralded his arrival in each city. Ballparks were jammed. Pitchers bore down as never before. "Stop DiMag" was the battle cry in American League dugouts.

Then somebody stole his bat. It happened between games of a doubleheader in Griffith Stadium, Washington. DiMaggio had hit safely in the first game, tying Sisler's record of 41 — but now the bat (36 ounces, 36 inches) was missing. He borrowed an identical model used by Tommy Henrich to break the record in the second game.

Ten days later, with the streak still alive but DiMaggio under a tremendous strain, an unidentified man phoned him in the Yankee clubhouse and said:

"I'm from Newark, New Jersey, and I know where your bat is. One of our guys pulled it from the rack for a souvenir. He didn't mean no harm. He loves you, Joe. He didn't mean no harm."

DiMaggio simply said: "I want it back." And when he arrived at the clubhouse the next day, it was there. And he kept hitting.

Les Brown and his Band of Renown were swinging to a new hit song ("Joltin' Joe DiMaggio"), and you could almost always find Bojangles Bill Robinson dancing on the Yankee dugout at home games, spreading what he called "Goofer Dust" over the roof to bring his favorite team good luck.

When the Yankees arrived in Chicago on July 13, a crowd of 50,387 turned out at Comiskey Park. DiMaggio got three hits in the first game and his streak now stood at 52. In the eighth inning of the second game, he singled to stretch it to 53.

On the next day, he was hitless in the sixth before topping a slow grounder toward third baseman Bob Kennedy (now Cubs' vice president). Kennedy, playing deep, had no chance to make the play, and the streak reached 54.

It was to be stopped by Ken Keltner and Lou Boudreau in Cleveland, just a few days later.

Twice Keltner made sensational stops at third base and barely nipped DiMaggio at first with strong throws. Then, in his final at bat against reliever Jim Bagby, Joe hit a sharp grounder toward second base. The shortstop, Boudreau, moved swiftly to his left, speared a bad hop and flipped to second baseman Ray Mack, who fired to first for a double play. The streak was finished.

DiMaggio had done it against 47 different pitchers and had carried the Yankees with him. They won 41 and lost 13 during Joe's torrid trip, and later teammate Bill Dickey was to say: "DiMaggio during this period gave the most consistent performance under pressure I have ever seen."

Afterward, somebody suggested that the Yanks change DiMaggio's number to 56. He refused because he said it would be like bragging. Somebody else said he could have made a financial killing with one more hit and a rumored contract with the Heinz 57 company.

But Joe got no financial reward. Not at that time — even though he immediately began another hitting streak of 17 games.

The Yankees, in fact, tried to cut his salary the following year by $2,500. He was earning only $37,500 at the time and, after a bitter period of haggling with management, he finally received a raise of $5,000.

DiMaggio played one more season, then served three years in military service. And though he returned to play another six years with the Yankees, there would never be another season for DiMaggio like 1941.

DANIEL'S DOPE

By Dan Daniel

CLEVELAND, July 18.—According to Joe Di Maggio, the hardest-hit ball of his long batting streak, which was ended by Al Smith and Jim Bagby under the floodlights in Cleveland last night, was the eighth-inning double to left off Elden Auker in the Stadium on June 26. That blow made it game No. 38 for Giuseppe.

Asked to designate the hit which, in his opinion, overcame the most serious obstacles in his continuing the spree, Joe replied, "That single I got off Johnny Rigney last Monday, when he broke our winning streak. I sure thought I was finished that afternoon. But in the sixth inning I topped a ball that stuck halfway to third base, and I beat it out easily."

However, in Joe McCarthy's book, the master stroke of the Di Maggio streak came in the second half of last Sunday's double-header in Chicago. Thornton Lee, left-hander, was pitching for the White Sox.

Lee was out to halt the Yankees and carried them into the 11th inning, while the Sox did not get a run off Red Ruffing. Eager as the southpaw was to stop the club, he seemed to be even more determined to snap the Di Maggio skein.

"The hit which Joe got off Lee in the sixth was a masterpiece," McCarthy said today. "Lee did not give Di Maggio a decent pitch all through the game. You will recollect that Joe grounded out to Knickerbocker in the first off a low ball and got a pass in the fourth.

"In his next time up Di Maggio waited for a good one in vain. Lee threw a high curve that hung there and Joe reached up, pulled that ball down and drove it into right-center. For my money that was the most artistic hit of the 90-odd he has made since May 15."

* * *

There is an interesting sidelight on Cleveland's chances for the pennant. At Detroit last week, when the American League repealed the rule which forbids the champion from making trades, the vote was 5 to 3. Supporting Washington and Philadelphia in the minority was, strangely enough, Cleveland. Baseball analysts say that if Alva Bradley had been loaded with confidence in the ability of the Indians to overhaul the Yankees he would not have voted to shackle the 1941 winner with that silly old rule.

* * *

Di Maggio's Streak Thrilled Customers.

Di Maggio's streak was a godsend to baseball in general and the American League in particular. It thrilled the customers all over the circuit and aroused the fans from coast to coast. Even last night the onlookers were strong for the Yankee streaker. They wanted to see the Indians win, but they were just as eager to see Giuseppe hit in his 57th straight game.

Interest in Joe's feat did not begin to develop into a major circumstance until he had hit in 30 games. Then the experts tumbled to the fact that this thing was serious. Di Maggio himself says he did not become aroused over the possibility of a record until he had hit in 33 games. Even then it took Mrs. Joe to make Di Maggio aware of the fact that he had before him a tremendous opportunity, a chance such as had not come to any ball player since Hank Greenberg came within two homers of Babe Ruth's all-time record of 60, in 1938.

Last night Di Maggio hit with more abandon than he had since the streak became a serious threat to the Sisler and Keeler records. It seemed that the continuous strain finally had made Giuseppe touchy. He had reached a point at which he was quite willing to toss the thing into the laps of the gods. Joe was out to shoot the works. He did not always wait for the good pitch. Perhaps he sensed that Al Smith was not going to risk anything, either as concerned Di Maggio or the ball game. Al was out to walk Joe rather than pitch to him.

* * *

While Di Maggio was on his streak the Yankees did some amazing hitting. They got homers in such cloisers, and with such profusion, as never before had been seen in the major leagues. Pitchers turned in deeds of derring do, fielders went daffy, as a club which had been seven lengths behind the Indians dashed into an incredible lead in so short a time.

But all these feats were submerged under the wave of popular excitement over the Di Maggio streak. Now the spotlight can be trained on this New York club as a machine. That Di Maggio mark is high enough. Perhaps no other hitter ever again will poke baseballs safely in 56 straight games.

The Crusher

YANKEES						INDIANS					
	ab	r	h	po	a		ab	r	h	po	a
Sturm, 1b	4	0	1	10	2	Weath'y, cf	5	0	1	4	0
Rolfe, 3b	4	1	2	2	3	Keltner, 3b	3	0	1	1	4
Henrich, rf	3	0	1	4	0	Boud'u, ss	3	0	0	0	2
DiM'io, cf	3	0	0	2	0	Heath, rf	4	0	0	0	0
Gordon, 2b	4	1	2	0	1	Walker, lf	3	2	2	1	0
Rosar, c	4	0	0	5	1	Grimes, 1b	3	1	1	12	0
Keller, lf	3	1	1	0	0	Mack, 2b	3	0	0	4	7
Rizzuto, ss	4	0	0	2	1	*Rosenthal	1	0	1	0	0
Gomez, p	4	1	1	2	1	Hemsley, c	3	0	1	5	1
Murphy, p	0	0	0	0	1	†Trosky	1	0	0	0	0
						Smith, p	3	0	0	0	0
						Bagby, p	0	0	0	0	0
						‡Campbell	1	0	0	0	0

Totals 33 4 8 27 10   Totals 33 3 7 27 14

*Batted for Mack in ninth inning.
†Batted for Hemsley in ninth inning.
‡Batted for Bagby in ninth inning.

Yankees ————— 1 0 0 0 0 0 1 2 4—4
Indians ————— 0 0 0 1 0 0 0 0 2—3

Runs batted in—Henrich, Walker, Gomez, Gordon, Rolfe, Rosenthal (2). Two-base hits—Henrich, Rolfe. Three-base hits—Keller, Rosenthal. Home runs—Walker, Gordon. Sacrifice—Boudreau. Double play—Boudreau, Mack and Grimes. Left on bases—Yankees, 5; Indians, 7. Bases on balls—Off Smith, 2; off Bagby, 1; off Gomez, 3. Struck out—By Gomez, 5; by Smith, 4; by Bagby, 1. Hits—Off Smith, 7, in 7 1-3 innings; off Bagby, 1 in 1 1-2; off Gomez, 6, in 8 (none out in ninth), off Murphy, 1 in 1. Passed ball—Hemsley. Winning pitcher—Gomez. Losing pitcher—Smith. Umpires—Summers, Rue and Stewart. Time—2:03. Attendance—67,468.

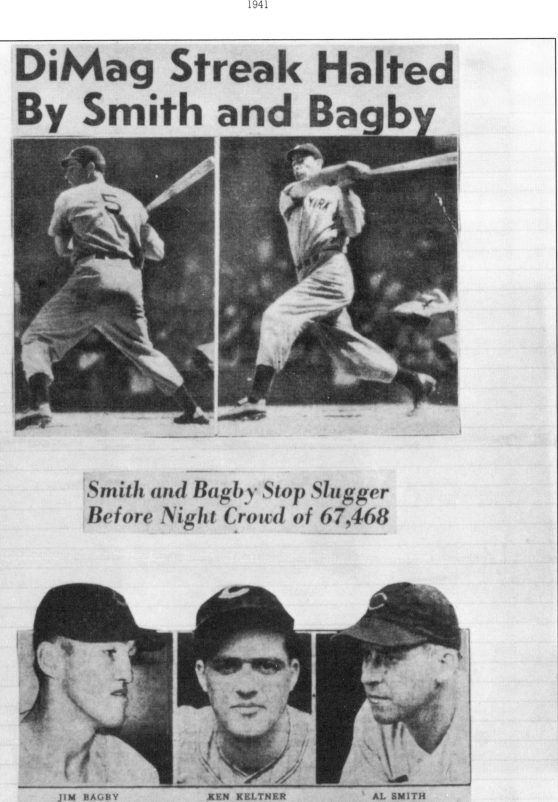

DiMag Streak Halted By Smith and Bagby

Smith and Bagby Stop Slugger Before Night Crowd of 67,468

JIM BAGBY   KEN KELTNER   AL SMITH

Here's trio of Cleveland Indians who stopped Joe DiMaggio's batting streak Thursday night at Cleveland. Smith and Bagby did the hurling against DiMag while sparkling fielding of Keltner stymied DiMag at 56-game mark of long string.

Those who stopped DiMaggio.

56 Games in Row

DiMag's Incredible Hitting Skein

BROEG ON BASEBALL

By BOB BROEG

ST. PETERSBURG, Fla.—No April Foolin', one of the most surprised players ever was Ted Williams in 1941, and not because he hit .406. Heck, 16 years later at 39, Ted hit .388.

Williams' surprise back there just before the attack on Pearl Harbor was because he didn't win the American League's Most Valuable Player award.

He didn't win it despite outhitting Joe DiMaggio by 49 points, homering seven more times (37) and logging only five fewer RBIs (120). Ted didn't make it even though Williams batted four points higher than DiMaggio (.412) during one stretch that prompted the MVP accolade for Joe, most definitely the better all-round player.

THE CLUE, OF course, is the year, 1941. That was the season DiMaggio put together the incredible 56-game hitting streak, perhaps the most amazing feat of sustained excellence in baseball history.

The 56 was so magic that back there in 1941, John Edward Wray, St. Louis Post-Dispatch sports editor, suggested that a "6" be added to DiMaggio's "5" as an enduring uniform number.

Just recently, talking to a gang of gaffers about single-season superlatives, I emphasized the high regard among present-day players for Hack Wilson's 190 RBIs in 1930. I pointed out they had been more impressed by that than by Rogers Hornsby's .424 average, George Sisler's 257 hits, Earl Webb's 67 doubles, Chief Wilson's 36 triples, Babe Ruth's 60 homers, Roger Maris' 61 round-trippers and Jack Chesbro's 41 victories.

"WHY," INQUIRED a geezer smarter than I, "didn't you throw DiMaggio's 56-game straight at 'em?"

H'mm, the same question Maris had asked when I polled the pennant-winning Cardinals 10 years ago. "Did you forget DiMag's streak?" asked Rog.

No, but I guess I'd thought of it as a CAREER achievement rather than a single-season feat.

And then just recently, "56" again was brought into focus by a television movie in which Robert Mitchum played private eye Philip Marlowe in a redo of Raymond Chandler's book, "Farewell My Lovely." Mitchum fretted through the mounting suspense of DiMag's streak 37 years ago.

THE YANKS were struggling, just like their 26-year-old super star in mid-May of 1941. DiMag was in a slump and so were the Bombers, playing only .500 ball and in fourth place, 5½ games behind the Indians, who had led the previous season until the Tigers caught them on the final weekend.

Then, on May 15, 1941, as the Yanks lost again, DiMaggio hit a run-scoring single off chunky Chicago southpaw Edgar Smith. For the next two months, the lithe, long-legged lad got at least one hit a day.

Over that span of 56 games, spurring the Yankees into the lead and World Series, DiMaggio hit .408. His 91 hits included 16 doubles, four triples and 15 homers for 160 total bases. He drove in 55 runs, walked 21 times and struck out in just seven of 223 trips.

The immigrant fisherman's son topped George Sisler's 19-year-old streak of 41 games and Wee Willie Keeler's string of 44 consecutive contests set in 1897.

ONLY A COUPLE of infield hits were included in DiMag's string. Only a time or two did players and fans strain to see what the official scorer would decide. Although DiMaggio could circle the bases with corner-cutting speed and long strides, he was not a fast man getting to first base. Most definitely not a leg hitter.

Cleveland's Al Smith and Jim Bagby combined to stop him July 17, a result of two brilliant stops by Ken Keltner at third base and a hot smash turned into a double play by Lou Boudreau at shortstop. Meanwhile, the Yankees had profited by playing at a .759 pace in the 56 games. They'd won 41, tied two and lost just 13.

Astonishingly, DiMaggio immediately hit in 17 more games in a row, giving him 73 out of 74 in a season in which he played in only 139 contests for the pin-stripers.

NINE YEARS before that, when DiMaggio was only 18, he put together a 61-game hitting streak with the San Francisco Seals of the Pacific Coast League. It attracted so much attention that even Papa DiMaggio became a baseball fan.

The day the future Yankee Clipper clipped the old PCL record by hitting in his 50th straight game, Mayor Angelo Rossi of San Francisco gave him a gold watch and gave his mother and young sister flowers. Joe's old Boys' Club, the Jolly Knights of North Beach, gave him a traveling bag and his Seals' teammates presented him with a check.

Pressure? Sure, Mr. Coffee of the distinguished, gray-templed present felt it then, but he thrived on it. Against the Seals' old rivals, the Los Angeles Angels, DiMag

Joe DiMaggio

threw out a runner from right field in the first inning. Then he prompted a five-minute standing ovation his first time up—by low-bridging Buck Newsom with a two-run single after Old Bobo had boasted how he'd stop the kid.

IN 1941, YANKEE teammates surprised him with a private party at which they gave him a handsome engraved silver cigarette humidor, one with his batting likeness on it, plus the record and the signatures of his appreciative comrades in pin stripes.

At pro baseball's centennial in 1969 at Washington, where it rained on Bowie Kuhn's parade, Joseph Paul DiMaggio was decreed the greatest living player. Ted Williams, then managing in Washington, wasn't at the dinner.

Ted hadn't forgotten the cruel coincidence by which the same year he'd become the LAST guy to hit .400, the other guy had become the ONLY fella to hit in 56 straight.

Sports of The Times

By ARTHUR DALEY

An Epic Accomplishment

JOE DIMAGGIO rifled a shot just inside the bag at third base. It should have been a double. But Ken Keltner of the Indians made an acrobatic backhand stab at the ball and threw out the runner at first. The Walls of Jericho had started to crumble. Later they crumbled still more when Keltner made almost as spectacular a seizure of another bid for a double. Thus ended at 56 consecutive games the hitting streak that had been fashioned by the Yankee Clipper.

The next day DiMadge was off on another tear. He was to rip through 16 more games of consecutive hitting and no one even noticed. But for two solid months, especially during the last month of mounting drama, the Jolter commanded a nation's attention. Day after day a waiting world was engrossed in the same question: Had DiMaggio hit safely? He had.

There are 158 pages of tightly packed records in the Little Red Book, the official compendium of baseball records. Some of the career marks have the weight of time to give them stature but it is doubtful that there is any sustained effort in the almanac that can quite match the epic accomplishment of the Yankee Clipper. He himself regards it as his most signal personal achievement, outranking in his estimation his three most-valuable-player awards and his two batting championships.

Highest Honors

The hitting streak was an important factor in Joe's election to the Hall of Fame and probably was the motivating influence in the new honors bestowed on him during the Baseball Centennial a few weeks ago. One of these was the designation as "the greatest living player." It will be in that role that DiMaggio will return to the Yankee Stadium on Saturday to receive the acclaim of the faithful during Old-Timers Day, when outstanding Yankees over the years will play an abbreviated game against outstanding opponents.

It's now 28 years since the Jolter compiled that glittering string and he himself even mar-

vels at it with an unbelieving shake of his head and a deprecatory grin. He got to talking about it again in Washington.

"There has to be an element of luck to it," he said modestly, "but the one thing that sticks in my mind is that whenever I kept the streak alive with a scratch hit, I always came through in that same game with an honest hit that could not be questioned. That's what made it so satisfying."

Joe DiMaggio in 1941
A 56-game streak takes luck

He had some close calls, of course. One was when he went into the last inning without a hit against tough Eldon Auker, the submarine ball pitcher, and DiMadge was to be the fourth hitter that inning. He wouldn't even get a swing unless a teammate got on base. With one out Red Rolfe walked and the thoughtful Tommy Henrich called time before returning to the

dugout for a brief conference with Manager Joe McCarthy.

"Joe," said Tommy, "If I hit into a double play, DiMadge won't even get to bat. Is it all right with you if I bunt?"

"Good idea," said McCarthy. "Drop down a bunt."

Henrich deftly sacrificed Rolfe to second and the Jolter slashed the first pitch to left for a double.

There was anxiety on DiMadge's part in a game against the Red Sox. One more hit would lift him past the record of 44 consecutive games established by Wee Willie Keeler, the legendary character who "hit 'em where they ain't."

Heber Newsome was pitching for the Bosox and he always gave the Clipper trouble. In the first at bat Joe lashed into one. But Stan Spence made a circus catch and Joe's heart sank. Then he hit one harder and farther the next time up. However, another supersensational catch was made in deepest center by Joe's little brother, Dom.

His Brother's Keeper

"It speaks well for the integrity of the game," said Joe on his return to the dugout, "but it wasn't diplomatic, especially when Dom is coming to my house for dinner tonight."

Two good shots against Newsome and two loud outs. It was more than par for the course and DiMadge worried. But then he hit one where no outfielder could catch the ball—a homer into the stand.

Once Johnny Babich of the Athletics walked the Clipper time and time again. In Joe's last at bat, Babich threw three wide ones. DiMadge looked despairingly for what had to be the take sign. Instead it was a green light. He could hit away.

"Good old Joe McCarthy," said DiMadge gratefully and exploded a hit that almost cut Babich's legs from under him.

Bob Muncrief of the old Browns could have halted him with a walk in the last inning but pitched away. DiMadge singled. The Brownie manager was critical of his pitcher for not stopping the Clipper with a walk.

"That wouldn't have been fair to him—or me," said Muncrief. "Hell, he's the greatest player I ever saw."

A lot of other people also think he's the greatest player they ever saw. They can look at him again at the Stadium on Saturday.

The Yankees today turned down the suggestion made in many quarters that Joe Di Maggio's number be changed from 5 to 56. . . . It had been proposed that Di Mag always bear a memento of his 56-game batting streak. . . . The Bombers have won 28, lost 12 and tied 1 in the Stadium this season. . . . The Yanks have a set of Japanese beetle traps in their dugout. . . . After

Joe Di Maggio

yesterday's game a fan made some nasty remarks to Cleveland players as they neared the Yankee dugout on their way to the clubhouse. George Susce, bullpen catcher, took up the issue and for a while it looked like a fight. . . . With his 22nd homer, Di Maggio made his runs-driven-in total tops for the majors, 84. Keller's 23rd drove in two and made his total 81. . . . It's a great race. . . . Bobby Feller said he did not feel right the first four innings on Tuesday and was inclined to blame a ride in an air-conditioned car the night before the battle. . . . In the seventh inning yesterday the Yanks got double play No. 113 when Rolfe,

Gordon and Sturm came to Russo's rescue after Trosky had doubled and Grimes had walked. . . . Grimes played second base, with Ray Mack benched for the first time in two seasons. . . . Russo gave himself a lift in the third when he picked Grimes off second. . . . The Yanks flopped twice with the bases loaded. . . . In the second, Russo hit into a double play with three on, and in the fifth Rosar failed. . . . The victory over Smith made the Yankee score against lefties 18 and 7. . . . Peck finally decided that Milnar could not beat the Bombers and kept him off the pitching list for the series which ends today.

* * *

DIMAGGIO FAILS AS DO YANKS FOR WORST DAY

Browns' Double Victory Smashes All Kinds of New York Streaks.

By HERBERT GOREN

Washington, Aug. 4.—Everybody in the American League has his own opinion as to whether Joe DiMaggio sparked the Yankees, or the Yankees sparked Joe DiMaggio. But on the eve of the McCarthymen's swing around the East, which starts here today, there was evidence of a negative nature which would indicate that DiMaggio carried the team.

Joe did not hit yesterday. He had his worst day of the season at bat, going 8 for 0. The Yankees were just as bad. They had their worst day, too, getting a total of six hits in two games with the Browns against the knuckle-ball pitching of Johnny Niggeling and the fast ball of Bob Harris.

Up to getaway day, DiMaggio had hit safely in seventy-two out of seventy-three games. No single pitcher had stopped him through nine innings since May 14. Both Niggeling and Harris horse-collared him yesterday, the latter with consummate ease.

DiMaggio hit in hard luck against the butterfly serves of Niggeling. Johnny Berardino, Brownie shortstop, took a hit away from him the first time he stepped to the plate with a diving catch. Later in the game, Roy Cullenbine went 400 feet to the bleacher wall in left center to pull down one of his towering smashes. This discouraged DiMaggio and hurt his average, for he lost nine points, dropping down to .373 to provide Ted Williams with a bigger batting lead than ever.

Real Streak Breakers.

The Browns really turned out to be streak bursters yesterday. They shattered Red Ruffing's nine-game winning spree. They stopped the run of scoreless innings by Yankee pitchers after it had reached thirty-five, six short of the record set by Cleveland in 1903. They plastered the Yankees with their first double defeat in ten twin bills this year.

The last time Ruffing had lost a game was on May 14. Mel Harder beat him. Harder that day stopped DiMaggio and Joe went on from there to a record-hitting streak. Ruffing pitched good ball yesterday, but he tired in the late innings when the breaks went against him and did not have enough in reserve to pitch out of difficulties.

Niggeling hurled remarkable ball against Ruffing. He was touched for four hits and two runs over the first three innings but that was the end of Yankee scoring, not only against Niggeling but also for the day. John's knuckler dipped and darted through six perfect innings.

Harris picked up from there. He blanked the Bombers with

two cheap hits in the nightcap. With better luck he might have had a no-hitter. Johnny Sturm, first batter to face him, dropped a pop fly double near the left field line. In the eighth Phil Rizzuto got a single when Outfielder Walt Judnich charged in and failed to hold a line drive off the grass tops. That was the sum total of Yankee power. The Bombers were a picture of futility.

Harris's two-hit shutout was the second pitched against the Yankees this season. The first was by another fellow named Harris—Mickey of the Red Sox—and it was unfolded in the afterpiece of a double header, as was the case yesterday.

DiMaggio's Hitting Weak.

Only two Yankees reached second base against Harris, and none reached third. The Brownie righthander walked three batters, Tommy Henrich twice, and it was very humiliating because DiMaggio, following Henrich, did not hit the ball with any great gusto in most of his appearances.

Atley Donald started for the McCarthymen. He just did not have it and was knocked out in the sixth inning. This was his third loss against five victories. The Brownies pummeled him for ten hits and all five runs before Ernie Bonham was rushed in from the bullpen.

Fortunately, the Yankees lost only one game in the day's doings, for the best the Indians could do against the Athletics was to gain an even break. Against the West on the home stand the Yankees won ten out of fourteen. They came to the Stadium with a lead of seven games. They left fully eleven and a half lengths out in front.

On the Line

——With CONSIDINE

NO ARGUMENT HERE

New York, Aug. 6.—All speculation over the identity of the highest salaried ball player should end next winter. Joe DiMaggio is going to ask for $80,000 for 1942. And even if he is belted down 10 or 20 thousand dollars less than that sum, he'll still be getting about twice as much as his nearest rival. Probably more than twice, because it looks as if Bobby Feller, who would have made $40,000 next year, will be making $21 a month on another kind of squad, when the 1942 season opens.

CONSIDINE

Babe Ruth reached his high-water mark of $80,000 in 1930 and held it there for two years before slipping back to $75,000. He was raised to his peak from $70,000, which sum he earned in 1927, 1928 and 1929. Looking at Babe's 1929 record, which more or less sponsored the pay raise to $80,000 in 1930, we find that Babe played in 135 games, went to bat 499 times, scored 121 runs, made 172 hits, smacked 46 home runs and batted .345.

Up until today's assignment in Boston, DiMaggio was hitting .372, had played in 105 games, had gone to bat 419 times, scored 100 runs, made 156 hits, belted 25 home runs and driven in 94 runs. Joe has about 50 games left to play, counting ties. There is little doubt that he will surpass Babe's 1929 mark in every department except home runs. Joe is either leading or contending in every department of the sizzling American batting race.

Joe's Arguments Will Be Strong

What Joe asks for and what he gets out of Ed Barrow usually are two different things. But he'll have one vastly important thing on his side next time he argues his case. For the first time he will have absolute proof that he draws customers personally. That was Ruth's great forte, of course, and the reason Babe made more money out of baseball than any other man ever did or probably ever will. Babe played on more colorful Yank teams than the present one, but nevertheless he remained the top lure. As attractive as were the old Yanks, there would be cancellations galore when word spread that Babe was going to be missing from the line-up—as he was on 19 occasions in 1929.

The Yanks couldn't win a pennant through the three-year period of Babe's highest salaries. Nor, curiously enough, was Babe named most valuable player in any of those years. In fact, he got that title only once, and that was in 1922.

DiMag's batting streaks and the way they have sparked the Yankees this season have not only taken the club to the top of the league race and insured a rich World Series but will attract more than a million and a quarter customers to the Yankee Stadium for regular league games this season. On the road the team will draw perhaps another million fans and share secondarily in the profits derived from same. The 1941 club, with a comparatively modest payroll, will make more money than the 1929 club.

He's the Clincher

The magic name DiMaggio has done most of this, granting the fact that he couldn't do it alone and duly allowing for the splendid comebacks of Keller, Ruffing, Gomez, Dickey and Rolfe, and the fine seasons being had by Rizzuto, Gordon and Henrich. But DiMag has been the clincher. The newspapers, radio and newsreels sing his praises because he is the one Yank the baseball public demands to read about, hear about and see. In St. Louis last month the management of the Browns bought advertising spreads in local papers to urge hibernating St. Louis fans to come out to the park to see if Joe could prolong his batting streak. P. S.—They came.

All this will be on Joe's side when he goes after more money than any ball player has dreamed of earning since the days of the immortal Babe—more money, of course, than F. D. R. makes. Joe has many profoundly good arguments on his side, including proof that he attracted at least $80,000—the sum he wants—in extra admissions during the span of a few days while he was making good his assault on the old batting marks of George Sisler and Willie Keeler.

There will be a few scattered grumbles, we dare say. We doubt if the Yankee management will take kindly to Joe's salary ambitions, in view of the fact that the executors of the estate are sort of looking to the Yanks to help with the huge tax demands on the late Jake Ruppert's fortune.

Injury List Claims Four Regulars—Pitchers Sag

Bombers May Find Range Again in Series Against Hard-Hitting Red Sox

By DANIEL,
World-Telegram Staff Writer.

BOSTON, Aug. 6.—As the Yankees today have lost three out of four for the first time since June 5, when they followed up a setback in Cleveland with two straight reverses in Detroit, an investigation was in order. This inquiring reporter discovered that quite a few of the Bombers were a bit the worse for wear, and that a few of them had been carrying on for some time with bruises and other handicaps.

After the 4-to-3 defeat which the Yankees suffered in their farewell to Washington, it was quite evident that they had begun to feel the pace. Just how long this natural letdown will linger, nobody can predict. The very sight of the socking Red Sox may rouse the Blasters out of the doldrums into which they sank in the superheated capital. And then again, this tired and bruised feeling may hang on long enough to begin giving Joe McCarthy a recurrence of his old insomnia.

After Doc Painter and his injury list, fever charts, liniments and nostrums had made the rounds on the New York club's arrival from Washington, it was discovered that these more important injuries threatened the happiness of the hitherto carefree pacemakers:

1. Charley Keller was nursing a swollen big toe, hurt in batting practice last Sunday, and which in the finale with the Senators prevented King Kong from doing anything more vital than pinch hitting, without success, in the ninth. With two out and two on and the game in his bat, he hoisted Senor Carrasquel's first pitch to Catcher Early.

2. Joe Gordon had a badly swollen and very stiff knee, having crashed into Early in a desperate fifth-inning effort to score.

3. Tom Henrich's right thigh was a mass of angry bruises. He got this accumulation of welts with his pads out of place on Monday.

4. Bill Dickey had an injured right arm, having been belted by a foul tip.

Di Maggio Could Stand Couple of Days Off.

On top of this, Joe Di Maggio undeniably has gone stale. No wonder. The reaction from that long batting streak was bound to come, and it took a lot of fortitude and zip to get going again for 16 games before bogging down. That heat in Washington didn't help, either.

Not that Giuseppe was collared by the astonishing Carresquel, who not only made his first start of the season, but pitched right through and held the Bombers to eight blows, the Venezuelan had fine control and issued just one pass. Joe got into the hit column, but with only one blow, and came into the Hub with an average of .372.

It would be a blessing for Di Maggio if he could take a couple of days off. But he is the one Yankee who cannot be spared, even for a game, and even in the face of the big lead the eased-up Bombers were enjoying.

This New York outfit is a highly-geared, sensitive machine, with all its power. Just missing Keller was enough to disarrange things in Washington. George Selkirk, making his first appearance in the outfield since June 3, got himself a hit. But Old Twink no longer is a powerhouse.

Russo Beaten, Pitching Also Shows Fatigue.

McCarthy's pitching, which not so many days back looked more than elegant, also has taken on that appearance of lassitude. Rube Russo, who started his campaign so brilliantly with a three-hit shutout in the Capital, was the fourth straight New York hurler who was not in at the finish. In the eighth, Johnny Murphy made his 26th appearance of the season.

Russo turned in a grand game against Cleveland, for his ninth victory. But against the Tigers he failed to last, Murphy getting credit for the triumph.

Yesterday the lefthander got off on the wrong foot, and the Senators belted him for three runs in the first. In the second errors by the pitcher and John Sturm helped the ultimate winners to another tally.

Thus Russo got his seventh defeat instead of his 10th victory, and that high promise of an 18-game season, which developed from his spring form, now must go a-glimmering. Big as he is, Marius does not seem to have the essential stamina.

Di Mag Out for Week with Turned Ankle

Injury Not Regarded Serious by Doctors

By JOE KING,
Staff Writer.

DETROIT, Aug. 20.—Joe Di Maggio took his ease in bed today with a strained left ankle benumbed beneath an ice pack and a sheaf of doctor's orders which indicate at least a week's absence from the Yankee lineup.

But the mishap to the star slugger, which might have cost the flag in a more troublesome season, adds very little to Joseph McCarthy's worries, which hadn't amounted to more than a small zero since the rest of the league folded.

Joe Di Maggio.

There simply isn't anything to worry about. The damage to Di Mag's underpinning, suffered in yesterday's split bill with the Tigers, can't be classed much higher than "trivial" after a complete going over by the medicos and the X-ray machine. The incident caused only a mild stir in the easy-going, free-wheeling New York camp, and the most important result may be merely to extend Di Maggio's unfortunate record of never having worked a full season.

The casual way the Yanks take Di Mag's accident matches the casual way it happened, in the fourth inning of the 8-to-3 second-game victory. The opener was lost by 12 to 3.

Joe doubled to left and pulled up at second. He didn't have to slide. Here's his explanation: "I landed on second with my left foot, but it didn't hit the bag squarely, so that it turned under when I put all my weight on it to make the extra stride with the right foot in order to stop. It didn't pain much and I don't think it is serious, although I can't feel a thing down there now with the ice pack on."

Di Mag advanced to third before George Selkirk subbed for him, and the centerfielder walked off the field with only a slight limp.

Provided the strain clears up quickly, as expected, the layoff may be beneficial to Frisco Joe, because he had been in his worst slump of the season. The accident-provoking double was his first honest hit in five games. His double in the opener was a gift, a long fly which dropped in front of Rip Radcliff as he and Barney McGosky played Alphonse and Gaston.

The enforced rest of the star centerfielder may fit in with McCarthy's plans at that. The manager is taking it easy, sparing the horses now, letting the club coast along until the time comes to speed up for the world series.

McCarthy used three replace-

N. Y. Batting

DODGERS.

Durocher	.383	Camilli	.282
Reiser	.327	Owen	.213
Walker	.325	Reese	.233
Wasdell	.315	Phelps	.233
Medwick	.311	Pranks	.225
Riggs	.314	Tatum	.167
Herman	.304	Coscarart	.130
Lavagetto	.302		

GIANTS.

Bartell	.294	Young	.262
Rucker	.292	Danning	.248
Jurges	.287	Whitehead	.233
Moore	.277	Hale	.232
Ott	.277	Orengo	.218
Hartnett	.269	O'Dea	.201
Arnovich	.263		

YANKEES.

Di Maggio	.350	Gordon	.264
Rosar	.318	Bordagaray	.260
Rizzuto	.315	Sturm	.217
Keller	.293	Crosetti	.242
Dickey	.285	Silvestri	.222
Henrich	.266	Priddy	.196
Rolfe	.265	Selkirk	.196

Slugger May Benefit By Enforced Rest

ments in yesterday's first game. He permitted Ken Silvestri the rare privilege of catching the entire game, subbed Frank Crosetti for Red Rolfe at third and Gerry Priddy at first for Johnny Sturm in the last three innings, after Detroit had salted down the game with an eight-run outburst which banished Marvin Breuer in the second. It was Priddy's first essay at first base, but there is nothing significant in the move. McCarthy is satisfied that second basemen do not make first basemen.

There wasn't any attempt to go all out trying to overcome the long Detroit lead in the opener. With two on base in the eighth, and none out, McCarthy did not even order a pinch hitter for Charley Stanceu, who had replaced Breuer in the second. Stanceu dribbled into a double play.

Clutch hitting was what the Yanks lacked most in the opener. Lefty Hal Newhouser allowed only five singles—three of them by Phil Rizzuto, for a perfect day. Rizzuto smashed three for four in the second game. But Newhouser also gave out 10 bases on balls, and only one of the recipients scored.

Marius Russo had command throughout the nightcap as his mates freely smacked Al Benton and Paul Trout. A scratch hit set up the first run off Russo in the seventh and errors by him and Joe Gordon helped the Tigers to two more in the eighth.

———

DiMag Starts Working Out

Priddy Sparkles at First Base
As Yanks Bump White Sox Twice

By JOE KING,
World-Telegram Staff Correspondent.

CHICAGO. Aug. 25.—The Yankee good news poured from a cornucopia today, as sunny and pleasant as it was gloomy and distressing on the first two stops of this trip. All goes well again and there is even an added encouraging development, the unveiling of Gerald Priddy as a capable reserve for the first base job.

The joyful items include the return of Joe Di Maggio with an ankle sufficiently healed to permit him to work out in the pasture. He will be ready to go again soon.

The double victory over the White Sox yesterday, 5–1 and 8–5, demonstrated anew the Yankee penchant for beating down the nearest foe, playing best against the closest contender. The twin defeat plunged runner-up Chicago 17 games off the pace. Of course, even Joe McCarthy admits his club is "in," but it still is heartening to see that the New Yorks have not lost their competitive fire, despite the lofty and untroubled perch they occupy.

Back again, too, is the home-run punch. It burst the Chicago team asunder, shook the Sox apart in the field as well as at the plate, when Tommy Henrich swatted his 24th and Charley Keller his 31st and 32nd to overwhelm Thornton Lee and his 3–1 lead in the second game. Ted Lyons was defeated in the opener by a cascade of singles in a ninth-inning four-run rally before 44,296 spectators.

But the surprise performance of Priddy stands above all. In the Saturday victory over Cleveland and again yesterday in the nightcap, the rookie second baseman, who never had played first as a pro. took over Sturm's position and handled it well.

McCarthy explained that Priddy and the other reserves were thrown into action because they needed the work, and should get it, now that the flag seemed assured. But Priddy's case carries more meaning than that. The high grade exhibition by the 21-year-old recruit from Kansas City signifies that McCarthy has gained a valuable new part for the Yankee infield.

Priddy may continue to play against left-handers in place of Sturm, but his more important use, looking ahead to the world series, will be as first base substitute in case Sturm must be lifted for a pinch-hitter in a close game. McCarthy several times in the pennant drive had to break up his keystone combination of Rizzuto and Gordon and shift the latter to first base, when he used a substitute batter for Sturm. Priddy, left in the cold at his nominal trade, second basing, when Gordon was returned to the post, ironically now looms

Joe Di Maggio.   Jerry Priddy.

most important at the job Gordon couldn't fill. He surely is a first-base prospect for 1942.

Tossing Priddy and the other bench riders into the game—Frank Crosetti, Frenchy Bordagaray, Ken Silvestri and George Selkirk—also serves to warm them up for possible use in the October fiesta. They have had very little work since spring. But that did not hinder them from sharing the victory spoils in the two games they played.

Both New York triumphs yesterday were works of art. They could not be faulted. There was polished, errorless fielding, and plenty of clutch hitting to protect adequate pitching by Red Ruffing in the opener and Spurgeon Chandler in the nightcap. Ruffing allowed a dozen blows, but had the stopper for the weak-hitting Sox in the pinch, especially in the ninth, when he had to retire the side with the bags loaded and one out. Chandler, who had a rocky start, needed help from Johnny Murphy in the eighth.

———

Yank Tribute to DiMaggio

Team Mates Pull Surprise Party on Jolting Joe, Who Receives Gift With Blushes.

By HERBERT GOREN.

Washington, Aug. 30—The pennant-bound New York Yankees let the world know how they rate Joe DiMaggio, as a man and ball player, when they paid their own sincere tribute to the outfielder on their arrival here last night. It was a tribute directly to DiMaggio and, indirectly, to the team's wonderful spirit.

The players were days in planning the little surprise party, and, in marked contrast to other surprise parties, this really came as a surprise to DiMaggio.

No sooner had the Yankees checked in at the Hotel Shoreham than George Selkirk was on the telephone calling players and newspaper men alike, telling them to be down to room 609D in thirty minutes.

Everybody got there on time; everybody, that is, except DiMaggio and Lefty Gomez. Lefty rooms with Joe. It was up to him to entice DiMaggio into the room without arousing any suspicion in Joe's mind. Gomez played his role to perfection. He said to DiMaggio:

"Say, Joe, I've got to pick up something in Selkirk's room. C'mon along."

DiMaggio balked. "I'll meet you in the lobby," he said.

"But it's right down the hall," said Gomez. "It will only be a minute."

"Okay," said DiMaggio, "but don't be long."

Surprise for DiMaggio.

The players were waiting. Selkirk was at the door, keeping an eye on the corridor, and when he spotted the pair he said:

"Here he comes."

Everybody had filled champagne glasses with sparkling Burgundy, and when DiMaggio and Gomez walked in, the Yanks hollered at Joe like mad parrots:

"Why don't you get here on time? What's the idea of being late?"

DiMaggio looked confused. He didn't know what to say. Then the Yankees, led by Art Fletcher, went through a loud and honest rendition of "For He's a Jolly Good Fellow," followed by a hip-hip hooray, with Frankie Crosetti as cheer leader.

Gomez presented a gift to DiMaggio. "Go ahead," he said, "open it up."

Joe did so slowly. It was a silver humidor. The top bore a likeness of DiMaggio finishing a swing. There were two numbers on either side. One was 56; the other 91. It was just a reminder of the number of successive games in which he hit safely and the number of hits he made. On the front was the following inscription:

"Presented to Joe DiMaggio by his fellow players on the New York Yankees to express their admiration for his consecutive game-hitting record. 1941."

Jolting Joe Blushes.

DiMaggio said: "This is swell, fellows. Thanks, only I don't know that I deserve it."

The humidor was filled with cigars and cigarettes and Joe lifted the box and added: "Cigars? Cigarettes?"

Everybody could see Joe blushing and flustered by the simple ceremony. Joe Gordon relieved the pressure, saying: "This is the first time in history that Gomez ever kept a secret."

Bill Dickey suggested a toast, and Johnny Murphy gave it. He said: "Joe, we want to let you know how proud we are to be playing on a ball club with you and that we think your great hitting streak spurred us on to a pennant."

The Yankees downed the Burgundy and then huddled in different parts of the room, each saying in his own little way what a wonderful player DiMaggio was and how happy they were to be doing this for Joe.

If ever there was any doubt in anybody's mind that the Yankees considered DiMaggio the driving force and inspiration in the pennant fight, that show of gratitude erased it. The gathering was a warm, human document in the history of the 1941 Yankees.

Di Maggio Adds to Long Homer Skein

Has 30 or More a Year For 5 Seasons in Row

By JOE KING.

All the hitting time Joe DiMaggio's lost through the years with injuries and such hasn't interrupted an extraordinary home run performance. DiMag claims 30 or more round-trippers for five straight seasons. He tacked 1941 on the string with his 29th and 30th off Phil Marchildon yesterday in Atley Donald's 7–2 defeat of the Athletics.

That is a feat of steady slugging which rates Joe among the best. Hornsby, Klein, York, Simmons and Greenberg didn't do it. Hank might have made it this year if he had had the chance. DiMaggio, though, still is far from a record. He ties Ott's best mark, but trails Ruth by three years and Gehrig by four. But far above all is that Sudlersville slugger of the Red Sox, Jimmy Foxx, who has planted 30 or more in the seats for a dozen years running.

* * *

Red Rolfe promises to return to third base tomorrow, ladies' day, in the Yankee double-header with the Senators. Rolfe lost five pounds during his illness and took plenty of punishment whipping his chassis back into condition this week. Red is satisfied now he is ready to go, and therefore is definitely in line for the series.

* * *

DiMaggio's two four-baggers give the Yankees a faint hope to attain that fabulous 100-homer outfield they aspired to in mid-season. DiMaggio, with 30, and Tommy Henrich, with 31, would have to clout six more in the four-game Senator series to reach the century. Charley Keller, tops with 33, reports extraordinarily fast healing for his damaged ankle but isn't likely to assist in the weekend homer quest.

* * *

ANYTHING CAN HAPPEN
IN BROOKLYN

There was always the saying around New York that anything could happen in Brooklyn. Well, that was true, especially in 1941. That year the Dodgers won the National League pennant, their first flag in 21 years. They had quite a team: with players like Pete Reiser, Pee Wee Reese, Dixie Walker, Joe Medwick, and Dolph Camilli, among others.

We had had little trouble taking the American League pennant, winning 101 games, 17 more than the second-place Boston Red Sox.

Then we met in the World Series. The fourth game was in Brooklyn: a classic, the one that involved the famous muff by catcher Mickey Owen. There were two outs in the ninth with the Dodgers ahead 4–3. Tommy Henrich was at bat, and swung and missed on a third strike that should have ended the game, but the ball got past Owen. I remember the police were already moving onto the field and Leo Durocher, the Brooklyn manager, was off the bench trying to shoo them out of the way. Henrich made it to first and so I got to bat and singled. Charlie Keller then doubled to score both Henrich and myself. We got two more runs before the inning was over and won the game 7–4. It put us ahead three games to one and we took the Series the next day in the same ballpark. Anything can happen in Brooklyn.

Joe DiMaggio

NEW YORK YANKEES 1941

JOSEPH PAUL DI MAGGIO, JR.
center fielder of the Yankees, achieved one of the greatest feats of baseball history this season—his sixth with the club —by hitting safely in 56 consecutive games. Giuseppe is listed among the greatest outfielders of the game's annals. Joe was born November 25, 1914, at Martinez, Cal. He was purchased by the Yankees from San Francisco for $25,000 and five players, and thus stands out as one of the greatest bargains the game has seen. It wasn't Joe's fault that the Yanks failed in 1940, as he won the batting championship of the league for the second consecutive year. He is married, and during the offseason manages his restaurant on Fisherman's Wharf, San Francisco.

JOSEPH EVANS GORDON
second baseman, quite generally is recognized as the best man at that position in the major leagues. He was born in Los Angeles on February 18, 1915. Joe was an all-around athlete at the University of Oregon, and joined the Yankee chain in 1936, with Oakland. Then he came to Newark and in 1938 Joseph succeeded Tony Lazzeri on the New York club. He is a righthanded hitter with home run propensities. His team mates call him Trigger and the scribes refer to him as Flash. Gordon is among the married majority on the McCarthy outfit. During the training season he shifted to first base and did a remarkably fine job until McCarthy decided to send Joe back to second.

WILLIAM DICKEY
catcher, quite generally is rated the best man of that trade in the game today, and one of the receiving nobility of all time. This hero goes back to the Yanks of the Ruth and Gehrig heyday. Dickey, of course, is a righthanded thrower. What catcher isn't. But he hits lefthanded and pulls the ball for the home run sector. He was born at Bastrop, La., on June 6, 1907, and spends his winters at Little Rock, Ark. He is married. Bill watched the Yankees beat the Cardinals four in a row in the 1928 world series and the following year became a regular. His achievements in five world series, in two of which he hit better than .400, are truly noteworthy.

PHILIP FRANCIS RIZZUTO
sometimes called The Flea, is one of the smallest players in the history of the Yankees. He stands only 5 feet 6 inches in height. But what he lacks in size, he makes up in skill, speed, acumen, ambition and fight. This is Rizzuto's first year in the majors, and already he is hailed as the standout rookie of the season. Rizzuto is a native New Yorker. He was born September 25, 1918. Phil makes his home in the Glendale section of Queens. He bats and throws righthanded and has the distinction of having been with a pennant winner every season of his professional career. He was with Kansas City in 1940. One of the few bachelors on the club.

**ARTHUR FLETCHER
COACH**

CHARLES ERNEST KELLER
is one of the college-bred Yankees. This stocky, powerful left fielder is an iron man. Those wrists of his are steel. Keller was born in Middletown, Maryland, September 12, 1916, and he still goes back there when the season is finished. He is married. Keller did big things at the University of Maryland and was with Newark for two seasons before he landed on the Yankees in 1939. He marked his first season in the majors with a .334 average and 11 homers. And he has been socking four baggers ever since. Keller is a lefthanded hitter with a marvelous arm. He suffered a tough break September 11, when he chipped an ankle bone sliding to second against the Tigers.

THOMAS DAVID HENRICH
right fielder, is a newly married man. Tom became a benedict in July. Henrich started out in baseball as a softball player, at Massillon, Ohio, where he was born February 20, 1916. Although he began in softball, American League opponents will agree that the balls he hits are anything but soft. The Cleveland club glimpsed his baseball possibilities, but eventually Judge Landis declared Henrich a free agent and he signed with New York in April, 1937, receiving a bonus of $20,000. Henrich is a lefthanded hitter of the home run type, and is a fleet fielder with a great arm. His team mates call him Baby Face. This is his fourth world series.

ROBERT ABIAL ROLFE
third baseman, came to the Yankee chain right out of Dartmouth College in 1931. He joined the Bombers in 1934, as a shortstop, but Joe McCarthy soon discerned his greater aptitudes at third and shifted him to a position in which he became the All-American exemplar. Rolfe was born at Penacook, N. H., on October 17, 1908. At college he was coached by Jeff Tesreau, one-time star pitcher for the Giants. Red's big year was 1939, in which he led the league in hits, with .213. Injuries kept him out of action at the end of this season, but he's back in uniform. He lives in Penacook, and likes bridge, cribbage, skating, basketball and skiing. Rolfe is married.

GEORGE ALEXANDER SELKIRK
surnamed Twink and Twinkletoes, was born in Canada—at Huntsville, Ont., on January 4, 1908. He got his nickname from the lightning-fast movements of his feet when in action. This outfielder long has been a well-liked and colorful member of the McCarthy entourage, which he joined in 1934, from Newark. George started out to be a professional wrestler, but after a season of mat competition decided that he wanted to be a catcher. However, when he landed at Cambridge, Md., he found the club already had a backstop, so he announced himself as a flychaser, and a flychaser he has been since. Twink is a man with a happy family.

The Sporting News

THE BASE BALL PAPER OF THE WORLD

REG. U. S. PAT. OFF.

VOLUME 112, NUMBER 8 — ST. LOUIS, OCTOBER 2, 1941 — TEN CENTS THE COPY 18c in Canada

NEW YANKS IN THE RANKS
They Bloom as Bombers
First Time in Classic Competition
Ten Added Since Series of '39,
Eight Coming Up This Season

Phil Rizzuto, as Ace Member of Novitiates, Along With Sturm,

Helped to Spark Return to Familiar Flag Atmosphere;

Newcomer Bordagaray Cut Pennant Teeth With Reds

By DAN DANIEL
Of the New York World-Telegram

STEVE PEEK

ERNEST BONHAM

WORLD'S SERIES eligibles among the Yankees include ten players who on October 1 will go into their first classic. For the most part, the roster of the Bombers is made up of men who are Series veterans, accustomed to nothing but the best in that competition, habitual grabbers of the winners' swag. But after the New York club's drop into third place in 1940, there came an infusion of new blood. Not exactly a transfusion, but enough to perk up the perhaps sated nobles, and give the Bombers more dash, more verve, the realization that nobody had a too tight hold on his job—a new incentive.

Of the ten players who never before were involved in the classic struggle with the Bombers, there are no fewer than eight who came to the team this year. These are Phil Rizzuto, shortstop; Johnny Sturm, first sacker; Gerald Priddy, general utility infielder; Frenchy Bordagaray, outfielder; Ken Silvestri, catcher, and Steve Peek, Norman Branch and Charley Stanceu, righthanded hurlers. Bordagaray was with the 1939 Cincinnati Red champions. The duo who came to the Bombers in 1940 and saw their club fail after having taken four consecutive world's championships, for an all-time record, are Marvin Breuer, righthander, and Tiny Bonham, forkball expert.

Breuer, possessing a remarkable curveball, was called in from Kansas City. That team also contributed Bonham, but he did not report until mid-August. Had he been requisitioned a month sooner, the Yankees, and not the Tigers, very probably would have gone into the World's Series, and who knows what would have happen-

ed to the Reds, who went seven games to take the title?

* * *

**Flea Hops Right Into
Place of Prominence**

OF THE eight recruits of the Class of 1941, the most important and interesting is Phil Rizzuto, The Flea. Here we have the Rookie of the Year in the American League, the only rival for the major first-year laurels of Pete Reiser of the Dodgers. Let it be emphasized that Reiser played in more than 50 games for Brooklyn last year, while Rizzuto put in

JOE DiMAGGIO

40th ANNIVERSARY

CLEVELAND, OHIO
JUL. 16 1981
USPO

Dahlia USA 18c

CONSIDERED THE GREATEST BASEBALL FEAT OF ALL TIME, NEW YORK YANKEE CENTER FIELDER JOE DiMAGGIO ESTABLISHED THE ALL-TIME MAJOR LEAGUE HITTING STREAK RECORD OF 56 GAMES ON THIS DATE IN 1941 AGAINST THE CLEVELAND INDIANS. THE YANKEE CLIPPER WAS ELECTED TO BASEBALL'S HALL OF FAME IN 1955 WITH A .325 CAREER AVERAGE AND 361 HOME RUNS.

Commemoratives: an envelope with a postmark from Cleveland, where Joe DiMaggio's 56-game hitting streak came to an end in 1941; and a collector's plate, a numbered edition entitled "The Yankee Clipper" from an original painting by Pablo Carreno.

The most treasured piece of memorabilia in Joe DiMaggio's possession is this sterling silver humidor, which was designed, purchased, and presented to him by the players on his team after Joe's unprecedented and hitherto unequalled 56-game hitting streak of 1941.

"Any ballplayer picks up a lot of presents in his career," DiMaggio later wrote. "Few ballplayers are ever lucky enough to get a present from their own teammates."

The presentation was on an evening in August 1941, in Washington, D.C. The Yankees had played and beaten the Senators that afternoon, and afterwards DiMaggio was planning to go to a movie with his roommate, pitcher Lefty Gomez. As they were leaving the Shoreham Hotel, Gomez insisted they stop by a room to deliver a message to fellow pitcher Johnny Murphy.

Inside the suite of rooms waited the rest of the Yankee baseball team. There, too, was the humidor, handcrafted in silver at Tiffany's and inscribed inside with the autographs of all Joe's fellow ballplayers and of manager Joe McCarthy. It was a perfect surprise, and a memorable one.

"When Gomez turned the handle of that door in the Shoreham, he paved the way for the greatest thrill I've ever had in baseball," DiMaggio later said.

Joe DiMaggio looks at the exhibit honoring his 56-game hitting streak at the National Baseball Hall of Fame in Cooperstown, New York. He was inducted into the Hall of Fame in 1955.

KENNETH SILVESTRI

PHILIP RIZZUTO

MARVIN BREUER

the entire 1940 season in the American Association.

Rizzuto's influence on the Yankees was not technical and physical, alone. Players are superstitious. Ball clubs represent a mass psychology that, despite protestations to the contrary, goes strong for hexes, Indian signs and various other features of the mystic, the occult and the dark sciences.

The Yankees of 1941 knew from the start that they could not lose, because of Rizzuto and Priddy, who in their four years in the Yankee chain never had failed to be with a pennant winner.

Rizzuto started with Bassetts, Va., and Priddy with Rogers, Ark. These teams won flags. In 1938, they were united with the Norfolk club. Another pennant. Then two years with Kansas City, still another championship outfit, and both seasons running.

Rizzuto's influence on the mechanical side of the Yankee picture cannot be overestimated. In the spring, he seemed to lack a pennant-winning arm. Soon both he and Priddy were benched, and Johnny Sturm went to first base, while Joe Gordon, who had been working at the job of filling Babe Dahlgren's shoes, returned to his more familiar duties at second, with a sharp rise in infield efficiency.

Eventually, Frankie Crosetti, who had regained his post at short, was cut on the hands by Hal Trosky's spikes, and Rizzuto returned to short. At once the Bombers began to move. At once, the Indians began to recede. Soon the race was turned topsy-turvy, and by late July, the Yankees were ten games in front and already as good as "in," with the pennant clinched on September 4.

Sturm's defensive skill around first base gave the rising club a tonic. Later on, Joe McCarthy started a series of experiments with Priddy, playing him now at first base, then around third, when the opportunity was created by Red Rolfe having to undergo a minor operation.

Of the eight newcomers on the Yanks this year, five came from Kansas City. In addition to Rizzuto, Priddy and Sturm, there were Stanceu and Bordagaray.

• • •

**Even Marse Joe Needs
Some Extra Soldiers**

STANCEU is a big, strong righthander who needs work every four days and who is bound to make the grade when he gets his regular labor. As an occasional relief, he could not show his true gait. Bordagaray, a veteran outfielder who still has considerable speed, filled in a while, did some base running and righthanded pinch-hitting.

Peek, a big knuckleball hurler, won 13 straight for Newark last year. In mid-season this year he was sent back to Newark, which needed him more than did the away-out-in-front Yanks. Joe McCarthy promised Steve he would bring him back for the Series, and the manager lived up to his word.

Silvestri is the only newcomer on the club who did not play in the George Weiss chain store system last year. Ken was obtained from the White Sox in exchange for Billy Knickerbocker.

Knickerbocker, Babe Dahlgren, Jake

GERALD PRIDDY

Powell, Bump Hadley, Oral Hildebrand, Arndt Jorgens, Monte Pearson, Steve Sundra and last, but certainly not least, poor soul, Lou Gehrig, were on the Yankees' World's Series list in 1939, and now are gone.

But the new Yankees, pennant winners on the earliest date of all Yankee pennant winners, carry on!

JOHN STURM

CHARLES STANCEU

NORMAN BRANCH

His Score Is 5 to 1

LOOPING
THE
LOOPS

=== By J. G. T. SPINK ===

A FRANK LOOK AT YANKS

WE YIELD to no man (except Larry MacPhail) in our admiration for the Dodgers. They are a game team, they have two outstanding pitchers, they have a hustling, scrappy manager. But, as a prognosticator, we are obliged to give priority to the American League pennant-winners in the clashes now under way. The Yankee Clippers are seasoned in World's Series competition, they went into the Series refreshed and relaxed, with the final standing in their own league testifying to their ability. They have deadly, long-distance bombing power and their feat of tying the major record for double plays is evidence of their defensive skill. And who can doubt the ability of their pilot?

You've heard about the Yankees' punch and fielding, their knack of coming through when the chips are down. Here are some sidelights on them as men, as individual personalities, based on what their mates and opposing players think of them. Starting with the head Bomber, we give you:

* * *

Joseph Vincent McCarthy, manager of the Yankees, is the very antithesis of Leo Durocher in temperament and in method. . . . Joe is not at all stolid, but he makes his plans and sticks to them. Leo plays hunches strongly and, lacking Joe's experience as a leader, is inclined to change with the trend of a game. . . Durocher listens to his coaches for advice, McCarthy gives the orders to his aides. . . . McCarthy finds World's Series old stuff, having been in one with the Cubs against the Athletics in 1929, and with the Yankees in 1932 and four years starting in 1936. . . . This, therefore, is Joe's seventh classic, but the first for Leo as a manager, though he was a player for the Yanks in 1928 and the Cardinals in 1934. . . . McCarthy's score of Series victories, as a manager, is 5 to 1. . . . Joe is quiet in dress and manner, never appears at night clubs, has a happy home life. . . . Mrs. McCarthy does not bother much with baseball, but is a fine cook. . . . Joe is one of those few major league leaders who never was a big circuit player. . . . He got no closer to the majors than signing with the Brooklyn Feds, just before that ill-fated league blew up.

* * *

Joseph Paul DiMaggio, center fielder, by many experts is rated the best ball player of today. . . . He set an amazing record this year by hitting in 56 consecutive games . . . Joe is married, was born in California, bats and throws righthanded, won American League batting championships in 1940 and 1939. . . . Has a marvelous arm, covers incredible territory. . . . Likes dark clothes and dark ties. . . . Slicks his hair down, crazy about music over the radio. . . . Rather shy, though not as much as he used to be.

* * *

BOMBERS GO INTO SERIES AS HEAVY CHOICE TO TAKE BATTLING DODGERS

'Overwhelming Sentiment Out of Line Considering 22-Win Pitchers in Wyatt, Higbe and Power of Reiser, Camilli,' Says Daniel; Terry Tests Recruits in Waning Days

NEW YORK, N. Y.—With the Yankees 1 to 2 favorites over the Dodgers, the thirty-eighth World's Series is under way. No matter who wins, Pop Knickerbocker will come out with a smile. He had had classics on a five-cent fare between the Bombers and the Giants, and had dreamed of the day when the Dodgers would move into a purely local competition with the American leaguers. Well, the drama has come true, the vision has been realized. New York feels that this Yankee-Dodger Series is not just a benefice to this city. It believes it is a terrific impetus to baseball interest all over the country. It believes the progress of the Dodgers was watched by fans from coast to coast and that the success of the have-not Brooklyns furnished a tremendous kick to the public. There is every indication that in money and attendance. if not in competitive thrills, this will be the Series of Series. The enthusiasm of Brooklyn fans is a byword all over the country, and the Bombers are not without backers of their own.

The Yankees went into the classic almost unanimously considered easy winners. Actually, there is no foundation for such overwhelming sentiment. The facts are the Dodgers were not shooed into the Series; they did not back into it. They outlasted the Cardinals by taking 11 out of 17 on their final journey around the

> WEEK SEPT. 22 TO CLOSE OF SEASON
> Giants Won 6-Lost 3   Yankees Won 3-Lost 3

circuit. In the last series in St. Louis, they snagged two out of three.

Brooklyn sent out a hard-hitting gang, which included a couple of 22-game pitchers in Whit Wyatt and Kirby Higbe; the batting champion of the league in Pete Reiser, and the home-run and runs-batted-in title winner in Dolph Camilli. There were very few features in individual, as well as team, excellence in which this Brooklyn team did not demonstrate its superlative qualities.

But the Yankees went into the classic the most relaxed outfit that yet had dashed into the inter-league competition. There was a question whether they had not let down too much, and would have trouble getting a fine competitive edge again.

'Twas a Dizzy Race for Dodgers

The Dodgers went into the Series tired physically, and frazzled mentally. They had taken part in the longest two-club race in the history of the majors. They took the lead on April 28, lost it in middle June, won it again and lost it again times innumerable. In fact, the Dodgers took first place no fewer than ten times. At no stage of the race was either club more than four games in front.

Could the Dodgers relax enough in the few days that followed the clinching in Boston? That was the big question as the Series got under way.

As the Yankees went into the Series there was keen speculation as to the place this team would be allotted in the all-time ranking of New York American League clubs.

The Series would have to furnish some clinching evidence not only as regards the team as a group, but on some of the individuals.

Just how good is this man Joe DiMaggio? How great a ball player is Charlie Keller? And how far under-rated has Tommy Henrich been?

As regards DiMaggio—well, that's an old discussion with the writer—one which has brought him plenty of hot words from fans around the country. But the fact that Ted Williams won the batting title over DiMaggio and hit over .400 did not change the writer's belief that Giuseppe is the greatest player in the game today.

Win, lose or draw in the World's Series, the Yankees will present a formidable layout for 1942. Too formidable for the rest of the American League.

Joe Gordon, of course, is set at second base. Phil Rizzuto is a fixture at short. The outfield is set, so is the catching. For that matter, so is the pitching. Of course, there will be more work next season for Charley Stanceu, Red Branch and Steve Peek. Johnny Lindell and Hank Borowy will come in from Newark, ready to work in the American League, and there may be some changes among the veterans. But it is too soon to begin speculating about that.

STANLEY BORDAGARAY

After a while, interest will center in the situations at first and third bases.

It may be that the New York club will go after a harder-hitting first sacker than Johnny Sturm. He did well enough—far better than had been expected—but the Yankees are accustomed to home-run power in Lou Gehrig's old job, and it would not surprise us if Joe McCarthy tried to make a deal.

At third base, there is evidence that Marse Joe will use Gerald Priddy. What that means for Red Rolfe we cannot conjecture as this time. Very likely, Rolfe will remain with the club, just as Frankie Crosetti remained when it was evident that Phil Rizzuto was the new shortstop.

Game 1 October 1 at New York

Brooklyn	Pos	AB	R	H	RBI	PO	A	E
Walker	rf	3	0	0	0	3	0	0
Herman	2b	3	0	0	0	0	6	0
Reiser	cf	3	0	0	0	4	0	0
Camilli	1b	4	0	0	0	7	2	0
Medwick	lf	4	0	1	0	4	0	0
Lavagetto	3b	4	1	0	0	0	0	0
Reese	ss	4	1	3	0	4	2	0
Owen	c	2	0	1	1	1	0	0
a Riggs		1	0	1	1	0	0	0
Franks	c	1	0	0	0	0	1	0
Davis	p	2	0	0	0	1	0	0
Casey	p	0	0	0	0	0	0	0
b Wasdell		1	0	0	0	0	0	0
Allen	p	0	0	0	0	0	0	0
Totals		32	2	6	2	24	11	0

a Singled for Owen in 7th.
b Fouled out for Casey in 7th.

Double—Dickey. Triple—Owen. Home
Run—Gordon. Double Plays—Rolfe to
Rizzuto, Gordon to Rizzuto to Sturm.
Hit by Pitcher—Sturm (by Allen).
Left on Bases—Brooklyn 6, New York 8.
Umpires—McGowan (A), Pinelli (N), Grieve (A),
Goetz (N). Attendance—**68,540.**
Time of Game—2:08.

Bkn.	0 0 0	0 1 0	1 0 0		2
N.Y.	0 1 0	1 0 1	0 0 x		3

New York	Pos	AB	R	H	RBI	PO	A	E
Sturm	1b	3	0	1	0	7	0	0
Rolfe	3b	3	0	1	0	2	2	0
Henrich	rf	4	0	0	0	0	0	0
DiMaggio	cf	4	0	0	0	5	0	0
Keller	lf	2	2	0	0	4	0	0
Dickey	c	4	0	2	1	6	0	0
Gordon	2b	2	1	2	2	0	2	0
Rizzuto	ss	4	0	0	0	3	5	1
Ruffing	p	3	0	0	0	0	0	0
Totals		29	3	6	3	27	9	1

Pitching	IP	H	R	ER	BB	SO
Brooklyn						
Davis (L)	5⅓	6	3	3	3	1
Casey	⅓	0	0	0	0	0
Allen	2	0	0	0	2	0
New York						
Ruffing (W)	9	6	2	1	3	5

1st Inning
Brooklyn
  Walker walked.
1 Herman grounded to third.
2 Reiser flied to center.
3 Camilli struck out.
New York
  Sturm singled to left.
1 Rolfe forced Sturm at second, Camilli
  to Reese.
2 Henrich forced Rolfe at second, Herman
  to Reese.
3 DiMaggio flied to left.

2nd Inning
Brooklyn
1 Medwick struck out.
2 Lavagetto grounded to short.
3 Reese flied to left.
New York
1 Keller flied to center.
2 Dickey grounded to second.
  Gordon homered into the lower left
  field stands.
3 Rizzuto flied to left.

3rd Inning
Brooklyn
1 Owen flied to left.
2 Davis flied to left.
3 Walker flied to left (Keller's 4th
  successive putout)
New York
1 Ruffing grounded to short.
2 Sturm grounded out, Camilli to Davis.
3 Rolfe struck out.

4th Inning
Brooklyn
1 Herman grounded to short.
2 Reiser fanned.
3 Camilli fanned.
New York
1 Henrich popped to short.
2 Medwick made a great catch of
  DiMaggio's fly at the low left field
  concrete wall.
  Keller walked.
  Dickey doubled off the right-center
  field wall, scoring Keller.
  Gordon intentionally walked.
3 Rizzuto grounded to second.

5th Inning
Brooklyn
1 Medwick flied to center.
2 Lavagetto flied to center.
  Reese singled to left.
  Owen tripled into left-center, scoring
  Reese.
3 Davis grounded to short.
New York
1 Ruffing flied to center.
2 Sturm grounded to second.
  Rolfe singled to center.
3 Henrich flied to right.

6th Inning
Brooklyn
1 Walker lined to center.
  Herman walked.
  Reiser walked.
2 Camilli struck out for the third time.
3 Medwick forced Herman at third, Rolfe
  unassisted.
New York
1 DiMaggio grounded to short.
  Keller walked.
  Dickey singled to center, moving Keller
  to third.
  Gordon singled to center, scoring
  Keller with Dickey stopping at second.
  For Brooklyn—Casey pitching.
2 Rizzuto flied to center.
3 Ruffing flied to right.

7th Inning
Brooklyn
  Lavagetto safe at first on Rizzuto's
  throwing error to first.
  Reese singled with Lavagetto going to
  second.
  Riggs, pinch-hitting for Owen, singled
  to center, scoring Lavagetto with
  Reese going to second.
1,2 Wasdell, pinch hitting for Casey,
  fouled to Rolfe who threw to
  Rizzuto covering third to double up
  Reese trying to advance after the
  catch.
3 Walker grounded to second.
New York
  For Brooklyn—Franks catching and Allen
  pitching.
  Sturm hit by a pitched ball.
1   Sturm caught stealing Franks to
    Reese.
  Rolfe walked.
2 Henrich flied to left.
3 DiMaggio flied to center.

8th Inning
Brooklyn
1 Herman grounded to short.
2 Reiser lined to short.
3 Camilli flied to center.
New York
1 Keller grounded to second.
2 Dickey flied to right.
  Gordon walked.
3 Rizzuto grounded to second.

9th Inning
Brooklyn
  Medwick beat out an infield hit.
1 Lavagetto fouled to Dickey.
  Reese singled (his third) sending
  Medwick to second.
2,3 Franks in his first at-bat hit into
  a double play, Gordon to Rizzuto to
  Sturm.

Game 2 October 2 at New York

Brooklyn	Pos	AB	R	H	RBI	PO	A	E
Walker	rf	4	1	0	0	4	0	0
Herman	2b	4	0	1	0	4	4	0
Reiser	cf	4	0	0	0	2	1	0
Camilli	1b	3	1	1	1	8	1	0
Medwick	lf	4	1	2	0	0	0	0
Lavagetto	3b	3	0	1	0	1	1	0
Reese	ss	4	0	0	1	2	4	2
Owen	c	2	0	1	1	6	1	0
Wyatt	p	3	0	0	0	0	1	0
Totals		31	3	6	3	27	13	2

Pitching	IP	H	R	ER	BB	SO
Brooklyn						
Wyatt (W)	9	9	2	2	5	5
New York						
Chandler (L)	*5	4	3	2	2	2
Murphy	4	2	0	0	1	2

*Pitched to 2 batters in 6th.

Bkn	000	021	000		3
N.Y.	011	000	000		2

New York	Pos	AB	R	H	RBI	PO	A	E
Sturm	1b	5	0	1	0	11	0	0
Rolfe	3b	5	0	1	0	1	2	0
Henrich	rf	4	1	1	0	0	0	0
DiMaggio	cf	3	0	0	0	4	0	0
Keller	lf	4	1	2	1	1	0	0
Dickey	c	4	0	0	0	5	1	0
a Bordagaray		0	0	0	0	0	0	0
Rosar	c	0	0	0	0	0	0	0
Gordon	2b	1	0	1	0	2	7	1
Rizzuto	ss	4	0	1	1	0	0	0
Chandler	p	2	0	1	0	3	5	0
Murphy	p	1	0	0	0	0	0	0
b Selkirk		1	0	1	0	0	0	0
Totals		34	2	9	2	27	15	1

a Ran for Dickey in 8th.
b Singled for Murphy in 9th.

Doubles—Henrich, Medwick.
Double Plays—Reese to Herman to Camilli, Gordon to Rizzuto to Sturm 2, Dickey to Gordon. Left on Bases—Brooklyn 4, New York 10. Umpires—Pinelli, Grieve, Goetz, McGowan. Attendance—66,248. Time of Game—2:31.

1st Inning
Brooklyn
1 Walker took a called third strike.
2 Herman grounded to second.
3 Reiser struck out on an outside pitch with a 3-2 count.
New York
1 Sturm looked at a third strike.
  Rolfe beat out a bunt for a single.
2,3 DiMaggio grounded into a double play, Reese to Herman to Camilli.

2nd Inning
Brooklyn
1 Camilli flied to second.
  Medwick singled to left-center.
2,3 Lavagetto bounced into a double play, Gordon to Rizzuto to Sturm.
New York
  Keller singled to center.
1 Dickey looked at a called third strike.
  Gordon walked.
2 Rizzuto grounded to second, advancing both runners.
  Chandler beat out a bounder to third for a single, scoring Keller, Gordon
3 was out also attempting to score, Camilli to Owen.

3rd Inning
Brooklyn
1 Reese flied to left.
2 Owen grounded to second.
3 Wyatt grounded to short.
New York
1 Sturm lined to Camilli.
2 Rolfe grounded to first.
  Henrich doubled off the right field wall.
  DiMaggio walked.
  Keller singled between first and second, scoring Henrich with DiMaggio going to third.
3 Dickey grounded to second.

4th Inning
Brooklyn
1 Walker grounded to second.
2 Herman grounded to third.
3 Reiser grounded to second.
New York
  Gordon singled to left.
1 Rizzuto lined to second.
2 Chandler forced Gordon at second, Reese to Herman.
  Sturm blooped a Texas League single into center and Chandler was out trying for
3 third, Reiser to Lavagetto.

5th Inning
Brooklyn
  Camilli walked on five pitches.
  Medwick doubled down the left field line, moving Camilli to third.
  Lavagetto walked loading the bases.
1 Reese forced Lavagetto at second, Rizzuto to Gordon scoring Camilli.
  Owen singled to left, scoring Medwick and sending Reese to third.
2,3 Wyatt grounded into a double play, Gordon to Rizzuto to Sturm.

5th Inning (continued)
New York
1 Rolfe grounded to first.
2 Henrich flied to center.
3 DiMaggio flied to right.

6th Inning
Brooklyn
  Walker safely to first on Gordon's throwing error.
  Herman singled to left, moving Walker to third.
  For New York—Murphy pitching.
1 Reiser fanned.
  Camilli singled to right, scoring Walker and advancing Herman to third.
  Medwick hit a slow roller to Rizzuto
2 who threw to the plate to nail Herman.
3 Lavagetto flew out to center.
New York
1 Keller flied to right.
2 Dickey flied to right.
  Gordon walked.
  Rizzuto singled to left, Gordon stopping at second.
3 Murphy fanned.

7th Inning
Brooklyn
1 Reese popped to short.
  Owen walked.
2,3 Wyatt was called out on strikes and Owen was doubled up trying to steal, Dickey to Gordon.
New York
1 Sturm fanned.
2 Rolfe grounded to short.
3 Henrich struck out.

8th Inning
Brooklyn
1 Walker grounded to second.
2 Herman lined to first.
3 Reiser fouled to Rolfe.
New York
1 DiMaggio flied to center.
2 Keller grounded back to the mound.
  Dickey got all the way to second on Reese's double error, fumbling the grounder then throwing over Camilli's head.
  Gordon intentionally walked.
  Bordagaray ran for Dickey.
3 Rizzuto forced Gordon, Reese to Herman.

9th Inning
Brooklyn
  For New York—Rosar catching.
1 Camilli flied to center.
2 Medwick flied to center.
  Lavagetto singled to left.
3 Reese grounded to third.
New York
  Selkirk, pinch hitting for Murphy, singled to right.
1 Sturm forced Selkirk at second on an attempted sacrifice, Owen to Reese.
2 Rolfe forced Sturm at second, Herman to Reese.
3 Henrich flied to right.

Game 3 October 4 at Brooklyn

New York	Pos	AB	R	H	RBI	PO	A	E
Sturm	1b	4	0	1	0	12	0	0
Rolfe	3b	4	1	2	0	1	2	0
Henrich	rf	3	1	1	0	2	0	0
DiMaggio	cf	4	0	2	1	2	0	0
Keller	lf	4	0	1	1	2	0	0
Dickey	c	4	0	0	0	4	1	0
Gordon	2b	3	0	1	0	2	4	0
Rizzuto	ss	3	0	0	0	2	3	0
Russo	p	4	0	0	0	0	4	0
Totals		33	2	8	2	27	14	0

Pitching	IP	H	R	ER	BB	SO
New York						
Russo (W)	9	4	1	1	2	5
Brooklyn						
Fitzsimmons	7	4	0	0	3	1
Casey (L)	⅓	4	2	2	0	0
French	⅔	0	0	0	0	0
Allen	1	0	0	0	0	0

		1	2	3	4	5	6	7	8	9		
N.Y.		0	0	0		0	0	0		0	2	0		2
Bkn		0	0	0		0	0	0		0	1	0		1

Brooklyn	Pos	AB	R	H	RBI	PO	A	E
Reese	ss	4	0	1	1	3	1	0
Herman	2b	1	0	0	0	0	1	0
Coscarart	2b	2	0	0	0	0	3	0
Reiser	cf	4	0	1	0	6	0	0
Medwick	lf	4	0	1	0	3	0	0
Lavagetto	3b	3	0	0	0	1	0	0
Camilli	1b	3	0	0	0	11	0	0
Walker	rf	3	1	1	0	2	0	0
Owens	c	3	0	0	0	2	1	0
Fitzsimmons	p	2	0	0	0	0	2	0
Casey	p	0	0	0	0	0	0	0
French	p	0	0	0	0	0	0	0
a Galan		1	0	0	0	0	0	0
Allen	p	0	0	0	0	0	0	0
Totals		30	1	4	1	27	8	0

a Struck out for French in 8th.

Doubles—Reiser, Walker. Triple—Gordon. Stolen Bases—Rizzuto, Sturm. Double Plays—Rizzuto to Sturm, Reese to Camilli. Left on Bases—New York 7, Brooklyn 4. Umpires—Grieve, Goetz, McGowan, Pinelli. Attendance—33,100. Time of Game—2:22.

1st Inning
New York
1 Sturm flied to center.
2 Rolfe flied to left.
3 Henrich popped to third.
Brooklyn
1 Reese bunted out to the mound.
Herman walked on a full count.
2 Reiser forced Herman at second, Russo to Rizzuto, Reiser just beating the throw to first.
3 Medwick flied to right.

2nd Inning
New York
DiMaggio singled to left.
1 Keller grounded to first, DiMaggio going to second.
2 Dickey foul popped to Camilli.
3 Gordon was retired for the first time in the Series, flying to right.
Brooklyn
Lavagetto walked.
1,2 Camilli grounded into a double play, Rizzuto to Sturm.
3 Walker grounded to third.

3rd Inning
New York
1 Rizzuto grounded to the pitcher.
2 Russo flied to left.
3 Sturm grounded to second and the Yanks were retired on 5 pitches.
Brooklyn
1 Owen flied to center.
2 Fitzsimmons flied to left.
3 Reese grounded to short.

4th Inning
New York
Rolfe singled to center.
1 Henrich forced Rolfe at second, Reese unassisted.
2 Henrich picked off first Owen to Camilli.
3 DiMaggio popped to first.
Brooklyn
1 Herman grounded to second (Herman hurting his side on the swing).
2 Reiser lined to second.
Medwick got the first hit off Russo a tap down the third base-line which he and Rolfe let go hoping it would roll foul but it stayed fair.
3 Lavagetto lined to second.

5th Inning
New York
For Brooklyn—Coscarart playing second.
1 Keller grounded to second.
2 Dickey flied to deep center.
Gordon tripled off the lower stand in left-center.
Rizzuto intentionally walked.
Rizzuto stole second.
3 Russo fanned.
Brooklyn
1 Camilli fanned.
2 Walker grounded to second.
3 Owen flied deep to center.

6th Inning
New York
Sturm singled on a blooper to short center.
Sturm stole second.
1 Rolfe pop fouled to Owen on an attempted sacrifice.
Henrich walked.
2 DiMaggio flied to right.
3 Keller grounded weakly to first.
Brooklyn
1 Fitzsimmons grounded to short.
2 Reese flied to left.
3 Coscarart's bounder was deflected by Russo to Rolfe who threw to first for the out.

7th Inning
New York
1 Dickey grounded to second.
Gordon walked.
2 Rizzuto grounded to second, advancing Gordon to second.
3 Russo's line drive caromed off Fitzsimmons' left leg to Reese for a pop out. Fitzsimmons had to be helped from the field.
Brooklyn
Reiser doubled off the right-center screen.
1 Dickey dropped Medwick's third strike and had to throw him out.
2 Lavagetto grounded to second with Reiser going to third.
3 Camilli took a called third strike.

8th Inning
New York
For Brooklyn—Casey pitching.
1 Sturm flied to center.
Rolfe singled to right.
Henrich beat out an infield hit.
DiMaggio singled to center, scoring Rolfe with Henrich going to third.
Keller singled to center, scoring Henrich with DiMaggio going to third.
For Brooklyn—French pitching.
2,3 Dickey grounded into a double play, Reese to Camilli.
Brooklyn
Walker lined a double into right.
1 Owen bounced back to the pitcher with Walker holding second.
2 Galan, pinch hitting for French, fanned.
Reese singled to right, scoring Walker.
3 Coscarart popped to third.

9th Inning
New York
For Brooklyn—Allen pitching.
1 Gordon flied to center.
2 Rizzuto lined to left.
3 Russo lined to center.
Brooklyn
1 Reiser struck out.
2 Medwick flied to short right.
3 Lavagetto grounded to second.

Game 4 October 5 at Brooklyn

N.Y.	1 0 0	2 0 0	0 0 4	7
Bkn.	0 0 0	2 2 0	0 0 0	4

New York	Pos	AB	R	H	RBI	PO	A	E
Sturm	1b	5	0	2	2	9	1	0
Rolfe	3b	5	1	2	0	0	2	0
Henrich	rf	4	1	0	0	3	0	0
DiMaggio	cf	4	1	2	0	2	0	0
Keller	lf	5	1	4	3	1	0	0
Dickey	c	2	2	0	0	7	0	0
Gordon	2b	5	1	2	2	2	3	0
Rizzuto	ss	4	0	0	0	2	3	0
Donald	p	2	0	0	0	0	1	0
Breuer	p	1	0	0	0	0	1	0
b Selkirk		1	0	0	0	0	0	0
Murphy	p	1	0	0	0	0	0	0
Totals		39	7	12	7	27	11	0

Pitching	IP	H	R	ER	BB	SO
New York						
Donald	*4	6	4	4	3	2
Breuer	3	3	0	0	1	2
Murphy (W)	2	0	0	0	0	1
Brooklyn						
Higbe	3⅓	6	3	3	2	1
French	⅓	0	0	0	0	0
Allen	⅓	1	0	0	1	0
Casey (L)	4⅓	5	4	0	2	1

*Pitched to 2 batters in 5th.

Brooklyn	Pos	AB	R	H	RBI	PO	A	E
Reese	ss	5	0	0	0	2	4	0
Walker	rf	5	1	2	0	5	0	0
Reiser	cf	5	1	2	2	1	0	0
Camilli	1b	4	0	2	0	10	1	0
Riggs	3b	3	0	0	0	0	2	0
Medwick	lf	2	0	0	0	1	0	0
Allen	p	0	0	0	0	0	0	0
Casey	p	2	0	1	0	0	3	0
Owen	c	2	1	0	0	2	1	1
Coscarart	2b	3	1	0	0	4	2	0
Higbe	p	1	0	1	0	0	1	0
French	p	0	0	0	0	0	0	0
a Wasdell	lf	3	0	1	2	2	0	0
Totals		35	4	9	4	27	14	1

a Doubled for French in 4th.
b Grounded out for Breuer in 8th.

Doubles—Camilli, Gordon, Keller 2, Walker, Wasdell. Home Run—Reiser.
Double Play—Gordon to Rizzuto to Sturm.
Hit by Pitcher—Henrich (by Allen).
Left on Bases—New York 11, Brooklyn 8.
Umpires—Goetz, McGowan, Pinelli, Grieve.
Attendance—33,813. Time of Game—2:54.

1st Inning
New York
1 Sturm grounded to short.
Rolfe singled into left.
2 Henrich flied to left.
DiMaggio walked.
Keller singled beyond first, scoring Rolfe with DiMaggio going to third.
3 Dickey grounded to second.
Brooklyn
1 Reese fouled to Dickey.
2 Walker out on his bunt toward third, thrown out by Donald.
3 Reised looked at a third strike.

2nd Inning
New York
1 Gordon grounded back to the mound.
2 Rizzuto flied to center.
3 Donald popped to short.
Brooklyn
Camilli doubled off the right-center field wall.
1 Riggs flied to short right.
2 Medwick grounded to third, Sturm making a good catch on Rolfe's high throw
Owen walked.
3 Coscarart fanned.

3rd Inning
New York
1 Sturm lined to right.
Rolfe singled to center.
2 Walker flied deep to Henrich in right-center
3 DiMaggio forced Rolfe at second, Reese to Coscarart.
Brooklyn
Higbe singled to center.
1 Reese forced Higbe at second, Gordon to Rizzuto.
2 Walker lined to left.
Reiser singled off Gordon's glove, advancing Reese to third.
3 Camilli grounded to first.

4th Inning
New York
Keller doubled to right-center.
Dickey walked.
Gordon singled to left, loading the bases.
1 Rizzuto forced Keller at the plate, Riggs to Owen (bases still loaded).
2 Donald struck out on three pitches.
Sturm singled to left, scoring Dickey and Gordon, Rizzuto going to second.
For Brooklyn—French pitching.
3 On a passed ball both Rizzuto and Sturm ran for the next bases with Rizzuto getting caught and tagged out by Reese.
Brooklyn
1 Riggs popped to second.
2 Medwick flied to DiMaggio in left-center.
Owen walked.
Coscarart walked.
Wasdell, pinch hitting for French, doubled into the left field corner, scoring Owen and Coscarart.
3 Reese grounded to short.

5th Inning
New York
For Brooklyn—Wasdell playing left, Allen pitching (batting 6th).
1 Rolfe flied to right.
Henrich hit by a pitched ball.
2 DiMaggio lined to left.
Keller singled off Coscarart's leg, moving Henrich to third.
Dickey walked, loading the bases.
For Brooklyn—Casey pitching.
3 Gordon flied to left.
Brooklyn
Walker doubled to left.
Reiser hit a two-run homer over the scoreboard.
For New York—Breuer pitching.
1 Camilli lined to right.
2 Riggs fanned.
Casey singled to center.
3 Owen lined to center.

6th Inning
New York
1 Rizzuto fouled to Camilli.
2 Breuer flied to right.
Sturm singled to right.
3 Rolfe popped to second.
Brooklyn
1 Coscarart grounded to third.
2 Wasdell grounded back to the mound.
3 Reese popped to second.

7th Inning
New York
1 Henrich popped to second.
DiMaggio singled on an infield hit to third.
2 Keller popped to second.
3 Dickey grounded to the pitcher.
Brooklyn
Walker singled to left.
1,2 Reiser grounded into a double play, Gordon to Rizzuto to Sturm.
Camilli singled through the box.
Riggs walked.
3 Casey looked at a called third strike.

8th Inning
New York
1 Gordon flied to right.
2 Rizzuto bunted for an out to the pitcher.
3 Selkirk, pinch hitting for Breuer, grounded to short.
Brooklyn
For New York—Murphy pitching.
1 Owen grounded to second.
2 Coscarart struck out.
3 Wasdell flied to right.

9th Inning
New York
1 Sturm grounded to second.
2 Rolfe grounded to the pitcher.
Henrich got to first on a strike out as Owen dropped his third strike for an error.
DiMaggio singled into left.
Keller doubled off the right field wall, scoring Henrich and DiMaggio.
Dickey walked.
Gordon doubled over Wasdell's head, scoring Keller and Dickey.
Rizzuto walked.
3 Murphy grounded to short.
Brooklyn
1 Reese fouled to Dickey.
2 Walker grounded to short.
3 Reiser grounded out, Sturm to Murphy.

YANKS WIN IN 9TH, FINAL 'OUT' TURNS INTO 4-RUN RALLY

Game-Ending Third Strike Gets Away From Dodger Catcher, Leading to 7-4 Victory

KELLER IS BATTING HERO

Double, His Fourth Safety, Puts New York in Front—Victors Now Lead in Series, 3-1

By JOHN DREBINGER

It couldn't, perhaps, have happened anywhere else on earth. But it did happen yesterday in Brooklyn, where in the short space of twenty-one minutes a dazed gathering of 33,813 at Ebbets Field saw a world series game miraculously flash two finishes before its eyes.

The first came at 4:35 of a sweltering afternoon, when, with two out and nobody aboard the bases in the top half of the ninth inning, Hugh Casey saw Tommy Henrich miss a sharp-breaking curve for a third strike that for a fleeting moment had the Dodgers defeating the Yankees, 4 to 3, in the fourth game of the current classic.

But before the first full-throated roar had a chance to acclaim this brilliant achievement there occurred one of those harrowing events that doubtless will live through all the ages of baseball like the Fred Snodgrass muff and the failure of Fred Merkle to touch second.

Makes Frantic Dash

Mickey Owen, topflight catcher of the Dodgers, let the ball slip away from him and, before he could retrieve it in a frantic dash in front of his own dugout, Henrich had safely crossed first base.

It was all the opening Joe Mc-Carthy's mighty Bronx Bombers, shackled by this same Casey ever since the fifth inning, needed to turn defeat for themselves into an amazing victory which left a stunned foe crushed.

For in the wake of that excruciating error came a blazing single by Joe DiMaggio, a two-base smash against the right-field barrier by Charley Keller, a pass to Bill Dickey by the now thoroughly befuddled Casey and another two-base clout by the irrepressible Joe Gordon.

Flatbush's Darkest Hour

Four runs hurtled over the plate and, though the meteorological records may still contend that this was the brightest, sunniest and warmest day in world series history, it was easily the darkest hour that Flatbush ever has known.

For this astounding outburst gave the Yankees the game, 7 to 4, and with this victory McCarthy's miraculous maulers moved to within a single stride of another world championship. Their lead, as the series enters the fifth encounter at Ebbets Field today, now stands at three games to one, and the Bombers need to touch off only one more explosion to bring this epic interborough struggle to a close.

Almost from the moment Mayor La Guardia threw out the first ball this battle was one that had the crowd seething and sizzling under an emotional strain that at times threatened to burst out the sides of the arena in the heart of Flatbush.

Higbe First to Go

Neither of the starting pitchers, Kirby Higbe for the Dodgers and Atley Donald, survived the fierce fighting under the blistering midsummer sun. Kirby, twenty-two-game winner of the National League champions, making his delayed first appearance in the series, was the first to go. He was driven to cover in the fourth inning, by which time the Yanks had run up a lead of 3 to 0.

But this merely provided the setting for the making of a couple of Brooklyn heroes who last night would have been the toast of the borough had victory remained where it momentarily perched at 4:35 o'clock.

One was Jimmy Wasdell, who hit a pinch double in the last of the fourth to drive in two runs. The other was Pete Reiser, freshman star of the Dodgers, who, finally coming into his own, whacked a homer over the rightfield wall with Dixie Walker on base in the fifth inning to give the Brooklyn host its 4-to-3 lead.

That blow finished Donald and, though Relief Pitchers Marvin Breuer and Johnny Murphy gave the Dodgers no more runs, they appeared to need no more to clinch this victory that would have squared the series at two games apiece. For Casey, the same round-faced Hugh whose brief relief turn had opened the floodgates for a Yankee triumph in Saturday's third game, looked this time to have the Bombers firmly in hand.

Casey replaced a wavering Johnny Allen in the fifth inning to repulse the Yanks with the bases full and he kept repelling them right on and up through the ninth until Owen's crowning misfortune turned the battle and the arena upside down.

Johnny Sturm, Yankee lead-off man, had opened that last-ditch stand in the ninth by grounding out to Pete Coscarart, who again was at second base for Brooklyn in place of the injured Billy Herman. Red Rolfe proved an even easier out. He bounced the ball squarely into Casey's hands and was tossed out at first with yards to spare.

Two were out, nobody was on, the Yanks looked throttled for the second time in the series and the Brooklyn horde scarcely could contain itself as it prepared to hail the feat with a tumultuous outburst of pent-up enthusiasm.

A Swing and a Miss

Casey worked carefully on Henrich and ran the count to three balls and two strikes. Then he snapped over a low, sharp-breaking curve. Henrich swung and missed. A great Flatbush triumph appeared clinched. But in the twinkling of an eye the victory was to become an even greater illusion.

As the ball skidded out of Owen's mitt and rolled toward the Dodger bench with Mickey in mad pursuit, police guards also came rushing out of the dugout to hold back the crowd which at the same moment was preparing to dash madly out on the field.

Owen retrieved the ball just in front of the steps, but Henrich, who the moment before had been at the point of throwing his bat away in great disgust, now was tearing like wild for first and he made the bag without a play.

The Yanks, of course, had not yet won the game. They were still a run behind and, though they had a man on first, Casey needed to collect only one more out to retain his margin.

But there was an ominous ring to the manner in which DiMaggio bashed a line-drive single to left that sent Henrich to second. A moment later Keller belted the ball high against the screening on top of the right-field fence. It just missed being a home run.

It was recovered in time to hold the doughty King Kong on second for a double, but both Henrich and DiMaggio streaked around the bases and over the plate. The dreaded Yanks were ahead, 5—4. To make matters even more excruciating, Casey had had a count of two strikes and no balls on Keller when King Kong pasted that one.

Down in the Brooklyn bullpen Curt Davis was warming up with great fury, but the Dodger board of strategy appeared paralyzed by the cataclysm and Manager Leo Durocher did nothing.

Casey pitched to Dickey and walked him. Again the Yanks had two on base. Casey stuck two strikes over on Gordon, then again grooved the next one. Ironically, Joe the Flash smacked the ball into left field, where Wasdell, who might have been one of the heroes, was left to chase it while Keller and Dickey raced for home with two more runs to make it four for the round.

This was enough, more than enough. Few clubs in major league history have ever had an almost certain victory snatched from them under more harrowing circumstances.

Snuffing out the final three Dodgers in the last half of the ninth was almost child's play for the relief hurler whom the Yanks affectionately call Grandma Murphy. Indeed, the kindly Grandma appeared motivated by only the most humane feelings as he put those battered Dodgers out of their misery.

Game 5 October 6 at Brooklyn

New York	Pos	AB	R	H	RBI	PO	A	E
Sturm	1b	4	0	1	0	9	0	0
Rolfe	3b	3	0	0	0	3	0	0
Henrich	rf	3	1	1	1	1	0	0
DiMaggio	cf	4	0	1	0	6	0	0
Keller	lf	3	1	0	0	4	0	0
Dickey	c	4	1	1	0	2	0	0
Gordon	2b	3	0	1	1	0	3	0
Rizzuto	ss	3	0	1	0	2	2	0
Bonham	p	4	0	0	0	0	1	0
Totals		31	3	6	2	27	6	0

Pitching	IP	H	R	ER	BB	SO
New York						
Bonham (W)	9	4	1	1	2	2
Brooklyn						
Wyatt (L)	9	6	3	3	5	9

N.Y.	020	010	000					3
Bkn.	001	000	000					1

Brooklyn	Pos	AB	R	H	RBI	PO	A	E
Walker	rf	3	0	1	0	0	0	0
Riggs	3b	4	0	1	0	1	3	0
Reiser	cf	4	0	1	1	2	0	0
Camilli	1b	4	0	0	0	9	1	0
Medwick	lf	3	0	0	0	0	0	0
Reese	ss	3	0	0	0	2	3	1
b Wasdell		1	0	0	0	0	0	0
Owen	c	3	0	0	0	9	1	0
Coscarart	2b	2	0	0	0	3	3	0
a Galan		1	0	0	0	0	0	0
Herman	2b	0	0	0	0	0	2	0
Wyatt	p	3	1	1	0	1	1	0
Totals		31	1	4	1	27	14	1

a Fouled out for Coscarart in 7th.
b Flied out for Reese in 9th.

Double—Wyatt. Triple—Reiser. Home Run—Henrich. Double Plays—Owen to Riggs, Reese to Coscarart to Camilli, Herman to Reese to Camilli. Wild Pitch—Wyatt. Left on Bases—New York 6, Brooklyn 5. Umpires—McGowan, Pinelli, Grieve, Goetz. Attendance—34,072. Time of Game—2:13.

1st Inning
New York
Sturm singled to center.
1 Rolfe forced Sturm at second, Reese to Coscarart.
Henrich walked, the fourth ball getting away from Owen rolling into the Yankee dugout however, Rolfe held second.
2,3 As DiMaggio went down swinging, Rolfe was caught trying for third, Owen to Riggs.
Brooklyn
1 Walker flied to left.
2 Riggs grounded to second.
Reiser tripled off the center field fence.
3 Camilli popped to short.

2nd Inning
New York
Keller walked (again Owen lost the ball).
Dickey singled to center moving Keller to third.
Keller scored and Dickey went to second on Wyatt's wild pitch.
Gordon singled to right, scoring Dickey.
1 Rizzuto forced Gordon at second, Riggs to Coscarart.
2 Bonham fanned.
3 Sturm bunted out to third.
Brooklyn
Medwick walked.
1 Reese flied to center.
2 Owen flied to left.
3 Coscarart grounded to the pitcher.

3rd Inning
New York
Rolfe walked.
1 Henrich flied to center.
2 DiMaggio struck out.
3 Keller grounded to second.
Brooklyn
Wyatt doubled into the left field corner.
1 Walker flied to center.
Riggs singled off Bonham's ankle, the ball rolling toward third and advancing Wyatt to third.
2 Reiser flied to very deep right, Wyatt scoring after the catch.
3 Camilli fanned.

4th Inning
New York
1 Dickey grounded back to the mound.
Gordon walked provoking a big argument by Wyatt and Durocher on plate umpire McGowan's calls.
Rizzuto walked.
2 Bonham fanned after a big protest by McCarthy and Bonham to McGowan on the second strike call.
3 Sturm grounded to first.
Brooklyn
1 Medwick lined to center.
2 Reese lined to left.
3 Owen fouled to Rolfe.

5th Inning
New York
1 Rolfe grounded out Camilli to Wyatt.
Henrich homered over the right field wall.
2 DiMaggio flied to deep center, a fight between Wyatt and DiMaggio was averted by the umps as both dugouts emptied on to the field.
3 Keller fanned.
Brooklyn
1 Coscarart flied to DiMaggio as objects from the stands were hurled at him.
2 Wyatt also flied to DiMaggio.
Walker walked.
3 Riggs fouled to Rolfe.

6th Inning
New York
Dickey got safely to first on Reese's error.
1,2 Gordon hit into a double play, Reese to Coscarart to Camilli.
Rizzuto singled to left.
3 Bonham fanned.
Brooklyn
1 Reiser grounded to second.
2 Camilli flied to left.
3 On only the fourth pitch of the inning Medwick grounded to short.

7th Inning
New York
1 Sturm grounded to second.
2 Rolfe popped to short.
3 Henrich looked at a called third strike.
Brooklyn
1 Reese popped to first.
2 Owen grounded to short.
3 Galan, pinch-hitting for Coscarart, fouled to Sturm (Bonham using only three pitches to retire the side, he only pitched seven balls in the course of two innings).

8th Inning
New York
For Brooklyn—Herman at second.
DiMaggio singled to center.
1,2 Keller grounded into a double play, Herman to Reese to Camilli.
3 Dickey grounded to second.
Brooklyn
1 Wyatt grounded to second.
Walker singled to right.
2 Riggs fouled to Storm.
3 Reiser fanned.

9th Inning
New York
1 Gordon grounded to third.
2 Rizzuto went down swinging.
3 Bonham also swung at a third strike.
Brooklyn
1 Camilli lined to short.
2 Medwick fouled to Rolfe.
3 Wasdell, pinch hitting for Reese, ended the Series flying to deep center.

Casey in the Box—1941

By MEYER BERGER

The prospects all seemed rosy for the Dodger nine that day.
Four to three the score stood, with one man left to play.
And so, when Sturm died, and Rolfe The Red went out,
In the tall weeds in Canarsie you could hear the Dodgers' shout.

A measly few got up to go as screaming rent the air. The rest
Were held deep-rooted by Fear's gnaw eternal at the human breast.
They thought with only Henrich, Hugh Casey had a cinch.
They could depend on Casey when things stood at the pinch.

There was ease in Casey's manner as he stood there in the box.
There was pride in Casey's bearing, from his cap down to his sox
And when, responding to the cheers, he took up his trousers' sag,
No stranger in the crowd could doubt, he had them in the bag.

Sixty thousand eyes were on him when Casey toed the dirt.
Thirty thousand tongues applauded as he rubbed his Dodger shirt.
Then while the writhing Henrich stood aswaying at the hip,
Contempt gleamed high in Casey's eye. A sneer curled Casey's lip.

And now the leather-covered sphere came hurtling through the air
And Henrich stood awaiting it, with pale and frightened stare.
Close by the trembling Henrich the ball unheeded sped.
"He don't like my style," said Casey. "Strike One!" the umpire said.

From the benches black with people there went up a muffled roar
Like the thunder of dark storm waves on the Coney Island shore.
"Get him!" "Get him, Casey!" shouted some one in the stand.
Hugh Casey smiled with confidence. Hugh Casey raised his hand.

With a smile of kindly charity Great Casey's visage shone.
He stilled the Faithful's screaming. He bade the game go on.
He caught Mickey Owen's signal. Once more the spheroid flew,
But Henrich still ignored it. The umpire bawled, "Strike Two!"

"Yay!" screamed the maddened thousands, and the echo answered,
    "YAY!"
But another smile from Casey. He held them under sway.
They saw his strong jaws tighten. They saw his muscles strain,
And they knew that Hughie Casey would get his man again.

Pale as the lily Henrich's lips; his teeth were clenched in hate.
He pounded with cruel violence his bat upon the plate.
And now Great Casey held the ball, and now he let it go.
And Brooklyn's air was shattered by the whiff of Henrich's blow.

But Mickey Owen missed this strike. The ball rolled far behind,
And Henrich speeded to first base, like Clipper on the wind.
Upon the stricken multitude grim melancholy perched.
Dark disbelief bowed Hughie's head. It seemed as if he lurched.

DiMaggio got a single. Keller sent one to the wall.
Two runs came pounding o'er the dish and, oh, this wasn't all.
For Dickey walked and Gordon a resounding double smashed.
And Dodger fans were sickened. All Dodger hopes were hashed.

Oh somewhere North of Harlem the sun is shining bright
Bands are playing in The Bronx and up there hearts are light.
In Hunts Point men are laughing, on The Concourse children shout.
But there is no joy in Flatbush. Fate had knocked their Casey out.

Tommy Henrich, as he approaches home plate after belting one out of Ebbets Field in the last game of the 1941 World Series against the Brooklyn Dodgers, is welcomed by Joe DiMaggio. The Yankees won the game 3–1, and took the Series 4 games to 1.

YANKS WIN SERIES AS BONHAM BEATS DODGERS, 3 TO 1

Gain Ninth World Title, 4 to 1, and Sixth Under McCarthy, Record for Manager

HENRICH SLAMS HOME RUN

Blow Crushes Brooklyn Fans —Two Tallies Off Wyatt in 2d—Losers Get 4 Hits

By JOHN DREBINGER

Sweeping irresistibly toward their goal in a manner to which they had long since become accustomed, the Yankees vanquished the Dodgers once more at Ebbets Field yesterday and, with this victory, achieved by a score of 3 to 1, again established themselves as undisputed baseball champions of the universe. The triumph gave Joe McCarthy's invincible Bronx Bombers the 1941 world series, four games to one.

In striking contrast to Sunday's cyclonic struggle, which saw the Yanks bludgeon their way out of the shadows of defeat with a four-run blast that exploded in the wake of Mickey Owen's imperishable error, the end came quietly yesterday at 3:45 P. M.

Oddly, the crowd, which totaled 34,072, was larger than either of the gatherings that had turned out for the two week-end games in Flatbush. The appearance of the additional few hundred in the sweltering arena doubtless was inspired by a desire to see whether the Dodgers could conceive of still one more way of losing a ball game.

Same Old Story

However, Leo Durocher's dashing Dodgers, apparently wearied of dashing their heads against an impenetrable wall, seemingly had run out of ideas. There was some snapping and snarling midway in the conflict, but in the closing rounds Brooklyn's so-called Beautiful Bums followed the pattern of almost all other National League champions whose luck it has been to be pitted against this flawless Yankee machine in a world series.

They quietly reconciled themselves to the futility of it all and retreated with as good grace as circumstances would permit. It was a sad spectacle for the thousands of die-hards who suffered excruciatingly in the intense heat, but there was no help from it.

Ernie Bonham, called Tiny because he scales about 220 pounds, took the mound as McCarthy's fifth starting pitcher in the series and by throttling the Brooklyn attack down to four meager hits, matched Marius Russo's stellar performance of last Saturday. Like Russo, he won his first world series game.

Too Much For Wyatt

The Dodgers, their perspiring backs practically to the mat after the calamitous happenings of Sunday's battle, found themselves practically forced to call again on their veteran right-hander, John Whitlow Wyatt, who had pitched them so gallantly to their only victory in the second encounter. Whit, though he hurled the entire distance and allowed only six hits, simply was not equal to the task of again preventing the McCarthy juggernaut from pursuing its relentless course.

The Yanks wrenched two runs from Wyatt in the second inning on a pass, singles by Bill Dickey and the rampant Joe Gordon and a wild pitch.

In the fifth, Tommy Henrich, the Massillon Mauler who is called Baby Face by his colleagues, sent a home run soaring over the right-field ramparts for no reason perhaps other than to let all Flatbush realize more reprisals were in store should the hapless Dodgers so much as wiggle their ears. A two-bagger by Wyatt in the third paved the way for the only Brooklyn tally.

Yanks' Twelfth Series

Thus for the ninth time in the twelve world series they have appeared in since 1921 the Yankees have stalked off with the winner's share of the spoils. McCarthy has led them to six of these triumphs in the last ten seasons. He now has won more world titles than any other manager. Before this year McCarthy was tied with the venerable Connie Mack of the Athletics.

The Yanks' last defeat in a world series was in 1926 when they lost a memorable seven-game struggle with the Cardinals. But in 1927 they started a string of records unparalleled in world series warfare, winning all eight world championships in which they appeared. Even more amazing perhaps is their feat of bagging thirty-two games during this stretch while losing only four.

Through four successive years, 1936 to 1939, they kept the banners of the American League aloft by sweeping past all National League opposition to come before them. Last year, after a torrid fight, they were shut out of their pennant race by the slender margin of two games.

This year they hammered their way back with an unprecedented rush. Tearing their league apart in midsummer, they clinched their flag on Sept. 4, the earliest in the history of circuit, and by the record margin of twenty games. With that they quietly settled back to await the outcome of the bitter National League struggle between the Dodgers and Cardinals.

Cards Held No Stronger

Once this was settled, they went to work again, and in the light of what followed few are likely to dispute that the vaunted Bombers would have polished off the Cards with the same ease and facility as they did the Dodgers.

The receipts yesterday were highest of the three games played in Brooklyn. They reached $161,-921 to bring the total for the five games to $1,007,762, making this the eleventh million-dollar world series.

In some respects this final game, coldly decisive as it was played, was more bitterly fought than any of the other four. For one thing, the scorching sun and insufferable heat were again performing at an all-time high for series competition, usually played in stinging autumnal atmosphere. This, along with the nerve-racking events of the previous afternoon, doubtless had tempers running a trifle short.

In the fourth inning the fiery Leo Durocher, who had kept singularly quiet and subdued through most of the series, came dashing out to launch a bitter protest against a ball called by Umpire Bill McGowan. A few moments later even the conservative, rarely seen Manager McCarthy came up to the plate to make a vigorous, though dignified kick against the same arbiter.

There Is a Joe McCarthy

The latter development, of course, may have been prompted solely by a desire on McCarthy's part to let the folk in Brooklyn see just what the leader of those invincible Bombers looks like. He comes so seldom into public view on a ball field that in some quarters in Flatbush there had been a suspicion that there never was a Joe McCarthy.

Perhaps the most surprising flare-up of the day came in the fifth when the usually imperturbable Joe DiMaggio and the equally silent Wyatt exchanged a few snappy lines that had the players of both sides tearing belligerently to the center of the diamond.

DiMaggio, who struck out on his first two times up to give the Brooklyn host its few chances to gloat, ducked a pitch which came perilously close to his head in the fifth. Then Jolting Joe went out on a long fly to Pete Reiser in center field, but matters did not end there.

As DiMaggio ended his futile run around the bases in the vicinity of second and jogged past the pitching mound on his way back to his dugout, he made a remark to Wyatt, who apparently answered in kind, for Joe spun sharply.

This proved the signal for a general outpouring from both benches, and the Brooklyn contingent in the stands, fretful enough over the disastrous turn things had taken in the series, suddenly perked up at the prospect of having matters enlivened perhaps by a good, old-fashioned neighborhood fight.

Owen Rushes Out

Catcher Owen was first to reach the scene of threatened hostilities, and as he rushed up on DiMaggio the latter struck a defensive attitude, as if he expected an immediate attack from a fresh quarter. But the four umpires also converged on the mound and quelled the uprising almost at once.

DiMaggio stalked off to his dugout, Wyatt resumed his pitching and the crowd, seemingly more annoyed than pleased, settled back to the less exciting business of watching the Dodgers continue their hopeless efforts against the Yanks.

In the eighth DiMaggio got his revenge by lashing a single to center, and later he gained the distinction of making the put-out that ended the game by catching Pinch Hitter Jimmy Wasdell's fly in center. With that catch, Jolting Joe set a world series record of nineteen put-outs for an outfielder in a series of less than seven games. DiMaggio had set the previous mark of eighteen in 1937.

34,072 Pay $161,921 At Final Series Game

Final Standing of Teams

	W.	L.	P.C.
Yankees	4	1	.800
Dodgers	1	4	.200

Fifth-Game Statistics

Attendance (paid) ...	34,072
Total receipts	$161,921.00
Advisory Council's share	24,288.15
Each club's share ...	34,408.21
Each league's share..	34,408.21

Statistics for Five Games

Attendance (paid)..	235,773
Total receipts	$1,007,762.00
Advisory Council's share	151,165.60
*Players' share	431,378.91
Each club's share...	106,305.94
Each league's share.	106,305.94

*Players on the winning club will divide $181,179.14 and those on the losing club will split $120,786.10, while $129,413.67 will be divided among the second, third and fourth place clubs of both leagues. These figures do not include radio rights.

Highlights

- The Yankees won their ninth world championship, almost twice the titles of the next most successful teams at that point, the Red Sox and the Athletics, who could claim five crowns apiece.
- Yank Red Ruffing tied the record for most career Series wins with six, sharing the record with Lefty Gomez, Waite Hoyt, and Chief Bender.
- The Dodgers batted only .187 as a team; their top hitter, Ducky Medwick, hit only .235, and the only Dodger homer came from Pete Reiser.
- Joe Gordon's average of .500 tied the record for a five-game Series set by Giant Larry McLean back in 1913. Gordon's slugging average of .929 also set a record.
- Gordon homered and drove in two runs to lead the Yanks to victory in Game 1.
- Dodger Dolph Camilli singled to send Dixie Walker home with the game-winning run in the sixth inning of Game 2.
- Back-to-back singles by Joe DiMaggio and King Kong Keller drove in two runs to provide the margin of victory in Game 3.
- Dodger catcher Mickey Owen recorded the most infamous passed ball in Series history when he let the third strike of the last out in the ninth inning of Game 4 get by him. The score had been 4–3 in favor of Brooklyn. As a result of Owen's error, Tommy Henrich got to first base and then the Yankees exploded for four runs. Instead of a Dodger win, which would have evened the Series at two games each, Brooklyn fell behind three games to one.
- In Game 4, King Kong Keller doubled in the ninth inning to drive in two runs to give the Yanks the lead. Joe Gordon followed with another double to drive in two more insurance runs.

Best Efforts

Batting

Average	Joe Gordon	.500	Hits	Joe Gordon	7
Home Runs	Joe Gordon	1		King Kong Keller	7
	Tommy Henrich	1	Runs	King Kong Keller	5
	Pete Reiser	1	RBIs	Joe Gordon	5
				King Kong Keller	5
Triples	Joe Gordon	1	**Pitching**		
	Pete Reiser	1	Wins	(five players)	1 game
	Mickey Owen	1	ERA	Johnny Murphy	0.00
Doubles	King Kong Keller	2	Strikeouts	Whit Wyatt	14
	Dixie Walker	2	Innings Pitched	Whit Wyatt	18

NEW YORK YANKEES
BROOKLYN DODGERS 1941

The Yanks Slip the Dodgers a Mickey

Reprinted, with permission, from
The World Series, A Complete
Pictorial History, by John Devaney
and Burt Goldblatt (Rand McNally
and Company, Chicago, © 1972).

In a Series filled with disappointments for the Dodgers, the Yankees won four games to one, manager Joe McCarthy winning his sixth World Series, breaking the record held by Connie Mack.

This would be no romp for the Yankees, however. In the first game Red Ruffing narrowly won his sixth Series game, 3-2, tying the number won by Chief Bender, Waite Hoyt, and Lefty Gomez. The Dodgers won the second game behind Whit Wyatt. In the third game Fat Freddie Fitzsimmons, now 40, went to the mound to try to win his first Series victory in four attempts. He and young Marius Russo pitched brilliantly for six shutout innings. With the score still 0-0 in the seventh, Russo came to bat and lined a pitch off Freddie's kneecap, chipping a bone. As his wife and daughter wept in a front-row seat, Fitz hobbled off the field, bent in pain, his last chance at a Series victory ended. The Yankees then went on to win, 2-1.

The ending of the fourth game was probably the weirdest of all Series games—and one of the most heartbreaking for a loser.

The Dodgers led, 4-3, in the top of the ninth, two men out, no one on base, victory seeming certain. With two strikes on Tommy Henrich, Hugh Casey threw a breaking ball. Henrich swung and missed for the third strike that would have ended the game. But catcher Mickey Owen missed the pitch. Henrich ran to first as Owen chased after the ball. A flood of cops burst out of the dugout, thinking the game was over, and they blocked whatever chance Owen had to throw to first.

At third base Brooklyn's Cookie Lavagetto thought to himself, "Oh, we can't give these guys a chance like that." He was right. The Yankees promptly blasted home four runs to win, 7-4.

After the game a white-faced Owen said, "I should have held the ball. It was my fault. I'm not sorry for myself. I'm sorry for what I've done to the other fellows."

Phil Rizzuto:
"It rocked old Ebbets Field"

I can still recall that look on Henrich's face when he struck out, said Phil Rizzuto, the former Yankee shortstop and now a CBS sportscaster. *He was looking back. He couldn't believe that Owen had missed it. I was sitting on the bench. I was holding the gloves of the guys who were batting that inning—DiMaggio, Keller, Dickey and [Joe] Gordon. In Brooklyn those kids would run down after the third out and take anything they could. When Henrich swung and missed that pitch, we all started for the runway in the dugout. Then all of a sudden—I couldn't believe it—people were jumping over the stands, Brooklyn fans. It looked like the third out and Brooklyn had won. Poor Casey, he had a hell of a spitball. Sure, that's what he threw. He threw that on the third strike. The ball exploded by Owen. When Henrich swung, Owen didn't get near the ball. He didn't even touch it. It exploded by him. Henrich couldn't believe it. It was a while before he started to run to first base. Then, when he ran, he had to run between people to get to first base. It took them a while to restore order. Then DiMaggio, Keller, Dickey and Gordon came up and what shots they hit—I never seen such shots in my life. That was exciting in itself but I'll never forget what happened the next day when Owen came to bat. The hand those Brooklyn fans gave him was unbelievable. They were telling him they didn't blame him. They stood and cheered. It rocked old Ebbets Field.*

Di Maggio, Williams, Camilli Top All-America Selections for 1941 •

Feller, Wyatt and Lee Top Pitching Selections, With Dickey Catching, In Ranking Major League Heroes For Past Season

By DANIEL M. DANIEL

YOU may search for it in vain in the Bible—that is, in these very words. Nevertheless, "He who goeth out on a limb, verily he is a sucker—yea, his progeny, unto the third generation." The man who values such shreds of reputation as he prides himself on being adorned with, and his peace of mind, yet boldly steps into the market place and announces an All-America baseball team, is a SUCKER.

But the fans expect the annual awards of laurels at the various positions, and the BASEBALL MAGAZINE's responsible editor says, "Go to work and let the chips fly where they may. Rather you than I."

The writer divided the 1941 season between the American and National Leagues, first covering the Yankees and then the Dodgers. Thus he saw the two World Series teams in action—and, of course, all the 16 clubs from which an All-America team must be selected.

He came out of the season with the impression that the most valuable players of the two circuits could be ranked in this way:

1—Joseph Paul DiMaggio, Jr., center fielder, Yankees.

2—Theodore Francis Williams, left fielder, Red Sox.

3—Dolf Camilli, first baseman, Dodgers.

4—Robert Andrew Feller, pitcher, Indians.

5—Whitlow Wyatt, pitcher, Dodgers.

6—Joseph Evans Gordon, second baseman, Yankees.

7—Enos Slaughter, right fielder, Cardinals.

8—Pete Reiser, center fielder, Dodgers.

9—Bill Dickey, catcher, Yankees.

10—Charley Keller, left fielder, Yankees.

Photo by Press Association

Dolf Camilli, first baseman of the Brooklyn Dodgers (left) and Joe DiMaggio, center fielder for the New York Yankees, two All-America players of 1941

There, we have gone and done it—gone and left ourselves wide open. But he who goes out to please everybody ends up by pleasing nobody.

We can hear the man in the fifth row shout, "Hey, aren't there any ballplayers except on the Yankees? You have named DiMaggio, Gordon, Dickey and Keller—four out of the first 10—from the Bombers. How come?"

Well, Chumley, in the light of what happened in the American League, in which the Yankees clinched their pennant on the earliest date in the history of the circuit—September 4; in view of the prominence of the four Bombers named in this remarkable feat; in the light of what the Yanks did in the World Series—there is evidence aplenty that we have not gone too far in honoring the two Joes, Bill and King Kong.

In picking our All-America team, we have given no fewer than eight of the 13 positions to players representing American League teams.

At first base, Jimmy Foxx, veteran of the Red Sox, who long held the top honors at that position, now loses out to Camilli, whom we have rated the most valuable player in the National League. The star of the Dodgers hit .285, drove in 120 runs, to lead his circuit, and hit 34 homers,

ALL-AMERICA BASEBALL TEAM FOR THE YEAR OF 1941

Position	Player	Club	League
First base	Dolf Camilli	Brooklyn	National
Second base	Joe Gordon	New York	American
Third base	Jimmy Brown	St. Louis	National
Shortstop	Cecil Travis	Washington	American
Right field	Jeff Heath	Cleveland	American
Left field	Ted Williams	Boston	American
Center field	Joe DiMaggio	New York	American
Catcher	Bill Dickey	New York	American
Pitcher	Bob Feller	Cleveland	American
Pitcher	Whitlow Wyatt	Brooklyn	National
Pitcher	Thornton Lee	Chicago	American
Pitcher	Ernie White	St. Louis	National
Pitcher	Elmer Riddle	Cincinnati	National

The two great hitters of '41: Joe DiMaggio hit safely in 56 straight games, batted .357, and led the league with 125 RBIs, while Ted Williams became the last .400 hitter with an average of .406.

The Sporting News

THE BASE BALL PAPER OF THE WORLD

REG. U. S. PAT. OFF.

VOLUME 112, NUMBER 14 ST. LOUIS, NOVEMBER 13, 1941 TEN CENTS THE COPY 18c in Canada

JOE DI MAGGIO, MOST VALUABLE IN A. L.

Yank Star Chosen by Scribes

Over Ted Williams, 291 to 254

Bob Feller Only Other Performer to Receive Votes From All in Competition for The Sporting News Trophy; Joe Becomes Fifth to Be Named More Than Once

By EDGAR G. BRANDS

JOE DI MAGGIO, center fielder of the New York Yankees, in winning the American League Most Valuable Player honor for the second time in three years, edged out Ted Williams of the Boston Red Sox in a close race. DiMag, named by a committee of the Baseball Writers' Association of America, will receive THE SPORTING NEWS trophy, emblematic of his selection. The Yankee star accumulated a total of 291 points in the balloting, to 254 for Williams—a much smaller margin than he had in 1939, when Jolting Joe gained the honor by topping Jimmie Foxx, 280 to 170. The two gardeners and Bob Feller, Cleveland pitcher, were the only players in a field of 29 to receive votes from all committeemen. DiMaggio rolled up his point total with 15 firsts and nine seconds, while Williams was given only eight first-place votes, along with 14 seconds and two thirds.

Feller did not receive any first or second-place ranking, but was placed third on 14 ballots, fourth six times, fifth and seventh once each and sixth on two voting slips, for 174 points. The other first-place selection was given to Thornton Lee, Chicago White Sox pitcher, who finished fourth, with 144 points.

Since the selections were inaugurated in 1911, when the choice was known as the Chalmers Award, four other American League players have been so honored more than once, the late Lou Gehrig leading with four nominations—in 1927, 1931, 1934 and 1936. Jimmie Foxx won the distinction three times, 1932, 1933 and 1938. Walter Johnson, in 1913 and 1924, and Hank Greenberg, in 1935 and 1940, were others selected twice. DiMaggio's acquisition of the honor marks the seventh time among the 24 awards in which a Yankee was designated.

That Joe was not considered the only important factor in the winning of the American League pennant is attested by the number of teammates who also figured in the voting, six other members of the champions being accorded considerable support, headed by Charlie Keller, who finished fifth. The Tigers ranked next to the Yankees in the number of representatives, five placing. The Red Sox had four, the Indians, White Sox and Athletics, three each, and Washington and Browns, two each.

Outfielders dominated the voting, 11 of them receiving a total of 797 points. Pitchers were next in favor, with eight gathering 380 points. Four shortstops registered 144 points; one second baseman, 60; two catchers, 21; two first basemen, 13; and a lone third baseman, 1.

Results of the Balloting

Results of the balloting, counting 14 points for first place, nine for second, eight for third and so on down to one for tenth, were:

1—Joe DiMaggio, New York	291
2—Ted Williams, Boston	254
3—Robert Feller, Cleveland	174
4—Thornton Lee, Chicago	144
5—Charlie Keller, New York	126
6—Cecil Travis, Washington	101
7—Joe Gordon, New York	60
8—Jeff Heath, Cleveland	37
9—Heber Newsome, Boston	32
10—Roy Cullenbine, St. Louis	29
11—Joe Cronin, Boston	26
12—Sam Chapman, Philadelphia	25
13—Bill Dickey, New York	18
14—Tommy Henrich, New York	16
15—Barney McCosky, Detroit	12
Ted Lyons, Chicago	12
17—Dick Siebert, Philadelphia	10
Lou Boudreau, Cleveland	10
19—Alton Benton, Detroit	8
20—Phil Rizzuto, New York	7
Emil Leonard, Washington	7
22—Bruce Campbell, Detroit	4
23—Rudy York, Detroit	3
Frank Hayes, Philadelphia	3
25—Taft Wright, Chicago	2
Charles Ruffing, New York	2
27—Elden Auker, St. Louis	1
Frank Higgins, Detroit	1
Dominic DiMaggio, Boston	1

By Joe Williams

Yankee Party
Put Seal on
Di Maggio Value

We think the jury, composed of baseball writers, returned a just and fair verdict. Put to a tough, ticklish task, they took Joe DiMaggio over Ted Williams as the most valuable player in the American League.

This was a difficult decision to make, and yet it wasn't. We feel if it had been up to Gus H. Fan and his sentimental cohorts the decision would have been reversed. Williams of the Boston Red Sox was a rarity, a .400 hitter. It had been years since the majors saw one of those things. He had outhit the Yankee star by some 50 points.

That's quite a wide margin. We can hear old Gus arguing: "How can them press-box bums give it to DiMaggio when Williams outhits him from here to Peoria?" But this wasn't a hitting proposition. It was a matter of team value. It simmered down to this: Was DiMaggio more valuable to the Yankees than Williams was to the Red Sox?

The baseball writers thought he was, and we find ourself readily agreeing with them. It has been charged that there is a weakness in the voting which almost invariably sees the award going to a member of a pennant-winning club. Perhaps that is so—but after all, the main thing is to finish first. There can be good seconds and good thirds, even good fourths, but only the pennant winners get into the world series.

We don't question for a second that the Red Sox would have finished a notch or two farther down if it hadn't been for Williams' tremendous hitting. It is entirely probable he could have switched places with DiMaggio and the Yankees still would have won as far off as they did. This, naturally, comes under the head of pure speculation.

* * *

Yank Players Gave Joe Credit.

But what did happen, and what is completely beyond the realm of speculation, is that the Yankees did win with DiMaggio, and they didn't start to win until DiMaggio started his unprecedented hitting streak in which he hit safely in 56 consecutive games. Records lend themselves to all sorts of interpretations, mostly influenced by casual whims and wishful thinking. In this case the records make out a good substantial case for DiMaggio. The Yankees were five and a half games behind when he started his streak. They were out in front with the pennant virtually clinched when he ended his streak. He was the spark, the inspiration, in short, the symbol of victory.

Who should know better than the Yankee players themselves who straightened them out and pointed their way to the white lights of success? Come to think of it, the Yankee players made it rather simple for the jury, the baseball writers, to arrive at their verdict. Near the end of the season—it was in Boston, we believe—they publicly acknowledged their gratitude to DiMaggio. They threw a party for him and gave him a present from the whole team. We don't recall that anything of this sort ever happened before in baseball. The implication of this gesture was unmistakable: It was the other Yankees telling DiMaggio he had won the pennant for them.

And at this point it should be noted that the jury created no precedent in ignoring a .400 hitter. That has been done before. For instance, there was Harry Heilmann of the Detroit Tigers who led the league with .403 in 1923. That year the most valuable award went to Babe Ruth of the Yankees. He had hit 41 homers and contributed mightily to the New Yorkers' pennant success. "As Ruth goes, so go the Yankees." That was never true of Heilmann and the Tigers. Up to now it hasn't been true of Williams and the Red Sox. Last season it very definitely was true of DiMaggio and the Yankees.

The plain truth is Williams isn't the ballplayer DiMaggio is. A better hitter, yes, but not too much of a better hitter. After all, .357 hitters don't grow on hallracks, either. But Williams won't throw or even run with DiMaggio, and from what we hear he isn't the team player the 'Frisco kid is, either. However, this isn't an item that concerns us greatly. He's still a youngster, he loves baseball and this type usually comes around to putting the welfare of the team ahead of individual exploits.

* * *

Williams Finishes Like Champ.

That's just what Williams' performance was this year—an individual exploit. This is not written in criticism. He could have hit .800 and the Red Sox would have trailed the Yankees. They weren't good enough to get up there and stay on the brilliance of one man. Under the circumstances Williams was entirely within his right in concentrating on a classic goal.

We liked the way he reached it, too, the hard way, the admirable, gallant way. This was the phase of his performance that made him stand out in our book, might have made us pause in writing out our ballot if we had been on the jury. It had been years since anybody hit .400. Bill Terry of the Giants in 1930 was the last big leaguer to do it. The abovementioned Heilmann was the last American Leaguer to do it, and that was all of 18 years ago.

Coming into Philadelphia for the last three games of the season, Williams was hitting .405. All he had to do was sit the rest of the season out. Nobody could take anything away from him, either the batting title or the coveted .400 mark. But he elected to play. His remark was characteristic: "Hell, that's what they pay me for."

In the first of the last three games he went to the plate four times, got one hit and his average dropped below .400. It was the first time since July 25 he had been under .400. Now the pressure was on. The stage was set for a panic. A blight has stolen across dreamland. There's a double-header the next day. So what does this frightened, nervous, timid youngster do? He just gets four for five in the first game and two for three in the second and winds up with .406! He came home like a champion. It's too bad there was a DiMaggio around.

DiMaggio Believes He Hasn't Reached Peak— Thinks '42 May Be His Big Season

By DANIEL.

Joe DiMaggio just had finished fixing his Christmas tree in his apartment at 400 West End Ave. He had done a lot of posing in a Santa Claus costume with 3-month-old Little Joe and Dorothy. He sat down and relaxed—and talked about the war.

"The first thing to do is to win this fight," said the Yankee who last season set an amazing record by hitting in 56 consecutive games and who now is reported to be seeking a contract for $50,000.

It was suggested to Joe that he take the lead in issuing an appeal to the players of the major leagues to support the Defense Bond campaign.

"It would be a presumption on my part to make that appeal, because every ballplayer sees his duty, and every player is sure to do it," DiMaggio replied. "For myself I can say that this week I purchased $5000 worth of bonds. And I intend to go right on buying them as the pay checks come in."

What about those pay checks? "Honest, I have not made any plans concerning my contract," DiMaggio said. "I have read that I would demand this and ask for that. But I have discussed it with nobody.

"This looks like a bad time to do any loose talking. All of us are marking time. We don't know what tomorrow will bring. I will receive my contract when it is mailed out with the rest of the Yankee agreements, and I will be right here to get it—and tell Mr. Barrow my reaction. Until I receive the papers why should I talk?"

DiMaggio looked thin. "No, I have not lost weight; I have picked up exactly one pound since the world series, scaling at 198," Giuseppe continued. "But this life is too soft, and I'll have to change my program soon.

"Right after the holidays I will begin working out at the New York A. C., very likely with Lefty Gomez, who should be back from Boston by then. I will remain in New York until the baseball writers' dinner on Feb. 1 and as soon as possible after that will take my family down to St. Petersburg. Little Joe needs some sun. And so does Big Joe, for that matter.

"I want at least a month of fishing, golfing, walking and swimming before I put on my baseball uniform.

"This should be the year if everything goes well. I have not yet reached my peak as a ballplayer. However, there is no sense in making predictions."

How did it feel to look back at that stretch of 56 games, in which he hit better than .400?

"It feels fine now, but I don't mind confessing it was a lot tougher than I admitted to any of you writers," Joe chortled.

"The strain was terrific. Now, in my first year with San Francisco, I hit in 61 straight games. But nothing bothered me then. Besides, it was in the minors, and nobody paid very much attention to me. There were no big crowds, no fans waiting outside the park, no writers interviewing me every day.

"If I say it myself, that 56 streak was a good trick. That's one job the boys are not going to beat while I am around."

DiMaggio discussed business. The war had hit San Francisco hard. The fishermen were beached by the War Department edict that none could go outside the Golden Gate. And DiMaggio's Grotto, on Fisherman's Wharf, was doing next to nothing. Brother Tom wrote that business there was at a standstill.

Going back to baseball, DiMaggio assumed no cocky attitude. Frankly, he was quite at sea. He asked how the major leagues had fared in 1917-1918. He asked about reactions to Connie Mack's suggestion that the players accept lower rates with clauses calling for bonuses if things turned out well.

DiMaggio was willing enough to state that, major losses to the services barred, the Yankees again would be far too good for their league.

Joe has a 3A rating with his San Francisco draft board, and while he would not discuss that situation, he indicated he did not expect any change.

However, there is a possibility that his younger brother, Dominic, of the Red Sox, may have his rating shifted from 3A to 1A. Dom was deferred because of wearing glasses.

It was a kick to see Joe so thoroughly domesticated. He beamed with joy over Little Joe, who is unusually big for his meager months and already has demonstrated his dad's fondness for food.

"Just hold back the bottle five minutes and will that guy holler!" Pop chuckled. Sounded like a warning to Ed Barrow.

Joe's .357 Boosts Average Two Points

L IFTING his major league batting average two points, from .343 to .345, Joe DiMaggio, New York Yankee center fielder, named the American League's most valuable player, hit the ball for a percentage of .357 in 1941, which placed him third in the circuit, behind Ted Williams, the leader, and Cecil Travis, the runner-up. Joe's complete batting figures for his three seasons and part of another in the minors, with San Francisco in the Pacific Coast League, and six in the majors, all with the Yankees, follow:

Year—Club.	League.	G.	AB.	R.	H.	2B.	3B.	HR.	RBI.	B.A.
1932—San Francisco	P. C. L.	3	9	2	2	1	1	0	...	.222
1933—San Francisco	P. C. L.	187	762	129	259	45	13	28	169	.340
1934—San Francisco	P. C. L.	101	375	58	128	18	6	12	69	.341
1935—San Francisco	P. C. L.	172	679	173	270	48	18	34	154	.398
1936—New York	A. L.	138	637	132	206	44	15	29	125	.323
1937—New York	A. L.	151	621	151	215	35	15	46	167	.346
1938—New York	A. L.	145	599	129	194	32	13	32	140	.324
1939—New York	A. L.	120	462	108	176	32	6	30	126	.381
1940—New York	A. L.	132	508	93	179	28	9	31	133	.352
1941—New York	A. L.	139	541	122	193	43	11	30	125	.357
Major League Totals		825	3368	735	1163	214	69	198	816	.345

AMERICAN LEAGUE'S FOREMOST PLAYER

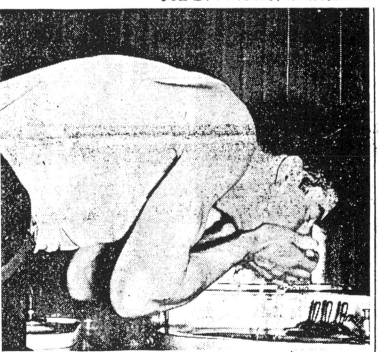

1941'S MOST VALUABLES....
DOLPH CAMILLI, *National* and
JOE DI MAGGIO, *American*....

Joe DiMaggio   The New York Times

ALWAYS MAKING A SPLASH

JOE DIMAGGIO FIRST FOR RUNS BATTED IN

Yankee Slugger's Drives Sent 125 Tallies Home—Heath, Indians, Totaled 123

TEAM HONORS TO RED SOX

American League Again Broke or Tied 37 Records in 1941, Champions Setting Pace

Although thwarted in his bid to retain his batting crown last Summer, Joe DiMaggio of the Yankees captured one of the major individual prizes of the 1941 campaign by carrying off top honors in runs batted in. Jolting Joe, according to the official American League statistics announced yesterday, led his circuit in this important department with a total of 125 runs driven in, a margin of two over Jeff Heath of the Indians, who placed second.

Charlie Keller of the Yanks, who appeared to have the prize all tucked away until a sprained ankle shelved him in the late weeks of the pennant race, finished third with 122, while directly behind him comes Ted Williams of the Red Sox with 120.

In all, ten players drove in 100 or more runs in the American League last Summer. In this group was Jimmy Foxx, the Red Sox vet-

eran, who with a total of 105 made this the thirteenth consecutive season in which he batted in 100 or more runs, thereby tying the major league record held by the late Lou Gehrig.

First in Fanning Again

Incidentally, by fanning 103 times, Foxx added another year to his somewhat unenviable record of most years leading in strikeouts. It was the seventh season in which he whiffed the greatest number of times.

In the matter of drawing passes, Williams finished far in front. The lanky Red Sox outfielder walked 145 times in 143 games.

Frankie Crosetti, after leading the loop for five straight years in being hit most by pitched balls, had to vacate this distinction last Summer because of his rather infrequent appearances in the Yankee line-up, and Dominic Di Maggio of the Red Sox carried off this honor by being clipped seven times.

Pete Suder and Frank Hayes of the Athletics shared the dubious honor of hitting into the most double plays. Each plowed into twenty-three twin killings to equal the major-league record set by Lou Boudreau of the Indians in 1940.

In a separate group of statistics, released for publication today, the American League reveals that the same number of records, thirty-seven, were broken or equaled in the circuit in 1941 as in 1940.

DiMaggio's Streak No. 1 Feat

Outstanding in the record feats of last Summer, of course, was Joe DiMaggio's phenomenal hitting streak in which the famous Yankee clipper connected safely in fifty-six consecutive games, stretching from May 15 until the memorable night game on July 17 in Cleveland, when Pitchers Al Smith and Jim Bagby finally brought him to a halt.

Joe DiMaggio Year's Outstanding Athlete

Wins Male Award by 2-1 Margin; Ted Williams of Red Sox Second; Joe Louis Third, Craig Wood Fourth

By ORLO ROBERTSON

New York, Dec. 17—(AP)—For breaking all major league consecutive hitting records with a string of 56 straight games, Joe DiMaggio was voted the outstanding male athlete of 1941 by a margin of more than 2 to 1 over his nearest rival.

Ted Williams Placed Second

The slugging New York Yankee outfielder, who batted .357, piled up a total of 157 points as 42 of the 82 sports experts participating in the Associated Press' annual poll placed him first on their list. He was given either second or third place on 20 other ballots.

Ted Williams, who in hitting .406 for the Boston Red Sox became the first major leaguer in many years to surpass the .400 mark, ran second to DiMaggio. Polling five first-place votes, Williams received a total of 74 on the basis of three points for first, two for second and one for third.

Joe Louis, heavyweight boxing champion, outscored Williams in the number of first places, receiving 10, but wound up third with 64 points for his unprecedented performance of successfully defending his title seven times during the year.

With Craig Wood, U. S. open golf king, finishing fourth with 27 votes, football was completely routed for the first time in three years.

Football Fails To Lead Poll

Tommy Harmon of Michigan won No. 1 honors last year and Niles Kinnick of Iowa in 1939 but this year the gridiron sport could do no better than fifth with Don Hutson, the Green Bay Packers' great end. He was given four firsts and a total of 23 votes, seven more than Minnesota's all-America back, Bruce Smith, who received three firsts and enough seconds and thirds to make 16.

Track was headed by Cornelius Warmerdam, world record holder in the pole vault, with 14 tallies.

Five coaches, four of them gridiron mentors, received consideration. They were Frank Leahy of Notre Dame, Earl Blaik of the Army, Burt Shotton, leader of the Columbus Redbirds of the American Baseball Association, Paul Brown of Ohio State and Bernie Bierman of Minnesota's unbeaten Gophers.

The complete voting:

	First	Points
Joe DiMaggio, baseball	42	157
Ted Williams, baseball	5	74
Joe Louis, boxing	10	64
Craig Wood, golf	1	27
Don Hutson, football	4	23
Bruce Smith, football	3	16
Cornelius Warmerdam, track	2	14
Frankie Sinkwich, football	3	12
Bill Dudley, football	0	7
Frank Leahy, football	1	6
Bud Ward, golf	1	5
Bob Feller, baseball	0	5
Bill Smith, swimming	1	5
Leslie MacMitchell, track	1	4

Three Points—Frankie Alberts, football (1); Earl Blaik, football (1); Billy Conn, boxing; Burt Shotton, baseball (1); Paul Brown, football (1); Steve Lach, football (1).

Two Points—Ray Robinson, boxing; Pat Harder, football; Ucurt Davis, baseball; Bob Reinhard, football; Bobby Riggs, tennis; Lem Franklin, boxing; Fred Fitzsimmons, baseball.

One Point—Edgar Jones, football; Willie Hoppe, billiards; Joe Platk, handball; Al Blozis, track; Endicott Peabody, football; Billy Hillenbrand, football; Gregory Rice, track; Elmer Riddle, baseball; Ned Day, bowling; Angelo Bertelli, football; Bernie Bierman, football; Kirby Higbe, baseball; Pete Reiser, baseball.

At ease at home. And why not? He won the MVP award for 1941 and glided through the World Series for the fifth time in his six years as a New York Yankee.